STALIN
A POLITICAL BIOGRAPHY

FROM THE LIBRARY OF

Dennis F. Giovanetti

STALIN
A POLITICAL BIOGRAPHY

ISAAC DEUTSCHER

SECOND EDITION

A Galaxy Book

NEW YORK   OXFORD UNIVERSITY PRESS   1967

First edition, Copyright 1949 by Oxford University Press, Inc.

Second edition, © Oxford University Press 1966

Preface to the second edition © Isaac Deutscher 1967

First published 1949

Second edition 1966

First published as a Galaxy Book 1967

Printed in the United States of America

I DEDICATE THIS BOOK
A LINK IN OUR FRIENDSHIP
TO
TAMARA

PREFACE TO THE SECOND EDITION

THIS edition of *Stalin* appears nearly twenty years after the book was written. When I was completing it, in the summer of 1948, Stalin was still at the summit of his power, admired and feared all over the world, and surrounded by a dizzy 'cult' in his own country. And the world looked very different then. The Soviet Union was not yet a nuclear power; the victory of the Chinese revolution was still some way off; and Stalin's break with Tito had only just begun making headlines in the newspapers. I introduced my assessment of Stalin's record, in the last pages of the book, with these words:

Here we suspend the story of Stalin's life and work. We are under no illusion that we can draw from it final conclusions or form, on its basis, a confident judgement of the man, of his achievements and failures. After so many climaxes and anti-climaxes, his drama seems only now to be rising to its pinnacle; and we do not know into what new perspective its last act may yet throw the preceding ones.

It is this 'last act' that I now relate in a new section of the book, the Postscript on Stalin's Last Years. After 1948 the drama of my chief character did indeed rise to its final culmination, which led to the subsequent crumbling of the Stalin cult. Yet the remark with which I prefaced my assessment of Stalin's role now appears perhaps to have been somewhat over cautious: Stalin's activity and behaviour in his last years, far from throwing his previous record into any new perspective, only added a sharper outline to the perspective I had drawn, when, in the concluding passages of the book, I anticipated the so-called de-Stalinization.

I am often asked whether I see no reason to revise my views in the light of the 'revelations' made by Khrushchev, Mikoyan, and others at the Twentieth Congress in 1956 and later. In truth those revelations have added nothing significant to the account I had given here of Stalin's rise to power, of his relationship with Lenin and other Bolshevik leaders, of his policies in the inter-war period, of his conduct of the Great Purges, and of his role in the Second World War and its aftermath. On all these crucial phases of Stalin's career my biography contains far more abundant information than that which is even now accessible to Soviet readers. And, incidentally, my *Stalin* still remains a forbidden book in the U.S.S.R., China, and the countries of Eastern Europe.[1]

Nor do I take all of Khrushchev's 'revelations' at their face value: I do not accept, in particular, his assertion that Stalin's role in the Second World War was virtually insignificant. This allegation was obviously meant to boost Khrushchev himself at Stalin's expense; and it does not accord with the testimonies of many reliable eye-witnesses, of Western statesmen and generals who had no reason to exaggerate Stalin's role, and of Soviet generals who have recently written on this subject in a sober and critical vein.[2]

There is only one aspect of Stalin's activity which has appeared to me in a clearer light as a result of Khrushchev's disclosures—namely, the extent to which Stalin, having suppressed the Trotskyists, Zinovievists, and Bukharinists, victimized his own followers, the Stalinists. In the new section of this book I analyse the consequences of that important fact, consequences which made themselves felt most strongly in the last phase of Stalin's rule and account in some degree for the character and style of the Khrushchevite de-Stalinization. Otherwise I have seen no reason to alter my narrative or interpretation of Stalin's career. The original text of the book is reproduced here with only a few minor corrections and stylistical revisions.

11 October 1966   I. D.

---

[1] It is possible, however, that my account of one of the Great Purges, the Tukhachevsky affair, may need some revision; but if so, Khrushchev and his successors have not provided the elements necessary for such a revision, despite the fact that they have rehabilitated Tukhachevsky and cleared him of the charge that he plotted against Stalin in Germany's interest, as Hitler's agent. In my account of the affair I emphatically refuted that accusation; but I related a version drawn from unimpeachably anti-Stalinist sources (quoted in a footnote on p. 380), according to which Tukhachevsky had indeed planned a *coup* against Stalin, in order to save the army and the country from the insane terror of the purges. This version may be mistaken; but Khrushchev and his successors have not revealed a single document or a single fact that would throw light on the affair and allow us to dismiss altogether the anti-Stalinist accounts which insisted on the reality of the plot.

[2] I gave a detailed analysis of Khrushchev's disclosures in a essay published in 1956, and reproduced in my *Ironies of History*, pp. 3–17.

FROM THE INTRODUCTION (1961)

I WROTE this biography thirteen to fourteen years ago as a book for the general reader rather than for the expert, and I did my best to state in it the essential facts about Stalin and his career as plainly and as non-controversially as possible. When I began planning the work, the public and the press in this country had not yet quite recovered from their war-time adulation of Stalin; when I was putting the finishing touches to it, the air-lift to Berlin roared on and Stalin was *the* villain of the cold war. These violent changes in the political climate did not, I think, affect my treatment of Stalin: I had never been a devotee of the Stalin cult; and the cold war was not my war. Yet shortly after publication a British critic could write that 'like its subject, the book has become the focus of an animated and at times ferocious controversy . . . no biography in recent years has aroused similar interest or evoked similar passionate resentment and hostility'. I should perhaps add that most British critics received the book open-mindedly and generously—nevertheless, the 'ferocious controversy' did in fact go on for years, especially abroad, on both sides of the Atlantic.

The book has been praised or blamed for the most contradictory reasons, either as a denunciation of Stalinism, or as an apology for it, and sometimes as both denunciation and apology. Thus, the late Moshe Pijade, Marshal Tito's friend and associate, once explained to me why the government of which he was a member refused to allow a Yugoslav edition of *Stalin*: 'You see,' he said, 'the trouble with your book is that it is too pro-Soviet for us whenever we quarrel with the Russians; and it is too anti-Soviet whenever we try to be friendly with them.' ('In any case,' he added with a twinkle in the eye, 'we cannot permit a Yugoslav edition to appear because if we did everyone would see at once from what source our great theorists have drawn most of their wisdom.')

According to an old, golden rule of portrait painting, a good portrait is one which does such justice to the complexity of the human character that every viewer sees in it a different face. Something might still be said for that rule; and judged by it

Stalin might be said not to have done badly. Almost every critic, hostile or friendly, has found in this portrait what he has wanted to find and has read into it what he has wished to read. Few have been those who have paid attention to the full complexity of the character depicted here and to the intricacy of a portrait which shows Stalin *en face* as the descendant of Lenin and in profile as the descendant of Ivan the Terrible. I admit that what I have striven for in this work is old-fashioned objectivity; and I must also admit that objectivity did not come to me easily, that I had to strive for it. Nothing would have been easier for me than to produce an accusatory biography of Stalin: I had been opposed to Stalinism ever since the early nineteen-thirties; I had denounced the cruelties of forcible collectivization while these were still being perpetrated (and not, as some of my critics did, twenty or twenty-five years after the event); I had been, at least since 1931, a stern critic of the Stalinist policy which facilitated the rise of Nazism; I exposed the mass terror, the purges, and the Moscow trials while these were staged; and so on, and so on.¹ Briefly, I had been a 'premature' anti-Stalinist; and if I had chosen to rehash all that I had written against Stalin and Stalinism in the course of nearly two decades the result would have been a book against which no one would have levelled the criticism that it was an apology for Stalin.

However, the one thing I was determined *not* to do was to write this book from intellectual inertia. I decided to take a fresh and critical look at the subject, so familiar to me, of my study. Some critics have remarked on my 'cool and impersonal' approach to Stalin. Yet the work on this book was to me a deeply personal experience, the occasion for much silent heart-searching and for a critical review of my own political record. I had belonged to those whom Stalin had cruelly defeated; and one of the questions I had to ask myself was why he had succeeded. To answer this question the partisan had to turn into an historian, to examine dispassionately causes and effects, to view open-

¹ In the last years of the Stalin era people in Poland, unknown to me, still reproduced clandestinely my brochure *The Moscow Trial*, which I had published in Warsaw in 1936 to expose the ill-famed trial of Zinoviev and Kamenev. In doing so, they risked life and liberty; and some were in fact sentenced to many years' imprisonment. I have learned about this only recently from the President of the Polish Supreme Court who in 1956 or 1957 quashed the sentences.

mindedly the adversary's motives, and to see and admit the adversary's strength where strength there was. The political fighter cannot allow himself to be too severely restricted by a deterministic view of the situation in which he acts, if only because some of the elements of that situation, and some of the chances, are as yet unknown and even undetermined; and because he can never be quite sure what will be the impact of his own action on any given situation. The historian, on the other hand, cannot help being a determinist, or behaving as one if he is not: he has not done his job fully unless he has shown causes and effects so closely and naturally interwoven in the texture of events that no gap is left, unless, that is, he has demonstrated the inevitability of the historic process with which he is concerned. The partisan deals with fluid circumstances: on all sides men still exercise conflicting wills, marshal forces, use weapons, and achieve or reverse decisions. The historian deals with fixed and irreversible patterns of events: all weapons have already been fired; all wills have been spent; all decisions have been achieved; and what is irreversible has assumed the aspect of the inevitable.

This, the approach from the historian's angle, accounts for the much-debated undertone of inevitability that runs through this book. As a partisan I had repudiated many of the deeds of my chief character which as a biographer I demonstrate to have been inevitable. The contradiction, however, is more apparent than real. In both my capacities I have argued from the same philosophical-political premisses, but from different and partly conflicting angles.

The objections to my method have been obvious enough. When I published *Stalin*, not all the situations narrated in it had receded into history and become irreversible. It was still possible to expect, as leading Western statesmen and commentators did, that, for example, Soviet power would be 'rolled back' from Eastern Europe, the industrial advance of the Soviet Union would be brought to a standstill by a failure of planned economy, and so on. By treating as irreversible the post-war revolutions in Eastern Europe, which at the time of my writing were still in progress, and by taking for granted the continued industrial ascendancy of the U.S.S.R. at a time, just after the war, when that country was still half in ruins, I admittedly ventured into the field of political judgements and predictions from which many an historian would have shied off. I trust that after so many years readers will forgive me this offence, and that in judging my explicit and implicit predictions they will consider whether these have or have not stood the test of time.

Another criticism, which may still be repeated, is that by showing Stalin's triumphs to have been inevitable I have after all justified his record. The criticism implies that reasonable men are or should always be reconciled to the inevitable. I do not accept this implication. Some of the proudest moments in man's history are those when he struggles against the inevitable; and this his struggle, too, is inevitable. The philosopher who claims that 'what is real is reasonable' also maintains that 'what is reasonable is real'. History runs its course on various levels, superficial and deep, of reality and necessity. The generation of Russian revolutionaries which perished in resisting Stalin's autocracy represented not less than he did an historic necessity, but one of a different kind. And I may perhaps remind critics that, having demonstrated the 'inevitability of Stalinism' and dwelt on its positive as well as negative aspects, I concluded my study, nearly eight years before Khrushchev's famous revelations about Stalin, with this emphatic forecast of the 'inevitability' of de-Stalinization: '. . . history may yet have to cleanse and reshape Stalin's work as sternly as it once cleansed and reshaped the work of the English Revolution after Cromwell and of the French after Napoleon.'[1]

---

[1] How some critics received this forecast can be seen in the following passages from Franz Borkenau's very long essay on *Stalin* published, as a special feature, in periodicals appearing in various countries under the auspices of the Congress for Cultural Freedom (*Der Monat, Preuves*, and others):

'Deutscher's perspective is utterly false. . . . Napoleon's person could be detached from the destinies of France; and the achievements of the revolution and of the Napoleonic period were indeed preserved. But it is more than doubtful whether Russia's destiny can be separated from Stalinism, even if Stalin were ever to die a natural death. The inner law of the Stalinist terror drives Stalin's Russia, not less, even if more slowly, than the law of the Nazi terror drove Hitler's Germany, to conflict with the world and thereby to total catastrophe not only for the terroristic régime, but also for the nation ruled by it. . . . The danger of Deutscher's book is that in place of this grave and anxious prospect it puts another one which is more normal and reassuring. According to Deutscher's conception there is nothing terrible to fear because in the main the terrors are already in the past. To this conception we oppose the opinion that the revolution of the twentieth century shows parallels to earlier revolutions only in its opening phase, but that later it ushers in a régime of terror without end, of hostility

Stalin appears in this edition as it was published originally, without change. If I were to write the book anew, I would probably do it in somewhat different style. But however differently in detail or with whatever shifts of emphasis I would now tell the story, it is, I think, better on balance to publish it as it stands. The fact that the book has over so many years been the object of so wide and animated a controversy has probably made of the original text something of a document with which even its author should not tamper. And, on the whole, I *do* stand by the interpretation of Stalin and Stalinism given here.

This biography was originally conceived as part of a trilogy including also Lives of Lenin and Trotsky. My work on the trilogy is still in progress; but two volumes of a study of Trotsky, *The Prophet Armed* and *The Prophet Unarmed*, have already appeared; and the third should soon be completed.[1] It is inherent in the design of such a work that certain strands of narrative and interpretation should remain only half-developed in one part of the trilogy, and that they should be taken up, expanded, and brought to the fore in another. And so, although *Stalin* is a self-contained work, which has been and still can be read independently, knowledge of the other parts of the trilogy would give readers a far more comprehensive idea of the subject matter of this study.

I. D.

24 April 1961

towards everything human, of horrors which carry no remedy, and which can be cured only *ferro et igni.*'
Borkenau was the leading light of a school of thought which for over a decade was unfortunately extremely influential in Western 'sovietology'.

[1] Since this Introduction was written, the third volume, *The Prophet Outcast*, has been published.

PREFACE TO THE FIRST EDITION

THIS narrative of Stalin's life ends somewhat indefinitely with the years 1945–6. This is as far as the biographer can at present carry his story. No documentary evidence is available on which a description of Stalin's role in the last two or three years could be based. I hope, however, that the closing chapters of this book do shed some light upon Stalin in the aftermath of war. A very short time ago it would have been almost impossible to carry the story beyond 1938 or 1939. Fortunately, however, the recently published official documents and the war memoirs of western ministers and generals have eased my task, but no comparable documents or war memoirs have been published in Russia. The writer who tries to consider the pros and cons of Stalin's case finds on one side the evidence of Messrs. Churchill, Hull, Byrnes, Harry L. Hopkins's White House Papers, and others. On the other he finds almost nothing, except a few coloured fragments of semi-official disclosures contained, strangely enough, in scripts for Russian films, such as Virta's *Stalingradskaya Bitva*, for this has been the only channel so far through which the Soviet leaders have chosen to convey to their people an infinitesimal part of the inner story of those great years. Clio, the Muse of History, has failed to obtain admittance to the Kremlin.

It is, indeed, a sad paradox that the nation which bore the greatest and the most heroic sacrifice in the Second World War should be the one that is allowed to know least about its diplomatic, military, and political background. Western writers and memoirists, as is only natural, tell their tale from their own peculiar national and political standpoints, and I hope that in using their evidence I have made sufficient allowance for inevitable bias. But the very diversity of outlook and judgement in those writings is in itself a means of assessing their relative trustworthiness; and it is surprising to find how great has been their consonance so far on the crucial facts and even the details that are relevant to an account of Stalin's role. I have, in addition, tried to fill part of the gap in the documentary evidence by drawing upon private impressions and accounts—

relating to this as well as to other periods of Stalin's career—given to me by statesmen, diplomats, and politicians of many nationalities and conflicting political views whose activities have at one time or another brought them into touch with Stalin. To these men, whose names I cannot mention, I gratefully acknowledge my debt.

I make no apology for calling this work a political biography. I admit that I am inclined to study the politics rather than the private affairs of public men. And altogether apart from this, it is impossible to narrate the private life of Stalin, since only one private letter of his has yet come to light, and this in the confiscated book by A. S. Alliluyeva, his sister-in-law.[1] Nearly all biographers who have been tempted to delve into this aspect of Stalin's life have had little of real interest to say, or have had to be content with unverifiable gossip. Even so shrewd an observer and so notable a writer as Trotsky, who sat with Stalin in the Politbureau for nearly ten years, was no exception to this rule.

As to the early and middle periods of Stalin's career, it is not the scarcity of documentary evidence but its abundance and contradictoriness that have troubled the biographer. Stalin's life-story is like an enormous palimpsest, where many scripts are superimposed upon one another, each script dating from a different period, each written by a different hand, each giving a different version of events. Even the scripts in Stalin's own handwriting contradict each other glaringly. I trust that the reader of this book will find in it an explanation of this bizarre circumstance. For more than twenty years I have watched the progress of this palimpsest and now I have examined it again, script after script, and compared, checked, and cross-checked the conflicting versions. Here I have set out my findings. I have tried to avoid encumbering this narrative unduly with an account of the involved processes of comparative analysis by which I have arrived at my conclusions. This, I am certain, would have wearied the reader beyond measure. Students and experts, however, will find the necessary clues in my footnotes, where references to sources hostile and friendly to Stalin frequently appear side by side.

[1] This letter is quoted on page 128. One cannot, of course, regard as private the few letters published for the first time in Stalin's *Sochinenya* in the last two years, for these he wrote, as a rule, *ex officio*.

This book is intended as the first instalment of a biographical trilogy to be continued and completed with a *Life of Lenin* and a study of *Trotsky in Exile*. The main study of pre-1917 Bolshevism and the history of such ideas as the dictatorship of the proletariat, the Soviets, the 'proletarian vanguard', and so on, must have their place in the biography of Lenin. In the present volume the growth and evolution of these ideas have been sketched only in so far as was necessary for an understanding of the chief character. The major part of *Stalin* deals, of course, with the outlook of Bolshevism since the revolution and the civil war.

I gratefully acknowledge my debt to friends and colleagues. Thanks are due in particular to Mr. Donald Tyerman and Miss Barbara Ward for constant and friendly encouragement and advice; to Professor E. H. Carr for expert critical comment; and to Mr. D. M. Davin and members of the editorial staff of the Oxford University Press for their infinitely patient scrutiny of my manuscript and most valuable stylistical suggestions. Mr. Jon Kimche very kindly helped me with books and documents. I alone, however, bear responsibility for the views expressed in the book and for its shortcomings.

More than to anyone else I am indebted to my wife, whose devoted assistance has made this work possible and whose critical sense has contributed to the shaping of every paragraph in it.

I. D.

CONTENTS

ILLUSTRATIONS

STALIN
A POLITICAL BIOGRAPHY

CHAPTER I

Childhood and Youth

Stalin's parents: Vissarion Djugashvili and Ekaterina Gheladze.—The birth (1879), childhood, and schooldays of Joseph Djugashvili (afterwards Stalin) at Gori in Georgia (Caucasus).—Influence of Georgian folk-lore.—Russians and Georgians. —Stalin at the Theological Seminary, Tiflis, 1894-9.—The Georgian struggle against Russification.—As 'Soselo' (Little Joe), Stalin publishes verses in 1895.— Clandestine reading.—Joins *Messame Dassy* (The Third Group) in 1898.—Industrial revolt in the Caucasus.—Stalin's apprenticeship as Socialist lecturer.—His expulsion from the seminary.—The stigmas of serfdom.

PERHAPS in 1875, perhaps a year or two before, a young Caucasian, Vissarion Ivanovich (son of Ivan) Djugashvili, set out from the village Didi-Lilo, near Tiflis, the capital of the Caucasus, to settle in the little Georgian county town of Gori. There he started a small shoemaker's business. Vissarion Djugashvili was the son of Georgian peasants who only ten years before had still been serfs. He himself had been born a chattel slave to some Georgian landlord. Had he remained so for the rest of his life, he would never have been free to leave his native village and become an independent artisan. Certainly none of his forefathers could have done anything of the sort. They had been tied to the soil, and at best they could pass only from the hands of one landlord to those of another. Even in the years of Vissarion's childhood Georgian newspapers still carried advertisements in which landlords offered for sale or sought to purchase, say, '500 or 1,000 acres of land with 50 or 150 souls'. The trade in chattel slaves had often been fraudulent; and in the archives of Georgian courts, cases were recorded in which the same peasant family had been sold to three or more buyers simultaneously.[1]

Vissarion, then, must have left his village in a mood of hopeful elation. He had become a free man, and now as an independent artisan he hoped to achieve some prosperity. In Gori he married a girl of similar humble origin—Ekaterina, the

[1] F. Makharadze, 'Gruzya v XIX veke' in *Trudy Pervoi Vsesoyuznoi Konferentsii Istorikov-Marksistov*, vol. i, p. 488.

daughter of the serf George Gheladze, of the village of Gambareuelli. Like many another daughter of poor peasants, she may have moved to the town to become a maidservant to an Armenian or Russian middle-class family. (The middle classes in the Caucasus were Russian, Armenian, or Jewish. There was almost no Georgian *bourgeoisie* yet—Georgians were either gentry or serfs.) When she married Vissarion Djugashvili, Ekaterina was only fifteen years old. Such early marriages were not rare in a country where human beings mature as rapidly as the grapes under a semi-tropical sun. The couple took a poor dwelling at the outskirts of Gori, the rent of which was one and a half roubles (roughly two shillings) a month. It consisted of only a kitchen and one other room. That room, covering not more than five square yards, was dim, for little light came through its one small window. Its door opened straight into a drab courtyard, from which mud and water would pour in on rainy days, since the floor of the dwelling was on a level with the courtyard and not separated from it by any steps. The floor was of bare brick, and a small table, a stool, a sofa, a plank-bed covered with a straw mattress were all the family's furniture.[1] The abode of the Djugashvilis, transformed into a museum, is now shown to crowds of tourists who visit the place. So is Vissarion Djugashvili's tiny workshop, with its old rickety chair, hammer, and lasts.

It was in that dark, one-and-a-half-rouble dwelling that Ekaterina gave birth to three children in the years from 1875 to 1878. All three died soon after birth. Ekaterina was hardly twenty when on 21 December 1879 she gave birth to a fourth child. By a freak of fortune this child was to grow into a healthy, wiry, and self-willed boy. At baptism he was given the name of Joseph; and so the local Greek Orthodox priest, who acted as registrar, recorded the appearance in this world of Joseph Vissarionovich Djugashvili, later to become famous under the name of Joseph Stalin.

. . . .

About his early childhood very little is known. At the age of six or seven he fell ill with smallpox; and his face remained pockmarked. He fell ill for a second time when a blood infection

---

[1] E. Yaroslavsky, *Landmarks in the Life of Stalin*, p. 7.

developed out of an ulcer on his left hand. He was to recollect later that he was near death. 'I don't know', he was to tell A. S. Alliluyeva, his sister-in-law, 'what saved me then, my strong constitution or the ointment of a village quack.' When he recovered he could not easily bend his left arm at the elbow. Because of this slight infirmity, the future Generalissimo was to be declared unfit for military service in 1916.[1]

He grew up amid the squalor and poverty into which he had been born. Vissarion Djugashvili made an attempt to climb up to the ranks of the lower middle class but was unsuccessful. His shoemaker's business did not earn him a living; and so his wife 'had to slave day and night to make ends meet . . . and was obliged to go out to work as a washerwoman'.[2] Even the one-and-a-half-rouble rent for their dwelling was paid from her earnings. From this, some of Stalin's biographers deduce that Vissarion Djugashvili must have been spending on vodka the little money he did earn, a conclusion for which there is some basis in the reminiscences of Stalin's schoolmates.[3] Drunkenness was indeed something like a shoemaker's occupational disease—the saying 'drunk as a cobbler' recurs in most eastern European languages. Vissarion, it is further claimed, was cruel to his wife and child. 'Undeserved and frightful beatings', writes Iremashvili, a friend of Stalin's childhood, 'made the boy as grim and heartless as was his father.' His defences against his father's heartlessness were distrust, alertness, evasion, dissimulation, and endurance. Life was to teach him, early, lessons—and some *ruses de guerre*—that would be useful later on.

This portrait of a drunkard and bully does not perhaps do full justice to Vissarion Djugashvili. He must have had better qualities as well, a spirit of enterprise and curiosity about the world. Otherwise he, the son of serfs, would hardly have exchanged the sluggish life of his native village for the uncertainties of urban existence. In eastern Europe the 'cobbler-philosopher' is as proverbial as is the 'drunken cobbler'. Both bywords describe occupational propensities which often go together. It was probably from his father that Stalin inherited a reflective mind, and

[1] A. S. Alliluyeva, *Vospominanya*, p. 167.
[2] E. Yaroslavsky, op. cit., p. 7.
[3] L. Trotsky, *Stalin*, pp. 6–7.

he has himself unwittingly given us a clue to the inner conflict which made his father grow sulky, bitter, and cruel to his family. Unsuccessful as an independent artisan, Vissarion left the town of Gori and his family, and went to Tiflis where he became a worker in the shoe factory of one Adelkhanov. His new position apparently humiliated him: his ambition had been to be his own master, and now he exchanged chattel-slavery for wage-slavery. He struggled against his lot as long as he could, even though he had ceased to be the family's breadwinner. Hence, probably, came his irritability and his outbursts. In one of his early pamphlets, Stalin illustrated a point of Marxian theory by the experience of his own father: 'Imagine', he wrote, 'a shoe-maker who had a tiny workshop, but could not stand the com-petition of big businesses. That shoemaker closed his workshop and hired himself, say, to Adelkhanov, at the Tiflis shoe factory. He came to Adelkhanov's factory not to remain a worker for ever but to save some money, to lay aside a small capital and then to reopen his own workshop. As you see, the position of that shoemaker is *already* that of a proletarian, but his conscious-ness is *not yet* proletarian, but petty-bourgeois through and through.'[1] There can be no doubt which shoemaker served the writer as the illustration for his thesis. The tiny workshop, the bad luck in business, even the name of the employer, all were part of Vissarion's story. What had warped Vissarion's mind was the conflict between his social position and his 'petty-bourgeois' ambition.

Vissarion did not succeed in 'laying aside a small capital' and reopening his workshop. He died at Tiflis in 1890, when his son was eleven years old. His death probably made no differ-ence to the material condition of his family, for the widowed washerwoman was accustomed to earn her and her son's liveli-hood. In Joseph's mind, later, the image of the deceased man became blurred—he hardly ever mentioned his father. Recol-lection of the 'heartless beatings' may, of course, account for Stalin's and his official biographers' extreme reticence about Vissarion.[2]

Much more is known about Ekaterina Djugashvili. There

---

[1] J. Stalin, *Sochinenya*, vol. i, pp. 314-15.

[2] In the memoirs of the Alliluyevs, which contain much information about Stalin's and his mother's personal life, his father is never mentioned.

was little to distinguish her from the great mass of her contemporaries, of whom a Russian poet said:

> Fate has had three ordeals in store,
> The first is to be married to a slave;
> The second, to be mother to the slave's son;
> The third, to obey the slave until death.
> And all these terrible ordeals
> Beset the woman of the Russian land.

Ekaterina possessed the infinite patience and submissiveness of the eastern peasant woman. She endured her lot with fortitude, bearing no grudge against her husband. She devoted all her tenderness to her only surviving son. She was deeply religious; in her trials she found her only consolation in church. She was also illiterate. Only in her old age was she to learn to read, and so prove herself worthy of her famous son. All who knew her agreed in admiration of her 'quiet, restrained dignity, which comes to people after a long life spent in worries, the bitterness of which has not warped her character'.[1] *Babushka* Keke (Grandma Kate) remained a modest peasant woman even after her son's ascendancy. When for a time she stayed with him in the Kremlin she longed to go back to her more familiar surroundings in the sunny Caucasus, and back she went. Yet, in her own half-comic but moving way, she tried to live up to the role of the great man's mother. Alliluyeva relates how at Borzhom, the Caucasian spa, she once met old Mrs. Djugashvili, dressed heavily and solemnly in black despite unbearable heat. Asked why she was so uncomfortably dressed, the old woman replied: 'I have to. . . . Don't you see, everybody around here knows who I am.'[2]

It was a truly heroic decision on Ekaterina's part to send her son, at the age of nine, to the ecclesiastical school at Gori. It was not rare for children of poor parents to become shoemakers' or carpenters' apprentices at this age, but that was not the career Ekaterina wished for her son, even though it might have eased her own lot. She wanted her Soso[3] to succeed where Vissarion had failed, and to rise above the humble standing of his parents. In her bolder flights of fancy she no doubt saw him

---

[1] A. S. Alliluyeva, *Vospominanya*, p. 81.   [2] Ibid., p. 82.
[3] Soso is the Georgian for Joe. Soselo is a more diminutive form.

as the parish priest respectfully greeted by the neighbours. The prospect was dazzling—only a few years before, ecclesiastical schools were still closed to children of peasant estate.

Soso attended the Gori school for five years, from 1888 till 1893. Usually he was one of the best or even the best pupil in his form. Teachers and schoolmates alike quickly noticed that the poor pockmarked boy had a quite extraordinary memory and learned his lessons almost without effort. They also noticed a streak of self-assertiveness, an eagerness to out-shine others that waxed the keener the more Soso grew aware that most of his schoolmates came from wealthier homes than his, and that some of them, also aware of the difference, looked down on him. Nevertheless, he had the advantage in the class-room, where he could recite his lessons with greater ease than the pampered offspring of wine or wheat merchants; while in the playground he excelled them so much in agility and daring that they let themselves be bossed and ordered about by the shoe-maker's boy. It was in this obscure parish school that the future Stalin had his first taste of class differences and class hatred.

There, too, he had his first glimpse of a problem that was to keep him preoccupied in his mature years—the problem of national minorities. Georgian was the Djugashvilis' native tongue. Ekaterina knew no Russian at all; and it is doubtful whether her husband had as much as a smattering of it. At school most lessons were taught in Russian—the curriculum provided for only a few lessons in Georgian every week. Soso absorbed the alien language with the ease natural to his age. But out of school and at home he went on talking Georgian. The native tongue of some of his classmates may have been Armenian, or Turkish, or some Caucasian dialect. At school all the vernaculars were silenced, and Russian reigned supreme. This policy of Russification, enforced by the Government, caused bitterness. Even boys in their early teens staged school strikes and other demonstrations in defence of their native tongue. In the seventies, school riots were frequent in Georgia: Russian teachers were assailed and beaten up and pupils set fire to schools.[1] In the years when Djugashvili attended the Gori school there was no such turbulence, but there must have been much simmering resentment.

[1] *Istorya Klasovoi Borby v Zakavkazi*, vol. i, Appendix, pp. 89–90.

Among the early influences in his life, nature and the tradition and folk-lore of his native town played their part. Gori lies at a point where three fertile wheat- and vine-growing valleys meet. The cliffs outside the town, the banks of the river Kura and two other rivers, the walls of an old Byzantine fortress, and the fields between the tortuous little streets in the town itself, which was half-village and half-town, all offered the boy plenty of space for playing freely and escaping from the drabness of the parental home. Nature itself made some amends to the young slum-dweller for the dullness and stuffiness of his home. The country-side abounded in animals, birds, plants, and fruit— not for nothing was it believed that this had been the land of the Golden Fleece. These healthy surroundings contributed to the strong physical constitution of the future Stalin. The country-side was also proverbially rich in romance and legend. Alexander the Great and Genghiz Khan had fought there. Tales of Persian and Turkish invasions were found in the school-books. Folk-song and story told of the famous Caucasian brigands. In folk-lore, these brigands were often national or popular heroes: Georgian noblemen who fought against the Russian Tsars, or leaders of serfs, people's avengers, with big and tender hearts for the poor and downtrodden and sly hatred for the rich. Their hiding-places were in the snow-capped peaks and in caves in the cliffs from which they would swoop down to the roads to trap and destroy their enemies. All this folk-lore was not far from the facts. The land around Gori was even in those days infested by highwaymen. There were multitudes of impoverished Georgian petty gentry around, who had no defined social standing and no regular incomes but still lived mentally in a fading world of clans and feuds. They would often engage in fanciful forays against one another or against other people who happened to hurt their pride or otherwise incur their enmity. The whole land would then resound with stories of the raids, exploits that bordered on banditry yet were not without romantic appeal. These local Robin Hoods offered examples that the boys 'playing brigands' in the cliffs and fields of Gori must have been eager to imitate.

The five school years at Gori were thus not altogether unhappy for young Djugashvili. But already there began to grow in him an awareness of the social and national inequalities that was to make of him the rebel and revolutionary of later years. It is impossible to say just how strong was this awareness. Official Soviet biographers and memoirists claim that already at Gori their hero had read Darwin and become an atheist. One may doubt whether he could have read Darwin at so early an age. But he may have acquired a vague notion of the new theory from popular summaries, and his mind may have turned against religion. The fact of his precocious mental development is established, for in 1895, only a year after he had left the Gori school, he was already publishing verses in a leading Georgian periodical. He must have tried his hand at verse-writing while at Gori. His official biographers also claim that it was there that he first acquainted himself with Marxian ideas. This seems highly improbable: by that time Marxism had won only a few converts at Tiflis, the capital of Transcaucasia, and its influence could hardly yet have spread to the Gori school.[1] Stalin's apologists are only too ready to project his 'Marxist-Leninist' orthodoxy almost into his childhood. Subsequent events seem to warrant no more than the following hypothesis: young Djugashvili left the Gori school in a mood of some rebelliousness, in which protest against social injustice mingled with semi-romantic Georgian patriotism. While in the upper forms, he had been much more impressed by the nostalgic nationalism of Georgian poetry than by any sociological ideas. 'In the upper classes of the Gori school', writes one of his school-fellows, Vano Ketskhoveli, 'we became acquainted with Georgian literature, but we had no mentor to guide our development and give a definite direction to our thoughts. Chavchavadze's poem "Kako the Robber" made a deep impression on us. Kazbegi's heroes awakened in our youthful hearts a love for our country, and each of us, on leaving school, was inspired with an eagerness to serve his country. But none of us had a clear idea what form this service should take.'[2] Since Djugashvili was careful to conceal his rebellious sentiments from his teachers they regarded him as an exemplary pupil and helped him to the next stage of his career.

[1] L. Berya, *On the History of the Bolshevik Organizations in Transcaucasia*, p. 11; F. Makharadze, *Istorya Rabochevo Dvizhenya v Gruzii*, pp. 114–28; S. T. Arkomed, *Rabocheye Dvizhenie i Sotsial-Demokratya na Kavkaze*, pp. 49–50.

[2] E. Yaroslavsky, op. cit., pp. 9–10.

That next stage was his matriculation, in the autumn of 1894, at the Theological Seminary of Tiflis. His mother's dream seemed to be coming true. As the poor washerwoman was unable to contribute to his upkeep at the seminary, the head-master of the Gori school and the local priest succeeded in obtaining a scholarship for him. The promising boy must have felt encouraged by the prospect opening before him. The mere change from the small dreamy county town to the sprawling and turbulent capital of the Caucasus was dazzling. At the age of fifteen he was mature enough to realize the advantages of his new position, advantages that not so long ago were unattainable to peasant children. He must have travelled the forty miles to Tiflis with an exhilarating sense of his own social advancement, infinitely more real than the one that had lured his father on the journey from Didi-Lilo to Gori some twenty years before.

. . . .

His stay at the Theological Seminary lasted from October 1894 till May 1899. For his intellectual development these were decisive, formative years. What broader influences were now to mould his mind?

In the last decade of the nineteenth century two problems agitated Georgian society: Georgian–Russian relations; and the consequences of the abolition of serfdom in the Caucasus.

Throughout the century Tsarist Russia was engaged in con-quering the Caucasus and consolidating the conquest. Georgia, which had been a Russian vassal since 1783, completely lost her independence. The lot of the Georgians was in some respects similar to that of the Poles. But unlike the Poles, who in every generation rose in arms to fight for their independence, the Georgians made no serious attempt to break away from Russia. With them anti-Russian feeling combined with a relative in-difference to national aspirations. Their grievance against Russia was tempered by the consciousness that Georgia had no chance of maintaining her independence in any case, and that of all her possible conquerors Russia was to be dreaded least. The last Georgian kings had surrendered to the Russian Tsar when Turkey and Persia had threatened to conquer their country. Religious considerations determined the choice—

Georgia, like Russia, belonged to the Greek Orthodox Church.[1] In Russian eyes the Caucasus was a *place d'armes* against the Ottoman Empire, second in importance only to the Danubian countries. Russia built the great Georgian military road and then the network of Caucasian railways, thereby stimulating industrial development in the province. This was one of the redeeming features of Russian domination.

Another was Russia's cultural influence upon Georgia. Although the Georgians prided themselves on their ancient civilization, which was much older than the Russian, their outlook was that of an oriental half-tribal and half-feudal community. *Vis-à-vis* Georgia, Russia represented Europe. 'Under the influence of western European and especially Russian civilization', writes the historian G. Khachapuridze, 'European customs and manners penetrated into the life of the upper classes of Georgia.'[2] The policy of the Tsars was full of contradictions. On the one hand, they strove to Russify the country. On the other, they tried to ensure the loyalty of the Georgian gentry and clergy. The last Georgian dynasties were deported either to central Russia or to Siberia; but the sons of the deported kings were allowed to do valuable cultural work for their people—from St. Petersburg. Some of them, such as the brothers Bagrationi, became the spokesmen of Georgian 'enlightenment', translated many European literary works into Georgian, and acquainted Russian society with Georgian literature and history. Tsar Nicolai I even appointed Teimuraz Bagrationi an honorary member of the Imperial Academy.

Parallel with these influences Russian revolutionary ideas spread into the Caucasus. The man who conquered the province for the Tsars was General Yermolov, the hero of the battle of Borodino in 1812. This 'pro-Consul of the Caucasus' showed some leaning towards the Decembrists, the leaders of the Liberal revolt which took place in St. Petersburg in December 1825.

---

[1] In 1899, Ilya Chavchavadze, the most prominent nationalist Liberal leader and Georgian writer, thus summed up the experience of a century of Russian domination: 'There was no other way out. George XII [the last king of eastern Georgia] had to lean either on Turkey or on Iran or on Russia in order to save Georgia.... He had to make the choice quickly. George naturally turned towards co-religionist Russia. This was dictated to him by the will of his ancestors, who had ever since 1491 repeatedly negotiated with Russia, hoping to obtain her support.' Quoted from G. Khachapuridze's essay on 'Georgia and Russia in the Nineteenth Century' in *Voprosy Istorii*, nos. 5–6, 1946.   [2] Ibid.

He sheltered great writers who had been mixed up with the rebels: Pushkin and Griboyedov, who was his minister and political adviser, Bestuzhev (Marlinsky), and others. A whole regiment which had taken part in the rebellion was deported to the Caucasus; and in it many cashiered officer-intellectuals served as privates. The deportees kept in touch with the few educated Georgians and strongly influenced them. They sympathized, of course, with Georgian patriotism, and, more advanced than their Georgian friends, they advocated the emancipation of the Georgian peasants.

These early contacts prepared the ground for a continuous influence of Russian liberal and revolutionary ideas. The Tsars themselves greatly, though unwittingly, contributed to this, inasmuch as they chose the Caucasus as one of the places to which political offenders were deported. In every generation new Russian revolutionaries, and new ideas, made their appearance at Tiflis, Kutais, and elsewhere in the province. The military rebels and writers of the early part of the century were succeeded by *Narodniks*, agrarian Socialists, from the ranks of the Russian aristocracy and civil service. Then came Polish insurgents and Russian terrorists, to be followed, towards the end of the century, by a quite new revolutionary type, Marxist factory workers deported from central Russia. Among the latter were Mikhail Kalinin, the future President of the Soviet Union, and Sergo Alliluyev, Bolshevik organizer and Djugashvili-Stalin's father-in-law.

While the Russian opposition thus exported its advanced ideas into the Caucasus, the Tsars did their utmost to keep the social structure of the country as backward as seemed compatible with strategic interest.[1] In Russia serfdom was abolished in 1861. The emancipation of the Georgian peasants was delayed until 1864–9, and even after that—and, indeed, until

---

[1] How difficult it is to strike a balance between Russia's beneficial and harmful influences upon Georgia can be seen from an incident, which was not without a pleasantly comic touch, at a Congress of Soviet historians in 1929. The prominent Georgian Marxist F. Makharadze gave a lecture in which he dwelt with some emphasis on the better aspects of Georgia's association with Russia. This provoked a protest from Professor Pokrovsky, then the leading Russian historian: 'Comrade Makharadze has shown us Russians far too much indulgence. In the past *we, the Russians*, and I am speaking as a Great Russian of the purest possible blood, in the past we, the Russians, have been the worst plunderers one can imagine.' *Trudy Pervoi Vsesoyuznoi Konferentsii Istorikov-Marksistov*, vol. i, pp. 494–5.

1912—serfdom, in the form of 'temporary servitude', lingered in Georgia. The Russian administration, anxious to retain the support of the Georgian gentry, postponed reform. It was compelled to tackle it only when news of the emancipation of the Russian peasants had spread into the Caucasian country-side. The serfs were in a rebellious mood; and in view of their long record of *jacquerie*, it was too dangerous to delay their emancipation any longer.[1] But reform there was much more favourable to the landlords than it was even in Russia. The peasants obtained personal freedom, but roughly half the land they had held as serfs was taken from them. They had to pay compensation altogether beyond their means for the land they were allowed to retain. The economic dependence of the peasants on their landlords presently expressed itself either in sharecropping, as it did in the South after the abolition of slavery in America, or in agreements on 'temporary servitude'. As late as 1911 an authority by no means inimical to Tsardom wrote: 'In Russia chattel-slavery is now remembered as a nightmare that has long passed into history. But in Transcaucasia, especially in Georgia, no law has yet been passed to stop temporary servitude. . . . The economic dependence of our peasants . . . has grown in the last fifty years and assumed a new form of serfdom.'[2]

Serfdom thus permeated the whole atmosphere in which the young Djugashvili lived. It weighed heavily not only upon the peasants directly affected by it but also upon human relations at large, upon family, Church, and school, upon psychological attitudes, upon the whole manner of life.[3] Up to a point this was, of course, true of the whole of the Tsarist Empire. Comparing the abolition of serfdom in Russia with the emancipation

---

[1] Peasant risings broke out in Georgia in 1804, 1811, 1812, 1820, 1830, 1837, 1841, 1857, 1866. At the time of the Crimean war Russian commanders were very uneasy about the attitude of the Caucasian serfs. It was claimed that the British envoy at Trebizond was arming them for rebellion. See P. I. Lyashchenko, *Istorya Narodnovo Khozyaistva SSSR*, vol. i, p. 557, F. Makharadze in *Trudy*, &c., vol. i, p. 485 ff., and G. V. Khachapuridze, 'Krestyanskoye Dvizhenie v Gruzii' in *Ocherki po Istorii Rabochevo i Krestyanskovo Dvizhenya v Gruzii*, pp. 13–105.

[2] The authority quoted is the *Kavkazkoye Khozyaistvo*, organ of the Imperial Institute of Agriculture. See *Istorya Klasovoi Borby v Zakavkazi*, vol. i, pp. 10–15.

[3] The Georgian poet G. Leonidze, who has written an adulatory epic poem on Stalin's childhood and youth, suggests that Stalin's serf-grandfather was tortured to death by his landlord. (The poem was translated into Russian by N. Tikhonov and published in book form in 1944.)

of the American negroes, Lenin pointed out that the Russian reform of 1861 had been much less thoroughgoing than its American counterpart: 'Therefore now, half a century later', he concluded, 'the Russians show *many more* marks of slavery than the negroes.'[1] In this bitter remark Lenin undoubtedly exaggerated. The exaggeration was natural to the revolutionary propagandist who was impatient to see Russian society shedding once for all the legacy of its feudal past. But what was not quite true of the Russians was still true of the Caucasians. Their social existence showed all too many and all too fresh 'marks of slavery'. Crude and open dependence of man upon man, a rigid undisguised social hierarchy, primitive violence and lack of human dignity, characterized the way of life that had grown out of serfdom. Dissimulation, deception, and violence were the chief weapons of the oppressed, who had been kept in darkness and were as a rule incapable of defending themselves by open, organized action.

. . . .

The Theological Seminary of Tiflis was a strange institution. It was the most important, though not the only, high school in Georgia and, indeed, in the whole of the Caucasus. It was the main breeding-ground of the local intelligentsia. It was also something like a spiritual preserve of serfdom. It was here that advanced social and political ideas most directly infiltrated and clashed with feudal-ecclesiastical habits of mind.

The seminary looked like a barrack. Inside, life was strictly regimented by austere monks. Once the door closed behind the entrant he was expected to sever himself entirely from the outside world. Seminarists were supposed to stay indoors day and night, though two hours' leave could be obtained on application to the monk in charge of the class. The day's programme was filled with lectures on scholastic theology and prayers, endless prayers.[2] Pupils from poor homes led a half-hungry existence, and twenty to thirty students were herded together in one dormitory. Spiritually, the school was half monastery and half barrack. 'Life was sad and monotonous', says an ex-student.

---

[1] Lenin, *Sochinenya*, vol. xviii, p. 508.

[2] 'The students were set essays on such subjects as "In what language did Balaam's ass speak?" ' alleges one of Stalin's biographers.

'Locked in day and night within barrack walls, we felt like prisoners who must spend years there, without being guilty of anything. All of us were despondent and sullen. Stifled in the rooms and corridors . . . youthful joy almost never asserted itself. When from time to time youthful temperament did break through, it was immediately suppressed by the monks and monitors.'[1] Students were not allowed to borrow books from secular libraries; only literature authorized by the monks was to be read. The seminary was, of course, also an instrument of Russification. Any infringement of regulations was punished by confinement to the cells. The monks assiduously spied on the thoughts and the doings of their pupils, searching their belongings, eavesdropping, and denouncing them to the Principal on the slightest suspicion.

This grim seminary was, however, also an important centre of political opposition. Many men who were to become national figures and leaders of public opinion, not only Georgian but Russian public opinion, spent their formative years within its walls. In 1930 the historical faculty of the Transcaucasian Communist University published the archives of the Tiflis *gendarmerie* containing reports on manifestations of 'political disloyalty' in the seminary. These reports, covering a period of twenty years, from 1873 up to the time when Djugashvili was admitted, give a good insight into the ferment of ideas among the students.[2]

As early as 1873 a colonel of the *gendarmerie* informed his superiors that intercepted letters showed that some of the students had read the works of Darwin, Buckle, Mill, and Chernyshevsky. A search was ordered and two more 'seditious' books were found: Renan's *La Vie de Jésus* and Hugo's *Napoléon le Petit*. It was ascertained that three teachers lectured to their classes 'in a liberal spirit', a crime for which the Principal dismissed them and denounced them to the *gendarmerie*. A number were convicted, some because they had known of the offences and refrained from informing against the culprits.[3] The report emphasizes that the offenders were animated by Georgian patriotism.

---

[1] Quoted in L. Trotsky's *Stalin*, p. 14.
[2] *Istorya Klasovoi Borby v Zakavkazi*, vol. i, Appendix, pp. 31–100.
[3] Ibid., p. 83.

The ferment led to a dramatic event in June 1886, when Joseph Lagiyev, a student expelled for his anti-Russian attitude, assassinated the Principal, Pavel Chudetsky. The assassin was the son of a priest in the county of Gori. The chief of the Tiflis *gendarmerie* reported: 'In comparison with the Russian seminaries the Tiflis Seminary finds itself in the most unfavourable conditions. The pupils who come to the seminary . . . often show . . . an anti-religious frame of mind and are hostile to the Russian element. It is often impossible to reform such pupils, because of the extreme irritability and the morbid *amour propre* of the natives.'[1] He added that several Georgian newspapers, just banned, had incited the public against Russia and made the seminary a rampart of Georgian patriotism. The seminary was closed for several months. A curious part was played in this incident by His Eminence the Exarch of Georgia, Paul, who suggested to the chief of the *gendarmerie* that the assassination was a deed not of an individual but of a secret organization. He mentioned a certain Sylvester Djibladze, who himself had assailed the Principal a year before, as the chief suspect. Djibladze was to become one of the founders of a Social Democratic organization and one of Djugashvili's political tutors. Among the students expelled in 1886 was also Mikhail Tskhakaya, the son of a priest and afterwards a friend of Lenin, a member of the Bolshevik Central Committee, and President of Soviet Georgia.

A formal strike of all Georgian pupils at the seminary occurred only a few months before Djugashvili's admittance. On 4 December 1893 General Yankovsky of the Tiflis *gendarmerie* cabled to St. Petersburg: 'The majority of pupils of the Orthodox Seminary has declared a strike, demanding the removal of several tutors and the establishment of a Chair for Georgian literature.'[2] The Exarch of Georgia spent a whole day with the pupils, trying in vain to dissuade them from the strike. The Principal asked the police for help. The police closed the seminary and compelled the pupils to return to their homes. But its chief reported uneasily that 'many intelligent people consider the closing of the seminary to be an act of injustice towards the pupils who defended their national interests, according to their ideas'. On leaving school, the students took an oath

[1] Ibid., pp. 89-90.　　　　　　　　　[2] Ibid., p. 92.

of solidarity. Eighty-seven of them, however, were expelled from the seminary before the end of the term. Mikhail Tskhakaya was again mentioned as the chief organizer of the revolt. Among the expelled was Lado Ketskhoveli, a former pupil of the Gori school, only three years older than Djugashvili, soon to become Djugashvili's political mentor.[1] In none of these reports is there any mention of Socialist propaganda. Outraged Georgian patriotism was the main motive of the demonstrations. .

When the fifteen-year-old Djugashvili appeared in the seminary, the echoes of the last strike were still very fresh. Pupils must have discussed the event and commented on the expulsion of the eighty-seven, and the new-comer could not but sympathize with the demand that his native literature be taught in the seminary. He was thus from the beginning affected by the political ferment. But as in Gori so here he concealed his feelings from his teachers. As in Gori so here he was a model pupil, able, diligent, attentive. Doubtless he watched his new surroundings with avid curiosity. The Principal was the Russian monk Hermogenes; the Inspector was the Georgian Abashidze, who, precisely because he was Georgian, was anxious to ingratiate himself with the Russian authorities by an extravagant display of servility. Here the young Djugashvili could observe at close quarters the workings of autocratic rule on a small scale. Those in authority themselves lived in tension and fear: the Russian Principal remembered his assassinated predecessor; the Georgian Inspector was as terrified at the slightest sign of his superiors' displeasure as at the thought of the plots that might be hatched in the corners of the long and dark corridors and in students' dormitories. Yet the closer the monks watched their pupils, the more assiduously they eavesdropped on them, the more frequently they searched the pupils' coats and cases for forbidden books, the more effectively did heresy spread within the walls of the seminary. The recently expelled students acquired a moral authority in the eyes of the younger pupils, and they somehow managed to keep in touch with their former colleagues and to make their influence felt inside the ecclesiastical fortress.

While he was still in the first form, Djugashvili must have

[1] *Istorya Klasovoi Borby v Zakavkazi*, p. 100; *Razkazy o Velikom Stalinie*, p. 79; S. Alliluyev, *Proidennyi Put*, p. 86.

made frequent half-stealthy excursions into town and got in touch with the members of the opposition. This can be seen from the fact that a poem by him was published in the Georgian periodical *Iberya*, edited by the liberal patriot Ilya Chavchavadze, on 29 October 1895, almost exactly a year after Djugashvili's arrival at Tiflis. He dedicated the verses, patriotic in character but coloured with social radicalism, to a well-known Georgian poet, R. Eristavi. It appeared under the signature 'Soselo' ('little Joe'), for the author must have been anxious to conceal his identity from the seminary authorities.[1] His other offence was to borrow books from a circulating library in town. Apart from Georgian poetry, the masterpieces of Russian and European literature were his favourite reading. Most of all he enjoyed the three great Russian satirical writers, Saltykov-Shchedrin, Gogol, and Chekhov, whom he afterwards frequently quoted in speeches and articles. Victor Hugo's novels and Thackeray's *Vanity Fair*, in Russian translations, figure among the foreign books he read. Of greater importance to his development were popular books on Darwinian biology, on economics and sociology. At that time positivist and materialist conceptions of nature and society exercised a strong influence upon young Liberals and Socialists.

Nearly all the memoirists, whether friendly or hostile to Stalin, agree with the impression of him given by G. Glurdjidze, one of his school-fellows, who in the thirties was still a teacher at Gori:

We would sometimes read in chapel during service, hiding the book under the pews. Of course, we had to be extremely careful not to be caught by the masters. Books were Joseph's inseparable friends; he would not part with them even at meal times. . . . When asked a question, Joseph would as a rule take his time in answering. One of our curious pleasures in the unbearably stifling atmosphere of the seminary was singing. We were always overjoyed when Soso arranged us in an improvised choir and, in his clear and pleasant voice, struck up our favourite folk-songs.[2]

Another writer, Iremashvili, stresses, however, a less pleasant

---

[1] Under this signature the verses were reprinted in two anthologies of Georgian poetry in 1899 and 1907. See M. Kelendjeridze, 'Stikhy Yunovo Stalina' in *Razkazy o Velikom Staline*, pp. 67–70.

[2] Quoted from E. Yaroslavsky, op. cit., p. 15.

aspect of Djugashvili's character. He, too, describes Djugashvili as one of the chief debaters among the seminarists, more knowledgeable than most of his comrades, and able to advance his argument with much stubbornness and polemical skill. But in his craving for prominence, Djugashvili could not easily bear to be overshadowed by others. He would become fretful whenever his arguments were effectively challenged, and would become incensed and sulky at the slightest set-back in debate. Sometimes, so a few of his class-mates were to recollect, he would nurse a grudge against a successful opponent and seek to revenge himself by malignant gossip and slander. Such behaviour, though not perhaps exceptional among boys of his age, made him a difficult companion.

It was only at the beginning of his third year at the seminary that the monks began to notice that their promising pupil was going astray. In November 1896 one of them made the following entry in the conduct-book: 'It appears that Djugashvili has a ticket to the Cheap Library, from which he borrows books. To-day I confiscated Victor Hugo's *Toilers of the Sea* in which I found the said library ticket.' The Principal acknowledged the report with the remark: 'Confine him to the punishment cell for a prolonged period. I have already warned him once about an unsanctioned book, *Ninety-Three* by Victor Hugo.'[1] Indeed, Hugo's famous novel on the French Revolution could hardly have helped to prepare its young reader for the career of a priest. Similar entries appeared in the conduct-book more and more frequently: 'At 11 p.m. I took away from Joseph Djugashvili Letourneau's *Literary Evolution of the Nations*, which he had borrowed from the Cheap Library. . . . Djugashvili was discovered reading the said book on the chapel stairs. This is the thirteenth time this student has been discovered reading books borrowed from the Cheap Library. I handed over the book to the Father Supervisor.' This was written in March 1897, only four months after the first complaint. The Principal decreed: 'Confine him to the punishment cell for a prolonged period with a strict warning.'[2] The complaints mention no socialist, let alone Marxian, books found on the delinquent. But, to judge from the reminiscences of his contemporaries and from his own subsequent doings, he must have made his first

---

[1] E. Yaroslavsky, op. cit., pp. 16-17.   [2] Ibid., p. 17.

acquaintance with Socialist and Marxian theories while he was in the upper forms. It was then, too, that he joined a secret debating circle within the seminary itself and a clandestine Socialist organization in town called *Messame Dassy*. He joined the latter in August 1898.[1] Socialist books were apparently too dangerous to be brought into the seminary. Nor were they readily available. Only one copy of Marx's *Capital* in a Russian translation, Yaroslavsky tells us, was then obtainable in Tiflis, and the young Socialists copied from it by hand. One may assume that Djugashvili read or scanned books and pamphlets by Socialist writers in those few hours which he managed to spend outside the seminary.

Messame Dassy, the organization he joined when he was nearly nineteen, was founded in 1893. This was one of the first Social Democratic groups in Tiflis, although its outlook was still tinged with Georgian patriotism. It assumed the name *Messame Dassy* (The Third Group) to distinguish itself from *Meori Dassy* (The Second Group), a progressive Liberal organization which had led the Georgian intelligentsia in the eighties.[2] Among the founders of *Messame Dassy* were Noah Jordania, K. Chkheidze, and G. Tseretelli, who were soon to become well known outside Georgia as the spokesmen of moderate socialism. One of the energetic promoters was Sylvester Djibladze, the same that had been expelled from the seminary for an assault on the Principal. The leaders of *Messame Dassy* expounded their views in the columns of the Liberal newspaper *Kvali* (The Furrow).

Much later Djugashvili himself thus recalled the motives of his adherence to socialism: 'I became a Marxist because of my social position (my father was a worker in a shoe factory and my mother was also a working woman), but also . . . because of the harsh intolerance and Jesuitical discipline that crushed me so mercilessly at the Seminary. . . . The atmosphere in which I lived was saturated with hatred against Tsarist oppression.' Events outside provided the final stimulus. In those years there were turbulent strikes by the Tiflis workers, the first

[1] *J. V. Stalin* (Kratkaya Biografya), p. 24.
[2] *Pirveli Dassy* (The First Group), supported by progressive men among the Georgian nobility, had advocated the abolition of serfdom even before 1865. L. Berya, op. cit., p. 203, and S. T. Arkomed, op. cit., pp. 172–9.

strikes in the capital of the Caucasus. Their effect on the working class and the radical intelligentsia can hardly be imagined now. In later years strikes were to become common; their sheer frequency was to deprive them of their exciting quality. But the first strikes were a revelation of unsuspected strength in Labour; they were a new weapon in the social contest; and, as new weapons usually do, they evoked exaggerated hopes and fears. Rulers and ruled alike saw in them the sign of great events impending and of dramatic changes—and, as far as Russia was concerned, they were not wrong.

Tiflis was then the centre of an industrial revolution on a small scale. Its life reflected the fresh impact of industrial capitalism on the oriental, tribal, and feudal Caucasus. 'The country, sparsely populated in the years after the Reform, inhabited by highlanders and staying aloof from the development of world economy, aloof even from history, was becoming transformed into a country of oil industrialists, wine merchants, grain and tobacco manufacturers.' Thus the still unknown Lenin described the state of the country by the end of the century. The oil industries at Baku and Batum were being developed with the help of English and French capital. To the industries enumerated by Lenin, the mining of the rich manganese ore of Chiaturi was soon to be added. In 1886–7 the total value of industrial production of two Georgian regions, Tiflis and Kutais, amounted to only 10 million roubles. Within four years its value was more than trebled. In 1891–2 it amounted to 32 million roubles.[1] In the same period the number of industrial workers rose from 12,000 to 23,000, not counting railwaymen. Tiflis was the main junction on the Transcaucasian railway connecting the Caspian coast with the Black Sea, Baku with Batum. The railway workshops became the main industry of Tiflis itself, and the most important nerve-centre in the clandestine Caucasian labour movement that was now springing up. These workshops and the noisy Asiatic bazaars were the two contrasting elements in the life of the town. The young Djugashvili may have spent some hours observing the ways and habits of Oriental traders—these were certainly to leave an imprint on his mind. Nevertheless, that

---

[1] F. Makharadze, *Trudy*, &c., vol. i, pp. 489–90, and *Ocherki po Istorii Rabochevo Krestyanskovo Dvizhenya v Gruzii*, pp. 115–28.

oriental world, 'aloof even from history', was not for him. He was attracted by the new element in Caucasian life.

Two or three of the would-be clerics, turned revolutionaries, had already become his mentors. Apart from Sylvester Djibladze, a leading figure among the adherents of *Messame Dassy* and too important to be the novice's intimate friend, he used to meet two others who were his tutors as well as friends. They were Sasha Tsulukidze and Lado Ketskhoveli. Tsulukidze, only three years older than Djugashvili, was already a man of letters of some standing among the *Messame Dassyists*. He served the cause with fervour but was himself devoured by the tuberculosis that was to kill him five or six years later. His essays and articles published in local Georgian newspapers showed his wide knowledge of sociology and were written with genuine brilliance and literary flair. Among his works there was a notable popularization of Marx's economic theory.[1] Together with Sasha Tsulukidze, Djugashvili sometimes visited the editorial offices of *Kvali* and listened, at first respectfully and later with a half-ironical smile, to the words of wisdom spoken by its semi-Liberal and semi-Socialist editors.

His other teacher-friend, Ketskhoveli, was no man of letters. His was an altogether more practical mind. Having embraced the new faith, Ketskhoveli was mainly interested in the steps needed to make others embrace it. He had already seen something of the world outside the Caucasus. One of the 'eighty-seven' expelled from the seminary in 1894, he then went to Kiev, an old centre of spiritual and political life, less provincial than Tiflis. There he spent several years and got in touch with clandestine groups of Socialists who had made contact with like-minded people in Petersburg and even with exiled leaders in Switzerland, France, and England. He had come back to the Caucasus eager to do something, to take the movement in his native province out of its swaddling-clothes. He looked round to see whether it would not be possible to set up a secret printing press, in his view the first solid base for any group of revolutionary propagandists. The local semi-Socialist and semi-Liberal Georgian newspapers were of no use: their editors had

---

[1] Stalin later recalled Tsulukidze's memory with gratitude. In 1927 he saw to it that the Soviet State publishers reprinted in book form Tsulukidze's essays, scattered over many little Georgian periodicals.

to look over their shoulders after every word they wrote, and to submit every article to Tsarist censorship. Such timid and emasculated propaganda as they were able to make could convince nobody and led nowhere. At all costs, they, the younger revolutionaries, must now gain their freedom from censorship. That meant a secret press. It was towards such practical matters that Ketskhoveli turned Djugashvili's mind when the latter became a member of *Messame Dassy*.

Ketskhoveli and Tsulukidze saw to it that the new apprentice to revolution was given a specific job, running a few workers' study circles. His task was to lecture on socialism to a few tobacco workers, masons, shoemakers, weavers, printers, and conductors of the local horse-trams. The workers would gather in small groups, a dozen or at most a score in each. Every volunteer student would be given a similar assignment, for the young organization badly needed people ready to enlighten those of its members who could not afford to read the books and brochures that expounded its doctrine. The circles met in the workers' own overcrowded slum-dwellings and filled the air with the biting smoke of *makhorka* and the smell of sweat and squalor, while one member watched the street outside to see that the safety of the others was not endangered by the police. The lecturing seminarist probably got a lot of moral satisfaction out of the work. His labours were rewarded by the satisfactory sense of his own promotion. Here he was, ostensibly one of the meek flock shepherded by the monk Abashidze, laying spiritual dynamite at the foundations of Empire and Church. He was respectfully listened to by workmen, often much older than himself, and accepted by them as their authority and guide.

After such a meeting it was hard and even humiliating to have to rush back to the sombre seminary, to explain himself to the monks, to invent excuses for his unusually long absence, to put on a pious mask, and join the rest of the flock at singing prayers in the chapel. This was a double life in a double sense. Not only had the disbeliever to pretend orthodoxy; the revolutionary, already a somebody in the town and beginning to comport himself like a public figure, had to relapse into the role of a pupil, not yet grown up, ordered about and bullied by superiors. How long could he go on?

During his last year or two at the seminary Djugashvili must often have pondered this question. He was deceiving the monks most impudently and hypocritically; but this gave him no scruples or qualms. He was only countering deception with deception. Were they not spying on him and searching his belongings in his absence? Were not their teachings one monstrous deception? His own hypocrisy was only an answer to theirs. In this duel of lies and hoodwinking he certainly came off the better; and no doubt his success and the amusement it afforded helped him to tolerate a situation that was almost unbearable. He might, of course, pack up one day and say good-bye to the monks. But what next? He had no livelihood outside the seminary. The organization was terribly poor and could not help him. He did not wish to become a burden on his mother. Nor was the prospect of becoming a factory hand or a clerk in any way attractive. Unpleasant as the seminary was, it still left him with enough time for arguing, dreaming, and reading; and these he would not easily give up. A more impulsive or idealistically ambitious young man would have banged the door of the seminary and damned the consequences. But he was the son of ex-serfs, and though he was now working to change the life of a whole people, he had inherited something of the peasant-like immobility and inertia, born from fear of change. It was true that remaining at the seminary demanded constant concealment and dissimulation; but these he had had to practise from childhood; and they came to him now almost as second nature.

Nevertheless, his position was becoming more and more difficult. The entries in the conduct-book, made in the last months of his stay at the seminary, contain no mention of any Socialist propaganda on his part. He apparently managed to conceal this side of his activities. But his conflicts with authority grew ever sharper. A report of 29 September 1898 stated: 'At 9 p.m. a group of students gathered in the dining hall around Joseph Djugashvili, who read them books not sanctioned by the Seminary authorities, in view of which the students were searched.' A few weeks later it was noted that 'in the course of a search of students ... Joseph Djugashvili tried several times to enter into an argument ... expressing dissatisfaction with the repeated searches . . . and declaring that such searches were never made in other Seminaries. Djugashvili is generally disrespectful and rude towards persons in authority. . . .'[1]

Not more than a few months after he joined *Messame Dassy* his dilemma was solved for him by the monks. On 29 May 1899 he was expelled from the seminary on the ground that for 'unknown reasons' he did not attend examination.[2] He himself later stated that he was turned out for 'propagating Marxism'. This was not the reason given by the authorities of the seminary; but they undoubtedly suspected political disloyalty. The outcast had few regrets as he left the half-monastery, half-barrack in which he had spent five important years.

. . . .

The fact that Djugashvili-Stalin's parents were born serfs distinguishes him from almost all the other leading figures in the revolution. Most of them came from quite different walks of life, from the gentry, the middle classes, and the intelligentsia. As an undergraduate Lenin, with acute intellectual curiosity, saw peasant life at close quarters. But he, the son of an ennobled school inspector, was neither in it nor of it. Trotsky first saw poverty and exploitation from the window of the home of an upstart Jewish landowner, whose son he was. Zinoviev, Kamenev, Bukharin, Rakovsky, Radek, Lunacharsky, Chicherin, and scores of others knew the evils against which they had themselves girded from a much greater distance. To most of them even capitalist exploitation, let alone serfdom, were sociological formulas into which they probed with varying degrees of penetration; the realities behind the formulas were no part of their own personal experiences. Some prominent Bolsheviks like Kalinin, Tomsky, and Shlyapnikov were workmen themselves; and like most Russian workers they still had roots in the country-side. But even of these almost none had in his youth breathed the atmosphere of serfdom as directly and painfully as did Djugashvili-Stalin.

The twenty-year-old Djugashvili had certainly risen high above his original environment. He now belonged to the intelligentsia, not, of course, to the settled and respectable layer that well knew its place and worth in society, but to the semi-nomad fringe of *déclassés*. Nothing, however, could take

---

[1] E. Yaroslavsky, op. cit., pp. 16–17.   [2] Ibid.

from him an almost sensuous feeling of closeness to those who
were at the very bottom of the social pyramid. The revolutionaries from the upper classes knew from personal contact only
an *élite* of the working class, intelligent workmen who were
susceptible to Socialist propaganda and eager to make friends
with idealistic intellectuals. They would describe the great inert
mass that was not so accessible to Socialist notions as the backward and unconscious sections of the proletariat. The Marxian
revolutionaries had some idea of the dead weight of that backwardness. They remembered the lot of upper-class revolutionaries of a previous generation who idealistically 'went to the
people' to work for their weal in their own midst, only to be
bestially massacred by suspicious peasants or betrayed by them
to the gendarmes. But the Marxists hoped that enlightenment
and political experience would eventually bring to socialism
even the backward and the unconscious. Meanwhile they, the
theorists and the propagandists, had really no common language with the still unawakened masses. On the other hand,
the first impulses that pushed young people from the upper
classes towards socialism were usually those of humanitarian
sympathy mixed with a sense of guilt. Such feelings made them
see the oppressed classes as the embodiment of virtue and
nobility of spirit.

The young Djugashvili must have had quite an exceptional,
an almost instinctive, sensitiveness towards that element of
backwardness in Russian life and politics, a sensitiveness that
was to grow even stronger in future years. Though he, too,
would now be chiefly interested in the advanced workmen,
because it was only through them that the backward mass could
be approached and shaken from its meekness and inertia, he
would not at heart give himself to sanguine hopes or idealistic
generalizations about the working class. He would treat with
sceptical distrust not only the oppressors, the landlords, the
capitalists, the monks, and the Tsarist gendarmes, but also the
oppressed, the workers and the peasants whose cause he had embraced. There was no sense of guilt, not a trace of it, in his
socialism. No doubt he felt some sympathy with the class into
which he had been born; but his hatred of the possessing and
ruling classes must have been much stronger. The class hatred
felt and preached by the revolutionaries from the upper classes

was a kind of secondary emotion that grew in them and was cultivated by them from theoretical conviction. In Djugashvili class hatred was not his second nature—it was his first. Socialist teachings appealed to him because they seemed to give moral sanction to his own emotion. There was no shred of sentimentalism in his outlook. His socialism was cold, sober, and rough.

These features of his character were to serve him well in the future. But they were also bound up with important handicaps. The revolutionaries from the upper classes came into the Socialist movement with inherited cultural traditions. They rebelled against the beliefs and prejudices of their native environment, but they also brought into the milieu of the revolution some of the values and qualities of their own milieu —not only knowledge, but also refinement of thought, speech, and manners. Indeed, their Socialist rebellion was itself the product of moral sensitiveness and intellectual refinement. These were precisely the qualities that life had not been kind enough to cultivate in Djugashvili. On the contrary, it had heaped enough physical and moral squalor in his path to blunt his sensitiveness and his taste. Few of the other leaders suffered any sense of social inferiority. Most of them, had they chosen more peaceful and sheltered paths, could have made brilliant and respectable careers for themselves. A man of Lenin's genius might have become a great national leader in any régime. Trotsky was a man of letters of the highest repute. A Kamenev, a Lunacharsky, or a Bukharin could have risen to high standing in the academic world. All were highly gifted orators or writers, thinkers with great *élan*, imagination, and originality, which they showed at a surprisingly early age. Young Djugashvili had plenty of acumen and common sense; but imagination and originality were not his characteristics. He could lecture coherently on socialism to small circles of workers; but he was no orator. Nor, as time was to show, was he a brilliant writer. In caste-ridden, official Russia the son of Georgian peasants could not climb high on the social ladder, even with much ambition, pertinacity, and good luck. In the Church he would, at best, have become another Abashidze. Circumstances inevitably bred in him a certain sense of inferiority, of which he would not rid himself even in the Socialist underground.

CHAPTER II

The Socialist Underground

Makers of the future Revolution.—Marxists versus *Narodniks* (Agrarian Socialists).
—Plekhanov and Lenin: their influence in the Caucasus.—Stalin becomes a clerk
at the Tiflis Observatory, 1899.—His revolutionary activities drive him into the
underground, 1901.—Edits *Brdzola* (The Struggle).—His first political prose work.
—Attitude towards the *bourgeoisie*.—'The people's curiosity' as a weapon against
tyranny.—Stalin leaves Tiflis for Batum, 1901.—Begins to use the pseudonym
Koba (The Indomitable).—Sets up a secret press.—Clash between workers and
military.—Stalin arrested, 1902.

DJUGASHVILI joined *Messame Dassy* in August 1898. Earlier in
the year, in March, a few Socialists, less than a dozen, gathered
in the town of Minsk in a secret conference to proclaim the
foundation of the Russian Social Democratic Workers' Party.
The coincidence of dates shows that Djugashvili joined the
Socialist ranks at a significant moment, when the movement
was approaching a turning-point. Nothing like a nation-wide
Socialist party existed in Russia at the time. There were only
small groups of propagandists consisting mostly of intellectuals.
The arguments and discussions going on among these little
groups were hardly noticed by outsiders; and even now they
would be regarded by superficial students as so much doctrinaire
irrelevance. But the 'sectarian' propagandists were real makers
of history, the scientists or artists of the future Revolution.

Throughout the century the bolder spirits among the Russian
intelligentsia were in revolt against the oppressive autocracy of
the Tsars; but it was only towards the end of the century that
Marxian socialism became the dominant trend in the revolutionary opposition. Until late in the eighties an agrarian brand
of socialism, represented by the *Narodniks* or Populists, predominated. The *Narodniks* believed that Russia, agrarian and
feudal, would avoid the evils of modern profit-seeking industrialism, and that she would achieve a Socialist order all of
her own, based on the *Mir* or *Obshchina*, the primeval community of land that had survived in the country-side. All that
was needed for the creation of social and spiritual freedom was,

in their view, the abolition of serfdom and autocracy. Once these were won, Russia's Socialist salvation was secure; and the peasantry, not any industrial proletariat, would then be the leading class, the creative force of the nation. Most of the *Narodniks* were revolutionary Slavophiles, opposed to the spread of European influence in their country.

But from their own ranks another trend emerged, itself influenced by western European Socialist thought. In the year of Djugashvili's birth, a secret conference of the *Narodniks*, held at Voronezh, split into two groups: one stuck to the traditional agrarian views; the other, led by George Plekhanov, soon began to graft the ideas of western industrial socialism on to the Russian revolutionary movement. Plekhanov himself came to the fore as the most gifted expounder of Marxist philosophy and sociology in Russia, the teacher of Lenin and of a whole generation of Russian revolutionaries. Plekhanov made the confident forecast that capitalist industrialism was about to invade Russia and destroy its patriarchal-feudal structure and the primitive rural communes on which the *Narodniks* wanted to base their socialism. An urban industrial working class, he argued, was about to grow up in Russia, and would fight for industrial socialism very much on the western European pattern. The vision of a peculiarly Slavonic rural socialism springing straight from pure feudalism was Utopian, and would soon vanish into thin air. Plekhanov concluded that the revolutionaries must now begin to organize the industrial working class.

He was well ahead of his time. Modern industry was only beginning to strike its first, feeble roots in Russia. Only a very bold thinker could see much significance in its modest beginnings and stake all social and political hope on an almost non-existent industrial proletariat. The Marxists and not the *Narodniks* seemed to preach Utopia.[1]

The fundamental dispute was widened by a controversy over tactics. The *Narodniks* strove either to raise the peasants against autocracy, an endeavour in which they were not successful, or to overthrow it by attempts on the life of the Tsar himself or his ministers and governors. Since they believed that their

---

[1] Curiously enough, Marx himself refused to support the Russian Marxists in their controversy against the *Narodniks*. See his letters to Vera Zasulich in *Perepiska K. Marxa i F. Engelsa s russkimi politicheskimi deyatelami*.

agrarian socialism was already virtually in existence under the hard crust of feudal autocracy, it was, from their point of view, only natural that they should try to smash the crust. They achieved a seeming triumph in 1881 when they succeeded in assassinating Tsar Alexander II. The terrorists were men and women of the highest moral and intellectual qualities—'a phalanx of heroes reared, like Romulus and Remus, on the milk of the wild beast'. Most of them were the sons and daughters of aristocratic or at least noble families who offered their lives for the sake of the people—one of the central figures in the conspiracy was Sophia Perovskaya, the daughter of the Governor-General of St. Petersburg. Yet their very triumph—the assassination of the Tsar—became the source of their disillusionment and decline. They had expected the hated order to crumble under the blow. In reality, they managed to kill an autocrat but not autocracy. Alexander II was succeeded by Alexander III whose tyranny was much more cruel. The Marxists would have nothing to do with the terroristic methods. The assassination of individuals, or 'individual terror' as they called it, was useless. What was needed, they argued, was the overthrow of a system, and a system was not dependent on a handful of individuals. They set their hopes on the industrial proletariat that would act against autocracy *en masse*; but, since that proletariat was still numerically far too weak to act, they had no choice but to wait until the growth of industry produced the big battalions of workers. Meanwhile, they could only make propaganda, enlist converts to socialism, and set up loose groups of like-minded people.

Time proved the Marxian forecasts sound. As the years went by, industry and with it the working classes grew in numbers and strength, and labour troubles multiplied. In the nineties the doctrines of the *Narodniks* looked time-worn and stale in the eyes of young revolutionaries. When in 1894, the year Djugashvili entered the seminary, young Lenin published his pamphlet, *Who are the Friends of the People?*, in which he attacked the *Narodniks*, this was a nail in their coffin, although another and more up-to-date version of agrarian socialism was still to make its appearance some years later.

There was a curious paradox in the thought of the Russian Marxists. In their polemics against the *Narodniks* they argued that for socialism to become possible in Russia, capitalism must first develop. To them socialism without modern industry was a contradiction in terms. In western Europe, Socialists might well work for the overthrow of capitalism, but in Russia all hopes still rested on its growth and development. Since they saw in capitalism an indispensable half-way house on the road from feudalism to socialism, they stressed the advantages of that half-way house, its progressive features, its civilizing influence, its attractive atmosphere, and so on. Many of the early writings of Russian Marxists, including those of Plekhanov and Lenin and to a lesser extent even of Stalin, read almost like apologies for Liberal western European capitalism. The paradox inevitably led to equivocation. Among the propagandists some put the stronger emphasis on the one part of the Marxist argument, some on the other. Some looked to the objective—socialism; others had their eyes fixed on the half-way house of capitalism. In other words, some were Socialists, while others were bourgeois Liberals using the Marxian idiom to plead for progressive capitalism. Whereas in western Europe socialism itself was the illegitimate offspring of liberalism, in Russia liberalism was in part the outgrowth of socialism. The closer the fellow travellers came to the half-way house, the more clearly their differences came into the open.

By the turn of the century the split between the Marxists and the so-called legal Marxists became unbridgeable. The 'legal Marxists' (so called because they preached the doctrine only in that abstract form in which it was acceptable to the Tsarist censorship) were grouped around a few eminent economists and sociologists—Struve, Tugan-Baranovsky, Bulgakov, and others—who used the Marxist method in sociological and economic analysis, but ignored or rejected outright the revolutionary aspects of Marxism.[1] The split caused confusion among the adherents of Marxism, the more so because for a long time Marxism undoubtedly attracted quite moderate people.[2] Its criticism of 'individual terror' and its rebuffs to the

[1] In later years, the legal Marxists became the spokesmen of conservative liberalism and monarchism. Tugan-Baranovsky was known in the West as the author of a Marxist history of British trade cycles in the nineteenth century.

[2] It was a current joke that 'in all the world the Marxists are the party of the working class, only in Russia they are the party of big capital'. M. N. Pokrovsky, *Brief History of Russia*, vol. ii, p. 72.

organizers of assassination and attempts at assassination had made it appear the more moderate of the current revolutionary doctrines. Plekhanov and Lenin (and their less eminent friends —Axelrod, Zasulich, Martov) had to work hard to overcome the confusion, to restate the revolutionary conclusions of their teaching and sort out the Liberals from the Socialists.

The controversy raged in books, pamphlets, and periodicals. It spread to every centre of political opposition in Russia; and Tiflis, too, was affected by it. *Messame Dassy* was a loose group of all who swore by Marxist principles; but the outlook of its moderate members was tinged with 'legal Marxism'. The controversy was in a fairly advanced phase when Djugashvili joined *Messame Dassy*. The right wing, led by Noah Jordania, got the upper hand. Djugashvili joined the left wing minority.[1]

This controversy was hardly over when a new one arose. The first strikes and labour troubles stimulated a new trend called 'Economism'. This peculiar label was used by Russian Socialists to describe what the French called Syndicalism, that is non-political Trade Unionism. The 'Economists' wanted to confine their activities to supporting workers' claims for higher wages and better conditions of work, without bothering about politics. They feared that 'wild' political talk against the Tsar and propaganda for socialism would antagonize the working classes, whom they believed to be interested in bread-and-butter problems, and in little else. The politically minded Socialists retorted that the 'Economists' took a rather low and contemptuous view of the working class. Events, they argued, would show that workers could become the most politically minded class, provided Socialist propaganda drove home to them the importance of politics. They would certainly not rise above the bread-and-butter level if their leaders themselves were afraid of talking politics.

As late as 1901 the 'Economists' were still in a majority at Socialist conferences held abroad. But the politicians were not discouraged; and they set out to convince the wavering against

[1] Incidentally, Noah Jordania, the leader of the majority, was not a typical 'legal Marxist'—he was later the recognized leader of the Georgian Mensheviks. After 1917 he was to be elected President of the Georgian Republic. He was driven out of his country by the Soviet invasion of Georgia, ordered by Stalin personally in February 1921. The disputes that took place in Tiflis at the turn of the century were thus something like a prologue to future drama.

the majority. In the Caucasus in particular, the 'Economists' were for a short time on top of the politicians. However, agents sent out to Tiflis by Plekhanov and Lenin did some spade work there, and the influence of 'Economism' began to wane. The people with whom young Djugashvili mixed, Tsulukidze, Ketskhoveli, and others, as well as he himself, supported revolutionary politics against 'Economism'.

Finally, two other inter-connected points were claiming the attention of the young Socialists. Their numbers were now growing quite rapidly. By 1900 there were several hundreds of them in Tiflis alone. More important still, in the underground groups there were more workers than intellectuals; they had firm connexions with the factories and they were now able to approach the great mass of workers. The time was clearly ripe to pass from merely lecturing on Socialist principles before a few dozen chosen individuals to systematic trade-union and political work among the masses. In the Russian idiom, this was called 'the transition from propaganda to agitation'. The meaning of the word propaganda was quite different then from what it has become to-day. The word did not mean stunning the general public with clever tricks of political advertisement, 'selling an idea' to the credulous, or the artificial boosting and building up of leaders. It meant the exact opposite, the modest and earnest discussion of principles in small study groups, a traffic in ideas rather than slogans. Now, at the turn of the century, most Russian Socialists felt that such propaganda was no longer enough. But for systematic political work on a mass scale they needed an organized party with a recognized national leadership that would have at its command enough moral and material resources to be capable of leading, instructing, and co-ordinating the activities of the various local groups. What was needed, in other words, was a nation-wide party of some coherence and striking power.

For more than twenty years after Plekhanov split the conference of the *Narodniks* at Voronezh, no such party had come into being. Only local groups guided by local leaders existed; and this was still the position when Djugashvili became a Socialist. The conference that took place at Minsk in 1898 was the first attempt to create the party. But nearly all the participants were rounded up by the police, and their resolutions were destined to remain on paper for some time after. The chief spokesman of Marxism, Plekhanov, was living in exile, in western Europe, and he was tending to lose touch with Russia. The need for the unification of the scattered groups was felt acutely by the younger Socialists. Far away in north-east Siberia, in a village somewhere in the Yenissei province, 300 miles away from the nearest railway station, Lenin, now thirty years old, was waiting impatiently for the approaching end of his three-year banishment. In Siberia he had written several essays and a copious and weighty economic treatise on *The Development of Capitalism in Russia*, which at once gained him the reputation of a leading Marxist writer. But the exile was not satisfied with his literary success. He was devoured by impatience to do something to build up a real Socialist party.

Released from Siberia, Lenin got into touch with his friends in Petersburg and Moscow. They held the view that they ought to consult 'the grand old man' Plekhanov and his associates and co-operate with them. Lenin was only too eager to do so. Within a few months he went abroad and established links between the old and the young Marxists. The outcome was not yet a party but an enterprise which, though it was seemingly much more modest, was to take its place in Russian and, indeed, in world history. In the last days of 1900 the first copy of a new periodical called *Iskra* (The Spark) was published in Stuttgart. The name of the paper was meant to be symbolical—from that spark the fire of the Russian Revolution was to be fanned. The editors were not content simply to confine themselves to journalistic comment on current events. They saw to it that their paper reached readers in Russia regularly; copies were smuggled across the frontier by members of the underground. There was nothing extraordinary or novel in this; all the many Russian periodicals which had for decades been published by exiles went into Russia in much the same way, though perhaps less regularly. The really new feature of *Iskra*, a feature which was to make it a unique venture in the whole history of journalism, was that the paper was also the organizing centre of the underground party inside Russia. The Editorial Board appointed a number of canvassers and agents who travelled secretly all over the country, got into touch with local groups or set up groups where none existed, and saw to it that those groups kept up a regular correspondence with the Editorial Board abroad and also acted on its advice. Thus all the threads of the still uncoordinated clandestine movement were soon to converge on the editorial offices of *Iskra*, which were shifted from Munich to Geneva and then to London, outside the reach of the Tsarist police. The editors of the paper soon acquired a good insight into the strength and inner life of the groups scattered all over the Russian Empire; and from a team of commentators and journalists they became something like the real executive of the underground. Now they were in a position to shape the sprawling and still formless movement, to weld it into a national party. All Socialists in Russia who shared their views called themselves *Iskrovtsy* or *Iskra*-men. The modest journal thus became a lever of revolution.

The Caucasus was not overlooked by the canvassers of *Iskra*. In Tiflis, young Socialists were quick to label themselves *Iskra*-men, and Djugashvili was one of them. Like others, he now awaited impatiently the successive copies of the paper arriving by clandestine mail at rather long intervals. The advent of a new copy was a festive event. Here was the intellectual authority on which he could confidently lean, for each copy of *Iskra* brought food for thought and plenty of solid arguments that would come in very usefully in debates with opponents. The periodical also reinforced the young man's self-confidence. He could now confound his opponents with pointed arguments and sharp phrases coined by the leading theorists abroad and get from the people on the spot some of the credit due to those who had briefed him. He was, of course, too young and too little educated, though knowledgeable by local standards, to make any contribution of his own to *Iskra*. But his mind was trained enough to absorb and assimilate the main lines, if not all the subtle shades, of the views it propounded. To the workers of whom he had political charge he would now expound not only the general ideas of socialism and the reasons why Tsardom and capitalist exploitation should be opposed: he could also recount the specific arguments against agrarian socialism, legal Marxism, and economism. All his mental activity was now based on these lines of reasoning and they formed the gist of his own first writings in Georgian.

The two years after his expulsion from the seminary thus

became a most important phase of his mental and political development. When he left the seminary his Socialist views still seemed vague. He was attracted by Marxist theory. But he had hardly been familiar with it, let alone assimilated it. His Georgian patriotism was giving way to a broader loyalty, to the belief that international socialism would put an end to national and racial oppression as well as to economic exploitation. But his patriotic mood must have still lingered on. About two years later, doubtless under the influence of the writings of Plekhanov, Lenin, and their associates, his mind was set, if one is to judge from his first political essays published in 1901. His leanings towards Georgian patriotism were overcome. His whole attention was absorbed by the 'social', as distinct from the 'national', problem; and he already spoke in the idiom of the convinced and 'uncompromising' Marxist.

. . . .

For several months after his expulsion from the seminary, from May till the end of 1899, Djugashvili could find no employment and had no definite dwelling. He spent some of that time with his mother at Gori, but then returned to Tiflis, where he probably lived with some of those class-conscious workers that attended his lectures. With the help of friends he managed to make some money, giving lessons in middle-class homes. By the end of the year he got a job as a clerk at the Tiflis Observatory. His salary was a mere pittance, but the job had important advantages. He was not tied down too much to his work; and he had a room to himself in the Observatory, his first taste of privacy. Now he could hold occasional meetings in his room and hope that the respectable cover of the Observatory would for a time protect him from the eyes of the police. This was important, for in the next few months the police arrested several members of *Messame Dassy*. He was not among them. He knew how to make himself inconspicuous. Cautious, taciturn, observant, and possessing great presence of mind, he was already, in many ways, the ideal underground worker.

During his first months at the Observatory, he was busy preparing, together with others, the first May Day demonstration in the Caucasus. This was a challenge to authority as well as an act of solidarity with the workers of Europe. The challenge was still somewhat timid. On the appointed day, four or five hundred workers slipped out of the town to assemble at the Salt Lake in the remote outskirts of Tiflis on which the police were not likely to keep a watch. There the demonstrators closed their ranks and hoisted red banners. Home-made portraits of Marx and Engels were raised aloft. The modest meeting was rather like an Orthodox religious procession with the icons, the holy pictures, replaced by the portraits of Marx and Engels. The meeting was addressed by Djugashvili—this was his first speech in public. There were two or three more speeches followed by the singing of Socialist hymns; and then the little crowd hurriedly dispersed. In retrospect, the incident may look completely unimportant; the behaviour of the demonstrators may seem extremely timid. But in the atmosphere of those days it looked quite different. In this way socialism was beginning to muster its strength; next May Day the demonstrators would defy the *Okhrana* right in the heart of the town.[1]

The other two events of some significance in an otherwise uneventful year were a strike at the railway workshop and the arrival at Tiflis of a friend of Lenin, Victor Kurnatovsky. To some extent Djugashvili was involved in the strike. No doubt he discussed with his comrades the strike tactics of the railwaymen and helped to produce leaflets. But the strike itself was led by the skilled railwaymen themselves, the deported Russians, Kalinin, Alliluyev, and others.[2] The arrival of Kurnatovsky gave a fillip to socialism in Tiflis. Lenin's friend and admirer must have told them something about the man himself, and about his ideas and plans. Lenin's emissary himself was, by all accounts, an attractive personality. Later he became a legendary hero of the Revolution of 1905. Djugashvili was greatly impressed by him. To Kurnatovsky he was one of the band of local leaders on whom he could rely, but there were no closer ties between the two.[3]

The year 1901 was to be eventful. May Day was the

---

[1] *Okhrana*, replacing the Third Department, was the political police set up in 1881, after the assassination of Alexander II. A description of this May Day demonstration is given in F. Makharadze i G. V. Khachapuridze, *Ocherki po Istorii Rabochevo i Krestyanskovo Dvizhenya v Gruzii*, pp. 164–5, and S. Alliluyev, *Proidennyi Put*, pp. 46–8.

[2] S. Alliluyev, op. cit., pp. 46–59. See also *Krasnyi Arkhiv*, no. 3, 1939.

[3] *Razkazy o Velikom Staline*, p. 91; L. Berya, op. cit., p. 22; S. Alliluyev, op. cit., pp. 74–80; L. Trotsky, *Stalin*, pp. 27–8.

Socialists' great venture; it was to be much more serious than the year before. Authority was to be challenged more directly and more sharply. 'The workers of the whole of Russia', stated a leaflet issued at Tiflis, 'have decided to celebrate May Day openly, in the best thoroughfares of their cities. They proudly tell the authorities that Cossack whips and sabres, torture by the police and the *gendarmerie* hold no terrors for them.'[1] The *Okhrana* of Tiflis decided to strike first. A month before May Day, on 21 March, Kurnatovsky and the most active among the local Socialists were imprisoned. Djugashvili's room at the Observatory was raided; at last the police had seen through the doings of the inconspicuous clerk. Djugashvili was not at home and so he escaped arrest. But he could not return to the Observatory. He had to say good-bye to his quiet job. Nor could he live elsewhere under his own name, because the police would then immediately trace him. Indeed, he could not exist legally any longer. He had to shed his identity. Even before, few of his comrades had known his real name; most had called him by various nicknames. From now on his whole existence would be screened by false passports and nicknames, of which he was to use nearly twenty in the next fifteen years. Hitherto he had existed on the borderline between clandestinity and legality. Now he was descending into the actual underground from which he was to emerge finally only in 1917, shortly before he became a member of the first Soviet Cabinet. For his living he would depend entirely on such assistance as the organization, rich in ambition and enthusiasm but poor in money, could give him, and on his comrades' private help. The decision to take this course was an informal vow of poverty, which in a sense terminated his novitiate to socialism. The ex-seminarist was now becoming one of that godless order of knight-errants and pilgrims of the revolution, to whom life offered little or no interest and attraction outside their service.

His first task after the arrests was to parry the *Okhrana's* blow. The May Day venture had to be seen through to its end. The *Okhrana* could not be given the satisfaction of real success. Apart from this, the arrest of the other leading members was his own opportunity. He had only to prove his mettle now to be automatically promoted to higher standing in the

[1] L. Berya, op. cit., p. 23.

underground. The challenge put out in the leaflet must be kept up at any cost. On May Day a crowd of workmen about 2,000 strong—four or five times stronger than the year before—gathered at the *Soldatsky Bazaar* near the Alexander Garden, in the centre of the city. Police and Cossacks were already on the spot. In the clash that ensued fourteen demonstrators were wounded and fifteen arrested. A few weeks later, the editors of *Iskra* commented upon the demonstration as upon an augury of greater things to come: 'The event that took place on Sunday, 22 April, at Tiflis is of historical importance for the entire Caucasus—that day marked the beginning of an open revolutionary movement in the Caucasus.'[1]

Hitherto Djugashvili had occasionally written short leaflets and proclamations as the need for them had arisen. He now tried his hand at revolutionary journalism. Ketskhoveli had gone to Baku and at last succeeded there in setting up the secret printing press about which he had dreamt so long.[2] He could now tackle the publication of an illegal journal in the Georgian language. The first copy of the paper called *Brdzola* (The Struggle) appeared in September 1901.

The programme of the journal was set out in a statement 'From the Editors' of which Stalin was to claim the authorship as late as 1946, when he included it in the first edition of his *Collected Works*. Stylistically, the statement was not much like his later writings. Probably it was written collectively by several hands, and Djugashvili made an essential contribution to it. The statement, lucid and simple, with no rhetoric in it, did not set out the general ideas of socialism; these its editors took for granted. Instead, they turned from the very beginning to indirect polemics against the moderate majority of *Messame Dassy*. They explained the reasons that impelled them to resort to illegal printing: 'We would regard it as a great mistake on the part of any worker to think that a legal newspaper . . . could stand for his, the worker's, interests. The Government, in its "concern" for the workers, has nicely coped with the legally published newspapers. A whole pack of officials, called censors,

---

[1] L. Berya, op. cit., p. 24.
[2] L. B. Krasin, *Dela Davno Minuwshykh Dnei*, pp. 14–17. Krasin, who was responsible for the whole technical side of the organization, calls Ketskhoveli an 'organizer of genius'.

has been put on to such newspapers. . . . Instruction after instruction goes out to the committee of censors: "nothing is to be said about the workers, nothing published about this or that event" and so on.'[1]

Brdzola was the first free paper, because it achieved freedom from censorship. What was even more characteristic was the editors' political modesty. They expressly stated that they had no ambition to make any policies of their own, because Georgian Labour ought to be part of the Labour movement of the whole of Russia. So their policies would inevitably be subordinated to those of the leaders of socialism in the Tsarist Empire. This again was more than a pinprick at the majority of *Messame Dassy* who were inclined to favour a Georgian party of their own, federated with the Russian party but not subordinated to it.

The next copy of *Brdzola* came out three months later in December 1901. It carried a fairly long, unsigned essay on 'The Russian Social Democratic Party and its Immediate Tasks'. Its author was Djugashvili. The essay was a summary of the views of *Iskra*, and quite especially of those of Lenin himself; but the future Stalin could unmistakably be traced in its style and method of exposition, in its vocabulary and even in the favourite metaphors that several decades later the author was to repeat time and again in quite different circumstances, when they would be reported all over the world and make history. There was a quaint forcefulness in his emphasis on the essential points of the argument, a somewhat boring repetitiveness also characteristic of Lenin's style—and a fondness for the sombre hyperbolic image smacking of an Orthodox Sunday sermon. 'Many storms, many streams of blood have swept western Europe in order that an end should be put to the oppression of the majority of the people by a minority; but the suffering has not yet been dispelled, the wounds have remained just as sore as before, and the pain is becoming more and more unbearable every day.'[2] Leaving the clumsy images behind, the author then gave a concise and popular summary of the history of socialism in Europe and Russia, such as most Socialist propagandists of the time would have made on the basis of Engels's *Utopian and Scientific Socialism* and of Plekhanov's or

---

[1] J. Stalin, *Sochinenya*, vol. i, pp. 3–10.   [2] Ibid., p. 11.

Lenin's writings. He used concrete examples from recent local events to point the conclusion that the Caucasus had lagged behind the rest of Russia in Socialist maturity. He then struck out against the Economists who wanted the workers to fight only for their bread and butter and not for socialism against autocracy. The Economists were as penny wise and pound foolish as the moderate Socialists in western Europe; for instance, the followers of Eduard Bernstein in Germany, who believed in petty reforms and gave up the great ideal of socialism. His references to disputes among Socialists in Germany were based on reports in *Iskra*, for the author knew no German; but they showed that he was watching the trends and currents in western European socialism though his evidence was second-hand. In western Europe, he went on to argue, the reformist Socialists could at least claim that they lived under a civilized capitalism, 'where human rights had already been won'; but how could one believe in piecemeal progress under despotic Tsardom? 'Only great aims can arouse great energies.' This was not to say that Socialists should have nothing to do with the workers' fight for bread and butter. On the contrary, Socialists should help in that fight, because in the course of it, however petty its immediate objectives, the workers were bound to muster their strength and eventually to clash with the State that represented nothing but the organized force of the possessing classes.

The second part of the essay began with a bitter and angry picture of oppressed Russia:

Not only the working class has been groaning under the yoke of tsardom. Other social classes, too, are strangled in the grip of autocracy. Groaning is the hunger-swollen Russian peasantry. . . . Groaning are the small town-dwellers, petty employees . . . petty officials, in a word, that multitude of small men whose existence is just as insecure as that of the working class and who have reason enough to be discontented with their social position. Groaning, too, is the lower and even middle *bourgeoisie* that cannot put up with the tsarist knout and bludgeon, especially the educated section of the *bourgeoisie*. . . . Groaning are the oppressed nationalities and religions in Russia, among them the Poles and the Finns driven from their native lands and injured in their most sacred feelings. Autocracy has brutally trampled over their rights and freedom that were granted to them by history. Groaning are the unceasingly perse- cuted and humiliated Jews, deprived even of those miserable rights that other Russian subjects enjoy—the right to live where they choose, the right to go to school, &c. Groaning are the Georgians, the Armenians and other nations who can neither have their own schools nor be employed by the State and are compelled to submit to the shameful and oppressive policies of Russification. . . . Groaning are the many millions of members of Russian religious sects who want to worship according to the dictates of their own conscience rather than to those of the Orthodox priests.[1]

The picture of that 'other', the oppressed Russia, made emphatic by crude and yet effective repetitions was calculated to impress the readers with the great possibilities of the approaching revolution. The working class, that most revolutionary of all classes, had allies in so many sections of society.

Here, however, the author sounded a sober note of warning: 'Alas, the Russian peasantry is still stunned by age-old slavery, misery, and dark ignorance; it is only now awakening, it has not yet grasped where is its enemy. The oppressed nationalities of Russia cannot even think of freeing themselves of their own accord as long as they have against them not only the Russian Government but even the Russian people still unaware that autocracy is their common foe.' But his more emphatic warning was against the duplicity of the bourgeois opposition to Tsardom: 'The *bourgeoisie* of all countries and nations know only too well how to appropriate the fruits of victories won by others; they know only too well how to stir a fire with other people's hands. They never wished to risk their own relatively privileged position in a struggle against a powerful foe, in a struggle not yet easily to be won. Though discontented, they are still quite well-off and therefore gladly cede to the working-class and to the ordinary people at large the right to expose their backs to

[1] J. Stalin, *Sochinenya*, vol. i, pp. 21–2. The sequence in which the author spoke about the 'groaning' nationalities is noteworthy. First came the oppressed classes in Russian society itself, then the Poles and Finns, then the Jews; and only after the Jews did the author mention *inter alia* the Georgians, his own nationality, to wind up with the persecuted *Russian* religious sects. This sequence was not accidental. It was calculated to put the Georgian problem in a wide international perspective, in which it appeared as only one, and not the most important, particular case of general, Empire-wide oppression. This manner of treating the Georgian problem in a Georgian newspaper was almost provocatively deliberate. The author was clearly determined to counteract the political self-centredness, so characteristic of any oppressed nationality, of which other political groups in Georgia were not free. The promise made by *Brdzola*, in its first issue, that it would treat Georgian socialism as an organic part of Russian socialism was scrupulously carried out here.

Cossack whips, to fight on barricades and so on.' The industrial working class therefore ought to assume the leadership. Any victory over autocracy would turn out a sham if it were to be achieved under bourgeois leadership, because the *bourgeoisie* would trample upon the rights of workers and peasants after these had 'picked the chestnuts out of the fire' for the *bourgeoisie*.[1] If autocracy was overthrown by the people led by proletarian Socialists, the result would be 'a broad *democratic constitution*, giving equal rights to the worker, the oppressed peasant and the capitalist'.

Read nearly half a century after it was written, this moderate democratic conclusion (equal rights even to the capitalists) must appear inconsistent with the bitter aspersions cast by the author on the *bourgeoisie*. But this 'inconsistency' was then common to all Russian Socialists. Their common assumption was that Russia was not ripe for socialism; and that all that the revolution could achieve in any foreseeable future was the replacement of feudal autocracy by democratic capitalism.[2] This was the now familiar paradox in the attitude of Socialists who as opponents of capitalism had nevertheless to fight for the victory of a capitalist democracy in their country. A few years later a fundamental split was to occur in their ranks in connexion with that paradox. The moderate Socialists, or Mensheviks, were to argue that in a revolution that was merely to replace feudalism by capitalism the Liberal middle class must inevitably play first fiddle; and that the Socialists having helped liberalism to defeat autocracy and to obtain power must subsequently assume the role of an ordinary Socialist opposition in a parliamentary capitalist republic. The Bolsheviks were to argue, just as Djugashvili was arguing in 1901, that bourgeois liberalism could not be relied upon to defeat autocracy; and

[1] J. Stalin, *Sochinenya*, vol. i, p. 23. In 1939 Stalin tried to justify in advance the agreement with Hitler he was then preparing by saying that after Munich the western powers wanted Russia to 'pull the chestnuts out of the fire for them'.

[2] In his foreword to his *Works*, written in 1946 (*Sochinenya*, vol. i, pp. xiv–xv), Stalin explained why he thought that Russia was not ripe for socialism at that time. He 'accepted then the thesis familiar among Marxists, according to which one of the chief conditions for the victory of the Socialist revolution was that the proletariat should become the majority of the population. Consequently in those countries in which the proletariat did not yet form the majority of the population, because capitalism had not yet sufficiently developed, the victory of socialism was impossible.'

that Socialists had to assume leadership in the anti-feudal revolution, even though in doing so they merely paved the way for some sort of democratic order that would remain capitalist in its economic structure. This political debate was to develop fully only on the eve of the Revolution of 1905. From then on the Bolsheviks' stock argument was to remain unchanged in its main features until 1917.

Thus, Djugashvili in the 'moderation' and democratic orthodoxy that led him to believe in equal rights for workers, peasants, and capitalists was true to the spirit of Russian socialism in those days. What is perhaps surprising is that at that early stage, several years before the split between Bolsheviks and Mensheviks, when he himself was only twenty-two, his outlook was already that of the future Bolshevik. He already spoke in the idiom in which Leninism was to speak until 1917. His political ideas had already crystallized to such an extent that the next ten or fifteen years were to change them but little. Lenin's influence on him had already been decisive even then, in spite of the fact that the founder of Bolshevism had only published his early writings, his influence being still mainly anonymous, since most of his essays and articles had appeared under various pen-names or altogether unsigned. This is not to say that the young Caucasian was equally impressed by all aspects of Lenin's complex and many-sided personality. Some of the master's preoccupations and ideas, and, even more, some of the undercurrents in his mind, were quite beyond the mental range of the pupil, and they were to remain so. But to those features of Lenin's thought which he could grasp, he responded keenly from the outset.

The young writer was no mere propagandist; he also showed himself to be a technician of the revolution, keenly interested in the specific means that would lead the party to the desired end. He analysed the various methods of action, their merits and demerits, and made a comparative study of the relative effectiveness of strikes, clandestine newspapers, and street demonstrations. The clandestine press could reach only a narrow circle of readers; this was its limitation. Strikes were more effective but risky; they tended to rebound upon the striking workers themselves. Street demonstrations were the most effective form of action so far. Djugashvili obviously had in mind the first successful May Day in the Caucasus which he had just helped to stage. Somewhat dizzy with success, he may have overrated its importance. But in his analysis there was a flash of shrewd insight into mass psychology and also into the mechanics of Tsardom's suicidal self-defence. Demonstrations staged by a handful of revolutionaries, he argued, stirred the curiosity of an indifferent public; and *nothing could be more dangerous to tyrannical authority than the people's curiosity*.[1] The street demonstration captures the mind of the neutral onlooker who cannot remain neutral for long. The police would brutally disperse the demonstrators and some onlookers would be in sympathy with the victims of oppression. In its stupid rage the police would fail to distinguish between onlookers and demonstrators; both would feel its knout. The ranks of the next Socialist procession would be swollen by some who had merely gaped at the previous one. Even the knout is becoming our ally, Djugashvili commented. At the end of the process, he prophesied, was 'the spectre of a people's Revolution'. About this he was so confident that he ventured a very specific forecast: it would take no more than two or three years for the 'spectre' to appear.[2] Rarely has a political prophecy been better confirmed than this one. Exactly three years passed and then followed the outbreak of the Revolution of 1905.

Whatever its political quality, the essay was not a literary feat. There was nothing scholarly in it. At Djugashvili's present age, twenty-two, Lenin had written economic and statistical treatises of which many a lecturer and even professor of economics would not have felt ashamed. Trotsky, born in the same year as Djugashvili, soon gained distinction as one of *Iskra's* important contributors. An essay like Djugashvili's would hardly have made its way into the columns of *Iskra*, let alone into those of the more highbrow journal *Zarya* (The Dawn), also published by Plekhanov and Lenin. Judged by such standards, his essay was too much the work of a disciple and imitator; his sociological reasoning was crude; his style, though forceful in its own way, was too pedestrian. The editors of *Iskra*, and especially Lenin, could easily have told on which of their own articles the provincial writer had been chewing and they could have traced the paragraphs he had borrowed from them, lock,

---

[1] J. Stalin, *Sochinenya*, vol. i, pp. 26-7.   [2] Ibid., p. 28.

stock, and barrel. But it would be unfair to judge Djugashvili's first writings by the standards of the highly sophisticated literary *élite* of Russian socialism, especially after *Brdzola* had modestly introduced itself to its readers as the Georgian mouthpiece of that *élite*. By local Caucasian standards, Djugashvili's essay was a feat. The student who reads it now, with the author's later writings in his mind, cannot help wondering at the comparative maturity of its style. The essay in *Brdzola* belongs to the best things its author was to write over nearly half a century; few were to be better, and many were to be much poorer in both content and style.

    .   .   .   .

A detailed account of Djugashvili's doings in the next few months or even years would make a monotonous tale. He was now leading the typical existence of a hunted Socialist agitator and organizer; the substance of this life consisted of strikes, street demonstrations, secret meetings, conferences, and so forth. His doings were so typical of people of his sort that most of them went unrecorded. Only thirty or forty years later was the limelight of research turned on them. Then every detail relating to his early activities was seized upon by both friend and foe, the one eager to show that even the youth of the great leader shone with extraordinary grandeur; and the other equally determined to trace back almost to the cradle the vices of the evil man. The apologetic and denunciatory volumes that have been written in the process have contributed little to a real knowledge of Stalin. Only a few indubitable facts can be picked out of the welter of irrelevant polemics.

In November 1901 he was formally elected as a member of the Social Democratic Committee of Tiflis. This body, consisting of nine persons, led the Socialist groups in the Caucasian capital, and for a time it was also the virtual Executive for the whole of the Caucasus. Djugashvili was thus placed in a position of vantage for the control of the movement in the whole province. Only two weeks after his promotion, however, he quitted Tiflis for Batum, the new centre of the oil industry on the Turkish border, which had only just been connected by pipeline with Baku. The central figure in the Tiflis Committee was Sylvester Djibladze, the same man who had once assaulted a Principal of the Theological Seminary and later became Djugashvili's tutor in socialism. The two men were not on good terms. Djibladze may have treated his pupil somewhat patronizingly and hurt his pride. In addition, he sided with the moderate wing of *Messame Dassy*. Political as well as personal antagonisms made their co-operation rather difficult. Djugashvili's departure for Batum was probably the most convenient way out for all—for Djibladze, for Djugashvili, and for the Tiflis Committee. Batum needed an energetic Socialist organizer, and the junior of the two rivals was bound to find an outlet there for his energy and ambition.[1] It was, incidentally, during his stay in that town, on the Turkish border, that Djugashvili began to use the pseudonym Koba, meaning 'The Indomitable' in the Turkish vernacular. Koba was also the name of a heroic outlaw, a people's avenger in a poem by the Georgian poet Kazbegi, one of Djugashvili's favourite writers in the years of boyhood. As Koba the revolutionary was to be best known among his comrades before he assumed the more famous pseudonym Stalin, and old Caucasian Bolsheviks were to call him Koba even much later.[2]

Batum was a much smaller town than Tiflis; its population was only 25,000, while Tiflis had 150,000. But as an industrial centre it was rapidly growing in importance, largely because of the influx of foreign capital. The chief oil works were already owned by the Rothschild concern; and more than one-quarter of all the industrial workers of the Caucasus lived in Batum. Though the town had already had its share of Socialist propaganda, it could not yet pride itself on the possession of a coherent clandestine organization. Koba was bent on making good this gap. A few weeks after his arrival he convened a conference of Socialists—ostensibly the gathering was merely a gay and harmless New Year's party—at which the Social Democratic Committee of Batum was elected. His next step was to set up a secret press, similar to Ketskhoveli's at Baku. The press was established in one little room that served him also as his private lodging. 'The type was laid out in match and cigarette boxes and on slips of paper', according to the memoirs of one of the printers who themselves were, of course, also Socialists. The

---

[1] L. Berya, op. cit., pp. 24–5; L. Trotsky, *Stalin*, pp. 29–30.
[2] A. S. Alliluyeva, *Vospominanya*, p. 110.

eyewitness was to remember Koba seated at a table in the middle of the printing shop, writing his leaflets and passing them on to the compositors.[1] Now and then Koba would make a trip to Tiflis, get in touch with the Committee men there, take part in their deliberations and report on his own achievements at Batum. The leaflets written by himself and produced in his own lodgings were finding their way to the oil works, the loading stations, and the factories, and their effect was soon felt in political ferment and labour troubles. A confidential report of the secret police stated : 'In autumn 1901 the Social Democratic Committee of Tiflis sent one of its members, Joseph Vissario-novich Djugashvili, formerly a pupil in the sixth form of the Tiflis Seminary, to Batum for the purpose of carrying on propaganda among the factory workers. As a result of Djugash-vili's activities . . . Social Democratic organizations began to spring up in all the factories of Batum. The results of the Social Democratic propaganda could already be seen in 1902, in the prolonged strike in the Rothschild factory and in street demonstrations.'[2] During one such demonstration the Cau-casian Rifle Battalion opened fire on the crowd and fifteen workers were killed and many wounded. The *Okhrana* now redoubled its efforts to discover the secret press and the Socialist agitators. On 5 April 1902 Koba was arrested at a meeting of the Batum Committee. The printing shop was not discovered.

His stay at Batum had lasted only four and a half months, but these were months of intense activity. One incident deserves to be mentioned, because it cast its shadow ahead on future events. Koba's doings at Batum evoked some sharp criticisms

[1] See the memoirs of S. Todrya and G. Kaladze in *Batumskaya Demonstratsya 1902 goda*, pp. 53, 73.

[2] See the police reports on Stalin's activities, ibid., pp. 177-90. A colourful description of the primitive oriental background of the Batum organization is found in *Stalin i Khashim*, pp. 14-32. Hunted by the police, Koba moved to an Abkhazian village near Batum. There he lived in the house of an old Moslem, Khashim, whither he transferred the printing press as well. Members of the organization coming to collect illegal leaflets disguised themselves as women and covered their faces with *chadras*, the traditional long veils worn by Caucasian women. Neigh-bours became suspicious, and the rumour spread that Koba was engaged in counterfeiting money. When the villagers began to demand a share in his profits the situation became dangerous. But Koba apparently succeeded in explaining the real nature of his work to the villagers and in gaining their confidence. He had, however, to promise Khashim that he would embrace the Moslem faith.

from the more moderate Socialists on the spot who were led by Nikolai Chkheidze. Chkheidze, an ex-seminarist like Koba, had cautiously sown the first seeds of socialism on the Black Sea coast and had been held in high esteem for his wide education and fine oratory. Apparently the propagandist later on grew timid over the setting up of an effective clandestine organization. He did not believe that such an organization had any chance of survival in a small place like Batum where secrecy would not easily be maintained and clandestine activity could be nipped in the bud by the *Okhrana*. He considered Koba's plans to be reckless, and implored him, personally and through friends, to desist and leave the local Socialists to go their own way. But Koba was not to be persuaded. Though denounced by his adversary as a 'disorganizer' and 'madman', he saw his plans through to the end and denounced Chkheidze's 'faint-heartedness'.[1] Later the two Georgians were to meet in bigger encounters. Ten years after, in 1912, Chkheidze was the great Menshevik orator in St. Petersburg and Chairman of the parliamentary representation of the Socialists in the Duma (the Tsarist quasi-Parliament), while Koba was one of the leaders of clandestine Bolshevism, pulling the wires behind the Bol-shevik deputies in the Duma. In 1917 Chkheidze was the Menshevik President of the Petersburg Soviet (a post in which, when the tide of Bolshevism was rising, he was succeeded by Trotsky); while Stalin was a member of the Bolshevik Central Committee. In that year of revolution the two Georgian ex-seminarists joined battle in the capital of the Tsars to the accompaniment of epithets not very different from those first exchanged at Batum.

[1] L. Berya, op. cit., p. 29; *Batumskaya Demonstratsya 1902 goda*, pp. 64–5, 187–90.

STALIN'S MOTHER

Sovfoto, New York

STALIN AS A SCHOOLBOY

STALIN'S BIRTHPLACE
The lower photograph shows the interior as now maintained as a Stalin
museum

CHAPTER III

The General Rehearsal

Stalin in prison at Batum.—Tsarist prisons as centres of education for revolution.—
Origins of Bolshevism.—Lenin: Paragraph I of the Party Statutes.—Stalin transported to Siberia, 1903.—Escapes and returns to Tiflis, 1904.—Conflict between
Bolsheviks and Mensheviks.—Stalin turns to Bolshevism late in 1904.—The 1905
revolution.—The Petersburg Soviet.—Peasant revolts and soldiers' riots in the
Caucasus.—Stalin as Lenin's disciple.—Emergence from the underground.—
Stalin (under the pseudonym Ivanovich) attends the national Party Conference
at Tammerfors (1905) and meets Lenin for first time.—Stalin makes his first
journey abroad, to the Stockholm Congress, 1906.—Differs from Lenin on land
reform.—The 'fighting squads'.—The Party Congress opposes 'expropriation'.—
Trotsky indicts the Bolsheviks.

WHEN, in the first days of April 1902, the doors of the Batum
prison closed behind Koba-Djugashvili he needed no exceptional
gift for martyrdom to endure his lot. The Tsarist prisons, ill-
famed as they were, seem mild, almost humanitarian to a
generation that knows the cruelties of a Himmler or a Yezhov
and the death camps of Belsen and Auschwitz. The régime in
Tsarist prisons and places of exile was a mixture of brutality
and 'liberal' inefficiency. There was enough brutality to confirm the prisoners in their hatred of the existing order, and
enough muddled inefficiency to allow the revolutionary work
to be effectively carried on even behind prison bars. For many
young Socialists, the prisons were their 'universities', where they
had a chance to get a solid revolutionary education, often under
experienced tutors. As a rule, the political prisoners, who
enjoyed certain 'privileges' not granted to criminals, organized
their communal life in a spirit of solidarity and mutual assistance. The prison was usually a great debating society. No
wonder that in their memoirs some of the ex-prisoners recall
the mild sadness they felt on leaving their cells for freedom.

Koba imposed upon himself a rigid discipline, rose early,
worked hard, read much, and was one of the chief debaters in
the prison commune. After many years ex-inmates remembered
him arguing against agrarian Socialists and other opponents of

Iskra. His manner in debating was logical, sharp, and scornful. Apart from such discussions, he was uncommunicative, self-possessed, and aloof. So far nearly all the writers of memoirs seem to agree, but they differ on other points. Friends remember him as a patient, sensitive, and helpful comrade, while opponents describe the self-confident debater as a dark intriguer, fond of reviling his critics and of inciting his fanatical followers against them.[1] From Batum, Koba was transferred to another prison at Kutais, and from there he was shifted back to Batum. Altogether he spent over a year and a half in Caucasian jails, until the end of November 1903. The prosecution had no specific evidence against him except reports of secret police agents which an ordinary judge would not accept as valid ground for conviction. Like most suspects on whom no offence could be pinned, Koba was 'administratively' condemned to deportation for a term of three years. He was to be exiled to the village Novaya Uda in the Irkutsk province of eastern Siberia. The prisoner could invoke no habeas corpus; no law whatsoever protected him against the arbitrary exercise of power by authority.

While Koba was imprisoned two events occurred: one was local in character and threw some light on his status in the underground; the other was of far greater importance for the future of Russia, world socialism—and Koba's career. In March 1903 the Social Democratic groups of the Caucasus formed an All-Caucasian Federation. In his absence Koba was elected a member of its Executive. It was very rare indeed for any conference to elect an imprisoned member to a leading body, unless his role in the underground was so eminent that it was worth the organization's while to take all the trouble of consulting him on a major issue in his prison. Much has since been written in order to belittle or to exaggerate Koba's role in those days. This suggests that at the age of twenty-two he was already some sort of 'grey eminence' in the underground of his native province. He was certainly not the undistinguished member of the rank and file, the nonentity, described by Trotsky. Nor was he the 'Lenin of the Caucasus', as his hagiographers see him; for this his personality was still too grey, even if eminent.

[1] E. Yaroslavsky, op. cit., p. 31; *Batumskaya Demonstratsya 1902 goda,* pp. 96–7.

The other, far more important, event began in July, in a back room of the Socialist *Maison du Peuple* in Brussels—a room packed with bales of wool and full of fleas—and ended in London in the latter half of August. In Brussels there assembled at last the All-Russian Congress of Social Democrats prepared by the *Iskra*-men. This was in fact the first real Congress of Russian Socialists, although out of deference to the miscarried gathering in Minsk in 1898 historians have called it the Second Congress. After a few days, the delegates found that their comings and goings were closely watched by Tsarist spies; and the Congress was hastily transferred from Brussels to London. The delegates hoped to consummate the work of *Iskra* and to achieve the final formation of an All-Russian party. But this was not to happen, for at that Congress began the split of Russian socialism into two factions, the Bolsheviks and the Mensheviks, the revolutionaries and the moderates or the 'hards' and the 'softs', as they were called at first. The session of the *Iskra*-men at which the first skirmishes took place was presided over by the twenty-three-year-old Trotsky, because the older leaders could not agree on the person of any other chairman. Fourteen or fifteen years after it began, the schism was to shake Europe and the world not less violently than did another schism initiated by Martin Luther 400 years before. Yet its beginnings seemed trivial in the extreme. The Wittenberg Cathedral certainly provided a less grotesque setting for the birth of the Reformation than the flea-infested bales of wool at the *Maison du Peuple* in Brussels for the birth of Bolshevism. Luther put his challenge to the Papacy in the ninety-five Theses he nailed to the door of the Cathedral. Lenin's challenge was at first contained in one small clause of one short paragraph. If Luther was surprised but comforted by the strength of the opposition to his ideas, Lenin was so upset by the cleavage he had provoked that immediately after the Congress he suffered a nervous breakdown.[1] Luther's Theses are said to have been known all over Germany within a fortnight of their publication—Lenin's First Paragraph of the Party Statutes was to remain unknown to any wide public. Yet the ball that he set rolling into history in July–August 1903 is still on the move.

Paragraph 1 of the Party Statutes was to define who should

---

[1] N. Krupskaya, *Memories of Lenin*, pp. 72–80; L. Trotsky, *Mein Leben*, p. 154.

be regarded as a member of the party. Seemingly, no matters of principle or even tactics were raised by it. Indeed, the Congress began discussing the point as an issue of pure organization, after a common programme and resolutions on tactics had been agreed upon. Two draft clauses lay before the delegates. Lenin's draft ran as follows: 'A member of the Russian Social Democratic Workers' Party is any person who accepts its programme, supports the Party with material means and personally participates in one of its organizations.' In the other draft, put forward by Martov, the words 'personally participates in one of its organizations' were substituted by 'personally and regularly co-operates under the guidance of one of its organizations'.[1] On the face of things, the two formulae were almost identical, and the controversy looked like an elaborate essay in hairsplitting. Underlying the wrangle, however, were two distinct and even conflicting ideas about the outlook and structure of the party. Lenin insisted that only people regularly participating in the underground organization should be regarded as members and have the formal right to influence the policy of the party. He would not include within the framework of the party the growing fringe of sympathizers and fellow travellers, whether intellectuals or workers. The members of the clandestine organization were to be the soldiers of revolution, voluntarily accepting its discipline and ready to act on the orders and instructions of a central leadership. The fellow travellers could not be reckoned upon as the steady and reliable soldiers of the revolution—they were its shapeless and wavering civilian reserve. The party, as Lenin saw it, was to be a coherent, closely knit and highly centralized body, endowed with unfailing striking power. Its strength would be diluted and its striking power blunted if the unsteady fringe of moody sympathizers were to be brought into it. Lenin argued that this was exactly the danger lurking in Martov's vague formula, which demanded from members merely 'co-operation under the guidance of the organization' instead of disciplined work in the organization itself.

The party was to be the instrument of revolution. So far only the shape of that instrument was a matter of controversy.

[1] Lenin, *Sochinenya*, vol. vii, pp. 55–69; F. Dan, *Proiskhozhdenie Bolshevizma*, pp. 266–80.

Both sides took it for granted that they were of one mind on the nature of the revolution itself. True, even before the Congress, the editors of *Iskra* were dimly aware of differences in outlook. Half jestingly they would label one another as 'hard' or 'soft'. Lenin's 'hardness' was beyond dispute. 'This is the stuff of which the Robespierres are made', remarked Plekhanov of his ex-pupil, who was now distinctly making his bid for leadership, in defiance of the Old Guard. Equally indisputable was Martov's 'softness'. But until now such differences had been looked upon as differences of individual disposition and temperament, natural in any team of men working for a common purpose; these temperamental differences had not yet had time to translate themselves into distinct political antagonisms. At the Congress the protagonists themselves were surprised and dismayed at the passionate nature of the dispute. They felt they were allowing their tempers to carry them much farther than sound reasoning could justify. They comforted themselves with the thought that the unexpected squall would be followed by more serene weather; and that the minor crack in their unity could easily be plastered over. On the immediate issue—Paragraph 1 of the Statutes—Lenin was defeated. Martov's draft was passed by 28 votes against 23. Lenin took his reverse with good grace. 'I do not think', he said, 'that our differences are so important as to be a matter of life or death for the party. We shall hardly perish because of one poor clause in our statute.'[1] All the actors seemed to shrink before their own roles and to mistake the prologue to the drama for its epilogue.

A new squall broke towards the end of the Congress, when delegates came to elect the leading bodies of the party and the editorial staff of *Iskra*. Unexpectedly Lenin's candidates were elected and Martov's defeated. The ballot was largely accidental. Some of the 'softer' delegates had left the Congress so that now only two-thirds of the initial number of delegates cast their votes. Lenin's candidates were elected by a majority of 2 votes only (19 against 17, with 3 abstentions). Lenin insisted on the legitimate character of the ballot, as he was formally entitled to do. But the 'minority' refused to accept defeat. From now on, Lenin's followers would be called the men of the

[1] F. Dan, op. cit., p. 281, and *2 Syezd R.S.D.R.P.*, p. 278.

majority, *Bolsheviki*. From this the incongruous term Bolshevism, with its cosmopolitan suffix ill-fitted to its Russian root, entered the vocabulary of politics. The followers of Martov were the men of the minority—*Mensheviki*. The new 'isms', reflecting not differences of principle but the accidental arithmetic of a single ballot, were as if designed to mark a superficial and transient division. In fact they marked a chasm which was to split the movement from head to foot.

After the Congress, the Mensheviks refused to acknowledge the authority of the Bolshevik Central Committee and declared a boycott of it. Lenin insisted on the letter of the decision made by the Congress. The majority that elected his candidates, he argued, was valid, and the Central Committee was the legitimate supreme authority of the party; the Menshevik boycott was an act of impermissible individualism and anarchism not to be tolerated. Out of this there developed anew, and with increased vigour, the dispute over the nature and the structure of the party. The Mensheviks protested against the 'state of siege' that Lenin was introducing into the party and against his idea of what the party ought to be. They charged him with foisting on socialism a lifeless barrack-like discipline. Gradually, the field of controversy widened, though it was many years before even Lenin grasped all its implications.

This much at least soon became clear: the different views on organization reflected different approaches to issues crucial for the revolution. The Mensheviks saw the party as a rather broad, and therefore somewhat loose, organization which should strive to embrace the working class and the Socialist intelligentsia and in the end to become identical with them. That conception was based on the belief that socialism was so congenial to the proletariat that the whole proletariat could be looked upon as the potential Social Democratic party. To Lenin's mind, this was naïve. He saw the working class as a vast heterogeneous mass, divided by differences of origin and outlook and split by sectional interests. Not all sections of the proletariat could, in his view, achieve a high degree of Socialist enlightenment. Some were deeply sunk in ignorance and superstition. If the party tried to embrace the whole, even most, of the proletariat, it would become heterogeneous like the proletariat itself—it would embrace its weakness as well as its strength, its ignorance as well as its Socialist longing, its backwardness as well as its aspirations. It would become an inert image of the working class instead of being its inspirer, leader, and organizer.[1] It was foolish, in Lenin's view, to rely on the spontaneous urge of workers towards socialism, because of their own accord they would attain no more than pure trade-unionism, which in itself was compatible with the capitalist order. Quoting the recognized authority on Marxist doctrine, Karl Kautsky, Lenin kept rubbing in the point that socialism had been brought into the Labour movement from outside by bourgeois intellectuals, by Marx, Engels, and others. This proved that it was no use relying on the 'inborn' socialism of the masses. The party must be a select body embracing only the most enlightened and courageous sections of the working class, its real vanguard which would not shrink from determined and disciplined action. To the Mensheviks this sounded like an ominous repetition of Blanquism, the doctrine of the leader of the Paris Commune, who had believed that the only method of achieving revolution was direct action by a small conspiratorial minority ignoring the will of the majority. Blanquism was anathema to all Marxists; and Lenin was anxious to clear himself of the charge. He explained that in his view revolution could win only if it was wanted and backed by a majority of the people —in this he differed from Blanqui. But the majority must be led by an active and highly organized minority—in this he differed from the Mensheviks and the western European Socialists who, like Kautsky and Rosa Luxemburg, sided with the Mensheviks.

Looking farther back in history for another analogy, the Mensheviks, especially Trotsky who at first was their vigorous spokesman, castigated Lenin for his 'Jacobinism'. Lenin took no umbrage at the label. He accepted it even with some pride and remarked only that, while the Jacobins were the party of the lower middle class, the petty *bourgeoisie*, he was a proletarian Socialist. But after all were the Jacobins not the makers of the French Revolution? And was it not odd that the revolutionaries should deem Jacobinism to be an insult? He concluded that his critics were merely the Girondins of their day, the imitators of those timid conciliators whom the revolution had

---

[1] Lenin, *Sochinenya*, vol. vi, pp. 456–9.

to sweep away in order to rise to its Jacobin climax.[1] At this point history seemed to move over the debate that raged in little brochures and obscure 'sectarian' periodicals. Trotsky was quick to remind Lenin that the Jacobin story did not end with the ascendancy of revolution; and that its epilogue was the mutual slaughter of the Jacobin leaders. The Jacobins, Trotsky wrote in 1903, 'chopped off people's heads—we want to enlighten human minds with socialism'. 'Jacobin Bolshevik tactics will eventually result in the indictment before a revolutionary tribunal of the whole international proletarian movement charged with conciliatoriness. The lion's head of Marx would be the first to roll under the blade of the guillotine.' To Lenin this sounded like empty and pretentious rhetoric. He was not impressed by speculative glimpses into a remote post-revolutionary epoch. His dynamic intellect and will were now entirely geared up to the more immediate task of preparing the revolution itself and forging the tools for the job. Trotsky and the other Mensheviks were not able to produce any satisfactory alternative to his scheme for the party—the party which they conceived would never be able to achieve revolution.

In the course of the next year, 1904, the first tremors of a political earthquake were felt throughout Russia. Tsardom suffered its first defeats in the war against Japan that had begun in February. Middle-class liberalism, emboldened by events, began openly to demand an end to autocracy and the establishment of a constitutional monarchy. What were the Social Democrats to do? The Mensheviks argued that they were bound in duty to support middle-class liberalism against autocracy because in a 'bourgeois' (that is anti-feudal, but not anti-capitalist) revolution, the middle class was anyhow destined to lead. Lenin objected to any alliance with middle-class liberalism, let alone to the acceptance of its leadership. The Liberals' newly-found courage was deceptive. They would not, he forecast, resist autocracy effectively and for long, because they were as much afraid of revolution as was Tsardom itself. The working class, that is the Socialists, had to assume leadership even though the revolution would not bring socialism.[2] At

---

[1] N. Trotsky, *Nashi Politicheskiye Zadachi*, pp. 90–102; Lenin, *Sochinenya*, vol. vii, p. 353.

[2] Lenin, *Sochinenya*, vol. ix, pp. 32–48, 74–85; F. Dan, op. cit., pp. 358–62.

this stage, all matters of tactics and even principle were thrown into the melting-pot. The split grew deeper, wider, and more bitter.

At the Second Congress Lenin had won the first round, but he soon lost the next one. He held fast to his views with such fanatical single-mindedness and fought his opponents so relentlessly that he failed to carry his allies or even his followers with him. The Menshevik rebels refused to go to Canossa and continued to boycott the Bolshevik Central Committee and the Editorial Board of *Iskra*. Plekhanov, who had supported Lenin at the Congress, was now eager to meet the Mensheviks half-way. The boycotted Central Committee itself felt ill at ease with its formal authority and refused to impose it on a reluctant membership. Lenin found himself almost isolated. He resigned from the Editorial Board of *Iskra*, leaving the paper in the hands of the Mensheviks. He thereby undid an important part of his initial success, for most of the threads to the underground in Russia were in the hands of *Iskra*. But having missed his opportunities immediately after the Congress, when ostensibly he was on strong ground, Lenin was undeterred by his isolation. On the contrary, his energy multiplied and he seemed to recover all his tactical resourcefulness, even though he stood almost alone, deserted by friends and derided by opponents. He shifted the weight of the struggle into the underground in Russia. He appealed to the local committees against the Mensheviks and those Bolsheviks who were anxious to conciliate them.

.   .   .   .

While the colonies of Russian émigrés in western Europe were seething with the new controversy, Koba-Djugashvili was shifted from prison to prison, until in November 1903 he was deported to Novaya Uda. Before the convoy of exiles, escorted by gendarmes, left the Black Sea coast for the long and dreary journey into the Siberian winter, he may or may not have heard the first vague tidings about the split. It was more than a month before Koba arrived at Novaya Uda. On the way, the convoy often halted to absorb more deportees. As they moved eastwards, the exiles felt more and more closely the breath of the impending Russo-Japanese war. There was far too much excitement and fever in the air for Koba to put up with the prospect of being cut off from politics for three long years. No sooner had he arrived at his destination than he began to prepare his escape. In the eve-of-war confusion, the vigilance of the authorities near the Manchurian frontier was weakened. The underground was able to organize escapes on a mass scale. On 5 January 1904 Koba began his journey back across the snowbound wastes of what is to-day the great industrial area of the Kuznetsk Basin but was then a lifeless wilderness. A peasant cart carried him westwards towards the Urals. On the way he suffered from frostbite, but by the end of January or the beginning of February 1904 he managed to reappear in Tiflis.

By now accounts of what had happened at the Congress had percolated down to the Caucasian organization. Three Caucasian delegates had returned from London where they had sided with Lenin. Naturally enough, in their accounts the Bolsheviks appeared in a favourable light. Leonid Krasin, the future diplomat, had also followed Lenin. His influence was very great in the Caucasus, where, as an outstanding technician holding high managerial posts in industry, he was able to render the underground discreet but valuable services. Shortly before Koba returned from Siberia, Tiflis was visited, too, by one of Lenin's youngest shield-bearers, Leon Kamenev, who also did his share of canvassing. But the initial success of Bolshevism in the Caucasus was quickly lost. And, in fact, it was Krasin himself who led the conciliatory Bolsheviks against Lenin. He was anxious not to allow the cleavage to wreck the young organization and he conducted its day-to-day activity as if no split had occurred. Much to Lenin's indignation, he handed the great and efficient clandestine printing shop of Baku, where *Iskra* had been printed, to the Mensheviks who were now in charge of the paper. In the ranks of the Mensheviks, too, conciliators and irreconcilables were at loggerheads.

Thus, the returning Koba ran straight into a confused and shifting array of factions and sub-factions. The outlines of the controversy were confused by these exasperating processes of fission. His first reaction to Bolshevism could not be other than vague. Many years later his official biographers were to claim that, in his apostolic clearsightedness, he had sided with Lenin even before he was deported to Siberia. This version was challenged by Trotsky, who asserted that Koba was at first a Menshevik.[1] In actual fact there is nothing to suggest either that Stalin ever was a Menshevik or that he declared himself to be a Bolshevik immediately after the split. Probably, he refrained at first from committing himself to any group, trying to find out the facts and their meaning amid a fog of conflicting reports. His hesitations, if this be the right word for his state of mind, did not last long. A few months after his escape from Siberia he made up his mind to support Lenin. Towards the end of the year 1904 he was already zealously agitating for Bolshevism.

His first journalistic statement on the split was his article 'The Class of Proletarians and The Party of Proletarians' written in Georgian by the end of the year and published, on New Year's Day 1905, in *Proletariatis Brdzola* (Proletarian Struggle).[2] The periodical, appearing at rather more than quarterly intervals, replaced *Brdzola*, in which he had made his début three years before. The article was a summary of Lenin's famous brochure *One Step Forward, Two Steps Back*. The party, Stalin stated, is 'the militant group of leaders'. Consequently it must be: (*a*) smaller in numbers than the working class; (*b*) superior in consciousness and experience; and (*c*) more coherent than any other working-class body. 'The party of the *fighting* proletarians cannot be an accidental agglomeration of individuals—it must be a coherent centralized organization.' 'Unity of views on programme, tactics and organization forms the basis on which our party is being built. If the unity of views crumbles, the party, too, crumbles.' Passive acceptance of the party's view was not enough. There was no lack of prattlers and twaddlers ready to accept any programme. Nor could the battles of the working class be won by free-lances. 'Until now our party has been like a hospitable patriarchal family, welcoming any sympathizer in its midst.' Now, however, 'we are changing altogether into a fortress, the doors of which will be opened only to the worthy.' How different was that fortress from the Socialist banqueting-hall that pleased the Mensheviks so much. Koba took the whole reasoning and even the similes from Lenin. Only

[1] L. Trotsky, *Stalin*, p. 50. Trotsky based this assertion on a single sentence contained in a police report written in 1911. The report is inaccurate in other points as well. It claims, for instance, that Stalin joined the Social-Democratic party only in 1902.

[2] J. Stalin, *Sochinenya*, vol. i, pp. 62–73.

in one point was he more original, namely in his insistence, already familiar from his first writings, on the need for absolute uniformity of views inside the party. He was aware that in this he was more emphatic and explicit than Lenin himself; but he trusted that he was dotting the i's and crossing the t's in harmony with Lenin's intentions. The Mensheviks, he stated,

speak only about the acceptance of the programme [as a condition for membership]. They do not say a word about tactics and organization. Yet, unity of views on tactics and organization is just as essential for the unity of the party as is unity of views on matters of programme. We shall be told that Lenin's formula does not mention this either. That is true. But there was no need for Lenin to discuss this in his formula. Is it not understood that he who works in one of the party's organizations, he who fights together with the party and submits to its organization cannot follow any tactics or principles of organization other than those held by the party?[1]

It did not occur to the writer that people might be members of a party, accept its programme and discipline and yet disagree with it on secondary issues of tactics or methods of organization. The ideal that he held out smacked of that 'monolithic' orthodoxy into which Bolshevism was to change after its victory, largely under Koba's own guidance. But that 'monolithism' was still a matter of the future. Not even Lenin thought that the split was irremediable. He still hoped for an eventual fusion of the factions, and believed that within the broad framework of the party there was room for various shades of opinion, provided that the unifying factors—community of principle, centralization, and self-imposed discipline—were strong enough to hold them together.

In the summer of 1904, Lenin's young lieutenant Kamenev, just released from a prison in Moscow, returned to Tiflis. Kamenev had already seen and learned more than Koba, though he was three years younger. He had behind him revolutionary activity at the Moscow University, trips to Geneva, Paris, and London, work abroad under Lenin's personal guidance, and debates with the other leading lights of *Iskra*. He could not fail to exert some influence on Koba. His present assignment was to prepare a regional conference of Caucasian

---

[1] J. Stalin, *Sochinenya*, vol. i, p. 71.

Bolsheviks—similar regional conferences were convened in northern and southern Russia. For unknown reasons Koba did not participate in the Caucasian conference that took place in November. The three regional conferences elected an All-Russian Bolshevik Bureau, headed by the future Soviet Premier Alexey Rykov and the future Commissar for Foreign Affairs Maxim Litvinov. The Bureau was Lenin's counterweight to the wavering Central Committee. He was now able to claim that his irreconcilable attitude *vis-à-vis* the Mensheviks was backed by the underground workers in Russia. He proposed the convening of a new Congress that would put an end to the ambiguous situation prevailing hitherto. The Bolshevik conciliators accepted the proposal. Koba was drawn into the campaign for the Congress, which filled the end of this and the beginning of the next year.

The general reasons why Bolshevik tactics appealed to Koba are not far to seek. By temperament he belonged to the 'hard' brand of revolutionaries—softness in any form was not one of his characteristics. Lenin's ideas appealed to him on their own merits. They were clear-cut and sharp-edged, very much to his liking. Apart from this, one aspect of Leninism, even in those early days, had a soothing effect on his own mental and emotional tensions. Menshevism seemed to belittle or even to degrade the role of men like himself, while Bolshevism seemed to exalt it. In Lenin's conception, the professional revolutionary, the hunted and poorly living full-time agitator and organizer was 'the salt of the earth'. It was he who was steadily infusing true socialism into the spontaneous Labour movement. The committee-men of Koba's type were the chosen men of the revolution. It is not difficult to imagine how much self-confidence and pride Lenin's theory must have given to Koba, who had no recognized standing in official society, who could not play a brilliant part even in the underground. He must have craved some sort of psychological compensation. And here was a theory by which he represented nothing less than the high principle of organization opposed to all-pervading chaos. In the mirror of the Leninist idea he could see himself as the Atlas on whose shoulders rested the future of mankind.

The underground was beginning to breed its caucus, its hierarchy, its bureaucracy. Neither Mensheviks nor Bolsheviks could do without them. That hierarchy was in no way inferior to the officialdom of any normal, respectable, western European party. In some respects—in idealism, devotion to its cause, and even in education—it was superior. In the Menshevik pattern of the party it had no definite place or role. In theory, though by no means in actual fact, it was put on an equal footing with everybody else, 'every striker and Socialist-minded intellectual'. Martov was an ideologue and a man of letters, not the head of any hierarchy. Not so Lenin. Although as an ideologue and propagandist he was second to none of his rivals, he was, even in those early years, also the head of a revolutionary administration. He felt and behaved as such without shyness or inhibition. He defined clearly the framework of that administration, and exalted its activities to the plane of the ideal.[1] In Koba's eager response to Lenin's attitude there was therefore a streak of unconscious gratitude for moral promotion.

.   .   .   .

While the Socialist underground was torn by the controversy and the factions were beside themselves with polemical frenzy, they hardly noticed the outbreak of the first Russian revolution. The Bolsheviks were preparing a new Congress to be convened in London in April 1905. Lenin, having withdrawn from *Iskra*, at last succeeded in publishing a new periodical in Geneva— *Vperyod* (Forward). The Mensheviks announced that they would boycott the Congress and convene a conference of their own. Meanwhile, the Russo-Japanese war ended with the fall of Port Arthur and Russia's defeat. On 9 January 1905, according to the old Orthodox calendar, a huge crowd of workers, led by the priest Gapon, marched towards the Winter Palace in Petersburg to submit a petition to the Tsar. The procession was meant to be peaceful. Its participants were inspired by faith in the Tsar, from whom, they believed, bad advisers had kept the truth about the plight of the people. The tone of their petition was plaintive and timid. The loyal character of the demonstration was stressed by the many church icons and portraits of the Tsar carried by the demonstrators. The Tsarist

---

[1] 'We ought to raise the calling and the importance of the member of the party higher, higher and still higher', thus at the Congress Lenin wound up his speech on Paragraph 1 (*Sochinenya*, vol. vi, p. 459). 'We should have created', he added later, 'a coherent, honest *Iskra-Ministry*' (ibid., vol. vii, p. 65).

Guards met them with bullets. The volleys fired into the crowd became the signal for revolution. Strikes spread throughout the country. Revolutionaries assassinated the Grand Duke Sergey, one of the leaders of the court camarilla.

The first wave of strikes had hardly subsided when peasant revolts broke out in various parts of the country. The fever spread to the fringes of the Empire. Strikes in the Polish city of Lodz led to an armed rising which lasted nearly a week. Barricades covered the streets and squares of Warsaw and Odessa. In the port of Odessa the crew of the cruiser *Potemkin* joined in the revolt. In some cities, strikers elected Councils of Workers' Delegates—the first Soviets that emerged from the maelstrom of the popular movement. The Tsar, shaken in his self-confidence, made a concession and promised to convene a *Duma*, a Consultative Assembly, in which the workers, however, were not to be represented. All parties of the opposition, from the Liberals to the Bolsheviks, protested against his edict. In October a general strike spread from Moscow and Petersburg throughout the country. All railways came to a standstill. The strikers in Petersburg elected a Council of Workers' Deputies, the Petersburg Soviet, which soon became the most spectacular centre of the revolution. For a short time the Petersburg Soviet was a virtual rival to the official administration—its orders and instructions commanded universal obedience. The Soviet called on the country to stop paying taxes to the Tsar. Its members, together with their young chairman Leon Trotsky, were arrested. New strikes broke out, which culminated in the December rising in Moscow, the real climax of the First Revolution. The rising was defeated, and, thereafter, the revolution began to subside. Although it was still capable of rallying, after each rally it grew weaker, until, finally, its impetus was spent. Throughout 1906 and even part of 1907 the ferment was still so strong that few political leaders noticed the actual ebbing of the movement. Nearly all Socialists looked forward to a new climax of the revolution. But the Tsar, gradually regaining his confidence, withdrew the semi-Liberal concessions he had made in his first panic. The *coup d'état* of 3 June 1907 marked the end of the revolution. On that day, the new Prime Minister Stolypin dispersed the 'second Duma', and arrested fifty-five of its deputies, all Social Democrats.

In later years Lenin described the revolution of 1905 as 'the general rehearsal' for the upheaval of 1917. How, it may be asked, did the chief actors of 1917 behave in the course of that general rehearsal? How and with what effect did they perform their roles? The answer is surprising: most of the chief actors did not appear on the stage at all. The future performer in the chief role, Lenin himself, was satisfied with the part of a prompter so distant from the scene that the real performers could hardly hear his voice. While the tide of revolution was rising, he remained in his exile in Geneva. Only towards the end of October 1905, nearly ten long months after the Petersburg procession, did he leave Switzerland. When at last he arrived in Petersburg, the great general strike was over, the course of events was set—the revolution was climbing to its next and last and hopeless climax, the rising in Moscow. There was little that the great architect of the revolution could do.

What kept Lenin away from Russia during the crucial months of the year? He had every reason to expect that the Tsarist police would be after him when he returned, as indeed they were in November when he made his appearance in Petersburg. But this could not have been why he delayed leaving Switzerland. He knew his value to the revolution, and he could have had no doubt as to the importance for him of being near the scene of action. When he did finally come back, he directed his followers from a clandestine hiding-place; he could have done the same much earlier. Did he then not grasp the full significance of the events he himself had so long expected and forecast? What he apparently did not yet realize clearly was the importance of time in a revolution. He must have thought that the process would be more protracted than it was; that the climax was not very near; and that the change from flood to ebb would not be as abrupt as it eventually proved to be. In this error he persisted even after the tide had definitely turned.

Meanwhile, he was anxious to use his time so as to work out his revolutionary tactics, to impress them on his followers, to teach them the art of insurrection, and so on. He was still experimenting in the laboratory of revolutionary politics when the revolution, not waiting for the results of his work, knocked at his door. What a dilemma for the scientist and practitioner of revolution! On the one hand he saw that the whole movement

TIFLIS
Above: Street in the old quarter
Below: Working-class district

STALIN IN EXILE, 1903

in Russia was spontaneous, driven forward by all sorts of accidental impulses, uncoordinated, shapeless, and lacking in leadership. He distrusted spontaneity. He wanted to prepare the party to assume leadership; and this, in his view, he would achieve only if he induced it to discard Menshevik conceptions. Even so, he might have had a better chance to influence events if he had emerged from his Swiss seclusion earlier in the year. The young Trotsky, the only man among the émigré leaders who did rush to the battlefield as soon as he could, became the chief leader of the First Revolution. By the time Lenin set his foot on Russian soil, Trotsky was about to become the President of the Petersburg Soviet. After 1905, Lenin must have reflected more than once on his missed opportunities. When the next opportunity came he was resolved not to waste it; and in 1917 he did not hesitate to undertake the journey across Imperial Germany, then at war with Russia, in order to appear in the Russian capital at an early stage of the Second Revolution.

Lenin's relative failure at the 'general rehearsal' was not an exception. There was not one of the great leaders of Menshevism and the lesser lights of Bolshevism who gave a better account of himself. The powerful tide of 1905 roared on, leaving Plekhanov, Martov, Axelrod, and others stranded on the shoals. Apart from Trotsky, the leaders of 1905 were nameless rankers swept forward by popular enthusiasm or indignation but possessing little revolutionary training and technique. Trotsky's performance came nearest to the role he was to play in 1917, again as President of the Petersburg Soviet. But nothing throws a sharper light on the 'immaturity' of the First Revolution than the contrast between his roles in 1905 and 1917. In the First Revolution he put his imprint upon events as an individual standing almost alone. In 1917 his immense personal gifts were backed up by the solid power of the Bolshevik party which he had joined in the meantime. In 1905 he spent himself in brilliant fireworks of oratory and somewhat theatrical gestures of revolutionary defiance, which had no immediate practical effect, although they appealed to the imagination of the masses and thereby furthered the cause. When Cossacks and gendarmes surrounded the Petersburg Soviet in session, it was Trotsky who ordered its armed members to break the locks of their revolvers and surrender, since armed resistance was hopeless. His inspired speech before the Tsarist court, glorifying the revolution and proclaiming its right to armed insurrection, sank into the minds of many workers and was one of the seeds for the next revolution. But in all this there was still a lot of inspired amateurishness, an amateurishness that was not to be found in the Trotsky of 1917, when, under his chairmanship, the Petersburg Soviet, far from symbolically breaking the locks of their revolvers, headed the successful October insurrection.

What was Koba-Djugashvili's performance in that 'year of revolutionary folly'? Throughout this whole period he played no national role. He remained one of the provincial, Caucasian leaders. The Caucasus, however, was a very important centre for this revolution. There were times when, though a province, it gave an example to the rest of the Empire; and it was the last to acknowledge defeat when the counter-revolution set in and the rest of Russia was succumbing to apathy. In December 1904, a few weeks before the procession to the Winter Palace in Petersburg, a stubborn and protracted strike of the oil workers of Baku had ended in the conclusion of a collective agreement between workers and employers. This was the first collective agreement to be signed in Russia. The industrialists were compelled to bargain with a committee of virtual outlaws, the clandestine leaders of the strike. In a sense these events in Baku were the real prelude to the revolution. Koba was just touring the province with lectures against Mensheviks, Anarchists, Federalists, Armenian Dashnaks (semi-nationalists and semi-Socialists), and others when the strike broke out. He interrupted his tour and hurried to Baku. He could not have led the strike himself, for he stayed in the city only a few days. But his counsel must certainly have carried weight with its leaders. From Baku and from his journeys in the province, where conscripts drafted into the army were protesting against their enrolment, he got a strong presentiment of the things that were to come.

With his ear so close to his native ground he did not miss the first rumblings of the revolution. As early as 8 January 1905, on the eve of the 'bloody Sunday' in the capital, the Caucasian Union of Social Democrats issued a proclamation under the title 'Workers of the Caucasus, the hour of revenge has struck'.[1]

---

[1] J. Stalin, *Sochinenya*, vol. i, pp. 74-80.

Its author was Koba. He affirmed that 'the Tsarist autocracy is losing its main prop—its reliable warriors', i.e. the army, which he considered to be turning against the Government. He overrated the strength of the movement. One of the reasons that enabled Tsardom to withstand and survive the shock of the First Revolution was precisely the reliability of its 'warriors'. On the whole, the army still allowed itself to be used against the revolutionary people. Eight or nine soldiers out of ten were mouzhiks, and the attitude of the army reflected this fact: for the peasantry was not whole-heartedly behind the revolution. Koba's error can easily be explained by the peculiar circumstances that prevailed in the Caucasus. In his native land, Georgia, the peasants were far worse off than in the rest of Russia. The hunger for land was much more acute there; and peasant revolts and soldiers' riots were more widespread there than elsewhere.[1]

In other respects, too, Koba tended to overrate the adversities with which Tsardom had to contend. He forecast that the Government would soon go bankrupt because it was losing credit in western Europe. In actual fact, the *Bourse* of republican France was generous with loans that helped the Tsar to put his finances into some order. Koba warned his readers that Tsardom was 'changing its skin snake-like', that in panic it was going to lay aside the knout for a change and to offer some sops to the people; but 'the time has come to *destroy* the Tsarist Government, and *destroy* it we shall. . . . Russia is like a loaded gun, at full cock, ready to go off at the slightest concussion.' 'Let us therefore join hands and *rally around the party Committees*! We should not forget for even a single moment that *only the party Committees can lead us in a worthy manner, that they alone* can light for us the road to the "Promised Land" that is called a Socialist world. The party that has opened our eyes and shown to us our enemies, organized us into an awe-inspiring army and led us into battle, the party that has never deserted us, whether in joy or in sorrow and has always marched ahead of us—is the Russian Social Democratic Workers' Party.' How strongly the ex-cleric lived on in the tough Committee-man!

[1] An official report claimed that the partisan groups in the Georgian countryside consisted mainly of 'temporary serfs'. See *Istorya Klasovoi Borby v Zakavkazi*, vol. i, p. 23.

In his vision of things, the people wandered through the desert to the Promised Land of socialism, the party, like the biblical pillar of fire, illumined the road ahead. Who else then should lead the people, 'whether in joy or in sorrow', if not the priests and the Levites of the party Committees? The proclamation ended with the slogan: 'Down with Tsarist autocracy! Long live a Popular Constituent Assembly! Long live the Democratic Republic! Long live the Russian Social Democratic Workers' Party!'

To counter the menace of revolution the Tsarist Ministry of Home Affairs let loose the Black Hundred gangs upon Socialists of all shades, Liberals, and Jews. At Baku the Black Hundreds began to operate soon after the oil-strike. What the Jews were in other parts of the Empire, the scapegoats on whom Tsardom tried to divert popular discontent, the Armenians were in the Caucasus. For in the Caucasus the racial and religious feud between Turks and Armenians was always simmering, and kept going by the passions which the slaughter of Armenians over the Turkish border aroused as well as by the hatred felt for the Armenian middle class on the spot. Nothing was easier for the Black Hundreds than to incite a Moslem mob to slaughter Armenians, and so to swamp the Caucasus in bloody tribal feuds. The ugly troubles of those days were vividly described in his memoirs by Sergo Alliluyev, Stalin's father-in-law:[1]

The authorities, actively supported by officials from all departments and of all grades, who were members of the Black Hundreds of Baku, and by town and county police, armed the thugs of the 'Russian People's Union'. First the gangs incited Armenian and Turkish children against one another. Then over the injured children there arose riotous quarrels among adults. The Black Hundreds killed Armenians and Turks from ambush and set fire to houses. Stirring the feuds by all sorts of tricks, the authorities achieved their desired objective; in August Armenians and Turks began a savage slaughter of one another. The town resounded with shots. Armenian shops were looted and dwellings ransacked. Corpses lay about on roads and pavements; and the groans of the bleeding wounded could be heard everywhere. Here and there soldiers and policemen stood by quietly and watched the slaughter. The Black Hundreds then set fire to factories and oil-wells and spread wild rumours that this had been done by the strikers. On the pretext of a 'fight against arson', bandits and assassins hunted our prominent party workers. . . .

[1] S. Alliluyev, op. cit., p. 130.

Life for all of us was a sort of inferno. The fires in the oil works became more and more threatening. Around us was the raging element, the awe-inspiring, savage and untameable flame; and there was death and destruction everywhere.

For a good many months the revolution was almost defeated or at a standstill in the multi-tribal cities of the Caucasus. Koba wrote leaflet after leaflet warning the working class against fratricidal strife and calling for international solidarity. He extolled the few instances in which crowds of Turks, Armenians, Persians, and Russians marched in fraternal processions from churches to mosques and cemeteries 'to take an oath to love one another'.[1] He urged the party to encourage such demonstrations and advocated agreements with any other parties and factions prepared to take common action against the slaughters and pogroms.

Concurrently with this, the Menshevik–Bolshevik controversy continued. In May Koba issued a pamphlet, *A Brief Survey of Party Differences*,[2] once again a repetition of Lenin's arguments, studded with the invariable metaphors about the Promised Land of socialism. The pamphlet, as well as his other articles, left no doubt that Koba was an irreconcilable Leninist. The Bolsheviks carried with them only a small minority of the Caucasian underground. Koba's native Georgia was the Menshevik stronghold *par excellence*. The point of view he took was that of a minority within the minority, since most of the Bolshevik leaders in the province were seeking a *rapprochement* with the Mensheviks. At this point Koba inevitably caught Lenin's attention. For Lenin had been suspecting that his case was not put across with enough vigour and conviction in the Caucasus; and it was with pleasant surprise that he learned from Maxim Litvinov about Koba's brochure, published in Russian, Georgian, and Armenian. Nadezhda Krupskaya, Lenin's wife and assistant, asked for a copy of the brochure and of the Georgian sheet in which Koba expounded Lenin's views. This was the first indubitable, though still indirect, contact between Lenin and his future successor. It is doubtful whether Koba would have caught Lenin's eye at this stage if the more prominent Bolsheviks of the province had supported Lenin whole-heartedly. It was characteristic of Lenin that whenever he felt that he

---

[1] J. Stalin, *Sochinenya*, vol. i, pp. 81–8.   [2] Ibid., pp. 89–130.

could not rely on the other Bolshevik leaders he sought to establish direct contact with those of secondary status and the rank and file, who were more determined to back him and whom he then encouraged, took into his confidence, and promoted to higher standing in his faction. The first signs of friendly attention from Lenin gave Koba a gratifying compensation for lack of success on the spot. The style of his polemics against the local bigwigs of Menshevism became more and more fanatical and bitter, reflecting both his sense of isolation among his comrades on the spot and the self-confidence imparted to him by the knowledge that he was marching in step with Lenin himself. His sense of isolation must have been the greater because of the passing of his two friends and mentors—Tsulukidze and Ketskhoveli. Both those leaders of the minority of *Messame Dassy* might well have been firm Bolsheviks like himself if they lived. But Ketskhoveli was shot by his jailers at the Metekhy Castle, the dreaded fortress prison of Tiflis; and Tsulukidze died of consumption.

. . . .

Meanwhile, Koba watched his master developing new variants of revolutionary technique. Already at the April conference in London, Lenin had put before his followers the question of armed insurrection.[1] Back in Geneva he went on to probe this question. Tsardom, he argued, would not willingly abdicate; it would have to be overthrown by an armed insurrection. This was a truism accepted by all Socialists. But many of them envisaged the insurrection as a spontaneous revolt of the people, as one of those elemental phenomena of revolution that were as inevitable and could just as little be prepared and planned as the risings and settings of the sun. Lenin treated such Socialists contemptuously as the romantic Micawbers of revolution. Insurrection, he argued, was an art to be learned and practised. He reminded the party of such elementary maxims as that insurrection could succeed only if it was constantly on the offensive and that defence was its death. He urged his followers to set up specialized military branches of the party.

Koba restated the argument in *Proletariatis Brdzola*:

[1] Lenin, *Sochinenya*, vol. viii, p. 336.

Many of our organizations have already practically solved the problem and directed part of their strength and resources towards arming the proletariat. Our struggle against autocracy has now reached the stage at which everybody admits the need to arm ourselves. But it is not enough to acknowledge that need—the practical task ought to be put squarely before the party. Our Committees ought at once to set out to arm the people on the spot, to form special groups entrusted with the job, to set up regional centres for the collection of arms, to organize workshops for the preparation of all sorts of explosives and to work out plans for the seizure of governmental and private stores of arms and arsenals ... quarrels between the various factions ought least of all to interfere with the unification of all Social Democratic forces for this purpose.[1]

Koba translated Lenin's instructions not merely into Georgian, but into action as well. He took part in building and guiding the provincial military organization, which had at its disposal a very efficient secret laboratory of explosives, set up by Krasin. True, Lenin's idea of a centrally planned and directed rising was not to materialize in the First Revolution. Even so, the fighting squads came to the fore in the many uncoordinated revolts of that year. In the Caucasus they resisted the Black Hundreds, protected working-class quarters against tribal feuds, and kept in touch with peasant guerrillas. Koba's role in the new branch of the party was not that of a combatant officer but of an organizer, administrator, and inspirer.

The new branch of the party had to be organized on a basis of exceptionally strict secrecy. Its hierarchy and its members were wrapped in even thicker layers of clandestinity than the rest of the party. Indeed, the contacts between the technical branch and the other branches were kept to a minimum.

In the hey-day of the revolution the ranks of the party were swollen with new and untried members. As the Tsarist terror diminished the party relaxed its rules and habits of secrecy. Before 1905 committees, executives, and party officers were, as a rule, appointed by higher committees at their own discretion—the organization was built from above; and the rank and file did not know who were the members of the various leading bodies. In the course of the First Revolution the method of organization was changed; the committees were

---

[1] J. Stalin, *Sochinenya*, vol. i, p. 134.

subjected to democratic control by the rank and file. Appointment of committees from above was replaced by elections from below.[1] The elective principle, however, could not be introduced into the technical branch. An important part of Koba's activities throughout the First Revolution, especially during its ebb, developed inside that most secret redoubt of the party, out of sight and beyond the control of ordinary members.

The armed insurrection, if successful, would result in the setting up of a Provisional Revolutionary Government. The outlook and functions of that government were Koba's next theme. Here, too, he followed Lenin closely: Russia was not ripe for socialism; and, therefore, the Provisional Revolutionary Government would not be a 'proletarian dictatorship'. Nor would it be a parliamentary government, since this was not possible in the middle of a revolution. Lenin's label for the Provisional Government was 'a democratic dictatorship of the proletariat and the peasantry'. That cumbrous and self-contradictory formula was never clearly explained either by its author or his disciples although it was the basis of all Bolshevik propaganda from 1905 till 1917; and in 1917 the lack of clarity on this point led to one of the most severe crises in the history of Bolshevism, so rich in internal controversies and crises.

These were the tasks of the Provisional Revolutionary Government as Koba saw them: it would disarm the 'dark forces' of the counter-revolution; it would lead in the civil war; it would then convene a Constituent Assembly, issuing from a general election. Between the emergence of the Revolutionary Government, deriving its power from no constitutional source, and the convocation of the Constituent Assembly, the Government would decree a series of radical reforms, none of which would go beyond the limits of bourgeois democracy. The reforms would include: the proclamation of the freedom of the Press and of assembly, the abolition of indirect taxes, the imposition of a progressive tax on profit and of progressive death duties, the setting up of revolutionary peasant committees to take charge of land reform, the separation of Church and State, the eight hours' working day, the introduction of social services and labour exchanges, and so on. Altogether the

---

[1] *V.K.P. (b) v Rezolutsyakh*, vol. i, p. 59; N. Popov, *Outline History of the Communist Party*, vol. i, p. 174.

programme was much more moderate than that that was to be adopted exactly forty years later by the moderate Labour Government in Britain. For Russia, however, in the beginning of the century, barely forty years after the abolition of serfdom, it spelt a thorough-going upheaval.[1]

Koba, like all Bolsheviks, argued that the programme just outlined could be put into operation only by an alliance of the Socialist working class with the individualistic peasantry, because the urban, Liberal middle class would not support the revolution. He realized that in the long run the working class and the peasantry were pursuing different aims, and that eventually their interests and policies were likely to clash. But the clash would arise only if and when the Socialists attempted to overthrow capitalism, and this was not the task of the revolution in Russia. Thus, the 'democratic dictatorship of the proletariat and the peasantry' was to be purely democratic because in its programme there was 'not an ounce' of socialism proper; it was to be a dictatorship because even so limited an objective as the establishment of a non-Socialist parliamentary republic would call for the suppression of the *ancien régime* by violent dictatorial means; it would be based on a coalition of two classes and this meant that representatives of different parties would sit in the Government. It followed from this that the Social Democratic party was bound in duty to enter the Government, to represent in it the interests of the working class and so to 'secure the hegemony of the proletariat'. In other words, the Socialists would give a lead to the party or the parties of the peasantry, which by definition were less advanced, less clear-sighted and determined than was the party of the proletariat.

The Mensheviks stuck to their view that the Liberal middle class would lead in the revolution. From this they drew the conclusion that the Social Democratic party ought not to participate in the Provisional Revolutionary Government, because it was not the task of Social Democrats to manage the business of a non-Socialist administration. In those years an overwhelming majority of Socialists all over the world, and even the moderate ones, still regarded the participation of Socialists in any coalition government as an act of impermissible opportunism, if not a direct betrayal of socialism. When the French

[1] J. Stalin, *Sochinenya*, vol. i, pp. 138–59.

Socialist Millerand accepted the portfolio of a bourgeois minister he automatically put himself outside the Socialist pale. The Mensheviks were now charging Lenin with Millerandism. In their view his advocacy of Social-Democratic participation in a non-Socialist Government came very close to mere opportunism. Koba counter-argued that the Mensheviks were confusing different types of government. A provisional government, issuing from a revolution and committed to radical reforms, was quite different from an ordinary administration whose task it was merely to conserve the existing order. 'What is a cabinet of ministers?', he asked. 'The result of the existence of a regular administration. And what is a Provisional Revolutionary Government? The result of the destruction of the regular administration. The former puts into effect the existing laws with the help of a regular army. The latter scraps the existing laws and promulgates the will of the revolution with the help of a people in insurrection. It is strange that the Mensheviks should have forgotten the ABC of revolution.' Lenin, as he interpreted him, was definitely not a smug ministerialist, a contemptible Millerand.

Another Menshevik criticism—and one that reflected more truly the critics' real apprehensions—was that Lenin's programme was a mockery of constitutional rule. For the Provisional Government, as he saw it, was to decree a series of root-and-branch reforms even before the convocation of a Constituent Assembly. The Assembly, so the critics forecast—and their forecast came true in 1918—would either have to put up with the accomplished facts of those reforms or be dispersed by the dictatorial Government. To Koba's mind such constitutional scruples were ludicrous.[1] He saw no reason why the Assembly should oppose the reforms decreed by the Provisional Revolutionary Government during a constitutional interregnum: the reforms, radically democratic but not Socialist, were bound to command the support of an immense majority of the people. Why argue whether or not the Provisional Revolutionary Government should defer the reforms until the Constituent Assembly met, when it should be clear as daylight that unavoidable civil war would delay elections to the Assembly and that in the meantime the Provisional Government

[1] J. Stalin, *Sochinenya*, vol. i, p. 156.

would be driven by the mood in the country to give land to the peasants, to decree an eight-hour day, and so on? The self-preservation of the revolution would dictate that course of action. 'Does not that [Menshevik] reasoning', asked Koba, 'flavour of rotten liberalism? Is it not strange to hear it from the mouth of a revolutionary? Do not the Mensheviks remind one of the convict who, when he was about to put his head into the hangman's noose, implored the hangman not to scratch the pimple on his neck?'

Both Bolsheviks and Mensheviks still held the same idea about the general objective of the revolution—it was to be 'bourgeois democratic' and no more. The difference was in tactics. The Mensheviks made their tactics suit the limited strategic objective, while Lenin's uninhibited revolutionary tactics were at cross-purposes with it. It was easy for the Bolsheviks to prove that the 'bourgeois-democratic' orthodoxy to which their adversaries stuck implied resignation from revolution. It was even easier for the Mensheviks to prove that the Bolshevik conception was a contradiction in terms. The criticisms made by each side were equally effective and flawless in their logic. The Menshevik case was undoubtedly more consistent; but in that consistency there was a disturbing undertone of quietist resignation that boded ill for the party if it were caught in the rapids of revolution. Lenin's argument was confused; in Koba's crude summaries it was at times even incoherent; but its tone reverberated with revolutionary will to power. Eventually—so some of Lenin's critics forecast—Lenin would have to bring his strategy and tactics into line with each other. He would either have to give up his extreme tactics or break out of the framework of a purely democratic, non-Socialist revolution and try an experiment in socialism. Lenin repeated that such an experiment in Russia would be a quixotic venture. The Socialist who in 1905 believed that the revolution, if victorious, could not help embarking upon the road of proletarian dictatorship and socialism, was Trotsky, whose prognostications were treated like the ravings of a lunatic by both Mensheviks and Bolsheviks.[1] At the 'general rehearsal' the chief actors, apart from Trotsky, not only failed to appear

[1] Trotsky's view was shared by Helphand-Parvus, whose role in the Russian revolution was only episodical.

during the most important acts—even their parts were different from those they were to play at the actual performance. This was, of course, true of Koba as well.

In October the Tsar issued his manifesto with a promise of constitutional freedom. The Liberals triumphed. They hoped to be able to transform Tsardom into a constitutional monarchy and they saw in the Duma, the newly convoked Parliament, the instrument for that transformation. Most Mensheviks and some Bolsheviks, too, thought that they should take part in the election. True, the franchise was to be limited, the working class was to be very poorly represented and the Duma was, therefore, certain to be dominated by the moderate Liberals. This, the Mensheviks argued, did not really matter. In the French Revolution the moderate Assembly had been forced by the popular movement to give place to the more radical Convention. Similar shifts in Russia would sweep away the Duma and replace it by a Convention. Koba did not share that view. He advocated a boycott of the election, because any election now 'on the eve of an all-Russian rising of the people' would merely divert the people's attention from direct revolutionary action. In an appeal which he wrote on behalf of the Tiflis Committee he stated: 'The proletariat does not ask the government for petty concessions such as the abolition of martial law and a stop to executions in some towns and villages. . . . He who now asks the government for such concessions does not believe in its death, while the proletariat breathes that belief.' 'Only on the bones of the oppressors can the people's freedom be founded—only the blood of the oppressors can fertilize the soil for the people's self-rule.'[1] Lenin, who sometimes approved such expressions of plebeian anger, the Russian versions of *les aristos aux poteaux*, himself never indulged in them. For this his taste was too refined. In the mouth of Koba, the son of ex-serfs, such words had a natural ring. In another of his proclamations he called for 'a fight without quarter against the Liberal enemies of the people', because the Liberals were making their deal with Tsardom. It was no far cry from this to decrying the Mensheviks, too, even though Bolsheviks and Mensheviks were still members of the same party. 'Either the bourgeois Liberals have become Mensheviks', Koba remarked, 'or else

[1] J. Stalin, *Sochinenya*, vol. i, pp. 189–90.

the Caucasian Mensheviks have changed into bourgeois Liberals.'

The Tsar's manifesto provoked a storm of protests. It was too half-hearted to satisfy the opposition; and it was so obvious a sign of weakness that it was bound to encourage fresh demands. The protests were followed by the general strikes and local risings. Two months after the Tsar had made his semi-Liberal gesture the superintendent of the police in the Caucasus reported to his chief in Petersburg as follows: 'The Kutais province is in a critical condition. . . . The insurgents have disarmed the gendarmes, made themselves masters of the western line of the railway and are themselves selling tickets and keeping order. . . . I am receiving no reports from Kutais; the gendarmes have been taken off the line and concentrated in Tiflis. The couriers sent out with reports are searched by revolutionaries and the documents are seized; the situation there is impossible. . . . The Vice-Regent has had a nervous breakdown; the situation is not yet hopeless. The Count is attending to reports of major importance but is very weak. If possible I shall send details by post; if not, by messenger.'[1]

The parties had emerged from the underground. Socialist dailies were published and sold openly. In Petersburg Litvinov and Krasin edited *Novaya Zhizn* (The New Life). Trotsky edited *Nachalo* (The Start), the most brilliant journalistic venture of the First Revolution, with a circulation of about half a million. In Tiflis Koba-Djugashvili and S. Shaumian[2] jointly edited a Bolshevik daily with a less symbolical name, *Kavkasky Rabochy Listok* (The Caucasian Workers' News-sheet). The newspapers were short-lived—they were suppressed by the police as soon as the risings fizzled out. Meanwhile, Koba was dividing his time between the editorial offices of the legally published daily, the half-clandestine Tiflis and Caucasian Social Democratic Committees, and the altogether clandestine technical branch of the party. Amid such varied activities he was also preparing the fourth conference of the Caucasian Bolsheviks, at which he himself was elected delegate to the party's

[1] L. Berya, op. cit., p. 80.
[2] Shaumian was the future Bolshevik commissar of Baku, one of the twenty-six commissars shot by Russian counter-revolutionaries during the British intervention in the Caucasus.

national conference, convened by Lenin for the first time inside Russia. In actual fact, the conference took place in the Finnish town of Tammerfors, because Finland enjoyed autonomy and greater freedom than the rest of the Tsarist Empire and the delegates felt safer there.

. . . .

This was the first time that Koba emerged from the half-Asiatic Caucasus into European Russia, from the backwater of Tiflis into a truly national gathering. At Tammerfors, too, he first met Lenin. Years later he described with characteristically vivid crudeness the impression his master made on him:[1]

I had hoped to see the mountain eagle of our party, the great man, great physically as well as politically. I had fancied Lenin as a giant, stately and imposing. How great was my disappointment to see a most ordinary-looking man, below average height, in no way, literally in no way, distinguishable from ordinary mortals. . . . Usually, a great man comes late to a meeting so that his appearance may be awaited with bated breath. Then, just before the great man enters, the warning goes round: 'Hush . . . silence . . . he is coming.' The rite did not seem to me superfluous, because it created an impression and inspired respect. How great was my disappointment to see that Lenin had arrived at the conference before the other delegates were there and had settled himself somewhere in a corner and was unassumingly carrying on a conversation, a most ordinary conversation, with the most ordinary delegates. I will not conceal from you that at that time this seemed to me to be rather a violation of certain essential rules.

Nothing could sum up Koba's parochial outlook at the time better than his own words. The descendant of serfs may have learned to use an elementary Marxist idiom and argue about the mechanics of the revolution. But he was still surprised to see that the leader of that revolution lacked all seigniorial manner. The ex-seminarist who had turned his back on the Church still fancied Lenin as the high priest or mandarin of socialism.

He gazed at Lenin, listened avidly to his speech, and watched every move and gesture. There were enough qualities in the man to impress the Tiflis delegate deeply: the overwhelming

[1] J. Stalin, *Sochinenya*, vol. vi, p. 54.

logic of his speech, his political fearlessness, the broad historical sweep of his views, the subtlety and simplicity of his conclusions, and—last but not least—his sober practical sense. The delegates had arrived at Tammerfors in a mood of exhilaration, dizzy with the hope of a quick overthrow of Tsardom, a hope that was stimulated by the first tidings of the Moscow rising.[1] Even Lenin was affected by the general optimism; and there were such comic-opera touches about the conference as, for instance, the intervals between its sessions when the delegates headed by Lenin went out to practise revolver-shooting in the woods. Nevertheless, Lenin's sobriety and circumspection were not swept away. At the opening session he proposed that, in spite of all that was happening in those 'days of liberty', the delegates should use pseudonyms instead of their real names. The *Okhrana* had not yet been defeated, he said, and it was too early to dispense altogether with clandestinity. Koba assumed the nickname of Ivanovich. His own role at the conference was as modest and unassuming as his nickname. No ties of close acquaintance, let alone friendship, arose between him and Lenin as yet. But he met a number of people who were to become important later on: Lozovsky, the future head of the Red Professional International (Profintern) and chief official spokesman during the Russo-German war of 1941–5; Yaroslavsky, future leader of the Society of the Godless; Borodin, who was to become Stalin's envoy and military adviser to General Chiang Kai-shek exactly twenty years later; Nadezhda Krupskaya, Lenin's wife; and several others.

It must have been with some surprise that Koba learned that a merger between Mensheviks and Bolsheviks was the main item on the agenda of the conference. Events had brought the two factions nearer to each other. The trend towards unification was stronger in central Russia than in the Caucasus, where the split was of no great practical importance because the Bolsheviks wielded little influence. Both factions felt that the split was weakening them and were anxious to put an end to it. At Tammerfors Lozovsky proposed that the local organizations should merge straight away, without waiting for formal agreement between the leaders. His motion was accepted.

---

[1] See the account of G. Kramolnikov in *Trudy Pervoi Vsesoyuznoi Konferentsii Istorikov-Marksistov*, vol. i, pp. 210–47.

Simultaneously with the Bolsheviks, the Mensheviks, too, were in conference and adopted a parallel decision in favour of union. The two conferences were to be followed by negotiations between the leaders in Petersburg.

The next issue discussed at Tammerfors was elections to the Duma. Ought the Social Democrats to take part in them or not? At the conference of the Caucasian Bolsheviks Koba had argued in favour of boycott. The place of the working class was on the barricades and not at polling-booths. Much to his surprise, however, at Tammerfors Lenin came out in favour of participation in the election, or at least in some of its phases, since the election was to be indirect. The tactics of boycott seemed to Lenin negative and barren; and the antithesis of barricades and polling-booths too crude to make good policy. Something could be said for the Menshevik view that a moderate Duma might under popular pressure be replaced by a radical Convention; and he believed in the maxim *les absents ont toujours tort*. Ordinary parliamentarism, with its oratory and habits of conciliation and bargaining, had no attraction for him; but he saw no reason why the cause of revolution should not be furthered from the parliamentary platform. In later years, he was to say that revolution could be preached even from a dungheap or in a pigsty—why not preach it in the 'pigsty' of the Tsarist Duma? To most delegates at Tammerfors, to the practical workers of the underground who came to the conference full of the sound and fury of the strikes and the risings, Lenin's reasonings sounded like pure Menshevik opportunism. Together with other provincial delegates, Koba strongly objected to his master's proposals. Together with others, he must have thought that the great leader, like many émigrés, had lost touch with life in Russia and underrated the impact of recent events. They, the practical workers, who studied the course of revolution not in the libraries of Geneva, London, or Paris but in the slums of Moscow, Kazan, or Baku, knew better. Lenin was shaken by the unexpected strength of the opposition. Perhaps, he said, the practical workers were right after all; and he jovially announced that he was 'withdrawing from his position in good order'. Koba-Ivanovich was elected to the commission that was to draft a resolution on the subject. This was his first success at a national party gathering. That he obtained it against Lenin could not but enhance his self-confidence.[1]

The conference ended on the last day of the eventful year. According to a report of the secret police, who had an agent among the delegates, on the morrow of the conference 'the Social Democratic Central Committee and a number of delegates, Menshevik and Bolshevik, met at No. 9 Zagorodny Prospect in Petersburg in order to discuss unity'. The report mentioned Ivanovich, the delegate of Tiflis, as one of those present. Koba witnessed a curious scene: Lenin and Martov spoke about current affairs in a most conciliatory vein. Martov even went so far as to accept Lenin's famous Paragraph 1 of the Party Statutes, the paragraph that had caused the split. Lenin might well have triumphed. Social Democracy seemed at last to reunite and to do so on his, Lenin's, terms.

In the first days of January 1906, while Koba was on his way back to Tiflis, the tide of revolution had already turned. The Moscow rising had been defeated. The risings in Georgia were only smouldering under the ashes. The Vice-Regent, by now recovered from his nervous breakdown, gave orders to suppress the *Caucasian Workers' News-sheet*. But the change in the situation made itself felt only gradually. The revolution's reverses were seen by the leaders as a mere zigzag in a complicated graph. In a pamphlet *Two Skirmishes*, Koba analysed the events of the year, from the Petersburg procession to the defeat of the Moscow rising:[2] the rising failed because it was on the defensive, when it should have been constantly on the attack. It lacked leadership; and this was due to the split inside Social Democracy. The events showed the need for unity, which would soon be happily achieved.

[1] 'The *Komitetchik* [Committee-man]', writes Krupskaya, 'was usually a fairly self-assured person, who realized what great influence the work of the Committees had over the masses; *he generally did not recognize any inner-Party democracy whatever.* "This democratism [which required that the Committees should be elected by the rank and file] only leads to us falling into the hands of the authorities . . . ," the *Komitetchiks* would say. And inwardly these Committee members always rather despised "the people abroad [i.e. the leaders in exile]. . . . They ought to be sent to work under Russian conditions" was their verdict. The *Komitetchiks* . . . did not like innovations. . . . In 1904–5 [they] . . . bore tremendous responsibilities . . . but many of them experienced the utmost difficulty in adapting themselves to . . . increasing opportunities for legal work and to the methods of open struggle' (*Memories of Lenin*, p. 93). Krupskaya's words undoubtedly reflected Lenin's opinion about the Committee-men. [2] J. Stalin, *Sochinenya*, vol. i, pp. 196–205.

But unity, that healing medicine, was being administered rather late in the day; and it was doubtful how far its ingredients corresponded to the label. The Mensheviks, who had allowed themselves to be carried away by the radical mood of the last months of the year, were now relapsing into their previous, more moderate or timid, attitude. The Bolsheviks were ensuring themselves against the risk of a merger and formed a secret Bolshevik Caucasian Bureau, a sort of party within the 'united party'. After these preliminary moves, the factions sent their delegates to attend the fourth Congress, which assembled in Stockholm in April 1906 in order to sanction the merger. Eleven delegates represented the Caucasus at the Congress—ten Mensheviks and one Bolshevik. The one Bolshevik was Koba-Ivanovich.

During this, his first, journey abroad, he had no time to observe life outside Russia. The Congress dragged on in a string of long sessions and interminable debates and squabbles. He spoke several times in defence of Lenin's views. On the crucial issue of the debate, however—land reform—he took an independent view.[1] The Mensheviks advocated dispossession of the landlords and the transfer of their land to municipal ownership. Lenin advocated nationalization of the land. The Mensheviks, as usual, saw the future Russian Republic dominated by the Liberal middle class and were eager to strengthen the more popular local government against the central administration. Lenin, thinking in terms of 'the democratic dictatorship of workers and peasants', wanted the ownership of all land to be vested in the central government. Koba-Ivanovich was equally opposed to nationalization and municipalization. The land reform for which he stood was simply the sharing out of the great estates among the peasants. Even before the Congress, he gave his views on land reform in the Georgian periodical *Elva* (Storm).[2] Against Lenin's policy of nationalization he set two arguments, one that sounded as if it had been borrowed from the Mensheviks, and the other characteristically his own. The future government, he stated, would be a bourgeois government; and it would be an error to strengthen it unduly by vesting it with the ownership of all the land. Koba did not even attempt to explain how this tallied with the 'democratic

[1] J. Stalin, *Sochinenya*, vol. i, pp. 236-8.   [2] Ibid., pp. 214-35.

dictatorship of workers and peasants' that he himself was propagating. But his main objection to both nationalization and municipalization was that neither would satisfy the peasants. He, the revolutionary of peasant stock, was more sensitive than others to the mouzhik's werwolf hunger for land. 'Even in their dreams', he wrote, 'the peasants see the landlords' fields as their own property.' 'Distributism', as this viewpoint came to be called, was branded by most Socialists as a reactionary concession to peasant individualism. Lenin thundered against 'the practical party workers', who were out to win favour with the backward mouzhik and, ignoring Socialist principle, played unscrupulously on his appetite for property. Ivanovich's answer was that the land reform he wanted would, of course, foster capitalism in the country-side, but this was precisely what, by common agreement, the revolution stood for. Small holdings and rural capitalism would certainly be an advance on feudalism. As the Mensheviks had a majority, Lenin in the end voted with the pro-mouzhik group in his own faction, hoping thus to defeat the Mensheviks; but he went on to vent his irritation on the narrowminded 'realists' of Koba's sort.

The incident was a significant, though remote, prelude to the agrarian revolution in Russia in 1917 and the land reforms that were to be carried out in eastern Europe and eastern Germany under the auspices of the Red Army in 1945. In 1917 the Bolsheviks actually divided the land among the peasants, though in theory it was nationalized. In 1945 the land of the Prussian Junkers and Polish and Hungarian landlords was shared out among the peasants, without even the theoretical pretence of nationalization. In Stockholm in 1906 the course such agrarian revolutions would take was mapped out in advance by Ivanovich more clearly than by Lenin, though this did not prevent Ivanovich-Stalin from crushing the 'rural capitalism' he had defended and replacing it by collective farming in 1930. Forty years later, in 1946, in the foreword to his *Collected Works*,[1] Ivanovich-Stalin tried to explain his Stockholm controversy with Lenin and self-critically he attributed it to the narrow-mindedness and lack of theoretical insight on the part of the 'practical workers' of whom he was one. We, he

[1] Ibid., pp. xi–xv.

confessed, the '*praktiki*', could not understand that Lenin was already then looking ahead to the Russian revolution, as it would be when it passed from its 'bourgeois democratic' to its Socialist phase. He, Stalin, thought that the two phases would be separated from one another by a long period of capitalist development, because he could not conceive of a Socialist revolution taking place before the working class grew to be the majority of the nation. A curious confession: on the strength of this principle, Russia should have remained a capitalist country until to-day. The confession offers a glimpse of the complex evolution of Bolshevism itself as well as of the groping manner in which its leaders, driven by events, were changing the direction of their revolutionary journey.

Back from Stockholm Ivanovich reported on the 'unity Congress' in a special pamphlet signed by 'Comrade K.'.[1] The Congress was in his eyes a failure. Its resolutions reflect~d the opportunistic spirit of the Menshevik majority. No wonder the middle-class Liberals were jubilant about its outcome.

. . . .

Among the many resolutions adopted by the Stockholm Congress there was one that had a close bearing upon Koba's discreet doings in the Technical Branch. On the initiative of the Mensheviks, the Congress condemned the raids made by the fighting squads on banks, treasury transports, and government troops. Lenin, believing that the revolution was still on the upgrade and that partisan raids were a good way of training the fighting squads for the expected nation-wide insurrection, fiercely opposed the resolution. The Mensheviks had not been in their element at all while the pandemonium of revolts and risings lasted. They were quicker than the Bolsheviks to realize that the revolution was now in retreat, though as yet nobody dared to say so in as many words. Plekhanov concluded his second thoughts on the December rising with the words: 'We should not have taken up arms.' To Lenin this was sheer blasphemy—he was in no mood to repent of the 'follies' of 1905. Many Mensheviks did not yet dare to endorse Plekhanov's second thoughts, but his saying aptly epitomized the mood that was taking hold of them.

[1] J. Stalin, *Sochinenya*, vol. i, pp. 250–76.

At first the controversy over the fighting squads was subsidiary to the wider dispute. If the December rising had been a bad mistake, the raids of the fighting squads were even worse. If, however, the revolution was still to advance then the fighting squads had an essential role to play. The Stockholm Congress outlawed 'partisan warfare' in principle, but it could not make up its mind to pass a categorical verdict.[1] It prohibited all forms of raids, with the exception of the seizure of arms and arsenals. The technical branches soon made the utmost of that loophole and continued to stage attack after attack on high Tsarist officials, banks, treasury transports, as well as arsenals. This was the most obscure, and perhaps also the most romantic, chapter of the First Revolution. It abounded in dramatic incidents and unheard-of exploits. Its heroes were fearless idealists, saints, and colourful adventurers: but there were also *agents provocateurs* and gangsters plying their trade under the banner of revolution. It was not easy to tell one type from another and to disentangle individual motives. It was long customary in western Europe to speak and write about this episode of Russian history as something peculiarly Russian, reflecting the mysteries of the Slav soul. According to their taste, western Europeans would express either admiration or abhorrence of the terrorists' deeds, though the sympathy of western European Liberals went out to the 'indomitable fighters against Tsarist tyranny'. But both those who extolled and those who condemned these deeds thought of them as of things so remote and exotic that they could never happen in a civilized western European environment. Unfortunately, or perhaps fortunately, western Europe was not spared that 'exotic' experience in the years when it was submerged by Nazi conquest. What the various movements of resistance, the *Maquis* and guerrillas did in France and Italy, Belgium and Norway, was exactly what the Russians had done nearly forty years before, only that the European Resistance was on a far larger scale, better financed, far more 'terroristic' and costly in human life. The Russian revolutionaries considered themselves at war with their own native autocracy; and in this they found moral justification for what they did. As in Nazi-occupied Europe, so in Tsarist Russia the heroic and idealistic core of the

---

[1] *Protokoly Obyedinitelnovo Syezda RSDRP v Stokholme v 1906 g,* pp. 262–7, 336–7.

movement was surrounded by dubious elements. The basic types—fighters, idealists, adventurers, heroes, and gangsters—were almost equally frequent in both movements, and many of the famous mysteries of the 'Russian soul' revealed themselves startlingly in French, Italian, Belgian, and Danish souls.

In spite of the moral justification which the revolutionaries believed they had for this particular method of opposition many Bolsheviks were uneasy. Guerrilla warfare could play only an auxiliary part in the revolution, just as forty years later it was auxiliary to the main war waged by the regular armies. The 'regular army', to which the Bolshevik fighting squads had to be subordinated was, in Lenin's eyes, the whole Russian people in insurrection. Unsupported by a general rising, left to itself and isolated, partisan warfare was certain to degenerate into a hopeless and demoralizing adventure. Logically, one would have expected Lenin to call off partisan warfare and disband the fighting squads as soon as it became clear that the ebb of revolution was not temporary and that years would pass before the next tide began to rise. At first, throughout 1906, Lenin clung to the hope that the revolution had not yet spent its force; and this may have accounted for the stubbornness with which he defended his fighting squads, even when the Central Committee of the united party, dominated by the Mensheviks, insisted on their disbandment.

But there was more to it than that. The defeat landed the Bolsheviks, as well as other factions, in great financial straits. In 1905 the membership of the party grew by leaps and bounds and so did its revenue from members' subscriptions. Wealthy sympathizers made important contributions to the treasury. After the counter-revolution had set in, in 1907 and 1908, the membership shrunk even more rapidly than it had grown; fellow travellers turned their backs on the defeated revolution; and so the party, whose apparatus had in the meantime been inflated to large dimensions, was left without financial means to carry on. Lenin, the real head of a revolutionary administration, was the last man to see that administration wrecked for lack of money. Even if this revolution was beaten, he thought, the next one had to be prepared; and he was determined to get the funds needed for that task. Who, if not the fighting squads, should provide the party with the means it needed to tide over the grim interval of counter-revolution and to emerge with flying colours into the Second Revolution? Lenin was fond of saying that if need be the revolutionary ought to be able to creep towards his goal with his belly in mud—he now ordered his fighting squads to creep in the mud to supply the revolution. Aware of the moral risk, he proposed to bring the squads under the strict control of the party so that they should be cleansed from dubious and unreliable elements.[1]

The Caucasus was the main area where the fighting squads operated. They were at first surrounded by an aura of romanticism that fitted only too well into the local tradition of chivalrous brigandage. Altogether 1,150 acts of terrorism were recorded in the Caucasus between 1905 and 1908.[2] The most famous seizure of treasury funds (or 'expropriation' as it came to be called) took place in one of the main squares of Tiflis on 23 June 1907. The scene of another was on board the steamship *Nicholas I* in the port of Baku. The Tiflis raid yielded a quarter of a million roubles which were duly transferred to the Bolshevik treasury abroad. As the prize consisted of banknotes of very large denominations it was not easy to exchange them in foreign banks which had been warned about their origin. Several important Bolsheviks, including the future Commissar of Foreign Affairs Litvinov, were arrested in western Europe while they were trying to exchange the money. The affair agitated the Russian and the European Press. The Mensheviks raised an outcry against Lenin and brought the issue before a party jury that was presided over by another future Commissar of Foreign Affairs, Litvinov's future boss and rival, Chicherin, then still a Menshevik. Trotsky made the charges against Lenin in the German Social Democratic newspapers and drew the attention of the Socialist International to what he called the danger of disintegration and demoralization of Russian socialism.[3]

Koba's role in all this was important, though it has never been clearly defined. He acted as a sort of a liaison officer between the Caucasian Bolshevik Bureau and the fighting squads. In this capacity he was never directly engaged in the raids. He would approve or disapprove of actions planned by

---

[1] *V.K.P. (b) v Rezolutsyakh*, vol. i, pp. 67–8; L. Trotsky, *Stalin*, p. 97.
[2] Ibid.   [3] L. Trotsky, *Stalin*, p. 105, and *Mein Leben*, pp. 209–10.

the fighting squads, advise them, take care of the 'logistics' of a major operation, and watch its execution from afar. The Tsarist police in their hunt for the perpetrators never suspected Koba of any connexion with them. His technique of dis-simulation was so perfect that this role of his was thoroughly concealed even from the eyes of the party. The two chief legendary commanders of the fighting squads were his pupils and henchmen—Ter Petrossyan ('Kamo') and Kote Tsin-tsadze, both big and warmhearted, romantic, resourceful, and untiring revolutionaries, who underwent inhuman torture when caught by the *Okhrana* without betraying any of their secrets.[1] Koba, who had a shrewd eye for the characteristics of his comrades, knew that he could trust these two, and he apparently confided his contacts to them, the safest of the safe. Nevertheless, the Caucasian Mensheviks apparently had an inkling of his true role, for they tried to impeach him before a party jury for contravention of the ban on raids imposed by the last Congress. But he somehow evaded the trial and moved from Tiflis to Baku.

In the oil city the Bolsheviks were stronger than in the capital of the Caucasus; and there, as the leader of the Baku Committee, he could defy his accusers. Because of his wire-pulling behind the fighting squads, his reputation among his political oppo-nents, never too high, fell even lower now. The familiar epithets 'madman' and 'disorganizer' were now thrown at him with unfailing regularity. Koba was not concerned with his reputation among political opponents—he knew that what he did had Lenin's approval. Let the local Mensheviks threaten him with expulsion from the 'united' party. To his mind that unity was, in any case, half-unreal. Nor was he perturbed by the lamentable effect that partisan warfare had upon the political atmosphere in the Caucasus. In the eyes of many the revolu-tion became associated with ordinary robbery. The raids pro-voked the authorities to savage reprisals, which struck fear into the people and, though they increased the general hatred of Tsardom, deepened the apathy on which the counter-revolution was thriving. The reckless tactics of the fighting squads were wasteful of human life and energy. In his memoirs S. Alliluyev gave a gloomy picture of that heroic wastefulness which reads

[1] L. Trotsky, *Stalin*, pp. 104–8.

like an unintentional indictment of the political leadership of the squads that was exercised, at least locally, by Koba, his future son-in-law.[1] All the difficult dilemmas of partisan warfare, with which an all-European underground was to grapple in the Second World War, arose before the Russian Socialists in those early days. Whether one analyses the way the dilemmas were solved four or forty years after the event, it is equally difficult to pass judgement, to glorify uncritically or to condemn the leaders, who, under the pressure of events and amid a thousand uncertainties, made their hazardous and perilous decisions.

The Bolsheviks were not alone in practising guerrilla warfare and 'expropriations'. In the Caucasus the Armenian Federalists, a much more moderate group, did the same; and even the Menshevik Georgians, loud in denouncing the Bolshevik raids, were not averse from making similar raids of their own or from sharing the booty of Bolshevik forays. In Poland it was the right rather than the left wing of the Socialists that specialized in revolutionary terrorism. The most celebrated Polish terrorist was the future marshal and dictator of Poland, Pilsudski. One of Pilsudski's chief assistants in organizing the raids was a Polish worker, Arciszewski, who was to be the Premier of the Polish anti-Soviet émigré government in London in 1945. Koba and Pilsudski then seemingly trod the same ground. But their methods, and even more so their motives, differed. Pilsudski, in his romantic nationalism, only thinly varnished with socialism, looked back to the risings of the quixotically brave Polish nobility in the eighteenth and nineteenth centuries, and saw himself as the descendant of a long line of Polish national heroes —Kosciuszko, Mieroslawski, and others. He did not place much hope on any popular, let alone Socialist, revolution, but he really did hope to deliver Poland from Russian dominance by guerrilla warfare. Koba did not share any illusions. His fighting squads were to remain merely the tools, and certainly not the decisive ones, of a great popular revolution.

This, incidentally, accounts for the different manner in which the two men treated their early partisan exploits when they became the rulers of their countries. In Pilsudskist Poland, the deeds of the fighting squads were surrounded by an official cult.

[1] S. Alliluyev, op. cit., pp. 159–66.

The anniversaries of every major raid were celebrated with solemnity and pomp. Every historical detail relating to Pilsudski's exploits was dug out and described in innumerable books and articles—and many a detail was manufactured *post factum* by obliging historians. In Russia, discreet official silence has surrounded Stalin's role in guerrilla warfare. All his official biographers have avoided even hinting at it, while Stalin himself has never uttered a single word either to confirm or to deny the current versions about that phase of his career. Even the very detailed Biographical Chronicle appended to his *Collected Works*, in which he himself has traced his own activity during the First Revolution month after month and week after week, contains not a single mention of the guerrilla campaign.[1] All that has been known about it has been disclosed by his opponents or selected by those who were his Caucasian subordinates long before his ascent to absolute power. In the light of the Leninist tradition, his connexion with the fighting squads lacked sufficient respectability to be brought back into the limelight. It amounted to something like a deviation or slip in Stalin's or even Lenin's career. What appears to be established is that in his first quasi-military performance Koba showed a distinct penchant for a reckless, wasteful method of warfare, a characteristic of his that would come to light more strongly and on a gigantic scale in the future.

In May 1907, Koba, assuming once again the nickname Ivanovich, went to London to attend a new Congress of the party. His delegate's mandate was questioned by the Mensheviks. Eventually he was admitted to the Congress but only with a consultative voice. His native province was now so much a Menshevik 'fortress' that he could not easily obtain credentials from any recognized Caucasian body. He consoled himself with the thought that the Bolsheviks swayed the organization in other parts of Russia, in Petersburg, Moscow, and elsewhere.[2] At the Congress the Bolsheviks gained a slight majority and managed to put their imprint on its decisions and resolutions. Partisan warfare inevitably came up for discussion. Martov inveighed against Lenin, who this time refrained from parrying the attack. The opposition to the fighting squads had spread to the Bolshevik faction itself. Most of Lenin's followers wanted to put a stop to their activities. On this point the Mensheviks carried the Congress without difficulty and passed a ban on all armed raids and 'expropriations'. Throughout the Congress Koba-Ivanovich prudently sat still and kept quiet, probably because he had been warned by Lenin not to expose himself. Lenin abstained from voting on the ban, though many delegates indignantly pressed him to show his hand. He undoubtedly was prepared to offend against this ban and to try a few more 'expropriations'. Otherwise, the debates were rather unreal, because both Mensheviks and Bolsheviks were still prophesying an imminent 'new revolutionary explosion', though the Mensheviks were already adapting their policies to the conditions of the counter-revolutionary era.[1]

On his return to Baku, Koba-Ivanovich described the Congress in the new clandestine paper *Bakinski Proletarii* (The Baku Proletarian).[2] Bolshevism, he stated, represented the aspirations of the advanced workers of central Russia who were mostly employed in heavy industry. The Menshevik predominance in his native land he explained by the 'backward and petty bourgeois' character of the province. The Mensheviks railed against Bolshevik bureaucracy, but at the Congress they had more party officials and fewer workers than Lenin's faction. In addition, there were few genuine Russians among the moderate Socialists—most of them were Jews or Georgians, whereas the overwhelming majority of the Bolsheviks were pure Russians. 'Somebody among the Bolsheviks remarked jestingly that since the Mensheviks were the faction of the Jews and the Bolsheviks that of the native Russians, it would become us to make a pogrom in the party.' Anti-semitism could hardly be read into this heavy jocular aside, because nobody had been more blunt than Koba in the condemnation of racial hatred. But the joke was ambiguous enough to grate on the ears of most Socialists.

Koba's report contained another characteristic remark. The Congress, so he related, was sharply divided into two factions. Trotsky, who joined neither, proved himself to be 'beautifully useless'. It was at the London Congress that Koba first met his future great rival. The ex-President of the Petersburg Soviet,

[1] *V.K.P.* (*b*) *v Rezolutsyakh*, vol. i, pp. 109–10; F. Dan, *Proiskhozhdenie Bolshevizma*, pp. 388–9.　　　　　　　　　　　　[2] J. Stalin, *Sochinenya*, vol. ii, pp. 46–77.

condemned to life-long exile in Siberia, had succeeded in escaping from his banishment just in time to join the Congress. He was very vocal in his indignation at Lenin's partisan warfare. Thus, at their very first meeting the future rivals were already arrayed against each other in a bitter controversy, though they did not directly exchange even a few words during the many gatherings in that Brotherhood Church in London, where the Congress was in session for nearly three weeks. Koba's personal stake in that controversy was his own standing with the party. He could not help being hurt by what Trotsky had to say about 'expropriations'. The phrase about Trotsky's 'beautiful uselessness' reflected the aesthetic impression of Trotsky's great oratory and probably also Lenin's impatience with it, for Koba, so it seems, repeated the phrase after Lenin. The two men, Koba and Trotsky, were stars of an altogether different magnitude and lustre in those days. It would hardly have entered anybody's mind that one day they would confront each other in the greatest feud in the whole history of Russia. Trotsky already enjoyed national and European fame, while Koba's star was shining only very dimly on the narrow Caucasian horizon. But already from that first meeting in a London church Koba could not have failed to carry away in his heart the first seed of resentment against the ex-President of the Petersburg Soviet.

CHAPTER IV

Koba becomes Stalin

Triumph of counter-revolution (1907–12).—'Liquidators' and 'boycotters'.—
Stalin's work in Baku (1907–10).—His imprisonment and deportation to Solvy-
chegodsk.—Escape and return to Baku (1909).—Stalin charges émigré leaders,
including Lenin, with 'aloofness from Russian reality'.—Stalin hiding among
Tartar oil workers.—His correspondence in the Russian Socialist Press.—His
second exile in Solvychegodsk (1910–11), and the end of his activity in the Caucasus.
Final split between Bolsheviks and Mensheviks.—Stalin becomes a member of the
Bolshevik Central Committee and issues the first copy of *Pravda* (April 1912).—
Stalin's part in the elections to the fourth Duma.—His journey to Cracow and
Vienna.—*The Problems of Nationalities and Social Democracy.*—Stalin meets Bukharin
and Trotsky in Vienna.—On his return to Russia is betrayed by an *agent provo-
cateur* and arrested.—Is exiled to sub-polar Siberia (1913–17).—The First World
War.—Lenin's 'revolutionary defeatism'.—Stalin's inactivity during the war.

'An era of counter-revolution has begun; and it will last some
twenty years, unless Tsardom is in the meantime shaken by a
major war.'[1] With these words Lenin parted from one of his
friends when, in December 1907, he made up his mind to return
to Geneva. The terror of the Stolypin Government, 'the régime
of June 3rd', raged in the country; and even in his hiding-place
in Finland Lenin was no longer safe. Nine years later he did
not yet believe the second revolution to be near. In January
1917, a few weeks before the downfall of Tsardom and a few
months before his own rise to power, he gave a commemorative
address on the first Russian revolution to young Swiss Socialists
and finished it with the assurance that though his generation
would not live to see the second revolution, they, the youth,
would certainly witness its triumph.[2] The interval between the
two revolutions lasted in fact less than ten years; and of these
only the first five could be described as the era of counter-
revolution proper. By 1912 there was a new upswing of the
revolutionary movement.

At the end of 1907, however, Lenin's pessimism seemed all
too justified. Tsardom was firmly back on its feet. The working
class was overcome by weariness and disillusionment. At the

---

[1] L. Krasin, *Leonid Krasin*, p. 37.   [2] Lenin, *Sochinenya*, 3rd ed., vol. xix, p. 357.

height of the revolution more than two million workers took part in strikes, most of them designed to promote political ends. In 1908 only 174,000 workers came out in strikes; only 64,000 in 1909, and 46,000 in 1910. The limited freedom of speech, of assembly, and of the Press largely disappeared. The parties of the underground were exhausted and demoralized. Defeat bred cynicism or scepticism among their members and followers. The prodigal sons of the intelligentsia recanted their radicalism and sought readmission to respectable society. The literary *Bohème* that had lived in reverie on the fringe of the underground now plunged into despondent mysticism, sexualism, or art for art's sake. The clandestine organizations were like pricked balloons. What was left of them teemed with *agents provocateurs*, who gave the *Okhrana* first-hand information about the personnel and the activities of the various factions. The agents of the *Okhrana* penetrated even into the leading centres of the various groups and did their utmost to exacerbate their inner feuds and to turn the underground into a morass of treacherous intrigue, fear, and suspicion.

An aversion from clandestine work was one typical reaction to such conditions. It was elevated to a political principle by Menshevik writers, who demanded that the party should wind up its underground activity, abandon its old habits, and transform itself into an ordinary opposition working for its ends openly, within the limits prescribed by the law—like the European Socialist parties. Those who preached this 'revaluation of values' were derogatorily labelled by Lenin 'the liquidators', the grave-diggers of the party. The mole of revolution, Lenin argued, must continue to burrow in the underground, despite the corrupted condition of the clandestine groups. In those days both Bolsheviks and Mensheviks still looked up in admiration to western European and especially German Socialism, with its powerful political and trade-union machines, its vigorous, popular Press, its impressive electoral campaigns and parliamentary representations. The greater the disgust with the disintegration of the Russian underground, the stronger grew the desire to europeanize the movement at home.

Yet the whole fabric of Russian society was un-European. Tsardom remained a half-Asiatic autocracy. True, even the régime of 3 June did not obliterate all the gains of the First

Revolution. After the most violent wave of terror was over, shaky islets of freedom were left here and there. The parties of the opposition resumed the open publication of periodicals, but, supervised by a severe and malevolent censorship, they could express their views only in a diluted form, resorting to Aesopian hints and allusions. As a rule the periodicals were short-lived. The fist of the *Okhrana* clamped down upon them under the slightest pretext. The same was true of the few legally existing trade unions and leftish educational clubs and associations. The position of the shadow parliaments, the Dumas, was not much better. All the four Dumas elected between the two revolutions were arbitrarily dissolved or prorogued by the Tsar; and in none of them did the Socialist deputies enjoy immunity—most of those deputies spent their parliamentary terms in Siberian banishment. Those who under such handicaps attempted to graft a European Labour Party on to the Russian body politic might as well have tried to grow tropical fruit in a sub-polar region. Several Menshevik leaders still wished to keep clandestine organizations in being but hoped to shift the main burden of the party's work to lawful forms of activity. Only Plekhanov, in many ways the most moderate Menshevik of all, continued to attribute to the underground the same importance as before. This provided the basis for the last political alliance between Lenin and Plekhanov, an alliance which came to an end only at the outbreak of the First World War.

Looking back to that period, Lenin wrote many years later: 'The revolutionary parties must complete their education. They had learnt how to attack. . . . They had got to learn . . . that victory was impossible . . . unless they knew both how to attack and how to retreat correctly. Of all the defeated opposition and revolutionary parties, the Bolsheviks effected the most orderly retreat. . . .'[1] Some of Lenin's colleagues and followers refused to learn the art of 'orderly retreat'. Lenin's tactics were to avoid hopeless clashes with autocracy and to economize the forces of the revolution. He defended the underground party against the 'liquidators', but he wanted the party to use lawful as well as clandestine forms of action. Even before the counter-revolution set in, he had given up boycotting parliamentary elections; and, seeing that his followers persisted in the tactics

---

[1] Lenin, *Sochinenya*, vol. xxv, p. 177.

of boycott, he did not-hesitate to cast his vote with those of the Mensheviks against his whole faction in order to send socialism to the polling-booth.[1] He also insisted that his followers should publish such periodicals, books, and pamphlets as the censorship permitted and that they should work in legally existing trade unions and educational associations. Only thus would the party be able to convey its ideas and views to a public much wider than that which was accessible to clandestine propaganda. Its open propaganda was, of course, bound to leave many things unsaid; but it would be supplemented by an uninhibited clandestine propaganda. The secret committees should direct and control all forms of activity, whether lawful or underground.

While disgust with the underground was the dominant mood among the Mensheviks, the Bolsheviks were reluctant to act in the open. Throughout 1907 and even 1908 'boycottism' swayed their mind. Lunacharsky, Bogdanov, Krasin, Gorky, the best writers, propagandists, and organizers, led the Bolshevik 'ultra-left'.

The content as well as the form of Socialist action was again at issue. Those who turned their backs on the underground willy-nilly preached a degree of conciliation with the existing order. It was impossible, for instance, to advocate the overthrow of Tsardom in publications that were meant to be passed by the Tsarist censorship. Therefore, Lenin argued, those who wanted the party to confine itself to forms of action permitted by authority were virtually abandoning the republican principle. Like the middle-class Liberals, in whom they saw the legitimate leaders of the opposition, the Mensheviks now placed their hopes on the gradual transformation of Tsardom into a constitutional monarchy. In Lenin's eyes such hopes were as unworthy of Social Democrats as they were hollow. The boycotters, on the other hand, were the sectarians and not the practitioners of the revolution. In making a fetish of the underground, in shying away from the broader opportunities for action, they tended to reduce the revolution to impotence. They were liquidators à rebours.[2]

. . . .

It was during the interval between the two revolutions that

---

[1] F. Dan, *Proiskhozhdenie Bolshevizma*, pp. 427–8; *VKP (b) v Rezolutsyakh*, vol. i, p. 113. [2] Lenin, *Sochinenya*, vol. xv, pp. 417–24.

GEORGIAN GUERRILLAS, 1905

STALIN, 1906

Koba became Stalin, and from a comparatively obscure Georgian underground worker rose to be one of the national leaders of Bolshevism. His rise appears the more puzzling as, of the ten years between 1907 and 1917, he spent nearly seven in prisons, on the way to Siberia, in Siberian banishment, and in escapes from the places of his deportation. His carefully collected political writings of that period add up to less than one slender volume of his *Works*. The most indulgent reader of that volume could hardly find in it any proof of striking intellectual or political attainment. The man who in the beginning of 1917 hurried back from Siberia to Petersburg to lead the Bolsheviks before Lenin's return from Switzerland had made little advance on the youthful author of the essays published in *Brdzola*. The clue to his promotion lay in his practical activities rather than in any talent for letters or journalism.

He remained at Baku while Lenin and the other leaders once again pitched their tents in western Europe. He was not one of those leaders whom the party needed abroad and could not leave within reach of the *Okhrana*. Nor was he one of those promising workers who were sent to complete their revolutionary education at the various party schools abroad. In Lenin's personnel files he ranked as fit to look after his own education. Except for two brief trips to Cracow and Vienna, he spent all those years in Russia, entrenched in the underground, immersed in the drudgery of the revolution's working day that was so different from its stormy, exciting festivals. This was to be the source of great strength as well as great weakness in him. He had no inkling of the broad international vistas that life in western Europe opened before the émigré leaders. Like every other Bolshevik he was, of course, an internationalist, though his internationalism was more a matter of dogma than of living experience. Its range was provincial. He knew the bloody feuds between the Caucasian tribes and nationalities in which the folly of self-centred nationalism demonstrated itself. What his internationalism lacked was any intimate understanding of the broad trends of European life, any sensitivity to the shades and colours of that dazzling rainbow which was called European civilization. On the other hand, he really drew his strength from his native soil. In it he was rooted, first by birth and upbringing and now by his political fortunes.

On 25 October 1907 he was elected a member of the Baku Committee. 'Two years of revolutionary work among the oil workers of Baku', he wrote later on, 'hardened me as a practical fighter and as one of the practical leaders. In contact with advanced workers of Baku . . . in the storm of the deepest conflicts between workers and oil industrialists . . . I first learned what it meant to lead big masses of workers. There in Baku I thus received my second revolutionary baptism in combat.'[1] In Baku, Europe and Asia met and interpenetrated even more closely than in Tiflis. The quickly expanding oil industry represented European methods of technical and economic organization. The transit trade with Persia was oriental in character. Forty-eight per cent. of the workers employed at Baku by that time were Russians and Armenians. Forty-two per cent. were Persians, Lezgins, and Tartars—most of the Persian labour was migratory. Ten per cent. were Turks. It was an extraordinary endeavour to try to bring all these patches of races and nationalities and religions, with their peculiar customs and habits, within the framework of a single Marxist organization. The Russians were the skilled workers, the pioneers of a modern way of life. The Moslems were the unskilled, pauper-like proletariat. The Tartars practised self-flagellation on the days of their festival *Shakhssey-Vakhssey*. The tradition of blood-feuds was only slightly less powerful than in the deserts in Arabia. In the Moslem quarters of the city each family lived a secluded inert life, completely devoid of the fever and curiosity for the world that animated the Russian and Armenian settlements. For this reason the Moslem quarter was well suited for clandestine work. There the Bolsheviks had their secret printing shop. There, too, Koba, having assumed the name of Gayoz Nisharadze, hid from the police.

But the atomized mass of Moslem labourers did not lend itself easily to propaganda or organization. And the Asiatic element was reflected not only in the composition of the working class; it also coloured the policies of the oil companies, although the shareholders were Europeans. The wage system was a curious combination of truck payment and of baksheesh or beshkesh, as Koba called it in his articles. The frauds of exploitation with which western Europe was familiar only in the

[1] J. Stalin, *Sochinenya*, vol. viii, p. 174.

early stages of the industrial revolution and all the cheating that oriental slyness could invent were used in 'rewarding' the labourers of the oil-fields. The wage system in the mechanical workshops, where the Russians and the Armenians were employed, was more European. But this again divided the workers and made it difficult for trade unionists to co-ordinate their demands. The truck system made even the Russians so dependent on the employers that in 1909 the Caspian Oil Company could allow itself to prohibit its workers to marry without the firm's permission. No wonder labour conflicts time and again acquired here an acute and explosive character, despite the heterogeneity and the backwardness of the working population.

At the end of 1904, it will be remembered, revolutionary stirring in Baku preceded the 'bloody Sunday' in Petersburg. Later on, political life here was swamped by bloody tribal feuds. Baku lived through a new revolutionary flare-up towards the end of 1907, after the ferment in the rest of Russia had fizzled out. The underground did not fall to pieces here as soon as it did elsewhere. At the end of September, in the primary elections to the Duma in which each estate chose its electors separately, the workers' *curia* elected Bolsheviks as its representatives, and Koba wrote the 'Instruction of the Baku Workers to their Deputy'.[1] The deputy, he stated, was to be a member of the party and was to carry out the instructions and the orders of its Central Committee. He was not to see his task as that of a legislator. He ought to state frankly in the Duma that no progressive legislation or peaceful reform would be of any use as long as Tsardom survived. He should remain an agitator of the revolution. This instruction was to be a model of Bolshevik parliamentary tactics.

After the election Koba turned to the labour conflicts in the oil industry. The workers in the oil-fields proper belonged to one union which was under Bolshevik influence, while those of the mechanical workshops were organized separately and led by the Mensheviks. What Koba now advocated came very close to the C.I.O. principle—the industrial union as opposed to the trade organization. The oil companies, he insisted, must bargain with the delegates of the whole industry. One trade must not allow itself to be bribed at the expense of another.

[1] Ibid., vol. ii, pp. 78–80.

The wage system must be changed. What the workers needed was not more baksheesh but a European system of wages. The workers stood for European methods against the Asiatic practices of the employers. In *Gudok* (The Signal), the legal newssheet of Bolshevik trade unionists, he expounded those ideas in a series of short articles signed K. Cato.[1] After the industrialists had agreed to bargain with the representatives of the whole industry, he called on the '50,000 Baku workers' to elect their delegates. The authorities promised immunity to the conference of the delegates. This was a success for the Bolsheviks, for the Mensheviks had argued in favour of starting negotiations with the oil companies without laying down any conditions beforehand, while the Social Revolutionaries and the Armenian Dashnaks had called for an unconditional boycott of the negotiations.

The delegates' conference was in session for several months, debating every point in the collective agreements, controlling strikes, and airing its political views. 'While all over Russia black reaction was reigning, a genuine workers' parliament was in session at Baku', wrote later Sergo Ordjonikidze, the future Commissar of heavy industry, one of Koba's closest friends in those days. There was daring and defiance in Baku's challenge to the régime of 3 June. Lenin followed the events with melancholy admiration: 'These are our last Mohicans of the political mass strike.'[2] He knew that Baku could not stir the rest of Russia to action. The revolution was merely fighting a rearguard battle in the Caucasus. But the Bolshevik leaders of Baku, the commanders of that battle, attracted his attention. Who were these men who still withstood the all-pervading apathy and resignation? Well, there was that Ivanovich-Koba whom he had seen at Tammerfors, in Stockholm, and London, the man connected with the Fighting Squads, whose proper name had not yet been marked down even in Lenin's secret files, Ordjonikidze, Voroshilov (the secretary of the oil-workers' trade union—the future Marshal), the brothers Yenukidze (one of whom was to become Vice-President of the Soviet Union), Spandarian, Djaparidze, and Shaumian, future Commissars of Baku. The dead silence in the rest of Russia was the sounding-board on which the 'signal' from Baku reverberated with

[1] J. Stalin, *Sochinenya*, vol. ii, p. 98.   [2] Lenin, *Sochinenya*, vol. xvi, p. 368.

unusual strength. One other fact made Koba's nickname gradually more familiar to Lenin. He had ceased to write in his native tongue—Georgian. There were few Georgians in Baku. The Russian language was, as it were, the unifying factor in the diversity of languages and vernaculars spoken there. *Gudok* and the clandestine *Bakinsky Proletarii*, edited or co-edited by Koba, were Russian newspapers. They were regularly dispatched to Bolshevik headquarters abroad, where Lenin sternly scrutinized every article and note printed by his followers. Koba's writings were neither numerous nor intellectually startling, but they were marked by fanatical devotion to the Bolshevik faction, as well as by a businesslike practical tone highly esteemed by Lenin. Thus, in going from Tiflis to the oil city on the Persian border, Koba was really moving from his native backwater into the main stream of national politics.

After eight or nine months of work on the Baku committee and many strikes in the oil-fields, Koba-Nisharadze and his friend Sergo Ordjonikidze were caught by the *Okhrana* and put in the Bailov prison. Long months of waiting for the orders of deportation were passed in prison politics, debates with inmates of different views, exchanges of secret messages and printed matter with comrades at large, writing for clandestine sheets, smuggling the writings out of the prison, and so on. The debates between the adherents of various factions were bitter with the exacerbation of defeat. Of the two spokesmen for the Bolshevik prisoners, Koba was cool, ruthless, and self-possessed, Ordjonikidze touchy, exuberant, and ready to fly off at a tangent into riotous affray. The discussions were poisoned by suspicion— the *Okhrana* had planted its *agents provocateurs* even in the prison cells. Time and again the prisoners, roused to feverish suspicion, would try to trace them and, in some cases, they would kill a suspect, since the code of the underground allowed or even demanded the killing of *agents provocateurs*, as a measure of self-defence. Harmless people unfortunate enough to have aroused suspicion may sometimes have suffered in these hunts; for they provided an outlet for phobias and even opportunities for settling private accounts. Each faction was quick to detect *agents provocateurs* among its opponents, and slow in unmasking them in its own ranks. Unfriendly memoirists who shared with Koba a cell in the Bailov prison have told a few stories in which

Koba is seen as slyly inciting others to witch-hunts and victimizing innocent people who had incurred his disfavour.[1] It is impossible to say how much truth or invention there is in such stories: they were told about many an underground worker and they reflect the all-pervading suspicion of those days.

In other respects, too, the Baku prison was markedly different from the comparatively quiet and easy-going Batum prison, in which Koba had been lodged a few years before. Convicts awaiting execution were often herded together with the rest. Executions took place in the courtyard. Nerves were strained to the limit when men saw their comrades, who might just have taken part in a debate, led to the gallows. In the tension of such moments Koba would, if an eyewitness is to be believed, fall sound asleep, astonishing his comrades by his strong nerves, or else he would go on with his unsuccessful attempt to master the intricacies of German grammar. Amid all the filth and the degradation, he still contrived to watch the conflicts in the oil industry and to keep up a running commentary in the *Gudok* and *Bakinsky Proletarii*.[2] But the tone of his comment was now less confident. He counselled his comrades not to count upon a general strike. 'Striking in individual concerns is the most expedient form of retreat, the form best suited for the present moment.' He urged the workers to be on guard against 'economic terror'—the acts of despair, assaults by individual workers on their employers or managers, that were becoming more and more frequent—for it would recoil upon organized labour. But when the local 'liberal' newspaper—'the mouthpiece of the oil magnates'—began to preach morals to Socialist trade unionists and blame them for indifference *vis-à-vis* economic terror, Koba retorted with an angry philippic on the wretched conditions of the oil proletariat which accounted for their despair and violence. He scorned a Menshevik suggestion that Socialists should up to a point co-operate with authority in prevention of economic terror. By its own means and in its own interests, concluded Koba, organized labour must curb despair and violence, but it would not denounce the culprits to authority. Nor would it fawn upon the self-righteous 'liberalism' of the oil magnates.

In November he received the order of deportation to a place

[1] L. Trotsky, *Stalin*, pp. 117–21.   [2] J. Stalin, *Sochinenya*, vol. ii, p. 98.

called Solvychegodsk, where he was to remain under police supervision for two years. Solvychegodsk, a little settlement founded in the fourteenth century by Russian pioneer-merchants as a centre of trade in salt and furs, lies in the northern part of the Vologda province, in European Russia. Its climate is less severe than that of the northern Siberian places of banishment. The terms of Koba's deportation were thus fairly mild. He was still successful at playing an inconspicuous part in the eyes of the *Okhrana* and had avoided being caught red-handed. On the northward trek from Vologda to Solvychegodsk he fell ill with typhus, but at the end of February 1909 he arrived. After four months he escaped. He travelled to the Caucasus via Petersburg, where he called on his future father-in-law Alliluyev and through him got into contact with the secret party headquarters. He was issued with a new false passport—in July he reappeared in Baku as Zakhar Gregorian Melikyants. At Petersburg headquarters he must have been given a hearty welcome—party workers still looked up to the 'indomitable fortress' of Baku. He also secured his informal appointment to be the Caucasian correspondent of the party's 'central' periodicals published abroad. In this role he was to attract Lenin's attention more closely than hitherto.

On his way from Petersburg to Baku he must have been given to unpleasant reflections on the things he had seen and heard in the capital. The organization there, which in 1907 still numbered 8,000 members, was now reduced to barely 300. There seemed to be an air of inefficiency about party headquarters. He had avidly asked for news from the Caucasus, but at headquarters they had no information. The contact between Petersburg and the émigré leaders was tenuous. The distribution of the clandestine Press was feeble. He could not help feeling an itch to lend his own hand to the job at Petersburg headquarters.

The condition in which, one and a half years after his imprisonment, he found the 'Baku fortress' was not encouraging either. Here, too, the organization had dwindled down to a few hundred members, two or three hundred Bolsheviks and a hundred Mensheviks. The following of the trade unions was not much bigger. The educational clubs ('Science' and 'Knowledge is Power') gave few signs of life. In the oil-fields working hours had been increased from eight to twelve; and, though a boom had begun in the oil industry, the workers were not taking advantage of their bargaining power. The organization had turned its back upon the Tartar proletariat. It ceased to approach them with leaflets or news-sheets in their tongue. The party's funds were exhausted—not even a copy of the clandestine Russian *Bakinsky Proletarii* had been published during the year since his deportation. Things still looked better here than elsewhere, but this was not the old defiant Baku.

The first thing that Koba-Melikyants did, after he settled down in a hiding-place inside the Balakhlana oil-field, was to revive the *Bakinsky Proletarii*. Three weeks after his return a copy of the paper was issued with his unsigned editorial 'The Crisis in the Party and our Tasks'.[1] He did not mince his words in diagnosing the crisis; and he made the analysis with an eye to party headquarters abroad as well as to readers at home. 'The party has no roots in the mass of the workers', he stated, recording some of the information he had brought from the capital. 'Petersburg does not know what is happening in the Caucasus, the Caucasus does not know what is going on in the Urals—each corner lives its own isolated life. Strictly speaking, that integrated party which lived one common life, that party of which we were so proud in 1905, 1906, and 1907, exists no longer.' The Menshevik and Bolshevik émigré centres were equally at fault, because their periodicals—here he mentioned Lenin's *Proletarii* as well as the Menshevik *Golos*—'do not and cannot link the scattered organizations inside Russia, they cannot infuse into them a common party life. It would even be strange to think that the foreign organs, aloof as they are from Russian reality, could integrate the work of the party that has since long outgrown the phase of small propagandist circles.'[2] The last part of the statement was beside the point. On the writer's own showing the underground was now not stronger than in the days when the old *Iskra* was assembling the small groups of pioneer propagandists into a party. But Koba was airing the impatience of the home-bred revolutionary with the émigré leaders 'aloof from Russian reality'; and he did not mean to exempt Lenin from his chidings. Various remedies, he went on, were suggested, such as the winding up of the

[1] J. Stalin, *Sochinenya*, vol. ii, pp. 146–58.   [2] Ibid., p. 147.

underground or the transfer of all functions in the underground to ordinary workers. The former would amount to the liquidation of the party, the latter would yield little improvement as long as the old system of organization remained in being 'with its old ways of work and "leadership" from abroad'. He put the word leadership in contemptuous inverted commas.

In his conclusion, however, he was more circumspect, for he did not demand the transfer of leadership to Russia. What was needed was a national newspaper published in Russia that would keep in touch with life there and integrate the dispersed elements of the party. It was for the Central Committee to set up and direct such a paper. 'It is the Central Committee that is anyhow under the obligation to direct the work of the party. But at present that obligation is poorly discharged. . . .' These were still days of a half-merger between the two factions. Inside the Central Committee there was a chronic deadlock between Bolsheviks and Mensheviks. Koba did not touch that point at all. His charge against the Central Committee as a whole was 'aloofness from Russian reality'. His idea of a national newspaper was a practical proposition; but it took another three years before *Pravda* (The Truth) was set up in Petersburg, with Koba as one of its editors. Meanwhile, the editor of the *Bakinsky Proletarii* was indirectly offering himself as a candidate for work at Petersburg headquarters. In an aside, he remarked that unlike most other branches, the Baku branch of the party 'had till now preserved its contact with the masses'.

In the same *Bakinsky Proletarii* he published a resolution of the Baku Committee, written by himself, on the dissensions among the Bolshevik leaders abroad. The resolution openly rebuked Lenin for splitting the faction over what Koba thought to be minor divergences of opinion.[1] For at this time the founder of Bolshevism was parting company with the radicals and boycotters, the philosopher and economist Bogdanov, the writer Lunacharsky, the feuilletonist Manuilsky, and several others. The radicals charged Lenin with betrayal of Bolshevism. By inducing his followers to combine underground work with lawful activity, Lenin encouraged them, in the critics' view, to dilute principles and to carry on an emasculated, Menshevik-like propaganda.

[1] Ibid., pp. 165–8.

The tactical differences were curiously complicated by a philosophical disputation. The radicals questioned some notions of Marxist philosophy and attempted to revise dialectical materialism in the light of neo-Kantian or empirio-critical philosophy. For a time Lenin detached himself from day-to-day politics and, to the grave embarrassment of his pupils, shut himself up in the Paris libraries in order to produce his philosophical *magnum opus, Empirio-criticism and Materialism*, in which he flayed the neo-Kantians, the God-seekers, and all the other questioners of Marxist philosophy.[1] The adversaries set up rival schools for party workers who were drawn into the disputation. Lenin's school was at Longjumeau near Paris. The radicals and God-seekers, whose school was patronized by Maxim Gorky, preached their ideas on the Italian isle of Capri. The schools vied with each other for pupils and funds. The workers who at great peril to themselves arrived from Russia, yearning to learn practical politics, political economy, and the technique of underground work, found themselves subjected to an intensive course in philosophy, called upon to choose between conflicting gnostic theories and to vote for or against the expulsion of heretics who also happened to hold views of their own on political tactics.

The leader of the Baku Committee, hiding among the Tartars of the Balakhlana oil-field, had little patience with the disputation between Longjumeau and Capri. The émigrés' aloofness from Russian reality, he must have reflected, had reached the limits of mental aberration. The Baku Committee should tell them off and try to bring them back to their senses. His motion expressed agreement with Lenin's tactical and political views as against the radicals, but it protested against the expulsion of Bogdanov by Lenin as well as against Bogdanov's disregard of party discipline. As the sub-factions were of one mind on all major political issues, they should work together; and Lenin ought to stop trampling upon the rights of the minority. Baku refused to take sides in the controversy between Longjumeau and Capri, about which it was not sufficiently informed. Lenin

---

[1] In his reminiscences Professor Pokrovsky related how the Bolsheviks sent a delegation to Lenin asking him to give up his philosophical studies and to return to practical politics. Pokrovsky himself was a member of that delegation. Lenin, however, refused to yield to his followers.

took notice of the reprimand. In his periodical he gently tried to explain to his Caucasian critic that he was not given to witch-hunting, but that he had had to expel the radicals solely because they refused to behave in a disciplined manner.[1]

Having brought pressure to bear upon headquarters abroad, Koba was careful not to embroil himself with Lenin. In November and December 1909 he wrote a series of 'Letters from the Caucasus' for the *Social Democrat* that was published in Paris and Geneva on behalf of the joint Bolshevik-Menshevik Central Committee. The editorial board consisted of Lenin, Zinoviev, Kamenev, Martov, and Dan. The 'Letters' gave an informative and solid survey of Caucasian affairs. The author discussed the position in the oil industry, local government, trade unions, relations between Caucasian nationalities, underground work, and lawful Socialist activities, contrasts between Tiflis and Baku—all in the same business-like and concrete though pedestrian style. Some 'Letters' in which he harshly criticized the Caucasian Mensheviks and their chief, Noah Jordania, evoked Martov's and Dan's objections and were published in the discussion-sheet to which such controversial matter was usually transferred; and one Letter was altogether withheld from publication. The Caucasian correspondent showed himself to be a stubborn Leninist. He refrained from giving as much as a hint of the criticisms of Lenin that he had voiced anonymously through the Baku Committee and the *Bakinsky Proletarii*. Lenin was glad to receive such succour from the Caucasian correspondent. Quick to take note of the mood of his followers in Russia, he also took up the demand for the setting up of operative national headquarters in Russia and pressed it on the reluctant Mensheviks. Meanwhile Baku put on more steam. In another resolution written by Koba at the beginning of 1910, Baku urged the 'transfer of the leading (practical) centre into Russia'. The demand was substantiated by the forecast, made in the opening phrase of the resolution, that 'the state of depression and torpor that gripped the motive forces of the Russian revolution is beginning to pass'.[2] In this Koba was, as on one or two previous occasions, ahead of most émigré writers, although, in Vienna, a similar forecast was at that time made by Leon Trotsky. The Baku Committee, now

---

[1] J. Stalin, *Sochinenya*, vol. ii, pp. 391-2.   [2] Ibid., pp. 197-200.

evidently working in close touch with Lenin, also asked for the final expulsion of the 'liquidators' and for a merger between the Bolsheviks and those Mensheviks who, like Plekhanov, stood for the underground.

In March, in the middle of preparations for a general strike in the oil industry, Koba-Melikyants was once again arrested. On the day of his imprisonment the secret printing shop issued his pamphlet written in honour of the working man August Bebel, the celebrated seventy-year-old leader of German Social Democracy, 'whose words made the crowned heads of Europe tremble'. After eight months of intensive work, he now had six months waiting once more in prison for the next 'administrative' verdict. It was not harsh this time either. He was ordered to complete his banishment at Solvychegodsk. After that he would be forbidden to live in the Caucasus and in the bigger cities of Russia for another five years. Then followed the now-familiar trek northwards. This time he stayed about nine months, till the end of his term, 27 June 1911, without any attempt at escape. This time, too, he had left the Caucasus for good. In future he would still make short trips to his native province, but only in order to inspect the local branches on behalf of the Central Committee. His Caucasian chapter was now closed.

. . . .

The forecast revival of the revolutionary movement did soon manifest itself. Street demonstrations at the funeral of Leo Tolstoy in 1910 marked its beginning. The movement gained real *élan* in 1912, when workers protested with widespread strikes against the shooting of several hundred strikers at the gold-mines of Lena in Siberia. Meanwhile the spurious unity of the Social Democratic party was breaking down irretrievably. In January 1912 Lenin convened in Prague a conference of Bolsheviks and a few Plekhanovites in order to proclaim the constitution of his faction as a separate party or, rather, in order to establish his faction as *the* party. This was to be his final break with the main body of the Mensheviks. Like the Congress in Brussels in 1903, so this conference, too, took place at a *Maison du Peuple*. The Czech Socialists acted as hosts to the Russian revolutionaries. It was at the Prague conference that Lenin placed Koba's name on the list of candidates to the Central

Committee which he submitted to the delegates. But Koba was not elected. His name still conveyed little or nothing to most delegates who had known one another from the various émigré colonies. Ordjonikidze, Koba's former assistant and his hot-tempered co-prisoner at Baku, was elected, probably because he had come straight from Lenin's school at Longjumeau, where he was still a pupil. But Lenin did not drop the matter at that. Under the statutes of the party, the elected Central Committee had the right to co-opt other members. At the instance of Lenin the Committee used that right in favour of Koba. The other members of the Central Committee were Lenin, Zinoviev, Ordjonikidze, and the Russified Pole Malinovsky who was the *Okhrana*'s *agent provocateur*.

What accounted for Lenin's leaning towards Koba? At the outset of the political revival Lenin was anxious to get for himself a maximum of elbow-room. He rid himself of the hamstringing connexion with the Mensheviks so that no compromises or considerations of unity should compel him to 'curtail' his propaganda and slogans. Now he was out to knock his organization into shape. In the preceding splits he parted company with his ablest colleagues. His latest decision to burn all boats behind him left him with few outstanding associates. Trotsky now headed a motley coalition of right-wing Mensheviks, radical Bolsheviks, anti-Mensheviks and anti-Bolsheviks, liquidators, boycotters, God-seekers, and simply Trotskyists in a ferocious journalistic onslaught on Leninism. Zinoviev and Kamenev were Lenin's closest aides-de-camp, but even Kamenev, Trotsky's brother-in-law, had begun to waver. Lenin turned his back on the émigré intelligentsia. He picked practical workers of the underground for the new Central Committee. Soon after its election, the Committee created a Russian Bureau which was to direct the party's activities inside Russia. The Bureau consisted of four members: Koba, Ordjonikidze, Spandarian, and a certain Goloshchekin. The first three had all been members of the Baku Committee. The Caucasian group came to be the pillar of the Bolshevik organization, and to play a role quite out of proportion to the importance of their province. The reputation that Baku derived from the strikes and demonstrations of 1908 was still very high, perhaps exaggeratedly so, in Lenin's eyes. The job ahead,

Lenin must have thought, required men of grit, pertinacity, and acumen, men like the leaders of Baku. In Krupskaya's files the code name for the Baku group had been 'The Horses'. Lenin now put his horses into harness.[1]

Koba's promotion did not come suddenly. From Caucasian workers abroad Lenin must have heard many an appreciative word about him. At the Longjumeau school Ordjonikidze canvassed Koba as the strong man of the Baku Committee. The candidate himself did not neglect to make a few discreet and well-calculated moves that would help him to advance. From exile, he kept in touch with influential party workers who at headquarters might throw in a word in his favour; and he tried to appear as amiable to everybody as possible. In a letter written from Solvychegodsk to a member of the Central Committee, Simeon Schwarz, he once again suggested the formation of a Russian Centre, obliquely offering his own services. The tone of the letter was extremely deferential towards the émigré Central Committee, full of devotion for Lenin and scorn for his opponents ('Lenin is a sensible muzhik knowing well where the crayfish hides in the winter'). The content of the letter could not have remained unknown to Lenin, who now had every reason to believe that his Caucasian admirer, so obviously impatient for promotion, would be a faithful executor of his ideas.[2]

By the end of June 1911 Koba had completed his term of banishment. As he was forbidden to live in any of the big cities, he chose the town of Vologda conveniently close to Moscow and Petersburg. After two months he dashed from Vologda to Petersburg and knocked once again at Alliluyev's door. Alliluyev's house was watched by *Okhrana* spies, but Koba, warned about this, got impatient with what seemed to him an excess of caution and suspicion. It so happened that this very day the Prime Minister Stolypin was assassinated in Kiev by a remorseful *agent provocateur*, Bagrov, who wanted to redeem himself in the eyes of the underground. The *Okhrana* was in a panic and rounded up all suspects. Koba, under a new alias (Chizhikov), was arrested.[3] He again spent a few

---

[1] L. Krasin, *Dela Davno Minuvshykh Dnei*, p. 16.
[2] J. Stalin, *Sochinenya*, vol. ii, pp. 209–12.
[3] A. S. Alliluyeva, *Vospominanya*, pp. 108–9.

months in prison, and was then deported back to Vologda for three years.

While he was on his way back delegates for the Prague conference were assembling abroad. He learned about the results of the conference only in the middle of February 1912 when Ordjonikidze, now a member and an emissary of the newly elected Central Committee, came to see him at Vologda. 'I have been to see Ivanovich', Ordjonikidze reported to Lenin, 'and have arranged everything with him. He was very pleased to hear how things had turned out. The news made a splendid impression on him.'[1] Koba apparently had no objection to Lenin's final break with the Mensheviks. Apart from considerations of principle, the fact that his own promotion was connected with that break would help commit him to follow Lenin's policy. The next thing was to flee from police supervision at Vologda and return to the capital. While preparing his escape he wrote a proclamation explaining the decisions of the Prague conference to Socialists in Russia. Under the document he put the signature of the Central Committee of the Russian Social Democratic Workers' party. For the first time he now spoke on behalf of the national leadership of Bolshevism.[2] Six thousand copies of the proclamation were circulated in the main industrial cities. The respectable Russian Press of those days hardly noticed the event. Yet Koba had now reached a decisive stepping-stone on his way to power. Five years later, after the Tsar's abdication, he would return from Siberia to Petersburg and, by dint of this formal seniority acquired in 1912, assume the leadership of the Bolsheviks, pending Lenin's arrival from Switzerland.

It would be mistaken to believe, however, that at this stage of his career Koba's standing among the Bolsheviks was second only to Lenin's, as his official biographers claim. Far from it. The turnover in the leading personnel of Bolshevism was continual. There was nothing stable in the hierarchy as yet, except for its central figure, Lenin, whose authority was based on his boundless intellectual and political resourcefulness, not on any formal claim to loyalty or obedience on the part of his followers. The galaxy of satellites around Lenin revolved capriciously and

[1] E. Yaroslavsky, *Landmarks*, p. 75.
[2] J. Stalin, *Sochinenya*, vol. ii, pp. 213–18.

erratically, perpetually losing old stars and gaining new ones. Quite a few men whose names have since fallen into oblivion held in the Bolshevik hierarchy ranks comparable to Koba's. It is only in the light of his subsequent career that his promotion in 1912 appears so significant. Unlike others, he came to stay. At the time, his elevation to the Central Committee looked like one of the many shifts in the party's personnel. The more so as the newcomer had not made his mark as an initiator of new ideas or a maker of policy. He was to be the strong arm of the Central Committee, not its brain or heart.

The incidental, almost fortuitous, nature of this turn in Koba's career was further underlined by the scantiness of his activity in the five years that were to elapse between his elevation and the second revolution. Only during the first of these years did he discharge the duties of a member of the Central Committee—for the next four he was to be deported to subpolar Siberia. Even in the course of that first year he was out of action for about five months, once again arrested and deported, and once again making his escape. His effective political work lasted altogether seven months, and only five at one stretch. This was just enough for him to try his hand at the job, to become familiar with the leading people of the party, perhaps to strengthen his own position, but not enough for him to gain much new experience or radically to alter his standing.

The short time ahead of him was one of dogged activity. Straight from Vologda he went to the south to get the ear of the Caucasian Bolsheviks for the decisions of the Prague conference. From the Caucasus he hurried to Moscow to exchange impressions with Ordjonikidze on the response of the various branches to Lenin's new 'line'. By the middle of April he was back in the capital in time to lend a hand with preparations for May Day. There followed his inevitable May Day proclamation, signed by the Central Committee but still echoing the accents of the Seminary:[1] 'Ever wider spreads the ocean of the workers' movement, engulfing ever new countries and states from Europe and America to Asia, Africa and Australia. . . . The sea of proletarian anger is rising in high waves and strikes ever more menacingly at the toppling rocks

[1] J. Stalin, *Sochinenya*, vol. ii, pp. 219–24.

BAILOV PRISON IN BAKU

SECRET MEETING PLACE IN BAKU, 1907

BAKU OILFIELDS

STALIN'S HOUSE OF EXILE, 1913-16

of capitalism. . . . Confident in their victory, calm and strong, the workers march proudly on the road to the promised land. . . . The Russian workers ought to say to-day that, like their comrades of the free lands [of Europe], they do not and will not worship the golden calf. . . .'

During his present stay in Petersburg—it lasted only twelve days till the next arrest—he established contact with the Bolshevik deputies to the Duma, whose moves he was to control on behalf of the Central Committee, edited with fresh gusto three copies of *Zvezda* (Star), filling most of its columns with his own articles, and prepared the publication of the first issue of *Pravda*. On 22 April 1912 *Pravda* at last appeared carrying Koba's editorial statement.[1] As the workers' response to Lenin's final break with the Mensheviks was not very favourable, Koba spoke the language of sweet reasonableness. *Pravda*, he promised, would not blur over the differences between the Socialists. 'We believe that a strong and full-blooded movement is unthinkable without controversy—full conformity of views can be achieved only at a cemetery.' Many more things united the various shades of Labour than divided them. *Pravda* would, therefore, call for Socialist unity in class struggle, 'unity at all cost'. 'Just as we ought to be irreconcilable *vis-à-vis* our enemies, so we must make concessions towards one another. War to the enemies of the workers' movement, peace and friendly collaboration inside the movement.' This was the text for the daily that would in the future be famous for its Stalinist conformity. On the day these words left the printing press, its author was lodged in a Petersburg prison. After three months came the routine order of deportation for three years, this time to the Narym province in western Siberia. Exactly two months later Koba fled from Narym to reappear in Petersburg just in time to lead his party in the election to the fourth Duma.

The campaign in the Labour *curia* proceeded through several stages: election of representatives in factories and workshops, election of electors, and finally the election of deputies. After the first stage the authorities annulled the results of the election in some of the biggest factories. Koba convened the Petersburg Executive of the Bolsheviks and moved it to proclaim a strike

[1] Ibid., pp. 248-9.

of protest. The Government retraced its steps. Throughout all the stages of the campaign, Bolsheviks and Mensheviks openly competed for the Labour vote. The assembly of the workers' electors in the capital passed Koba's 'Instruction for the Labour Deputy',[1] very much on the lines of the Instruction he had written at Baku during the previous election. The Labour deputy was required to publicize the workers' claims ('the uncurtailed programme of 1905'), to act as the spokesman of revolution, and 'not to indulge in the empty game of legislation in the Tsarist Duma'. Lenin, who inspired the campaign and watched it from Polish Cracow, was delighted with the bluntness of the Instruction and with Koba's success. In the workers' *curia* the Bolsheviks had the upper hand. Eventually thirteen Social Democrat deputies were elected, six Bolsheviks, and seven Mensheviks. But all the Bolshevik deputies were elected in the Labour *curia*, whereas most Mensheviks came from middle-class constituencies. The working class, so Lenin inferred, supported Bolshevism in its first open contest with the moderate wing. In his articles in *Pravda* and his correspondence to the *Social Democrat*, Koba mildly curbed Lenin's optimism, pointing out that, while the radical Bolshevik slogans appealed to the workers, the open split between the Socialist factions did not.

Immediately after the election, in November 1912, Koba went for a few days to Cracow where the Central Committee met to take stock of the situation. Lenin vehemently pressed for an open split between the Bolshevik and Menshevik deputies in the Duma. He was confident that eventually the workers would see the justification for the split, but he was prepared to draw a clear dividing line between Bolshevism and Menshevism even if this were to prove unpopular. On his return to Petersburg, Koba blunted the edges of Lenin's policy. The Bolshevik deputies themselves were not willing to expose an inner Socialist cleavage before a Duma that was dominated by the extreme right. To his indignation, Lenin found that *Pravda*, too, shirked the split. He may have asked himself whether the Caucasian whom he had brought into the inner councils of his party was not now letting him down. In his biography of Stalin Trotsky described the incident as one of Koba's vicious plots against

[1] J. Stalin, *Sochinenya*, vol. ii, pp. 250-2, 398-9.

his teacher.[1] Lenin hardly saw it in that light. He looked upon it as upon an awkward but only passing discord which he hoped to smooth over in the shrewd and tactful manner that was peculiarly his. He called a joint conference of the Central Committee and of the six Bolshevik deputies at Cracow, and prepared to overhaul the editorial board of *Pravda* in a way that would give no offence to Koba.

By the end of December 1912 Koba left Russia for about six weeks—the longest stay abroad in his whole career.[2] His doings in that brief time were of consequence for his future. The immediate differences were ironed out smoothly and left no ill feeling between master and disciple. Lenin managed to induce the six deputies to separate themselves from their Menshevik colleagues. He chided *Pravda* for its conciliatory tone and quietly dispatched to Petersburg a certain Jacob Sverdlov to take charge of the paper. Sverdlov (the future President of the Soviet Republic) overruled the editorial staff on the spot— among them was the young undergraduate Skryabin-Molotov

---

[1] Lenin, *Sochinenya*, vol. xviii, pp. 398–401; A. E. Badayev, *Bolsheviki v Gosudarstvennoi Dume*, pp. 194–211; L. Trotsky, *Stalin*, pp. 143–9. An account of these events is contained in the reports of the omniscient *Okhrana*, published in the *Krasnyi Arkhiv*, no. 1, 1939, pp. 77–80. From Sverdlov's correspondence, intercepted by the *Okhrana*, it is clear that the Bolshevik cadres were not favourably impressed by the way Stalin edited *Pravda*.

[2] Stalin described his journey to Cracow to A. S. Alliluyeva, his sister-in-law. He travelled without passport. In 'the little town on the frontier between Russian and Austrian Poland, he knew nobody, but he made a casual acquaintance with a poor man living there:

On the way they talked. . . . He was a Pole, a cobbler. . . . They came to his home. The host bid him to rest and share a meal. . . . Kind-hearted and discreet . . . , he only asked whether his guest had come from afar.

"From afar", Stalin answered and, looking at the shoemaker's tools and stool in the corner, he said: "My father, too, was a shoemaker, over there, at home, in Georgia."

"In Georgia?" the Pole repeated. "You are a Georgian, then? Heard of your country, it's nice there—mountains, vineyards. And Tsarist gendarmes just as in Poland. . . ."

"Yes, just as in Poland", said Stalin, "no schools in our own tongue, but plenty of gendarmes." They looked at each other. "Can I trust him?" Stalin reflected. And having made up his mind, he said: "I must cross the frontier to-day."

The man asked no more questions. "All right," he said, "I will take you across, I know the way. . . ." At the frontier Stalin wanted to pay him . . . but the guide pushed away Stalin's hand. "No", he said firmly, "don't. . . . We are sons of oppressed nations and should help one another." ' A. S. Alliluyeva, *Vospominanya*, pp. 185–7.

—and put new wind into *Pravda*'s sails. Lenin abundantly sweetened the pill for Koba by giving him a few important assignments in Cracow and Vienna.

Undoubtedly at this stage Lenin wished to acquaint himself with his protégé more closely. What was his mental make-up? How well was he grounded in Marxist doctrine? Which were his strong features and which his weaknesses? Lenin was a connoisseur of men and had a truly Socratic way of approaching them. At first he certainly questioned Koba on all sorts of things: the course of the election in Petersburg, the condition of the underground, the races and nationalities of the Caucasus, and so on. The examination, it may be guessed, was not over-pedantic. The examiner must have known the limitations of his disciple already. But he found the result satisfactory. The young man—Koba was now thirty-three—though no independent thinker, was open-minded, shrewd, and very well informed on things that mattered practically. He was, for instance, exceptionally well versed in the involved affairs of the Caucasian nationalities. Soon the talks between the two men centred on that point. Lenin had his ideas about the problem, while Koba, drawing on his experience, was able to give flesh and blood to his master's schemes. In the course of one such discussion Lenin suggested that Koba should write an essay on the subject for *Prosveshchenye* (Enlightenment), the party's solid sociological journal.

The suggestion was flattering, for hitherto Koba had not dared to enter the field of sophisticated theory. But the problem of nationalities was much wider than the racial tangle of his native Caucasus. Here in Cracow, the medieval capital of Poland, the city of kings and poets, it was impossible to overlook the national aspirations of the Poles. Almost at a stone's throw from Lenin's home, Pilsudski was then preparing the cadres of his Legion for an insurrection against Russia. 'The Poles hate Russia,' said Lenin, 'and not without reason. We cannot ignore the strength of their nationalist feeling. Our revolution will have to treat them very gently and even allow them to break away from Russia if need be.'[1] Then there were the complex relations between the various races and nationalities of the Austro-Hungarian Empire: Magyars, Germans,

[1] Stalin related this to General W. Sikorski in 1941.

Czechs, Southern Slavs. The Austrian Socialists had worked out a programme for those nationalities. It would certainly be worth while to compare the Bolshevik and the Austrian policies. Discreetly, without hurting his disciple's *amour propre*, Lenin probably suggested to him the synopsis of the essay, its main argument and conclusions. The essay required a few weeks of work for which Vienna, the capital of the multi-national Empire of the Habsburgs, was the most suitable place. An emissary of the Central Committee had to go to Vienna anyhow to arrange certain technical matters, the printing of party resolutions and the party mail from Paris to Cracow, and so Koba might as well kill two birds with one stone. This was the origin of the essay *The Problems of Nationalities and Social Democracy* that appeared under the signature K. Stalin (the man of steel). Largely because of the reputation of being an expert on these matters that the essay brought him, its author was to become the Commissar of Nationalities in Lenin's Government five years later.

Meanwhile, after the deputies and the other members of the Central Committee departed, Koba stayed on in Cracow for a couple of weeks. Sitting at Lenin's feet he must have reflected on his own jibes at the émigré's 'aloofness from Russian reality'. What sort of a man was Lenin, after all? The disciple could not fail to examine his master. Lenin did not seem to be aloof from reality at all. He had an amazingly sure grip of the facts and essentials of each situation at home. His insight into the workings of the underground overwhelmed the most home-bred and hard-bitten Bolshevik. His mastery of men was superb. He was now in his early forties—his judgement and will-power, steeped in experience, were perfectly integrated in a matured and well-balanced personality. As a chief of a revolutionary administration he had no rival at all among the brilliant men who led Russian socialism. This trait of Lenin's certainly appealed to Koba-Stalin more strongly than any other. Why then did the man of action so often waste his energy on sectarian squabbles and doctrinaire hair-splitting? What made this genuine leader of the clandestine caucus indulge in such futile and bitter controversy as that between himself and the philosophers of Capri?

Koba-Stalin, like nearly all practitioners of Bolshevism, was sufficiently immersed in Marxist habits of thought to be aware of the political implications of a philosophical dispute. The Marxist outlook was emphatically monistic. In it science, philosophy, sociology, politics, and tactics were closely knit into a single system of ideas. Yet the interest of practitioners of Stalin's type in matters of philosophy and theory was strictly limited. They accepted certain basic formulas of Marxist philosophy, handed down to them by the popularizers of the doctrine, as a matter of intellectual and political convenience. These formulas seemed to offer wonderful clues to the most complex problems—and nothing can be as reassuring to the half-educated as the possession of such clues. The semi-intelligentsia from whom socialism recruited some of its middle cadres enjoyed Marxism as a mental labour-saving device, easy to handle and fabulously effective. It was enough to press a knob here to make short work of one idea, and a knob there to dispose of another. The user of labour-saving gadgets rarely reflects upon the difficult research that preceded their invention. Nor does he reflect upon the disinterested and seemingly unpractical research that will one day make his gadget obsolete. The users of the intellectual gadgets of Marxism, perhaps not unnaturally, treated their possession in the same narrowly utilitarian fashion. Unlike many of his followers, Lenin was the critical student in the laboratory of thought. In the end he always turned his findings to some political use; and his findings never shook him in his Marxist convictions. But while he was engaged in research, he pursued it with an open and disinterested mind. When on occasion it seemed to him that he ought to fill an important gap in his knowledge, he did not hesitate to take a year off from practical politics, entrench himself in the British Museum or in the Bibliothèque Nationale and assimilate a wealth of new material before he spoke his mind on a debatable issue. In such moments the users of the Marxist gadgets, including Stalin, grew somewhat impatient with the scrupulous thinker. The scholar in Lenin was indifferent to their fretfulness, the party boss was not. On the other hand, the disciples would contain their irritation at the theorist, because of their boundless confidence in the boss. Inevitably there was a mental barrier between Lenin and his disciple as they met in Cracow. By encouraging his junior colleague to tackle a major problem of political theory Lenin tried to reduce that barrier. He was not only the thinker and the party boss. He was also the subtle and attentive teacher who appreciated the hard conditions that had moulded his pupil. Undeterred by his mental uncouthness, Lenin helped him to bring his best qualities into the open.

In the second half of January 1913 Koba left for Vienna. He stayed there about a month, during which he wrote his work on the national minorities, a few articles and proclamations, and arranged for technical liaison between the various Bolshevik centres. He also met a few important exiles then in Vienna: Nikolai Bukharin, the future leader of the Communist International, Alexander Troyanovsky, the future Soviet Ambassador to the United States, and—Leon Trotsky.[1] Bukharin, still in his early twenties, was already making his mark as a talented and scholarly writer. At this time he was working on his Critique of the Viennese economic school of marginal utility of which Professor Böhm-Bawerk had been the most outstanding representative. The young man must have acted as cicerone to the gruff Caucasian, who, with his very rudimentary German, would feel awkward in the Austrian capital. Bukharin may have helped him to look up the books and quotations he needed. Bukharin dissented from Lenin on crucial points of Marxist theory and politics, among others on nationalities. While Lenin advocated their right to self-determination and interpreted that right in the sense that Poles, Ukrainians, Letts, and so on were entitled to secede from the Russian Empire and constitute themselves as independent nations, Bukharin disputed that view and saw in it a superfluous concession to Polish, Ukrainian, and other nationalisms. He believed that the revolution would cut across existing national divisions. Bukharin's argument left no mark on Stalin's essay, which was consistently Leninist. Nevertheless, the two men seem to have parted in a friendly manner. Their meeting in Vienna was the prologue to their close political partnership ten years later, a partnership that was to end in Bukharin's destruction by Stalin.

Neither Trotsky nor Stalin has described their meeting in Vienna. Trotsky merely recalled the 'glint of animosity' in Stalin's 'yellow eyes'. There was nothing surprising in that 'animosity'. Several years before, in denouncing the Bolshevik

[1] L. Trotsky, Stalin, p. 158.

fighting squads, Trotsky had unknowingly trodden upon Stalin's toes. The old grudge still rankled; and a new one was added to it. Trotsky's campaign against Lenin's final break with the Mensheviks had just reached its peak. In his views on the tasks of the revolution Trotsky was neither Menshevik nor Bolshevik. He did not share the Menshevik leanings towards middle-class liberalism. Nor did he share Lenin's view that the revolution would not be Socialist in character. In opposition to both, he preached proletarian dictatorship for Russia and forecast that the revolution would quickly pass from the anti-feudal to the anti-capitalist stage, or rather that the two stages would be intertwined in the actual course of events. But, as Russia was not 'ripe for socialism', its salvation would lie in a European upheaval. The Russian revolution would stimulate revolution in the rest of Europe, now ripe for Socialist transformation. This was, in a nutshell, his theory of 'permanent revolution', which in many respects placed him to the left of both Mensheviks and Bolsheviks. In the controversy inside the party, however, Trotsky stood between the two factions in so far as he preached the unity of all Socialists. His polemical thunder was now directed almost exclusively against Lenin, because it was Lenin who frankly discarded the idea of unity and deliberately split the party. Trotsky denounced the Prague conference as a 'fraud and usurpation'. Yet it was precisely to that 'usurpation' that Stalin owed his rise in the Bolshevik hierarchy.

But it was not only in matters of principle that the future rivals were at cross-purposes. For the second time now Trotsky, without knowing it, was hitting hard at Koba's personal standing with the underground. As in a Greek tragedy there was a streak of fatalistic consistency in the circumstances and accidents that created the first elements of conflict long before the real drama began. Stalin was in charge of the Bolshevik *Pravda* in Petersburg. Trotsky fired his broadsides against Leninist 'disruption' in his own Viennese *Pravda*. During the recent elections to the Duma Trotsky fed the newspaper of the Menshevik 'liquidators' in Petersburg with his articles. Summing up the results of the election shortly before his trip to Vienna, Stalin wrote in his *Pravda*: 'The practice of the movement dispels Trotsky's childish plan for merging the unmergeable. . . .

From the propounder of a fantastic unity Trotsky has turned into a helpmeet of the liquidators. . . . Trotsky has done his utmost to see that we should have two competing newspapers, two competing programmes, two rival conferences—and now that champion with faked muscles has come to chant to us his song on unity.'[1] Similarly, in a letter to the *Social Democrat*, under which the signature Stalin appeared for the first time (12 January 1913), he wrote:[2] 'It is said that Trotsky with his campaign for "unity" has brought a new current into the affairs of the liquidators. But this is not true. Regardless of all his "heroic" efforts and "terrible threats", he has proved himself to be a common noisy champion with faked muscles, for after the five years of his "labours" he has not succeeded in uniting anybody except the liquidators.' Five years later Trotsky would be hailed by the Bolsheviks as the leader of the revolution second only to Lenin, the builder of the Red Army and the victor in the Civil War. But the sneer about the 'noisy champion with faked muscles' would still flash across Stalin's mind. For all the coarseness of the phrase, its author clearly grasped Trotsky's weakness—his ineptness at the tactical game and manœuvre, at which Stalin was to prove himself a past master. Trotsky, on the other hand, must have watched with curiosity the unknown member of Lenin's new Central Committee. The imperious thinker and aesthete could hardly have been impressed by the uncouth man who spoke poor Russian with a pronounced Georgian accent and contributed no imaginative idea to a discussion. He certainly missed the shrewd, practical sense and the unbending spirit in his grey interlocutor. 'With what dull and sluggish people Lenin is now keeping company'—he may have murmured to himself. Shortly afterwards he wrote to Chkheidze, the leader of the Mensheviks in the Duma (the same who at Batum, in 1901, branded Koba as 'madman' and 'disorganizer'): 'What a senseless obsession is the wretched squabbling systematically provoked by the master squabbler Lenin . . . that professional exploiter of the backwardness of the Russian labour movement. . . .'[3] In

---

[1] J. Stalin, *Sochinenya*, vol. ii, pp. 259–60.

[2] Ibid., pp. 271–84.

[3] Quoted from N. Popov, *Outline History*, vol. i, p. 289. Trotsky never denied the authenticity of the letter.

Trotsky's eyes Stalin must have been a sample of that 'backwardness'.

By the middle of February Stalin was already on his way home. He was in high spirits. His work on the national minorities met with Lenin's enthusiastic appreciation. Almost certainly the 'old man' pruned the essay of the stylistic and logical incongruities with which the original must have bristled. But he could not help admiring the skill with which his disciple, surveying the mosaic of eastern European nationalities, marshalled a great mass of facts and crowned his analysis with a pithy and lucid statement of the Bolshevik programme. In a letter to Gorky[1] Lenin mentioned, with some pride in his protégé, the work of the 'wonderful Georgian'. The annoyance over recent differences was forgotten; and Lenin was only too glad to see his disciple winning the spurs of a theorist. Koba had secretly nurtured that ambition for a long time. With no chance to satisfy it, he had sometimes gladly hid his frustration under the exaggerated posture of the narrow-minded man of action. Presently, he could do without that posture. His formal rank in the party was enhanced by intellectual distinction.

A week after his return to Petersburg, on 23 February, his activity was interrupted by the political police. This time his arrest resulted in his banishment for a full four years. The circumstances of his disappearance were grotesque. He was betrayed to the *Okhrana* by his colleague on the Central Committee, the Bolshevik deputy for Moscow, Malinovsky. The *agent provocateur* had reported every detail of the Cracow conference to the head of the secret police Beletsky who in his turn passed on the information to the Minister of Home Affairs, Makarov. The nets were spread for the returning members of the Central Committee. On the day of his arrest Stalin attended a harmless musical matinée organized by the Bolsheviks but authorized by the police—one of the many lawful, educational activities through which the party kept in touch with its sympathizers. The unsuspecting Stalin asked Malinovsky whether there was any risk in his attending. The *agent provocateur* plausibly reassured him and immediately told the *Okhrana*. Sensing danger, Stalin's comrades tried to lead him

---

[1] W. I. Lenin, *Briefe an Maxim Gorki*, p. 74.

out of the trap and dressed him in a woman's coat to deceive the spies of the *Okhrana*. But the stratagem failed.[1]

Lenin was distressed by the news but hoped to arrange for Stalin's quick escape. The person asked to prepare it was— Malinovsky: for he was not only a member of the Central Committee, but belonged also to a small body in charge of eliminating *agents provocateurs* and organizing the important escapes. Lenin, Krupskaya, and Malinovsky jointly worked out elaborate codes of clandestine conduct, code names, &c. Thus Lenin called on 'Number Three' to bring out Vassil. But 'Number Three' (Malinovsky) saw to it that the *gendarmerie* in the northern Siberian province of Turukhansk kept a closer watch on 'Vassil' (Stalin) and removed him farther and farther into the sub-polar tundra.[2] Meanwhile Lenin was in despair, for all his important emissaries, among them Jacob Sverdlov, editor of *Pravda*, disappeared in a similar way. Yet he would permit no suspicion of Malinovsky, though the Mensheviks had repeatedly aired their distrust of him. Later, Malinovsky resigned his seat in the Duma because the new chief of the *Okhrana* was afraid of scandal. The Liberal Speaker of the Duma, Rodzianko, knew about the affair but kept it secret from the Duma. Even after Malinovsky's resignation, Lenin refused to doubt his integrity and expelled him from his party merely on grounds of undisciplined behaviour. Only in 1917, when the archives of the *Okhrana* were opened, did the bizarre truth come to light.[3]

More than a year after his arrest, in March 1914, Stalin was shifted to the settlement of Kureika on the lower reaches of the Yenissey. About 10,000 Russian and native settlers were scattered there over a land of the size of Scotland. They lived in tiny hamlets, separated from one another by tens or hundreds of miles of ice-bound wilderness. The winter there lasted eight or even nine months and the summer was short, hot, and dry. In the summer the inhabitants, Ostyaks, lived in tents of reindeer skin; for the winter they retired into half-huts and half-caves. The frozen soil yielded no food. The Ostyaks lived by

[1] A. E. Badayev, op. cit., pp. 283-4.

[2] Malinovsky's role has been described by Badayev, op. cit., pp. 100-2; Krupskaya and Pyatnitsky in *Prazhskaya Konferentsya RSDRP*, pp. 173-88. See also *Y. M. Sverdlov (Sbornik, Vospominanya)*, pp. 42-4.

[3] A. E. Badayev, op. cit., p. 285.

hunting and fishing and kept warm with furs and vodka. Only since the Five-Year Plans have their sources of livelihood had help from the petrol engine and from modern agricultural methods. In the years of Stalin's banishment the land was a howling wilderness.

The health of the exile who had grown up in the sub-tropical Caucasus stood the test. The solitude and inactivity were lightened by books and newspapers, which friends sent and which an erratic postman delivered once in a few months. At first the two ex-editors of *Pravda*, Stalin and Sverdlov, shared a room. Sverdlov thus described their common life:

There are two of us here, for I share the room with the Georgian Djugashvili; he is a good chap, but too much of an individualist in daily life, while I cannot do without at least some appearance of order. That is why I am nervous at times. . . . What is worse, there is no getting away from the houseowner's family. Our room is next to theirs and has no separate entrance. They have children and the kids naturally spend many hours with us. Sometimes they are in the way. Apart from this, people from the settlement pop in. They come, sit down, keep silent for half an hour and then suddenly get up and say 'Well, I have got to go, good-bye'. As soon as one man has gone, another one pops in and it is the same all over again. As if in spite, they come in the evening hours, the best time for reading. . . . There is no kerosene here; and we have to read by the light of candles. . . .[1]

The two men apparently did not get along well. . . . Sverdlov was soon transferred to another settlement and Stalin remained alone, fishing, hunting, and reading for the remaining few years. At first the idea of an escape still occupied his mind, but it gradually faded as the watch on him grew closer, until the outbreak of the war put it out of his head for good—with martial law in Russia the exiles preferred to stay where they were. At first Stalin pursued his study of the national minorities, wrote a new essay on the topic, and dispatched it to Lenin through the inestimable Alliluyev who still lived in Petersburg.[2] It was never published; either it was lost on the way or it was not up to the standard of his previous work and did not please Lenin. For the rest of his stay at Kureika he wrote almost nothing. In

---

[1] Quoted by L. Trotsky in *Stalin*, p. 171. See also A. S. Alliluyeva, op. cit., p. 115.   [2] A. S. Alliluyeva, op. cit., p. 118.

his *Collected Works* there is a gap between February 1913 and March 1917 which the publishers try to explain by the circumstance that Stalin's writings of that period 'had not yet been recovered'.[1] Since Stalin was freed from banishment by the revolution and his writings could not have been destroyed by the *Okhrana*, the explanation does not sound plausible. It is more likely that while he was cut off from practical activity he did not take to the pen. He was the practitioner of the revolution, not its man of letters.

It was in his solitude at Kureika that he learned about the outbreak of the First World War. The event was not a bolt from the blue, but it confounded Russian as well as European socialism. In previous years international Socialist congresses had addressed strong anti-militaristic appeals to the working classes of the world, but few of the leaders really believed in the imminence of war. In the two years before its outbreak Lenin, immersed in factional affairs, wrote scarcely anything which suggests his awareness of the danger. When the war did break out, he was taken aback by the behaviour of European socialism. On reading in Swiss newspapers that the parliamentarians of German socialism came out in support of the Kaiser's war, he refused to believe his eyes and at first treated the report as a kite flown by the German General Staff to fool the working class into acceptance.[2] So great and simple had been his belief in the strength of Socialist internationalism. For a brief spell he was so downcast that he thought of leaving politics altogether. But then he recovered and decided to 'wage war on war'. He was no pacifist. His answer to war was revolution. He pilloried the trusts, cartels, and banks as the real culprits, denounced the patriotic truce between the classes preached by most Socialists in the belligerent countries, and launched the slogan 'turn the imperialist war into a civil war'. Undismayed by the charge that, by promoting revolution in his country, he might provoke its defeat, he frankly described himself as a revolutionary defeatist. The defeat of Tsardom, he argued, would be the least evil in any circumstances; and if it speeded up the revolution, then all the better. After all, all the parties of the opposition in Russia, including the middle-class Liberals, had taken

---

[1] J. Stalin, *Sochinenya*, vol. ii, p. vi.
[2] L. Trotsky, *Mein Leben*, pp. 226–7.

up a defeatist attitude only ten years before, during the Russo-Japanese war. He went a step farther and refused to have any truck with Socialists who did not share his views. There could be no unity with those Labour leaders who had become vile purveyors of cannon fodder to the General Staffs of Europe. In his eyes they were traitors to socialism; and any association with them was treacherous. The Second (Socialist) International was dead—nothing was left but to begin again and to build the Third International from the foundations.

As sometimes in the past so now Lenin ran far ahead of most of his disciples and followers. This is not to say that they, too, were carried away by war-time chauvinism. They remained true to their anti-militaristic conviction and opposed the war. But it seemed to them that Lenin had dangerously overstated his case. They were perplexed to see how emphatically he and Zinoviev stressed their defeatist views in their writings in Switzerland. About the same time Trotsky in Paris preached 'neither victory nor defeat', but revolution; and many Bolsheviks saw more common sense in that. They were also dumbfounded by Lenin's call for a break with the whole Second International to which they had been accustomed to look as to the embodiment of all Socialist dreams and hopes. Between the Socialists that supported the war (the 'social-patriots' or the 'defensists') and those who opposed it there was a large body of floating Socialist opinion, which was dismayed by the deeds of the 'social-patriots' but reluctant to embark upon irrevocable schism.

Most of the Bolshevik leaders inside Russia were afraid that if they strictly adhered to Lenin's policies they would cut themselves off from this wavering but bulky section. At the beginning of the war the Tsarist Government put the Bolshevik deputies into prison and charged them with treason. With them Kamenev, who since Stalin's deportation inspired their policies and edited *Pravda*, took his place in the dock. The prosecution used Lenin's defeatist declarations as evidence against the defendants. Kamenev and some of the deputies then dissociated themselves from Lenin, partly because they really objected to the latter's defeatism and partly because they were anxious to parry the prosecution's blows. The deputies and Kamenev were deported to Siberia to the settlements in the Yenissey province. Their arrival gave rise to confused and angry debates among the exiled people. Lenin's followers—the defeatists—reproached them with lack of political principle and undignified conduct before the court. The exiles used to travel hundreds of miles in dog- or reindeer-drawn sleighs to a meeting-point in one of the settlements, where the debates took place. Stalin, too, attended a few such meetings. What he said there and with whom he sided has remained unknown. His official biographers say that he was the chief spokesman of the revolutionary defeatists—the canons of Stalinist orthodoxy forbid admitting that their hero could on any occasion have dissented from Lenin. The anti-Stalinist biographers have been equally categorical in underlining the dissension. In all probability Stalin hedged, since this was what he was still doing in 1917, immediately after his return to Petersburg.

At all events, he did not take the controversy much to heart. He was thousands of miles away from any scene of political action; and thrashing out principles for their own sake, without the faintest chance for their immediate application, was not his pet occupation. The more sanguine exiles or those who were more given to speculative thought were agitated, argued and wrote treatises and theses all through two or three long arctic winters. Stalin kept more and more aloof, until in the end he withdrew into hermit-like solitude.

. . . .

There is very little that can be said about Stalin's private life, although he was now already in his middle thirties. He himself was later unwilling to shed any light upon it. Apart from this, the existence of a professional revolutionary left only the narrowest margin for 'private life'. In his youth he was married to Ekaterina Svanidze, the sister of one of his Socialist schoolmates at the Tiflis Seminary. She died during the First Revolution, leaving a son who was brought up by his grandparents in the Caucasus. Stalin was not to marry again until 1918. But he was already in close friendship with the family of Sergo Alliluyev, his future father-in-law; and the Alliluyevs often looked after him. It was they who sent him parcels of food, clothing, and books during his banishment.

In his lonely existence on the Yenissey there must have been some bitterness. The cause to which he had devoted himself seemed to have been thwarted. As he looked back upon the many years of his labours in the underground, he could not derive much comfort from their results. His private life was empty and frustrated. He expressed some of his loneliness in a letter to Olga Evgeyevna Alliluyeva, his future mother-in-law. This, incidentally, is Stalin's only private non-political letter we know. He thanked the Alliluyevs for their parcels and asked them to spend no more money on him, for they themselves needed it. All he wanted was picture post-cards, because where he was, on the Yenissey, nature in its 'dull ugliness' offered nothing to the eye, except the frozen endlessness of the tundra. 'In this accursed country . . . I have been overcome by a silly longing to see some landscape, be it only on paper.'[1]

[1] A. S. Alliluyeva, op. cit., pp. 117–18.

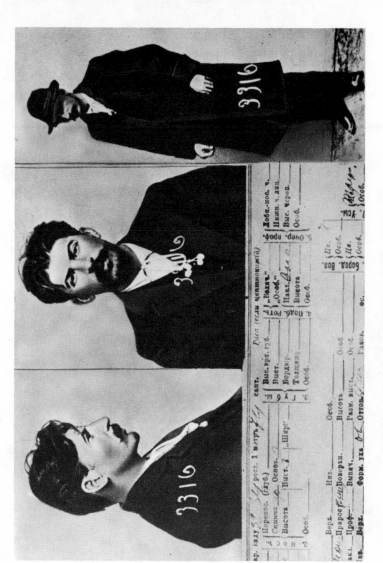

POLICE RECORD OF STALIN, 1912

CHAPTER V

1917

Stalin unfit for military service.—The February Revolution.—Councils of Workers'
and Soldiers' Deputies (Soviets).—Stalin and Kamenev return to Petersburg on
12 March and curb the Bolshevik left led by Molotov and Shlyapnikov.—Lenin's
return on 3 April and his 'April Theses'.—Crisis in Bolshevik party.—Stalin
retraces his steps and sides with Lenin.—Elected to the Central Committee, he
devotes himself to organizing the party.—The ups and downs of the revolution.—
Stalin's role during the 'July days'.—Stalin urges Lenin to go into hiding and
directs the Sixth Congress of the party.—Trotsky joins the Bolsheviks.—General
Kornilov's mutiny.—Bolsheviks win majority in Soviets.—Lenin's plans for an
insurrection.—Split in the Central Committee.—The first Politbureau is elected
on 10 October.—Stalin's attitude in the controversy between the adherents and
opponents of insurrection.—The October Revolution.—Trotsky's leadership in the
insurrection.—Stalin absent from headquarters.—His editorial work on *Pravda*.—
His attack on Maxim Gorky: 'The revolution is incapable either of regretting or of
burying its dead.'

AT the end of 1916 Tsardom was completely exhausted by the
war. The flower of Russian manhood lay wasted in the mud
of innumerable fronts; and now even the political deportees in
Siberia were being called to the colours. In the last days of the
year Djugashvili-Stalin left the settlement of Kureika for Krasnoyarsk to appear before a military medical commission.
Because of the defect in his left arm which he had had from
childhood, the future Generalissimo was found unfit for military
service.[1] In February he was allowed to settle for the rest of
his term in the vicinity of Krasnoyarsk; but these were already
the last days of Tsardom.

A week later Russia heard the death-knell of the old order.
Strikes and demonstrations in the capital which began on the
anniversary of the 'bloody Sunday' of 1905 culminated in a
spontaneous uprising, in which the garrison went over to the
side of the people. The revolution was there; it came from the
people itself. But it had been stimulated and helped by a
palace revolt, in which a part of the court camarilla, Liberal
middle-class leaders, and British diplomacy joined hands against

[1] A. S. Alliluyeva, *Vospominanya*, p. 167.

the Tsar, in the hope that his overthrow would free Russian policy from the influence of the pro-German cliques at the Court and enable Russia to wage the war more vigorously. On 2 March the Tsar abdicated in favour of his brother, Grand Duke Michael. A day later the Grand Duke resigned from the throne. The Tsar's ministers were under arrest. The Liberal monarchist Prince Lvov formed a Provisional Government with the Liberal professor Miliukov as Foreign Minister and the left-ish ex-deputy Kerensky as Minister of Justice. The constitutional title-deeds of the Government were dubious: it was formed on the initiative of a few members of the last Duma, the discredited quasi-parliament which had, moreover, been disbanded by the Tsar. Even so, the Provisional Government began its existence amid popular enthusiasm. It was willingly supported by the Petersburg Council of Workers' and Soldiers' Deputies (or Soviet) that sprang into existence a few days before the Tsar's abdication.

The members of the Soviet were elected in factories, workshops, and later on also in the barracks of the regiments that were stationed in the capital. In a similar way, Soviets came into being in all the greater towns of Russia, and later in the country-side. Because of the mode of their election they did not represent the nobility and the numerically weak middle classes. They were 'people's parliaments' *par excellence*, from which the upper classes were by definition excluded. In the absence of any parliamentary institutions, they were the broadest and the most representative bodies that Russia possessed in 1917. Deputies to the Soviets were not elected for any fixed term—the electorate had the right to replace them by other men at any time. The composition of the Soviets was therefore renewed through frequent by-elections, so that they became a very sensitive reflection of the changing popular mood. This was the source of their unrivalled moral authority. Apart from giving quasi-parliamentary representation to the lower classes, they were also the *de facto* executive power, for which the discredited normal administration was no match. The writ of the Soviet ran in factory, railway depot, post office, and regiment alike. From the first hours of its existence the Provisional Government was unable to carry out a single important decision unless it was endorsed by the leaders of the Petersburg

Soviet. Thus the Government was the virtual prisoner of the Soviet, though neither the Soviet nor the Government were as yet aware of this. The conflict, now latent, now open, between the two was to underlie the whole course of the revolution. Meanwhile, the people were still enjoying the honeymoon of the revolution: the conflicts which the future held were still hidden and, for the time, the prevailing mood was one of exhilaration. Liberty had been seized, even though this had happened amid the terrors of war.

Groups of political prisoners and exiles returned from Siberia, greeted and fêted all the way. From a Siberian town three returning exiles cabled their 'fraternal greetings' to Lenin in Switzerland. They were Stalin, Kamenev, and the Bolshevik ex-deputy Muranov. Memories of past discord had faded; all three were anxious to greet their teacher in the first hours of freedom. On 12 March Stalin and his companions arrived in Petersburg, where they were welcomed as the senior leaders of the party on the spot—the émigré leaders had not yet come home. In Petersburg a temporary bureau of the Central Committee had directed the Bolshevik organization during the February Revolution. It had been composed of three very young men: Vyacheslav Skryabin-Molotov, the contributor to *Pravda* before the war, Alexander Shlyapnikov, and Peter Zalutsky, two energetic and self-educated workmen. The trio had not enough political knowledge or experience to formulate any clear policy that would fit the unforeseen circumstances of revolution. The party was in a state of confusion—Bolsheviks of the right and left were at loggerheads; no group had leaders with enough authority to sway the whole party. The trio represented the Bolshevik left. It was discontented with the composition of Prince Lvov's Government, where bourgeois liberalism had the upper hand, and with the moderate policy of the Soviet, in which the Mensheviks and the agrarian Socialists or the Social Revolutionaries predominated. The trio viewed with hostility the Government's avowed intention to go on with the war 'till a victorious conclusion' and the patriotic attitude or the 'defensism' of the Mensheviks.[1] *Pravda*, edited

---

[1] A. Shlyapnikov, *Semnadtsatyi God*, vol. ii, pp. 170–88. See also Molotov's account (Lenin i Partya za Vremya Fevralskoi Revolutsii) in *U Velikoi Mogily*, pp. 533–4.

by Molotov, called for the immediate overthrow of Prince Lvov and the transfer of all power to the Soviets. A right wing of the Bolsheviks, led by Voytinsky, preached support for Prince Lvov, 'defensism', and the reunion of Bolsheviks and Mensheviks in one party. With Kamenev's return the right groups were strongly reinforced. Stalin, cautiously feeling his way, kept at an equal distance from the opposed groups and tried to bridge the gap between them.

On the ground of his formal seniority as a member of the Central Committee of 1912, he 'deposed' the Petersburg trio and, together with Kamenev, took over the editorship of *Pravda*.[1] For about three weeks, until Lenin's return from Switzerland on 3 April, he exercised the actual leadership of the party. His middle-of-the-road attitude made him more or less acceptable to both its wings. His name meant nothing to the mass of workers, but neither did the names of most leaders of the underground, who had been compelled to hide in anonymity. Even their anonymity was a personal and political asset—it suggested a record of devoted and unselfish service. When, a few days after his return, he appeared at a session of the Executive of the Petersburg Soviet as one of the Bolshevik representatives on that body, he was greeted as an old acquaintance only by a few Georgian Mensheviks who, like Chkheidze, were now very prominent in the capital. To the rest he was an unknown soldier of the revolution.

The change in the Bolshevik leadership did not pass unnoticed. In the Soviet as well as in *Pravda* the Bolsheviks struck a more conciliatory tone. Kamenev was the chief exponent of moderation. Stalin's articles were a good many degrees more to the left than Kamenev's, but they were not quite as radical as Molotov's. Two days after his return he published a short essay on the role of the Soviets.[2] The Soviets embodied the alliance of two classes, workers and peasants, which—in keeping with the old Bolshevik conception—he regarded as the guarantee of the final victory of the revolution. But the links between the two classes were not yet sufficiently solid. The task was to 'strengthen the Soviets . . . to link them under the guidance of a Central Soviet . . . as an organ of Government by the revolutionary people'. Here he clearly anticipated what

[1] A. Shlyapnikov, op. cit., pp. 175–88.   [2] J. Stalin, *Sochinenya*, vol. iii, pp. 1–3.

was to become the Bolshevik watchword after Lenin's return to Russia: 'All Power to the Soviets'. This seemed to imply stiff opposition to the Government of Prince Lvov. But Stalin was satisfied with stating his positive principle, and refrained from drawing its negative implication. He put the programme of the revolution in a nutshell: 'Land for the peasants, protection of labour for the workers, and the democratic republic for all citizens of Russia'. In other words, the revolution was still to be anti-feudal, but not anti-capitalist; it was to be 'bourgeois democratic', not Socialist.

His next article 'On the War' similarly combined radicalism in the general principle with vagueness in practical conclusions.[1] The war was imperialist in character; and it remained so even after the overthrow of Tsardom: 'We are deeply convinced that the course of events in Russia will demonstrate the falsity of the cries about "liberty in danger". The patriotic smoke-screen will fade away and the people will clearly see the genuine urge of the Russian imperialists towards the Straits . . . towards Persia.' This was a leaf from Lenin's book. But—'the bare slogan "down with the war" is altogether unsuitable . . . it leads practically nowhere'. With some reservations, Stalin welcomed the semi-pacifist and semi-defensist Manifesto of the Petersburg Soviet to the Peoples of the World, but he doubted whether its appeal would at all reach the workers of the belligerent countries. Workers, peasants, and soldiers must press the Provisional Government to state its willingness to start peace negotiations at once. This sounded almost like a demand for separate peace with Germany. But in the next sentence the writer urged the Provisional Government 'to come out openly and in the hearing of everybody with an attempt to persuade *all* belligerent powers to start immediate peace negotiations. . . .' On balance, the argument was heavily weighted on the 'anti-imperialist' side, but it implied that the defensists, Menshevik or even Liberal, acted in good faith, an implication that Lenin would soon laugh to scorn.

A few days later Stalin commented on a statement of the Foreign Minister Miliukov about Russia's war aims: 'The readers of *Pravda* know that those war aims are imperialist: the conquest of Constantinople, the acquisition of Armenia, the

[1] Ibid., pp. 4–8.

dismemberment of Austria and Turkey, the acquisition of northern Persia. . . . It turns out that Russian soldiers are shedding their blood on the battlefields not to "defend their fatherland", nor for "liberty", as the venal bourgeois press assures us, but for the conquest of foreign lands. . . .' The leftish Minister of Justice Kerensky had declared that Miliukov had expressed his private views and not those of the Government. 'Either—or', remarked Stalin, 'either Kerensky did not speak the truth, or else Miliukov must go.' (It could hardly have occurred to the writer that nearly thirty years later he himself would rehash some of Miliukov's war aims and that Miliukov himself would then, from his death-bed in his Parisian exile, generously applaud his former critic.)

A note of acute disquiet over the prospects of the revolution crept into one of Stalin's articles written barely a week after his return from Siberia. By now he had grasped with clarity the latent conflict between the Soviets and the Provisional Government. The revolution was based primarily on the capital, on the Petersburg Soviet. The Provisional Government drew its strength from the provinces. The dualism of power could not last long. The Provisional Government represented the moderate *bourgeoisie* that was frightened out of its wits by the 'excesses' of the revolution even before the revolution had got into its stride. Such a Government might become the shield for a feudal-bourgeois counter-revolution. The revolution must rally the provinces. The workers must be armed as Red Guards. The Army 'stands between revolution and counter-revolution'; but in an emergency the Soviets could not rely upon it because it was constantly shifted from place to place and in a state of dislocation. Finally, the revolution needed the sanction of a Constituent Assembly which would undoubtedly be more radical than the Provisional Government.

At the end of March an All-Russian conference of Bolsheviks, the first to take place since the Tsar's abdication, met in Petersburg, in a luxurious palace that had been requisitioned from the Tsar's mistress and court danseuse Kshesinskaya and transformed into the Bolshevik headquarters. The conference was characterized by an uneasy muddle and malaise.[1] The dele-

---

[1] The official account of this conference was published by Trotsky in *The Stalin School of Falsification*, pp. 231–301.

gates tried to deduce a policy from the Bolshevik scheme of revolution, as it had been preached by Lenin before the war. Yet history seemed to have played havoc with that scheme. The actual events could not be fitted into it. It had been assumed that the revolution would be democratic but not Socialist and that it would result in a democratic republic of workers and peasants but not in a proletarian dictatorship. Everybody still stuck to that assumption. So much so that, when a delegate half-jokingly questioned that axiom, he was deprived of the platform by the chairman. It had further been assumed that the Liberal middle class would back Tsardom through thick and thin, that the working class would lead in the democratic upheaval, and that the Provisional Revolutionary Government would be a coalition of the parties of workers and peasants in which the revolutionary Marxists would play first fiddle. Instead, the Liberal sections of the nobility and the middle class deserted the Tsar and stood at the helm of the Republic. The Menshevik conception seemed to have been more realistic. What was to be the role of the proletarian Socialists? Were they to remain in opposition to the Liberal Government and guard the interests of the industrial working class, as the Mensheviks had suggested ever since 1905? But history was playing tricks on the Menshevik scheme, too, for the Mensheviks were heading towards a coalition with the middle-class Liberals. The moderate Bolsheviks wanted their party to give qualified support to the administration of Prince Lvov.

To the more radical groups, steeped in the party's spirit of plebeian extremism, this sounded too incongruous to believe. They argued that the anti-feudal revolution had not yet really won, that, though the Tsar had gone, the landed aristocracy still lorded it over rural Russia; that Prince Lvov would not expropriate his own class in favour of the peasantry; and that only the working class, the Soviets, could sponsor the agrarian revolution. In this scheme of things, however, the industrial workers were to carry the main burden of the revolution, while the peasants were to be the main beneficiaries. The worker would hardly find much inspiration in a policy that expected him to be merely the peasants' political keeper. The logic of the situation demanded that the workers' stake in the upheaval should be as clear or as high as the peasants'; that socialization of industry should be linked with the breaking up of the land-lords' estates; that the revolution should be anti-capitalist as well as anti-feudal. But this would have meant throwing over-board the old axiom that Russia could not start a Socialist revolution. None of Lenin's disciples had the courage to carry out so drastic a revision in matters of doctrine. They continued to argue themselves into the impasse of a strictly anti-feudal revolution, in which the moderate Bolsheviks saw no use for radicalism and the radicals found insufficient scope for their revolutionary *élan*.

For about a week Stalin presided over the wrangle with cautious and helpless cleverness. As the chief spokesman of the rump Central Committee, he was less concerned with solving the basic dilemma than with providing the formula that would veil it, shelve a solution, and so forestall an incipient split in the party. Referring to 'the two Governments', the administration of Prince Lvov and the Soviet, he stated:

There is and there ought to be friction and struggle between them. The roles have been divided. The Soviet of Workers' and Soldiers' Deputies has in fact taken the initiative in effecting revolutionary transformation. The Soviet is the revolutionary leader of the people in insurrection, an organ of control over the Provisional Govern-ment. On the other hand, the Provisional Government has assumed the role of the fortifier of the conquests of the revolutionary people. The Soviet mobilizes the forces and exercises control, while the Provisional Government, balking and muddling, assumes the role of the fortifier of the people's conquests. . . . Such a situation has its advantages as well as disadvantages. It would not be to our ad-vantage at present to force events and thus antagonize all the sooner those bourgeois layers who will inevitably desert us in the future. It is necessary for us to gain time by putting a brake on the splitting away of those layers so that we may prepare ourselves for the struggle against the Provisional Government. . . .[1]

He shifted the emphasis of his argument according to the changing pressures, now proposing qualified support for the Government and now denying it any backing, or evasively suggesting that what mattered was not whether or not the Government should be supported but whether the Government would support the revolutionary initiative of the Soviet.

[1] L. Trotsky, *The Stalin School of Falsification*, pp. 237–8.

A new three-cornered fight arose over the proposal for unification with the Mensheviks. One group favoured unification without any strings attached to it. On behalf of the radicals Molotov spoke against it and argued that unity was possible only between those who accepted a clear-cut anti-war programme. Stalin urged that negotiations on unity be started at once on the basis of adherence to 'the principles of Zimmerwald and Kiental', principles, that is, established by international Socialist conferences that took place in two Swiss towns, which Lenin regarded as lacking in revolutionary spirit. Stalin waived Molotov's objections: 'There is no use running ahead and anticipating disagreements. No party life is possible without disagreements. We will live down minor divergencies of views within the Party.'[1] But he reassured the left by saying that the negotiations would be tentative and that their results would not be binding on the party. The negotiations, in fact, began right away and were interrupted only after Lenin's return.

As soon as Lenin returned, Stalin withdrew to the wings or behind the scenes. The few weeks of his leadership had been just enough for him to show his hand. He was of the party and in it, but not ahead of it. He shunned the extreme groups and stuck to the middle trend, even though that meant marking time and shilly-shallying. He led because he followed the prevailing mood and expressed it in a grey patchwork of formulas. He did not try to mould it into any new shape. Such leadership can keep any normal party, working within an established order, afloat; but it was not the type of leadership under which Bolshevism would have become the parent of a new revolution.

On 3 April, after his famous journey 'in the sealed train'[2]

---

[1] L. Trotsky, *The Stalin School of Falsification*, p. 275.

[2] Lenin arranged for that journey through the medium of well-known French, Swiss, Swedish, and German Socialists. The only obligation which he took *vis-à-vis* the German Government was to do his best to ensure that a group of German civilians were allowed out of Russia, as a *quid pro quo*. The German Government, aware of his opposition to the war, certainly hoped to benefit from his propaganda inside Russia. Lenin had his scruples before he decided to avail himself of the facilities to travel through Germany. The scruples gave way to his main preoccupation, which was to find himself as quickly as possible at the centre of the revolution. He would rather have gone to Russia via England, but the British Government refused him transit. On his arrival nobody reproached him for the journey. The leaders of the moderate parties welcomed him as one of the old and proven leaders. A few weeks later Martov and other Mensheviks followed his example and journeyed home by the same route, without ever meeting with any

across Germany, Lenin returned to Petersburg, where he was welcomed by crowds of workers, sailors, and soldiers. From the railway station he drove triumphantly in a convoy of armoured cars through the streets of the capital.[1] He could hardly contain his boredom at the many garrulous, good-natured speeches of welcome to which he was subjected. He was burning with impatience to meet his comrades and followers. His mind and will-power were strung up for the *coup* which he had to carry out in his own party before his party would be capable of carrying out a new revolution in the country. He had hardly recovered from the unexpected welcome when he dotted down in a hasty telegraphic style ten Theses. These—his confession of faith, his new scheme for revolution, his new charter of Bolshevism—he presented to the Bolshevik conference the day after his arrival.

His followers were about to meet the Mensheviks at a unity conference, when Lenin hit them over the head with his Theses.[2] He prefaced their presentation by an indignant fling at the political idyll he had found on the spot. On his way to Russia, he said, he expected to be taken straight from the railway station to the fortress of Peter and Paul, the dreaded prison for political offenders. Instead, he was greeted by the enemies and traitors of socialism. Something had gone wrong. 'Defensism' was victorious in Russia as elsewhere. The *bourgeoisie* and the Mensheviks were deceiving the proletariat. 'What is peculiar in Russia is the gigantically swift transition from savage violence to the most delicate deceit', by which the masses were led to believe in the righteousness of their rulers' war-aims. The Bolsheviks must have no truck with defensists and semi-defensists. Their task was to establish proletarian dictatorship. In February the working class had virtually all the power in its hands, but not knowing what to do with it it simply ceded it to the *bourgeoisie*. 'Even our Bolsheviks show confidence in the Government. That can only be explained by intoxication

reproach or criticism. Only later on, when Lenin's influence began to grow, was the 'sealed train' played up by some of his opponents into a sinister compact between the German General Staff and the Bolsheviks. N. Sukhanov, *Zapiski o Revolutsii*, vol. iii, pp. 10–13. Lenin, 'How we arrived', *Collected Works*, vol. xx, book 1, pp. 91–3. *Leninskii Sbornik*, vol. ii, pp. 376–406, 410–12, 448–57.

[1] N. Sukhanov, op. cit., vol. iii, pp. 26–7.
[2] Lenin, *Collected Works*, vol. xx, book 1, pp. 95–111.

incidental to revolution. That is the death of socialism. You, comrades, have confidence in the Government. If that is your attitude, our ways part. I prefer to remain in the minority.' One revolutionary like the German anti-militarist Karl Liebknecht was better than a whole pack of Mensheviks, social-patriots, and defensists. 'If you are in sympathy with Lieb-knecht and extend even a finger to the "defensists", this will be a betrayal of international socialism.'

Careful to refrain from personal taunts, preferring to let his misguided disciples quietly retrace their steps, Lenin, neverthe-less, flayed *Pravda* without pity: '*Pravda* demanded of the Government that it renounce annexations. To demand of the Government of the capitalists that it renounce annexations was nonsense . . . flagrant mockery . . . a fog of deception. . . . It is high time to admit the mistake. . . . Have done with greetings and resolutions! It's time to get down to business.' The revolutionary phrases of the Mensheviks were mere 'flattery of the revolutionary people'. He was not advocating any imme-diate seizure of power, because the Bolsheviks were still in a minority in the Soviets. As long as they were not a majority, they should patiently explain their policy to the masses that still trusted the Mensheviks, until they persuaded the majority of the working people of the need for a new revolution. Mean-while they had to tell the people that what they strove for was 'not a parliamentary republic . . . but a republic of Soviets . . . abolition of the police, of the [standing] army and of official-dom'. The peasants want land '. . . they will not ask your per-mission . . . we shall take the land and the landlord will never be able to take it back'. But this was not all. The revolution had entered the Socialist phase. All the banks ought to be merged into a single national bank, controlled by the Soviets. Industry could not be socialized immediately, but production and distribution must be placed under workers' control. It was high time to change the antiquated programme of the party, and even its name: '. . . I propose that . . . we call it the Com-munist Party . . . the majority of the official Social Democrats have betrayed socialism. . . . Are you afraid to go back on your old memories? But to change our linen, we have got to take off the dirty shirt and put on a clean one.' His last thesis fore-shadowed the foundation of the new, the Third International.

He wound up with a warning that if his comrades were not ready to follow him, he would not falter. . . . He would rather remain alone, like Liebknecht in Germany, and fight against them in the sure knowledge that the future was his.

A non-Bolshevik writer, who by chance was present at the conference, described later the impact of Lenin's words: 'I shall never forget that thunderlike speech, startling and amazing not only to me, a heretic accidentally present there, but also to the faithful, all of them. I assert that nobody there had expected anything of the kind. It seemed as if all the elements and the spirit of universal destruction had risen from their lairs, knowing neither barriers nor doubts, nor personal difficulties nor personal considerations, to hover through the banquet chambers of Kshesinskaya, above the heads of the bewitched disciples.'[1]

In the next few days Lenin continued his *tour de force*. Kamenev, Kalinin, and others held out against him his own formulas and schemes, his own categorical statements that Russia was not ripe for proletarian dictatorship and socialism. He retorted with bitter invective against 'the old Bolsheviks who more than once played a sad role in the history of our Party', because they conservatively stuck to old formulas they had learned by heart, instead of reviewing them critically in the light of new experience. He admitted that Russia, considered in isolation from the rest of Europe, was not ripe for a Socialist order. But Europe as a whole was; and Russia was called upon to make the beginning in a European Socialist revolution. This was Trotskyism not Leninism, grumbled the Leninists, once again referring back to old disputes. After a few days of intense argumentation, Lenin carried the bulk of the party with him. One group of Bolsheviks, the extreme right, left the party altogether, snubbing their former leader as an anarchist plotter, a new Bakunin. The radical groups, however, for whom Molotov and Shlyapnikov had acted as ineffective mouthpieces, were very receptive. They found in Lenin's Theses a systematic rationalization of their own mood. The framework of the purely democratic revolution, from which they themselves had been too timid to break out because it had had the sanction of the party doctrine, but which, they dimly felt, unduly constricted their revolutionary ambition, was now broken open by the

[1] N. Sukhanov, op. cit., vol. iii, pp. 26–7.

author of the doctrine himself. Lenin's *coup* was so astonishingly effective because it answered a psychological need in his own party. It gave boldness and a sense of direction to groping and befogged men. To his opponents the change seemed so wild and abrupt that this alone condemned it, in their eyes, to futility. Kamenev, Kalinin, and others stuck to their guns, hinted that Lenin's prolonged absence from Russia had made him lose touch with Russian reality and hoped that the party would sooner or later recover from its infatuation with the new Leninism and steer back to milder and less adventurous policies. Throughout the year of the revolution, and especially on the eve of the October rising, the tug-of-war between the new and the old Leninism would still strain the unity of the leaders; and the controversy was to break out anew after Lenin's death in the fight over his succession. But from April on, Bolshevism was geared for the steep and dangerous climb to a second revolution.

The hail of Lenin's argument and invective drove Stalin into protective silence. This was not the first time his cautious mind demurred at a hazardous stroke of his master. Yet he could not suspect Lenin of light-mindedness or quixotry—he knew him too well already. Though it was not always easy for him to follow the flights of his master's bold political imagination, he had developed an implicit faith in Lenin's realism. The thing cannot be sheer fantasy if Lenin stands for it, he must have said to himself. He swallowed Lenin's taunts at *Pravda*, though it must have been humiliating for him to be given such a rap over the knuckles just after he had played the leader of the party. He was not too badly exposed to Lenin's criticism, however, once he had decided not to parry it. After all, he had not been one of the open 'conciliators' like Kamenev. He had oscillated between conciliators and radicals carefully enough to be able to accept Lenin's Theses without much loss of face. His shilly-shallying had reflected his own embarrassment; and it was now a relief to be freed from it. Nor was Lenin bent on making those who led the party in his absence lose face once they had given up the fight. Stalin remained the editor of *Pravda*; and Lenin helped him adjust himself. Barely ten days after Lenin came out with his Theses, Stalin hastened to demonstrate, in *Pravda*, his solidarity with Lenin.

His signed editorial 'Land for the Peasants' was a rebuttal of the things which he himself had just advocated.[1] The Minister of Agriculture, Shingarev, had forbidden the peasants to till the estates of landlords who, frightened by the spirit of *jacquerie* in the country-side, had fled to the towns and forsaken their property. The Minister urged the peasants to wait patiently until the Constituent Assembly initiated a land-reform. 'Since the date for the convocation of the Assembly remains unknown,' commented Stalin, 'since the Provisional Government is delaying it . . . so the land is actually to remain untilled, the landlords are to retain their estates, the peasants are to go without land and Russia—workers, peasants and soldiers—without enough bread.' He called on the peasants to take justice into their own hands, to 'form peasant committees and till the land in an organized fashion, without waiting for any permission', without paying heed to reactionary ministers, 'who put spokes into the wheels of revolution'. A few days before, he had argued that the Bolsheviks ought not yet to force events because that would antagonize bourgeois progressives. Now he branded the same view as 'reactionary utopia'. 'The victorious march of the Russian Revolution will sweep them [the bourgeois progressives] aside like useless rubbish agreeable and pleasing only to the enemies of revolution.' A few days before he had doubted whether workers in western Europe would lend their ears to any propaganda against the war. Now he maintained firmly (in the May Day proclamation which he wrote on behalf of the Central Committee)[2] that 'under the thunder of the Russian Revolution the workers in the West, too, rise from their slumber. . . . The ground is burning under the feet of the capitalist robbers—the Red banner of the International is rising again over Europe.' Gone were the hopes for unity with the moderate Socialists, for the latter were now 'tired of the Revolution'. 'Those who try to halt in a Revolution will inevitably lag behind; and he who lags behind will receive no mercy—the Revolution will throw him into the camp of the counter-revolution.'

By the end of April another national conference of Bolsheviks elected a new Central Committee of nine members, among them Lenin, Zinoviev, Kamenev, Stalin, Sverdlov. This was

[1] J. Stalin, *Sochinenya*, vol. iii, pp. 34–6.   [2] Ibid., pp. 37–8.

the first time Stalin was confirmed in leadership by a large vote in a direct, open election. To the cadres of the party he was now a familiar figure, although to outsiders he was still a name only. At the conference he was the *rapporteur* on the problem of nationalities.[1] The Provisional Government had just come into conflict with the Finns who were breaking away from Russia. 'It is unthinkable', said Stalin, 'that we should acquiesce in the forcible keeping of any nation within the framework of any state.' If we did that, 'we ourselves would be the continuers of Tsarist policy'. He, the Georgian, did not want the separation of the Caucasus from Russia; but should the Caucasian peoples desire it, nobody had the right to hold them back. When the Pole Felix Dzerzhinsky, the future founder of the Bolshevik political police, objected that the separatist aspirations of the various nationalities were reactionary, Stalin retorted: 'But is not the fight of the Irish against the English revolutionary?' The issue, so he argued, was very big indeed, for it involved the fate of all the colonial peoples. To support the national aspirations of those peoples was 'to cast a bridge between East and West', and to secure a vast Asiatic backing for the Socialist Revolution in Europe. The editor of *Pravda* was confirming his reputation as the party's foremost expert on these matters.

Meanwhile, the tide of Bolshevism began to rise. The 133 delegates at the national conference represented about 76,000 members.[2] (In the days of the February revolution the membership of the party amounted to 30,000 at the most.) This was still a 'handful' that would have weighed little in the scales of any normal parliamentary election. But it was not in such scales that the weight of social and political influences was measured in the year of revolution. The 'handful' of Bolsheviks consisted of well-organized and disciplined 'key-men' operating from decisive vantage points in industry and transport, in the army and in the Soviets. Most of them were shop-stewards and delegates of factories and regiments wielding a steadily growing influence over the mass of workers and soldiers. They were the 'activists', the 'revolutionary vanguard', behind which there moved into battle a genuine political *levée en masse*. In each Soviet the Bolsheviks acted as a compact body; and as in the successive by-elections their numbers increased, their actual

[1] Ibid., pp. 49–57.　　　　[2] N. Popov, *Outline History*, vol. i, p. 364.

weight grew out of proportion to their numbers. Somebody had to look after that vast mass of agitators, shop-stewards, and members of the Soviets. Somebody had to keep in touch with them from day to day, convey to them the decisions of the Central Committee and instruct them how to vote in the Soviets and behave *vis-à-vis* the other parties. This arduous job was carried out by Stalin and Sverdlov. The chaos in transport and the circumstance that Petersburg was the focus of revolution made it impossible for members of the Central Committee regularly to canvass the provincial branches of the party. Every now and then delegates would come to the capital to attend the national conferences of the Soviets, meetings of army committees, and trade unions' or peasants' rallies. The two chief organizers of the Central Committee would use such opportunities to instruct and muster the delegates either at the Kshesinskaya palace, the party's headquarters, or at the Tauride Palace, the original seat of the Petersburg Soviet. While Lenin, Zinoviev, or Kamenev took the platform and engaged in battles of words and resolutions, Stalin and Sverdlov acted as the indefatigable and invisible conductors of the Bolshevik groups in the assemblies, making the rank and file behave and vote in unison with the leaders. The tenacious and skilful organizer to whom Lenin had assigned so crucial a role in his scheme of the revolution now had to prove himself, not within the narrow confines of an underground but in the middle of an open and swelling popular movement. Yet, by its nature, his role remained as anonymous and modest as it had been. Not for him the popularity and fame which the revolution was generously and rapidly bestowing upon its great tribunes and master-orators.

In those days Bolshevism acquired a new tribune in Leon Trotsky, who by his courage, political *élan*, and oratorical brilliance soon outshone the gifted leaders who day after day spoke to the country from the platform of the Petersburg Soviet. Trotsky returned to Russia straight from a Canadian internment camp, a month after Lenin. He was anxious to close his long controversy with the founder of Bolshevism and to join hands with him.[1] The war had in part changed his outlook. He gave up his long-cherished ambition to unite Bolsheviks and

---

[1] N. Sukhanov, op. cit., vol. iv, pp. 185–94; L. Trotsky, *History of the Russian Revolution*, vol. ii, pp. 313–14.

Mensheviks. He had hoped that under the impact of revolution the Mensheviks would swing to the left and the Bolsheviks rid themselves of what he regarded as their characteristic sectarian narrowness. He now saw that under that impact the Mensheviks had swung to the right and become 'defensists'. On the other hand, the Bolsheviks seemed to him to have become more open-minded since they had emerged from the underground. He was willing to admit that in the controversy over the nature of the revolutionary party, its structure and discipline, not he but Lenin had proved right. He consoled himself with the thought that in his April Theses, the founder of Bolshevism had adopted the view, expounded by Trotsky long before, that the Russian revolution must aim at proletarian dictatorship—not for nothing did old Bolsheviks raise their eyebrows over Lenin's unexpected 'Trotskyist deviation'.

In Petersburg Trotsky led a small group of very gifted and influential Socialists known as the *Mezhrayontsy* (The Inter-Borough Organization), which joined the Bolshevik party in July. To that group belonged men like Lunacharsky, the future Commissar of Education, Pokrovsky, the great historian, Ryazanov, the biographer of Marx, and the future diplomats Manuilsky, Yoffe, Karakhan, Yureniev, and others. Even before their formal adherence, Trotsky and some of his colleagues acted in agreement with Lenin and often spoke on behalf of the Bolsheviks in and outside the Soviet. A whole Pleiad of great and ardent tribunes of revolution, such as Europe had not seen since the days of Danton, Robespierre, and Saint-Just, came forward into the limelight—while Stalin continued to do his job in the twilight of the *coulisse*.

During May and June the revolutionary fever in Petersburg continually mounted. Municipal elections in the capital exposed the weakness of Miliukov's Constitutional Democrats (Cadets), the party that predominated in the Government. Half the vote went to the moderate Socialists, leaving the two extreme parties, Cadets and Bolsheviks, as influential minorities. The predominantly Cadet Government gave way to a coalition of Cadets, Mensheviks, and Social Revolutionaries. But the new Government as it tried to ride the storm showed few signs of real strength. The Bolsheviks were becoming the masters in the working-class suburbs of Petersburg. From the army came the ever louder clamour for peace, while Russia's western allies were pressing the Russian Supreme Command to start an all-out offensive against the Germans. The Bolsheviks met the new coalition with grim hostility; but in opposing it they displayed a tactical imagination and subtlety which could not fail to yield massive and quick rewards. They did not simply shout down the whole Government, for they knew that the working class was still favourably impressed by the fact that Socialist parties were now in office, for the first time in Russian history. But the working classes were also suspicious of the middle-class Cadets, the senior partners in the coalition. Lenin therefore pressed the moderate Socialists to break up the coalition and form a Government of their own, based on the Soviets. In the Red suburbs of the capital hosts of Bolshevik agitators raised two plain slogans: 'Down with the Ten Capitalist Ministers!' and 'All Power to the Soviets!' The first slogan stirred the widespread suspicion of the Cadets common to the Menshevik and Bolshevik rank and file. The demand that all power be transferred to the Soviets was equivalent to the demand that the moderate Socialists should take power alone, since they wielded a majority in the Soviets; and so that slogan, too, had its appeal to the ordinary Menshevik worker. Throughout May and June, legions of Menshevik workers were converted to Bol-shevism. On 18 June half a million workers and soldiers marched in the streets of the capital in a procession which was nominally called by the Menshevik leaders of the Soviets. The vast mass of demonstrators carried placards and banners with almost exclusively Bolshevik slogans. The first All-Russian Congress of Soviets was just then in session; and the delegates from the provinces, among whom the Bolsheviks were still a minority of one-sixth, could not help being impressed by this demonstration of Bolshevik influence in the capital.[1]

At the Congress of the Soviets there occurred a significant incident. When one of the Socialist ministers was apologetically explaining the need for a broadly based government and arguing that no party could cope single-handed with the disintegration and chaos engendered by the war, Lenin, from the floor, interrupted the speaker with a curt statement that his party was

---

[1] L. Trotsky, *History of the Russian Revolution*, vol. i, pp. 446–68; N. Sukhanov, op. cit., vol. iv, pp. 282–375.

ready to assume the whole power.[1] Lenin's words were received with loud, derisive laughter; but the mass processions in the streets of the capital imparted to them a deadly earnestness.

In fact, the Bolsheviks were not yet ready to take power. They continued to regard the Soviets as the legitimate source of revolutionary authority; and, as long as his party was in a minority in the Soviets, Lenin ruled out any attempt on its part at seizing power. But he had to work hard to keep on a leash the impatient, semi-anarchist groups of workers, soldiers, and sailors who fretted at his prudent tactics. He saw that his scheme of action was imperilled by the uneven rhythm and impetus of the revolution. While his policies were still too extreme for the provincial working class, a large section of the garrison and the proletariat in the capital was already beginning to suspect the Bolsheviks, too, of excessive moderation or of insufficient revolutionary pluck. In *Pravda* Stalin was compelled to warn the Red suburbs against the anarchist and semi-anarchist agitators who urged the workers to 'come out' prematurely. In the next few months Bolshevism uneasily balanced between the hazards of delaying the revolution and the risks of premature action.

The hazards and risks were increased by the fact that the counter-revolution, too, was preparing for a show-down. Monarchist generals, leagues of patriotic officers, associations of ex-service men and the Cadet middle class, all took notice of the meaning of the June demonstration and made up their minds to throw back the mounting tide of Bolshevism by a violent *coup*. The moderate Socialist leaders were intimidated and vaguely played with the idea that such a show-down would rid them of their rivals on the left, against whom they themselves were more and more helpless. Lenin and his colleagues were determined not to allow themselves to be driven into premature insurrection. They were fairly confident that, basing themselves on the proletarian masses of the capital alone, they could seize power immediately; but they were equally convinced that they could not hold it against the opposition of the rest of the country.[2] They were also aware that every major

---

[1] N. Sukhanov, op. cit., vol. iv, p. 232.

[2] L. Trotsky, *History of the Russian Revolution*, vol. ii, pp. 73–95; J. Stalin, *Sochinenya*, vol. iii, p. 122.

demonstration in the streets of Petersburg was now more likely than not to degenerate into street fighting. The workers were armed. Soldiers were reluctant to march in any demonstration without their rifles. Each unarmed procession offered a shooting target to the bands of the counter-revolution. The Central Committee of the Bolshevik party therefore banned all demonstrations. It was, however, unable to enforce the ban—the revolutionary temper in the suburbs and barracks had grown beyond its control. This was the background to the grave crisis of the 'July days', in which Stalin played a curious role, and which ended in a severe though temporary setback for Bolshevism.

A vivid and apparently truthful account of the events was given by Stalin himself in a report to the sixth Congress of the party which met a couple of weeks after the 'July days'.[1] On 3 July, in the afternoon, a delegation from one of the regiments burst into the city conference of the party and declared that their regiment and others had decided to 'come out' that same evening, that they had already sent messengers to other regiments and factories calling everybody to join in the revolt. Volodarsky, the leader of the Petersburg Committee, sternly reminded the soldiers that the party expected them, as its members, to observe the ban on demonstrations. The Central Committee, the Petersburg Committee, and the Bolshevik Military Organization then met, once again confirmed the ban, and sent agitators to the factories and barracks to enforce it there. At the same time the Central Committee delegated Stalin to inform the Executive of the Soviets, which was controlled by the Mensheviks, about the new development. Two hours after these events had begun to unfold, Stalin was carrying out his mission. But the avalanche was already on the move. Towards evening, crowds of workers and a number of regiments, fully armed and flying their colours, assembled in front of the offices of the Petersburg Committee of the party. Bolshevik speakers urged the crowd to disperse peacefully, but they were interrupted by hoots and catcalls. The raging elements of revolution struck over their heads. They then proposed that the demonstrators march towards the Tauride Palace, the seat of the Soviet, and submit

---

[1] J. Stalin, *Sochinenya*, vol. iii, pp. 156–68.

their demands to the Soviet Executive. To the tune of the *Marseillaise* the procession moved on. All through the night the crowd virtually besieged the Tauride Palace, waiting in vain for an answer to their main demand that the Soviet leaders disown the Provisional Government and themselves assume power.

Mensheviks and Social Revolutionaries were biding their time, meanwhile, in the expectation that they would soon be rescued by 'loyal' government troops. So far the meetings and processions were peaceful, but with every hour the excitement was boiling up to an explosion. The Minister of Agriculture, Chernov, was recognized by the crowd and 'placed under arrest' by a group of thugs—only thanks to Trotsky's presence of mind and his courageous intervention was the Minister, himself an old revolutionary, saved from violence and released.[1] Long after midnight, from the balcony of the Tauride Palace, Zinoviev tirelessly argued in his high-pitched voice with the crowd, trying to achieve the impossible: to persuade the multitude to go home and yet not to damp its revolutionary temper but, on the contrary, to keep it hot. The Bolshevik Central Committee was in permanent session, struggling with the awkward dilemma. In the end it decided that the party should take part in the demonstration in order to lead and direct it into peaceful channels. The risk was that they would not succeed in doing so; that a battle would not be avoided; and that it might end in a major defeat that would swing the scales in favour of the counter-revolution. Defeat in such a show-down was the more probable as the Bolsheviks pulled their punches all the time. The other course of action open to them was to dissociate themselves from the demonstrators and let events run their own way. The party of the revolution, however, could not show such equanimity. The masses, left to themselves, to their own passion and impatience, were sure to walk into the trap of civil war. They would never have forgiven the Bolsheviks what would have amounted to a desertion at a time of crisis. The Bolsheviks could not afford to discredit themselves in the eyes of those very people on whose confidence and support their ultimate victory depended.

[1] N. Sukhanov, op. cit., vol. iv, pp. 422–7; L. Trotsky, *History of the Russian Revolution*, vol. ii, pp. 51–2.

In the next few days the demonstrations, growing in size and turbulence, led to sporadic clashes and bloodshed. But the worst fears of the Bolsheviks did not materialize—the clashes did not lead to regular civil war. The whole movement spent its impetus and petered out. Almost simultaneously a counter-movement was gathering momentum. To the relief of the upper and middle classes armed groups of the right wing came into action. The Bolshevik headquarters and the offices of *Pravda* were wrecked. In the middle of all this turbulence came the news of the collapse of the Russian offensive on the front. The Bolsheviks were blamed; and a cry of vengeance went up. Agitators of the right branded Lenin and his followers as German spies. A popular newspaper published faked documents purporting to prove the charge. Government troops were engaged in punitive expeditions in the Red suburbs.

Throughout the 'July days' Stalin, on behalf of the Central Committee, parleyed with the Executive of the Soviets and did his best to bring unwieldy elements under control. At the outset he brought the Bolshevik decision against the demonstration to the knowledge of the Executive, only to learn later on that the decision had been reversed. He then presumably had to report the change to the Soviet leaders and explain its reasons. In the ruling circles of the Soviets, Stalin's good faith was apparently taken for granted, for later on when the Government issued writs for the arrest of most Bolshevik leaders, he, though a member of the Central Committee, was not molested. It also fell to him to carry out the final act in the winding up of this semi-insurrection, the surrender by the rebels of the powerful Peter and Paul fortress. Accompanied by a Menshevik member of the Soviet Executive, Stalin went to the fortress, which was situated on an island opposite the Bolshevik headquarters, just at the moment when those headquarters were being occupied by government troops. The garrison of the fortress consisted of fiery Kronstadt sailors, the machine-gunners who had initiated the revolt, and civilian Red Guards, all refusing to surrender and preparing for a long and bloody siege. It is easy to imagine how difficult and delicate was Stalin's mission. He was helped by official assurances that the rebels would not be penalized; but they still persistently refused to surrender. In the end Stalin shrewdly persuaded them to capitulate to the Executive of the Soviets, which sounded more honourable than a surrender to the Government. A blood-bath was avoided.[1]

The Bolshevik setback was superficial, as events would prove. Immediately after the 'July days', however, the setback was exaggerated by all parties. Most Bolshevik leaders, including Lenin, thought themselves more thoroughly defeated than they actually were.[2] The baiting of Bolsheviks grew. Lenin and Zinoviev were indicted as spies in German pay. The moderate Socialists knew the accusation was false, but their grudge against the Bolsheviks was strong enough to prevent them from defending Lenin and his colleagues against it. Many of them suspected Lenin of having made a serious attempt, in the 'July days', to seize power.

The Central Committee now discussed whether Lenin and Zinoviev should hand themselves over to the authorities or whether they should go into hiding. Lenin and Zinoviev were hesitant: they feared that to avoid trial would confirm, in the eyes of uninformed opinion, the charges levelled against them. This was at first also the view of Lunacharsky and Kamenev. Stalin, on the contrary, advised them to go into hiding. It would be folly, he said, to trust the justice of the Provisional Government. An anti-Bolshevik hysteria was being so unscrupulously whipped up that any young officer or ensign escorting the 'German spies' into prison, or from prison to court, would think it an act of patriotic heroism to assassinate them on the way. Lenin still hesitated to follow Stalin's advice. Stalin then approached the Executive of the Soviets and told them that Lenin was prepared to face trial if the Executive guaranteed his life and personal safety from lawless violence. As the Mensheviks and Social Revolutionaries refused to shoulder any such responsibility, Lenin and Zinoviev finally made up their minds to go into hiding.

On 8 July Lenin disappeared, no doubt remembering the example of Robespierre who, shortly before his rise to power, was similarly hunted and found refuge with a Jacobin carpenter. Lenin's 'carpenter' was the workman Alliluyev, Stalin's old

---

[1] J. Stalin, *Sochinenya*, vol. iii, pp. 111–12, 161.

[2] Lenin, *Sochinenya*, 3rd edition, vol. xxi, p. 26; G. Zinoviev, *Sochinenya*, vol. xv, p. 41; *6 Syezd RSDRP*, pp. 113–15.

friend. In his house Lenin lived for a few days.[1] On 11 July Stalin and Alliluyev escorted Lenin through the darkening streets of the city to the Maritime Station where Lenin left to hide first in the villages near the capital and then in Finland. From now on until the October Revolution he remained underground, inspiring the strategy, if not the tactics, of his party through the pamphlets, articles, and letters which he showered on the Central Committee. Together with Lenin departed Zinoviev. A few days later Kamenev was imprisoned. So were Trotsky—after he had openly declared his solidarity with Lenin —Lunacharsky, and others. The great leaders and tribunes were dispersed. At that critical moment Stalin once again stepped to the fore to lead the party. His relative anonymity stood him in good stead; for his name did not arouse the anger and the hatred inspired by the others.

Soon after Lenin's departure he published under his full signature ('K. Stalin, member of the Central Committee', &c.) an appeal 'Close the ranks', addressed to the defeated but not routed party.[2] He repeated that in the 'July days' the hands of the Bolsheviks were forced by events, that the counter-revolution had gone over to the attack, and that the 'conciliators' burdened themselves with a heavy responsibility. The offensive of the counter-revolution was not yet over—'from the attack on the Bolsheviks they are now passing to an attack on all Soviet parties and the Soviets themselves'. He forecast a new political crisis: 'Be ready for the coming battles. . . . Our first warning is: do not lend yourselves to counter-revolutionary provocation, arm yourselves with endurance and self-control, save forces. . . . Our second warning is: draw closer around our party . . . encourage the weak, rally those who lag behind.' He repeated the same instructions to the city conference of the Bolsheviks, which had begun before the 'July days' and was now half-secretly resumed. The conference adopted a manifesto written by Stalin in a style that was a peculiar mixture of the revolutionary and the oriental, sacerdotal idiom:

Those gentlemen evidently hope to confound our ranks, to sow

---

[1] N. Krupskaya, *Memories of Lenin*, p. 272; S. A. Alliluyeva, *Vospominanya*, pp. 183-4. Alliluyeva describes Stalin acting as Lenin's barber. He shaved off Lenin's beard and moustache to make him unrecognizable.

[2] J. Stalin, *Sochinenya*, vol. iii, pp. 104-7.

doubt and confusion amid us and to make us distrust our leaders. The wretches! They do not know that never have the names of our leaders [i.e. the names of Lenin, Trotsky, Zinoviev, Kamenev] been as dear and near to the working class as they are now when the impudent bourgeois rabble is slinging mud at them. The venal traitors! They do not even guess that the heavier the slander of bourgeois hirelings the deeper the love of the workers for their leaders. . . . The shameful stigma of slanderers . . . take that stigma from the hands of 32 thousand organized workers of Petersburg and carry it to your grave. . . . And you, gentlemen capitalists and land-lords, bankers and profiteers, priests and agents of the counter-espionage . . . you are celebrating your victory too early. You have taken too early to burying the great Russian Revolution. The Revolution is alive, and will yet let you feel it, Messieurs the grave-diggers.[1]

The Bolsheviks, indeed, quickly recovered from the blow. By the end of July they were able to hold half-secretly a national Congress at which 240,000 members, three times as many as in April, were represented. Stalin and Bukharin were the chief spokesmen for the Central Committee. A high light of the Congress was a debate between Stalin, Bukharin, and Preobrazhensky on the character of the approaching revolution. In part the debate was an echo of the controversy over Lenin's April Theses; in part it was an anticipatory flash of a more dramatic controversy in years to come. Stalin tabled a motion to the effect that the victorious Russian Revolution would direct its power 'in alliance with the revolutionary proletariat of the advanced countries towards peace and the Socialist reconstruction of society'.[2] Preobrazhensky, a young Marxist economist, tabled an amendment saying that the revolutionary government should 'direct its power towards peace and—if proletarian revolution materializes in the west—towards socialism'. In both versions the 'alliance' between the Russian revolution and the western European proletariat was taken for granted. In Preobrazhensky's view, however, Russia could not embark upon Socialist construction unless western Europe, too, was revolutionized. Failing this, the revolution could only achieve peace (and presumably the consolidation of the democratic order). Bukharin defined the objectives of the revolution in much the same way. Stalin saw no reason why Russia could

[1] J. Stalin, *Sochinenya*, vol. iii, pp. 141–2.   [2] Ibid., pp. 186–7.

not start building socialism, regardless of whether there was a revolution in the west or not:

'You cannot rule out the possibility', so he argued against Preobrazhensky, 'that precisely Russia will be the country that paves the way to Socialism. . . . The base of the revolution is broader in Russia than in western Europe, where the proletariat stands alone against the *bourgeoisie*. With us the working class is supported by the poor peasantry. . . . In Germany the apparatus of state power works with incomparably greater efficiency. . . . We ought to discard the obsolete idea that only Europe can show us the way. There exists a dogmatic Marxism and a creative one. I am opting for the latter.'[1]

Paradoxically enough, at that stage, Stalin's view appeared to be identical with Trotsky's; for Trotsky, too, argued that Russia would *begin* the Socialist revolution before Europe. Stalin did not yet expound the idea of Socialism in one country, the view that Russia by herself, in isolation from the rest of the world, could build to the end the edifice of socialism. Only seven or eight years later would he formulate that view jointly with Bukharin and against Trotsky. But already now there was a stronger emphasis in his words on Russia's peculiar Socialist mission than either in Trotsky's or in Lenin's. In Trotsky's and Lenin's writings of those days that emphasis could also be found but it was offset by their equally categorical insistence on the *ultimate* dependence of the fate of socialism in Russia on proletarian revolution in the west. Russia could and would begin the building of socialism before the other more advanced countries, but she could not carry it far all by herself—argued Lenin and Trotsky. Stalin tended to repeat the first half of the thesis but not the second. His words did in fact breathe an implicit, only half-conscious faith in Russia's revolutionary self-sufficiency. In July and August 1917 nobody was aware of these meaningful hints at future schism.

There is a touch of irony in the circumstance that at a Congress run by Stalin, Trotsky's group formally merged with the Bolshevik party and that the still-imprisoned Trotsky was elected to its new Central Committee. The other members were Lenin, Stalin, Kamenev, Zinoviev, Sverdlov, Rykov, Bukharin, Nogin, Uritsky, Miliutin, Kollontai, Artem, Krestinsky,

[1] J. Stalin, *Sochinenya*, vol. iii, p. 187.

Dzerzhinsky, Yoffe, Sokolnikov, Smilga, Bubnov, Muralov, Shaumian, Berzin. The Congress paid its homage to the persecuted leaders by electing Lenin, Trotsky, Zinoviev, Lunacharsky, Kamenev, and Kollontai to the 'honorary presidium'.

Meanwhile, the man who directed the party in the absence of the great ones produced no great ideas. There was no sweep of original thought in his speech. His words were dry and lacked fire. But he had the confidence of a man who had in the middle of battle stepped wittingly into a breach. His steadfastness and reliability were enough to quell any incipient panic in the ranks. While he was making his report to the Congress news was received of punitive expeditions against the Bolsheviks in various towns, including Tsaritsyn (the future Stalingrad) and of virtual martial law in various parts of the country. The Congress did not stir. Like the Koba of the old Baku days, during the ebb of the First Revolution, the Stalin of these was still able calmly to weather the storm.

After the Congress, when the imprisoned leaders, first Kamenev and then Trotsky, Lunacharsky, and others were gradually released, Stalin again withdrew into the twilight of the *coulisse*.

At the end of August the capital was alarmed by the revolt of General Kornilov, the Commander-in-Chief, against the Provisional Government, a revolt that confirmed the persistent Bolshevik warnings of an imminent counter-revolution. The origin of the *coup* was obscure. The Prime Minister Kerensky had contemplated a final show-down with the Bolsheviks and had asked General Kornilov to send reliable forces to the capital. The General was not content with the plan to suppress Bolshevism—he wanted to rid the country of the Soviets, the moderate Socialists, and Kerensky himself as well. Inflated with self-confidence and the sense of his own mission as 'saviour of society', he made no bones about his intentions, withdrew allegiance from the Government, and, having surrendered Riga to the Germans, ordered his troops to march on Petersburg.

The Government, the Soviets, the Menshevik and Social Revolutionary Committees and Executives were now in a panic. They were not in a position to defeat Kornilov's *coup* without help from the Bolsheviks, without arming the workers who followed Lenin, without reviving the Soviets and calling back to life the Red Guards suppressed in the 'July days'. Kerensky himself asked the Bolsheviks to induce the sailors of Kronstadt, who had been so active in the July mutiny, to 'protect the revolution'. Keeping their own grievances and resentments under control, the Bolsheviks responded to the appeal and fought 'in the first ranks' against Kornilov. The counter-revolution overreached itself and drove all Socialist factions to form a 'united front', which spelt its doom. The Bolsheviks, on the other hand, were careful not to commit a similar mistake. When the sailors of Kronstadt visited Trotsky in his prison and asked him whether they should not 'deal' with Kornilov and Kerensky at one stroke, Trotsky advised them to tackle their adversaries one by one. After a few days the Kornilov *coup* collapsed.

The abortive counter-revolution gave Bolshevism the impetus it needed for the last lap on its road to power. The Bolsheviks emerged from the crisis with the halo of the most determined, if not the only, defenders of the revolution. When, after the suppression of Kornilov's revolt, Lenin openly called upon the Mensheviks and Social Revolutionaries to break up their partnership with the Cadets, Kornilov's accomplices, to take the reins of government into their own hands, and to base it exclusively on the Soviets, promising that if his advice was followed the Bolsheviks would play the role of a legal, constitutional opposition within the framework of the Soviets; and when the Mensheviks and Social Revolutionaries rejected that advice, they irretrievably discredited themselves in the eyes of the working classes.[1] The popularity of the Bolsheviks grew in the army together with their ever louder clamour for peace and for land for the peasants. The simple and incisive style of the Bolshevik agitation in those days can be exemplified by Stalin's unsigned editorial in *Rabochyi* (of 31 August)—and Stalin's writings were really the small change of Bolshevik propaganda:

The counter-revolution of landlords and capitalists has been broken, but not destroyed.

The Kornilovite generals have been beaten. But the triumph of the revolution has not been secured.

Why?

[1] L. Trotsky, *History of the Russian Revolution*, vol. ii, pp. 322–3; Lenin, *Sochinenya*, vol. xxi, pp. 132–6.

Because the conciliators parley with our enemies, instead of ruthlessly fighting them.

Because the defensists make deals with the landlords and capitalists, instead of breaking with them.

Because the Government invites them into the ministries, instead of outlawing them.

In the south of Russia General Kaledin raises a revolt against the Revolution. Yet they have appointed his friend, General Alexeyev, to be the Chief of the General Staff.

In the capital of Russia Miliukov's party has openly backed the counter-revolution—yet its representatives, the Maklakovs and Kishkins, are invited to join the ministry.

It is time to put an end to this crime against the Revolution.

It is time to state firmly and irrevocably that *one fights enemies and does not seek agreement with them.*

Against the landlords and capitalists, *against* the generals and bankers, *for* the interests of Russia's peoples, *for* peace, *for* freedom, *for* land—this is our watchword.

To break with the *bourgeoisie* and the landlords—such is the first task.

To form a government of workers and peasants—such is the second task.[1]

A few days after the arrest of General Kornilov, an important event occurred in the Petersburg Soviet. As a result of recent by-elections, the Bolsheviks became the majority party. Similar shifts occurred in the Soviets of Moscow and other towns. Soon Trotsky, released on bail, was elected President of the Petersburg Soviet, the post he had held in 1905. Under his guidance the Soviet demanded from the Central Executive, still dominated by the moderate Socialists, that the second All-Russian Congress of Soviets should be called and all power transferred to it. Logically, this resolution was the prelude to insurrection. As long as Mensheviks and Social Revolutionaries were in a majority, the Bolshevik clamour 'all power to the Soviets' could have no immediate practical consequences. What that slogan meant was that the Soviet majority, Mensheviks and Social Revolutionaries, should take full power. It was up to that majority to follow or not to follow that course of action. But presently 'all power to the Soviets' implied power for the Bolsheviks, the new majority party. And what—the question inevitably arose—if the Provisional Government refused to

[1] J. Stalin, *Sochinenya*, vol. iii, pp. 266–7.

yield to that demand and efface itself in favour of the Soviets? Then, the Soviets would be under the political obligation to assert their claims against the Provisional Government, to overthrow it, and to put an end to the existing dualism of power. This could be achieved only through insurrection.

By the middle of September Lenin had reached this conclusion and decided to urge the Central Committee to prepare for an uprising.[1] As he was unable to attend its sessions in person, he communicated with his colleagues through a series of letters, which (together with fragmentary records of the Central Committee) offer a unique insight into the preliminaries of the insurrection and more especially into the dramatic controversy among the Bolshevik leaders which preceded it. The letters were delivered by messenger to the house of Sergo Alliluyev, where Lenin had hidden after the 'July days' and into which Stalin had moved soon after his departure. It was Stalin's function to maintain liaison between Lenin and the Central Committee. On 15 September he brought with him to the session of the Committee two memoranda by Lenin: 'The Bolsheviks must take Power' and 'Marxism and Insurrection'.[2] 'To treat the insurrection in a Marxist manner', Lenin wrote, 'that is like an art, we must without waiting a minute organize a staff of the insurgent detachments, distribute forces, move reliable regiments to the most important points, surround the Alexandrinsky Theatre [where the so-called Democratic Assembly was just sitting], seize the Peter and Paul Fortress, arrest the General Staff and Government . . . seize the telegraph and telephone exchanges, locate our insurrectionist staff at the central telephone exchange, connect it by phone with all factories, regiments, outposts, &c.'[3]

This first scheme of the rising had very little in common with its eventual course. Lenin was not concerned with the political setting for the rising, or the authority with whose sanction it would be proclaimed. He was too far from the scene of action to work out any operative plan. In the light of the actual rising his first sketch looks like a somewhat naïve essay in adventure.

[1] Lenin, *Sochinenya*, vol. xxi, pp. 193–4.

[2] J. Stalin, *Sochinenya*, vol. iii, p. 421; L. Trotsky, *History of the Russian Revolution*, vol. iii, pp. 125–66; Lenin, *Sochinenya*, vol. xxi, pp. 193–9.

[3] Lenin, ibid., vol. xxi, p. 199.

It was received with shrugging of shoulders by Trotsky, Stalin, and the other members of the Committee. Lenin himself treated it only as a tentative suggestion. His intention was to impress his colleagues with the urgency of the matter, to warn them against amateurish calculations on a spontaneous 'people's rising', to remind them that insurrection must be treated like an art and so to stir them to immediate action. The Central Committee was divided. Trotsky agreed with Lenin's emphasis on urgency, but mooted a plan of his own more artfully thought out both in its political and in its military aspects. He opposed the idea that the party alone should shoulder the responsibility for the uprising and wanted to associate the Soviets with it, because the moral authority of the 'workers' parliament' stood undoubtedly higher in the eyes of the workers than that of the party. This political and psychological consideration dictated the timing of the rising. The All-Russian Congress of the Soviets was to meet in the capital in the latter part of October; and so the rising was to coincide with the Congress.

Strategically, Trotsky was in agreement with Lenin; tactically, he was opposed to him. Kamenev and Zinoviev were opposed to him on the strategic principle itself. When Lenin's first letters on insurrection were read out at the session of 15 September Kamenev was so afraid that the party would compromise itself by the course of action suggested by Lenin that he proposed to burn the letters. Six members of the Committee voted for Kamenev's proposal. Stalin proposed that the letters should be submitted to the major organizations for discussion, which suggested that he supported Lenin, since any wide discussion of the matter would have tended to commit the party to pass from argument to action. In Trotsky's view, Stalin hoped that by referring the matter to the provincial organizations he would shelve it, because the provincials were even more timid than the Central Committee.[1] This may or may not have been so—in any case, Stalin's proposal was not accepted.

In the next few weeks adherents and opponents of the insurrection were arrayed against one another in the Central Committee of the party and in the lower circles of the caucus. Soon they had the opportunity to test their strength in connexion with the convocation by the Government of the so-called

[1] L. Trotsky, *Stalin*, p. 222.

Pre-parliament, a pathetically belated and feeble attempt by Kerensky to prop up his régime by some sort of a representative body opposed to the Soviets. The Pre-parliament was to be merely a consultative assembly; and the Government itself was to appoint its members. Should the Bolsheviks accept their appointments and participate in the Pre-parliament or should they boycott it? The question was not entirely identical with the other one concerning the insurrection; but it was connected with it. The determined adherents of the insurrection thought that they had nothing to look for in a pseudo-parliament, the days of which would, anyhow, be numbered. Those who shrunk before Lenin's plans favoured participation in the Pre-parliament. The question was put to a vote at a national conference of the party, at which Trotsky and Stalin spoke in favour of boycott. This was one of the few occasions on which the future rivals shared the same viewpoint. Kamenev and Rykov, however, who argued for participation, carried the majority of the conference with them. Thus, barely one month before the insurrection, the insurrectionist party displayed a mood which Lenin indignantly castigated as a 'deviation from the proletarian revolutionary road'.[1]

Meanwhile the country was sinking ever deeper into defeat and chaos. For a time the Government and the General Staff contemplated evacuating Petersburg and transferring the ministries to Moscow. Rumours about this put new wind into Bolshevik sails, for the plan was interpreted as a counter-revolutionary plot. It was said that by surrendering the Red capital the Government hoped to decapitate the revolution. The threat brought the city's Soviet to its feet and impelled it to assume responsibility for defending Petersburg. As power began to come within their reach the Bolsheviks had gradually switched over from unconditional opposition to the war to a quasi-defensist attitude; they now called for the defence of Petersburg as the capital of the revolution, not of the empire. The ordinary traditional defensism of the moderate Socialists coincided for the moment with the new defensism of the Bolsheviks. Thus the decision of the Soviet to assume responsibility for the defence of the capital had the support of all parties represented in it.

[1] Lenin, *Sochinenya*, vol. xxi, p. 287.

By taking this initiative the Soviet lifted itself to a new prominence and authority which would eventually enable it to undo
the Provisional Government. Trotsky, who as President of the
Soviet dominated all its activity, succeeded in presenting this
crucial preliminary to the revolution as a measure dictated by
the national needs of the Republic. The Soviet then asserted,
first in principle and then in actual fact, its right to control the
movement of troops in the capital and in the provinces around
it; the right, that is, to control the military commands and
staffs. The popular distrust of the officers corps, extremely acute
since the Kornilov revolt, strengthened the hands of the Soviet
for any conflicts that might come. The body which took charge
of these matters on behalf of the Soviet was the Military
Revolutionary Committee, appointed by the Executive of the
Soviet on 13 October.[1] The President of the Soviet was at the
same time the chairman of that Committee which was, by its
nature, the General Staff of the insurrection.

What was extraordinary in this development was that the
organ of the insurrection was no clandestine, self-appointed
group or clique of conspirators but a body openly elected by a
broad representative institution like the Soviet. The conspiracy
was, so to speak, wrapped up in Soviet legality, a circumstance
that half paralysed the opposition of moderate Socialists. The
Mensheviks and the Social Revolutionaries stayed in the
Soviet as helpless and bewildered witnesses of, and up to a point
accomplices in, their own undoing. Trotsky—all the threads of
the insurrection were now in his hands—succeeded in giving to
the rising the appearance of a defensive operation designed
to forestall or rather to parry a counter-revolution, a tactical
stratagem which brought over the hesitant sections of the
working class and the garrison to the side of the insurgents.
This is not to say that the defensive character of the rising was
altogether a false pretence. The Government and, behind its
back, monarchist generals and right-wing politicians were preparing a come-back: on the eve of the uprising Kerensky outlawed the Revolutionary Military Committee, issued new writs
for the arrest of Bolshevik leaders, and attempted to mobilize
loyal troops and suppress the Bolshevik press. But, in the race
between revolution and counter-revolution, the former had a

---

[1] L. Trotsky, *History of the Russian Revolution*, vol. iii, pp. 92–5.

very long start indeed; and the start was made even longer by the shrewdness with which the leader of the insurrection kept up its defensive appearance to the end.

While Trotsky was thus gaining one vantage point after another in the Soviet, Lenin, from hiding, directed his efforts towards overcoming Zinoviev's and Kamenev's opposition in the Central Committee. He contrived to persuade his followers to withdraw from Kerensky's Pre-parliament, as Trotsky and Stalin had counselled. On 7 October the Pre-parliament heard the rumblings of the approaching revolution in Trotsky's fiery and thunderous statement on the secession of the Bolsheviks from 'this council of counter-revolutionary connivance', and in his cry: 'Petersburg is in danger! The Revolution is in danger! The people are in danger!', to the accompaniment of which the Bolsheviks left the chamber.[1] On 8 October Lenin secretly returned from Finland to Petersburg. Two days later the Central Committee met to take its final decision. Zinoviev and Kamenev made their most eloquent plea: 'Before history, before the international proletariat, before the Russian Revolution and the Russian working class, we have no right to stake the whole future on the card of an armed uprising.' They urged the Central Committee to wait for the Constituent Assembly which the Government now promised to convene and which, they hoped, would be swayed by a radical majority. They conceived the new state as a combination of a Soviet republic and parliamentary democracy. They gave their warning that Lenin's policy would lead to the final *débâcle* of the revolution: 'There are historical situations when an oppressed class must recognize that it is better to go forward to defeat than to give up without battle. Does the Russian working class find itself at present in such a situation? *No, and a thousand times no!!!!*'[2] They opposed the insurrection for two reasons, one of which was soon to be refuted by the events, whereas the other was to be confirmed in the future. The advocates of the insurrection, they said, overrated their own strength and underrated that of the Provisional Government. They also took too sanguine a view of the proximity of proletarian revolution in western Europe.

[1] L. Trotsky, *History of the Russian Revolution*, vol. iii, pp. 68–70.

[2] Quoted from English edition of Lenin's *Collected Works*, vol. xxi, book 2, pp. 328–32.

Lenin impatiently brushed aside all scruples about the Constituent Assembly; the Government had shelved it so many times—where was the guarantee that it would not do so again? To delay the insurrection meant giving the Kornilovite generals time to stage a *coup* and establish their dictatorship. Lenin regarded his opponents' pessimistic view of the relationship of forces as the counsel of faint-heartedness. The Bolsheviks had behind them the majority of the Russian working classes; and all 'proletarian Europe' was certain to support them.[1] Of the twelve members present at this session ten, including Stalin, voted for insurrection. Two, Zinoviev and Kamenev, cast their votes against it. After the vote a Political Bureau was elected, on Dzerzhinsky's proposal, 'for the purpose of political guidance during the immediate future'. Its members were: Lenin, Zinoviev, Kamenev, Trotsky, Stalin, Sokolnikov, and Bubnov.[2] Thus the institution that was eventually to tower mightily above state, party, and revolution was called into being. At the same session, 20 October was fixed as the day of the insurrection.

The Political Bureau was unable to fulfil the task assigned to it. Zinoviev and Kamenev refused to submit to the decision on the insurrection and did their utmost to achieve its reversal. Lenin, who had appeared at the sitting of 10 October in disguise, wearing a wig, went back into hiding and could not take part in the day-to-day preparations. All his energy was absorbed in his sustained and almost desperate effort to overcome the 'shameful vacillation', the 'astounding confusion and cowardice' of the two men who were his closest friends and disciples.[3] Trotsky was too busy with the Soviet and the Revolutionary Military Committee to attend much to the business of the Central Committee. Apart from this Lenin's schemes for the uprising did not appeal to him. Discarding his first plan for a *coup* in Petersburg, Lenin suggested that the blow be struck in Moscow first. Then he proposed that the rising should begin in Helsinki and develop into an offensive against Petersburg.[4] Trotsky continued to shrug his shoulders at these 'counsels of

---

[1] Ibid., pp. 108–28.   [2] Ibid., p. 328.
[3] *The History of the Civil War*, vol. ii, p. 193.
[4] See Lenin's Letters in the English edition of his *Collected Works*, vol. xxi, book 2, pp. 65, 70, 103–4.

an outsider', as Lenin himself called them. So did Stalin, who some time later recollected, not without irony, Lenin's variants of the uprising: 'We thought that we, the practical workers, could see better all the ravines, pitfalls and holes on our road. But Ilyich [Lenin] is great, he is not afraid of ravines, pitfalls or holes on his road, he is not afraid of dangers and says: "Get up and go straight to your goal". But we, the practical workers, reckoned that it was not convenient so to act, that it was necessary to obviate the obstacles so as to be able then to take the bull by the horns. And, regardless of all Lenin's demands, we did not follow him.'[1] Apart from their military incongruities, Lenin's plans had one major political fault in common: they tended to narrow the political base for the insurrection, to deprive the uprising of the sanction of the Soviet, to reduce what Trotsky staged as a popular act into a narrower affair of the Bolshevik party. They also tended to strip the insurrection of its defensive wrapping and to give it that undisguised offensive character that would have appeared provocative even to well-wishers of the revolution.

Another meeting of the Central Committee on 16 October, which was attended by prominent non-members of the Committee, confirmed the previous decision in favour of insurrection. On the morrow Zinoviev and Kamenev carried the struggle against Lenin into the open and warned public opinion against the insurrection in Maxim Gorky's newspaper *Novaya Zhizn* (New Life), which stood half-way between Bolshevism and Menshevism. Lenin, furious at the indiscretion, branded his two colleagues as 'strike-breakers', 'traitors to the revolution', and demanded their immediate expulsion from the party.[2] The penalty seemed too harsh to the other members of the Committee. Stalin published Lenin's denunciation in the Bolshevik newspaper, but softened its effect by a conciliatory editorial comment meant to bridge the gap between the opposed viewpoints.[3] At the session of the Central Committee on 16 October, he himself had argued against Zinoviev and Kamenev: 'What Kamenev and Zinoviev propose leads objectively to the opportunity for the counter-revolution to prepare and organize. We

[1] J. Stalin, *Sochinenya*, vol. iv, pp. 317–18.
[2] Lenin, *Collected Works*, vol. xxi, book 2, pp. 127–37.
[3] *Rabochyi Put* (*Pravda*), 20 October 1917.

shall endlessly retreat and lose the revolution. . . . There is need now for more faith. . . . There are two policies here: one policy is to steer towards the victory of the revolution and to look to Europe; the other policy has no faith in the revolution and hopes that the party will remain merely an opposition party. . . . The Petersburg Soviet has already embarked upon the road to insurrection.'[1]

This last sentence meant that while the Central Committee was wasting time, the Soviet, under Trotsky's guidance, had passed over to action. Why then did Stalin now protect his two indiscreet colleagues who were to all intents and purposes putting spokes in the wheels of the insurrection? Was he anxious to arrest a rift in the party? Or did Kamenev's and Zinoviev's warnings and cries of panic make him, too, somewhat hesitant? Or was he perhaps, as Trotsky asserts, cynically re-insuring himself against failure without openly deserting the ranks of the insurrectionists? At the next session of the Central Committee Stalin again defended Kamenev when the latter announced his resignation from the leadership. The resignation was accepted; and then Stalin, too, having drawn Lenin's criticism upon his editorial attitude, tendered his resignation. This, however, was not accepted by the Central Committee which was wary of driving the editor of the party's newspaper into the arms of the opponents of the rising. Pardoned for his editorial slip, Stalin in his turn was now eager to show that he was really of one mind with the advocates of the insurrection. He proposed that the two most determined leaders of the insurrectionist majority, Lenin and Trotsky, should be the party's chief spokesmen at the forthcoming All-Russian Congress of the Soviets, the Congress of the Revolution.[2]

Meanwhile, the Menshevik Executive delayed the opening of the Congress by another five days, till 25 October. It was in these few days that the crucial preparations for the uprising were completed. On 21 October a conference of the regimental committees of Petersburg officially recognized the Military Revolutionary Committee as the real master of the garrison— no order was to be obeyed unless countersigned by a representative of the Committee, by Trotsky or his assistants

[1] J. Stalin, *Sochinenya*, vol. iii, pp. 381–2.
[2] L. Trotsky, *History of the Russian Revolution*, vol. iii, pp. 163–4.

Antonov-Ovseenko, Podvoysky, or by duly authorized commissars. On 23 October the Revolutionary Military Committee appointed its commissars with almost every detachment stationed in and around the capital, thus securing liaison with all the forces virtually under its command. Orders from official headquarters aiming at a reshuffling of the garrison were ignored. Detachments scheduled to leave the capital refused to budge. Officers failing to submit to the authority of the Soviet were removed from their posts, and a number of them were arrested.

Finally, on 24 October, the Government decided to strike back, thereby providing the pretext for the uprising. Governmental troops occupied the offices of the newspaper of which Stalin was the editor, and closed its printing press. A delegation of workers from the press asked the Revolutionary Military Committee to send its troops to the offices of the paper and to ensure publication. This was done. 'A piece of official sealing wax', wrote the leader of the rising later, 'on the door of the Bolshevik editorial room as a military measure—that was not much. But what a superb signal for battle!'[1] The battle rapidly extended to bridges, railway stations, post offices, and other strategic points: all were occupied without a shot by the troops under Trotsky's command. The only real fight developed in the course of the assault of the insurgents upon the Winter Palace, the seat of the Provisional Government. Even that operation, led by Antonov-Ovseenko, the future Soviet Ambassador in Poland and in Spain during the civil war, was not devoid of comic touches like the bombardment of the Palace with duds from the cruiser *Aurora*. The Provisional Government was politically so isolated and the insurgents enjoyed such overwhelming support that they were able to elbow the Government out of existence by a slight push. When on 25 October the second All-Russian Congress of the Soviets assembled, the rising was nearly complete; and the Bolshevik majority of the Congress immediately sanctioned the upheaval.[2]

In the days of the upheaval Stalin was not among its main

[1] L. Trotsky, *History of the Russian Revolution*, vol. iii, p. 205.
[2] Up to this point the dates have been given according to the old Russian calendar which was in force before the revolution. From now on the dates are given in accordance with the new calendar.

actors. Even more than usual, he remained in the shadow, a fact that was to cause embarrassment to his official biographers and perhaps justified Trotsky in saying that 'the greater the sweep of events the smaller was Stalin's place in it'. In part this was the result of the ineffectiveness of the Central Committee, within which Stalin's own weight was much greater than outside it. At the critical session of the Central Committee on 16 October Stalin and four other members (Sverdlov, Bubnov, Dzerzhinsky, and Uritsky) were delegated to represent the party on the Revolutionary Military Committee of the Soviet. If the Chairman of the Committee, Trotsky, is to be believed, however, Stalin's contribution to the work of that organ of the insurrection was nil.[1] Trotsky's testimony might be dismissed because of its partisan character, if it were possible to find among the welter of documents on the rising at least a few recording Stalin's direct connexion with it. But none have been found.

Since Stalin's rise to absolute power the name of Trotsky has been assiduously and systematically expunged from all official histories of the revolution—it is mentioned only as the name of the 'traitor' and the 'saboteur' of the actual rising. All the official histories and text-books speak of the leadership of Lenin and Stalin or ascribe those of Trotsky's deeds and words that can in no way be omitted to the anonymous Revolutionary Military Committee. But in spite of their best intentions and indubitable zeal, the official Soviet historians have not been able to write Stalin's name into the blanks left by the deletion of Trotsky's. Even the all too unscrupulously compiled *History of the Civil War in the U.S.S.R.*, edited by Stalin himself, Zhdanov, Voroshilov, Molotov, Gorky, and Kirov, does not contain a single document or concrete fact which would support the bare statements about Stalin's leading role in the Revolutionary Military Committee, unless one were to class among historical documents the rather cheap and strikingly false paintings of a Svaroga or Vladimirsky, paintings made many years after the event, in which an oddly handsome daredevil Stalin is depicted as issuing instructions to the insurgents. Stalin's own detailed Biographical Chronicle is equally uninformative on this point.[2] Surprisingly enough, he was not

---

[1] L. Trotsky, *Stalin*, p. 234.
[2] See Biographical Chronicle in vol. iii of Stalin's *Sochinenya*, p. 423.

even present at the session of the Central Committee that took place on the morning of the insurrection. 'Not that he was a coward. There is no basis for accusing Stalin of cowardice,' (this is Trotsky's comment) 'he was simply politically non-committal. The cautious schemer preferred to stay on the fence at the crucial moment. He was waiting to see how the insurrection turned out before committing himself to a position. In the event of failure he could tell Lenin and me and our adherents: "It's all your fault!" One must clearly reeapture the red-hot temper of those days in order to appreciate according to its deserts the man's cool grit or, if you like, his insidiousness.'[1]

Trotsky's explanation seems self-contradictory: the insidiousness which he attributes to his rival appears after all to be tinged with cowardice. It is impossible to accept Trotsky's interpretation for yet another reason: Stalin did in fact commit himself as early as 10 October, when the first vote on the insurrection was taken in the Central Committee. He then voted with Lenin and Trotsky. On 16 October he again voted and spoke for the insurrection, this time not in the narrow conclave of the Central Committee but at a much wider conference at which were present delegates from the Petersburg organization, the party's military branch, the trade unions, and the Petersburg Soviet as well as delegates from factory committees, railroad workers, &c. A 'cautious schemer preferring to stay on the fence at the crucial moment' would hardly have stepped down so heavily on Lenin's side before the eyes of a gathering of that sort. It is not possible to find any alternative explanation for Stalin's absence or inactivity at the headquarters during the rising. But the queer and undeniable fact remains.

The one post at which he undeniably did his duty throughout the critical period was the editorial offices of *Rabochyi Put* (Workers' Road), as *Pravda* had been renamed. There he spoke with the voice of the party, mainly in anonymous editorials. He did not, of course, openly call for insurrection. Like Trotsky in the Soviet, Stalin in his newspaper gave defensive cover to an essentially offensive policy—this was the cautious camouflage of the insurrection. On 10 October, even before the Central Committee took its first vote on the uprising, he wrote: 'The first Kornilovite conspiracy has

---

[1] L. Trotsky, *Stalin*, p. 234.

been frustrated. But the counter-revolution has not been crushed. . . . The second Kornilovite conspiracy, which is now being hatched, ought to be destroyed at the roots, so that any danger may be averted from the revolution for a long time to come. . . . Let the Soviets and the Committees take every measure to smash the second attempt of the counter-revolution with all the might of the revolution.'[1] Three days later he became more explicit: 'The moment has come when the watchword "All Power to the Soviets!" ought at last to be put into effect.' On the morning of the rising itself he thus summed up the course of the revolution: 'After the victory of the February Revolution, power remained in the hands of the landlords and capitalists, bankers and speculators, profiteers and marauders— therein lay the fatal error of the workers and peasants. . . . That error ought to be corrected at once.'[2] As if echoing Lenin and hinting at Zinoviev's and Kamenev's opposition, he went on: 'The moment has come when further delay threatens to destroy the whole work of the revolution. . . . The present self-appointed Government, neither elected by the people nor responsible to it, must be replaced by a Government . . . elected by representatives of workers, soldiers, and peasants and responsible to them.' Fourteen years later Trotsky thus described the mood of the insurgents: 'All those taking part in the insurrection, from top to bottom—in this lay its power, in this also at times its Achilles heel—were imbued with absolute confidence that the victory was going to be won without casualties.'[3] Stalin's words, written a few hours before the rising, breathed precisely that confidence: 'If only you act in a spirit of comradeship and steadfastness nobody will dare to oppose the people's will. The old Government will the more peacefully make place for the new one the stronger and the better organized you come out.'[4]

Perhaps the most authentic projection of the man's emotions and mood on the eve of the great event can be found in an article in which he dealt with the many captious or merely anxious questions about the Bolshevik plans and intentions that were asked from all sides. Stalin's reply was a masterpiece of abusive evasiveness or evasive abuse:[5]

[1] J. Stalin, *Sochinenya*, vol. iii, pp. 362-3. [2] Ibid., p. 388.
[3] L. Trotsky, *History of the Russian Revolution*, vol. iii, p. 221.
[4] J. Stalin, *Sochinenya*, vol. iii, p. 390. [5] Ibid., pp. 383-6.

Here is the reply. As for the *bourgeoisie* and its 'apparatus': with them we shall settle our accounts separately. As for the agents and hirelings of the *bourgeoisie*: these we refer to the counter-espionage. There they can 'enlighten' themselves and in their turn 'enlighten' others about the 'day' and the 'hour' of the *coup*, the schedule of which has already been concocted by the *agents provocateurs* of the *Dyen*. . . . To those heroes [the moderate socialists] who have sided with . . . the Government against the workers, soldiers and peasants we owe no explanation. But we shall see to it that those heroes at blacklegging be brought to book by the Congress of the Soviets.

His most vicious invective was reserved for Maxim Gorky, the famous writer and revolutionary, Lenin's fellow traveller for many years, the man whom Stalin himself would one day anoint as the prophet of a new civilization. Gorky's newspaper, the same in which Zinoviev and Kamenev had spoken against insurrection, had also asked Lenin and his colleagues to 'put their cards on the table'; and Gorky himself attacked the Bolsheviks in an article under the title 'I cannot keep silent', borrowed from an old anti-Tsarist writing by Tolstoy. Stalin retorted with a hot gush of spite:

As for the neurasthenics of the *Novaya Zhizn* [Gorky's paper] we are at a loss to understand what it is that they actually want from us. If they wish to know the 'day' of the insurrection so as to be able to mobilize in advance the forces of the frightened intellectuals for a timely . . . escape, say, to Finland, then we have only . . . praise for them, for we are 'generally' for mobilization of forces. If they are asking about the 'day' of the uprising in order to calm their 'steel-like' nerves, then we assure them that even if the 'day' of the rising had been fixed and the Bolsheviks whispered it into their ears, our neurasthenics would not get the slightest relief from that: there would be new questions, hysterics, &c.

Other Bolshevik leaders, too, were annoyed with Gorky; but none assailed him and his colleagues in such a personal and venomous vein, suggesting cowardice, treachery, and so on. Even more unjust and coarse was Stalin's taunt:

Does not this account for Gorky's 'I cannot keep silent'? This is incredible but true. They sat and kept silent when landlords . . . drove their peasants to despair and hunger 'riots'. They sat and kept silent when the capitalists and their hangers-on were preparing an all-Russian lock-out for the workers. . . . But these people, so it appears, cannot keep silent when the vanguard of the revolution, the Petersburg Soviet, has stood up in defence of the cheated workers and peasants! And their first word is one of reproach addressed not to the counter-revolution but to that same revolution about which they talk with enthusiasm over a cup of tea but from which they flee as from the plague in the most critical moments.

The attack culminated in the following pregnant words:

The Russian Revolution has overthrown not a few authorities. Its power expresses itself, among other things, in that it does not bow to 'great names'. The revolution has enrolled them in its service, or thrown them into nothingness if they have not been willing to learn from it. Of such great names thrown away by the revolution there is a whole legion. Plekhanov, Kropotkin, Breshkovskaya, Zasulich and generally all those old revolutionaries who are remarkable only because they are *old*. We fear that the laurels of those 'pillars' do not let Gorky sleep. We fear that they, those antiquities, have had a deadly pull on Gorky. Well, everyone is his own master. . . . The revolution is incapable either of regretting or of burying its dead.'

To the author of these lines, the descendant of Georgian serfs and the member of the Bolshevik caucus, the revolution was obviously not only the vindication of the oppressed classes. It was also the triumph of the obscure, anonymous committee-man over the 'great names' of Russian socialism. He had no attachment to and no organic tie with any tradition, not even Socialist tradition. In this he was very unlike the other leaders and especially Lenin who, even in the heat of the most frantic polemic, would never have brought himself to say of his former teacher Plekhanov that he was 'remarkable only because he was old'. It is not difficult to feel behind Stalin's unrestrained railings the pent-up frustration of a man whose peculiar gifts were such that they had earned him no 'great name' even while he was reaching the threshold of power. Yet the revolution, though it had thrown some great names 'into nothingness', did create new ones that shone with even greater brilliance and were engraved in the hearts and the minds of the people.

Later events were to impart to Stalin's words the meaning of an unconscious or perhaps half-conscious challenge to those new names. For the moment the revolution was turning only one of its faces towards the world—the one that was radiant with enthusiasm and noble hope. Its other face, the one of the monster devouring its own children, was still hidden. Yet it was that other face that Stalin seemed to worship already in those days. 'The revolution is incapable either of regretting or of burying its dead'—what a text for the great purges which he was to stage nearly twenty years later.

CHAPTER VI

Stalin in the Civil War

Introduction: dilemmas of revolution.—Stalin appointed Commissar of Nationalities.—Lenin's first Government.—Coalition of Bolsheviks and left Social Revolutionaries.—Stalin goes to Helsinki to proclaim the independence of Finland.—His
views on the 'self-determination' of small nations.—His sketch of the first Soviet
Constitution (1918).—The peace of Brest Litovsk (3 March 1918).—Stalin votes
with Lenin for peace and fights the 'left Bolsheviks' who urge 'revolutionary war'
against Germany.—Terror and counter-terror.—Stalin conducts peace negotiations with the Ukrainian *Rada* at Kursk, May 1918.—The spread of civil war.—
Stalin's mission to Tsaritsyn (Stalingrad) in June 1918. He supports Voroshilov
and Budienny against Trotsky.—The origin of the great feud.—Stalin asks for
plenary powers on the southern front.—Lenin attempts to reconcile Stalin and
Trotsky.—Conflicting accounts of the defence of Tsaritsyn.—Stalin recalled to
Moscow, October 1918.—His reaction to the 1918 revolutions in Europe: *Ex
Oriente Lux*.—Stalin defends Petersburg, May 1919.—Trotsky and Stalin awarded
Orders of the Red Banner.—Stalin as administrator.—His role in the Russo-Polish
war of 1920.—The Kronstadt rising and the New Economic Policy (1921).—The
single-party system and the ban on Bolshevik opposition groups.—Stalin benefits
from the growing influence of the Bolshevik caucus.

THE October upheaval—a mild, bloodless event—was followed
by a cruel civil war and foreign intervention which lasted nearly
three years. The new revolutionary state formed itself less under
the influence of ideas preached by the Bolsheviks when they
seized power than under the harsh exigencies of civil war.
Events compelled the party of the revolution to give up some of
its aspirations, hopes, and illusions in order to save the essential
framework of the revolution. In the process, the party itself,
its leaders and followers, underwent a profound spiritual and
political change.

One broad aspect of that change has been common to all
revolutions so far. Each great revolution begins with a phenom-
enal outburst of popular energy, impatience, anger, and
hope. Each ends in the weariness, exhaustion, and disillusionment of the revolutionary people. In the first phase the party
that gives the fullest expression to the popular mood outdoes its
rivals, gains the confidence of the masses, and rises to power.
Even the most revolutionary party is sometimes not revolutionary enough in the eyes of the most extreme section of the people.

It is driven forward by the swelling tide to overcome all the obstacles in its way and to challenge all conservative powers. Then comes the inevitable trial of civil war. The revolutionary party is still marching in step with the majority of the nation. It is acutely conscious of its unity with the people and of a profound harmony between its own objectives and the people's wishes and desires. It can call upon the mass of the nation for ever-growing efforts and sacrifices; and it is sure of the response. In this, the heroic phase, the revolutionary party is in a very real sense democratic, even though it treats its foes with dictatorial relentlessness and observes no strict constitutional precept. The leaders implicitly trust their vast plebeian following; and their policy rests on that trust. They are willing and even eager to submit their policies to open debate and to accept the popular verdict. Though they aspire to lead the masses, they also allow themselves to be led.

This happy relationship between the party of the revolution, whether it be called Independent, Jacobin, or Bolshevik, and the mass of the people does not last long. It hardly survives the civil war. Many of the devoted and energetic supporters of the new order perish in the civil war. Others rise from their modest and unpretentious existence to power and often also to privilege. The party of the revolution emerges triumphant, with tremendous pride and self-confidence, but also with inner weariness and enervation. The weariness of the people is even deeper. The country, ravaged by civil war and intervention, has sunk into a misery that may be worse than that against which the people had risen in revolt. In 1920 Russia suffered worse hunger and privation than in 1917. The ruthlessness of the new rulers, a ruthlessness dictated by circumstances and the needs of self-preservation, provokes a reaction. The reaction may be strongest among those who have previously urged the party to pursue the course that has made that ruthlessness inevitable.

The anti-climax of the revolution is there. The leaders are unable to keep their early promises. They have destroyed the old order; but they are unable to satisfy the daily needs of the people. To be sure, the revolution has created the basis for a higher organization of society and for progress in a not very remote future. This will justify it in the eyes of posterity. But the fruits of revolution ripen slowly; and of immediate moment are the miseries of the first post-revolutionary years. It is in their shadow that the new state takes on its shape, a shape that reveals the chasm between the revolutionary party and the people. This is the real tragedy which overtakes the party of the revolution. If its action is to be dictated by the mood of the people, it will presently have to efface itself, or at least to relinquish power. But no revolutionary government can abdicate after a victorious civil war, because the only real pretenders to power are the still considerable remnants of the defeated counter-revolution. Abdication would be suicide. It would entail, too, a reversal of the vast work of the revolution by which society has been transformed but which has not yet been consolidated. The political mechanics of a régime around which all the passions of revolution and counter-revolution have been let loose has no feature like those political revolving doors provided by any stable parliamentary order, through which governments come or go more or less politely without chopping off one another's heads. The party of the revolution knows no retreat. It has been driven to its present pass largely through obeying the will of that same people by which it is now deserted. It will go on doing what it considers to be its duty, without paying much heed to the voice of the people. In the end it will muzzle and stifle that voice.

At first the party of the revolution is by no means clearly aware of all the implications of the new phase. It has assumed office as a government of the people, by the people, and for the people. It now forfeits at least one of its honourable attributes— it ceases to be government by the people. The whole party may still hope that its discord with the mood of the country is transient; and that honest exertion in one direction or another will allow it to fire anew the imagination of the people and to recapture the recent heroic past. But the chasm is growing wider and deeper. The rulers acquire the habits of arbitrary government and themselves come to be governed by their own habits. What had hopefully begun as a great, warm-hearted popular venture gradually degenerates into a narrow and cold autocracy. In the transition, the party of the revolution is split between those who have promoted the new outlook, or made peace with it, and those who have not. Some of its leaders point in alarm to the divorce between the revolution and the people. Others justify the conduct of the party on the ground that the divorce is irremediable. Still others, the actual rulers, deny the fact of the divorce itself: for to admit it would be to widen further the gap between the rulers and the ruled. Some cry in alarm that the revolution has been betrayed, for in their eyes government by the people is the very essence of revolution—without it there can be no government for the people. The rulers find justification for themselves in the conviction that whatever they do will ultimately serve the interests of the broad mass of the nation; and indeed they do, on the whole, use their power to consolidate most of the economic and social conquests of the revolution. Amid charges and counter-charges, the heads of the revolutionary leaders begin to roll and the power of the post-revolutionary state towers hugely over the society it governs.

In this broad scheme of revolutionary development much must seem simplified and confused. Historical truth consists less in the broad generalizations than in the complex sequence of events, different in each revolution. Some features which appear only dimly in the picture of one revolution are very clear and distinct in that of another. Processes, for instance, by which Jacobinism was consumed and destroyed within a few months, have developed in Bolshevism slowly, over whole decades; and their results, too, have in many respects been vastly different. But what is important in this context is the general trend of events; and this has been common to all great revolutions so far. It is in this broad perspective that the metamorphosis of triumphant Bolshevism, and Stalin's own fortunes, can best be understood.

. . . .

Few men have known a transition from obscurity, poverty, and persecution to power and fame as sudden and sharp as that by which the leaders of Bolshevism became the rulers of Russia. A few moments after he had taken off his make-up, his wig, and big spectacles, and met his friends at the Smolny on the night of the insurrection, Lenin ironically confessed to a sense of dizziness caused by that transition. A similar feeling must have taken hold of Stalin when on 26 October 1917 he heard Kamenev reading out to the Congress of the Soviets the names of the men who formed the first Soviet Government, the first

Council of the People's Commissars. The list included the name of Joseph Vissarionovich Djugashvili-Stalin—'Chairman of the Commissariat for Nationalities'.

The Government of which he became a member was boycotted by all non-Bolshevik parties. Of its fifteen members eleven were intellectuals and only four workers. Lenin was its Premier and Trotsky its Commissar of Foreign Affairs. Rykov was in charge of Home Affairs, Miliutin of Agriculture, and Shlyapnikov of Labour. Military and Naval Affairs were entrusted to three men: Antonov-Ovseenko, revolutionary and ex-officer, Krylenko, ex-ensign and lawyer, and F. Dybenko, a huge, half-illiterate, crude, and good-natured sailor who distinguished himself as revolutionary leader in the Baltic Fleet. The 'God-seeker' and savant, A. Lunacharsky, was responsible for Education. The new Government was to do away with the traditional habits and paraphernalia of authority. Its flair for demonstrative innovation showed itself even in its name and in the replacement of the title Minister by that of Commissar. Each Commissariat was to be ruled by a Committee or a Collegium, of which the Commissar was the Chairman. The organization of the Government reflected its democratic radicalism. It cannot be said that the outlook of that first team of commissars corresponded to those standards of 'ruthless determination' or 'fanatical zeal' which later came to be associated with the very term Bolshevism. On the contrary, the 'soft-heartedness' of most commissars very soon placed the Government in quite a number of tragi-comic situations. Only two or three characteristic episodes can be recounted here.

While the Bolshevik rising in Moscow was still on, a rumour went around that the Kremlin had suffered destruction in the fighting. The Commissar of Education, Lunacharsky, resigned from his post in protest against the 'vandalism' of the Red Guards. 'Comrades,' he cried in a proclamation, 'that which is happening in Moscow is a horrible, irreparable misfortune.... The People in its struggle for power has mutilated our glorious capital. ... It is particularly terrible in these days of violent struggle, of destructive warfare, to be Commissar of Public Education. ... Even the most ignorant will awake and understand what a source of joy, strength and wisdom is art. ...'[1]

---

[1] Quoted by John Reed in *Ten Days that shook the World*, p. 304.

The rumour proved grossly exaggerated; and with some difficulty Lenin succeeded in persuading the sensitive commissar to resume office.

From the first day of its existence the Government was boycotted by the civil servants who refused to obey the orders of the new masters. 'Alexandra Kollontai', relates an eyewitness, '. . . appointed Commissar of Public Welfare . . . was welcomed with a strike of all but forty of the functionaries in the Ministry. Immediately, the poor of the great cities . . . were plunged in miserable want; delegations of starving cripples, of orphans with blue, pinched faces, besieged the building. With tears streaming down her face, Kollontai arrested the strikers until they should deliver the keys of the office and the safe.'[1] The revolution was still breaking the sabotage of its enemies with tears streaming down its face.

One of the first decrees of the Council of Commissars abolished the death sentence, in spite of Lenin's protests. The Cossack General Krasnov who marched on Petersburg to overthrow the Bolsheviks and disperse the Soviets was taken prisoner by the Red Guards and released on his solemn pledge that he would not resume the fight. Later Krasnov headed one of the White armies in southern Russia. It took time before the revolution, amid the gruelling experiences of civil war, wiped away its tears, ceased to trust the pledges of its foes, and learned to act with that fanatical determination which gave it some new and repulsive features, but to which it owed its survival. We shall soon find the 'man of steel' among those who weaned the revolution from its sensitive—or was it sentimental?—idealism.

In his own department Stalin met no sabotage by civil servants: for no special department dealing with the affairs of the various non-Russian nationalities had previously existed. He had to build up his Commissariat from scratch. At first the whole 'machinery' of his department consisted of a single table —in a room in the Smolny—on which a piece of cardboard had been pinned with the high-sounding name of the Commissariat. Later he secured a more impressive abode for his Commissariat through a strong-handed intervention in a somewhat comic scramble between the commissars for accommodation. Then he gathered around him a staff of assistants, Georgians, Poles,

[1] J. Reed, op. cit., pp. 220-1.

Ukrainians, and Jews, people competent to deal with the problems of his Commissariat.[1]

He had hardly begun the job when the first Council of People's Commissars ceased to exist. The right wing of the party, the former opponents of the insurrection, strongly represented in the Government, worked behind the scenes for a reconciliation with the Mensheviks and Social Revolutionaries. They urged their party to share power with the moderate Socialists. The demand was supported by Rykov, the Commissar of the Interior, Miliutin, the Commissar of Agriculture, Nogin, the Commissar of Industry and Trade, Lunacharsky, Kamenev (who had in the meantime been elected President of the Republic), and Zinoviev. These commissars resigned and so compelled Lenin to open negotiations with the other parties.[2] The attempt at reconciliation failed, however, because the Mensheviks insisted that Lenin and Trotsky, the two inspirers of the insurrection, should not be included in the coalition government. There was some hesitation about that condition in the Bolshevik Central Committee; but the majority saw in it an attempt 'at beheading the Bolshevik party' and rejected it. Stalin voted against the exclusion of Lenin and Trotsky and for bringing negotiations with the Mensheviks to an end. A new series of resignations from the Government and the Central Committee followed, which was only stopped when the recalcitrants were threatened with expulsion from the party. Lenin, Trotsky, and Stalin were the first to sign the statement containing the threat. The crisis did nevertheless lead to the formation of a new government which included the left wing of the Social Revolutionaries. This group, the only one willing to co-operate with Lenin and Trotsky, did so primarily in order to carry to its end the agrarian revolution.

It is difficult to understand the crucial role which Stalin came to play in the Soviet Government from its inception, unless due allowance is made for the effect that the 'softness' of most Bolshevik leaders had on Lenin. Their vacillations filled him with apprehension and alarm. He saw his Government confronted with almost insuperable adversities: internal chaos, economic paralysis, inevitable counter-revolution, and a legacy of war. He looked round to see which of his colleagues in the

[1] L. Trotsky, *Stalin*, p. 256.   [2] J. Reed, op. cit., pp. 223-4.

Government and in the Central Committee could be relied upon to form a close nucleus capable of the determined and swift action which would be needed in the emergencies to come. He thought of setting up an inner Cabinet rather than of any dictatorial triumvirate. Soon after the revolution, the Bolshevik Central Committee had appointed an executive of four members: Lenin, Stalin, Trotsky, Sverdlov. After the formation of the Bolshevik-left Social Revolutionary coalition, the Government delegated important and urgent business to an inner Cabinet which consisted of five commissars, three Bolsheviks and two Social Revolutionaries. The three Bolshevik members were Lenin, Trotsky, and Stalin.[1]

We have seen how Stalin became a member of the Central Committee in 1912. Lenin was then in disagreement with his most prominent colleagues (some of whom, incidentally, rejoined his party in 1917). The selection of a new Bolshevik hierarchy had been dictated by their elimination or self-elimination; and the intellectual leaders were replaced by the practical workers of the underground, mainly the committeemen of Baku. Something similar happened now. Stalin's promotion was due to the dissidence of so many members of the Central Committee. True, this time the dissidents did not leave the party, were not expelled, and even regained, later, their influence in the inner councils of Bolshevism. But they remained in reserve for the time being. This is not to say that Stalin was completely immune from the doubts and vacillations of the more moderate leaders; he had had his moment of hesitation on the eve of the October rising. But he was essentially Lenin's satellite. He moved invariably within Lenin's orbit. Every now and then his own judgement and political instinct tempted him to stray; and on a few important occasions his judgement was sounder than Lenin's. But, at least in the first years after the revolution, the master's pull on him was strong enough to keep him steadily within the prescribed orbit. Lenin was undoubtedly aware of this; and he was not averse from making full use of it. In matters of ideology and principle he would take the views of almost any other member of the Central Committee more seriously than Stalin's; but in day-to-day business of the Government, in its vast administrative work, he would

---

[1] L. Trotsky, *Stalin*, p. 241.

appreciate Stalin's assistance perhaps more than anybody else's. Though he himself showed no resemblance to Don Quixote, he was glad to have a Sancho Panza. It was by Lenin's side that Stalin spent the night from 27 to 28 October at Petersburg military headquarters, watching the measures taken to repel General Krasnov's march on the capital. He was by Lenin's side a few days later, when Lenin told the Commander-in-Chief, General Dukhonin, to offer an armistice to the German Command and to order the cease-fire, and when, after General Dukhonin's refusal, Lenin dismissed him and appointed Krylenko Commander-in-Chief. This was the beginning of Stalin's military activity which was to grow in scope and importance with the progress of the civil war.

. . . .

He made his first public appearance as the Commissar of Nationalities at the Congress of the Finnish Social Democratic Party at Helsinki, three weeks after the Bolshevik *coup*. For the Finns this was an unusual and memorable occasion: the representative of the new Russian Government proclaimed the independence of their country from Russia. The gradual absorption of Finland by the Tsarist Empire had begun under Tsar Alexander I, after the Napoleonic wars. Kerensky's democratic Government, which considered itself the legitimate heir to the Empire, insisted upon its sovereignty over Finland even while its sovereignty over Russia was becoming a hollow pretence. Now at last an old wrong was righted. The scene at the Helsinki Congress was the more unusual in that the man who, on behalf of the Russian Government, carried out the solemn act of historical justice was himself not a Russian, but a member of another small nation that had suffered Tsarist oppression. The buoyant phrasing of his speech contrasted queerly with its phlegmatic and ineffective delivery. The speaker almost mumbled his bald Russian sentences, pronouncing them with a marked foreign accent. But this only added another touch of sincerity to the occasion by divesting it of all pomposity. 'Full freedom to shape their own life is given to the Finns as well as to the other peoples of Russia! A voluntary and honest alliance between the Finnish and the Russian peoples! No tutelage, no control from above over the Finnish people! These are the guiding principles of the policy of the Council of People's Commissars.'[1] This was the message of the new Russia, which the son of southern Georgia brought to the free citizens of northern Finland. On 18 December 1917 the Soviet Government officially decreed the independence of Finland. The decree carried the signatures of Lenin and Stalin.

This magnanimous act harmonized with the programme which Stalin had outlined in his treatise on *Marxism and the Nationalities* in 1913. In it he championed the right of the peoples oppressed by the Tsarist Empire to self-determination; and he interpreted that principle in the sense that every oppressed people should be free to break away from Russia and constitute itself an independent state. It was true that socialism did not favour national separatisms and the formation of numberless small states all lacking viability. Its ultimate objective was international Socialist society. Real social and economic progress demanded, in the Socialists' view, the abolition of the barriers that kept nations apart. But international Socialist society could be founded, so Stalin had argued, only by voluntary agreement of the peoples that would form it; and voluntary agreement implied that each nation should first regain its complete freedom. Lenin defended this view in a witty comparison between that freedom and the freedom of divorce which was advocated by Socialists. 'We hardly mean', said Lenin, 'to urge women to divorce their husbands, though we want them to be free to do so.' Similarly, the Bolsheviks pleaded for the right of the non-Russian peoples to secede from Russia, without encouraging separatist aspirations. A week after the revolution, on 2 November, these principles were embodied in 'The Declaration of the Rights of the Peoples of Russia'. The Declaration, of which Lenin and Stalin were the authors, was one of the documents intended to demonstrate to the world the principles of the revolution. 'The Council of People's Commissars', it stated, 'has resolved to adopt . . . the following principles as the basis for its activity: 1. the equality and sovereignty of the peoples of Russia; 2. the right of the peoples of Russia to free self-determination, even to the point of separating and forming independent states; 3. the abolition of any and all national and national-religious privileges and

---

[1] J. Stalin, *Sochinenya*, vol. iv, pp. 1–5.

disabilities; 4. the free development of national minorities and ethnographic groups inhabiting the territory of Russia.'[1]

The Bolshevik leaders hoped that the non-Russian nationalities would follow the Russian example and carry out their own revolutions; and that having obtained the right to divorce they would after all rejoin Russia in a free union of Socialist nations. But the right of the Finns, Ukrainians, Balts, and others to secede from Russia was not made dependent on the régime they established in their own countries. On 22 December 1917 Stalin thus pleaded before the Central Executive of the Soviets, to which he had submitted his decree on the independence of Finland: 'If we look attentively at the picture . . . we see that the Council of People's Commissars has, regardless of its intention, given freedom not to the people, not to the representatives of the working class of Finland, but to the Finnish *bourgeoisie*, which . . . has seized power and received independence from the hands of the Socialists of Russia.' 'The lack of determination and the incomprehensible cowardice' of the Finnish Social Democrats was to be blamed for this; but 'nothing in the world would make the Council of People's Commissars disregard its own pledges' to recognize Finland's independence. Although the Council was blamed for its policy, it would treat the claims of the Finnish *bourgeoisie* with 'perfect impartiality'.[2]

The policy was indeed criticized from various sides. The anti-Bolshevik parties raised an outcry about the 'sell-out' of Russia. Bolsheviks like Bukharin and Dzerzhinsky saw in Stalin's policy a purposeless concession to the bourgeois nationalism of the smaller nations, a concession made at the expense of the Russian revolution. But Stalin, backed by Lenin, stuck to his precept.

Soon, however, it became clear that the precept tended to clash with reality. In all the borderlands of Russia new governments sprang into existence. All were anti-Bolshevik; and all insisted on their complete separation from Russia. Lenin and Stalin were taken at their word. The Ukraine presented the most serious issue. Its newly established Provisional Government, the so-called *Rada*, came into conflict with the Soviets. Ataman Petlura, 'Commander-in-Chief of the Ukrainian armed

---

[1] Lenin i Stalin, *Sbornik Proizvedenii k Izucheniu Istorii VKP (b)*, vol. ii, pp. 17–19.
[2] J. Stalin, *Sochinenya*, vol. iv, pp. 22–4.

forces', issued orders calling on all Ukrainian units to leave the fronts and to return to the Ukraine. From the Bolshevik viewpoint this was self-determination reduced to an absurdity. In an official statement Stalin explained the background of the incipient conflict.[1] The Bolsheviks admitted that each nation had the right to have its own army; but they were not yet in a position to regroup the armed forces so as to do justice to the Ukrainian demand. They were anxious to end the war and conclude peace with Germany; and they had already secured a short armistice and started peace negotiations at Brest Litovsk. But they could not possibly break up the army, dislocate the front, and disorganize the transport system before peace was concluded. In the old Tsarist army there had been no segregation of soldiers according to nationality; and to start such a segregation now would mean to disarm the Russian revolution in the face of a German army which still obeyed the Kaiser's orders. Here then was the dilemma between nationalist Ukrainian aspirations and the interests of the Russian revolution.

The dilemma reappeared under several forms. In the south of Russia the Cossack General Kaledin gathered a counter-revolutionary army and began the civil war. The Soviet Government was anxious to dispatch troops to the south, where the Red coal-mining district of the Donetz was exposed to Kaledin's offensive. The Ukraine, like a wedge, separated northern from southern Russia. The Ukrainian *Rada* refused to allow the passage of Red troops through its territory. Should the Soviets now bow to the *Rada*'s decision in deference to the Ukraine's right of self-determination, even though this might deliver southern Russia to the White armies? The dilemma did not end here. The Soviet revolution was, in fact, spreading to the Ukraine, too; and a strenuous fight developed there between the Ukrainian Soviets and the *Rada*. The *Rada* was dispersing the Soviets by armed force. Should Red Petersburg stand by and do nothing while Red Kiev and Kharkov were submerged by their native counter-revolution?

The Commissar of Nationalities did not hesitate long. He described the dilemma to the third All-Russian Congress of the Soviets, which met in January 1918, and advocated a revision of policy: the principle of self-determination for the small

[1] J. Stalin, *Sochinenya*, vol. iv, pp. 6–14.

nations 'ought to be understood as the right of self-determination not of the *bourgeoisie* but of the toiling masses of a given nation. The principle of self-determination ought to be used as a means in the struggle for socialism and it ought to be subordinated to the principles of socialism.'[1] On behalf of the Mensheviks Martov criticized the Commissar of Nationalities. Why, he asked, did the Bolsheviks grant independence to the Finnish *bourgeoisie* but not to the Ukrainian? Why did Stalin urge support for the Ukrainian Soviets, while Trotsky, already negotiating for peace at Brest Litovsk, asked only that plebiscites be held in Poland and the other German occupied borderlands? Stalin's answer was that there was no difference between his and Trotsky's view-points; but no Soviets existed in Poland and the other borderlands; and the Bolsheviks had no intention of 'inventing' them or of creating them artificially. But in the Ukraine the Soviets were already in existence and the Bolsheviks could not go back from the Soviets to 'bourgeois parliamentarism'. The Congress agreed with the Commissar of Nationalities.

Another revision of principle was contained in a sketchy motion which Stalin submitted to the same Congress on the constitution of the Soviet State. The motion provided for a federal organization of the Soviets.[2] In his treatise on the nationalities Stalin had, like Lenin, opposed federalism. The oppressed peoples, so he then argued, were free to break away from Russia altogether; but if they chose to remain part of Russia they would have to accept the centralized structure of the new state, because modern economy required a high degree of power at the centre and because barriers between various nationalities in the same state were politically undesirable. This was Stalin's view in 1913. At the beginning of 1918 it became clear that the Soviets could not afford the separation of all the smaller nations. A federal Constitution of the new state seemed to strike the most convenient balance between the needs of Bolshevik Russia and the demands of the small nations.

．　　．　　．　　．　　．　　．　　．　　．

However, the time for real Constitution-making had not yet come. The Soviet Government was not yet master in its own

---

[1] Ibid., pp. 31-2.　　　　　　　　[2] Ibid., pp. 32-3.

home. It had just been compelled to carry out another *coup* in order to retain power. In the first days of January 1918 it dispersed the Constituent Assembly which had refused to endorse its revolutionary measures: the establishment of workers' control over industry, nationalization of banks, expropriation of landlords, and the appeal for the immediate opening of peace negotiations that had been addressed by Trotsky to all belligerents. The Assembly, elected on the basis of a law that had been worked out under Kerensky, probably did not reflect the swing in the mood of the country that took place on the eve of the October revolution. Its dispersal presented no difficulty. The Assembly was incapable of rallying any section of the people in its defence. By dispersing it, the Bolsheviks and the left Social revolutionaries pulled up the first Russian shoot of parliamentary democracy by its root. The Soviets remained the only representative institution and the only repository of power.

A much graver crisis developed over the problem of war and peace. The Bolsheviks had hoped that the revolution would spread over Europe like wildfire and bring hostilities to an end. This did not happen. In spite of all the 'fraternization' in the trenches between Russian and German troops, a practice encouraged by the Bolsheviks in the hope that it would make the Germans catch the germ of revolution, the Kaiser's army had so far lost little or nothing of its fighting capacity. Great Britain, France, and Italy, encouraged by the entry of the United States into the war, were in no mood to talk peace. Russia was unable to continue the fight. Her list of casualties was prodigious; and the equipment and armament of her forces was worse than miserable. The new Government was pledged to end the war at once; and it would be judged by whether it kept that pledge or not. The agrarian revolution dealt the final blow to the armies in the field. The mouzhiks deserted the trenches and rushed home to take part in the share-out of the landlords' estates. 'They voted for peace . . . with their feet', according to Lenin's saying. The Soviets could do nothing but sue for a separate peace.

Peace could be obtained only on German terms. These included the annexation by Germany, in one form or another, of Poland, the Baltic states, and part of the Ukraine, the lands that had anyhow been occupied by German forces. Yet the Bolsheviks had committed themselves to the conclusion of a peace 'without annexations and indemnities'. This had been one of the stock slogans of their agitators. They had gone even farther and often said that they would make peace only with a revolutionary German Government, not with the servants of the Kaiser. Once again ideals and reality were in irreconcilable conflict.

Lenin did his best to drive home to his colleagues the absolute hopelessness of the situation and to persuade them to accept peace. They had to bow, he argued, to the impositions of German imperialism in order to save their young, unconsolidated Republic. The revolution in Germany and in the rest of Europe was delayed; and it would be nipped in the bud if in the meantime the Russian revolution were to be crushed by the weight of German arms. The survival of the Soviets, even if bought at the price of humiliation and a seeming negation of principle, would eventually encourage the European proletariat to revolt. The ground now ceded would not be lost for long, because they would use the dearly bought respite to prepare themselves for the return match.

At first, Lenin's exhortations fell on deaf ears. The overwhelming majority of his colleagues and followers stood for 'revolutionary war against German imperialism'. Bukharin headed the party of war or the left Communists, as they came to be called. He argued that peace would untie the hands of the Kaiser's Government for the struggle against incipient revolution at home. The Russian revolution would disgrace itself if, to save its own skin, it betrayed German and international socialism, and acquiesced in the annexation of foreign lands by the Hohenzollern Empire. Even if the Soviets were to go under in unequal battle, their defeat and destruction would still be preferable to their existence in shame and treachery. Their example would inspire others to resume or continue the fight as did the heroic example of the Paris Commune half a century before. Lenin, they argued, was urging the Bolsheviks to sacrifice life's only end for the sake of mere living.

Trotsky, who conducted the peace parleys at Brest Litovsk, remained outside the two factions. He agreed with Lenin that the Soviets were incapable of waging a revolutionary war; but he also agreed with Bukharin that they would disgrace themselves if they accepted the peace terms. At Brest Litovsk he dragged out the negotiations in the hope that in the meantime the German revolution might begin to stir. He produced before the amazed and irritated German and Austrian generals and diplomats his most brilliant fireworks of revolutionary oratory designed to expose the wickedness of the German Diktat and to shock the conscience of the German working classes. But the harvest of his revolutionary propaganda was slow in ripening; and meanwhile the life and death dilemma had to be solved. Trotsky succeeded in persuading the Central Committee to reverse its vote in favour of revolutionary war and to adopt his own formula: 'Neither war nor peace.' Events were soon to expose the escapist nature of that formula. The Soviets had to opt either for war or for peace. To 'choose neither' was a gesture becoming the propagandist and the journalist, but not the statesman and the politician.

Where did Stalin stand in this dramatic controversy? He was unmoved by the exhortations of the left Communists and by their preachings on revolutionary morality. The idea that the Russian revolution should sacrifice itself for the sake of European revolution was completely alien to him, even though Lenin, for all his realism, was chary of dismissing it lightly. To the man who had spent most of his active life in Baku and Tiflis, European revolution was a concept too hazy and remote to influence his thinking on matters which might determine the life and the death of the Soviet Republic, that same Republic whose still feeble but tangible reality he himself had helped to create. Nor was he impressed by Trotsky's attitude. He could only shrug his shoulders or mock at the idea that the appeals to the German proletariat made by Trotsky from Brest Litovsk would in any way affect the balance of forces at the fronts. He voted with Lenin and his tiny faction for peace. Lenin derided the left Communists as people who said 'we bank on the international Socialist movement; and we are therefore free to commit stupidities'. He compared Bukharin and his followers to the Polish nobleman—the *szlachcic*—'who dying in a beautiful posture, with the sword by his side said: peace is shame, war is honour. They argue from the view-point of the *szlachcic*. I am speaking from the view-point of the peasant', said Lenin.[1] Who could understand such language better than the son of Georgian peasants?

Stalin was not prominent in the debates which raged for the next two months in the Central Committee, the Government, at the fourth Congress of the Soviets, and at the seventh Congress of the party. (He was, incidentally, rather inconspicuous at any of the great debates, the true tournaments of ideas, in which the party periodically indulged during Lenin's lifetime.) But he said enough at a session of the Central Committee to show which way his mind worked: 'In accepting the slogan of revolutionary war we play into the hands of imperialism. Trotsky's attitude is no attitude at all. There is no revolutionary movement in the west, there are no facts [indicating the existence] of a revolutionary movement, there is only a potentiality; and we in our work cannot base ourselves on a mere potentiality. If the Germans begin to advance this will strengthen the counter-revolution in this country. . . . In October we talked about a holy war against imperialism, because we were told that the one word "peace" would raise revolution in the west. This has not been borne out. . . .'[2] Though he voted with Lenin there was a subtle difference in the emphasis of their arguments. Lenin, as usual, kept his eye on the facts and the potentialities of the situation and spoke about the delay in the development of the revolutionary movement in the west. Stalin grasped the facts and dismissed the potentialities—'there is no revolutionary movement in the west'. True, he added that if Trotsky's 'neither peace nor war' were to be accepted 'this would create the worst possible conditions for the revolutionary movement in the west', thereby implying that he, too, was concerned with that aspect of the problem. But in the context of his reasoning, this was hardly more than a casual tribute to obligatory Bolshevik parlance. The real weight of his argument was in his denial of the actuality of the revolutionary movement in the west and in his sour remark about the exploded illusions of October.

After many ups and downs in the stormy controversy which at times threatened to tear the party to pieces, after a break-

---

[1] *The Essentials of Lenin*, vol. ii, pp. 304–5.
[2] J. Stalin, *Sochinenya*, vol. iv, p. 27.

down of the armistice and a rapid new advance by the German army almost to the gates of Petersburg, after the signing of a separate peace with Germany by the Ukrainian *Rada*, after a merciless exposure of the military impotence of the Soviets, after Lenin's many rousing appeals and cries of alarm, after all this, the majority of the Central Committee and of the rank and file finally swung over to support the peace party. On 3 March Sokolnikov, who had replaced Trotsky as the head of the Soviet delegation at Brest Litovsk, signed the peace terms. Lenin made no effort to embellish the act. Nobody was more outspoken than he in denouncing its 'shamefulness'. He compared the treaty of Brest Litovsk to the humiliating and unjust peace of Tilsit which Napoleon imposed upon Prussia in 1807, and which progressive Prussian statesmen had used to carry out sweeping reforms at home and to prepare Prussia's triumph.[1] He prophesied a revolutionary war in the near future. By the end of the year the German and Austrian monarchies with all their military might had crumbled into dust; and a revolution-ized German army was evacuating the Ukraine. So the peace of Brest Litovsk was automatically annulled.

The controversy over Brest Litovsk had a complex after-math. Its political consequences were manifold. The left Communists were unreconciled. Though they were defeated over the immediate issue, they represented a significant mood in the party, an ideological malaise, an uneasiness with the compromises and the opportunism into which the victorious revolution had been and still would be driven more than once. They represented the unsophisticated, quixotic or Utopian fidelity to first principles, the unreasoning purity of revolu-tionary faith. Suppressed or defeated at one stage, that mood would reappear at the next; and, constantly changing its form and expression and even its mouthpieces, it would long trouble the Bolshevik mind.

A more specific consequence of Brest Litovsk was the break-up of the coalition between the Bolsheviks and left Social Revolutionaries. The latter resigned from the Government in March. Their motives were in part identical with those of the left Communists; in part they were dictated by ordinary nationalism. From now on power would be exercised by a

---

[1] *The Essentials of Lenin*, vol. ii, pp. 290–5.

single party. Government by a single party had hitherto not been a plank in the Bolshevik programme. But the course of events was such that the Bolsheviks could not help becoming the country's sole rulers after their partners had refused to share responsibility for the peace. Alone in office, they still refrained from suppressing their opponents, except for the extreme right the initiators of the civil war. Only in June 1918, when the civil war was already in full swing, were the Mensheviks and the right wing Social Revolutionaries temporarily outlawed, on the ground that some of their members sided with the White Guards. The Mensheviks were again permitted to come into the open in November of the same year when they pledged themselves to act as a loyal opposition within the framework of the Soviet régime.

But already in July the left Social Revolutionaries provoked the first real outburst of Bolshevik terror. In an attempt to disrupt the peace and to force the Bolsheviks back into war against Germany, the left Social Revolutionary Jacob Blumkin assassinated the German Ambassador Count von Mirbach. A series of insurrections staged by the same party broke out in various places including Moscow, to which the Government transferred its seat after the conclusion of peace. On 30 August Lenin was wounded and two other Bolshevik leaders, Uritsky and Volodarsky, were assassinated by Social Revolutionaries. Trotsky narrowly escaped an attempt on his life. The Bolsheviks officially retorted with mass reprisals; and their self-defence was at least as savage as the onslaught to which they had been subjected. The spirit of those days can be gauged from a dispatch which Stalin sent to Sverdlov from Tsaritsyn, the future Stalingrad, whither he had gone as a political commissar: 'The War Council of the Northern Caucasian Military Region, having learned about the wicked attempt of capitalist hirelings on the life of the greatest revolutionary, the tested leader and teacher of the proletariat, Comrade Lenin, answer this base attack from ambush with the organization of open and systematic mass terror against the bourgeoisie and its agents.'[1] The message was signed by Stalin and Voroshilov, the Commander of the Tsaritsyn army. The Cheka (the Extraordinary Commission), the forerunner of the O.G.P.U., directed by the

[1] J. Stalin, *Sochinenya*, vol. iv, p. 128.

Pole Dzerzhinsky, began a feverish activity which did not shrink from the shooting of hostages. The party responsible for the attempts and assassinations was, of course, outlawed. Such were the passions let loose by the peace of Brest Litovsk and such were its sombre consequences. Where he was posted, at Tsaritsyn, Stalin kept his word. The Red terror in the town, which was to bear his name, soon became a byword, just as the atrocities of the young Jacobin Fouché in Lyons were a byword in France nearly 130 years before. Terror and counter-terror inexorably grew in a vicious and ever-widening spiral.

Another less important consequence of the Brest Litovsk controversy concerned the personal standing of the various Bolshevik leaders. Lenin emerged with enormous moral credit. He had shown that undogmatic logic and courage of conviction which enabled him to defy the party's prevailing mood, and the extraordinary power of persuasion which enabled him in the end to sway the mind of the party. The party and the country which had seen and heard him but little during the actual upheaval in October could now gauge his real stature, the rare virtues of his mind and character. During the crisis the 'deserter and strike-breaker' of October, Zinoviev, rallied to his side; and Lenin was as quick in forgetting an old grievance as he had been ruthless in voicing it. On the other hand, Trotsky suffered a temporary eclipse. He had laid bare an important weakness of his—a certain lack of plain realism, a propensity to verbal solutions and theatrical gestures in a situation which brooked neither. His eclipse was not serious. His moral authority was still second only to Lenin's. He resigned from the Commissariat of Foreign Affairs, where he was replaced by Chicherin, and became the Commissar of War. In his new post he soon rose to a new climax of fame as the founder and builder of the Red Army. But among the leaders his attitude during the Brest Litovsk crisis was not forgotten; and it would be brought up against him several years later, in the bitter struggle over the succession to Lenin.

Stalin's position was correspondingly enhanced, though since the break-up of the coalition Government the Bolshevik triumvirate of the inner Cabinet ceased to exist. Since Stalin did not mount the rostrum to speak for peace in public, he made no gain in popularity. But he made himself even more indispensable to Lenin in his fight against the 'knights of the romantic phrase' and the ultra-revolutionary dreamers. 'Use the respite', 'discipline and organize yourselves'—these were now Lenin's instructions to his followers. In this prosaic new endeavour he believed he could rely upon the Commissar of Nationalities.

The price for the respite had not yet been fully paid. The Republic still lived in fear of war which Germany might renew. The peace treaty had to be implemented, clause by clause, each more humiliating than its predecessor. One clause provided for the separation of the Ukraine from Russia. It was with this in mind that on 2 April 1918, soon after the signing of the peace, Stalin urged the Soviet Government at once to open peace negotiations with the Ukrainian *Rada*: for with it the Soviets were still at war.[1] The Council of the People's Commissars hesitated for nearly a month. The reason for its hesitation was this: just before the signing of the peace the Bolsheviks had staged a *coup* in the Ukraine and formed a Government of their own, a rival to the *Rada*. Stalin himself had officially kept in touch with the Ukrainian Soviets and even instructed them to send their delegates to Brest Litovsk. His present motion amounted to a disavowal of the Ukrainian Soviets in favour of the *Rada*. This must have seemed to the Council of Commissars to be expediency carried too far; and so for a month no decision was taken. Meanwhile the German Command ordered the military occupation of the whole of the Ukraine. On 27 April the Council of Commissars finally agreed to open negotiations with the *Rada* and appointed Stalin head of the Soviet delegation which was to meet the Ukrainian envoys at Kursk. The negotiations had hardly begun when the news came that the German Command had deposed the mildly Socialist *Rada* and substituted a puppet Government headed by the monarchist Hetman Skoropadsky. German forces now occupied, in addition to the Ukraine, the purely Russian industrial areas on the Black Sea, Taganrog and Rostov-on-Don as well as the Crimea.

The cease-fire on the Ukrainian front, ordered by Lenin and Stalin on 5 May, came too late to retrieve the situation. Stalin

---

[1] See Biographical Chronicle, op. cit., p. 447, and *Leninskii Sbornik*, vol. xviii, pp. 64–8.

returned from Kursk to Moscow to consult the Government. The question arose whether the Bolsheviks should parley with Skoropadsky's puppet Government which was highly unpopular in the Ukraine. Stalin was not tormented by scruples. In an interview with the *Izvestya*, he stated that 'so far the present upheaval in the Ukraine has not adversely affected the peace parleys. On the contrary, one may assume that the upheaval in the Ukraine does not rule out the possibility of peace being concluded between the Soviet and the Ukrainian Governments.'[1] The events, he went on, had only demonstrated the futility of the *Rada* which tried to take up a half-way position between German imperialism and Bolshevism. Skoropadsky, the open counter-revolutionary and German puppet, so Stalin carefully hinted, might even prove a more solid partner for peace negotiations. He was rapidly learning his lessons in the school of expediency.

.   .   .   .

As all the western borderlands of Russia had been occupied by German forces, the scope of the work which Stalin could perform as the Commissar of Nationalities shrank to insignificance. Even in his native Caucasus he could do but little. The Germans occupied Georgia, without a protest from the Georgian Menshevik Government. The Turks moved into Batum. Events in the Caucasus confirmed Stalin in his conviction that the small nations, between the hammer of German militarism and the anvil of Bolshevism, were in no position to preserve even nominal independence. While the Bolsheviks let them use their right of self-determination, they were one after another falling a prey to German imperialism. For a while Stalin turned his attention to the uncivilized, backward tribes which inhabited the east of Russia, the borderland between Europe and Asia. To bring those races and tribes within the framework of the Soviets was in some respects much easier, and in others much more difficult, than to sovietize the more advanced nationalities on Russia's western fringe. The political aspirations of Tartars, Bashkirs, or Turkmens were very primitive. No strong separatist tendencies developed among them. It was, however, a formidable task to adjust their pre-capitalist,

[1] J. Stalin, *Sochinenya*, vol. iv, p. 83.

often pre-feudal and even nomad ways of life to the Marxist, Communist policies of the central Government. Stalin made a first attempt at tackling the job when, in the middle of May 1918, he sponsored the Republic of Tartars and Bashkirs, which was to be part of the Soviet Russian Federation.

No sooner had the attempt been made than it had to be abandoned because of the new dangers that beset the Soviets. In the spring and summer of 1918 the White Armies scored great successes which for a time reduced the area over which the Soviet writ ran to the Grand Duchy of Muscovy. In the east the Czechoslovak Legion, composed of former prisoners of war, made common cause with the White Guards and in a lightning advance occupied within a few weeks all the vital strategic and economic centres in Siberia, in the Urals, and on the middle reaches of the Volga. The newly formed Tartar-Bashkir Republic was already lost to the Soviets. In August the Whites seized Kazan, which created a direct threat to Moscow. In the south General Krasnov's Cossacks attempted to advance northwards and to join hands with the White forces at Kazan. In their advance they cut the rail connexion between Tsaritsyn and Moscow. The Soviet capital was thus cut off from the northern Caucasus which was, after the loss of the Ukraine and Siberia, its only granary. The bread ration for workers in Petersburg and Moscow went down to about one ounce a day. At the same time, Allied forces, still locked in combat on the western front, began operations against the Bolsheviks. American troops disembarked in Siberia. The British occupied Archangel in the north and Baku in the south. It was while the military strength of the Soviets was at its nadir that the revolts of the Social Revolutionaries and the attempt on Lenin's life took place.

At that moment of supreme danger, nearly all members of the Government left Moscow and hurried to the most vital sectors of the front. At the Kremlin Lenin with a few technical assistants directed the entire struggle, keeping in constant touch with the men on the spot. Two men were sent to retrieve the position where it looked most menacing. To try to save the capital from the military threat the Commissar of War, Trotsky, set out in his armoured train, which was to become legendary in the civil war, to Svyazhsk, near Kazan. Stalin, accompanied by an armed guard of nearly battalion strength, went to Tsaritsyn on the Volga to try to save the capital from the starvation that threatened it. He was to arrange the transport of grain from the northern Caucasus to Moscow. His assignment, which was essentially civilian, was expected to last a short time, after which he was to proceed farther south to Baku. But his stay at Tsaritsyn was prolonged by unforeseen circumstances; and the longer it lasted the deeper did he involve himself in the conduct of the civil war in the south and in a controversy with Trotsky, until in the end his trip to the Volga town became a landmark in his career.

The day after his arrival, on 7 June, he reported to Lenin on his first moves.[1] He found a 'bacchanalia of profiteering' in the Volga area and his first step was to decree the rationing of food and control of prices at Tsaritsyn. The Soviet official in charge of trade would be arrested. 'Tell Schmidt [the Commissar of Labour] not to send such rascals any more.' This was the language of the energetic administrator with a penchant for control and repression—both, given all the circumstances, probably justified. He had no liking for the ultra-democratic chaos that was left over from the revolution. 'Railway transport has been completely disorganized by the joint efforts of a multitude of Collegiums and revolutionary Committees.' After they had deposed the old managements in industry and administration, the Bolsheviks first tried control by committee. They were now engaged in scrapping that ultra-democratic but unworkable system and re-establishing individual management and individual responsibility. The left Communists passionately objected to the change. Stalin left no doubt where he stood. He appointed commissars to overcome the chaos in transport.

After a month at Tsaritsyn he asked for special military powers on the southern front. In view of the operations of Krasnov's Cossacks, the provisioning of Moscow had become primarily a military matter. In reply to a communication from Lenin on the outbreak of the Social Revolutionary mutinies, he assured Moscow that 'everything will be done to prevent possible surprises here. Rest assured that our hand will not tremble.'[2] The rail connexion between Tsaritsyn and the farming land of the northern Caucasus 'has not yet been restored.

---

[1] J. Stalin, *Sochinenya*, vol. iv, pp. 116–17.   [2] Ibid., p. 118.

I am driving and scolding everybody who needs it. Rest assured that we shall spare nobody, neither ourselves nor others, and that we shall deliver the bread. . . .' In his messages practical soberness mixed with a queer relish for expressions of ruthless determination.

The same message in which he asked for military powers gave the first hint of his conflict with Trotsky. It contained the following remark: 'If only our war "specialists" (the shoe-makers!) had not slept and been idle, the line would not have been cut; and if the line is restored this will be so not because of the military but in spite of them.'[1] This was the point over which the famous Tsaritsyn dispute started.

A few months before, after the complete disintegration of the old army, Trotsky had begun to build up the Red Army, first with volunteers and then with called-up workers and peasants. As the new army had no staff corps, Trotsky put officers of the old Tsarist army in charge of newly formed divisions and regi-ments; but, since the political reliability of the ex-officers was doubtful, he attached to them Communists as political com-missars. The 'military specialists' were to train the army and lead it in battle, while the commissars were to watch the con-duct of the officers, prevent, if need be, treason on their part, and 'educate politically' the rank and file. Each military order had to be signed by the commander and the commissar; and both were to enforce military discipline. The novel and bold experiment was at first viewed with apprehensive scepticism by the leaders of the party; it aroused the most violent opposi-tion on the part of the left Communists. Lenin himself dropped his doubts only when he learned from Trotsky that about 40,000 'specialists' had already been employed in the Red Army and that the whole military machine of the Republic would crumble if they were to be dismissed. Impressed by the shrewdness of the experiment, he threw the weight of his influence behind Trotsky, describing his move as the building of socialism with the bricks left over from the demolished old order, an indis-pensable method of building.[2]

Indispensable as it was, the experiment did not work smoothly.

---

[1] Ibid., pp. 118–19.
[2] Lenin, *Sochinenya*, vol. xxiv, pp. 65–6; L. Trotsky, *Kak Vooruzhalas Revolutsya*, vol. i, pp. 154–73.

Cases of treason by ex-officers were frequent; and they were the more frequent the poorer the military chances of the Soviets looked in the eyes of the officers. At the height of the civil war commanders of regiments, divisions, and even armies, went over to the White Guards, sometimes followed by their troops. Each case of treason strengthened the opponents of Trotsky and Lenin. There was nervous tension and suspicion at all levels of the military command, from company headquarters up to the General Staff, where a former Tsarist Colonel Vatzetis was promoted by Trotsky to be Commander-in-Chief. Relations between commissars and officers were exacerbated by the suspiciousness of the former, often expressed in rude, boorish forms, and the hurt pride of the latter. The issue was only part of a wider controversy. Trotsky was bent on merging a multitude of loose partisan detachments and Red Guards into a uniform army with an effective system of central command, administration, and supply. The transition was obstructed by many leaders of the Red guerrillas who had already distinguished themselves in the civil war and to whom subordination to conservative officers was, naturally enough, most repugnant. The more sophisticated left Communists objected on principle to centralization of military authority. They reminded Lenin and Trotsky of the emphatic promises they had made before the seizure of power that the Soviets would abolish the standing army (as well as the political police) once for all and replace it by people's militias. Like many other Bolshevik pledges made before October, this promise, too, had to be abandoned.

Tsaritsyn was the centre of bitter opposition to the new military policy. The commander of the Tenth Army which had its headquarters there was Klim Voroshilov, the worker who, ten years before, was Stalin's colleague on the Bolshevik Committee of Baku and led the trade union of the oil workers. Voroshilov himself had been a non-commissioned officer during the war. Another commander on the spot was Budienny, an ex-sergeant-major, a regular in the cavalry and a distinguished guerrilla leader. Ordjonikidze was political commissar with the Tenth Army. On his arrival Stalin found himself amid old friends bound together by memories of old fights. It was almost as if the old Baku Committee had been transferred to the headquarters of the Tenth Army. This alone must have disposed him sympathetically towards the 'Tsaritsyn group', even if he had viewed their doings with a critical eye.

The Tsaritsyn group refused to submit to the authority of the commander of the southern front, Sytin, a former Tsarist officer. Complaints about Voroshilov's insubordination were repeatedly wired from the command of the southern front to the General Staff and from the General Staff to Trotsky. Trotsky, in his turn, showered exhortations, injunctions, orders, and remonstrances on the Tsaritsyn headquarters. Several instances of treason committed by 'specialists' on the spot increased the obstinacy of the 'N.C.O.s' opposition', as Trotsky labelled the Tsaritsyn group.[1]

Stalin's sympathy with the opposition is at first sight puzzling, even if allowance is made for his old connexion with Voroshilov. In the Government and the Central Committee he stood for central authority and discipline. His own capacity for enforcing by stern means discipline on confused and semi-anarchist elements was one of the chief qualities for which he was valued. What then disposed him to comply with the defiance of authority at Tsaritsyn? The plebeian distrust of the Tsaritsyn group for the old intelligentsia, for the 'gentry' to whom the ex-officers belonged, probably struck a chord in the commissar of Georgian peasant stock. Nor were all the rights in the controversy on one side and all the wrongs on the other. Budienny, for instance, urged the High Command to form a Red Cavalry and to use it in large massed formations or even as a separate army. The imaginative idea of the ex-sergeant-major was cold-shouldered by the military specialists in much the same way as other specialists dismissed proposals for the use of tanks in mass formation at the beginning of the Second World War. Budienny's idea was at first rejected also by Trotsky, who feared that the cavalry would have to consist mainly of the Cossacks, Russia's born horsemen, who were unfriendly towards the Soviets. Only some time later did Trotsky issue his order: 'Proletarians to horse', which embodied the idea and started the most romantic legend of the civil war, the legend of the Red Cavalry and its commander Budienny.[2] Meanwhile, at Tsaritsyn, the ex-

---

[1] L. Trotsky, *Kak Vooruzhalas Revolutsya*, vol. ii, pp. 59–65, 92–6, and K. Voroshilov, *Lenin, Stalin i Krasnaya Armya*, pp. 70–5.

[2] K. Voroshilov, op. cit., p. 56; L. Trotsky, *Stalin*, p. 274; E. Wollenberg, *The Red Army*, p. 97.

sergeant-major vented his frustration and resentment towards the General Staff and the Commissar of War; and he found a willing and attentive listener in Stalin.

The chief reason for Stalin's patronage of the Tsaritsyn group, however, lay elsewhere—in the incipient rivalry between himself and Trotsky. For several years to come the public was to hear nothing about it, because the antagonism was to develop and grow in bitterness behind the closed doors of the Polit-bureau. Even in the Politbureau, under Lenin's watchful eyes, the antagonists comported themselves with relative discretion so that even the initiated missed the whole ferocity and bitter-ness of the rivalry. Yet the set-up in the Government before the break up of the coalition with the Social Revolutionaries almost invited this rivalry. In the inner Cabinet the Bolsheviks were represented by Lenin, Trotsky, and Stalin. Stalin was the junior member of that trio. The two senior members were enveloped in fame and popular affection. In common parlance their names were hyphenated. The Government was usually referred to as the Government of Lenin-Trotsky. The party, too, was first in Russia and then all over the world referred to as the party of Lenin-Trotsky by friend and foe alike. The appearance of the two men at congresses and meetings was invariably greeted with rapturous ovations. The enthusiasm of the young Republic spontaneously centred on the two leaders who needed no official claque to bolster them up. The junior member of the trio remained unknown. The contrast between his power and his obscurity would have been galling even to a person of lesser ambition and pride. It was unbear-able to the man who for all his extraordinary career had never since his early youth been able to still his yearning for distinc-tion, the man whose nagging sense of inferiority had been perversely stirred even by his promotions, in which there was usually a strong element of chance. Lenin's superiority gave him no hurt. He had been accustomed to take it for granted as an immutable circumstance, like their difference in age. But Trotsky's ascendancy could not but rouse in him a sour resentfulness. His rival was his contemporary—they had been born in the same year. Only a few years before, Stalin had, with Lenin's whole-hearted approval, attacked Trotsky in the most contemptuous manner as 'the champion with the faked muscles', 'the grandiloquent poseur', 'the abject ally of the Menshevik liquidators'. There was an unpleasant irony in a situation in which he was so hopelessly overshadowed by Trotsky and had to see Trotsky constantly hailed as the great champion of the revolution and to hear his grandiloquence acclaimed by enthusiastic Bolshevik crowds. His resentment must have risen when, after the break with the Social Revolutionaries, the Government was overhauled and the trio dissolved. Stalin's influence in the Government now diminished as fortuitously as it had risen, while that of Trotsky grew with the steady increase in importance of the Commissariat of War, which, as the civil war developed, became the hub of Government. The seeds of his resentment and envy began to sprout at Tsaritsyn.

Thus, the greatest and most violent feud in Russian history was trivial in its origin. It seems almost incongruous that the mighty current of events should have had its source in petty grudge and envy. Yet this is the undeniable fact. To be sure, much wider and more powerful motives, ideological and political, accounted for the conflict between Stalin and Trotsky in its later stages. Personal rivalry by itself would not have assumed the dimensions of that great drama in the course of which the whole life of the Soviet Republic and of the Communist International were gradually to be remoulded. But at its earliest stage the rivalry was purely personal; and because of this it was narrow. There was at first nothing unusual or extravagant in it. In no way did it differ from the personal animosities that are usually found among leaders of the same party or Government in any country, and which provide the stuff for the gossip columns of the popular Press. The most pedantic student of their careers will not find any serious difference of principle dividing the Commissar of War and the Commissar of Nationalities at this point. (Even in the controversy over military policy, Stalin in the end openly sided with Trotsky or, rather, with Lenin who backed Trotsky.) Each of them in his way and in his own field worked for a common purpose. Both strained their very different abilities and energies to wrest the revolution from defeat. They were only human if, in following their revolutionary vocation, they did not divest themselves of personal ambitions and passions.

In his unfriendly attitude towards Trotsky, Stalin was not alone. The old workers of the underground, Lenin's professional revolutionaries and organizers, had a distinct *esprit de corps*. To many of them Trotsky was a new-comer. His exceptional status in the party vaguely offended their collective sentiment. No caucus likes the brilliant outsider who joins the party, wins the heart of its following by storm, and towers high above the men of the caucus. True, in 1917, when Trotsky joined the Bolsheviks, he was received by them with open arms. But the party was then only striving for power; and Trotsky joined it in the days of the July crisis, when it was cornered by all its foes and did not know whether its next move would be to descend underground or to ascend to power. The adherence of a man of Trotsky's stature gave a fillip to the party's temporarily waning self-confidence. The perils of civil war again cemented the ranks of the Bolsheviks, whose future, in so far as it was at all dependent on any individual, depended on the success or failure of the Commissar of War. The force of events still kept the caucus in its place. But there were always enough committee-men about with long memories of past feuds, whom it would not be difficult to turn against Trotsky, especially when new grievances gave new strength to old memories.

The food transports from the northern Caucasus arrived in Moscow as Stalin had promised. Thus the Council of People's Commissars had reason to be grateful to its envoy at Tsaritsyn. Stalin, having failed to receive an answer to his first and somewhat timid request for special military powers, insistently repeated his demand in a cable to Lenin dated 10 July 1918. The message, which was first published only in 1947, contained a violent attack on Trotsky, an attack which by implication was also a remonstrance with Lenin. If Trotsky continued to send his men to the northern Caucasus and the Don without the knowledge of the people on the spot, Stalin stated, then 'within a month everything will go to pieces in the northern Caucasus and we shall irretrievably lose that land. . . . Rub this in to Trotsky. . . . For the good of the cause military plenary powers are indispensable to me here. I have written about this but received no reply. All right, then. In that case I alone shall, without any formalities, dismiss those commanders and commissars who ruin the job. . . . The lack of a paper mandate from Trotsky will, of course, not stop me.'[1]

Technically, Stalin's interference with military matters was illegal. His demand that no appointments be made by central headquarters without the knowledge of himself and Voroshilov was also beyond his terms of reference. However, matters of food and military operations were now interconnected; and Stalin felt that as a member of the Government and one of the top leaders of the party he was entitled to act as he did, whatever his formal standing vis-à-vis the army. Trotsky, on his part, insisted that as long as Stalin was attached to Tsaritsyn headquarters he was subordinate to the higher military command and should not use his position in the Government or in the Central Committee to undermine military authority.[2] Though Trotsky's insistence on this was technically correct, it was psychologically unrealistic. Stalin had a strong sense of his high place in the hierarchy. He refused to climb down in front of his old friends. Lenin, whatever he may have thought about the tone of Stalin's dispatches, was careful not to add fuel to the quarrel. He valued the work of both men, though he measured each of them with a different yardstick, and he was anxious to eliminate friction between them. Without showing Stalin's most offensive dispatches to Trotsky and without transmitting all of Trotsky's criticisms to Stalin, he tried to curb the one and placate the other. With Trotsky's agreement, Stalin was granted the plenary powers he had asked for. He was, on the other hand, left in no doubt of the support given by Lenin to measures designed to strengthen the authority of the central command.

It would be a dull matter to follow out the Tsaritsyn squabble in detail. The compromise proposed by Lenin did not remove friction. The direct wire between Moscow and Tsaritsyn continued to tap out orders, threats, complaints, and exhortatory messages. On one of Trotsky's orders, Stalin wrote down the remark: 'To be disregarded.'[3] In September Voroshilov drove the White Guards back beyond the Don. Stalin reported the success to the Council of Commissars: 'The enemy has been

[1] J. Stalin, Sochinenya, vol. iv, pp. 120–1.
[2] L. Trotsky, The Stalin School of Falsification, pp. 206–8.
[3] K. Voroshilov, op. cit., p. 47; E. Yaroslavsky, Landmarks, p. 115.

routed, the situation of Tsaritsyn is firm, the offensive continues.'[1] Soon afterwards, during Stalin's visit to Moscow, Lenin and Stalin sent a joint message with 'fraternal greetings to the heroic commanders and troops of the Tsaritsyn front'.[2] The confident tone of these messages was ill founded, however, for Tsaritsyn was soon again surrounded by the White Guards. Stalin's trip to Moscow was caused by Trotsky's repeated complaints. 'I insist categorically on Stalin's recall', Trotsky cabled Lenin. 'Things are going badly at the Tsaritsyn front in spite of superabundant forces. Voroshilov is capable of commanding a regiment, not an army of 50,000. However, I shall leave him in command of the Tenth Army, provided he reports to the commander of the Army of the South, Sytin. Thus far Tsaritsyn had not even sent reports of operations. . . . I have asked that reports on reconnoitring and operations be sent twice daily. If that is not done by to-morrow, I shall remand Voroshilov . . . to court martial and shall publish the fact in an army order.'[3] Trotsky repeated that threat in a personal interview with Voroshilov who at last gave way.

Trotsky's low view of the competence of the future Commissar of War and Commander-in-Chief was shared by most Soviet generals in later years; and it was confirmed in 1941, when Voroshilov, as well as Budienny, utterly failed as commander in the war against Germany. Meanwhile, called to explain his attitude before the Revolutionary Council of War, Stalin shrewdly dissociated himself from the 'N.C.O.s' opposition' and sought, at least outwardly, reconciliation with Trotsky. On 11 October 1918, just before the town was again surrounded by the Whites, he was sent back to Tsaritsyn. A few days later the besiegers were once again repulsed, and this time for good.

It was this victory at Tsaritsyn that subsequently gave rise to an interminable controversy over the credit that should be claimed for it. In Trotsky's version, a version that was upheld by most Soviet generals before the great purges of the thirties, the laurels were due to the Command of the southern front, whose forces broke the ring around Tsaritsyn from outside. Stalin, Voroshilov, and Budienny claimed the laurels for themselves. This was one of those futile military squabbles which

---

[1] J. Stalin, *Sochinenya*, vol. iv, p. 129.   [2] Ibid., p. 130.
[3] L. Trotsky, *Stalin*, p. 288, and *Kak Vooruzhalas Revolutsya*, vol. i, pp. 350–1.

it is hardly possible or worth-while to resolve, and which derive an exaggerated importance only from the political setting in which they take place. In the Kremlin, the claims of the Tsaritsyn group were apparently dismissed, for it was precisely after the lifting of the siege on Tsaritsyn that Lenin finally yielded to Trotsky's demand, recalled Stalin from the southern front, and gave Trotsky a free hand in dealing with Voroshilov.[1] Years later the controversy was to be renewed by the Tsaritsyn group, whose claims formed part of Stalin's military legend, itself an important though subsidiary point in Stalin's much wider claim to supreme power. About five years after the event Tsaritsyn was renamed Stalingrad. In 1942, when Stalin resolved to fight the decisive battle of the Second World War on the approaches and in the streets of Stalingrad, he was actuated not only by the strategic realities of the situation. He was also prompted by what one might call a 'Tsaritsyn fixation': he defended before history his first legend, while creating a second that was much closer to fact.

By the end of the summer of 1918 the danger that threatened Moscow from the east had been removed. As long as it existed the General Staff attached only secondary importance to the southern front. But in October the Czechs had been thrown back to the Urals, and Trotsky could turn his whole attention to the south, brooking no interference with his battle orders. The southern front was now too small for both antagonists. One of them had to go, and it was Stalin. Lenin did his best to sweeten the pill. He sent the President of the Republic Sverdlov to bring Stalin back to Moscow in a special train with all the necessary honours. The episode was characteristic of Lenin's handling of the man: he had a shrewd eye for his weaknesses and was very careful not to offend needlessly his touchiness and *amour propre*. Trotsky's manner was the exact opposite. He underrated his opponent, made no allowance for his ambition, and offended him at almost every step. This flowed from his natural manner rather than from deliberate intention. On its way to Moscow the train that carried Sverdlov and Stalin met Trotsky's train which was bound for Tsaritsyn. Prepared by Sverdlov's diplomatic labours, a meeting between the antagonists took place in Trotsky's carriage. According to

[1] L. Trotsky, *Stalin*, p. 289.

Trotsky's version, Stalin somewhat meekly asked him not to treat the 'Tsaritsyn boys' too severely. Trotsky's answer was sharp and haughty: 'The fine boys will ruin the revolution which cannot wait for them to grow up.' Subsequently Voroshilov was transferred from Tsaritsyn to the Ukraine.

Stalin arrived in the capital just before the celebration of the first anniversary of the revolution. He wrote for *Pravda* a brief and dry summary of last year's events:

From beginning to end [he stated], the insurrection was inspired by the Central Committee of the party, with Comrade Lenin at its head. Lenin at that time lived in Petersburg on the Vyborg side in a secret apartment. On 24 October, in the evening, he was called out to Smolny to assume general charge of the movement. All practical work in connexion with the organization of the uprising was done under the immediate direction of Comrade Trotsky, the President of the Petersburg Soviet. It can be stated with certainty that the party is indebted primarily and principally to Comrade Trotsky for the rapid going over of the garrison to the side of the Soviet and the efficient manner in which the work of the Military Revolutionary Committee was organized.[1]

Thirty years after it was written, Stalin's appreciation of Trotsky's role in the revolution sounds fantastically eulogistic. It was cut out by the author from his *Collected Works* in 1947. In the last twenty years no Soviet historian or writer has dared to quote it—so dangerously heretical have Stalin's own words become. But at the time they were written they sounded like anything but a eulogy. Their purpose was subtly to belittle Trotsky's role and to portray him, not quite in accordance with the facts, as a mere executor—a very able one, to be sure—of Lenin's idea. This was the extreme limit to which Stalin could then go in venting his grudge; he could hurt his rival only with a thorn concealed in a bouquet.

.   .   .   .

A few days after the first anniversary of the Russian revolution, Germany and Austria were aflame with their own revolutions. The First World War came to an end. The thrones of the Hohenzollerns and the Habsburgs lay in the dust. Councils

---

[1] This appreciation of Trotsky's role has been omitted in Stalin's *Sochinenya*, vol. iv, p. 154, published in 1947. It is quoted from the official English edition of his *October Revolution*, p. 30.

of Workers' and Soldiers' Deputies—Soviets—sprang into existence in Berlin and Munich, Warsaw and Riga. Moderate Socialists took the reins of power in the defeated countries. The Bolsheviks were confident that the process would end in a European, if not a world-wide, 'October'; that the Governments of the moderate Socialists would soon, very soon, be overthrown by the Socialists of the extreme left, just as Kerensky had been overthrown in Russia. Within weeks or months at the most the Russian revolution would be freed from isolation; and the foundations would be laid for international socialist society. The advanced, industrialized, and civilized countries of the west would lead the majestic movement and tow 'backward, semi-Asiatic Russia' towards a higher civilization. Intoxicated with illusion, the Bolshevik leaders, all of them, watched in hopeful suspense the course of events in the west. Those who, like Lenin, Trotsky, Kamenev, Lunacharsky, Zinoviev, Kollontai, Bukharin, and others, had spent many years as émigrés in western Europe, read the auguries and interpreted them to their own people. Russia's eyes were fixed on the west.

In the nineteenth century one of the great divides in Russia's spiritual and political life was that between the Westerners and the Slavophils, between those who strove to europeanize Russia and those who believed in Russia's peculiar mission to develop a civilization of her own, either independent from or distinctly opposed to that of western Europe. Russian Marxism was originally an offshoot of the 'Western' trend. In Bolshevism the two strands merged. As far back as 1913, on the occasion of the Chinese Republican Revolution, Lenin wrote about 'Backward Europe and Progressive Asia'.[1] Viewing the urge for revolution and socialism as the most progressive feature of modern civilization he described the west, entangled in imperialism and conservatism, as 'backward' and the east, stirring with social change, as 'advanced'. In so far as he applied this criterion, he may be said to have represented the 'eastern' trend, although his east, unlike that of the Slavophils, was not confined to Russia or the Slav peoples—it included the coloured races, the awakening colonial peoples. But Lenin remained a 'Westerner' in several senses. Progress to him meant the acceptance by the east of Marxism, the offspring of German

[1] Lenin, *Sochinenya*, vol. xix, pp. 77-8.

philosophy, English political economy, and French socialism. Moreover, he did not think that the east by itself could achieve final emancipation. The west, because of its industrialization and higher organization was, after it had done away with imperialist capitalism, predestined to lead the east. According to circumstances, the one or the other strand in his thought came to the fore. Now when the dawn of revolution seemed to rise over Europe, the 'western' element in Leninism assumed the greater weight. It was in those days that the Communist International, based, apart from the Bolsheviks, on the extreme left wing of western European socialism, was hastily formed.

How did Stalin react to the new situation? He had little to say about the events in the west. This was the domain of the émigré leaders who spoke from their knowledge of the west and from their long study of its problems. Stalin's contribution to the debate consisted, significantly, of two articles, one of which bore the title 'Do not forget the East', and the other—'Ex Oriente Lux'.[1] The man who had grown up among Russian, Tartar, and Persian oil workers and Georgian peasants on the borderline between Europe and Asia intimately identified himself with the 'eastern' strand in Bolshevism. The fact is the more remarkable because the two strands were not at all distinct; and none of the leaders, certainly not Stalin, was then aware of any potential disharmony between them. Any suggestion of a rationalized preference on the part of Stalin for the eastern element in the Bolshevik outlook at that stage would fly in the face of historical facts. His predilections were purely instinctive. In his view, too, it was 'primarily there, in the west, that the chains of imperialism that have been forged in Europe and are strangling the whole world, will be broken'.[2] But the remark on the importance of the west for the revolution, though sweeping in form, was merely incidental. It was meant to give point to his warning: Do not forget the east. There was a touch of political jealousy for the attention which the west was now monopolizing in his words: 'In such a moment the East with the hundreds of millions of peoples enslaved by imperialism, automatically fades from our view and is forgotten.' Speaking about a conference of Moslem Communists

[1] J. Stalin, *Sochinenya*, vol. iv, pp. 171–3, 177–82.
[2] Ibid., p. 171.

STALIN, LENIN, AND KALININ, 1919   E. N. A.

LENIN AND TROTSKY, 1920

STALIN, 1920

who were out to start propaganda in Persia, India, and China, he insisted: 'Once and for all you must learn the truth that he who wants the triumph of Socialism cannot afford to forget the East.' His other article, which dealt with the new upsurge of Bolshevism in the Ukraine, he wound up with the words: '*Ex Oriente lux*. The west with its imperialist cannibals has become the centre of darkness and slavery. The task is to destroy that centre to the joy and jubilation of the toilers of all countries.' This was the *cri de cœur* of the Baku committee-man installed in the Kremlin. In terms of Bolshevik strategy his insistence on the importance of the east was certainly legitimate; and his 'anti-western' tone was vague enough not to cause any objection. Nevertheless, the image of the revolutionary Socialist west was much dimmer in his mind than that of the west as the 'centre of darkness and slavery'. It would become even dimmer later on, during the Anglo-French intervention against the Bolsheviks, when Stalin wrongly dismissed the opposition to intervention inside Britain as a mere 'trick', designed, in fact, to further hostilities against Soviet Russia.[1] The 'trick' resulted in nothing less than the embargo placed by British dock workers on the shipment of munitions to Poland during the Soviet-Polish war in 1920.

It is interesting to compare Stalin's statements with, say, the Order of the Red Army and Navy—order no. 159—which was issued by Trotsky on 24 October 1919, during Yudenich's advance on Petersburg when the anti-British mood in Russia was at its strongest:

Red fighters, on all fronts you are meeting with the hostile artifices of the English. It is from English guns that the counter-revolutionary troops fire at you. It is munitions of English make that you have found at the camps of Shenkursk and Onega, on the southern and western fronts. The prisoners you take have English equipment on them. The women and children of Archangel and Astrakhan are murdered and mutilated by English airmen and English high explosives. English ships shell our coasts.

But even now, at the moment of the most bitter fight against England's hireling Yudenich, I call upon you: never forget that this is not the only England that exists. Apart from the England of profits, violence, bribery and bloodthirstiness, there exists the

[1] Ibid., p. 319.

England of labour, of spiritual power, of great ideals and international solidarity. It is the England of the Stock Exchange, the vile and honourless England, that fights against us. Toiling England, its people, is with us.[1]

How different were the tones and accents that mingled in the voice of Bolshevism in those days! For the time being the western accents heavily overlaid the oriental ones; but it was to the oriental ones that the future belonged.

．　．　．　．　．　．　．　．

The civil war reached its climax in 1919. This was the year of the most intensive intervention of the western powers. Early in the year the White troops of Kolchak again advanced from the east and captured Perm. No sooner had Kolchak been repulsed than Denikin started his offensive in the south, seized Kiev and Kursk and pressed on towards Moscow. Almost simultaneously, in May, Yudenich marched on Petersburg, hoping to capture the city with the help of a 'fifth column' in the command of its garrison. Stalin was sent to the former capital to take charge of its defence. He unmasked the conspirators, directed the military operations, and saved the city for the Soviets. In October Yudenich made another attempt at seizing Petersburg, an attempt which brought him right into its suburbs. This time Trotsky saved the city for the Soviets.

It was in October that the situation was most critical, because both Moscow and Petersburg seemed to be within the grasp of the White Guards. The White forces were backed to the hilt by the British and the French. Kolchak, who proclaimed himself dictator of Russia, was officially recognized by the Allied Supreme Council in Paris. Denikin was assisted by the Allied navies which had sailed into the Black Sea. French troops occupied Odessa. The British navy helped Yudenich in the Bay of Finland. Churchill in Great Britain and Clemenceau in France were the most determined protagonists of intervention. But neither the White generals—each of whom wished to reserve the role of Russia's saviour exclusively for himself—nor the western powers were able to concert their actions; and so the Bolsheviks disposed of their enemies one by one. In November 1919 the White armies were in disorderly retreat on

[1] Quoted from L. Trotsky, *Mein Leben*, p. 416.

all fronts. For the Revolution the civil war was virtually won. Its last act, the campaign against General Wrangel in the south, which followed the Russo-Polish war in 1920, was minor beside the previous campaigns. In November Red Moscow celebrated its triumph, awarding Trotsky and Stalin Orders of the Red Banner.

Throughout the civil war, and indeed until 1925, Trotsky remained at the head of the Red Army; and he was acclaimed as the father of victory. Stalin, though awarded the highest order, was no more popular by the end of the civil war than at its beginning. The many histories and memoirs written by participants hardly ever mentioned his name. But it would be wrong to base on this fact alone conclusions about the part he played. By the light of the secret military correspondence of those days—some small proportion of which Stalin has published and another small proportion Trotsky—his role looms much larger than it did in the writings published while Trotsky was in power, though not nearly as large as in the official histories of the Stalinist era.

About the strategic controversies of those days a whole literature has been written, designed mainly to promote the legends of various claimants to power. As is only natural, none of the leaders was infallible. Each of them had shown shrewd judgement on some occasions and committed gross mistakes on others. Trotsky's strategy against Kolchak was cautious to the point of timidity. When Kolchak's troops were demoralized by defeat he refused to pursue them across the Urals; and it was on the insistence of Stalin, among others, that the Red Army resumed the pursuit and cleared most of Asiatic Russia of the White Guards. On the other hand, Trotsky's plan for the campaign against Denikin in the south was, as events proved, brilliant in all respects. He proposed an offensive based on the mining area of the Donetz, the population of which was friendly towards the Red Army. The General Staff, however, supported by Lenin and Stalin, preferred to fight their campaign in the Don area inhabited by counter-revolutionary Cossacks. As during the October upheaval so now Trotsky had the sharper eye for the interplay of the social and the military factors in civil war. His plan was disregarded by his colleagues until Denikin's advance to Orel compelled them to change their mind. Again, when Yudenich was advancing on Petersburg for the second time, Lenin overrated the strength of the attacker and, to ensure that the defence of Moscow was adequate, pleaded for the surrender of Petersburg. Both Trotsky and Stalin stubbornly opposed this proposal and the event proved them right. These disputes did not reflect opposed political or strategic principles; they were caused by differences of views on what was militarily expedient.

Stalin's secret messages and reports from the various fronts show him in a different light from the one given by his public speeches and journalistic writings. The contrast between the styles of his public and his confidential statements is remarkable. It was on the platform and in the newspaper that his weaknesses were most apparent. His language betrays an astonishing barrenness of imagination, rare even among politicians. It was dull, dry, colourless—'soporific', as Trotsky called it. His arguments were unbearably repetitive, sprawling, and bristling with illogicalities. His images and metaphors were as a rule wildly incongruous. Happily, they were few and far between: not more than perhaps a score of metaphors occurred in all his writings over nearly twenty years; and not many more were to occur in the next thirty. Once his mind had seized an image he chewed upon it and returned to it over and over again with a monotony that revealed the narrowness of his vision. Face to face with a mass audience he was incapable of striking a spark either in himself or in the audience. This was not merely a literary or oratorical failing. The man felt ill at ease under public scrutiny, with the result that in public his voice acquired an uncannily ventriloquist ring. There was a rigid artificiality in his manner and style, the artificiality of utterly ineffectual histrionics.

But what a different man emerges from his confidential service messages. Their style was most often clear and cutting, concise and precise. Here spoke the great administrator, free from the inhibitions that public appearance imposed upon him. Almost no trace of his wearisome repetitiveness, of his bizarre incongruities and miscarried metaphors. Here the sober investigator, the inspector of danger spots, reported on his findings in straight and business-like terms. One could almost see him at the job: he had just arrived at his destination and was casting a cool and disillusioned glance at the scene, at the weak joints of the military machine, at the confused array of commands, party committees, local Soviets, and so on. He formed his first opinion and reported it to Moscow. Now he began 'chasing and scolding' those around him, continuing the investigation, finding out new shortcomings or omissions either on the spot or in higher commands. Then he would form a small closely knit group of men on whom he felt that he could rely, promote these, dismiss others, court-martial still others, arrange for supplies, and again report to Moscow. In the tail of almost every message there was a sting for Trotsky.

This was roughly the pattern of his messages from Perm, Petersburg, Smolensk, Serpukhov, and other places, a summary of which would have its place in a history of the civil war rather than in his biography. Perhaps the most remarkable of his inspections was that of Perm in the beginning of 1919. He went there together with Felix Dzerzhinsky, the head of the newly formed political police, to investigate the causes of a recent *débâcle* in the Third Army.

In our view [their Report, written by Stalin, stated] the weakness lies not only in the Third Army but also: 1. in the General and Regional staffs which . . . sent . . . notoriously unreliable units to the front; 2. in the All-Russian Bureau of Political Commissars which sends children and not Commissars to the units formed in the rear; and 3. in the Revolutionary Military Council of the Republic which upset with its so-called directives and orders the administration of the fronts and the armies.[1]

The semi-White reserves sent from the centre . . . could not be of any real help to the Third Army. Yet during the retreat the weariness and exhaustion of the Third Army were such that whole groups of soldiers lay down on the snow and begged the commissars to shoot them: 'We have not enough strength to stand up, let alone march, we are worn out, finish with us, comrades.' We must put an end to waging a war without reserves. . . . Reserves will be forthcoming only if the old system of calling up . . ., favoured by the General Staff, is radically changed and the personnel of the General Staff itself renewed. [This was an attack on Trotsky's protégé, the Commander-in-Chief Vatzetis. Vatzetis was soon to be replaced by Stalin's protégé Kamenev, who, like his predecessor, had been a Tsarist staff officer.]

[1] J. Stalin, *Sochinenya*, vol. iv, p. 190.

Unreliable people sit in the [local] Soviets; the committees of poor peasants are in the hands of well-to-do peasants [kulaks]; party organizations are weak, unreliable, unconnected with the centre; party work is neglected; and the local leaders try to compensate the general weakness of the party and Soviet institutions by the intensified work of the Chekas [political police], that have become the sole representatives of Soviet power in this province. . . . The newspapers of the party and the Soviets at Perm and Vyatka work badly. . . . (You would find nothing in them, except empty phrases about "world social revolution"). . . . Yet, . . . out of 4,766 officials of Soviet institutions of the town of Vyatka, 4,467 held the same jobs in the district administration under Tsardom. . . .[1]

The numerous technical and political suggestions for reform culminated in a proposal that a special Commissariat be formed to control and supervise all the other branches of the administration. The proposal was soon to be accepted and Stalin was to be put in charge of the new Commissariat.

Lenin studied the messages with a discerning eye. He took the criticisms of Trotsky with a grain of salt. When Trotsky, annoyed at the charges, resigned, the Politbureau passed a unanimous motion solemnly entreating him to stay in office. (Stalin, who had obliquely asked for Trotsky's dismissal, also cast his vote for the motion.) Stalin's reputation as a great administrator, however, was enhanced by his numerous inspections. When, some time after his appointment to the Commissariat of the Workers' and Peasants' Inspectorate, a prominent party man criticized the accumulation of so many important jobs in Stalin's hands, Lenin replied: 'We must have someone to whom any national representative can appeal. . . . Where is such a man to be found? I do not think Preobrazhensky can point to anyone but Stalin. It is the same with the Workers' and Peasants' Inspectorate. The job is enormous. To cope with it there must be a man with authority at its head.'[2]

The campaigns against Denikin and Yudenich were followed by the Russo-Polish war, during which Stalin was political commissar on the southern sector of the front. In May 1920, the Polish army under the command of Marshal Pilsudski advanced into the Ukraine and seized Kiev. Pilsudski's victory was short-lived. His army operated under a decisive handicap:

[1] J. Stalin, *Sochinenya*, vol. iv, p. 208.
[2] Lenin, *Sochinenya*, vol. xxvii, pp. 263-4.

it was met with hostility by the Ukrainian peasantry, who suspected that the victory of the Poles would lead to the re-establishment of the domination of the Polish landed gentry over the Ukrainian country-side. In June the Poles evacuated Kiev, hotly pursued by Tukhachevsky in the north and Yegorov and Budienny in the south. In a lightning offensive the Red Army reached the River Bug, which roughly separates ethnographic Poland from the Ukraine. Should it cross the Bug, carry the offensive into purely Polish lands and try to seize Warsaw? This was the question debated in the Politbureau. Lenin urged a continuation of the offensive, while Trotsky was in favour of offering peace to the Poles. Stalin at first shared Trotsky's view, but then sided with Lenin.

The issues at stake were momentous. Lenin hoped that the entry of the Red Army into Poland would spur on the Polish working class to Communist revolution. His main interest, however, was not in Poland but in Germany, which at the time was in a state of revolutionary ferment. His objective was to effect a junction between the Russian and the German revolutions. He played with the idea that communism in the west, not yet strong enough to seize power by itself, might be decisively strengthened by the advance of the Red Army. He wanted 'to probe Europe with the bayonets of the Red Army',[1] an idea which strikingly conflicted with his own warnings about the inadmissibility of attempts at carrying revolution abroad on the points of bayonets. His attitude reflected his despair at the continued isolation of the Soviets; and it was an attempt to break out from it. Lenin was supported by Zinoviev and Kamenev, who, now as in 1917, saw little hope for communism in Russia without a revolution in the west. Underlying their policy was a gross under-estimation of the resistance which the Polish people, including the Polish working classes, enjoying the honeymoon of their national independence, were to put up to Soviet invasion.

A clearer view of the mood in Poland prompted both Trotsky and Stalin to oppose talk about a march on Warsaw. Even before the recapture of Kiev by the Reds, Stalin warned the party in *Pravda* that 'the hinterland of the Polish forces is . . . to Poland's advantage, very different from that of Kolchak

---

[1] Klara Zetkin, *Reminiscences of Lenin*, pp. 19–21.

and Denikin. . . . It is *nationally* uniform and coherent. . . . Its predominant attitude is . . . patriotic. . . . If the Polish forces were to operate in Poland it would undoubtedly be difficult to fight against them.'[1] He repeated the warning in much blunter terms after the beginning of the Russian offensive: 'I think that the bragging and the harmful complacency of some comrades are out of place: some of them are not content with the successes on the front but shout about a "march on Warsaw"; others, not satisfied with defending our Republic against hostile aggression, boastfully declare that they could make peace only with "Red Soviet Warsaw". I need not point out that this bragging and complacency conform neither with the policy of the Soviet Government, nor with the balance of forces on the front.'[2] After all these sober warnings, he cast his vote with the 'bragging and complacent' adherents of the offensive. The opponents of the march on Warsaw, Trotsky and the two Poles Dzerzhinsky and Radek (the famous Polish-German revolutionary pamphleteer who had joined the Bolsheviks) were defeated. As sometimes in the past, so now, Stalin was swayed by his master's view, this time against his own better judgement.

He returned to his headquarters on the southern front on 12 July, when the whole front was irresistibly moving forward. Within a few weeks Tukhachevsky's army was approaching the outskirts of Warsaw. But lines of communication were dangerously stretched, the men were tired, and reserves depleted. Pilsudski, assisted by the French General Weygand, began to mount a counter-offensive on Tukhachevsky's southern flank. The Soviet Supreme Command ordered the commanders of the southern army, Yegorov and Budienny, to strike northwards in the direction of Warsaw so as to paralyse Pilsudski's counter-blow. But the commanders of the southern army had aims of their own. They wanted to seize Lvov at the same time as Tukhachevsky would enter Warsaw. Just as at Tsaritsyn, Stalin disregarded the orders from the centre and encouraged Yegorov and Budienny to forge ahead for Lvov. Then the scales of the war suddenly swung back. The Poles won the famous battle on the Vistula. By the time Stalin, Yegorov, and Budienny had changed their minds and rushed to the succour of Tukhachevsky,

---

[1] J. Stalin, *Sochinenya*, vol. iv, p. 323.   [2] Ibid., p. 333.

it was too late. The Red Army was already in disorderly retreat from Warsaw.

Now followed the inevitable argument over the mistakes that contributed to the defeat. Trotsky and Tukhachevsky blamed the southern command for their delay in changing direction from Lvov to Warsaw. Stalin repeated his familiar charge that Trotsky and the General Staff had failed to build up strong reserves behind the fighting lines. The mutual criticisms were well justified, though the chief cause of the defeat lay not so much in the mistakes committed during the offensive as in the very decision to carry it deep into Poland.[1]

.   .   .   .

After the Polish war and a quick campaign against Baron Wrangel, whose forces were driven from the Crimea and pushed into the sea at the Perekop Isthmus, peace at last returned to Russia. Soviet power was now consolidated, the ruling party sat firmly in the saddle, and the leaders paraded their laurels. But the country was devastated, hungry, and sick.

Over and over again emergencies had driven the ruling party to act against its original intentions, to contradict and over-reach itself. The Bolsheviks had pledged themselves to abolish the police and the standing army. Instead the political police, 'the sword of the revolution', grew to become, as Stalin wrote from Perm, 'the sole representative of Soviet power' in many parts of the country. At first the Bolsheviks tried to display tolerance towards their opponents. At the congresses of Soviets and trade unions, Menshevik, Social Revolutionary, Syndicalist, and Anarchist spokesmen freely and severely criticized the Government. A restricted but still wide freedom of expression existed. The ruling party itself was continually alive with open controversy, in which ideas were vigorously thrashed out and no authority was spared. Its members were free to form them-

---

[1] Lenin admitted his error in his talks with Klara Zetkin, quoted above. Trotsky's viewpoint is found in *Mein Leben*, pp. 439–44, and in his *Stalin*, pp. 328–30. The Stalinist viewpoint is given by Voroshilov in *Lenin, Stalin i Krasnaya Armya*, p. 58. See also E. Wollenberg, *The Red Army*, pp. 121–48. Tukhachevsky expounded his own view in an interesting essay on 'Revolution from without', reprinted in his *Voina Klassov* (pp. 50–60) and in lectures on the 1920 war. A Polish translation of these appeared as an appendix in J. Pilsudski's *Rok 1920*, which, like W. Sikorski's *Nad Wisłą i Wkrą*, analyses the war from the official Polish viewpoint.

selves into separate groups and factions in order to promote their views inside the party. There was no clear-cut or stable line of division between the groups and factions that fluctuated with events and with the issues as they arose. The libertarian spirit of the revolution survived the climax of the civil war until well into the year 1920. It was in the latest phases of the struggle, when victory was virtually assured, that it began to vanish, that the parties of the opposition were denied legal existence, and that even the ruling party found its freedom hemmed in by restrictions and coercion.

The reason for this paradoxical state of affairs was that the gravest danger to the régime arose only after the last shots of the civil war had been fired. The revolution had crushed its enemies; but it had also lost most of its friends. To feed the starved towns and to secure provisions for its armies, the Government ruthlessly requisitioned food from the peasants. In the heat of the civil war orderly requisitioning degenerated only too easily into downright plunder. The peasants, who had secured the victory of Bolshevism in 1918 and 1919, turned against it in 1920; and they did so the more resolutely the more they became confident that the power of the landlords and the White generals had been broken. Peasant revolts spread over the country. Nor was the régime sure of support from the industrial workers who had been the most active supporters of Bolshevism. It was in their name that the dictatorship was exercised. Yet their ranks were terribly thinned. The most vigorous and idealistic among them had perished. The survivors were weary and driven to despair by hunger, unemployment, and monetary inflation that made the rouble completely worthless. Industrial activity was less than one-fifth of normal.[1] The steel-works produced only 5 per cent. of their pre-war output. In those factories and workshops which by some miracle kept going, the workers received their wages in kind and then had to waste their energy and time on bartering away their wages for food. The industrial working class became *déclassé*—it had been uprooted from the orderly industrial

---

[1] See Lenin's description of the economic situation in *The Essentials of Lenin*, vol. ii, pp. 710–24, and in Trotsky's *The Revolution Betrayed*, pp. 28–30. See also Rykov's speech in *Tretii Syezd Profsoyuzov*, pp. 79–86, and L. Kritsman, *Gervicheskii Period Velikoi Russkoi Revolutsii*, pp. 149–62.

environment and thrown into the all-pervading chaos of black markets. The 'proletarian dictatorship' had been more or less consolidated; but in the process the proletariat itself had vanished as a class-conscious element and an organizing factor.

In order to put industry back to work, the Government gradually embarked upon militarization of labour. At first the armies which enjoyed a respite from fighting were employed on essential work such as the felling of timber and the transportation of fuel and food. They were reorganized into 'Labour Armies'. This had been Trotsky's idea. Stalin, as the political commissar on the Ukrainian front, became Chairman of the Ukrainian Council of the Labour Army. Later on the method was used on a wider scale and in a sense reversed: not only were conscripted soldiers used for industrial work, but industrial workers were conscripted for labour like soldiers. In 1920 Trotsky pleaded for the militarization of labour before the annual Congress of the trade unions.[1] Despite Menshevik opposition, the trade unions consented to act as the agents of militarization. Thus the party that had promised to abolish the standing army was transforming the working population into an army.

During the civil war there was little else that the Government could do. But then the rulers made a virtue of the dire necessity. They asked the people to accept what they did, not as emergency measures but as true socialism, as the new style of life, the higher civilization of Soviet society. This was the main illusion of the so-called War Communism. While Lenin and Trotsky argued that the labour armies were an indispensable feature of socialism, Bukharin extolled the galloping inflation and devaluation of money as the foretaste of a true Communist economy without money.[2] These notions contrasted sharply with the deliberate slowness and caution with which the Bolsheviks had begun to nationalize large-scale industry after the revolution, when they were acutely aware of the complexity of the transition from Russia's semi-feudal condition to a Socialist economy. But in the atmosphere of civil war the ruling party seems to have exchanged its original realism for

---

[1] *Tretii Syezd Profsoyuzov*, pp. 87–95.
[2] This was the view expressed by Bukharin in his *Dengi v Epokhe Proletarskoi Diktatury*.

a stubborn and quixotic passion to achieve Utopia. As Karl Radek put it, the Bolsheviks hoped to force their way by a short cut, rifle in hand, into a perfect classless society. Above all, they acquired the habit of military command and persisted in that habit when they were confronted with an economic and social chaos out of which no military command could create order.

In March 1921 the restive mood of the country suddenly flared up in the rising of Kronstadt which coincided with the tenth Congress of the party. 'This was the flash', said Lenin, 'which lit up reality better than anything else.'[1] There was a bitter irony in the fact that the scene of the rising was Kronstadt, the Bolshevik stronghold of 1917. White Guards sympathizers, Anarchists, and even Bolsheviks fought side by side against the Red troops which, on Tukhachevsky's orders, rushed across the frozen surface of the Bay of Finland to suppress the rising. A measure of the alarm that the rising caused in the ruling party can be seen in the fact that on receiving the news about its outbreak the Congress of the party interrupted its debates and sent most of its delegates to participate in the storming of Kronstadt. At no critical moment of the civil war had there been any comparable panic.[2]

The insurgents of Kronstadt demanded an end to the dictatorship of the Bolshevik party and the restitution of genuine government by Soviets such as the Bolsheviks had promised to establish. They also demanded an end to economic and political oppression. Some of the leaders were Anarchists and left Communists; and their watchwords were borrowed from the slogans of the Bolsheviks in the early days of the revolution. Yet, in spite of its extreme left colouring, the rising stirred new hope in the ranks of the defeated counter-revolution. The dictatorship had reached a point, familiar from other revolutions, when, having defeated the adherents of the *ancien régime*, it drove Right and Left, conservatives and revolutionaries, into a common bitter opposition. For a while, the shadow of the tumbrils which amid the rejoicing of the Parisian plebs and aristocracy carried Robespierre to the guillotine must have appeared before Lenin's eyes.

---

[1] *The Essentials of Lenin*, vol. ii, p. 693.
[2] L. Trotsky, *The Revolution Betrayed*, p. 96.

The rising was defeated, and from it Lenin drew the following conclusion: '. . . we had advanced too far . . . we had not secured a sufficient base . . . the masses had sensed what we ourselves could not as yet consciously formulate . . . namely, that the direct transition to purely Socialist forms, to purely Socialist distribution, was beyond our strength, and that, unless we proved able to retreat and to confine ourselves to easier tasks, we would be threatened with disaster.'[1] The system of War Communism was scrapped and replaced by the so-called New Economic Policy. The N.E.P., as that policy came to be known, established a mixed economy. Large-scale industry and transport remained state-owned. Private enterprise was allowed in small and medium-sized industry and in trade. Foreign concerns were invited to restart business in Russia, even in large-scale industry. The requisitioning of food in the country-side was stopped; it was replaced by ordinary agricultural taxation, first in kind and then in money. Later on, the rouble was stabilized. The prime purpose of these sweeping reforms was to re-equip industry almost from scratch, to renew the exchange of manufactures for food and raw materials, in a word, to re-establish a functioning economy with the help of private capital. The state reserved for itself, apart from the ownership of large-scale industry, the over-all economic control.

In this scheme the Socialist and private 'sectors' of the national economy were to compete with each other on a commercial basis. It was hoped that in that competition the Socialist sector would gradually expand, while the private one would shrink. The eventual victory of socialism was, in Lenin's view, made probable, though not certain, by the superiority of large-scale industry over the small business and by the Government's mildly protectionist policy in favour of the Socialist sector. Essentially, however, the competition was to be peaceful and genuinely commercial. Socialism had to prove its worth in an economic contest.[2] Some crucial points in the programme were, naturally enough, left vague or open; and the controversy over these points was to become part of the struggle for power after Lenin's death. Stalin made no contribution to the original programme of the N.E.P., which was entirely Lenin's creation. Nor did its adoption give rise to any special differences of view.

[1] *The Essentials of Lenin*, vol. ii, pp. 813-14.   [2] Ibid., pp. 777-80.

The reform was carried out on the spur of the Kronstadt rising, without any preliminary debate.

Almost simultaneously another, less conspicuous, act was carried out in the political field, an act the implications of which were hardly clear to its authors. While the economic dictatorship was radically relaxed, the political dictatorship was tightened. During the later stages of the civil war the parties of the opposition, Mensheviks and Social Revolutionaries, were finally suppressed. The next step was to forbid the formation of any opposition groups inside the ruling party itself. Unknowingly, almost gropingly, Bolshevism now reached the threshold of what was later to be called the totalitarian state. It is necessary to stop here for a moment to contemplate once again the outlook of Bolshevism and to analyse the impulses and the motives of its leaders in order to obtain a clue both to the further evolution of the Soviets and to Stalin's subsequent ascendancy.

The ban on opposition groups inside the ruling party was passed by the tenth congress after a dramatic debate over the role of the trade unions in the Soviet system. Three or four viewpoints emerged in the great controversy which flared up on the eve of the Kronstadt rising. The Workers' Opposition, led by the former Commissar of Labour Shlyapnikov and Alexandra Kollontai, demanded the syndicalization of the state—the transfer of all economic power to the trade unions. Curiously enough, the chiefs of the trade unions, Tomsky and Rudzutak, were not among the leaders of the Workers' Opposition; for it expressed not the aspirations of the trade union leadership but the discontent of many rank-and-file Bolsheviks with the party's economic dictatorship. The opposition criticized the growing economic bureaucracy and its rough treatment of the rights and interests of the workers. The trade unions, so Shlyapnikov and Kollontai argued, as the direct representatives of the working class should be made responsible for planning and directing the national economy; and they should be built up into a counter-weight to the Politbureau and the Government, both dominated by the same personalities.[1] Another group of malcontents, the faction of 'Democratic

---

[1] *Desyatyi Syezd RKP*, pp. 41, 54-5. See also A. M. Kollontai, *The Workers' Opposition in Russia*, p. 31.

Centralism', took up some of the same points and charged the leadership of the party with fostering 'bureaucratic centralism'.[1] This group, whose main demand was for freedom inside the Soviets and the party, was in many respects the forerunner of later and much more influential oppositions.

The extreme of 'bureaucratic centralism' was represented at the congress by Trotsky and his followers, who demanded that the trade unions be integrated in the machinery of the Government. Trotsky pointed out that the trade unions had outlived their old functions. The state was a workers' state. By definition, its Government represented the general and common interest of the proletariat, as distinct from the sectional interests of various groups of workers, for which the trade unions had always stood. The sectional demands of the workers should not be opposed to their common and general interest. The trade unions should now co-operate with the Government in the implementation of its economic plans rather than defend individual workers or groups of workers against the workers' state. While Shlyapnikov and Kollontai wished the state and the party to surrender its economic powers to the trade unions, Trotsky asked the trade unions to give up their independence and capitulate to state and party.[2]

Lenin, supported by twelve members of the Central Committee including Stalin, tried to strike a balance. He repudiated Trotsky's and Bukharin's demand for the absorption of the trade unions by the state. The Soviets, he argued, were not, strictly speaking, a workers' state. They represented two classes: workers and peasants; and, in addition, they suffered from 'bureaucratic deformation'. At his dialectical best, he argued that the workers had to defend that state, but that they also had to defend themselves against that state through the trade unions, which consequently should enjoy a measure of independence *vis-à-vis* the Government. Moreover, the workers, too, should have some independence *vis-à-vis* the trade unions; and they should be free to join or not to join them.

The main fight, however, was not between Lenin and Trotsky. Both made common cause against the Workers' Opposition and the group of Democratic Centralists, for it was

---

[1] *Desyatyi Syezd RKP*, pp. 339–41.
[2] Ibid., pp. 192–4.

from that side that the authority of party and Government was most directly threatened. The seriousness of the threat was matched by the unusual bitterness of Lenin's attacks on the 'Anarcho-Syndicalists', as he labelled his opponents, describing even their views, let alone their deeds, as 'a direct political danger to the very existence of the proletarian dictatorship'.[1] This was the motive for the ban on oppositional groups inside the party. What seemed so dangerous to Lenin in the Workers' Opposition was not so much its specific views on the trade unions, as the underlying desire to assign to the party a more modest role than it had come to play. Lenin made a half-hearted attempt to soften the rigour of the ban: members of the party were to be enabled to air differences of opinion in a special Discussion Bulletin; and some of the chief spokesmen of the Opposition were re-elected to the Central Committee. But he himself undid the effect of his liberal gestures when he persuaded the Congress to state that 'the propaganda of [Anarcho-Syndicalist] ideas is incompatible with membership of the Russian Communist party'.[2] The congress empowered the Central Committee to expel from the party leaders elected by the congress, thereby cracking a whip over the spokesmen of the Workers' Opposition who had just been re-elected. The three able, educated, and independent secretaries of the party, Krestinsky, Serebriakov, and Preobrazhensky, who showed a leaning or a leniency towards the Opposition, were removed from office and replaced by 'reliable' people like Molotov and Yaroslavsky. The new secretaries were Stalin's close associates. Trotsky voted for the ban, without suspecting that one day the ban would become a death-trap for his own opposition.

The idea that a single party should rule the Soviets was not at all inherent in the Bolshevik programme. Still less so was the idea that only a single party should be allowed to exist. The proscription of the other parties, wrote Trotsky, was 'obviously in conflict with the spirit of Soviet democracy' and 'the leaders of Bolshevism regarded [it] not as a principle but as an episodic act of self-defence'.[3] For a party with such a record of free and uninhibited inner controversy, the ban on internal opposition

---

[1] *The Essentials of Lenin*, vol. ii, p. 685.
[2] Ibid., pp. 683–6.
[3] L. Trotsky, *The Revolution Betrayed*, p. 96.

groups was a most drastic departure from its own time-honoured custom. The party was now at loggerheads with its own nature, it contradicted itself while it was trying to assert itself.

Towards the end of the civil war Bolshevism was in conflict with the classes that had supported it. The discontent of peasants and workers was voiced by Mensheviks, Social Revolutionaries, and Anarchists, whose criticisms of the Bolsheviks were now as convincing and effective as they had been ineffective between 1917 and 1919. If the mechanism of Soviet democracy had been allowed to function, if the Soviets had been freely elected and free to elect the Government, they would almost certainly have swept the Bolsheviks out of office and returned to power the same parties on whom they had previously turned their backs. The Bolsheviks were determined to forestall this. To their mind the revolution was safe only if the party of the revolution was in power. All their recent experience confirmed them in that view. The revolution had conquered in spite of and against all the doubts, hesitations, and obstructiveness of the Mensheviks and the Social Revolutionaries. The moderate Socialists had not the pluck and the fibre to wage a civil war. Their return to power could, in the Bolshevik view, be no more than an episode ending in the return of the White Guards and the restoration of the *ancien régime*. True enough, from weariness and exhaustion, the masses were now inclined to back Mensheviks or Anarchists; but should the masses be allowed to jeopardize the whole work of the revolution? Should the Soviets be given back their freedom of action when they were almost certain to use it for their own undoing? This was a situation in which, in Dante's words, 'the people shouted: "Death to our life! Life to our death!"'; and most of the Bolshevik leaders refused to listen.

Yet, while the mouthpieces of popular discontent were removed or silenced, the discontent was not. Nor could the conflicting interests of the various classes, especially those of the peasants, be conjured out of existence by the repression of their spokesmen. Now the mind of the ruling party itself, of that lonely victor on the political battlefield, began to be invaded by moods of frustration and discontent. Now this and now that section of the party began to air familiar grievances and complaints. The cleavages existing in the country threatened to cleave the ruling party itself and it had now to be kept together with iron bands. The sensitiveness of the party had to be blunted, its sight dimmed, and its hearing dulled in order to make its mind immune from undesirable influences. The need for all this seemed to become even more urgent in connexion with the reforms of the N.E.P. Capitalist groups and interests were allowed new scope in the economic domain; but no party was left to represent them in the political field. It was only natural that they should seek channels of expression, and that they should seek them amid the only political party left in existence. Only absolute insulation could prevent the party from splitting into a number of hostile parties.

The task Bolshevism now set itself, however, was little different from squaring a circle. To save the revolution's conquests it had to suppress the spontaneous rhythm of the country's political life. But in doing so, the party was mutilating its own body and mind. From now on its members would fear to express opinions which might, on analysis, be found to reflect 'the pressure of alien classes'. Only the highest authority could decide which view was Bolshevik and proletarian and which was not. Matters of ideology became mysteriously elusive; and the Politbureau became the sole repository of revolutionary wisdom. Most leaders were gradually losing touch with the feeling of their followers since the traffic of ideas moved only one way—from the Politbureau downwards. The party was gradually to transform itself into a bureaucratic machine. It was true enough that concern for the revolution compelled Bolshevism to take the road chosen by the tenth congress; but it was also true that as it moved along that road Bolshevism was losing more and more of its original self. In order to save the revolution the party ceased to be a free association of independent, critically minded, and courageous revolutionaries. The bulk of it submitted to the ever more powerful party machine. It saw no other solution. Those who handled the levers of the machine and were most intimately associated with it, those to whose upbringing and temperament the new bureaucratic outlook was most congenial, automatically became the leaders of the new era. The administrator began to elbow out the ideologue, the bureaucrat and committee-man eliminated the idealist. Who could be favoured by this evolution and who could favour it more strongly than Stalin, the committee-man *par excellence*, the committee-man writ large?

This trend of events did not very rapidly become apparent. It developed gradually, in contradictory zigzags, always at odds with the inertia of earlier habits. Nor was the cleavage between administrator and idealist hard and fast. There was no lack of idealism in the administrators; and the ideologues at first willingly surrendered to the bureaucrats or even vied with them in fostering the new discipline. Thus, in the debate over the trade unions, the ideologue Trotsky so overreached himself in promoting bureaucratic aspirations that he shocked even the staunchest bureaucrats and incurred considerable unpopularity. In Lenin the different characters were almost perfectly blended. That is why he was so ideally suited to preside over the transition of his party from one stage to the other. For the time being his moral authority enforced a temporary and shaky compromise on the conflicting tendencies, a compromise that was bound to break down after his death. But even in his lifetime the weight of the bureaucratic caucus grew steadily, if imperceptibly, with every month that passed by; and so did Stalin's role inside the caucus.

CHAPTER VII

The General Secretary

Accumulation of power in Stalin's hands.—His role as Commissar of the Workers' and Peasants' Inspectorate.—His position inside the Politbureau.—Stalin appointed General Secretary of the Central Committee (3 April 1922).—The functions of the General Secretariat and of the Central Control Commission.—Stalin conducts the first 'purges'.—Lenin's illness.—Stalin's conflict with Georgian Bolsheviks opposed to dictation from Moscow.—Reassertion of 'Great Russian chauvinism'.—Stalin as author of the 1924 constitution.—His conflict with Lenin. —Lenin's will.—Lenin attacks Stalin as Commissar of the Workers' and Peasants' Inspectorate (January–February 1923).—Stalin's success at twelfth congress of the party.—The triumvirate: Zinoviev, Kamenev, and Stalin.—The controversy of 1923.—The struggle between the triumvirs and Trotsky.—The origin of the Leninist cult.—Lenin's death (21 January 1924).—Stalin's oath of fealty to Lenin. —Lenin's will, advising Stalin's dismissal, read at a session of the Central Committee (May 1924).—Zinoviev saves Stalin.—A profile of Stalin in the middle twenties.—His tactics vis-à-vis his opponents and partners.—The 'literary debate' in the autumn of 1924.—Stalin defends Zinoviev and Kamenev against Trotsky.— Stalin against 'socialism in a single country' (spring 1924).—He changes his mind in the autumn.—Trotsky's permanent revolution'.—The psychological background of 'socialism in one country'.

FEW important developments in history are so inconspicuous and seem so inconsequential to their contemporaries as did the amazing accumulation of power in the hands of Stalin, which took place while Lenin was still alive. Two years after the end of the civil war Russian society already lived under Stalin's virtual rule, without being aware of the ruler's name. More strangely still, he was voted and moved into all his positions of power by his rivals. There was to be an abundance of sombre drama in his later fight against these rivals. But the fight began only after he had firmly gripped all the levers of power and after his opponents, awakening to his role, had tried to move him from his dominant position. But then they found him immovable.

Three of the offices he held immediately after the civil war were of decisive importance: he was the Commissar of Nationalities, the Commissar of the Workers' and Peasants' Inspectorate, and a member of the Politbureau.

As Commissar of Nationalities he dealt with the affairs of nearly half the population of the Russian Soviet Federative Socialist Republic, as the state that had replaced old Russia was now called. Sixty-five millions of its 140 million inhabitants belonged to non-Russian nationalities. They represented every possible level of civilization, from the quasi-European way of life of the Ukrainians to the primitive, tribal existence of 25 million Turkmen-shepherds. Byelorussians, Kirghizians, Uzbeks, Azerbaidjans, Tartars, Armenians, Georgians, Tadzhiks, Buriats, and Yakuts, and a host of others for which there seem to be no names in the English tongue, found themselves in various intermediate phases of development between tribal community and modern society. Bolshevism, eager to attract all these nationalities and to wipe away their memories of Tsarist oppression, offered autonomy and self-government to all of them. Few such groups had any degree of 'national' consciousness. Fewer still had acquired the minimum of education indispensable for self-government. For the management of their affairs they were dependent on help from outside: that is, from the Commissariat of Nationalities. To most of them the doctrinal problems of communism were as remote as the theories of Einstein were to the Khans of Bokhara. In their lands the revolution meant the freeing of the primitive communities from the dominance of Emirs, Khans, and Mullahs, and a degree of europeanization.

Apart from the Ukraine, ruled by an independent-minded government under Christian Rakovsky, the Commissariat of Nationalities faced primarily Russia's vast, inert, oriental fringe. None of the leaders who had spent most of their adult life in western Europe was as fit to head that Commissariat as Stalin. His first-hand knowledge of the customs and habits of his clients was unsurpassed. So was his capacity to deal with the intricacies of their 'politics', in which blood feuds and oriental intrigue mixed with a genuine urge towards modern civilization. His attitude was just that mixture of patience, patriarchal firmness, and slyness that was needed. The Politbureau relied on this and refrained from interfering.

The Asiatic and semi-Asiatic periphery thus became his first undisputed domain. Immediately after the revolution, when the leadership of the nation belonged to the turbulent and radical cities of European Russia, in the first place to Petersburg and Moscow, the weight of that periphery was not much felt. With the ebb of revolution, the primitive provinces took their revenge. They reasserted themselves in a thousand ways, economic, political, and cultural. Their spiritual climate became, in a sense, decisive for the country's outlook. The fact that so much of that climate was oriental was of great significance. Stalin, who was so well suited to speak on behalf of Russian communism to the peoples of the oriental fringe, was also well suited to orientalize his party. During his years at the Commissariat he made and widened his contacts with the Bolshevik leaders of the borderlands, on whose devoted support he could count, and of whom so many were to be found in his entourage at the Kremlin later on.

He was appointed Commissar of the Workers' and Peasants' Inspectorate in 1919, on Zinoviev's proposal. The Rabkrin, as the Commissariat was called, was set up to control every branch of the administration, from top to bottom, with a view to eliminating the two major faults, inefficiency and corruption, which the Soviet civil service had inherited from its Tsarist predecessor. It was to act as the stern and enlightened auditor for the whole rickety and creaking governmental machine; to expose abuses of power and red tape; and to train an *élite* of reliable civil servants for every branch of the government. The Commissariat acted through teams of workers and peasants who were free at any time to enter the offices of any Commissariat and watch the work done there. In the end, teams of the Rabkrin regularly attended private departmental conferences and even the meetings of the Council of Commissars. This system was devised as a method of training an *élite* for the civil service; but as a result of it the Rabkrin was able to keep its eye on every wheel of the governmental machine.[1]

The whole bizarre scheme of inspection was one of Lenin's pet ideas. Exasperated by the inefficiency and dishonesty of the civil service, he sought to remedy them by extreme and ruthless 'control from below', and the Commissariat was to be the means. The choice of Stalin for the job gives a measure of Lenin's high confidence in him, for the Inspectorate was to be a sort of a super-government, itself free from every taint and blemish of officialdom.

---

[1] See Lenin, *Sochinenya*, vol. xxvii, pp. 14–20; *Letters of Lenin*, pp. 455–6, 474–5. Zinoviev's speeches in *8 Syezd RKP (b)*, pp. 162–3, 501, 225–6, and 290–1; and *Kratkii Otchet Narkom. R.K.I.*

Lenin's cure proved as bad as the disease. The faults of the civil service, as Lenin himself frequently pointed out, reflected the country's appalling lack of education, its material and spiritual misery, which could be cured only gradually, over the lifetime of at least a generation. The Rabkrin would have had to be a commissariat of angels in order to rise, let alone raise others, above the dark valley of Russian bureaucracy. With his characteristic belief in the inherent virtues of the working classes, Lenin appealed to the workers against his own bureaucracy. The mill of officialdom, however, turned the workers themselves into bureaucrats. The Commissariat of the Inspectorate, as Lenin was to discover later on, became an additional source of muddle, corruption, and bureaucratic intrigue. In the end it became an unofficial but meddlesome police in charge of the civil service. But let us not run ahead of our story. Suffice it to say here that, as the head of the Inspectorate, Stalin came to control the whole machinery of government, its working and personnel, more closely than any other commissar.

His next position of vantage was in the Politbureau. Throughout the civil war, the Politbureau consisted of five men only: Lenin, Trotsky, Stalin, Kamenev, and Bukharin. Ever since the break between Bolsheviks and Social Revolutionaries, this had been the real government of the country. Lenin was the recognized leader of both government and party. Trotsky was responsible for the conduct of the civil war. Kamenev acted as Lenin's deputy in various capacities. Bukharin was in charge of press and propaganda. The day-to-day management of the party belonged to Stalin. The Politbureau discussed high policy. Another body, which was, like the Politbureau, elected by the Central Committee, the Organization Bureau (Orgbureau), was in charge of the party's personnel, which it was free to call up, direct to work, and distribute throughout the army and the civil service according to the demands of the civil war. From the beginning of 1919 Stalin was the only permanent liaison officer between the Politbureau and the Orgbureau. He ensured the unity of policy and organization; that is, he marshalled the forces of the party according to the Politbureau's directives. Like none of his colleagues, he was immersed in the party's daily drudgery and in all its kitchen cabals.

At this stage his power was already formidable. Still more was to accrue to him from his appointment, on 3 April 1922, to the post of General Secretary of the Central Committee. The eleventh congress of the party had just elected a new and enlarged Central Committee and again modified the statutes. The leading bodies of the party were now top-heavy; and a new office, that of the General Secretary, was created, which was to co-ordinate the work of their many growing and overlapping branches. It was on that occasion, Trotsky alleges, that Lenin aired, in the inner circle of his associates, his misgivings about Stalin's candidature: 'This cook can only serve peppery dishes.'[1] But his doubts were, at any rate, not grave; and he himself in the end sponsored the candidature of the 'cook'. Molotov and Kuibyshev were appointed Stalin's assistants, the former having already been one of the secretaries of the party. The appointment was reported in the Russian press without any ado, as a minor event in the inner life of the party.

Soon afterwards a latent dualism of authority began to develop at the very top of the party. The seven men who now formed the Politbureau (in addition to the previous five, Zinoviev and Tomsky had recently been elected) represented, as it were, the brain and the spirit of Bolshevism. In the offices of the General Secretariat resided the more material power of management and direction. In name the General Secretariat was subordinate to the illustrious and exalted Politbureau. But the dependence of the Politbureau on the Secretariat became so great that without that prop the Politbureau looked more and more like a body awkwardly suspended in a void. The Secretariat prepared the agenda for each session of the Politbureau. It supplied the documentation on every point under debate. It transmitted the Politbureau's decisions to the lower grades. It was in daily contact with the many thousands of party functionaries in the capital and the provinces. It was responsible for their appointments, promotions, and demotions. It could, up to a point, prejudice the views of the Politbureau on any issue before it came up for debate. It could twist the practical execution of the Politbureau's decisions, according to the tastes of the General Secretary. Similar bodies exist in any governmental machinery but rarely acquire independent authority.

[1] L. Trotsky, *Mein Leben*, p. 450.

What usually prevents them from transgressing their terms of reference is some diffusion of power through the whole system of government, effective control over them, and, sometimes, the integrity of officials. The over-centralization of power in the Bolshevik leadership, the lack of effective control, and, last but not least, the personal ambitions of the General Secretary, all made for the extraordinary weight that the General Secretariat began to carry barely a few months after it had been set up.

The picture would be incomplete without mention of another institution, the Central Control Commission, that came to loom large in Bolshevik affairs. Its role *vis-à-vis* the party was analogous to that of the Commissariat of the Inspectorate *vis-à-vis* the governmental machine: it audited party morals. It was formed at the tenth congress, in 1921, on the demand of the Workers' Opposition, with which the congress had otherwise dealt so harshly. It was in charge of the so-called purges. These, too, were initiated by the tenth congress, on the demand of the Opposition. They were intended to cleanse the party periodically of careerists, who had climbed the band-wagon in great numbers, of Communists who had acquired a taste for bourgeois life, and commissars whose heads had been turned by power. Lenin adopted the idea and intended to use it in order to stop his followers departing from the party's puritanic standards. But he also turned one edge of the purges against 'anarcho-syndicalists', waverers, doubters, and dissidents, against the real initiators of the new practice.

The procedure of the purges was at first very different from what it became in later years. The purges were no concern of the judiciary. They were conducted by the party's local control commissions before an open citizens' forum, to which Bolsheviks and non-Bolsheviks had free access. The conduct of every member of the party, from the most influential to the humblest, was submitted to stern public scrutiny. Any man or woman from the audience could come forward as a witness. The Bolshevik whose record was found to be unsatisfactory was rebuked or, in extreme cases, expelled from the party. The Control Commission could impose no other penalties than these.

The original motive behind the purges was almost quixotic. It was to enable the people to crack periodically a whip over their rulers. But, since the ruling party was convinced that in all essentials of policy it could not really submit to popular control, these new devices for reviving popular control were *a priori* irrelevant and could not but prove ineffective. They illustrated the party's already familiar dilemma: its growing divorce from the people and its anxiety to preserve its popular character; the dilemma that underlay Lenin's pathetic experiments with his party in the last two years of his political activity. The purges were to serve as a substitute for real elections; they were to remove corrupted members, without removing the party, from power.[1]

The Central Control Commission in Moscow soon became the supreme court of appeal for the victims of the purges all over the country. Originally, it was to be independent from the Central Committee and the Politbureau. Later it was put on an almost equal footing with the Central Committee; and the two bodies regularly held joint sessions. The General Secretariat was the co-ordinating link between them. Thus, unofficially, Stalin became the chief conductor of the purges.

Lenin, Kamenev, Zinoviev, and, to a lesser extent, Trotsky, were Stalin's sponsors to all the offices he held. His jobs were of the kind which could scarcely attract the bright intellectuals of the Politbureau. All their brilliance in matters of doctrine, all their powers of political analysis would have found little application either at the Workers' and Peasants' Inspectorate or at the General Secretariat. What was needed there was an enormous capacity for hard and uninspiring toil and a patient and sustained interest in every detail of organization. None of his colleagues grudged Stalin his assignments. As long as Lenin kept the reins of government they looked upon him merely as Lenin's assistant; and all of them readily accepted Lenin's leadership. Neither they nor Lenin noticed in time the subtle change by which Stalin was gradually passing from the role of assistant to that of coadjutor.

. . . .

Less than two months after Stalin's appointment to the post

[1] The purges provided a good cover for all sorts of private vendettas. In May 1922, Lenin wrote in a letter to Stalin: '. . . the purging of the party revealed the prevalence, in the majority of local investigation committees, of personal spite and malice. . . . This fact is incontrovertible and rather significant.' In the same letter Lenin complained about the lack of partymen with 'an adequate legal education . . . capable of resisting all purely local influences'. See *The Essentials of Lenin*, vol. ii, p. 809.

of General Secretary, the reins of government slipped from Lenin's hands. By the end of May 1922, he suffered his first stroke of arteriosclerotic paralysis. Almost speechless, he was taken out of the Kremlin to the country-side, near Moscow. Not until the middle of the autumn did he recover sufficiently to return to office; and then his activity was very short. At the end of the autumn a second stroke put him out of action; and at the end of the winter, in March 1923, a third stroke removed him finally from the political scene, though his body still wrestled with death until 21 January 1924.

The impact of Lenin's illness on the Bolshevik leadership can hardly be exaggerated. The whole constellation ceased, almost at once, to shine with the reflected light of its master mind or to move in the familiar orbits. Lenin's disciples and satellites (only Trotsky belonged to neither of these categories) began to feel for their own, independent ways. Gradually they were shedding those characteristics of theirs that were merely imitative, their second, and better, nature. The negative side of Lenin's overwhelming and constant influence on his followers now became strikingly apparent. Just how overwhelming it had been can be seen from the circumstance, attested by Trotsky, that during the years of their apprenticeship with their leader, Zinoviev and Kamenev had acquired even Lenin's handwriting. They were now to go on using his handwriting without the inspiration of his ideas.

Stalin was in a sense less dependent on Lenin than were his colleagues; his intellectual needs were more limited than theirs. He was interested in the practical use of the Leninist gadgets, not in the Leninist laboratory of thought. His own behaviour was now dictated by the moods, needs, and pressures of the vast political machine that he had come to control. His political philosophy boiled down to securing the dominance of that machine by the handiest and most convenient means. In an avowedly dictatorial régime, repression often is the handiest and most convenient method of action. The Politbureau may have been thrown into disarray by Lenin's disappearance; the General Secretariat was not. On the contrary, since it had no longer to account for what it did to the vigilant and astute supervisor, it acted with greater firmness and self-confidence. The same was true of the Workers' and Peasants' Inspectorate.

Both the Secretariat and the Inspectorate drew upon themselves criticisms from Trotsky, who proposed the complete disbandment of the latter.[1] But his proposal merely irritated the members of the Politbureau—the institution had, anyhow, had Lenin's blessing. Trotsky's criticisms of the Secretariat were no more effective. The General Secretary knew how to justify each act of repression against malcontent Bolsheviks in the light of the party statutes as they had, on Lenin's initiative and with Trotsky's support, been amended by the tenth and eleventh congresses. He was careful to explain every step he made as an inevitable consequence of decisions previously adopted by common consent. He packed the offices with his friends, henchmen, and followers, the men of Baku and Tsaritsyn. Dismissed malcontents complained to the Politbureau, where Trotsky took up their cases. In reply, Stalin referred to the commonly agreed division of responsibilities: the Politbureau was to pass decisions on matters of high policy; the General Secretariat and the Orgbureau were in charge of the party's personnel. The Politbureau was only bored with Trotsky's carping criticisms.

The gravest single charge was laid against Stalin in connexion with his doings in his native country, Georgia. The not too edifying antecedents of this conflict must be briefly told here. Until February 1921 Georgia was ruled by a Menshevik Government, though the rest of the Caucasus had gradually come under Soviet control. Moscow somehow put up with the Menshevik régime at Tiflis, though the fact that Jordania and Ramishvili, his old opponents of the days of Messame Dassy, ruled Tiflis could not but cause irritation to Stalin. The Politbureau bided its time, confident that Menshevik Georgia would not hold out long in a sovietized Caucasus, on which it was dependent for its bread and fuel. The popularity of the Menshevik Government began, in fact, to wane. But Stalin's patience waned even more rapidly. In February 1921 detachments of the Second Red Army invaded Georgia from the northern Caucasus and forced the Menshevik Government to flight.

True enough, the nationalism of the Georgian Mensheviks was not very genuine. Neither under the Tsar nor under Kerensky did they ever claim independence for their country— a degree of self-rule, within federal Russia, was the most they

[1] L. Trotsky, *Stalin*, pp. 346-7.

aspired to. Under Kerensky they were bitterly opposed to the separation of any borderland, be it Finland or Georgia, from Russia. Their newfangled patriotism was merely a form of their opposition to Bolshevism. Nevertheless, the invasion of the Red Army was resented by the Georgian highlanders. Stalin, who, three years before, had given the Finns the pledge: 'No tutelage, no control from above over the Finnish people!', now issued the marching orders for the invasion of Georgia. His old friend Sergo Ordjonikidze was the political commissar with the invading army. Preparations for the campaign were up to the last moment kept secret from the Commissar of War; but at the last moment the move was backed by Lenin and the Politbureau, who had been told that a Communist rising had broken out at Tiflis, and that the Red Army would merely give the scales a final tilt in favour of the Reds, whose assured success might be more costly if they were left to fight it out alone. A Communist revolt had in fact broken out at Tiflis; but its popular backing was not wide enough to secure its victory.[1]

Stalin had hardly fought his vendetta against his Menshevik compatriots to an end when he involved himself in a quarrel with the Bolsheviks of Tiflis. A few months after the invasion, he went to Tiflis to direct the work of the Caucasian committee of the party. In the autumn of 1921 he sponsored, with Lenin's support, the idea of a Caucasian Federation of Soviet Republics.[2] But the idea evoked little enthusiasm in Tiflis. Georgian Bolsheviks preferred their country to remain a truly autonomous Soviet Republic, loosely associated with a wide All-Russian Federation; they were unwilling to resign sovereignty in favour of a much closer, regional, Caucasian organization.

It is difficult to establish the rights and the wrongs of the dispute. The Caucasus was riddled with blood feuds between Georgians, Armenians, and Tartars, all in varying degrees opposed to the Russians. Cossacks, Chechens, Ossetians, and other minor tribes of highlanders were engaged in a merciless mutual massacre, which Stalin had tried to stop by their transfer and resettlement, a method which a quarter of a century later he was to apply, on a gigantic scale, to Ukrainians, Poles, Germans, and other nationalities.[3] It may well be that the Georgian

[1] L. Trotsky, *Stalin*, p. 267.   [2] J. Stalin, *Sochinenya*, vol. v, p. 428.
[3] Ibid., vol. iv, pp. 399–401.

Bolshevik leaders who opposed the Caucasian federation, Budu Mdivani and Philip Makharadze, were themselves, as Stalin claimed, infected by 'local nationalism'. But it is more probable that they felt that a Caucasian federation would not work in the heated atmosphere of blood feuds. They may also have wanted to preserve more than a semblance of their independence, especially because during the three years of Menshevik rule the Georgians' old, half-extinct nostalgia after their own statehood had again become a live and popular sentiment. That sentiment had been hurt by the invasion. It was hurt again by dictation from the Commissariat of Nationalities in Moscow and the activities of Russian agents of the political police, who had been dispatched to Tiflis to 'mop up' the local Mensheviks. Some of the Georgian Bolsheviks protested against the persecution of the Mensheviks on whom they still looked as on old comrades, in spite of all subsequent differences and all the persecution they themselves had suffered under Menshevik rule.

All these new policies roused the old Georgian fear of Russian domination. It mattered little that their inspirer was himself a Georgian; and that he addressed the crowds of Tiflis in their native tongue. He spoke with the voice of Moscow. The circumstance that the old Djugashvili was still alive in the dignitary of the Kremlin made matters even worse. Any other envoy of the central government might have viewed local disputes and squabbles with reserve and detachment. Stalin was soon up to the eyes in local passions and—memories of his youth. All over again he was the frustrated radical who had once been nearly driven from Tiflis by the petty-bourgeois majority of Messame Dassy. While he was thus, as Djugashvili, settling out-dated accounts a few hundred yards away from the old seminary, he also claimed for himself the obeisance due to Stalin. This he did not get.

On 6 July 1921 he addressed a meeting of party members at Tiflis,[1] at which he attacked his opponents. He described the economic plight which Georgia would be in as an 'isolated' state and the advantages of co-operation with the rest of the Caucasus. Georgia, he said, would get oil from Baku without payment. The Caucasian republics would receive a loan of several million roubles in gold from Russia. Holding out these gifts,

[1] J. Stalin, *Sochinenya*, vol. v, pp. 88–112.

he went on to attack 'local nationalism'. He was shocked, he said, by the local chauvinisms that had so wildly grown up in the Caucasus; and he contrasted these with a somewhat highly coloured picture of the 'full brotherly solidarity' in which the Caucasian working classes had lived in his Caucasian days. The next task of Georgian Communists was 'ruthless struggle against local nationalism'. They had to burn out 'the nationalist survivals with hot iron', and 'smash the hydra of nationalism'. The party must purge its ranks of local patriots. They should not be afraid of purges. The Russian mother party had only 700,000 members; it could easily have had seven million, if it had been concerned with numbers and not quality. Because of the quality of its membership, the Russian party had been able to make the revolution and to withstand all the onslaughts of world imperialism. Here then was a model worthy of imitation.

From a purely local, Georgian viewpoint, Stalin's strictures on the 'nationalists', as far as they went, were probably justified and sound. They would have sounded unexceptionable if they had come from one of the local leaders. But as Stalin spoke with the voice of Moscow, there was inevitably an undertone of 'Great Russian chauvinism' in what he said. In Tsarist days the peoples of the borderlands had had all their vital affairs settled by the central Russian Government. They now wondered whether the revolution had really brought any change in this respect. The Georgians had more ground than anybody else to be sceptical, if not cynical. Stalin's present sermons on their vicious self-centredness merely confirmed them in their cynicism. It was as if a member of a British Cabinet censured a Dublin audience, with long memories of British imperialism, on the 'hydra' of Irish nationalism. Even if that minister had been of Irish extraction, even if he had spoken on behalf of a revolutionary British government that had proclaimed the complete dissolution of the Empire, his words would still have jarred, especially if he had uttered them shortly after a new English invasion. This was roughly the effect of Stalin's utterances at Tiflis.

Unperturbed by the lack of response, Stalin then instructed Ordjonikidze to purge the party of the opponents of federation, the local patriots, and those who had a soft spot for the Mensheviks. No savage repressions were needed. It was enough to expel from the party some of the 'local patriots' and to pack conferences with those willing to accept Ordjonikidze's guidance. Those who hesitated or merely doubted, toed the line when they were told that the Politbureau had unanimously endorsed the idea of the Caucasian federation. This was indeed true.[1] In the end the leaders of the Bolshevik opposition, Mdivani and Makharadze, found themselves regularly outvoted at every conference and meeting. Outvoted, they went on to protest against the 'Great Russian chauvinism' of the Commissar of Nationalities.

The evolution which had brought the former Georgian Socialist into a position where he could be associated with 'Great Russian chauvinism' was remarkable. It was more so than either the process by which the Corsican Bonaparte became the founder of a French Empire or that by which the Austrian Hitler became the most aggressive leader of German nationalism. The Corsicans had had few grievances against the French; Napoleon's father had even been an adherent of the 'French party' in Corsica. Pan-Germanism had always been a powerful influence in Austria, kept in check only by the decaying dynastic interest of the Habsburgs. In Georgia there was not, and there could not have been, even a trace of any pan-Russian sentiment. Grievances against Russia rankled strongly, though not nearly as strongly as, say, in Poland. It was only through Bolshevism that Stalin became a Russian by adoption; and Bolshevism had attracted men like himself by its internationalism, especially by its sensitive attitude towards the oppressed nationalities. Though the charges of Russian nationalism have since been laid against Stalin more than once, he was not, either then or even in later days, prompted by any of the ordinary emotions and prejudices that go with nationalism. What he represented was merely the principle of centralization, common to all modern revolutions. To that principle

[1] Lenin accepted the idea on its merits, but in an appeal to his Caucasian followers he urged them 'to understand the necessity of not copying our tactics, but of thoughtfully varying them in accordance with the difference in the concrete conditions'. 'More mildness, caution and readiness to make concessions to the petty bourgeoisie, to the intelligentsia, and particularly to the peasantry.' 'Apply in your republics not the letter but the spirit, the sense, the lessons of the experience of 1917–21.' *The Essentials of Lenin*, vol. ii, pp. 698–9.

he gave an exaggerated and brutal expression. But whatever his motives, the practical effects of his doings were the same as if he had acted from Russian chauvinism.

There is evidence to show that now and then this paradoxical situation gave him a queer, not unpleasant sensation. Who has not met naturalized Englishmen, whose self-confidence is heightened when they can say 'We English' or, better still, 'We, the British Empire . . .'? It was in some such vein that Stalin, in one of his addresses to Moslem Communists, stated that nationalist sentiments among the Russians had never been a serious matter: 'Having been a ruling nation, the Russians generally, and the Russian Communists in particular, have not known any racial oppression and have, generally speaking, not had to deal with nationalist tendencies in their own milieu, apart from some inclinations towards "great power chauvinism"; they have therefore not had to overcome such tendencies.'[1] This was a startling assertion. It must have shocked many Bolsheviks when it appeared in *Pravda*; and Stalin never again repeated it. That in modern times the Russians did not know the kind of touchy nationalism which is bred by alien oppression is true enough. Theirs had been the oppressors' nationalism, callous, savage, and much more dangerous. Lenin warned his followers about its dangers, urging them to behave patiently and indulgently even towards the exaggerated pretensions of formerly oppressed peoples, because the memories of Tsarist rule would be lived down only very slowly. Great Russian chauvinism was the main evil to be fought by the Russian Communists, while the duty of their comrades in the borderlands was to counteract the manifestations of ebullient local patriotism. It was not easy to reconcile Lenin's generous injunctions with the demands of that centralized government for which he also stood. His policies tended to clash with one another; and only a very subtle and judicious administrator might have kept balance between them. Stalin obviously erred in the direction of over-centralization.

In his error, if this be the right word here, he reflected the drift of ideas, moods, and aspirations in the Russian civil service, as it had been recast and remoulded after the revolution. The drift was towards ever more centralization in government and even

[1] J. Stalin, *Sochinenya*, vol. v, p. 2.

towards the reconstitution of a 'great and indivisible' Russia. Communists stood for centralization because of its economic and administrative advantages. But the Communists were, in Lenin's words, merely 'drops in the ocean'.[1] They had carried out 'a great, universal agrarian revolution . . . with an audacity unexampled in any other country, and at the same time the imagination was lacking to work out a tenth-rate reform in office routine'.[2] The revolution could save itself from all-pervading chaos only by re-enrolling the old Tsarist bureaucracy, which, incompetent as it was, beat the ex-revolutionaries at administrative routine. After the promulgation of the N.E.P., Conservatives and Nationalists from the professional classes offered their services to the new rulers. They were received with open arms. Even among the White émigrés, the hope that Mother Russia was coming back into her own was very strong. It was rationalized by Professor Ustrialov, an ex-member of Kolchak's government, into a political programme. Ustrialov urged his followers to reconcile themselves with the Soviet régime and to work, inside it, for its gradual evolution, through the N.E.P., towards capitalism and nationalism. In the early twenties the old civil service already formed a very solid element of the new one.[3] It was especially strong in the higher grades, where experts were badly needed. Relations between the Communists and the ex-Tsarist officials were uneasy; the Communists regarded their 'fellow-travellers' with a mixture of suspicion and respect. The 'fellow-travellers' tutored the Bolsheviks with a feeling in which fear or contempt mingled with patriotic dutifulness. For all the conflict between them, which at times was brutal, they exercised a constant and organic influence upon one another.

Nothing was more natural for the old civil servants than to promote, directly and indirectly, the idea of 'great and indivisible' Russia in their new environment. In this they found justification before their own conservative consciences for their submission to the revolution. Acts like the invasion of Georgia and the reunion of other outlying provinces with Russia they

---

[1] *The Essentials of Lenin*, vol. ii, p. 790.
[2] Ibid., p. 851.
[3] About half a million of former Tsarist officials were employed by the Soviet Government shortly after the civil war.

acclaimed as *their* ideological triumph. The authentic Leninists, on the other hand, approved those acts as conquests for the revolution, not for Russia. In their eyes Russia herself was merely the first domain, the first rampart, of international revolution: her interests were to be subordinated to the supernational strategy of militant socialism. For the time being, however, the boundaries of both Russia and victorious socialism were the same. The Leninists still believed that socialism demanded equality between nations; but they also felt that the reunion of most, if not all, of the Tsar's dominions under the Soviet flag served the interests of socialism. At this point the line of division between Leninism and Ustrialovism became blurred. Between the two there was plenty of room for equivocation. The new, half-spurious and half-genuine, nationalism insinuated itself into the political thinking of the party, as Stalin was shortly to admit.[1] He himself, more than the other leaders, was in, and of, that amalgamated civil service. He registered its contradictory moods with an almost seismographic sensitivity. In the Georgian affair his own bent and bias concurred with the much wider, impersonal pressures that were making themselves felt in the state.

In the summer of 1922 his Commissariat was involved in a new conflict, this time with the Ukraine. The Ukrainian Government, too, protested against his interference. Its leaders, Rakovsky, the influential descendant of an aristocratic revolutionary Bulgaro-Rumanian family; and Skrypnik, a veteran Bolshevik, stuck to the letter and the spirit of the party's pledges about the independence of the outlying republics; and they demanded that the pledges be honoured, even though Stalin's interventions in Kiev or Kharkov were not even remotely as drastic as they had been in Tiflis. The Ukrainians and the Georgians joined hands and decided to challenge him in the forthcoming debates on constitutional reform.

It would, however, be false to exaggerate the importance of these conflicts. There was a brighter side, too, to Stalin's

---

[1] J. Stalin, *Sochinenya*, vol. v, p. 239. Professor Ustrialov himself wrote in 1921, when he was still an émigré: 'The Soviet Government will strive with all means to re-unite the outlying lands with the centre—in the name of world revolution. Russian patriots will fight to achieve the same objective—in the name of great, indivisible Russia. For all the ideological differences, they practically take the same road.' N. V. Ustrialov, 'Patriotica' in *Smiena Vekh*, p. 59.

activity. He worked with great vigour and determination on one of the most difficult problems that the revolution had inherited. It will be remembered that in 1918 he called to life the self-governing republic of Bashkirs. In the spring of 1920 an autonomous Soviet republic of the Tartars was founded. In October of the same year Kirghizian self-government followed. After the civil war a Daghestan republic was constituted, comprising a multitude of tribes speaking thirty-six languages and vernaculars. Karelians, Yakuts, and others went ahead with forming their own administrations. None of these republics was or could be really independent; but all enjoyed a high degree of self-government and internal freedom; and, under the guidance of Stalin's Commissariat, all tasted some of the benefits of modern civilization. Amid all the material misery of that period, the Commissariat helped to set up thousands of schools in areas where only a few score had existed before. Schemes for the irrigation of arid land and for hydro-electrical development were initiated. Tartar became an official language on a par with Russian. Russians were forbidden to settle in the steppes of Kirghizia, now reserved for the colonization of native nomads. Progressive laws freed Asiatic women from patriarchal and tribal tyranny. All this work, of necessity carried out on a modest scale, set a pattern for future endeavours; and even in its modest beginnings there was an *élan* and an earnest concern for progress that captivated many an opponent of Bolshevism.

In the summer of 1922, soon after Lenin's first stroke, the Politbureau began to discuss a constitutional reform that was to settle the relations between Russia and the outlying republics. Stalin was the chief architect of the reform. Throughout the second half of 1922 he expounded the principles of the new constitution. These were, briefly, his ideas: the federation of Soviet Republics should be replaced by a Union of Republics. The union should consist of four regional entities: Russia, Transcaucasia, the Ukraine, and Byelorussia.[1] (It was in connexion with this scheme that he pressed the Georgians to join the Transcaucasian federation.) He was opposed to the idea that the union should be formed directly by the constituent republics; and he insisted on the need for intermediate links between

[1] J. Stalin, *Sochinenya*, vol. v, pp. 152–3.

the central administration and the individual republican governments. His motive was that central control would be more effective if it were exercised through four main channels than if it were dispersed in a much greater number of direct contacts between Moscow and the local administrations. The Commissariats were to be classed into three categories: (a) Military Affairs, Foreign Policy, Foreign Trade, Transport, and Communication were to be the sole and exclusive responsibility of the Government in Moscow. The governments of the various republics were not to possess any commissariats dealing with those matters. (b) In the second category were the departments of Finance, Economy, Food, Labour, and the Workers' and Peasants' Inspectorate. These were not to be subordinate to the central government, though they were to be subject to a measure of co-ordination from Moscow. (c) Home Affairs, Justice, Education, and Agriculture belonged to the third category and were to be administered by the provincial governments in complete independence. Sovereign power was to reside in the All-Union Congress of Soviets and, between the congresses, in the Central Executive Committee. The latter was to be composed of two chambers: the Supreme Council and the Council of Nationalities. All ethnical groups were to be represented by an equal number of delegates in the Council of Nationalities. The Central Executive Committee appointed the Council of People's Commissars, the Government.

During his first convalescence Lenin was consulted on the scheme and endorsed it. The Politbureau once again pressed the Georgians to join the Transcaucasian federation. The Ukrainians demurred at Moscow's intention to conduct foreign policy on their behalf and refused to wind up their own Commissariat for Foreign Affairs. Nominally, however, the scheme left the republics with a very wide measure of self-government. It allowed them to manage independently their home affairs, security, and police, under the circumstances by far the most important department. But the actual practice of the Government was already in flagrant conflict with the letter of the prepared reform.[1] This was the circumstance that gave rise to a conflict between Lenin and Stalin, the first and the last really

---

[1] When the constitution was finally adopted, it actually provided for the control by Moscow of the political police in all the republics.

bitter disagreement in the course of their long and friendly association.

. . . .

In the second half of the year, while Lenin was slowly recovering in the country-side, Stalin paid him several visits and kept him informed about current events. From his impression of one of those visits published in *Pravda*, an impression overflowing with adoration for the sick leader, the party learned that Lenin would shortly be back at his work. The discussions in the Politbureau, Trotsky's attacks on the Commissariat of the Inspectorate, the project of the new constitution, and the oppositions in Georgia and the Ukraine must have been some of the main points in their talks. Lenin apparently accepted whatever was Stalin's version of the events, for he gave his unreserved backing to the General Secretary. Even later, in October, after he had resumed office, he persisted in that attitude and did his utmost to enhance the General Secretary's prestige. He angrily admonished the recalcitrant Georgians; he dismissed the criticisms against the Inspectorate; and he was getting ready to come out in defence of Stalin's constitutional scheme before the tenth congress of the Soviets in December. His implicit trust in his lieutenant seemed unshaken.

Then, in November, or at the beginning of December, something happened that shook that trust irretrievably. In all probability, the change was not caused by any single incident but by a coincidence of many. The leaders of the Georgian opposition replied to Lenin's charges with a full statement of their views, which may have given Lenin food for reflection. About that time an investigation commission headed by Dzerzhinsky, the chief of the political police, returned from Georgia, and Dzerzhinsky reported to Lenin on its findings. It was from him that Lenin learned about some of Ordjonikidze's brutalities. Infuriated, he demanded that his former pupil of the Longjumeau school be suspended from membership of the party and from office. He was wary of relying solely on Dzerzhinsky's report, however. The chief of the political police, a man of the highest integrity and idealism but a muddle-headed fanatic, had suspiciously meddled with the work of other governmental departments, for which Lenin had publicly rebuked him at a party congress.[1] He also supported Stalin's policy in Tiflis. Lenin now asked his own private secretaries to prepare for him a full brief on Georgia.

It was not only the Georgian affair that began to trouble Lenin's mind. Back in office, he sensed a vague and yet unmistakable change in the atmosphere around him. The creaking of the administrative machine had got worse during his absence. It had become more difficult to get straight and quick answers to queries. People grumbled about rudeness in some offices, red tape in others, and abuses of power in yet others. His own instructions and orders often got stuck in unidentified places, without reaching their destination. He had the feeling of obscure happenings behind his back. Even before his illness he had confided to the party his uncanny sensation that the whole governmental machinery had been moving in a direction different from the one he, the man at the wheel, had believed. That sensation grew in him even more strongly now. Trying to trace the source of the change, he ran straight into the offices of the General Secretariat. Georgia, disagreements in the Politbureau, complaints against Stalin, all began to appear in a somewhat different light.

In the middle of December Lenin suffered his second stroke. After a week he recovered enough to be able to dictate notes; but he felt the nearness of death. On 25 December 1922 he dictated to his secretary a brief memorandum in lieu of a will. He opened with his fear of a split in Bolshevism. 'Our party rests upon two classes'—peasants and workers; and 'if there cannot exist an agreement between those classes, its fall is inevitable. . . . No measures would prove capable of preventing a split.'[2] But this danger was 'remote and improbable'. The current disagreements in the Politbureau, so Lenin implied, did not reflect the fundamental antagonism between the two classes. Even so, he reckoned with the danger of a 'split in the near

---

[1] *The Essentials of Lenin*, vol. ii, p. 793.

[2] Lenin's will is quoted here from L. Trotsky's *The Real Situation in Russia*, pp. 320–1. The text of the will was never published in Russia, but official writers often quoted fragments from it against Bukharin, Zinoviev, and Kamenev in terms identical with those given by Trotsky, thus confirming indirectly Trotsky's version. See, for instance, N. Popov, *Outline History*, vol. ii, p. 264. In effect nearly the whole will was quoted officially, with the exception of parts unfavourable to Stalin and favourable to Trotsky.

future'. At this point Lenin's Marxist, sociological line of reasoning came to an abrupt end; and Lenin did not even try to hint what was, in his view, the social background to the discord in the Politbureau. Instead, he went on to state, briefly and with extreme caution, his views on his successors, as if implying that their discord was still due to personal animosities only, though it might acquire wider significance in the future. He had no hesitation in pointing to Stalin and Trotsky as the chief antagonists, 'the two most able leaders of the present Central Committee', an opinion which surprised nearly all of Lenin's colleagues and disciples when they first heard it. Trotsky disdainfully looked down upon his rival; and to his last days treated him as a 'dull mediocrity'. Nor would any of the other members of the Politbureau have subscribed to Lenin's view; each of them felt his own intellectual superiority to the General Secretary. Lenin himself had no doubt which of the rivals was the more able. 'Personally . . . Comrade Trotsky . . . is, to be sure, the most able man in the present Central Committee.' Yet Lenin by no means took it for granted that Trotsky's greater gifts would secure his ascendancy. The whole testament was permeated with uncertainty about the outcome of the struggle and anxiety to stop it before it was too late.

'Comrade Stalin, having become General Secretary, has concentrated an enormous power in his hands; and I am not sure that he always knows how to use that power with sufficient caution.' Each word here was carefully weighed. Lenin vented the misgivings and suspicions that had grown upon him before his relapse; but he did not feel that they were sufficiently grounded in the facts to warrant any straight condemnatory judgement. By comparison with what he had said about Stalin, his characterization of Trotsky was more critical, in spite of the tribute to his greater talents. Lenin recalled a recent instance of Trotsky's 'struggle against the Central Committee', in which Trotsky displayed 'too far-reaching a self-confidence and a disposition to be too much attracted by the purely administrative side of affairs'. If the party were to choose between the 'two most able men' on the basis of these remarks only, the odds might have been slightly in Stalin's favour. Not only were Trotsky's shortcomings stressed with the greater emphasis; Lenin also hinted at Trotsky's inclination to oppose himself to the Central Committee, a grave fault in the leader of a party which was bred in discipline, team-work, and was suspicious of 'individualism'. Lenin was careful not to impute evil intentions to either of the rivals—they 'might lead to a split quite innocently. If our party does not take measures to prevent it, a split might arise unexpectedly.'

About the other leaders he had less to say. He reminded his followers that Zinoviev's and Kamenev's opposition to the revolution in October 1917 'was not accidental', a discreet but firm expression of his conviction that his two closest disciples lacked revolutionary audacity and character. But 'the October episode . . . ought as little to be used against them personally as the non-Bolshevism of Trotsky' against Trotsky. In other words, the party should remember their old vices, but it should not bring up those vices against them. The reminder of Trotsky's non-Bolshevik past showed that it had, at any rate, not been forgotten. The testament ended with brief remarks on two younger leaders: Bukharin ('the greatest and most valuable theoretician', 'the favourite of the whole party', in whom there was, unfortunately, 'something scholastic') and Piatakov ('very able but not to be relied upon in a serious political matter').

As a last will and testament Lenin's remarks were disappointingly inconclusive. His premonition of the schism in his party contrasted with his utter helplessness to offer any practical guidance. His only advice was 'to raise the number of members of the Central Committee to 50 or 100', advice that was bound to prove completely irrelevant. Contrary to Lenin's expectations, the power of the Politbureau and the General Secretariat did not decrease in the enlarged Central Committee—it increased.

While Lenin was meditating over his will, Stalin guided the work of the tenth All-Russian Congress of the Soviets, which adopted in principle the constitutional reform. He extolled the reform as a 'decisive step on the road towards uniting the toilers of the whole world into a World Soviet Socialist Republic'.[1] Three days later, on 30 December, at the foundation congress of the Soviets of the Union of the Soviet Socialist Republics (U.S.S.R.), he praised the reform as an achievement

[1] J. Stalin, *Sochinenya*, vol. v, p. 155.

as important as was the building up of the Red Army in the civil war. This was, of course, an exaggeration, which meant: 'I have achieved no less than Trotsky.' 'This', he went on, 'is the day of the triumph of the new Russia over the old one, over the Russia that was the gendarme of Europe and the hangman of Asia. . . . Let this congress demonstrate to those who have not yet lost the capacity to understand that Communists are as good at building new things as they are at destroying old ones.'

Lenin, who in those days wrote some of his last powerful essays, refrained from uttering in public a single word about the celebrated event. On 30 December, the day when the congress of the Soviets of the U.S.S.R. opened, he dictated notes on the conflict in Georgia:

I think the hastiness and administrative impulsiveness of Stalin played a fatal role here, and also his spite against the notorious 'social chauvinism'; spite in general plays the worst possible role in politics. I fear also that Dzerzhinsky . . . distinguished himself by his true Russian disposition (it is well known that russified people of foreign birth always overshoot themselves in the matter of the true Russian disposition). . . . It is necessary to distinguish the nationalism of the oppressing nations from the nationalism of the oppressed. . . . It behoves us to hold Stalin and Dzerzhinsky politically responsible for this genuine Great Russian nationalistic campaign.[1]

In the course of the five days that had elapsed since Lenin dictated his will, his suspicions had hardened into a certainty of Stalin's guilt; and he now passed from cautious criticisms to uninhibited indictment. It may be that during those five days he received visitors from the provinces who had come to Moscow for the congress; or that his secretaries had put before him their brief on the Georgian problem; or that he himself had an unpleasant encounter with the General Secretary; or that all these things happened together. Enough that his views were now set and that he was having second thoughts on his testament. On 4 January 1923 he dictated a postscript to it, full of the anger of a man who felt that he had been deceived by his favoured assistant.

Stalin, is too rude, and this fault . . . becomes unbearable in the office of General Secretary. Therefore, I propose to the comrades to find a way to remove Stalin from that position and appoint to it

[1] L. Trotsky, *The Real Situation in Russia*, pp. 322-3.

another man . . . more patient, more loyal, more polite and more attentive to comrades, less capricious, &c. This circumstance may seem an insignificant trifle, but I think that from the point of view of preventing a split and from the point of view of the relations between Stalin and Trotsky which I discussed above, it is not a trifle, or it is such a trifle as may acquire a decisive significance.[1]

Apart from Lenin's wife, Krupskaya, and his secretaries, nobody knew about his will. Fearing complete paralysis or sudden death, Lenin hastened to put on record his charges against Stalin and his advice to the party. Soon afterwards his health again seemed to improve; and so he himself set out to attack the General Secretary, at first cautiously and then with increasing vigour. Part of the description of this incident is based on Trotsky's subsequent revelations, the truthfulness of which may be questioned by the sceptic. But the essential part of the story is based on Lenin's own statements in *Pravda*, which have been reprinted in all editions of his writings; and these not only fit in with Trotsky's revelations but lend them powerful support. No other version of the events has, at any rate, ever been presented either by Stalin or his apologists.

On 25 January 1923 *Pravda* published Lenin's first criticism of the Workers' and Peasants' Inspectorate, still mild in tone and muddled in its practical conclusions.[2] In the first week of February[3] Lenin dictated his article 'Better less but better', a devastating attack on Stalin as the Commissar of the Inspectorate. The article, his last in *Pravda*, did not appear in print until 4 March, four weeks after it had been written. In the interval vain attempts were apparently made either by Stalin or by his friends to dissuade Lenin from launching his attack.

'Let us say frankly', these were Lenin's words, 'that the People's Commissariat of the Workers' and Peasants' Inspectorate does not enjoy the slightest prestige. Everybody knows that a more badly organized institution than our Workers' and Peasants' Inspectorate does not exist and that under present conditions nothing can be expected from this Commissariat.'[4] Stalin's name was not once mentioned, but although he had

---

[1] L. Trotsky, *The Real Situation in Russia*, pp. 322-3.
[2] *Essentials of Lenin*, vol. ii, pp. 841-3.
[3] See *Lenin* (Official biography), p. 188.
[4] *Essentials of Lenin*, vol. ii, p. 846.

recently resigned from the Commissariat, the personal implications of the attack were obvious, for the Commissariat was Stalin's creation and he had directed it for over three years. 'Indeed,' Lenin continued, 'what is the use of establishing a People's Commissariat which carries on anyhow, which does not enjoy the slightest confidence and whose work carries scarcely any weight? . . . Our main object . . . is to change all this.' 'We must really set to work . . . to create something really exemplary, something that will win the respect of all and sundry for its merits, and not only because of its rank and title.' Lenin's remarks on the virtues that should reside in a reformed Commissariat were as many reflections on its vices under Stalin's leadership: 'Let us hope that our new Workers' and Peasants' Inspectorate will not suffer from . . . ridiculous primness or ridiculous swank . . . which plays entirely into the hands of our Soviet and party bureaucracy. Let it be said in parenthesis that we have bureaucrats in our party offices as well as in Soviet offices.' Lack of civilized manners was at the root of the trouble. 'People dilate at too great length and too flippantly on "proletarian" culture. We would be satisfied with real bourgeois culture for a start, and we would be glad, for a start, to be able to dispense with the cruder types of pre-bourgeois culture, i.e. bureaucratic or serf culture, &c. In matters of culture, haste and sweeping measures are the worst possible things.' The Commissariat which had to audit the workings of the whole administration, was itself apparently wallowing in 'bureaucratic and serf culture'.

This was Lenin's first, publicly delivered, blow. Behind the scenes he prepared for a final attack at the twelfth party congress, convened for April; and he agreed with Trotsky on joint action. On 5 March, the day after *Pravda* had at last published his criticisms of Stalin's Commissariat, he had a sharp exchange with Stalin. He then dictated a brief letter to Stalin, telling him that he 'broke off' all personal relations with him. The next day, 6 March, he wired a message to the leaders of the Georgian opposition, promising to take up their case at the congress: 'I am with you in this matter with all my heart. I am outraged by the arrogance of Ordjonikidze and the connivance of Stalin and Dzerzhinsky.'[1] He again communicated

---

[1] L. Trotsky, *The Stalin School of Falsification*, pp. 68-9.

with Trotsky about their joint tactics in the Georgian business; and he briefed Kamenev who was to depart for Tiflis with a special commission of inquiry. Just in the middle of all these moves, on 9 March, he suffered the third attack of his illness, from which he was not to recover.

Stalin had no exact knowledge of Lenin's moves; but he sensed danger. He knew his formidable opponent well enough to realize that his whole career was in the balance. He could not but receive the news of Lenin's relapse with mixed feelings, to say the least.[1] That Lenin would not be there to impeach him before the congress relieved him beforehand from the greater part of his embarrassment. He still had ground to suspect an attack from Trotsky, who might also be a dangerous critic but who might equally prove a 'champion with faked muscles'. He set out to lull Trotsky into inactivity. At the session of the Politbureau which discussed new arrangements for the congress, the first congress in the whole history of the party that was not to be guided by Lenin, Stalin proposed that, in place of Lenin, Trotsky should address the congress on behalf of the Central Committee, as its chief *rapporteur*.[2] The scene which then took place, as related by Trotsky, was a farce in which it is difficult to say which of the two rivals played the more insincere part. Trotsky refused to act in Lenin's customary role, lest people should think that he was advancing his claim to leadership even before Lenin was dead. His apprehension

---

[1] This is the most that can be said about Stalin's attitude towards Lenin's death. Trotsky suggests that Stalin may have poisoned Lenin. But this is no more than a vague surmise, as Trotsky himself states; and it sounds unreal in view of the fact that Trotsky never levelled that charge, or even hinted at it, during the many years of his struggle against Stalin up to 1939–40, when he raised it for the first time (L. Trotsky, *Stalin*, pp. 372–82). Apparently, Trotsky projected the experience of the great purges of the late thirties back to 1924. Yet such a projection contradicts Trotsky's own characterization of Stalin. 'If Stalin could have foreseen', says Trotsky, 'at the very beginning where his fight against Trotskyism would lead, he undoubtedly would have stopped short, in spite of the prospect of victory over all his opponents. But he did not foresee anything' (ibid., p. 393). Thus even after he had charged Stalin with poisoning Lenin, Trotsky still treated the Stalin of 1924 as an essentially honest but short-sighted man, a characterization that can hardly be squared with the accusation. There is also the fact that Stalin did not dispose of Trotsky himself in a similar manner, while the latter was in Russia, an act of which he would certainly have been capable if he had been capable of assassinating Lenin. The whole story of the relations between Lenin and Stalin at that time, however, seems to justify the conclusion that Lenin's death must have relieved Stalin of a grave apprehension.

[2] L. Trotsky, *Stalin*, p. 366.

was certainly genuine. But then he went on to propose that Stalin, as General Secretary, should *ex officio* act in place of Lenin. The latter, too, was cautious enough to refuse. In the end Zinoviev accepted the risky honour.

Meanwhile, Stalin displayed modesty and simple-minded devotion to Lenin. Such postures shielded him from a good half of the charges levelled against him. A few days after Lenin's new stroke he published an essay on 'Communist Strategy and Tactics',[1] full of reverential references to the sick leader. ('This essay is just a condensed and schematical exposition of Comrade Lenin's essential views.') Even if the story of their sharp clash had leaked out from the Kremlin, it would have sounded incredible to most people. He continued his vague overtures to Trotsky. At the sessions of the Politbureau he was yielding and conciliatory, readily accepting every amendment to the motions he was preparing for the congress. He almost welcomed every opportunity for making some verbal concession to his critics. Eventually, his motion on policy towards the small nationalities betrayed much more of Trotsky's style than of his own. Its burden was in the reprobation of 'Soviet officials in the *centre* and in the provinces' who chauvinistically interpreted the Union of Soviet Republics as 'the beginning of the reconstitution of "great and indivisible" Russia'. An amendment also explicitly provided for the possible scrapping of his own celebrated constitutional reform and for leaving the independent republics with their fully fledged governments, until the Russian bureaucracy had learned to give 'truly proletarian and truly fraternal consideration to the needs and demands of the backward nationalities'.[2] But Stalin obtained a condemnation also of the 'local nationalisms', a loophole for the justification of his own policies.

Frederick the Great once said that he had concluded an agreement with his people, under which they were free to say what they liked and he was free to act as he pleased. As long as he could act as he pleased, Stalin was at this stage willing to talk as Trotsky liked. After all his concessions, the Politbureau decided not to communicate Lenin's notes on the Georgian affair to the congress, on the ground that it was not clear what

---

[1] J. Stalin, *Sochinenya*, vol. v, pp. 160–80.
[2] Ibid., p. 190.

use Lenin had intended to make of them. This was Stalin's first tactical success. The next one was that Trotsky refrained from delivering, at the congress, the prepared attack on the General Secretary. (Only one member of the Politbureau, Bukharin, openly backed the Georgian and Ukrainian oppositions.) Hoping for Lenin's recovery and believing that their joint action would be more effective than his own solitary effort, Trotsky bided his time. Meanwhile Stalin acted.

. . . .

It was about this time that a triumvirate, composed of Stalin, Zinoviev, and Kamenev, formed itself within the Politbureau. What made for the solidarity of the three men was their determination to prevent Trotsky from succeeding to the leadership of the party. Separately, neither could measure up to Trotsky. Jointly, they represented a powerful combination of talent and influence. Zinoviev was the politician, the orator, the demagogue with popular appeal. Kamenev was the strategist of the group, its solid brain, trained in matters of doctrine, which were to play a paramount part in the contest for power. Stalin was the tactician of the triumvirate and its organizing force. Between them, the three men virtually controlled the whole party and, through it, the Government. Kamenev had acted as Lenin's deputy and presided over the Moscow Soviet. Zinoviev was the chairman of the Soviet of Petersburg, soon to be renamed Leningrad. Stalin controlled most of the provinces. Zinoviev was, in addition, the President of the Communist International, whose moral authority in Russia was then great enough to make any pretender strive for its support.

Finally, the three men represented, as it were, the party's tradition. Their uninterrupted association with Bolshevism dated back to the split of 1903; and they held seniority in leadership. Of the other members of the Politbureau, apart from Trotsky, Bukharin was considerably younger, and Tomsky, the leader of the trade unions, had only recently become a member of it. Seniority carried with it the halo of a heroic past, distinguished by unflagging devotion to Bolshevism. The three men refused now to follow that 'ex-Menshevik', Trotsky, who, after an association with the party which had lasted only five years, had come to be commonly regarded as

Lenin's successor. This motive, the only one that made for their solidarity, impelled them to act in concert. As the other members of the Politbureau walked each his own way, the triumvirs automatically commanded a majority. Their motions and proposals, on which they usually agreed before every session of the Politbureau, were invariably carried. The other members were bound hand and foot by the discipline of the Politbureau—any attempt by one of them to discuss their inner controversies in public would have appeared as an act of disloyalty.

With the scene so set, Stalin had little to fear from the congress. He had against him only second-rate opponents, who failed to carry the mass of the delegates. Many delegates were already dependent for their political standing on the General Secretariat. The degree of that dependence was indicated by Stalin himself when he described to the congress the work of the personnel department in the General Secretariat. His account shed light on the manner in which the party was securing its control over every field of public life. The year before only 27 per cent. of the regional leaders of the trade unions were members of the party. At present 57 per cent. of them were Communists. The percentage of Communists in the management of co-operatives had risen from five to fifty; and in the commanding staffs of the armed forces from sixteen to twenty-four. The same happened in all other institutions which Stalin described as the 'transmission belts' connecting the party with the people. Not a single public institution was to be left outside the system of these transmission belts.[1]

To be able to marshal its forces, the personnel department kept solid files with the most detailed records of the party's 'key-men'. The party had now, after the first purges, about 400,000 ordinary members and about 20,000 officials. So far the personnel department had compiled the records of the upper and medium layers, including 1,300 managers of industry. The investigation, Stalin disclosed, was still on. The files were compiled with special attention to every member's professional skill and specialization, political reliability, and moral bearings. Every blemish in a member's record was duly registered. 'It is necessary to study every worker through and through', said

[1] J. Stalin, *Sochinenya*, vol. v, p. 197 and *passim*.

Stalin, 'in every detail.'[1] 'Otherwise policy loses sense and becomes meaningless gesticulation.'[2] Since the personnel department had to meet or help in meeting any demand for officials, it had spread a network of branches throughout the country. It had the power to order members to change their occupation and place of residence at the shortest notice, to shift from the capital to the wilderness of Siberia or to an embassy abroad, in order to carry out any assignment. An assignment, even an honourable one, might be a pretext for the punishment of a somewhat restive member. Few persons, whatever their merits, could have been quite sure that if their politics displeased the General Secretariat, some *faux pas* committed by them in the past would not now be publicly held out against them. But, so far, this had not become common practice.

The General Secretary was also responsible for appointments of provincial party leaders. He spoke about this with specious sadness. It was time, he told the congress, that provincial organizations elected their secretaries, instead of getting them appointed from above. Unfortunately, the lack of qualified men was so acute that local branches were all the time pestering the General Secretariat to send them people from the centre. 'It is very difficult to train party leaders. This requires five, ten, or even more years. It is much easier to conquer this or that country with the help of Comrade Budienny's cavalry than to train two or three leaders from the rank and file.' He defended the provincial committees that had so often been attacked and ridiculed in the newspapers. He spoke for the whole phalanx of his secretaries; and he excused even their squabbling and intriguing, which had their good as well as their bad sides, because they helped in the crystallization of 'coherent nuclei of leaders'.[3] In other words, the provincial committees were miniature replicas of the Politbureau with their own little triumvirates and duumvirates and their groups of oppositionists.

At the congress Stalin, in reply to a critic, made his first public admission of the existence of the triumvirate and declared its solidarity against any opposition. 'Osinsky', these were Stalin's words, 'has praised Stalin and praised Kamenev,

[1] Ibid., p. 221. [2] Ibid., p. 210.
[3] Ibid., p. 216.

but he has attacked Zinoviev, thinking that for the time being it would be enough to remove one of them and that then would come the turn of the others. His aim is to break up that nucleus that has formed itself inside the Central Committee over years of toil. . . . I ought to warn him that he will run into a wall, against which, I am afraid, he will smash his head.'¹ To another critic,² who demanded more freedom of discussion in the party, Stalin replied that the party was no debating society. Russia was 'surrounded by the wolves of imperialism; and to discuss all important matters in 20,000 party cells would mean to lay all one's cards before the enemy'. Amid prolonged applause he concluded thus: 'It is long since I have seen a congress as united and as inspired by a single idea as this one. I am sorry that Comrade Lenin is not here. If he had been here, he could have said: "Twenty-five years I have nursed the party and I have brought her up to be great and strong." '³ At no other congress before had Stalin spoken with anything approaching his present self-confidence.

The malcontents, leaderless and helpless, were defeated at the congress. Three months later, in August 1923, the Politbureau was alarmed by a sudden outbreak of many strikes in industry. Since the promulgation of the N.E.P. in 1921, Russia's economy was beginning to recover. But the process was slow and painful. Industry was still unable to meet the country's most essential needs. It failed to supply the countryside with the goods that would induce peasants to sell food. Low wages, unemployment, and starvation were driving the working class to despair. Since trade unions refused to take up the workers' demands, discontent exploded in 'unofficial' strikes. The restive mood penetrated into the ruling party. Clandestine opposition groups were discovered within its ranks. Some of these groups were half Menshevik; others were wholly Bolshevik and consisted of remnants of the oppositions that had been banned in 1921 as well as of new elements. Their main plank was the demand for freedom of criticism inside the party. Some of the dissenters were expelled, others

¹ The critic who used the pen-name Osinsky was Prince Obolensky, a very prominent Bolshevik economist.
² That other critic, Lutovinov, was soon to commit suicide.
³ J. Stalin, *Sochinenya*, vol. v, p. 235.

imprisoned. These were the first instances of clandestine opposition among Communists. So far, the secret groups had acted without concert and lacked leadership. The triumvirs feared a link-up between their rivals and the discontented rank and file.[1]

They reacted to the crisis in a self-contradictory manner. They put before the Central Committee a motion about the need to restore democracy and freedom of discussion for the members of the party. On the other hand, they mobilized the political police against the secret oppositions. The police found that ordinary Bolsheviks often refused to co-operate in tracing the opposition groups. Dzerzhinsky asked the Politbureau to authorize the police to take action against uncooperative Bolsheviks, too. At this point the fight between Trotsky and the triumvirs entered a new phase. Without making it quite clear whether he thought that Dzerzhinsky's demand should be granted, Trotsky attacked the triumvirate. What had happened, he stated, was symptomatic of the party's state of mind, its sense of frustration, and its distrust of the leaders. Even during the civil war 'the system of appointment [from above] did not have one-tenth of the extent that it has now. Appointment of the secretaries of provincial committees is now the rule.' He granted that there was a grain of demagogy in the demands for a workers' democracy, 'in view of the incompatibility of a fully developed workers' democracy with the régime of the dictatorship'. But the discipline of the civil war ought to have given place to 'a more lively and broader party responsibility'. Instead, 'the bureaucratization of the party machine had developed to unheard of proportions; and criticism and discontent, the open expression of which was stifled, were driven underground, assuming uncontrollable and dangerous forms'.[2]

The triumvirs evaded the issues raised by Trotsky and charged him with malevolence, personal ambition, neglect of his duties in the Government, and so on. They accused him of trying to establish himself as Lenin's successor.[3] This last charge was, in a sense, true, for the fight over the succession was inherent in the situation. Yet this as well as the other charges

[1] Ibid., pp. 354-61; N. Popov, Outline History, vol. ii, pp. 194-204.
[2] M. Eastman, Since Lenin Died, Appendix IV, pp. 142-3.
[3] N. Popov, Outline History, vol. ii, pp. 144-96.

were beside the point, for the crisis in the party, as Trotsky diagnosed it, was a fact.

In the middle of this exchange forty-six prominent Communists issued a declaration the gist of which was identical with Trotsky's criticisms.[1] Among the signatories were: Piatakov, one of the two ablest leaders of the young generation mentioned in Lenin's testament, Preobrazhensky and Serebriakov, former secretaries of the Central Committee, Antonov-Ovseenko, the military leader of the October revolution, Smirnov, Osinsky, Bubnov, Sapronov, Muralov, Drobnis, and others, distinguished leaders in the civil war, men of brain and character. Some of them had led previous oppositions against Lenin and Trotsky, expressing the *malaise* that made itself felt in the party as its leadership began to sacrifice first principles to expediency. Fundamentally, they were now voicing that same *malaise* which was growing in proportion to the party's continued departure from some of its first principles. It is not certain whether Trotsky directly instigated their demonstration. So far he conducted his dispute with the triumvirs behind the closed doors of the Politbureau. The party at large was under the impression that he had all the time been whole-heartedly behind the official policy. He thus had the worst of both worlds: he had been burdened with responsibility for a policy to which he had been opposed; and he had done nothing to rally in time those who might have supported him.

In November the alarm caused by the crisis led the triumvirs to table a motion in favour of democratic reform in the party. As in the Georgian affair, so now Stalin agreed to make any verbal concession to Trotsky. The motion was carried by the Politbureau unanimously. Trotsky had no choice but to vote for it. On 7 November, the sixth anniversary of the revolution, Zinoviev officially announced the opening of a public discussion on all issues that troubled the Bolshevik mind. The state of siege in the party, so it might have seemed, was at last being lifted.

This was not the case. The state of affairs against which the opposition rose was not merely the result of Stalin's or the other triumvirs' ambition and ill will. It had deeper roots. The revolution had saved itself by building up a massive political machine. The apathy, if not the hostility, of the masses drove

[1] N. Popov, *Outline History*, vol. ii, pp. 144-96.

it to rely increasingly on rule by coercion rather than by persuasion. Who could say with any certainty that the time had now come to reverse all this, to scrap or even curb the political machine, and to rely on the soundness of popular opinion? Who could be sure that this would not have impaired the safety of the revolution? If a workers' democracy was needed, did that mean that the Mensheviks and the Social Revolutionaries were to be allowed to come back? Most of Stalin's critics, including Trotsky, agreed that the Mensheviks should remain outlawed. In their view, the time had not yet come to lift the state of siege in the republic—they wanted it to be lifted in the party only. But was it at all possible that the party should be an island of freedom in a society doomed, for good or evil, to dictatorial rule? Apart from all this, the massive dictatorial machine had now a vested interest in self-perpetuation, which it was able to identify with the broader interest of the revolution. Both sides in the dispute were aware of the dilemma; but while to one of them, the opposition, that awareness was a source of weakness, to the other it was a source of strength.

Trotsky consequently demanded not more than a limited reform, to be promulgated from above, a degree of administrative liberalism. He had been careful so far to refrain from any appeal to public opinion, even Communist opinion, against the rulers. Yet he felt the need for bringing the dispute into the open. The official inauguration of a public discussion gave him the opportunity to do so, the opportunity, that is, to appeal to public opinion against the rulers and to do so with the rulers' own formal permission. His inconsistency, real or apparent, was dictated by deeper considerations. He believed that it should be possible to strike a balance between dictatorship and freedom, that it should be possible to restrict or broaden the one or the other, according to circumstances. He hoped that with Russia's economic recovery and the progress of socialism, the régime would be able to rely less and less upon coercion and more and more upon willing support. The revolution should be able to recapture its own youth. The divorce between the revolution and the people, he thought, was of a temporary character. The triumvirs, and especially Stalin, were far less hopeful.

Here we touch the root of most of the differences between

Trotskyism and Stalinism. Both insisted on their basic loyalty to the Marxist outlook; and there is no reason to doubt the sincerity of their professions. For both factions to claim allegiance to Marxism and Leninism was as natural as it is for Protestants and Catholics to swear by Christianity. In the one case as in the other the professions of faith, common to both sides, offer almost no clue to their antagonism. What underlay Trotsky's attitude was a cautious and yet very real revolutionary optimism, a belief that, if only the rulers pursued the right Socialist policy, the working classes would support them. This belief had indeed been implicit in the Marxist philosophy; and Stalin never openly contradicted it. But between the lines of his policies there is always present a deep disbelief in the popularity of socialism, and even more than that: an essentially pessimistic approach to man and society. In the last instance the revolutionary optimist sets his hope on his frank appeal to the people, even when he may seem to hope against hope. The pessimist in power distrusts those whom he rules. The Communist pessimist treats his own doctrine as a piece of esoteric knowledge. He does not believe that the working classes are really capable of accepting it, unless it is, brutally speaking, pushed down their throats. Both the optimist and the pessimist are convinced that communism is the only remedy for the evils of capitalist society. But whereas the former is convinced that sooner or later—and sooner rather than later—the patient himself, if properly enlightened, will ask for the remedy, the latter is inclined to order the cure without much regard for the patient's wish. However, this digression perhaps runs ahead of our story.

A few weeks after Zinoviev had officially opened the public debate, Stalin addressed the Communists of Krasnaya Presnya, a working-class district in Moscow, on the meaning of the 'New Course'.[1] He frankly admitted that the party was in a state of ferment and that it had lost touch with the mood in the country. The reason for this he saw in the organizations on the spot, which had ceased to discuss public affairs and had abandoned elective practices in favour of nomination from above. The fault of the leadership, if there was any, was that it had not discovered these abnormal conditions in time. 'In 1917', he went on, 'we

[1] J. Stalin, *Sochinenya*, vol. v, pp. 354–70.

fancied that we were going to form a commune, an association of toilers, that we were going to finish off bureaucracy. . . . This is an ideal from the attainment of which we are still far off. . . . What is needed to free the state from bureaucratic elements . . . is a high degree of civilization in the people, a completely secure, peaceful condition all round, so that we should not need large military cadres . . . which put their imprint on the other governmental institutions. . . .'[1] The evils of this state of affairs could in part be remedied by the New Course. But the party should be wary of taking too much advantage of freedom. They should go back to elective practices, but the restrictions on election must also remain in force. There was to be freedom of expression, but the previously imposed limitations must still apply. The sting of his story was in its tail. Some critics, Stalin said, quoted Trotsky in their support. He, Stalin, did not know what right they had to do so, for he knew Trotsky (here his tone became almost reverential) as one who insisted that the party was no debating society, that it must have discipline in action. He thus gave his audience the impression that Trotsky stood behind the policies of the General Secretariat. In the light of the preceding exchange of letters between Trotsky and the triumvirs, his suggestion was undoubtedly meant to provoke Trotsky to a public debate.

Three days later, on 5 December, Trotsky retorted with an open letter to the Communists of Krasnaya Presnya.[2] Taking his stand on the Politbureau's latest decisions, he emphatically warned the rank and file that without their vigilant pressure on the leaders, those decisions would remain a dead letter. 'Certain conservatively disposed comrades [he did not mention names] incline to over-estimate the role of the machine and under-estimate the self-activity of the party, take a critical attitude to the resolution of the Politbureau. They say the Central Committee is undertaking an impossible task, the resolution will only spread false illusions and lead to negative results.' This was not his, Trotsky's, view. He thought it was time the party regained its initiative and self-rule, which it had abdicated in favour of the machine. 'The party shall subordinate to itself

---

[1] Ibid. This was, of course, a subtle intimation that the source of the evil was not in the party caucus but in the army, i.e. in Trotsky's department.
[2] Appendix VI in M. Eastman, *Since Lenin Died*, pp. 146-7.

its machine, not for one instant ceasing to be a centralized organization.' It should exercise its right to criticism 'without fear and without favour. . . . And first of all ought to be removed from the party positions those who at the first voice of criticism, of objection, of protest, are inclined to demand one's party ticket for the purpose of repression. The New Course ought to begin with this, that in the machine all should feel, from top to bottom, that nobody dares to terrorize the party.' Trotsky appealed to the youth; and, as if pointing to the triumvirs, the 'old guard' of Bolshevism, he warned the party that revolutionary 'old guards' had not rarely degenerated into bureaucrats. This had happened with the leaders of reformist socialism in Europe; and it might happen with Bolsheviks, too. It was from this letter that the public got the first inkling of the cleavage in the Politbureau.

The triumvirs took up the challenge instantly. The impulsive Zinoviev proposed that Trotsky be immediately arrested. Stalin, more circumspect and aware of Trotsky's immense popularity, opposed such a step. Curiously enough, at this stage, and even later, he was at pains to appear as the most moderate, sensible, and conciliatory of the triumvirs. His criticisms of Trotsky were less offensive than Zinoviev's or Kamenev's. Aware that the party resented the belittlement of Trotsky, he left his partners to go through the crudest forms of mud-slinging, from which their own as well as Trotsky's prestige was bound to suffer. He himself concentrated on a more discreet job, the handling of the party machine. Accustomed to attach due importance to the technical aspects of party life, he was anxious to obtain a formal verdict against the opposition from a national Communist assembly. It was still too risky to refer the controversy to an elected congress. It was therefore decided to convoke a national conference at which the local branches were represented by their secretaries, officials, and appointees of the General Secretariat. An assembly of that sort could be relied upon to oblige the triumvirate; and its verdict against Trotsky was, in its turn, certain to impress the rest of the party. The conference was convened for January 1924.

Meanwhile, at the end of December, Stalin joined in the affray with a public broadside, directed primarily against the extremists of the opposition and only in the second instance against Trotsky. His argument, bristling with solecisms and *non sequiturs*, was nevertheless very effective, because it brought to light the opposition's mental reservations and inconsistencies. Did the opposition demand that Lenin's rules, which banned factions and groupings inside the party, should be abolished? Yes or no? It was precisely on this point that the opposition could not answer with a definite yes or no. Trotsky, at any rate, was at cross-purposes with himself: he wanted Lenin's rules, that he himself had endorsed, to stand; but he claimed that they had been abused. It was on this point that Stalin concentrated his fire, compelling Trotsky to retreat, to vacillate, to give up one position after another, and then to attempt to regain the lost ground when it was too late, when Trotsky's followers had already been confused and disheartened.

.   .   .   .

It was in this debate, while Lenin was on his death-bed, that the cult of Leninism was actually initiated. To demand, directly or indirectly, that any measure that had been inspired by Lenin should be cancelled was now an unpardonable offence against an unwritten code of behaviour. When Preobrazhensky declared that the party longed to regain the 'Leninist' freedom of discussion which it enjoyed before 1920, in the controversy over Brest Litovsk, Stalin rejoined that the customs and habits of that time were hardly worthy of imitation. Did not, he asked, Preobrazhensky and his like, the left Communists, then plan to depose Lenin's government and replace it by their own? This was true in part. Yet during the Brest Litovsk controversy, and even later, it would have occurred to nobody that there was anything reprehensible in such an idea. The left Communists, the opponents of peace with Germany, had at one time carried the majority of the Central Committee; and it was natural for them to consider whether they themselves should not take over the government and assume responsibility for the conduct of a war to which Lenin was opposed.[1] This did not prevent them and Lenin from working together after the Brest Litovsk controversy was over. But now, in 1923, the episode of 1918

[1] Bukharin certainly mooted the idea. This was the grain of truth in the charge of a conspiracy against Lenin, levelled against him in the purge trials of the thirties. In 1923-4 Stalin refrained from mentioning Bukharin in this context, for Bukharin had just become his ally against Trotsky. See *15 Konferentsya Vsesoyuznoi Kom. Partii*, p. 558.

looked like a sinister conspiracy or an act of blasphemy. The party, so Stalin suggested, should beware of those who advocated a return to such pernicious practices.

In the light of the Leninist cult, Trotsky's position was most vulnerable. He had warned the party about the danger of a 'degeneration' of the old Bolshevik guard; and he had used in this context the first person plural: 'We, the old Bolsheviks', a phrase which was justified inasmuch as more than ninety per cent. of the present members of the party had joined it only after the October revolution.[1] 'I must defend Trotsky from Trotsky', Stalin replied sarcastically: for surely he was not of the old, now allegedly degenerating, guard. The degeneration of the old Bolsheviks, he went on, was a figment of Trotsky's imagination. There were elements of decomposition in the party; but these were in the Mensheviks, who had joined its ranks but remained alien to its spirit.[2] The innuendo needed no elaboration.

The debate, with all its diversions and red herrings, was only part of the preparation for a show-down at the forthcoming conference. Simultaneously the General Secretariat weakened the opposition by dispersing its leaders. Trotsky, ill and hampered by mental reservations, was not very active. Rakovsky was found to be badly needed on the staff of the Soviet Legation in London, in connexion with the establishment of Russo-British diplomatic relations in February 1924. Krestinsky had been sent on a diplomatic mission to Germany, Yoffe to China. The opposition could not protest against the assignments, which could be justified on their merits. The newly appointed diplomats could not meddle in the inner affairs of the party. The Ukraine had been a stronghold of the opposition under Rakovsky's premiership; and the General Secretariat now delegated the former leather-worker Lazar Kaganovich, a tough administrator, to clear this hornets' nest. In Moscow Trotsky's articles and pamphlets were virtually withdrawn from circulation; hesitant or doubting members had hardly a chance to acquaint themselves with both sides of the argument. The provincial functionaries were left in no doubt what were the wishes of the triumvirs; and the outcome of the conference was a foregone conclusion.

At the conference Stalin stated his views more bluntly than

---

[1] J. Stalin, *Sochinenya*, vol. vi, p. 202.   [2] Ibid., vol. v, pp. 384-5.

hitherto: 'I shall say but this, there will plainly not be any developed democracy, any full democracy.'[1] People were forgetting that 'there are moments when it is impossible and it would make no sense to adopt it', even within the very narrow limits of the party. Economic prosperity, military security, and a civilized membership, such were the conditions under which a workers' democracy would function; these conditions were lacking. Though the party was not democratic, it was wrong to charge it with being bureaucratic. His argument was muddled; his picture of the organization which was neither democratic nor bureaucratic was confused; but the strength of his argument lay precisely in its muddled character, calculated to satisfy hesitant minds. He then listed 'six mistakes' committed by Trotsky. Trotsky had voted for the Politbureau's motion on the New Course and then come out criticizing the Politbureau—he was placing himself above his colleagues and assuming the pose of a superman. He had refused to say clearly whether he was with the Central Committee or with the opposition. Trotsky, the 'patriarch of the bureaucrats', incited the party against its machine and the young people against the party. He had set himself up as the mouthpiece of the petty bourgeois intelligentsia, while the other leaders spoke for the proletariat. He had blamed the régime in the party for the emergence of secret factions and groups, whereas Marxists knew that the variety of groups reflected divergent class interests. The party must be of one piece, a party of steel, monolithic. Two hundred thousand workers 'from the bench' should be admitted into it at once; they would bring with them a sound proletarian spirit, immune from petty bourgeois individualism—this was the so-called Leninist call-up. Finally, Stalin created a sensation by making public a secret clause of Lenin's resolution to the tenth congress, which allowed the Central Committee to expel its own members guilty of factional work. He asked the conference to reaffirm that clause. All his proposals were accepted. The conference condemned the opposition as a 'petty bourgeois deviation from Leninism'.

. . . .

Three days later, on 21 January 1924, Lenin died. Despite all the miseries and disappointments of recent years, he was

[1] J. Stalin, *Sochinenya*, vol. vi, pp. 7–11.

mourned by the people as very few leaders in history have been mourned. In the popular mind his name still stood for the great promise of the revolution, the society of equal and free men. The mourning crowds were already turning uneasy eyes on his disciples: which of them would take his place at the helm of the state? In spite of recent squabbles and excommunications, the thoughts of many went out to Trotsky. But he was not to be seen at Lenin's bier, at which the crowds paid their last homage to the deceased leader as he lay in state, or at the numerous memorial meetings. Trotsky had gone to the Caucasus to have his illness treated; and, if his own testimony is to be believed, he failed to return for the funeral in Moscow because Stalin had misinformed him about its date. On the scales of history, it may be said, the incident weighed but little.[1] But the fact is that in those days the triumvirs, and not Trotsky, impressed themselves upon a popular imagination stirred by prolonged and elaborate funeral ceremonies. Skilful stage-management turned the limelight on the triumvirs as they were symbolically stepping into the breach. Stalin's own 'Biographical Chronicle'[2] tells the story in characteristic detail, day by day, even hour by hour:

21 January: 6.50 a.m. Lenin dies at Gorky. 9.30 a.m. Stalin and other members of the Politbureau arrive at Gorky.

22 January: Stalin co-edits a manifesto 'To all toilers of the U.S.S.R.', and sends out messages to the provincial branches of the party, calling them to keep faith with the teachings of the dead leader.

23 January: 9 a.m. Stalin and other leaders carry the coffin with Lenin's body from Lenin's home at Gorky; 1.30 p.m. Stalin and his friends carry the coffin from the Paveletsky Station to the House of the Trade Unions in Moscow, where Lenin lay in state for the next four days; 6.10 p.m. Stalin stands in the guard of honour at the bier.

25 January: Stalin calls upon the party to collect relics of Lenin for the newly founded Lenin Institute.

---

[1] Lovers of historical analogy may recall that in the train of events that led to the downfall of Danton, the incident of his illness and departure from Paris played a not dissimilar role. 'On 12 October [writes a biographer of Danton] he went for a holiday to Arcis-sur-Aube to restore his health. This was an excellent opportunity for his enemies—for Billaud Varenne and Robespierre—to prepare his downfall. When he returned to Paris in November, it was soon obvious that quitting his post had cost him his position.'   [2] J. Stalin, *Sochinenya*, vol. vi, pp. 418–19.

26 January: 8.24 p.m., at the second congress of the Soviets, Stalin reads an oath of allegiance to Lenin.

27 January: 8 a.m. Stalin takes his place in the guard of honour at Lenin's bier; 8.30 a.m. Stalin moves to the head of the bier; 9 a.m. Stalin and others carry the coffin out of the House of the Trade Unions; 4 p.m.—end of the funeral procession at the Red Square—Stalin and others carry the coffin into the crypt of the future Mausoleum.

28 January: Stalin addresses a memorial meeting.

The elaborate ceremony was altogether out of keeping with the outlook and style of Lenin, whose sobriety and dislike of pomp were almost proverbial. The ceremony was calculated to stir the mind of a primitive, semi-oriental people into a mood of exaltation for the new Leninist cult. So was the Mausoleum in the Red Square, in which Lenin's embalmed body was deposited, in spite of his widow's protest and the indignation of many Bolshevik intellectuals. To myriads of peasants, whose religious instincts were repressed under the revolution, the Mausoleum soon became a place of pilgrimage, the queer Mecca of an atheistic creed, which needed a prophet and saints, a holy sepulchre and icons. Just as original Christianity, as it was spreading into pagan countries, absorbed elements of pagan beliefs and rites and blended them with its own ideas, so now Marxism, the product of western European thought, was absorbing elements of the Byzantine tradition, so deeply ingrained in Russia, and of the Greek Orthodox style. The process was inevitable. The abstract tenets of Marxism could exist, in their purity, in the brains of intellectual revolutionaries, especially those who had lived as exiles in western Europe. Now, after the doctrine had really been transplanted to Russia and come to dominate the outlook of a great nation, it could not but, in its turn, assimilate itself to that nation's spiritual climate, to its traditions, customs, and habits. Imperceptibly, the process had been going on for some time. Nobody had had a deeper insight into it and felt more embarrassed by it than Lenin. His own death was the catharsis, which relieved many of his disciples from the inhibitions of pure Marxism. It revealed the degree of the mutual assimilation of doctrine and environment that had taken place so far.

It was perhaps natural that the triumvir who had spent his

formative years in a Greek Orthodox seminary should become the foremost agent of that change, that he should give the fullest expression to it. The oath to Lenin, which he read at the second congress of the Soviets, remains to this day the fullest and the most organic revelation of his own mind. In it, the style of the Communist Manifesto is strangely blended with that of the Orthodox Prayer Book; and Marxist terminology is wedded to the old Slavonic vocabulary. Its revolutionary invocations sound like a litany composed for a church choir:

Comrades, we Communists are people of a special cut. We have been cut out of peculiar stuff. . . . There is no loftier title than that of a member of the party, of which Comrade Lenin has been founder and leader. It is not given to everyone to be a member of such a party. It is not given to everyone to endure the hardships and storms that go with the membership of such a party. Sons of the working class, sons of misery and struggle, sons of incredible privation and heroic endeavour, these, above all, ought to be the members of such a party. . . .

In leaving us, Comrade Lenin ordained us to hold high and keep pure the great title of member of the party. We vow to thee, Comrade Lenin, that we shall honourably fulfil this thy commandment. . . .

In leaving us, Comrade Lenin ordained us to guard the unity of our party like the apple of our eye. We vow to thee, Comrade Lenin, that we shall fulfil honourably this thy commandment, too. . . .

In leaving us, Comrade Lenin ordained us to guard and strengthen the dictatorship of the proletariat. We vow to thee, Comrade Lenin, that without sparing our strength we shall honourably fulfil this thy commandment, too. . . .

In leaving us, Comrade Lenin ordained us to strengthen with all our might the alliance of workers and peasants. We vow to thee, Comrade Lenin, that we shall fulfil honourably this thy commandment, too. . . .

In leaving us, Comrade Lenin ordained us to strengthen and broaden the Union of the Republics. We vow to thee, Comrade Lenin, that we shall honourably fulfil this thy commandment, too. . . .

In leaving us, Comrade Lenin ordained us to keep faith with the principles of the Communist International. We vow to thee, Comrade Lenin, that we shall not spare our lives in the endeavour to strengthen and broaden the alliance of the workers of the whole world—the Communist International.[1]

[1] J. Stalin, *Sochinenya*, vol. vi, pp. 46–51.

In view of all that had recently passed between Lenin and Stalin, it might be thought that this half-mystical oath was a piece of sheer hypocrisy. Such a conclusion would seem to over-simplify the matter, though it can hardly be doubted that Stalin's exalted valediction contained its streak of insincerity. Yet he was undoubtedly sincere in his belief that he had the right to regard himself as Lenin's orthodox pupil. His adherence to Bolshevism had lasted twenty years; he had been a member of Lenin's Central Committees for ten years; and more than half of that time, for six difficult and stormy years, he had served directly under Lenin, with energy and devotion. Could their brief and violent conflict have obliterated their long, close association? Stalin still felt entitled to think of his clash with Lenin as of an awkward episode, a misunderstanding, which, if Lenin had recovered, might have been smoothed out to their mutual satisfaction. He was certainly convinced that his atti-tude towards the body of doctrine bequeathed by Lenin was beyond reproach. In all probability he was not aware that the Leninist cult, and in particular his own half-religious oath, sounded like a mockery of the real Lenin.[1]

Presently, he expounded Leninism, as he understood it, to the Communist youth and the undergraduates of the Sverdlov university, where the party was bringing up its new intellectual *élite*.[2] What he had to say on the subject was so unoriginal and dull that it hardly deserves to be summarized. The only original side of his exposition was its form. He presented Lenin's doctrine, which was essentially sociological and experimental, as a series of rigid canons and flat strategic and tactical recipes for mankind's salvation, all listed and enumerated with the precision of a book-keeper. He codified and formalized Lenin-ism in that style of spurious simplicity and lucidity that is highly attractive to the mind with little sociological training. He sup-ported every contention of his with a quotation from Lenin, sometimes irrelevant and sometimes torn out of the context, in

[1] Lenin bitterly scoffed at any attempt to introduce ritual form or quasi-religious parlance into socialism. On one occasion he was asked whether it was proper for a Socialist to say that socialism was his religion. 'If an ordinary worker said this [Lenin answered] then it only meant that that worker was abandoning religion in favour of socialism. But if a socialist leader or an intellectual was claim-ing socialism as his religion, he was abandoning socialism in favour of religion.'

[2] J. Stalin, *Sochinenya*, vol. vi, pp. 69–188.

the same way that the medieval scholastic sought sanction for his speculations in the holy writ. True, Lenin had also sometimes backed his arguments with all too frequent references to Marx. But Stalin carried the mannerism to such absurd perfection that in the end he might have paraphrased Archimedes: 'Give me a quotation from Lenin and I will move the earth.'

Meanwhile the one text of Lenin that might have removed the earth from under Stalin's feet, his will, was still unknown to the party and to himself. Only in May, four months after Lenin's death, was it read out at a plenary session of the Central Committee, which was to decide whether the document should be made public at the forthcoming congress of the party. 'Terrible embarrassment paralysed all those present', so an eyewitness describes the scene.[1] 'Stalin sitting on the steps of the rostrum looked small and miserable. I studied him closely; in spite of his self-control and show of calm, it was clearly evident that his fate was at stake.' In the atmosphere of the Leninist cult, it seemed almost sacrilegious to disregard Lenin's will. At this, for him, fateful moment he was saved by Zinoviev. 'Comrades', so Zinoviev addressed the meeting, 'every word of Ilyich [Lenin] is law to us. . . . We have sworn to fulfil anything the dying Ilyich ordered us to do. You know perfectly well that we shall keep that vow.' (Many among the audience drop their eyes—they cannot look the old actor in the face.) 'But we are happy to say that in one point Lenin's fears have proved baseless. I have in mind the point about our General Secretary. You have all witnessed our harmonious co-operation in the last few months; and, like myself, you will be happy to say that Lenin's fears have proved baseless.' Kamenev followed with an appeal to the Central Committee that Stalin be left in office. But if this was to happen it was not advisable to publish Lenin's will at the congress. Krupskaya protested against the suppression of her husband's testament, but in vain. Trotsky, present at the meeting, was too proud to intervene in a situation which affected his own standing too. He kept silent, expressing only through his mien and grimaces his disgust at the scene. Zinoviev's motion that the testament should not be published, but only confidentially communicated to picked delegates, was then passed by forty votes against ten. Stalin could now wipe

[1] B. Bazhanov, *Stalin, der Rote Diktator*, pp. 32-4.

the cold sweat from his brow. He was back in the saddle, firmly and for good.

The solidarity of the triumvirs stood this extraordinary test because both Zinoviev and Kamenev were as convinced that they had nothing to fear from Stalin as they were afraid of Trotsky. Zinoviev, the President of the Communist International, was still the senior and the most popular triumvir. Kamenev was conscious of his intellectual superiority over his partners. Both looked upon Stalin as upon their auxiliary; and, though they were sometimes uneasy about a streak of perversity in him, neither suspected him of the ambition to become Lenin's sole successor. Nor, for that matter, did any such suspicion enter the mind of the party as a whole. It was not, on the other hand, very difficult to arouse in the party distrust of Trotsky. The agents of the triumvirate whispered that Trotsky was the potential Danton or, alternatively, the Bonaparte of the Russian revolution. The whispering campaign was effective, because the party had, from its beginnings, been accustomed to consult the great French precedent. It had always been admitted that history might repeat itself; and that a Directory or a single usurper might once again climb to power on the back of the revolution. It was taken for granted that the Russian usurper would, like his French prototype, be a personality possessed of brilliance and legendary fame won in battles. The mask of Bonaparte seemed to fit Trotsky only too well. Indeed, it might have fitted any personality with the exception of Stalin. In this lay part of his strength.

The very thing which under different circumstances would have been a liability in a man aspiring to power, his obscurity, was his important asset. The party had been brought up to distrust 'bourgeois individualism' and to strive for collectivism. None of its leaders looked as immune from the former and as expressive of the latter as Stalin. What was striking in the General Secretary was that there was nothing striking about him. His almost impersonal personality seemed to be the ideal vehicle for the anonymous forces of class and party. His bearing seemed of the utmost modesty. He was more accessible to the average official or party man than the other leaders. He studiously cultivated his contacts with the people who in one way or another made and unmade reputations, provincial secretaries, popular satirical writers, and foreign visitors. Himself taciturn, he was unsurpassed at the art of patiently listening to others. Sometimes he would be seen in a corner of a staircase pulling at his pipe and listening immovably, for an hour or two, to an agitated interlocutor and breaking his silence only to ask a few questions. This was one of his qualities that seemed to indicate a lack of any egotism. The interviewer, glad of the opportunity to get his troubles off his chest, rarely reflected on the fact that Stalin had not revealed his mind in the conversation. For Stalin, to quote his secretary,[1] 'did not confide his innermost thoughts to anybody. Only very rarely did he share his ideas and impressions with his closest associates. He possessed in a high degree the gift for silence, and in this respect he was unique in a country where everybody talked far too much.'

His private life, too, was beyond reproach or suspicion. 'This passionate politician [says Bazhanov] has no other vices. He loves neither money, nor pleasure, neither sport, nor women. Women, apart from his own wife, do not exist for him.' In the middle of the civil war he married for the second time. His wife, Nadezhda Alliluyeva, the daughter of the workman in whose home Lenin hid in the July days of 1917, was twenty years younger than himself. She had been one of Lenin's secretaries after the revolution and went to Tsaritsyn in 1919. There the love between the Commissar and the Communist girl began. Now they had a small lodging in what used to be the servants' quarters in the Kremlin; and Nadezhda Alliluyeva was earnestly studying at a technical college in Moscow. The air of plainness and even austerity about the General Secretary's private life commended him to the puritanically minded party, which was just beginning to grow apprehensive at the first signs of corruption and loose life in the Kremlin.

Nor did Stalin at that time impress people as being more intolerant than befitted a Bolshevik leader. He was, as we have seen, less vicious in his attacks on the opposition than the other triumvirs. In his speeches there was usually the tone of a good-natured and soothing, if facile, optimism, which harmonized well with the party's growing complacency. In the Politbureau, when matters of high policy were under debate,

---

[1] B. Bazhanov, *Stalin, der Rote Diktator*, p. 21.

he never seemed to impose his views on his colleagues. He carefully followed the course of the debate to see which way the wind was blowing and invariably voted with the majority, unless he had assured his majority beforehand. He was therefore always agreeable to the majority. To party audiences he appeared as a man without personal grudge and rancour, as a detached Leninist, a guardian of the doctrine who criticized others only for the sake of the cause. He gave this impression even when he spoke behind the closed doors of the Politbureau. In the middle of the struggle Trotsky still described Stalin to a trusted foreign visitor as 'a brave and sincere revolutionary'.[1] A few descriptions of scenes in the Politbureau give a vivid glimpse of Stalin, the good soul:

When I attended a session of the Politbureau for the first time [writes Bazhanov] the struggle between the triumvirs and Trotsky was in full swing. Trotsky was the first to arrive for the session. The others were late, they were still plotting. . . . Next entered Zinoviev. He passed by Trotsky; and both behaved as if they had not noticed one another. When Kamenev entered, he greeted Trotsky with a slight nod. At last Stalin came in. He approached the table at which Trotsky was seated, greeted him in a most friendly manner and vigorously shook hands with him across the table.[2]

During another session, in the autumn of 1923, one of the triumvirs proposed that Stalin be brought in as a controller into the Commissariat of War, of which Trotsky was still the head. Trotsky, irritated by the proposal, declared that he was resigning from office and asked to be relieved from all posts and honours in Russia and allowed to go to Germany, which then seemed to be on the brink of a Communist upheaval, to take part in the revolution there. Zinoviev countered the move by asking the same for himself. Stalin put an end to the scene, declaring that 'the party could not possibly dispense with the services of two such important and beloved leaders'.[3]

He was slowly stacking his cards and waiting. The opposition, though again condemned by the thirteenth congress in May 1924, was still a factor to be reckoned with. The attitude of the Communist International had also to be considered. The

---

[1] M. Eastman, *Since Lenin Died*, p. 55.
[2] B. Bazhanov, *Stalin, der Rote Diktator*, p. 21.
[3] Ibid., p. 52.

leaders of European communism, Germans, Poles, and Frenchmen, had either protested against the discrediting of Trotsky or attempted to persuade the antagonists to make peace. It took Zinoviev a lot of wire-pulling to silence those 'noises off'. He had behind him the prestige of the only victorious Communist party, the international myth, so to say, of the October revolution, from which only very few Communists dared to break away. He also had at his disposal the treasure of the International, to which the Russian party was the greatest single contributor and on which some European parties were, up to a point, dependent. Enough that by using all means of pressure, after the expulsion or demotion of many Communist leaders, the triumvirate succeeded in extracting a pronouncement against the Russian opposition from the fifth congress of the International, which sat in Moscow in June and July 1924. Stalin, who had so far kept aloof from the Comintern, addressed in private its Polish commission and castigated the Poles for their bias in favour of Trotsky.[1]

Dissension among the triumvirs was yet another reason for Stalin's caution. Not until a year later, in 1925, did they fall out; but even now personal jealousies troubled their relations. Zinoviev and Kamenev began to feel that Stalin was tightening his grip on the party machine and excluding them from control. Stalin was envious of their authority in matters of doctrine. Shortly after the condemnation of Trotsky, he made his first public attack, irrelevant in content, on Kamenev's doctrinal unreliability.[2] Each of the triumvirs had enough ground to think that a split between them might drive one of them to join hands with Trotsky against the others. This motive did not impel Zinoviev and Kamenev, who eventually were to coalesce with Trotsky, to soften their attacks on him; but it did enter into Stalin's tactical calculations. As a tactician he proved himself superior to his partners.

Finally, he was still waiting for the adversary to make the blunders that were inherent in his attitude. Trotsky had accepted the Leninist cult, even though his rational mind and European tastes were outraged by it. The uniform of Lenin's disciple was, anyhow, too tight for him. The Leninist *mystique*, however, had already grown too powerful for anybody who

---

[1] J. Stalin, *Sochinenya*, vol. vi, pp. 264–72.   [2] Ibid., p. 257.

wanted to get the hearing of a Communist audience to ignore it, let alone challenge it. Trotsky thus involved himself in fighting on ground where he was weak. The triumvirs hurled at him old anti-Trotskyist quotations from Lenin and, what was even more embarrassing to him, his own strictures on Lenin which he had uttered twelve or fifteen years ago. In the mind of the young Communist, the selection of such quotations added up to a picture of Trotsky malevolently opposing Lenin at every turn of events, from the split in 1903 to the debates over Brest Litovsk and the trade unions. In the light of the Leninist dogma, Trotsky stood condemned.

For Trotsky to reject the dogma would have meant to appeal against the party to non-communist opinion. This was the one thing that Stalin could be quite sure Trotsky would not do. Outside the party, formless revolutionary frustration mingled with distinctly counter-revolutionary trends. Since the ruling group had singled out Trotsky as a target for attack, he automatically attracted the spurious sympathy of many who had hitherto hated him. As he made his appearance in the streets of Moscow, he was spontaneously applauded by crowds in which idealistic Communists rubbed shoulders with Mensheviks, Social Revolutionaries, and the new *bourgeoisie* of the N.E.P., by all those indeed who, for diverse reasons, hoped for a change.[1] Precisely because he refused to rally in his support such mixed elements, he showed timidity and hesitancy in almost every move he made. He could not stop opposing the triumvirs who had identified themselves with the party; and yet even in his rebellion he still remained on his knees before the party. Every move he made was thus a demonstration of weakness. Stalin could afford to wait until his rival defeated himself through a series of such demonstrations.

It is here that the knot was tied which was to be cut only in the tragic purge trials twelve and thirteen years later. It is here, too, that the most important clue to the understanding of those trials is to be found. At the congress in May 1924, Trotsky, facing the implacably hostile phalanx of party secretaries, was on the point of surrendering to his critics and abjuring the opposition. Krupskaya, Radek, and others exhorted the antagonists to make peace. Zinoviev, however, was not to be

[1] M. Eastman, *Since Lenin Died*, p. 128, and B. Bazhanov, *Stalin, der Rote Diktator*.

persuaded. He demanded that Trotsky should surrender in his thoughts as well as in his deeds, that he should admit that he had been wrong in his criticisms. In the history of Bolshevism this was the first instance where a member of the party was vaguely charged with a 'crime of conscience', a purely theological accusation. Its motive was tactical, not theological: Trotsky, submitting to party discipline but not recanting, still seemed to the triumvirs a formidable foe. Zinoviev therefore added to the terms of his submission an obviously unacceptable point, which would compel Trotsky to go on waging the unequal struggle. Thus, the first suggestion of a 'crime of conscience' against the party was made by the man who, twelve years later, was to go to his death with appalling recantations of his own 'crimes of conscience'. Stalin, at least in appearance, had nothing to do with that. He repeatedly stated that the only condition for peace was that Trotsky should stop his attacks. He repeatedly made the gesture that looked like the stretching out of his hand to his opponent.

Trotsky's reply to Zinoviev was pregnant with the tragedy that was to overwhelm Zinoviev and Kamenev even more cruelly than himself:

The party [Trotsky said] in the last analysis is always right, because the party is the single historic instrument given to the proletariat for the solution of its fundamental problems. I have already said that in front of one's own party nothing could be easier than to acknowledge a mistake, nothing easier than to say: all my criticisms, my statements, my warnings, my protests—the whole thing was a mere mistake. I, however, comrades, cannot say that, because I do not think it. I know that one must not be right *against* the party. One can be right only with the party, and through the party, for history has created no other road for the realization of what is right. The English have a saying: 'Right or wrong—my country.' With far greater historic justification we may say: right or wrong, on separate particular issues, it is my party. . . .[1]

These words of the leader of the opposition resembled less the words a patriotic Englishman might use than those of a medieval heretic, confessing his heresy, rueful and yet stubborn in his conviction, able to see no salvation beyond the Church and yet none in the Church either. Stalin sarcastically dismissed

[1] *13 Syezd Vsesoyuznoi Komunisticheskoi Partii*, pp. 166 and 245. See also M. Eastman, *Since Lenin Died*, pp. 88–9.

Trotsky's statement, saying that the party made no claim to infallibility.

.   .   .   .

The next stage in the struggle was the so-called 'literary debate' in the autumn of the same year. Trotsky opened it with a book, *The Lessons of October*, which shifted the polemic to new topics, ostensibly unconnected with the issues on which it had centred so far. The book was a study of the mechanics of revolution and the role of determined leadership in it. The gist of its argument was that a 'revolutionary situation' is a fleeting opportunity, which the revolutionary party is bound to miss if it is unaware of it or reluctant to seize it. It is true that a revolution cannot be arbitrarily staged; it is the outcome of a long and relatively slow disintegration of the old order—this is its 'objective' aspect. But, once that disintegration has reached a decisive stage, the role of the 'subjective' factor, of leadership, begins. The revolutionary situation is, by its nature, dynamic; its ups and downs follow in rapid succession. The class struggle passes from stationary warfare to lightning movement and manœuvre, in which everything hangs on the initiative and quick decision of the general staff of the revolution. Even the most revolutionary party suffers from a certain amount of conservative inertia. Its right wing fails to think and act in the strategic terms that suit the circumstances. It shrinks before action at the decisive place and at the decisive moment, being unaware of the importance of time and hoping for an indefinite prolongation of the opportunity which history offers perhaps only once in an epoch. Illustrating his thesis by the experience of 1917, Trotsky emphatically reminded his readers of Lenin's sharp discord with Zinoviev and Kamenev on the eve of the October rising.

It looked, then, as if Trotsky's book was merely a cool, almost academic study of the lessons of recent history. Yet, to the overwhelming majority of the party, those who joined its ranks only after the revolution, his version of the events of 1917 sounded like a sensational, almost indecent, indiscretion. Trotsky branded the two senior triumvirs as the spokesmen of a right wing, the 'strike breakers' (in Lenin's words) of the revolution. In the preface to his book he brought his argument up to date and contrasted the Bolshevik strategy of 1917 with what the Communists did in Germany in 1923, in the middle of the turmoil provoked there by the French occupation of the Ruhr.[1] In the autumn of 1923, Trotsky argued, Germany was ripe for proletarian revolution; but the revolutionaries missed their opportunity because they succumbed to the same inert timidity shown by Zinoviev and Kamenev in 1917. Ostensibly, his attack was directed against the leaders of German communism. Actually, it aimed at the triumvirs, especially at Zinoviev, who, as president of the Comintern, inspired the policy of its German branch.

The triumvirs parried the blow. They produced their own version of the history of the revolution, in which they minimized or even denied their hesitations, bogglings, and disagreements with Lenin. They also did their best to play down Trotsky's role in 1917. This was the first of a very long series of those bizarre 'revisions' and 'corrections' that, in the end, were to make the history of the revolution an almost illegible palimpsest, where countless and conflicting narratives were superimposed upon one another. In addition, all Trotsky's epithets about Lenin and all Lenin's rejoinders, dating from before 1917, were once again lifted from the archives and republished. The rank and file of the party were disgusted with the spectacle, which seemed to bear no relation to the country's misery and the constructive tasks of government and party. The leaders, many thought, were making an inexplicable exhibition of their own irresponsibility.

Stalin was the only man whose prestige was not impaired. Trotsky, whatever the merits of his views, had to take the blame for having initiated what looked like a squabble over bygones.[2] The endless recollections of his anti-Bolshevik past were not without their effect. On the other hand, his own scathing reminders of Zinoviev's and Kamenev's behaviour in 1917 did a lot to compromise the two. Trotsky could say little or nothing against Stalin, except in obscure hints; for, whatever Stalin had done or said in 1917, he had as a rule done it anonymously or in his usual elusive manner. Unwittingly, Trotsky now helped him to his ascendancy over Zinoviev and Kamenev. The latter were now in desperate need of a favourable testimony from the

---

[1] See L. Trotsky, 'The Need to Study "October"', in *The Errors of Trotskyism*, pp. 29–119.   [2] J. Stalin, *Sochinenya*, vol. vii, p. 6.

General Secretary, who alone seemed to be able to speak as a disinterested witness in the matter. Indeed, in November 1924, Stalin publicly bore witness to the Leninist rectitude of his partners.[1] Zinoviev and Kamenev, he stated, were good Leninists—Bolsheviks. Their disagreement with the party had been episodic only. He himself had made some mistakes before Lenin's return to Russia in 1917. But only somebody who was in the party but not of it, who viewed the party with the ill will of an outsider, could now rehash old differences and make so much play with them. As to Trotsky, he had 'played no special role' in the October revolution. True, he 'did fight well', but only as an agent of the Central Committee; and, incidentally, even the left Social Revolutionaries, who later on turned against the revolution, had fought well then. The actual leadership of the rising belonged to a 'party centre', of which Trotsky was not even a member. This was Stalin's first contribution to the 'revision' of history, a contribution that startled those who remembered the actual course of the rising.[2] Yet, on the whole, Stalin's argument sounded plausible, while Trotsky's revelations, in which the leadership of the party was seen as a sluggish body constantly whipped into action by Lenin, could not but hurt the party's *amour propre*. Even Lenin's widow, who knew the truth, was persuaded to come out with a dignified defence of her husband's two closest disciples; and for the rank and file her testimony settled the matter.[3]

The 'literary debate' still dragged on. Stalin published a collection of his own articles written in 1917 and added a topical preface. The debate shifted back to current affairs; and it had undertones of new significance which found their full expression in Stalin's theory of socialism in one country.

Stalin first formulated his ideas on socialism in one country

[1] J. Stalin, *The October Revolution* (English edition), pp. 68–94.

[2] The 'centre' to which Stalin referred consisted of five members of the Central Committee (Stalin, Sverdlov, Dzerzhinsky, and two others), who were delegated to serve on the Revolutionary Committee of the Soviet, over which Trotsky presided. As a separate body, the 'centre' never existed; and it played no part in the leadership of the October revolution. Only after Stalin's ascendancy did the legend of that 'centre' invade the history books; but even there it was not supported by a single document. See Chapter V, pp. 167–8.

[3] See N. Krupskaya, 'The Lessons of October', in *The Errors of Trotskyism*, pp. 365–71.

in the autumn of 1924. Belief in socialism in one country was soon to become the supreme test of loyalty to party and state. In the next ten or fifteen years nobody who failed that test was to escape condemnation and punishment. Yet, if one studies the 'prolegomena' to this article of Stalinist faith, one is struck by the fact that it was first put forward by Stalin almost casually, like a mere debating point, in the 'literary discussion'. For many months, until the summer of the next year, none of Stalin's rivals, neither the other triumvirs nor Trotsky, thought the point worth arguing. Nor was Stalin's own mind fixed. In his pamphlet *The Foundations of Leninism*, published early in 1924, he stated with great emphasis that, though the proletariat of one country could seize power, it could not establish a Socialist economy in one country.

But the overthrow [these are Stalin's words] of the power of the *bourgeoisie* and establishment of the power of the proletariat in one country does not yet mean that the complete victory of socialism has been ensured. The principle task of socialism—the organization of socialist production—has still to be fulfilled. Can this task be fulfilled, can the final victory of socialism be achieved in one country, without the joint efforts of the proletarians in several advanced countries? No, it cannot. To overthrow the *bourgeoisie* the efforts of one country are sufficient; this is proved by the history of our revolution. For the final victory of socialism, for the organization of Socialist production, the efforts of one country, particularly of a peasant country like Russia, are insufficient; for that, the efforts of the proletarians of several advanced countries are required.[1]

In his *Problems of Leninism*, however, which he wrote later in the same year, Stalin corrected himself and asserted the opposite. He withdrew the first edition of his *Foundations of Leninism* from circulation and renounced it as apocryphal. He was at first hardly aware of the weight that circumstances were soon to give to his 'socialism in one country'. He reached his formula gropingly, discovering, as it were, a new continent, while he believed himself to be sailing for quite a different place.

His immediate purpose was to discredit Trotsky and to prove for the *n*th time that Trotsky was no Leninist. Searching in Trotsky's past, the triumvirs came across the theory of 'perma-

[1] This quotation is taken from the English edition of J. Stalin, *Problems of Leninism* (p. 157), published in Moscow in 1945.

nent revolution', which he had formulated in 1905. They started a polemic against it; and it was in the course of that polemic that Stalin arrived at his formula. Since his 'socialism in one country' thus originated as a counter to Trotsky's 'permanent revolution', it is proper to sum up and analyse the two formulas in their bearing upon each other.

Trotsky had borrowed his theory from Marx and applied it to the Russian revolution.[1] He spoke of the 'permanency' of the revolution in a double sense: the revolution, he foresaw, would be driven by circumstances to pass from its anti-feudal (bourgeois) to its anti-capitalist (Socialist) phase. Contrary to the then accepted Marxist view, not the advanced western European countries but backward Russia would be the first to set out along the road to socialism. But Russia alone would not be able to advance far upon that road. The revolution could not stop at her national frontiers. It would have to pass from its national to its international phase—this was to be the second aspect of its 'permanency'. Under the impact of Russia western Europe, too, would become revolutionized. Only then could socialism be established on a broad international basis. The progress of mankind, so Trotsky argued, was now hampered not only by the capitalist mode of production but also by the existence of nation-states. The final outcome of the revolutionary transformation could only be One World, one Socialist world. There was, however, a disquieting question mark in this prognostication. What will happen—Trotsky asked in 1906— if the revolution fails to spread from Russia to western Europe? His grim answer was that it would then either succumb to a conservative Europe or become corroded in its economically and culturally primitive Russian environment.

Until 1917, it will be remembered, this theory was Trotsky's personal contribution to Marxist thought, rejected by Bolsheviks as well as by Mensheviks. On one or two occasions Lenin vaguely sketched a not dissimilar view of the future; but, on the whole, his policy was firmly based on the premiss that the Russian revolution would confine itself to its anti-feudal

---

[1] Trotsky first developed his theory in his famous pamphlet: *Itogi i Perspektivy Ruskoi Revolutsii*, published in 1906. He gave the most complete exposition of his theory in *Permanentnaya Revolutsya*, written in 1928, after his deportation to Alma Ata, and published abroad in 1930.

objectives. It was on this point that he denied its 'permanency'. Nevertheless he, too, did believe that the bourgeois revolution in Russia would stimulate a Socialist revolution in western Europe; and that then, but only then, might Russia also, with the help of the 'advanced countries', move forward towards socialism.[1] What Lenin denied was not the international character of the revolution but Russia's intrinsic capacity to embark upon socialism before western Europe. He reproached Trotsky with 'overlooking' the peasantry, because only if one ignored the peasantry's attachment to individual property could one assume that a peasant country like Russia would by itself pass from the bourgeois to the Socialist revolution.

In 1917, it will be remembered, Lenin changed his mind. In all essentials the thesis of the permanent revolution (though not, of course, its somewhat bookish nomenclature) was adopted by his party. The revolution did in fact pass from the anti-feudal to the anti-capitalist phase. To the very last Lenin and his followers expected it also to spread beyond Russia. Meanwhile they looked upon their own country as upon a besieged fortress, spacious and powerful enough to hold out. They believed that an important advance could be made in organizing the internal life of that fortress on Socialist lines. Spurring on his followers to the job, Lenin (and Trotsky) emphatically pointed to the possibilities of Socialist experiment opening before them. But essentially Lenin thought of Socialist society in international terms. We have seen that early in 1924 Stalin, too, was still arguing that 'for the final victory of socialism, for the organization of Socialist production, the efforts of one country, particularly of a peasant country like Russia, are insufficient'. He now stated that the efforts of Russia alone would suffice for the *complete* organization of a Socialist economy. A Socialist economy—this had so far been taken for granted—was conceivable only as an economy of plenty. This presupposed a highly developed industry capable of ensuring a high standard of living for the whole people. How then, the question arose, could a country like Russia, whose meagre industry had been reduced to rack and ruin, achieve socialism? Stalin pointed to Russia's great assets: her vast spaces and enormous riches in raw materials. A proletarian government

[1] Lenin, *Sochinenya*, vol. ix, pp. 64–5 and *passim*.

could, in his view, through its control of industry and credit, develop those resources and carry the building of socialism to a successful conclusion, because in this endeavour it would be supported by a vast majority of the people, including the peasants.

This, the most essential, part of Stalin's formula was very simple. It proclaimed in terms clear to everybody the self-sufficiency of the Russian revolution. It was true that Stalin begged many a question. He did not even try to meet the objections to his thesis that were raised later by his critics. One objection that most peasants, attached as they were to private property, were certain to put up the strongest resistance to collectivism, he simply dismissed as a heretical slander on the peasantry. Nor did he seriously consider the other argument that socialism was possible only on the basis of the intensive industrialization already achieved by the most advanced western countries; and that Russia by herself would not be able to catch up with those countries. According to his critics, socialism could beat capitalism only if it represented a higher productivity of labour and higher standards of living than had been attained under capitalism. The critics deduced that if productivity of labour and standards of living were to remain lower in Russia than in the capitalist countries then socialism would, in the long run, fail even in Russia. Nor did Stalin ever try to refute their forecast that in an economy of scarcity, such as an isolated Russian economy would be, a new and glaring material inequality between various social groups was certain to arise.

But, whatever the flaws in Stalin's reasoning, flaws that were obvious only to the most educated men in the party, his formula was politically very effective. It contained, at any rate, one clear and positive proposition: we are able to stand on our own feet, to build and to complete the building of socialism. This was what made the formula useful for polemical and practical purposes. It offered a plain alternative to Trotsky's conception. For a variety of reasons, however, Stalin did not present his thesis in that plain and clear-cut form. He hedged it round with all sorts of reservations and qualifications. One reservation was that the victory of socialism in Russia could not be considered secure so long as her capitalist environment threatened Russia with armed intervention. Socialism in a single state could not be beaten by the 'cheap goods' produced in capitalist countries of which his critics spoke; but it might be defeated by force of arms. In the next few years Stalin himself constantly held that danger before Russia's eyes and thereby seemed to weaken his own case. Moreover, he went on to express, though with ever decreasing confidence, a belief in the proximity of international revolution. He proclaimed the absolute self-sufficiency of Russian socialism in one half of his thesis and disclaimed it in the other.

The strangeness of that passionate ideological dispute does not end here. As the controversy developed, Stalin ascribed to his critics the view that it was not possible to build socialism in Russia. He then presented the issue as one between those who believed in the 'creative force' of the revolution and the 'panic mongers' and 'pessimists'. Now the issue was not as simple as that. His critics were beyond question not guilty of the things imputed to them. They, too, asserted that it was possible and necessary to organize the country's economy on Socialist lines. Trotsky in particular had, since the end of the civil war, urged the Politbureau to begin gearing up the administration for planned economy; and in those early days he first sketched most of the ideas that were later to be embodied in the five-year plans.[1]

The student of the controversy may thus often have the uncanny feeling that its very object is indefinable; that, having aroused unbounded passion and bitterness, it simply vanishes into thin air. Stripped of polemical distortions and insinuations, the debate seems in the end, to the student's astonishment, to centre on a bizarre irrelevancy. The point was not whether socialism could or should be built but whether the building could be *completed* in a single isolated state. Metaphorically speaking, the antagonists did not argue whether it was possible or desirable to erect the edifice they wanted; nor did they dis-

---

[1] N. Bukharin in his *Kritika Ekonomicheskoi Platformy Oppozitsii*, entirely devoted to a criticism of Trotsky's, Piatakov's, and Preobrazhensky's economic ideas, quotes Trotsky's letter to the Central Committee (8 October 1923), in which Trotsky summed up his policy as follows: 'Planned economy; severe concentration of industry; severe reduction of costs' (p. 54). In his *Novyi Kurs*, published later in the year, Trotsky urged the subordination of financial and monetary policy to the needs of industrialization (ibid., pp. 71-2). This brought upon him the charge that he advocated the 'dictatorship of industry' and 'super-industrialization'. See N. Bukharin, op. cit., pp. 3, 53-4.

agree about the materials of which it was to be built or even about its shape. Ostensibly, the only point at issue was whether it would be possible to cover the edifice with a roof. Stalin's yes was as emphatic as his opponents' no.[1] Both sides still agreed that the 'roof' was not to be laid for a very, very long time yet, that classless socialism would not be achieved within the lifetime of one or even two generations. Both sides also agreed that hostile forces might wreck the building at any stage of their work on it—they constantly saw the shadow of war falling across Russia. Finally, Stalin, like his critics, professed to believe that long before the time came to put on the roof, the problem he had posed would cease to exist, because revolution in the west would free Socialist Russia from isolation.

It might seem then that it was preposterous for the disputants, who were men of action, to pose the problem as they had posed it; and that, on their own showing, they could have travelled a very, very long way together, leaving their differences to professional scholastics to thrash out. Was the whole dispute, then, a mere smoke-screen for a clash of personal ambitions? No doubt the personal rivalries were a strong element in it. But the historian who reduced the whole matter to that would commit a blatant mistake. He would still have to explain why 'socialism in one country' split the ranks of Bolshevism from top to bottom, why it became an issue of such deadly earnest for a whole Russian generation, why it determined the outlook of a great nation for a quarter of a century. The other suggestion which is often made, that socialism in one country was invented to allay the suspicions of foreign governments, alarmed by 'subversive' activities directed from

[1] At a later stage of the debate, in January 1926, Stalin thus formulated his view: 'We mean the possibility of solving the contradictions between the proletariat and the peasantry with the aid of the internal forces of our country, the possibility of the proletariat assuming power and using that power to build a complete socialist society in our country, with the sympathy and the support of the proletariat of other countries, but without the preliminary victory of the proletarian revolution in other countries.

'Without such a possibility, the building of socialism is building without prospects, building without being sure that socialism will be built. It is no use building socialism without being sure that we can build it, without being sure that the technical backwardness of our country is not an *insuperable* obstacle to the building of a complete Socialist society. To deny such a possibility is to display lack of faith in the cause of building socialism, to abandon Leninism.' See J. Stalin, *Problems of Leninism* (English edition), p. 160.

Moscow, is even more pointless. When Stalin formulated his thesis, his name was still almost unknown abroad; and, even later on, the desire to allay foreign suspicions did not prevent him from making statements on communism in Europe that made the flesh of many a Conservative abroad creep.

As sometimes happens in important disputes, where both sides are strongly committed to certain common principles, so in this controversy, too, its explanation cannot be found in the literal meaning of the disputants' words, certainly not in their zealous reiteration of 'common' principles, but must rather be sought in the subtle, often imperceptible, shifts in the emphasis of their arguments. The explanation is further to be found in the state of mind and the moods of the milieu in which the disputants act and which they address. In the last resort, the doctrinal controversy grows out of those moods; and they—the moods—form the sounding-board that imparts a significant ring to the seemingly undistinguishable formulas that are bandied about. The audience that listens to the disputants is left unmoved by their professions of common principle; it treats these as part of a customary ritual. But it pricks up its ears at the different hints and allusions thrown out by either side; and it avidly absorbs all their undertones and unspoken conclusions. It quickly learns to tell the operative part of any formula from the reservations and escape clauses that seem to contradict it.

Now the operative part of Stalin's thesis, the thing that was really new and striking in it, was the assertion of the self-sufficiency of the Russian revolution. All the rest was a repetition of traditional Bolshevik truisms, some of which had become meaningless and others embarrassing, but all of which had to be repeated, because they had the flavour of doctrinal respectability. The thing that was new in Stalin's argument represented a radical revision of the party's attitude. But the revision was undertaken in a manner that seemed to deny the very fact of revision and to represent it as a straight continuation of an orthodox line of thought, a method familiar from the history of many a doctrine. We shall not lead the reader further into the thick of this dogmatic battle. Suffice it to say that Stalin did his best to graft his formula on to the body of doctrine he had inherited from Lenin.

More important than the dogmatic intricacies is the fact that now, in the seventh and eighth years of the revolution, a very large section of the party, probably its majority, vaguely and yet very definitely felt the need for ideological stocktaking and revision. The need was emotional rather than intellectual; and those who felt it were by no means desirous of any open break with Bolshevik orthodoxy. No revolutionary party can remain in power seven years without profound changes in its outlook. The Bolsheviks had by now grown accustomed to running an enormous state, 'one-sixth of the world'. They gradually acquired the self-confidence and the sense of self-importance that come from the privileges and responsibilities of power. The doctrines and notions that had been peculiarly theirs when they themselves had been the party of the underdog did not suit their present outlook well. They needed an idea or a slogan that would fully express their newly won self-confidence. 'Socialism in one country' did it. It relieved them, to a decisive extent, of a sense of their dependence on happenings in the five-sixths of the world that were beyond their control. It gave them the soothing theoretical conviction that, barring war, nothing could shake their mastery over Russia: the property-loving peasantry, the industrial weakness of the nation, its low productivity and even lower standard of living, all these implied no threat of a restoration of the *ancien régime*. Whoever, like Trotsky, and later on Zinoviev and Kamenev, dwelt on the dangers to the revolution inherent in all those circumstances, offended the complacency of the party.

Below this psychological attitude, which was confined to the rulers, there was a much broader undercurrent: the party and the working classes had grown weary of the expectation of international revolution which had been the daily bread of Bolshevism. That expectation was dashed in 1917, 1918, and 1920. It rose again in 1923, during the turmoil in Germany. This time the deferment of hope made the heart of the party sick. 'The European working classes are letting us down; they listen to their social democratic leaders and tremble over the fleshpots of capitalism'—such was, roughly, the comment of many a politically minded worker on the daily news from the west. It was a galling thought, one which was inseparable from Trotsky's 'permanent revolution', that in spite of all this the fortunes of Russian communism should still be regarded as ultimately dependent on the victory or defeat of communism abroad. There was something that hurt the national *amour propre* in the usual talk about 'backward' Russia and 'advanced' Europe, even though party speakers illustrated such talk with weighty comparative statistics on Russian poverty and western wealth. The average Bolshevik wished for nothing more than to push such thoughts off his mind; and Stalin, as it were, did that for him.

What Stalin told the party was, roughly, this: Of course we are looking forward to international revolution. Of course we have been brought up in the school of Marxism; and we know that contemporary social and political struggles are, by their very nature, international. Of course we still believe the victory of the proletariat in the west to be near; and we are bound in honour to do what we can to speed it up. But—and this was a very big, a highly suggestive 'but'—do not worry so much about all that international revolution. Even if it were to be delayed indefinitely, even if it were never to occur, we in this country are capable of developing into a fully fledged, classless society. Let us then concentrate on our great constructive task. Those who tell you that this is utopia, that I am preaching national narrow-mindedness, are themselves either adventurers or pusillanimous Social Democrats. We, with our much despised *muzhiks*, have already done more for socialism than the proletariat of all other countries taken together; and, left alone with our *muzhiks*, we shall do the rest of the job.[1]

Stripped of its terminological pretensions and pseudo-dialectical profundity, Stalin's theory reduces itself to this plain and 'sound' colloquialism. But it was as its author that Stalin now established himself as an ideologue in his own right. He was no longer just the General Secretary, the administrative magician of the party: he was the author of a new dogma as well. To old, educated Bolsheviks this was the surprise of their life. When, at one of the party meetings of those days, Stalin involved himself in a theoretical argument, he was interrupted by a half-amused and half-indignant remark from the old Marxist scholar Ryazanov: 'Stop it, Koba, don't make a fool of yourself. Everybody knows that theory is not exactly your field.' The condescending irony of the educated Marxists did

---

[1] J. Stalin, *Sochinenya*, vol. vii, p. 21.

not, however, prevent 'socialism in one country' from becoming the national creed. For all its triteness, Stalin's innovation had its weight and its *raison d'être*. Doctrines may, broadly speaking, be classed into two categories: those that, starting from a long train of intellectual ideas, strike out boldly into a remote uncharted future; and those that, though they are neither deeply rooted in ideas nor original in their anticipations, sum up a powerful and hitherto inarticulate trend of opinion or emotion. Stalin's theory obviously belonged to that second category.

The truly tragic feature of Russian society in the twenties was its longing for stability, a longing which was only natural after its recent experiences. The future had little stability in store for any country, but least of all for Russia. Yet the desire at least for a long, very long, respite from risky endeavours came to be the dominant motive of Russian politics. Socialism in one country, as it was practically interpreted until the late twenties, held out the promise of stability. On the other hand, the very name of Trotsky's theory, 'permanent revolution', sounded like an ominous warning to a tired generation that it should expect no Peace and Quiet in its lifetime. The warning was to come true, though not in the way its author expected; but it could hardly have been heeded.

In his argument against Trotsky, Stalin appealed directly to the horror of risk and uncertainty that had taken possession of many Bolsheviks. He depicted Trotsky as an adventurer, habitually playing at revolution. The charge, it need hardly be said, was baseless. At all crucial moments—in 1905, 1917, and 1920—Trotsky had proved himself the most serious strategist of the revolution, showing no proneness to light-minded adventure. Nor did he ever urge his party to stage any *coup* in any foreign country, which cannot be said of Stalin.[1] Trotsky firmly believed that western European communism would win by its own intrinsic momentum, in the ordinary course of the class struggle, in which outside initiative or assistance, though important at times, could play only a subordinate role. In weighing the chances of communism in the west, Stalin was more sceptical; and his scepticism was to grow as the years passed by. Be that as it may, the epithet 'adventurer' stuck to the ideologue of the 'permanent revolution'. Stalin went further

[1] See Chapter X.

and charged Trotsky with a fondness for terror which had allegedly horrified Lenin. This charge, too, was unfair, especially in Stalin's mouth. Trotsky had not shrunk from using terror in the civil war; but he can be said to have been as little fond of it as a surgeon is fond of bloodshed. Yet in the circumstances just described the charge had a vague and yet distinct eloquence. People afraid of the continuation of the terror were led to believe that the man who had laid the charge against Trotsky was himself at least liberal minded.[1]

The remarkable trait in Stalin was his unique sensibility to all those psychological undercurrents in and around the party, the untalked of hopes and tacit desires, of which he set himself up as a mouthpiece. In this he was very different from the other triumvirs. At the beginning of the controversy over 'permanent revolution' they acted in unison; towards its end they were already poles apart. As Zinoviev and Kamenev admitted later, they started the campaign in order to discredit Trotsky with outdated quotations from Lenin against the 'permanent revolution'; at heart they had no quarrel with its basic tenets, which had become the household ideas of the party. Their attacks upon Trotsky's theory were therefore strangely unreal; they were confined to pointless quibbling over long-forgotten episodes of the days of pre-revolutionary exile. They did not even dream of opposing Trotsky with a positive doctrine of their own. It was otherwise with Stalin. What for him, too, had begun as ideological shadow-boxing developed into a real ideological struggle. The debating-point became the issue. He came to feel a real hatred for his opponent's views; and because of this he had to counter with something positive. He sensed which of his arguments evoked the strongest response from the mass of party officials and workers, that vast human sounding-board which was his *vox dei*. The sounding-board proved un-expectedly responsive to 'socialism in one country'. As happens with revelationists, a figment of his mind, the vision of socialism in one country, took possession of him; but it did so because it corresponded to the things that were latent in so many other minds.

For a long time Zinoviev and Kamenev were unaware of the change that had occurred in their partner. They shrugged their

---

[1] J. Stalin, *The October Revolution*, pp. 88 and 92.

shoulders over his quaint insistence on the possibility of fully fledged socialism in a single country; but they treated the whole thing as a mere stick with which their intellectually inferior partner chose to beat Trotsky; and they did not bother to have a close look at it. They did not object even when, in March and April of 1925, Stalin asked the fourteenth conference of the party to give formal sanction to this thesis and obtained it. It was only next autumn, nearly a year after he had put forward his view, that they awakened to its significance and criticized it as the abandonment of traditional Bolshevism in favour of national communism. Trotsky did not challenge the dogma until 1926, when it had already gained wide acceptance.

The practical implications of Stalin's doctrine were not yet clear. Bolshevism had now reached a most important landmark of its post-revolutionary history; but so far the change affected its attitude of mind rather than its attitude in action. The broad lines of the change can be summed up as follows: hitherto Bolshevism looked upon Russia as upon a periphery of modern civilization. On that periphery the revolution started; there socialism had found its practical pioneers. From there came the impulses for revolutionary change in west and east. Russia's role in the world-wide transformation of society was seen as that of the powerful initiator of the whole movement. But western Europe still remained the real centre of modern civilization; and, in the old Bolshevik view, it was there in the centre and not on the periphery that the forms of a new social life were eventually to be forged. The whole process was seen in terms of a double impact: first of Russia upon the west and then of the Socialist west upon Russia.

In Stalin's doctrine Russia no longer figures as a mere periphery of the civilized world. It is within her own boundaries that the forms of a new society are to be found and worked out. It is her destiny to become the centre of a new civilization, in all respects superior to that capitalist civilization that is defending itself, with so much power of resistance, in western Europe. This new view of the future undoubtedly reflected the exasperation of Russian communism at its own isolation; but it gilded that isolation with dazzling prospects. Exhausted and disillusioned, Bolshevik Russia was withdrawing into her national shell, feasting her sore eyes on the vistas of socialism in one country.

CHAPTER VIII

The 'Great Change'

Introduction: Stalin as the man of the golden mean.—Trotsky's defeat and the end of the triumvirate (1925).—The emergence of a right wing, led by Bukharin, Rykov, and Tomsky.—Stalin supports the pro-*muzhik* policy.—Conflicting views on world capitalism.—Zinoviev and Kamenev turn against Stalin (1925) and join hands with Trotsky (1926).—The Frunze incident.—Stalin defends Bukharin and Rykov against Zinoviev and Kamenev.—His victory at the fourteenth congress of the party (1925): 'Leninist Central Committee united around Stalin'.—Zinoviev's and Kamenev's revelations about Stalin.—Trotsky's 'Clemenceau statement'.—The fifteenth congress expels Trotsky and his followers.—Zinoviev and Kamenev 'capitulate' to Stalin.—Stalin versus Bukharin, Rykov, and Tomsky (1928–30).—The peasantry threatens to starve the towns.—Stalin starts the collectivization of farming.—Politbureau decides to expel Trotsky from Russia (1929).—Demotion of right-wing leaders. 'Stalin is the Lenin of to-day'.—Stalin orders 'offensive against the *kulak*' (end of 1929), and announces the plan to transform Russia into an industrial power (June 1930).—Confusion and virtual civil war in country-side. —General view of the Soviet scene during the first five-year plan (1929–32).—Stalin and Cromwell.—Stalin's appeal to nationalist sentiment.—Political ferment in Stalin's *entourage*.—The suicide of Nadezhda Alliluyeva, Stalin's wife, in November 1932.—Stalin's social policy.—Direction of labour, forced labour, and the fight against levellers.—The achievements of industrialization.—The 'primitive accumulation' of socialism in one country.

IN 1929, five years after Lenin's death, Soviet Russia embarked upon her second revolution, which was directed solely and exclusively by Stalin. In its scope and immediate impact upon the life of some 160 million people the second revolution was even more sweeping and radical than the first. It resulted in Russia's rapid industrialization; it compelled more than a hundred million peasants to abandon their small, primitive holdings and to set up collective farms; it ruthlessly tore the primeval wooden plough from the hands of the *muzhik* and forced him to grasp the wheel of a modern tractor; it drove tens of millions of illiterate people to school and made them learn to read and write; and spiritually it detached European Russia from Europe and brought Asiatic Russia nearer to Europe. The rewards of that revolution were astounding; but so was its cost: the complete loss, by a whole generation, of spiritual and political freedom. It takes a great effort of the imagination to gauge the enormousness and the complexity of that upheaval for which hardly any historical precedent can be found. Even if all allowance is made for the different scales of human affairs in different ages, the greatest reformers in Russian history, Ivan the Terrible and Peter the Great, and the great reformers of other nations too, seem to be dwarfed by the giant form of the General Secretary.

And yet the giant's robe hangs somewhat loosely upon Stalin's figure. There is a baffling disproportion between the magnitude of the second revolution and the stature of its maker, a disproportion which was not noticeable in the revolution of 1917. There the leaders seem to be equal to the great events; here the events seem to reflect their greatness upon the leader. Lenin and Trotsky foresaw their revolution and prepared it many years before it materialized. Their own ideas fertilized the soil of Russia for the harvest of 1917. Not so with Stalin. The ideas of the second revolution were not his. He neither foresaw it nor prepared for it. Yet he, and in a sense he alone, accomplished it. He was at first almost whipped into the vast undertaking by immediate dangers. He started it gropingly, and despite his own fears. Then, carried on by the force of his own doings, he walked the giant's causeway, almost without halt or rest. Behind him were tramping the myriads of weary and bleeding Russian feet, a whole generation in search of socialism in one country. His figure seemed to grow to mythical dimensions. Seen at close quarters, it was still the figure of a man of very ordinary stature and of middling thoughts. Only his fists and feet contrasted with his real stature—they were the fists and the feet of a giant.

Our narrative of Stalin's life has reached the years 1925–6. Since then Stalin's Communist opponents have repeatedly described him as the leader of an anti-revolutionary reaction, while most anti-Communists have seen and still see the haunting spectre of communism embodied in his person. Yet, among the Bolshevik leaders of the twenties, he was primarily the man of the golden mean. He instinctively abhorred the extreme viewpoints which then competed for the party's recognition. His peculiar job was to produce the formulas in which the opposed extremes seemed reconciled. To the mass of hesitating members of the party his words sounded like common sense itself. They accepted his leadership in the hope that the party would be reliably steered along the 'middle of the road' and that 'safety first' would be the guiding principle. It might be said that he appeared as the Baldwin or the Chamberlain, the Harding or the Hoover of Bolshevism, if the mere association of those names with Bolshevism did not sound too incongruous.

It was neither Stalin's fault nor his merit that he never succeeded in sticking to the middle of any road; and that he was constantly compelled to abandon 'safety' for the most dangerous of ventures. Revolutions are as a rule intolerant of golden means and 'common sense'. Those who in a revolution try to tread the middle of the road usually find the earth cleaving under their feet. Stalin was repeatedly compelled to make sudden and inordinately violent jumps now to this now to that extreme of the road. We shall see him over and over again either far to the right of his right-wing critics or far to the left of his left-wing critics. His periodical sharp turns are the convulsive attempts of the man of the golden mean to keep his balance amid the cataclysms of his time. What is astounding is how well he has kept his balance—each of his many jumps would have broken the neck of any less resilient leader.

Thus, for all his inclination towards the reconciliation of conflicting Bolshevik viewpoints, he was no man of compromise. Apart from the fact that those viewpoints were mutually exclusive, his personal characteristics were not those of the conciliator. The only trait he had in common with any man of compromise was his distrust of extremes. But he lacked the suavity, the flair for persuasion, and the genuine interest in narrowing gaps between opposed views which make the political peacemaker. His temperament was altogether averse to compromise; and the conflict between his mind and his temperament underlay much of his behaviour. He appeared before the party with formulas, some parts of which he had borrowed from right-wing Bolsheviks and some from left-wing Bolsheviks. But these were strange compromise formulas: their purpose was not to bring the extremes together but to blow them up and to destroy them. He did not mediate between those who seemed to walk to the right or left of him; he annihilated them. He personified the dictatorship of the golden mean over all the unruly ideas and doctrines that emerged in post-revolutionary society, the dictatorship of the golden mean that could not remain true to itself, to the golden mean.

. . . .

We left Stalin as he was advancing the dogma of socialism in one country. Let us now quickly follow his next steps in the struggle over the succession to Lenin. In January 1925 he at last brought Trotsky to resign from the Commissariat of War. As the chief of the armed forces, Trotsky had still held a most formidable trump. If he had chosen to stage a military *coup d'état* he might perhaps have defeated the triumvirs. But he left office without the slightest attempt at rallying in his defence the army he had created and led for seven years. He still regarded the party, no matter how or by whom it was led, as the legitimate spokesman for the working class. If he were to oppose army to party, so he reasoned, he would have automatically set himself up as the agent for some other class interests, hostile to the working class. He would have entered the path of Bonapartism which he refused to tread. Having resigned from the Commissariat of War, Trotsky devoted his energy and talent to such minor jobs in the economic administration as Stalin assigned to him. He still remained a member of the Politbureau, but for more than a year he kept aloof from all public controversy.

After Trotsky had thus effaced himself, the only bond that kept the triumvirs together snapped. Up to the last moment Zinoviev clamoured for harsher reprisals against Trotsky, even for his arrest. Stalin countered his demands with a public statement to the effect that it was 'inconceivable' that Trotsky should be eliminated from the leadership of the party.[1] Soon afterwards he took the initiative in breaking up the triumvirate: he refused to consult his partners or to concert with them his moves before the sessions of the Politbureau. To all intents and purposes he was the indisputable master of the party, even though Kamenev was still entrenched in the organization of Moscow, while Zinoviev still led the Bolsheviks of Leningrad. Yet, powerful though Stalin's grip on the party was, he could assert his leadership only in a constitutional way, as the spokesman of a majority of the Politbureau. The totalitarian evolu-

[1] *Pravda*, 18 December 1924.

tion of the party had not yet gone far enough for its members to submit to the undisguised dictatorship of any single leader. Indeed, Stalin's stock phrase at that time was that not a single one of Lenin's disciples was worthy of Lenin's mantle and that only as a team could they aspire to leadership.[1] That team was organized in the Politbureau; and the will of the Politbureau was constitutionally expressed through majority vote. In 1925 that body consisted of seven members: Stalin, Zinoviev, Kamenev, Trotsky, Bukharin, Rykov, and Tomsky. Having put an end to the triumvirate, Stalin was now entirely dependent on the backing of three members: Bukharin, Rykov, and Tomsky.

The new alinement coincided with the crystallization of a right wing in the party and the Politbureau. The process began in the first half and was completed in the second half of 1925. Bukharin, Rykov, and Tomsky were the chief spokesmen of the new trend, while Zinoviev and Kamenev came to head the left wing. The new alinement had little or nothing in common with the previous ones. During much of the Leninist period, Bukharin had led the left Communists, while Zinoviev and Kamenev had, during the revolution, spoken for the most moderate group. In Lenin's days the lines of division between various factions were neither stable nor clear cut. Factions emerged and dissolved on a shifting political scene; individuals moved from one group to another, as situations, issues, and attitudes changed. Yesterday's lefts were to-day's moderates; and vice versa. There was then little sense of loyalty to group, coterie, or clique. The present alinement was of an altogether different kind. It had its stable points of controversy and rigid divisions; it bore all the marks of irrevocable finality. Left and right now confronted each other with conflicting programmes and slogans covering almost every aspect of Bolshevik policy.

Stalin belonged neither to the one nor to the other wing. Tactical reasons compelled him to join hands with the spokesmen of the right, on whose vote in the Politbureau he was dependent. He also felt a closer affinity with the men of the new right than with his former partners. Bukharin, Rykov, and Tomsky accepted his socialism in one country, while Zinoviev

[1] J. Stalin, *Sochinenya*, vol. vii, pp. 390-1.

and Kamenev denounced it. Bukharin may justly be regarded as the co-author of the doctrine. He supplied the theoretical arguments for it and he gave it that scholarly polish which it lacked in Stalin's more or less crude version.[1] Temperamental affinities also made for Stalin's alliance with the leaders of the right. Zinoviev and Kamenev were, first of all, ideologues. So was, to be sure, Bukharin, too. But Rykov and Tomsky were, like Stalin himself, primarily administrators. Rykov was now chairman of the Council of People's Commissars, the Soviet Premier. Tomsky was the leader of the trade unions. Both managed huge administrative machines with great caution, with a strong, though narrow, sense of reality, and with indubitable integrity. They and Stalin spoke in the same idiom, the idiom of the administrators. Nevertheless, Stalin felt uneasy in his new alliance. The only middle-of-the-roader in the Politbureau, he was in a sense his allies' prisoner. He used the first opportunity to strengthen his own position. After the fourteenth congress, in December 1925, Molotov, Voroshilov, and Kalinin were elected to the Politbureau. They formed the actual Stalinist 'centre', although Voroshilov and Kalinin were more attracted by the right than suited Stalin. Molotov, slow-minded, dull, but endowed with enormous patience and capacity for work, had followed Stalin like a faithful shadow from the days when, in 1913, he had helped Stalin to issue the first copy of *Pravda*. Stalin exercised upon him the fascination which an astute and ruthless man often exercises upon people lacking such qualities.

The main issue on which the new controversy centred was the practical interpretation that was to be given to the policy of the N.E.P. Under the N.E.P. the country had a mixed economy. State-owned industry formed its 'Socialist sector'. In commerce and small-scale industry private enterprise prevailed. Private ownership ruled supreme in farming. It was still commonly accepted that socialism could be attained only by the gradual expansion of the Socialist sector in competition with the private one.

The question arose, Within what limits should that com-

[1] Until the early thirties Russian and European Communists used to draw their arguments from Bukharin's writings rather than from Stalin's. Bukharin's two books, *The ABC of Communism* (written jointly with Preobrazhensky) and his *Historical Materialism*, were the two most important standard books of Communist propaganda.

petition be allowed; and what forms should it take? Everybody agreed that the country needed a degree of harmony and co-operation between the two sectors. The Socialist industry could not function without buying foodstuffs and raw materials from the individual farmers and without selling part of its own produce to them. The distribution of goods was dependent on private traders. But the competition of the two sectors also implied a degree of antagonism between them. The peasantry clamoured for more and cheaper industrial goods, demanding high prices for its own produce. Industry, only slowly rising from ruin, produced few goods and at high prices and clamoured for cheap food and raw materials. Broadly speaking, the 'Bukharin group' put the greater emphasis on harmonious co-operation between the various sectors of the national econ-omy, while Zinoviev and Kamenev stressed the conflict of their interests.

The general problem resolved itself into two more specific issues: the tempo of Russia's industrialization; and the Govern-ment's attitude towards private farming. The left Bolsheviks saw the chief danger to socialism in the slow recovery of industry and pressed for rapid industrialization. The right wing thought the position of socialism to be secure, even if industrialization were to proceed slowly, 'at a snail's pace' as Bukharin put it.[1] Industrialization, on the need for which everybody agreed 'in principle', required funds. These had to be levied to a large extent from private enterprise and private farming. Bukharin feared that such levies would discourage private initiative and thereby upset a precarious economic balance. The left argued that the farmers and the traders did not deliver the goods any-how; and that they would be induced to sell more food and raw materials if more and cheaper industrial goods were thrown on the market.

Meanwhile, the peasantry clamoured for an extension of the concessions made to it under the N.E.P. It asked for a reduction of agricultural taxation. Well-to-do peasants pressed for the abolition of restrictions on the hiring of farm labourers. Since the sale of land had been forbidden, they also pressed for long-term leasing of land to be permitted, for the freedom to invest

---

[1] N. Popov, *Outline History of the C.P.S.U.*, vol. ii, p. 268, and *14 Syezd Vsesoyuznoi Kom. Partii*, p. 135.

capital in agriculture, and so on. The ruling party claimed to stand for an 'alliance' with the poor and 'middle' peasants but not with the big farmers, the so-called *kulaks*.[1] In practice it had to appease the *kulaks* also, who only too often withheld food from the towns and induced other peasants to do likewise. In the middle twenties the farmers sold to the towns only one-third of the food they used to sell before the war.

In the summer of 1924 a rising of peasants broke out in Georgia. In part this was a delayed reaction of the Georgians' offended national sentiment to the invasion of 1921. In part the rising was provoked by economic grievances. Stalin convened the secretaries of the rural Communist organizations and warned them that 'what had happened in Georgia could happen in the whole of Russia'.[2] The party, he concluded, had lost contact with the peasantry; and it had to approach the *muzhik* with more attentiveness and confidence than hitherto.

But declarations of confidence in the *muzhik* were not enough. The Politbureau could not easily make up its mind what to do next. At first, the issue gave rise to no clear-cut division. Zinoviev urged that the peasants be given a bigger and more real share in running the Soviets. Trotsky argued about the need to offer them economic incentives. The division crystallized later when Bukharin, Rykov, and Tomsky came to voice a definite pro-*muzhik* policy. They wanted the Government to stimulate the development of prosperous farms capable of supplying the towns with food, since the poor and even the middle peasants produced only just enough to feed themselves. The logic of this attitude demanded that the party should abandon its hostility towards the well-to-do farmers, who could, in Bukharin's view, constitute no danger to socialism as long as the Government was master over industry, transport, and banking, the 'commanding posts' in the national economy. In the end, Bukharin believed, even the *kulak* would be more or less painlessly absorbed in the Socialist economy, though the convoy of socialism would have to move forward at the pace dictated

[1] The peasantry was divided into these three groups by the following rule of thumb method: 'Strong' farmers who hired labour were classed as *kulaks*. Those who had their small holdings but also hired themselves as labourers were regarded as poor peasants (*byednyaks*). The middle peasant (*serednyak*) was the self-supporting smallholder, who neither employed labourers nor hired his labour to others.

[2] J. Stalin, *Sochinenya*, vol. vi, p. 309.

by its slowest, that is its rural, section. Bukharin frankly called upon the peasants to 'enrich' themselves.

Stalin listened to the debates in the Politbureau and at first avoided committing himself. He was inclined to accept the policy of the pro-*muzhik* group, as a matter of practical convenience. But he had his mental reservations, especially when the right wing openly advocated the appeasement of well-to-do farmers. He tried to prevail upon his partners to exercise more discretion; and he disavowed Bukharin's frank appeals to the rural *bourgeoisie*. When at last he spoke his mind, his utterances were eclectic. In practice he opted for the course advocated by Bukharin; but he was anxious to appear as the devotee of Bolshevik orthodoxy.

In April 1925 a party conference drew up the balance of recent debates.[1] The agricultural tax was reduced. Restrictions upon the leasing of land, the hiring of labour, and the accumulation of capital were largely removed. The pro-*muzhik* group scored its first point. It stood for this course not because it favoured capitalist farming for its own sake, but because it saw in it the decisive factor in improving the provisioning of the towns.

Simultaneously with this swing in domestic policies, a new view on the international situation came to be accepted. Stalin and Bukharin told the party that in Europe the period of revolutionary strain and stress had come to an end and that foreign capitalism had achieved a degree of stabilization which made it certain that Soviet Russia would remain isolated for a long time to come. The spokesmen of the right wing forecast a period of stability and prosperity in the capitalist countries similar perhaps to that which prevailed before 1914.[2] Stalin carefully stressed the circumstances which might upset the 'stabilization'; but the general tenor of his argument also led to the conclusion that the capitalist world had recovered from the war and that the prospects of any new revolutionary crisis abroad belonged to a more or less remote future.[3] In retrospect, these prognostications, which were made a couple of years before the great depression of 1929, appear startling. They form a

[1] N. Popov, *Outline History of the C.P.S.U.*, vol. ii, p. 227.
[2] Ibid., pp. 282 and *passim*; and Zinoviev's report in *14 Syezd Vsesoyuznoi Kom. Partii*, p. 642.　　　　[3] J. Stalin, *Sochinenya*, vol. vii, pp. 52-3 and *passim*.

curious *pendant* to socialism in one country and to the 'gradual-ist', almost Fabian, trend in Soviet politics at that time.

It was against this Soviet Fabianism that Zinoviev and Kamenev rose in opposition. They denounced the pro-*muzhik* policy, saying that the stronger the big farmers grew the easier it would be for them to withhold food from the urban popula-tion and to wrest more and more concessions from the Govern-ment; the easier, in a word, it would be for them to undermine the Soviets and work for the restoration of capitalism. The Government should have reduced taxation for middle and poor peasants, but increased it for the well-to-do. The country was threatened by a chronic food crisis. In old days the supply of food was secured by the landlords' large estates, which were now split up. Before the revolution Russia had 16 million farms—it had 24 or 25 millions of them now. The Government should set out to create large farms, producers of marketable grain; but these should be large collective farms and not the large farms of the *kulaks*.

There was no question, in the view of the left Bolsheviks, of driving the peasants into collective farms by force. The switch-over from private to collective farming was to be carried out gradually, with the peasants' own consent. The masses of poor peasants would be only too glad to join in the collective farms if the Government offered them proper inducements: tractors, fertilizers, seeds, and so on. These would greatly increase the yield of agricultural labour and convince other smallholders of the benefits of collective farming. Such inducements would be forthcoming only if and when industry expanded. In addition, the *muzhik* had to be taught to handle machines. The trans-formation of agriculture would admittedly take much time; but the Government, so the left concluded, should at least make a determined start with the reform.

The left Bolsheviks also refused to accept Stalin's and Bukharin's views on the stabilization of capitalism. They repeated after Lenin that the First World War had opened a general crisis of the capitalist order, an epoch of world-wide revolutionary transformation. The temporary ebb and flow of the Communist tide abroad did not, in their view, affect the basically revolutionary character of the times. The left Bol-sheviks pointed to the revolution in China, which had just begun, and to the first rumblings of a grave social crisis in Great Britain.

In the autumn of 1925 the debate spread from the Polit-bureau into the press and public meetings. Zinoviev published his essay *The Philosophy of an Epoch* and his book *Leninism*. In October the leaders of the left submitted to the Central Committee a memorandum in which they asked for a free debate on all controversial issues. The memorandum, resembling Trotsky's previous interventions, was signed by Zinoviev, Kamenev, Krupskaya, and Sokolnikov, the Commissar of Finance.

The real controversy was between the two extreme wings. Stalin contributed to it not a single idea of his own. He looked askance at the bold plans for industrialization and collectivization and dubbed his former partners adherents of 'super-industrialization', even though their schemes were almost timid compared with those he himself was to promote a few years later. He charged them with attempting to disrupt the alliance between the proletariat and the peasantry, even though the 'anti-*muzhik*' measures proposed by the left Bolsheviks were very mild compared with the collectivization of 1929-30. The course advocated by the right seemed to him to be much safer and to promise much more immediate advantage.[1]

But he took pains to appear before the party as an advocate of the middle course. He spoke for the *muzhik*, that is for the poor and the middle peasants but against the *kulaks*. He reproached Zinoviev and Kamenev with preaching hostility not just to the *kulak* but to the middle peasants. Branding them as super-industrializers, he nevertheless included industrialization in the programme of his own which he presented to the fifteenth congress of the party. For nearly three years, until late in 1928, industrialization was actually shelved while the programme of the right wing was being carried out. But Stalin's vague intermediate formulas served their purpose. They sanctioned the policies of the right wing; and they put at ease those who, if they had to make a straight choice between right and left, might have opted for the left.

.   .   .   .

Meanwhile, Stalin benefited from the circumstance that

[1] J. Stalin, *Sochinenya*, vol. viii, pp. 281, 287, and *passim*.

Trotsky and the two ex-triumvirs hesitated to join hands against him, although they now had many points in common. From his position of vantage, he watched his divided opponents, their shy mutual overtures, their jealousies and resentments. He added to the confusion in their ranks by his own vague advances to Trotsky. Agents of the General Secretariat assiduously reminded Trotsky's followers that Zinoviev, not Stalin, had exhibited the worst virulence in the fight against them. Stalin himself in his book *Problems of Leninism*, which was published in January 1926, turned all his polemical zest against Zinoviev and Kamenev and refrained from making a single unfriendly remark about Trotsky. Some of the leading Trotskyists, for instance Antonov-Ovseenko and Radek, urged their friends to coalesce with Stalin. Others wished a plague on both the General Secretary and his former partners. Mrachkovsky, one of Trotsky's closest friends, laconically described the risk of any coalition: 'Stalin will deceive us and Zinoviev will sneak away.'[1] On the other hand, Zinoviev's followers had been so strongly indoctrinated against Trotsky that for them it was the irony of history that they should now repeat many of his arguments. Meanwhile, the heavy hand of the General Secretary bore down upon the new dissidents as it had done upon the old ones. Zinoviev's followers were removed from positions of responsibility. Ordinary workers who remembered that a vote for the previous opposition had cost some of them their jobs were non-committal—there was too much unemployment under the N.E.P. for anybody but the most courageous to brave the risk. The doubters and the waverers responded to the invocations of 'iron discipline' which the General Secretariat showered upon them.

A strange incident which happened in those days, in November 1925, shows how the party's reflexes had become conditioned to respond even to the most irrational demands of that 'iron discipline'. Frunze, Trotsky's successor in the Commissariat of War, fell ill. Some of his doctors advised him to undergo a surgical operation, while others feared that he was too weak to survive it. The Politbureau settled the matter, ordering the Commissar to submit to the surgical knife. Frunze reluctantly obeyed; and he died during the operation. Later on, Trotsky

---

[1] L. Trotsky, *Mein Leben*, p. 505, and *Bulleten Oppozitsii*, nos. 54–5.

suggested that Stalin got subservient physicians to express an opinion in favour of the operation to the Politbureau; and that he thus virtually condemned to death the Commissar who had sided with Zinoviev.[1] It is difficult to say what were the facts. What is certain and most significant in the story is that the Politbureau could arrogate to itself the right to take decisions on so personal a matter. The individual Bolshevik, whether he was the commander-in-chief or the secretary of a provincial committee, belonged in his entirety to the party. He had no existence and no will beyond it. Even the most intimate side of his private life was open to inspection by his superiors. It goes without saying that where a Frunze submitted, the average member could hardly dare to assert himself. As a body, the party lay supine under the knife of its implacable surgeon, the General Secretary.

It was, therefore, not surprising that, at the fourteenth congress, Stalin defeated his ex-partners, even though Zinoviev succeeded in rallying the delegates of Leningrad for a turbulent dramatic engagement. Both he and Kamenev protested vehemently against the rule of the General Secretary and made a belated attempt to bring Lenin's testament to the party's notice. Stalin now levelled against them all the charges from which he had defended them the year before, when these were made by Trotsky. They were the 'deserters' and 'strike-breakers' of October. He stood by his new partners, Bukharin, Rykov, and Tomsky, in the same way in which he had previously stood by Zinoviev and Kamenev, saying that it was grotesque to imagine that the party could be led without them.[2] He told the story how he had been put and kept in his office by his present critics and how many times he had wanted to resign. The shouts of the Leningraders, 'Resign now!', were drowned by outbursts of indignation on the part of the majority and by thunderous ovations for Stalin and 'the Leninist Central Committee united around him'. It was now that this characteristic phrase came into use. Nominally the party was still led by a team, the 'Leninist Central Committee', but the team was already 'united around Stalin'. Constitutionally, the General Secretary could

---

[1] L. Trotsky, *Stalin*, p. 418.
[2] Stalin 'refused' to give 'Bukharin's blood' to the opposition. *Sochinenya*, vol. vii, pp. 365, 384, and 387; *14 Syezd V.K.P. (b)*, pp. 504-5.

claim no status above that of any other member of the Central Committee; but he already was recognized as *primus inter pares*. In theory this was still to be his status many years later, after the Central Committee had been reduced to his mere shadow.

His next step, after the congress, was to dislodge the opposition from its stronghold in Leningrad. The voice of 'Lenin's city' carried too much weight to be allowed to speak for the opposition. The man whom Stalin sent to oust Zinoviev from Leningrad was Sergei Kirov—his assassination in 1934 was to become the starting-point for the terror of the late thirties. Hitherto the secretary of the organization of Baku, one of the lesser lights among the old Bolsheviks, Kirov was an energetic organizer and an able orator. Armed with plenary powers, he appealed to the Leningraders' sense of discipline;[1] and he quickly achieved his objective, at least in appearance. The city continued to sympathize with the opposition, but it submitted to orders from the General Secretariat.

It was only after they had been beaten, in the spring of 1926, that Zinoviev and Kamenev at last threw in their lot with Trotsky. Meanwhile, Trotsky, too, had further weakened his position by renouncing his supporters abroad, who had published Lenin's testament. He even went so far—and all in the name of discipline—as to describe the document as apocryphal. The union of the two oppositions represented therefore little more than the joint wreckage of their former separate selves.

Stalin received the news about the compact of his opponents with the brief sarcastic remark: 'Ah, they have granted themselves a mutual amnesty.' All he needed to do in order to cover his three rivals with ridicule was to recall what they had only recently said and written about one another.[2] The party also heard from Zinoviev and Kamenev the 'inside story' of their and Stalin's plot against Trotsky. The revelations could not reflect credit upon either of the plotters. They sounded incredible to people who were wont to think of the Politbureau as of the repository of all virtue, especially of unselfish devotion to the revolution. The fact that Zinoviev and Kamenev now

---

[1] S. Kirov, *Izbrannye Stati i Rechi*, pp. 35–95.
[2] N. Popov, *Outline History of the C.P.S.U.*, vol. ii, p. 275.

had an obvious axe to grind cast a shadow on their trust-worthiness. The things which they confided to Trotsky and his close friends were, indeed, startling. They allegedly warned Trotsky that his life was in danger; and they revealed that, on breaking with Stalin, they themselves had taken the precaution of making their wills. They portrayed the General Secretary as a sly, revengeful sadist, obsessed with vanity and lust of power; but they failed to explain why, if such were his vices, they had been his close partners for three years. Nor did their outbursts of panic prevent them from entertaining the most sanguine hopes about their own chances of success. 'It will be enough [said Kamenev to Trotsky] for you and Zinoviev to appear together on the platform in order to reconquer the whole party.'[1]

Soon afterwards Stalin exploded their illusions. He knew that the amalgamated opposition could not but founder on the scruple that had already defeated Trotsky, that it would not carry the struggle beyond the ranks of the party. The opposition would not even dream of constituting itself into a separate party: for it accepted the axiom that only a single party could exist in the Soviet state and that if two parties were to compete for influence one of them was bound to play a counter-revolutionary role. Yet the logic of the situation drove the opposition into the role of a separate party. Every step that it made in that direction filled its leaders with remorse and horror. Every such step was retracted and recanted, only to be followed by another that was again to be regretted and retraced. Such an attitude appeared as insincere and dishonest in the eyes of most Bolsheviks; and it could not but dishearten the adherents of the opposition.

The most delicate issue of all was the opposition's behaviour in the army. After Frunze's death, Voroshilov was appointed Commissar of War, as if to crown the revenge of the Tsaritsyn group on Trotsky.[2] But Lashevich, Zinoviev's friend and supporter, was still Voroshilov's deputy. Unlike the opposition of 1924, the present opposition, after much hesitation, began to carry the struggle into the armed forces. In July 1926 Stalin exposed before the Central Committee Lashevich's doings, the semi-secret organization of the sympathizers of the opposition

---

[1] L. Trotsky, *Mein Leben*, p. 505.   [2] See Chapter VI, pp. 204–5.

among the military. This was a shattering blow for the opposition. Lashevich was dismissed from his military post and expelled from the Central Committee. Zinoviev, his protector, lost his seat on the Politbureau.

For the first time Stalin now kept the threat of expulsion from the party suspended over his opponents. Anxious to avert it, they retreated. On 4 October Trotsky, Zinoviev, Kamenev, Piatakov, Sokolnikov, and others signed a statement admitting that they were guilty of offences against the statutes of the party and pledged themselves to disband their party within the party. They also disavowed the extremists in their ranks who were led by Shlyapnikov and Medvedev, the chiefs of the 1921 opposition. However, having admitted their offences against the rules of discipline, Trotsky and his associates restated with dignified firmness their political criticisms of Stalin and Bukharin.

Now it was again Stalin's turn to act. Towards the end of October 1926 he expelled Trotsky from the Politbureau. Not a single representative of the opposition now sat on that body. He deposed Zinoviev from the presidency of the Communist International and then indicted him before the Executive of the International, which confirmed the demotion. A Russian party conference endorsed the changes in the Politbureau; and it also granted the requests of Shlyapnikov and Medvedev for readmission to the party, after their exemplary recantation. Thus a pattern was set for future expulsions, recantations, and readmissions.

These events were followed, in the first half of 1927, by a spurious truce, the last before the denouement. In the summer the struggle flared up again, in connexion with critical developments in international politics. On 12 May the British police raided the premises of the Soviet trade delegation in London; and two weeks later Great Britain broke off diplomatic relations with Russia. On 7 June Voikov, the Soviet envoy in Warsaw, was assassinated by a Russian émigré. About the same time General Chiang Kai-shek turned against the Chinese Communists, who had hitherto supported him and had been affiliated to the Kuomintang. Stalin had been severely criticized by the opposition for the support of Chiang Kai-shek, to which he had committed Russian and Chinese communism;

and Chiang Kai-shek's new move gave him now considerable embarrassment. So did the breakdown of the agreement between the Soviet and the British trade unions, which he had also upheld against the opposition.[1] In the warlike tension caused by these events, eighty-three leaders of the opposition issued an eloquent declaration, in which they blamed Stalin and Bukharin for all recent failures.

It was in the course of that debate, in the summer of 1927, that Trotsky made his so-called Clemenceau statement, the clue to many of the events that took place ten years later, when the Second World War was really casting its shadow ahead. The crux of Trotsky's statement was his assertion that, if Russia were to find herself at war, the opposition would adopt towards the ruling group an attitude similar to that which Clemenceau took *vis-à-vis* the French Government of Caillaux and Malvy in the crisis of 1917. (Clemenceau had charged that Government with inefficiency and virtual defeatism before he himself took power and waged the war against Germany to victorious conclusion.) Trotsky, in other words, charged Stalin, Rykov, Bukharin, and Voroshilov with lack of foresight, efficiency, and determination; and he gave notice that in an emergency he would strive to achieve a change of government, so that the country might be rallied and its resources efficiently organized for defence.[2] By the normal standards of any régime allowing for alternative government, Trotsky's attitude was unexceptionable. Indeed, on the eve of the Second World War, Churchill, in a sense, successfully applied 'Clemenceau tactics' in Great Britain. In a régime admitting no alternative to the Government in power, however, Trotsky's statement seemed to smack of treason. The General Secretariat replied to it with counter-statements about a 'united anti-Soviet front from Chamberlain to Trotsky'.

To all intents and purposes the opposition was now outlawed, even though Trotsky and Zinoviev, already expelled from the Politbureau, were still members of the Central Committee. The General Secretariat refused to authorize the publication of the memoranda which they had prepared for the next con-

---

[1] A more detailed account of these events is given in Chapter X, dealing with Stalin's foreign policy.

[2] L. Trotsky, *Stalin School of Falsification*, pp. 175-6.

gress of the party, and the members of the opposition printed them semi-clandestinely. For this the leaders were expelled from the Central Committee. On 7 November 1927, during the official celebration of the tenth anniversary of the October revolution, Trotsky and Zinoviev led their followers in separate processions through the streets of Moscow and Leningrad. Though the processions were of a peaceful character and the banners and slogans carried by the demonstrators were directed against the ruling group only by implication, the incident brought the struggle to a head. Trotsky and Zinoviev were immediately expelled from the party. In December the fifteenth congress declared 'adherence to the opposition and propaganda of its views to be incompatible with membership of the party'.[1] Kamenev's and Rakovsky's pleas for the opposition were drowned in a continual, hysterically intolerant uproar from the floor. 'Enough, comrades,' Stalin said, 'an end must be put to this game. . . . Kamenev's speech is the most lying, pharasaical, scoundrelly and roguish of all the opposition speeches that have been made from this platform.'[2] The congress demanded from the leaders of the opposition that they renounce and denounce their own views—this was to be the price for their continued membership of the party. In vain did Kamenev and Rakovsky try to argue that such demands contradicted the traditions of Bolshevism; and that if they yielded they would only humiliate themselves without earning the respect of members.[3] On 18 December the congress expelled seventy-five leading members of the opposition, in addition to many others already expelled or imprisoned.

A day later the opposition split. Its Trotskyist section refused to yield to the demands of the congress. Trotsky was deported to Alma Ata, Rakovsky to Astrakhan. Zinoviev, Kamenev, and their followers, however, issued a statement in which they renounced their views. The opposition was defeated by this defection no less than by Stalin's reprisals. And with the defection the humiliation of those who had capitulated was only beginning. The congress refused to accept their unconditional surrender and left the decision of their readmission to the discretion of the General Secretariat. Stalin's triumph over his

---

[1] *15 Syezd V.K.P. (b)*, p. 1318. [2] Ibid., p. 372.
[3] Ibid., pp. 252–3.

ex-partners was far more complete than his victory over Trotsky.

.   .   .   .

The story which followed shows in many points so monotonous a resemblance to the one that preceded it that it is hardly worth while to tell it in great detail. Stalin's partnership with Bukharin, Rykov, and Tomsky broke down soon after the defeat of their adversaries exactly as the triumvirate had fallen apart after Trotsky's resignation. And, though the social and political background to the new phase was vastly different, the personal ambitions of the chief actors, their fears and afterthoughts, their belated searches for new alinements and so on, were almost the same.

It is astonishing how grossly Stalin was still underrated by his adversaries, old and new; and how quickly they were to learn of their error. At the fifteenth congress the defeated opposition forecast that now, after the left had been removed, the leadership would pass from Stalin to Bukharin, Rykov, and Tomsky.[1] Trotsky ceaselessly warned the party about an imminent and decisive 'swing to the right' which might end in the restoration of capitalism. Bukharin, Rykov, and Tomsky, too, felt that they were the winners. The Politbureau elected after the congress seemed so composed as to guarantee their predominance. It consisted of nine members. Stalin was sure of four votes: his own, Molotov's, and those of the two new-comers, Kuibyshev and Rudzutak. Bukharin, Rykov, and Tomsky counted on the support of Voroshilov and Kalinin. But, when it came to the show-down, both Voroshilov and Kalinin cast their votes for Stalin. 'Stalin has some special hold on them [Bukharin said later] that I do not know of.'[2] The deputy-members of the Politbureau, Kirov, Kaganovich, Andreyev, Mikoyan, and others, with the exception of one man, Uglanov, were Stalin's supporters. Relying on his majority, Stalin began to oust Bukharin's followers from influential positions in the administration and the party caucus, refraining for the time being from any open fight against his adversaries of the Politbureau.

The drive against the right began against the background of a grave social crisis which developed exactly as Trotsky and Zinoviev had predicted. Hardly a week had passed since the

[1] 15 Syezd V.K.P. (b), pp. 1248–50.
[2] B. Souvarine, Stalin, p. 484.

congress had pronounced sentence on them when the cities and towns of Russia found themselves threatened with famine. In January 1928 government purchases of grain from the peasants fell short by two million tons of the minimum needed to feed the urban population.[1] The Politbureau ordered 'emergency measures' which, in Stalin's own words, were characterized by 'administrative arbitrariness, violation of revolutionary law, raids on peasant houses, illegal searches'.[2] Contradicting all his recent statements, Stalin now asserted that, by withholding grain from the Government, the 'kulak was disrupting the Soviet economic policy'.[3] In June new emergency measures were announced; and in July Stalin called upon the party 'to strike hard at the kulaks'.[4] Such injunctions were not willingly followed by Bolsheviks in the country-side: for in the last three years the importance of the 'alliance with the peasantry' had been impressed upon them and they had been taught that hostility towards the muzhik was the distinctive mark of the Trotskyist heresy. Throughout March, April, May, and June the General Secretariat directed a 'spring cleaning' in the party, dismissing functionaries who obstructed the emergency measures.

Behind the closed doors of the Politbureau, Bukharin, Rykov, and Tomsky tried in vain to put a stop to the new course and to protect the victims of the purge. But they were careful not to carry the controversy into the open. In the eyes of the country they bore their share of responsibility for the emergency measures. Stalin derived every benefit from their discretion and assured the party that the emergency measures and the purge had been unanimously decided upon by the Politbureau. 'There are no right-wingers in the Politbureau', he said in October.[5] 'We in the Politbureau [he repeated a month later] are united and shall remain so till the end.'[6] At the plenary session of the Central Committee he limited himself to an attack on one of Bukharin's lieutenants, the new Commissar of Finance, Frumkin, who had stated that 'the country-side, with the exception of the small section of the poorer peasants, is opposed to us' and that 'the main mass of the peasantry is in gloom and despair'.[7]

---

[1] J. Stalin, Leninism, vol. ii, p. 128. [2] Ibid., p. 129.
[3] J. Stalin, Problems of Leninism, 'On the Grain Front', pp. 206–16.
[4] J. Stalin, Leninism, vol. ii, p. 128.
[5] J. Stalin, Problems of Leninism, speech on the 'Right Danger', p. 236.
[6] J. Stalin, Leninism, vol. ii, p. 183. [7] Ibid., pp. 168 ff.

Only in April 1929, more than a year after the struggle had begun, did Stalin for the first time publicly mention Bukharin as the leader of the right opposition.

The previous oppositions had at least wrestled with Stalin before they were defeated. The Bukharin group was not even capable of taking up his challenge. At an early stage of the controversy, in July 1928, Bukharin turned for support to Kamenev in much the same way in which Kamenev and Zinoviev had once turned to Trotsky. In both cases the 'revelations' which Stalin's erstwhile partners made were exactly the same; and they were made in the same mood of panic mingled with vague hope. Zinoviev and Kamenev had spoken about the danger to their and Trotsky's lives. '*He* will strangle us', Bukharin now whispered in terror to Kamenev.[1] 'He is an unprincipled intriguer who subordinates everything to his appetite for power. At any given moment he will change his theories in order to get rid of someone.' 'We consider Stalin's line fatal to the revolution. This line is leading us to the abyss. Our disagreements with Stalin are far, far more serious than those we have with you.' As if to inspire confidence, Bukharin enumerated the organizations and the influential men who would back the opposition. But in the same breath he implored his interlocutor to drop no hint of their secret conversation, because they were both closely watched by the political police; and he parted from Kamenev speaking in awe about the 'Genghiz Khan' of the General Secretariat. Trotsky and the two ex-triumvirs had joined hands against Stalin too late. For Bukharin and Kamenev it was already too late to try to join hands.

One reason for this pathetic state of affairs lay, of course, in the almost automatic growth of the pressure which Stalin exercised upon the whole political life of the country. The defeat of each successive opposition violently narrowed the margins within which the free expression of opinion was possible. The leaders of each opposition could not get for themselves more elbow room than that to which they themselves, in coalition with Stalin, had reduced their adversaries. After each show-down, actions hitherto regarded as unimpeachable were

[1] B. Souvarine, *Stalin*, p. 485. The document from which Souvarine quotes fragments of Bukharin's revelations was seen by the author of this book also. In Russia it was circulated clandestinely.

classed as unpardonable. On formal grounds Stalin could not expel Trotsky from the party for his 'Clemenceau statement', even though it implied the threat of an overthrow of the Government. Only specific offences against discipline, clandestine printings, and unauthorized street demonstrations, offences into which Stalin had provoked his adversaries, could justify reprisals against the opposition in 1927. Less than a year later a whispered conversation between a member of the Politbureau and a repentant leader of the opposition, the conversation between Bukharin and Kamenev, was already a grave offence, for which Bukharin tearfully begged pardon from the Politbureau.[1] The alternative to submission was an ostracism doubly unbearable; for it was pronounced against the 'offender' not by a class enemy but by his associate in the revolution, and it left the 'offender' incapable even of crying in the wilderness.

There was yet another reason for the paradox that Stalin's opponents grew the more helpless the more numerous they became. 'Our disagreements with Stalin', Bukharin told Kamenev, 'are far, far more serious than those we have with you.' What Bukharin had in mind was the manner in which Stalin was asserting himself, his despotism, his lack of scruple, his disregard of public opinion, and his contempt for the intellectual *élite* of the party. On this point all oppositions, old and new, were, indeed, of one mind. But this was not enough to knit them into a single, coherent body. On the contrary, Stalin's latest moves, his departure from the pro-*muzhik* policy, made the confusion in the ranks of his critics worse confounded. He stole Trotsky's thunder. Agents of the General Secretariat now visited many of the exiled leaders of the old opposition and lured them back into the fold. Stalin, they argued, has after all adopted the ideas for which you stood. He strikes at the *kulak* and is out to industrialize the country. He is engaged in a fight against Bukharin, Rykov, and Tomsky, your and his real opponents. What is the use of your staying out in the political wilderness when your experience and talents are now badly needed by the party? You say that you are entitled to open rehabilitation. But why should you ask the leadership of the party to put itself in the wrong at so critical a moment, when its prestige should be upheld at any cost? Personal pride is not

[1] Ibid., p. 518.

a Bolshevik virtue. Besides, you know that you did commit offences against discipline. All that the party demands from you is a formality, the repudiation of an attitude that has anyhow become outdated. In return it will enable you to resume your honourable service for the revolution.

Trotsky and Rakovsky were unrepentant and unyielding. Zinoviev, Radek, Piatakov, Sokolnikov, Smilga, and hosts of others were goaded on 'to sin in loving virtue'. Throughout 1928 and 1929 there was a steady traffic of 'repenting' members of the opposition from their places of exile to Moscow. The rueful oppositionists believed that Stalin's sudden swing to the left would put wind into their sails and that in good time they would regain their hold on the party. Meanwhile, they repudiated their friends who preferred exile or imprisonment to an intricate and undignified tactical game. Thus, while he was dealing his blows to the new opposition, Stalin was assured of the temporary benevolence of many adherents of the old one. Some of its leaders, discouraged by their own failures, now warned Bukharin and his associates not to allow themselves to be rushed into hopeless conflict. The pro-*muzhik* group cautiously played for time. It believed that Stalin was leading the country into a deadlock, in which his dismissal would become inevitable. All that mattered was to be prepared for the critical moment and to seize the reins when these would slip from his hands.

Towards the end of 1928 the symptoms of such a crisis did, indeed, multiply. But Stalin saw through the hopes and the tactical games of his rivals. He knew that his most dangerous opponent was still Trotsky, whose unbending attitude won him new respect from friend and foe alike. On 18 January 1929 he proposed to the Politbureau that Trotsky be expelled from Russia. The proposal was passed, against Bukharin's protests. This incident again allows us to gauge the gradualness with which the conflict was mounting towards its bloody climax. In 1929 Stalin still shrank from the imprisonment of Trotsky in Russia—seven years later he would not hesitate to pass a death sentence on him as well as on the whole 'Old Guard'.

After he had finally removed Trotsky from the Russian scene, he hastened to rout the leaders of the right wing. Rykov was deposed from the Premiership of the Soviet Government, in which he had succeeded Lenin. Tomsky was ousted from the leadership of the trade unions, on the ground that he had used his influence to turn the unions against industrialization. Bukharin was dismissed from the leadership of the Communist International, where he had replaced Zinoviev, as well as from the Politbureau. Before the year 1929 was out, Bukharin, Rykov, and Tomsky repudiated their own views and thus bought a few years of spurious breathing space.

Stalin's ascendancy was now complete. The contest for power was at its end. All his rivals had been eliminated. None of the members of the Politbureau would dream of challenging his authority. In the last days of the year Moscow celebrated his fiftieth birthday as if it had been a great historic event. From every corner of Russia tributes were addressed to the Leader. His virtues were praised, immoderately and crudely, by every party secretary in the country. The walls of Moscow were covered with his huge portraits. His statues and busts of all possible sizes filled the squares, the halls of public buildings, and the windows of every shop down to the humblest barber's shop. 'Stalin is the Lenin of to-day', the propagandists shouted themselves hoarse. Some of the older people recalled Lenin's fiftieth birthday. It had been a small and modest occasion, which Lenin reluctantly attended only to remonstrate with his admirers for their growing fondness for pomp and ceremony. The new Stalinist cult was now visibly merging with the old Leninist cult, and overshadowing it. When, on ceremonial occasions, Stalin appeared at the top of the Lenin mausoleum in the Red Square, Lenin's colossal tomb appeared to be only the pedestal for his successor.

. . . .

It would be easy for the historian to pass unqualified judgement on Stalin if he could assume that in his fight against Bukharin, Rykov, and Tomsky he pursued only his private ambition. This was not the case. His personal ends were not the only or the most important stakes in the struggle. In the tense months of 1928 and 1929 the whole fate of Soviet Russia hung in the balance.

On the face of things, the opening of the crisis was so undramatic as to appear irrelevant. The peasants had failed to deliver a few million tons of grain to the towns. Prosaic as the event was, there was real drama in it. In refusing to sell food, the peasants had no clear political motives. They did not aim at the overthrow of the Soviets, although some of the politically minded elements among the well-to-do peasantry hoped for such an ending. The mass of the peasants was driven to apply that peculiar form of 'sabotage' by economic circumstances. Most of the small farms did not produce more than was needed to feed their owners. After more than ten years the agricultural upheaval of 1917 was now taking its revenge. The splitting up of large estates into tiny holdings had given the Bolsheviks the support of the peasantry in the civil war; but in consequence the productivity of farming, or rather its capacity to feed the urban population, deteriorated. The big farmers, on the other hand, demanded high prices for food, prices intolerably burdensome to the townspeople; and they also pressed for further concessions to capitalist farming. Stalin was, indeed, confronted with a most complex dilemma. If he yielded more ground to the peasants he would dangerously antagonize the urban working classes, which, on the whole, now again stood behind the Government, especially after the Government had, about 1927, succeeded in rebuilding industry to its pre-war condition. But the refusal to yield to the peasantry also entailed the threat of famine and unrest in the towns. The problem demanded a radical solution. If the Government had begun to curb the big farmers and to encourage gradual collectivization earlier, as Trotsky and Zinoviev had counselled, it might not have needed now to resort to drastic emergency measures in order to obtain bread. As things stood, Stalin acted under the overwhelming pressure of events. The circumstance that he was not prepared for the events precipitated him into a course of action over which he was liable to lose control.

The unpremeditated, pragmatic manner in which he embarked upon the second revolution would have been unbelievable if, during the preceding years, from 1924 until late in 1929, Stalin had not placed his views on record. Up to the last moment he shrank from the upheaval, and he had no idea of the scope and violence which it was to assume. In this he was not alone. Not a single Bolshevik group, faction, or coterie thought of an industrialization so intensive and rapid or of a collectivization of farming so comprehensive and drastic as that which Stalin now initiated. Even the most extreme of the left Bolsheviks conceived collectivization as a mild, gradual reform. The only man who had propagated the idea of a 'second revolution' in the country-side was Yuri Larin, a second-rate economist, once a right-wing Menshevik. He wrote about it as early as 1925; and Stalin then ironically treated his view as a cranky idea.[1] He fulminated against those Bolsheviks who thought of 'fanning class struggle in the country-side':[2] 'This is . . . empty chatter . . . old Menshevik songs from the old Menshevik Encyclopaedia.' When students of the Sverdlov University put to him the captious question, 'How can one fight against the *kulaks* without fanning the class struggle?', he replied in the same tone, brooking no contradiction, that the party 'was not interested in fanning class struggle' in the country-side and that that slogan was 'quite inappropriate'.[3]

Three years later, in May 1928, when the emergency measures against the *kulaks* were already in operation, he still insisted that the 'expropriation of *kulaks* would be folly'.[4] He did not expect more than a small fraction of agriculture to be reorganized on collective lines within the next four years.[5] The first five-year plan, approved by the end of the year, provided for the collectivization of, at the most, 20 per cent. of all farms by 1933. Even in the spring of 1929, while he was already openly accusing the Bukharin group as the promoters of capitalist farming, Stalin still maintained that 'individual . . . farming would continue to play a predominant part in supplying the country with food and raw materials'.[6]

A few months later, 'all round' collectivization was in full swing; and individual farming was doomed. Before the year was out Stalin stated: 'We have succeeded in turning the bulk of the peasantry in a large number of regions away from the old capitalist path of development.'[7] The Politbureau now expected that state-owned and collective farms would already

---

[1] J. Stalin, *Sochinenya*, vol. vii, p. 373, speech at the fourteenth congress.
[2] Ibid., p. 103.   [3] Ibid., pp. 179 and 334-8.
[4] J. Stalin, *Problems of Leninism*, p. 221, 'On the Grain Front'.
[5] 'There are people,' he said in July 1928, 'who think that individual farming is at the end of its tether and is not worth supporting. Such people have nothing in common with the line of our party' (J. Stalin, *Leninism*, vol. ii, p. 131).
[6] J. Stalin, *Problems of Leninism*, p. 267.   [7] Ibid., p. 293.

supply half of all the food for the towns. In the last days of the year Stalin's orders for an all out 'offensive against the *kulak*' rang out threateningly from the Kremlin. 'We must smash the *kulaks*, eliminate them as a class. . . . Unless we set ourselves these aims, an offensive would be mere declamation, bickering, empty noise. . . . We must strike at the *kulaks* so hard as to prevent them from rising to their feet again. . . .'[1] Far from denouncing expropriation of well-to-do farmers as folly, he now argued: 'Can we permit the expropriation of *kulaks*. . . ? A ridiculous question. . . . You do not lament the loss of the hair of one who has been beheaded. . . . We must break down the resistance of that class in open battle.'[2]

A brief recapitulation of his crucial statements on industrialization reveals equally striking contradictions. In the middle twenties Russian industry, recovering to its pre-war condition, increased its output by 20 to 30 per cent. per year.[3] The Politbureau argued over the rate at which output could be expanded after all the existing plants and factories had been made to operate at full capacity. Everybody agreed that once this point had been reached, the annual increases would be smaller. Zinoviev, Trotsky, and Kamenev thought that it would still be possible to raise output by somewhat less than 20 per cent. a year. Stalin dubbed them 'super-industrializers'. When his opponents advanced the project for the Dnieprostroy, the great hydro-electrical power station on the Dnieper, he shelved it, allegedly saying that for Russia to build the Dnieprostroy would be the same as for a *muzhik* to buy a gramophone instead of a cow.[4] His report to the fifteenth congress, in December 1927, was full of contentment with the industrial condition of the country; but he already took a leaf from the opposition's book—and suggested that in the next few years industrial output should be increased at the annual rate of 15 per cent.

A year later his contentment with the condition of industry vanished; and he found that the Russian plants and factories were technically 'beneath all criticism'.[5] He now began to

[1] J. Stalin, *Problems of Leninism*, p. 318.   [2] Ibid., p. 325.
[3] J. Stalin, *Sochinenya*, vol. vii, pp. 308 and 315.
[4] *The Case of Leon Trotsky*, p. 245, and *Bulleten Oppozitsii*, no. 27 (March 1932).
[5] J. Stalin, *Leninism*, vol. ii, p. 151.

urge more rapid industrialization. Referring to a precedent in the minds of many of his listeners he argued: 'When Peter the Great, having to deal with the more advanced countries of the west, began feverishly to build factories and workshops, in order to supply his armies, . . . none of the old classes . . . could successfully solve the problem of overcoming the backwardness of the country.'[1] But the new structure of Russian society created incomparably better conditions for industrialization. Even now Stalin's projects were moderate. At a plenary session of the Central Committee he wrangled with the Commissar of Finance, Frumkin, who would not allocate in the budget more than 650 million roubles for capital investments. The Supreme Economic Council asked for 825 million roubles; and Stalin pleaded in favour of the higher appropriation.[2]

The actual investments in the next year, the first of the five-year plan, amounted to 1,300 million roubles, nearly 500 million more than Stalin's highest estimate. The radical and decisive turn towards industrialization occurred by the middle of 1929, when the appropriation for capital investments was suddenly raised to 3,400 million roubles, five times as much as the Commissar of Finance had allowed and four times as much as Stalin himself had demanded. Soon the Politbureau worked itself up into a real frenzy of industrialization. In June 1930 the sixteenth congress was dumbfounded by Stalin's triumphant statement: 'We are on the eve of our transformation from an agrarian into an industrial country.'[3] He predicted that in many branches of industry the plan would be fulfilled in three or even two and a half, instead of in five, years. He told the congress that in the current year industry was ordered to raise its output by nearly 50 per cent., an exertion which really belonged to the realm of super-industrialist fantasy.[4]

He was now completely possessed by the idea that he could achieve a miraculous transformation of the whole of Russia by a single *tour de force*. He seemed to live in a half-real and half-dreamy world of statistical figures and indices, of industrial orders and instructions, a world in which no target and no

---

[1] Ibid., p. 153.   [2] Ibid., p. 172.   [3] Ibid., p. 328.
[4] To be accurate, the increase was to be by 47 per cent. Stalin himself later admitted to a conference of industrial managers that it was only 25 per cent.; and even this figure is doubtful. Cf. *Leninism*, vol. ii, p. 385, and *Problems of Leninism*, p. 351.

objective seemed to be beyond his and the party's grasp. He coined the phrase that there were no fortresses which could not be conquered by the Bolsheviks, a phrase that was in the course of many years repeated by every writer and orator and displayed on every banner and poster in every corner of the country.

Here is a striking illustration of the feverish character of the endeavour: Iron and steel form the basis of industrial power. In 1928 Russia produced only three and a half million tons of pig iron. She was to produce ten million tons by the end of 1933, under the five-year plan. Stalin, not satisfied with putting the time limit for the whole plan a year or two earlier, told the sixteenth congress that 'ten million tons of pig iron . . . is not enough. . . . At all costs we must produce seventeen million tons in 1932.'[1] He branded the economists and business managers who feared that so high a target could not be attained as 'right-wing opportunists' and 'wreckers', even though their objections were very well founded. In 1941, when Hitler attacked Russia, the Russian output of pig iron was only just approaching the target which, according to Stalin's orders, it should have reached ten years earlier.[2]

.   .   .   .

We have seen how Stalin was precipitated into collectivization by the chronic danger of famine in 1928 and 1929. Some of his opponents suggested that the danger might be averted if food were imported. But the means of payment were lacking; and the Government could not hope to obtain foreign credits— the financial boycott of Russia, which had started after the revolution, was virtually still on. Apart from this, if the scarce funds of foreign currency and gold were to be spent on foreign food, industry could not develop even on the modest scale on which it had progressed so far. Industrial stagnation was bound to entail an even graver food crisis and more dangerous tension between town and country-side later on.

The ransacking of the barns of the well-to-do peasants and

---

[1] J. Stalin, *Leninism*, vol. ii, p. 375.
[2] N. Voznesensky, *Economic Results of the U.S.S.R. in 1940*, pp. 10 and 13. See also *Planovoye Khozyaistvo*, no. 5, 1947; A. Kursky, *Sotsialisticheskaya Industrializatsia S.S.S.R.*, p. 35.

the requisitioning of hidden stocks seemed to offer a simpler way out of the predicament, one that was not necessarily more unfair than the threat of starvation with which the country-side confronted the towns. But the administration, even assisted by party and police, was hardly capable of coping with the task. The peculiar gifts of peasants for evading regulations and controls imposed upon them by a more or less remote urban administration is notorious. Such regulations and controls, let alone requisitions, are most effective when they are enforced by a section of the rural population on the spot. Stalin therefore appealed to the poor peasants against the well-to-do farmers. He could not turn to the mass of the poor *muzhiks* empty-handed. He had to offer them tangible rewards for co-operation. And what reward could be more alluring to the destitute *muzhik*, the owner of a tiny plot, who tilled his land with a wooden plough (*sokha*), who possessed neither horse nor cow and was constantly at the mercy of the *kulak* and village usurer, what reward could be more tempting to the multitude of such *muzhiks* than a collective farm, which the Government promised to endow with some of the *kulaks'* agricultural implements and cattle as well as with tractors?

It is not known exactly how many of the 25 million private farmers belonged to that most destitute class. Their numbers were given as 5 to 8 millions—at least 5 millions of the smallest holdings were tilled with wooden ploughs.[1] At the other end of the scale there were $1\frac{1}{2}$ or perhaps 2 million prosperous farmers. In between there were the 15 to 18 millions of 'middle peasants'. Thus, only a minority of the peasantry, though a very substantial one, could be relied upon to welcome wholeheartedly the 'great change'. If Stalin had limited the reform to the pooling of the poorest holdings and to a moderate redistribution of wealth between the most prosperous and the most destitute sections of the peasantry, the collectivization would hardly have become the bloody cataclysm which in the event it did become. If the collective farms had, further, been endowed with tools and machines, assisted by governmental credits and technical advice, if they had then succeeded in visibly improving the living of their members, they would probably

---

[1] L. Trotsky, *The Real Situation in Russia*, pp. 64-7; and J. Stalin, *Problems of Leninism*, 'On the Grain Front', pp. 206-16.

have attracted many of the so-called middle peasants, who in fact led a miserable existence on the shifting borderlines of poverty.

About the middle of 1929 Stalin was carried away by the momentum of the movement. The beginning of collectivization was an indubitable success. As encouraging progress reports piled up on the desks of the General Secretariat, Stalin began to press the collectivization beyond the limits originally set. He dispatched thousands and thousands of agents to the country-side, instructing them to 'liquidate the *kulaks* as a class' and to drive the multitudes of reluctant middle peasants into the collective farms. The spirit of his instructions can be recaptured from a speech he gave to the party's rural agents in December 1929.[1] He used the bluntest words to dispel the scruples of his listeners, who apparently felt that a revolution may and must deal ruthlessly with a handful of exploiters but not with millions of small proprietors. Stalin quoted with vague irony the following lines from Engels: 'We stand decisively on the side of the small peasant: we will do everything possible to make his lot more tolerable and to facilitate his transition to the co-operative, if he decides to take this step. If he cannot as yet bring himself to this decision, we will give him plenty of time to ponder over it on his holding.' Engels's 'exaggerated circumspection', Stalin told his listeners, suited the conditions of western Europe; but it was out of place in Russia. The small peasant was not to be given time to ponder over collectivism on his own holding. The *kulaks*, Stalin elaborated his point, must not only be expropriated; it was ridiculous to suggest, as some Bolsheviks did, that after they had been expropriated they should be allowed to join collective farms. He did not tell his audience what should happen to the two million or so *kulaks*, who with their families may have numbered eight or ten million people, after they had been deprived of their property and barred from the collective farms.

Within a short time rural Russia became pandemonium. The overwhelming majority of the peasantry confronted the Government with desperate opposition. Collectivization degenerated into a military operation, a cruel civil war. Rebellious villages were surrounded by machine-guns and forced to sur-

[1] J. Stalin, *Problems of Leninism*, pp. 301 ff.

render.[1] Masses of *kulaks* were deported to remote unpopulated lands in Siberia. Their houses, barns, and farm implements were turned over to the collective farms—Stalin himself put the value of their property so transferred at over 400 million roubles.[2] The bulk of the peasants decided to bring in as little as possible of their property to the collective farms which they imagined to be state-owned factories, in which they themselves would become mere factory hands. In desperation they slaughtered their cattle, smashed implements, and burned crops. This was the *muzhik*'s great Luddite-like rebellion. Only three years later, in January 1934, did Stalin disclose some of its results. In 1929 Russia possessed 34 million horses. Only 16·6 millions were left in 1933—18 million horses had been slaughtered. So were 30 millions of large cattle, about 45 per cent. of the total, and nearly 100 million, or two-thirds of all, sheep and goats.[3] Vast tracts of land were left untilled. Famine stalked the towns and the black soil steppe of the Ukraine.

The *tour de force* in farming impelled Stalin to attempt a similar *tour de force* in industry. Rapid mechanization of agriculture now became a matter of life and death. Large-scale farming demands a technical basis much higher than that on which small farming, especially that of the antediluvian Russian type, can exist. The tractor must replace the horse. Before the great slaughter of livestock, economists thought that complete collectivization would require at least a quarter of a million tractors and an enormous mass of other machinery. When the upheaval began only 7,000 tractors were available in the whole of Russia. By an extraordinary exertion Stalin secured nearly 30,000 tractors more in the course of 1929.[4] This was a drop in the ocean. Without machines and technical advice no

---

[1] In that critical period the author travelled in Russia and the Ukraine. He remembers a striking account of the collectivization given to him, in a railway carriage on the way from Moscow to Kharkov, by a colonel of the G.P.U. The colonel was completely broken in spirit by his recent experiences in the country-side. 'I am an old Bolshevik,' he said, almost sobbing, 'I worked in the under-ground against the Tsar and then I fought in the civil war. Did I do all that in order that I should now surround villages with machine-guns and order my men to fire indiscriminately into crowds of peasants? Oh, no, no!'

[2] J. Stalin, *Leninism*, vol. ii, p. 344.

[3] J. Stalin, *Problems of Leninism*, p. 480.

[4] Ibid., p. 483.

rational organization and division of agricultural labour was possible. Many of the collective farms threatened to disintegrate and fall asunder as soon as they had been formed. It was now imperative that industry should, within the shortest possible time, supply fantastic masses of machinery, that the oil wells should produce the millions of tons of petrol by which the tractors were to be driven, that the country-side be electrified, that new power stations be built, and last, but not least, that millions of peasants be trained in handling and driving engines. But the plants and factories to produce the stuff did not exist. The output of coal, steel, oil, and other materials was desperately inadequate. And the men who were to teach the illiterate *muzhiks* to handle a tractor were not there either.

The whole experiment seemed to be a piece of prodigious insanity, in which all rules of logic and principles of economics were turned upside down. It was as if a whole nation had suddenly abandoned and destroyed its houses and huts, which, though obsolete and decaying, existed in reality, and moved, lock, stock, and barrel, into some illusory buildings, for which not more than a hint of scaffolding had in reality been prepared; as if that nation had only after this crazy migration set out to make the bricks for the walls of its new dwellings and then found that even the straw for the bricks was lacking; and as if then that whole nation, hungry, dirty, shivering with cold and riddled with disease, had begun a feverish search for the straw, the bricks, the stones, the builders and the masons, so that, by assembling these, they could at last start building homes incomparably more spacious and healthy than were the hastily abandoned slum dwellings of the past. Imagine that that nation numbered 160 million people; and that it was lured, prodded, whipped, and shepherded into that surrealistic enterprise by an ordinary, prosaic, fairly sober man, whose mind had suddenly become possessed by a half-real and half-somnambulistic vision, a man who established himself in the role of super-judge and super-architect, in the role of a modern super-Pharaoh. Such, roughly, was now the strange scene of Russian life, full of torment and hope, full of pathos and of the grotesque; and such was Stalin's place in it; only that the things that he drove the people to build were not useless pyramids.

In his own mind he saw himself not as a modern Pharaoh

but as a new Moses leading a chosen nation in the desert. For the mind of this atheistic dictator was cluttered with biblical images and symbols. Among the few metaphors and images scattered in his dull and dreary writings, the phrase about the march 'to the promised land of socialism' recurred perhaps most frequently, even while he led only a few 'committee-men' of Tiflis or Baku.[1] How much more real must that phrase have sounded in his own ears now. For all the distance of centuries and national character that separated him from Cromwell, and his followers from the Puritans, much of Macaulay's characterization of Cromwell and his men might easily have been written about Stalin:

That singular body of men was, for the most part, composed of zealous republicans. In the act of enslaving their country, they had deceived themselves into the belief that they were emancipating her. The book which they most venerated furnished them with a precedent which was frequently in their mouths. It was true that the ignorant and ungrateful nation murmured against its deliverers. Even so had another chosen nation murmured against the leader who brought it, by painful and dreary paths, from the house of bondage to the land flowing with milk and honey. Yet had that leader rescued his brethren in spite of themselves; nor had he shrunk from making terrible examples of those who contemned the proffered freedom, and pined for the fleshpots, the taskmasters and the idolatries of Egypt.

When Stalin put his programme before the people, demanding exertions and sacrifices, he could not simply explain it in terms of immediate economic needs. He tried to impart to it a more imaginative appeal. For the first time he now openly appealed to the nationalist as well as to the Socialist sentiments in the people. That double appeal had, it is true, been implied in the doctrine of socialism in one country; but so far he had refrained from openly stirring nationalist pride or ambition. Bolshevik hostility towards these sentiments had been fresh in the minds of the people; and any open departure from it would have been highly embarrassing to Stalin so long as he was exposed to criticism from his rivals. Nor is it certain that the nationalist train of thought was sufficiently crystallized in his own mind in earlier years. The new tone rang out with extraordinary

---

[1] See p. 67.

force in one of his famous speeches to business executives, in February 1931. He was arguing interminably against those who pleaded for a slower tempo of industrialization; and he was explaining the international and national motives of his policy. Industrialization was essential for socialism; and the Soviet Government was in the eyes of the world proletariat in duty bound to build socialism. These international obligations, he said, he placed even higher than the national. But he spoke about the international Socialist aspect of the problem in clichés so lifeless that they make one feel clearly that the speaker's heart was not in them. His words began to pulsate with emotion and assumed colour only when he turned to the national, the purely Russian motives for his policy:

No, comrades, . . . the pace must not be slackened! On the contrary, we must quicken it as much as is within our powers and possibilities. This is dictated to us by our obligations to the workers and peasants of the U.S.S.R. This is dictated to us by our obligations to the working class of the whole world.

To slacken the pace would mean to lag behind; and those who lag behind are beaten. We do not want to be beaten. No, we don't want to. The history of old . . . Russia . . . she was ceaselessly beaten for her backwardness. She was beaten by the Mongol Khans, she was beaten by Turkish Beys, she was beaten by Swedish feudal lords, she was beaten by Polish-Lithuanian *Pans*, she was beaten by Anglo-French capitalists, she was beaten by Japanese barons, she was beaten by all—for her backwardness. For military backwardness, for cultural backwardness, for political backwardness, for industrial backwardness, for agricultural backwardness. She was beaten because to beat her was profitable and went unpunished. You remember the words of the pre-revolutionary poet: 'Thou art poor and thou art plentiful, thou art mighty and thou art helpless, Mother Russia.'

. . . We are fifty or a hundred years behind the advanced countries. We must make good this lag in ten years. Either we do it or they crush us.[1]

---

[1] J. Stalin, *Problems of Leninism*, p. 356. To grasp how novel Stalin's words sounded in Russia, when they were spoken, one has to note the extent to which they rehabilitated the Tsarist past. In Stalin's summary of Russian history, Russia invariably appears as the victim of foreign conquerors and oppressors. Hitherto Bolshevik historians and writers specialized in exposing the seamy side of Russian history, in throwing light on the conquest and the oppression of weaker nations by the Tsarist Empire. Stalin gave short shrift to that anti-nationalist conception which had since the revolution been inculcated into the young generation. The

Stalin's call for industrialization at first fired the imagination of the urban working classes. The younger generation had long cherished the dream of Russia becoming 'another America', a Socialist America. The schemes of Dnieprostroy and Magnitogorsk and a host of other ultra-modern, mammoth-like industrial combines conjured up before its eyes the vistas of a new civilization, in which man would subject the machine to his will instead of himself being subjected to the machine and its owner. Multitudes of young workers, especially members of the Komsomol, volunteered for pioneering work in the wilderness of remote lands. They ardently greeted the vision of the new world, even if that world was to be built on their own bones. Less idealistically minded people welcomed industrialization because it put an end to the unemployment that had harassed the Russian worker all through the period of N.E.P.

Here again Stalin was carried away by the momentum of the movement until he overreached himself to an extent to which no experienced economic administrator would have done. But, strange as this may seem, Stalin was still utterly inexperienced in economic matters. He was no economist by training, though the Marxist outlook gave him a closer grasp of economics than that possessed by average politicians. Under Lenin his part in framing economic policy was as insignificant as his role in the political administration was great. In addition, in those years the economic condition of Russia was so backward and primitive that there was no room for any really complex decisions. In later years he was immersed over his ears in marshalling the Bolshevik caucus against his rivals; and he had little opportunity and time to concern himself with more than the general direction of political affairs. He thus initiated an industrial revolution, being more or less unaware of the limits to which the national resources and the endurance of the people could be stretched without disastrous effects. All his experience had bred in him an excessive confidence in the power of a closely knit and ruthless administration. Had he not got rid of all his once so powerful rivals merely because he was able to

most prominent expounder of the anti-nationalist view of Russian history, Professor Pokrovsky, was excommunicated some time later; and his books were banned. The rehabilitation of the nationalist tradition was to reach its climax only in the years of the Second World War.

turn that power against them? Had he not been able to tame a party, once so untameable, and to reduce it to a body of frightened and meek men always ready to do his bidding? Why then should he not succeed in dealing with the scattered, un-organized masses of *muzhiks* according to his ideas? Why should he not be able to make the directors of industry produce the quantities of coal, and steel, and machinery laid down in the plans? The main thing was that they should be subjected to ceaseless and relentless pressure from him and the Politbureau. He was unsurpassed at bringing that pressure to bear upon his subordinates and at making them convey it to all grades of the administration. He was the arch-intimidator, the arch-prodder, and the arch-cajoler in the whole business.

When at last he became aware of the results of the reckless drive in the country-side, he was anxious to appease the peasants and to free himself from the odium. On 2 March 1930 he tried to kill the two birds in a statement on 'Dizziness with Success'.[1] He threw the blame for what had happened on to over-zealous officials. He admitted that half the number of all the farms had already been collectivized; that in many cases force had been used; and that some of the collective farms were not viable. Three months before, while he was pressing the rural agents of the party not to allow the small peasants any more time to 'ponder' over collectivism 'on their own holdings', he himself gave his last unequivocal signal for forced collectivization. Now he intimated that his instructions had been misunderstood: 'Collective farms cannot be set up by force. To do so would be stupid and reactionary.' He railed at 'opportunists', 'block-heads', 'noisy lefts', 'timid philistines', and 'distortionists'; and he called for a halt to 'excesses'. His appearance in the role of the protector of the *muzhik* took the Politbureau and the Central Committee by surprise. He had not consulted them. He had made his appeal to the peasantry over the heads, as it were, of the men who had merely been his accomplices and whom he now made to appear as the main culprits.[2] Even the meek

---

[1] J. Stalin, *Problems of Leninism*, pp. 326–31.

[2] The statement on 'Dizziness with Success' seemed to appeal to the familiar popular belief about the 'good' ruler and his 'bad' advisers. Whether the appeal was effective is another question. The comment of an old Ukrainian peasant, questioned by the author, was roughly this: 'Things were very bad in our collective farm, but have been easier since *Stalin* got over *his* dizziness from success.'

Central Committee of those days protested against being used in this way as the lightning conductor for popular anger. Stalin then issued another statement saying that his call for a halt to violence represented not his personal view but the attitude of the whole Central Committee.[1]

Whatever the truth of the matter, he put a powerful brake on the collectivist drive. In the next three years only 10 per cent. more of all farms were pooled, so that by the end of the five-year plan six-tenths of all holdings were collectivized. The character, too, of the collective farm was altered. At first nearly all the farmers' belongings were declared collective property; and the members of the collectives were to receive for their labour no more than workmen's wages. In the early and middle thirties a whole series of 'Stalin reforms' made important concessions to the peasants' individualism. The *kolkhoz* was to be a co-operative (*artel*), not a commune. Its members shared in the farm's profits. They were allowed to own privately small plots of land, poultry, and some cattle. In the course of time a new social differentiation developed: there were 'well-to-do' and poor *kolkhozes* and 'well-to-do' and poor members in each *kolkhoz*. Authority came to favour the 'prosperous *kolkhozes*'. Stalin ordered the winding up of most state-owned farms (*Sovkhozes*) and made a gift to the collective farms of more than forty million acres of their land.[2] Thus a new, though not very firm, balance between private and collective interests was created, which enabled the Government to collectivize more slowly than at first nearly all the holdings without provoking bitter resistance. The costly and bloody lesson of 1929 and 1930 was not entirely wasted. In the late thirties the new social structure of rural Russia achieved a measure of consolidation, despite all the shakiness of its foundations at the beginning of the decade.

The ups and downs of the industrial revolution were not less abrupt and violent. In 1930, it will be remembered, Stalin demanded that the output of iron and coal be increased by nearly half within the year. The actual increase was, as he himself admitted next year, only 6–10 per cent.[3] The slow

---

[1] Ibid., p. 329.
[2] Professor F. Koshelev, *Stalinskii Ustav-Osnovnoi Zakon Kolkhoznoi Zhizni*, p. 28.
[3] J. Stalin, *Problems of Leninism*, p. 359.

progress of mining hampered the manufacturing and engineering industries. Stalin tenaciously pressed on with the development of new gigantic and modern iron- and coal-mines in the Urals and in Siberia, paying little or no heed to obstacles. 'In Magnitogorsk I was precipitated into a battle', wrote an American eyewitness and participant. 'I was deployed on the iron and steel front. Tens of thousands of people were enduring the most intense hardships in order to build blast furnaces, and many of them did it willingly, with boundless enthusiasm, which infected me from the day of my arrival.' 'I would wager' [the writer concludes] 'that Russia's battle of ferrous metallurgy alone involved more casualties than the battle of the Marne.'[1]

Immense as was the waste of human life, energy, and of materials, the achievement, too, was enormous. True, the targets of the first five-year plan were not attained;[2] and never again, except in the years of the war against Hitler, did Stalin demand from industry exertions like those to which he had spurred it at first. In the second five-year plan the annual rate of increase in industrial output was 13–14 per cent.; and it was under that more modest plan, in the years 1932–7, that the progress in industrialization was actually consolidated.[3]

. . . .

Only an absolute ruler, himself ruled neither by nerves nor by sentiments, could persist in this staggering enterprise in the face of so many adversities. There is something almost incomprehensible in the mask of unruffled calmness which Stalin showed in those years. Behind that mask there must have been tension and anguish. But only once did he seem to have been on the point of breakdown. Throughout 1932 adversities and frustrations piled up one upon another; and he sulked in his tent. His popularity was at its nadir. He watched tensely the waves of discontent rising and beating against the walls of the Kremlin. He could not fail to catch gleams of hope mixed with anxiety in the eyes of his defeated opponents, Bukharin, Rykov, Tomsky, Zinoviev, and Kamenev, whose hands were

[1] John Scott, *Behind the Urals*, p. 9.
[2] When Stalin drew up the balance of the first five-year plan, in January 1933, he claimed that only 93·7 per cent. of the plan had been fulfilled. Even this was probably an exaggeration. See his *Problems of Leninism*, pp. 398–402.
[3] Ibid., p. 406.

stayed only by the perils threatening Bolshevism, in all its shades and factions. The old division between the right and the left wings of the party had almost gone, giving place to a common longing for change, which began to affect even some of Stalin's hard-bitten followers. Memoranda about the need to depose him circulated in his immediate entourage. They were signed by Syrtsov and Lominadze, two men who had helped him in defeating the Trotskyists and the Bukharinists—Syrtsov had even replaced Rykov as Premier of the Russian Soviet Socialist Republic.[1] A similar memorandum was signed by Riutin, chief of propaganda, and others. These men were charged with conspiracy and imprisoned. Strictly speaking, they had not engaged in any plot. They merely urged the members of the Central Committee to depose Stalin in a constitutional manner; and, nominally, Stalin never questioned the constitutional right of the Central Committee to depose its General Secretary. The Ukraine, too, was seething with despair and hidden opposition. One of Stalin's confidants, Postyshev, went there to purge the Ukrainian Government which had supposedly consisted of devoted Stalinists. The purge led to the suicide of Skrypnik, the Ukrainian Commissar of Education, a veteran Bolshevik.

As a climax to these developments, tragedy visited the dictator's own home. His own wife, Nadia Alliluyeva, the daughter of the workman Alliluyev, hitherto blindly devoted to her much older husband, began to doubt the wisdom and rightness of his policy. One evening, in November 1932, Stalin and his wife were on a visit at Voroshilov's home. Other members of the Politbureau were there too, discussing matters of policy. Nadia Alliluyeva spoke her mind about the famine and discontent in the country and about the moral ravages which the Terror had wrought on the party. Stalin's nerves were already strained to the utmost. In the presence of his friends he burst out against his wife in a flood of vulgar abuse. Nadia Alliluyeva left Voroshilov's house. The same evening she committed suicide.[2]

The newspapers spoke about sudden and premature death [says V. Serge, a French ex-communist writer, who spent those years in Russia]. The story told by the initiated was that the young woman

---

[1] Syrtsov was the head of the Government of the Russian republic, as distinct from the Government of the U.S.S.R. That had, since Rykov's dismissal, been headed by Molotov.   [2] A. Barmine, *One who Survived*, p. 264.

suffered because of the famine and the terror, because of her own comfortable life in the Kremlin and the sight of the pictures of the General Secretary covering whole buildings on the public squares. She was worn down by fits of melancholy. . . .

There was the man of steel, as he had called himself, . . . face to face with that corpse. It was about that time that he rose one day at the Politbureau to tender his resignation to his colleagues. 'Maybe I have, indeed, become an obstacle to the party's unity. If so, comrades, I am ready to efface myself. . . .' The members of the Politbureau—the body had already been purged of its right wing—glanced at one another in embarrassment. Which of them would take it upon himself to answer: 'Yes, old man, that's that. You ought to leave. There is nothing better for you to do.' Which one? The man who would have said such a thing, without being backed by the others, would have risked a lot. Nobody stirred. . . . At last Molotov said: 'Stop it, stop it. You have got the party's confidence. . . .' The incident was closed.[1]

This seems to have been the only instance in which Stalin's self-reliance broke down for a moment. A few weeks later, in January 1934, after months of sullen silence, he again addressed a plenary session of the Central Committee. His speech, though still apologetic in tone, testified to his regained confidence: 'The party whipped up the country and spurred it onwards. . . . We had to spur on the country. . . . It was a hundred years behind and faced with mortal danger. . . .'[2] He virtually admitted that the first five-year plan had not been fulfilled, but explained this on the ground that industry had had to switch over to the production of munitions, because of the threat of war in the Far East. These were the days of the Japanese conquest of Manchuria. It is doubtful whether Stalin himself had thought the danger of a Japanese attack on Russia so imminent as to call for a drastic remaking of economic plans. Now, at any rate, just on the eve of Hitler's coming to power, he assured the country that the danger was over and that there was no need for the exacting tempo of industrialization any longer. The task before Russia within the next two or three years was to consolidate her gains and to master industrial technique.

A few days later he was again on the platform, describing

---

[1] V. Serge, *Portrait de Staline*, pp. 94–5.
[2] J. Stalin, *Problems of Leninism*, pp. 404–6.

the dangers with which the situation in the country-side was fraught. He startled the party by saying that the collective farms might become even more dangerous to the régime than private farming. In the old days the peasantry was scattered and slow to move; it lacked the capacity for political organization. Since the collectivization the peasants were organized into compact bodies which might support the Soviets but might also turn against them more effectively than the individual farmers could. To secure the party's close control over them, the rural Political Departments were established.[1] Parallel with these measures another amazing job was tackled. A year later Stalin reported to the seventeenth congress that two million *muzhiks* who had never handled a machine had in the meantime been trained to be drivers; that almost as many men and women had been trained in the administration of collective farms; and that 111,000 engineers and agronomists had been dispatched to the country-side. The number of illiterate people had dwindled to a mere 10 per cent.[2] This so-called cultural revolution was also carried through in feverish haste; and consequently it was extremely superficial. But it did mark the beginning of a momentous transformation in the outlook and habits of the nation.

. . . .

The description of Stalin's role in the second revolution would be incomplete without a mention of the new social policy which he inspired perhaps more directly than any other part of the 'great change'. It is in this field that the lights and the shadows of his policies contrasted most sharply. At the end of 1929 he initiated a new labour policy in terms so obscure and vague that their significance was almost entirely missed.[3] Under the N.E.P. labour policy had been characterized by a very high degree of *laisser faire*: workers had been free to choose their jobs, even though the scourge of unemployment made that freedom half-illusory; managers had been more or less free to hire and fire their men. But rapid industrialization at once created an acute shortage of labour, and that meant the end of *laisser faire*. This

[1] Ibid., pp. 431-5.
[2] Ibid., p. 484. In actual fact illiteracy was still widespread.
[3] Ibid., pp. 304-5 and 360-1.

was, in Stalin's words, the 'end of spontaneity' on the labour market, the beginning of what, in English-speaking countries, was later called direction of labour. The forms of direction were manifold. Industrial businesses signed contracts with collective farms, by which the latter were obliged to send specified numbers of men and women to factories in the towns. This was the basic method. It is an open question whether the term 'forced labour' can fairly be applied to it. Compulsion was used very severely in the initial phase of the process, when members of collective farms, declared redundant and deprived of membership, were placed in a position not unlike that of the unemployed man whom economic necessity drives to hire himself as a factory hand. Once in town, the proletarianized peasant was free to change his job. Stalin aimed at securing by decree the reserve of manpower for industry which in most countries had been created by the chronic and spontaneous flight of impoverished peasants to the towns.

Forced labour, in the strict sense, was imposed on peasants who had resorted to violence in resisting collectivization. They were treated like criminals and were subject to imprisonment. Here history played one of its malignant and gloomy jokes. Soviet penitentiary reforms of earlier years, inspired by humanitarian motives, viewed the imprisonment of criminals as a means to their re-education, not punishment. They provided for the employment of criminals in useful work. The criminals were to be under the protection of trade unions; and their work was to be paid at trade-union rates. As the number of rebellious peasants grew, they were organized in mammoth labour camps and employed in the building of canals and railways, in timber felling, and so on. Amid the famine and misery of the early thirties the provisions for their protection were completely disregarded. 'Re-education' degenerated into slave labour, terribly wasteful of human life, a vast black spot on the picture of the second revolution.

When Stalin then claimed that in Soviet Russia labour 'had from a disgraceful and painful burden been transformed . . . into a matter of glory, valour and heroism', his words sounded like mockery to the inmates of the labour camps. They did not sound so to those more fortunate workers to whom industrialization spelt social advance. Industrial labour and technical

STALIN IN THE 1930's   E. N. A.

Wide World Photo
NADEZHDA ALLILUYEVA, STALIN'S SECOND WIFE

WITH WOMEN COLLECTIVE FARMERS DURING
'LIBERAL SPELL'

efficiency were surrounded by unusual glamour, which made them attractive to the young generation. Press, theatre, film, and radio extolled the 'heroes of the production front', the way famous soldiers or film-stars were exalted in other countries. The doors of technical schools of all grades opened to workers from the bench; and such schools multiplied with extraordinary rapidity. 'We ourselves', Stalin urged the Bolsheviks, 'must become experts, masters at our business.'[1] 'No ruling class has managed without its own intelligentsia.'[2] Throughout the thirties the ranks of that new intelligentsia swelled, until Stalin spoke of it as of a social group equal, or rather superior, in status to the workers and the peasants, the two basic classes of Soviet society. The cultural and political qualities of the new intelligentsia were very different from those of the old one, which had kindled the flame of revolution under the Tsars and guided the workers' and peasants' republic in its early days. The new intelligentsia was brought up to spurn political ambition. It lacked the intellectual subtlety and the aesthetic refinement of its predecessors. Its curiosity about world affairs was damped or not awakened at all; it had no real sense of any community of fate between Russia and the rest of the world. Its chief interest was in machines and technical discoveries, in bold projects for the development of backward provinces, in administrative jobs, and in the arts of business management. In all these fields, too, it showed a crudeness which sometimes made it the laughing-stock of foreign experts. But it combined that crudeness with an extraordinary eagerness to learn, with great shrewdness and receptiveness of mind, the characteristics of pioneers. This was, indeed, the generation of Stalin's 'frontier men'.

At the same time the old intelligentsia suffered degradation. Stalin distrusted its critical mind and the cosmopolitan or internationalist outlook of many of its members. Old technicians and administrators viewed his projects with cool scepticism and even open hostility. Some sided with the one or the other opposition. A few persisted in an attitude of defeatism which led them to obstruct or even to sabotage the economic plans. At first Stalin displayed towards the technicians and administrators of the older generation the exaggerated respect which is often so characteristic of proletarian new-comers to the busi-

---

[1] J. Stalin, *Problems of Leninism*, p. 354. [2] Ibid., p. 369.

ness of government. Then, as his self-confidence grew and as he involved himself in clashes with economists and administrators, who were too strongly attached to their inert routine or too sober and realistic to keep pace with the industrial revolution, Stalin's respectful attitude towards them changed into its opposite. He scorned them and humiliated them. He used the offences or crimes of a few to surround them all with intense suspicion. A few demonstrative trials of 'wreckers' and 'saboteurs', at which scientists and academicians like Professor Ramzin and his associates were put in the dock, sufficed to make workmen and foremen look distrustfully upon their managers and technicians. The results were disastrous for industry. Moreover, the training of the new intelligentsia was dependent on the willing co-operation of the old one. In the end Stalin himself had to protect the members of the latter. His speeches on the subject bristled with contradictions which reflected his own phobias, vacillations, and belated attempts at retrieving the situation.

Perhaps the most important aspect of his social policy was his fight against the equalitarian trends. He insisted on the need for a highly differentiated scale of material rewards for labour, designed to encourage skill and efficiency.[1] He claimed that Marxists were no levellers in the popular sense; and he found support for his thesis in Marx's well-known saying that even in a classless society workers would at first be paid according to their labour and not to their needs. Nevertheless, a strong strand of equalitarianism had run through Bolshevism. Under Lenin, for instance, the maximum income which members of the ruling party, even those of the highest rank, were allowed to earn equalled the wages of a skilled labourer. That the needs of industrialization clashed with 'ascetic' standards of living and that the acquisition of industrial skill was impeded by the lack of material incentives to technicians, administrators, and workers can hardly be disputed. But it is equally true that,

---

[1] Stalin initiated that policy in his famous speech on the 'six conditions' for industrialization (23 June 1931). After that he emphatically reasserted it in almost every one of his speeches. At the seventeenth congress, in 1934, he decried the equalization of wages and salaries as a 'reactionary, petty-bourgeois absurdity worthy of a primitive sect of ascetics but not of a Socialist society organized on Marxian lines'. Only 'leftist blockheads . . . idealize the poor as the eternal bulwark of Bolshevism' (*Problems of Leninism*, p. 502).

throughout the thirties, the differentiation of wages and salaries was pushed to extremes, incompatible with the spirit, if not the letter, of Marxism. A wide gulf came to separate the vast mass of unskilled and underpaid workmen from the privileged 'labour aristocracy' and bureaucracy, a gulf which may be said to have impeded the cultural and industrial progress of the nation as a whole, as much as the earlier rigidly equalitarian outlook had done.

It was mainly in connexion with Stalin's social policy that his opponents, especially the exiled Trotsky, denounced him as the leader of a new privileged caste. He indeed fostered the inequality of incomes with great determination. On this point his mind had been set long before the 'great change'. As early as 1925 he enigmatically warned the fourteenth · congress: 'We must not play with the phrase about equality. This is playing with fire.'[1] In later years he spoke against the 'levellers' with a rancour and venom which suggested that in doing so he defended the most sensitive and vulnerable facet of his policy. It was so sensitive because the highly paid and privileged managerial groups came to be the props of Stalin's régime. They had a vested interest in it. Stalin himself felt that his personal rule was the more secure the more solidly it rested on a rigid hierarchy of interest and influence. The point was also so vulnerable because no undertaking is as difficult and risky as the setting up of a new hierarchy on ground that has just been broken up by the mighty ploughs of social revolution. The revolution stirs the people's dormant longings for equality. The most critical moment in its development is that at which the leaders feel that they cannot satisfy that longing and proceed to quell it.[2] They get on with the job which some of their opponents call the betrayal of the revolution. But their conscience is so uneasy and their nerves are so strained by the ambiguity of their role that the worst outbursts of their temper

---

[1] J. Stalin, *Sochinenya*, vol. vii, p. 376.

[2] 'The basis of bureaucratic rule is the poverty of society in objects of consumption, with the resulting struggle of each against all. When there is enough goods in a store the purchasers can come whenever they want to. When there is little goods the purchasers are compelled to stand in line. When the lines are very long, it is necessary to appoint a policeman to keep order. Such is the starting-point of the power of the Soviet bureaucracy. It "knows" who is to get something and who has to wait' (L. Trotsky, *The Revolution Betrayed*, p. 110).

are directed against the victims of that 'betrayal'. Hence the extraordinary vehemence with which a Cromwell, a Robespierre, or a Stalin, each hit out against the levellers of his time.

.   .   .   .

It was only in the late thirties that the fruits of the second revolution began to mature. Towards the end of the decade Russia's industrial power was catching up with Germany's. Her efficiency and capacity for organization were still incomparably lower. So was the standard of living of her people. But the aggregate output of her mines, basic plants, and factories approached the level which the most efficient and disciplined of all continental nations, assisted by foreign capital, had reached only after three-quarters of a century of intensive industrialization. The other continental nations, to whom only a few years before Russians still looked up, were now left far behind.[1] The industrial revolution spread from central and western Russia to the remote wilderness of Soviet Asia. The collectivization of farming, too, began to yield positive results. Towards the end of the decade agriculture had recovered from the terrible slump of the early 'thirties; and industry was at last able to supply tractors, harvester-combines, and other implements in great numbers and the farms were achieving a very high degree of mechanization. The outside world was more or less unaware of the great change and the shift in the international balance of power which it implied. Spectacular failures of the first five-year plan induced foreign observers to take a highly

---

[1] A detailed description of the achievements of the planned economy can hardly have its place in Stalin's biography. Only a brief statistical summary can be given here, in which the strength of Russian industry in 1928–9 is compared with that of 1937–8, i.e. towards the end of the second and the beginning of the third five-year plan. In the course of that decade the output of electricity per annum rose from 6 to 40 billion kwh., of coal from 30 to 133 million tons, of oil from 11 to 32 million tons, of steel from 4 to 18 million tons, of motor-cars from 1,400 to 211,000. The value of the annual output of machine-tools rose from 3 billion to 33 billion roubles (in 'stable prices'). (In 1941 the total output of the Soviet machine-building industry was 50 times higher than in 1913.) Between 1928 and 1937 the number of workers and employees rose from 11·5 million to 27 million. Before the revolution the number of doctors was 20,000; it was 105,000 in 1937. The number of hospital beds rose from 175,000 to 618,000. In 1914, 8 million people attended schools of all grades; in 1928, 12 million; and in 1938, 31·5 million. In 1913, 112,000 people studied at university colleges; in 1939, 620,000. Before the revolution public libraries possessed 640 books per 10,000 inhabitants; in 1939, 8,610 (*Strany Mira*, statistical yearbook for 1946).

sceptical view of the results of the second and the third. The macabre series of 'purge' trials suggested economic and political weakness. The elements of weakness were undoubtedly there; and they were even greater than may appear when the scene is viewed in retrospect from the vantage point of the late forties. But the elements of strength were also incomparably greater than they were thought to be in the late thirties.

The achievement was remarkable, even if measured only by the yard-stick of Russian national aspirations. On a different scale, it laid the foundations for Russia's new power just as Cromwell's Navigation Act had once laid the foundation for British naval supremacy. Those who still view the political fortunes of countries in terms of national ambitions and prestige cannot but accord to Stalin the foremost place among all those rulers who, through the ages, were engaged in building up Russia's power. Actuated by such motives even many of the Russian White émigrés began to hail Stalin as a national hero. But the significance of the second revolution lay not only and not even mainly in what it meant to Russia. To the world it was important as the first truly gigantic experiment in planned economy, the first instance in which a government undertook to plan and regulate the whole economic life of its country and to direct its nationalized industrial resources towards a uniquely rapid multiplication of the nation's wealth. True enough Stalin was not the originator of the idea. He borrowed so much from Marxist thinkers and economists, including his rivals, that often he might well be charged with outright plagiarism. He was, nevertheless, the first to make of the abstract idea the practical business of government. It is also true that an important beginning in practical planning had been made by the German Government and General Staff in the First World War; and that Lenin had often referred to that precedent as to a pointer to future experiments.[1] What was new in Stalin's planning was the fact that it was initiated not merely as a war-time expedient, but as the normal pattern of economic life in peace. Hitherto governments had engaged in planning as long as they had needed implements of war. Under Stalin's five-year plans, too, guns, tanks, and planes were produced in great

[1] *The Essentials of Lenin*, vol. ii, pp. 90–3, 104.

profusion; but the chief merit of these plans was not that they enabled Russia to arm herself, but that they enabled her to modernize and transform society.

We have seen the follies and the cruelties that attended Stalin's 'great change'. They inevitably recall those of England's industrial revolution, as Karl Marx has described them in *Das Kapital*. The analogies are as numerous as they are striking. In the closing chapter of the first volume of his work, Marx depicts the 'primitive accumulation' of capital (or the 'previous accumulation', as Adam Smith called it), the first violent processes by which one social class accumulated in its hands the means of production, while other classes were being deprived of their land and means of livelihood and reduced to the status of wage-earners. The process which, in the thirties, took place in Russia might be called the 'primitive accumulation' of socialism in one country. Marx described the 'enclosures' and 'clearings' by which the landlords and manufacturers of England expropriated the yeomanry, the 'class of independent peasants'.[1] A parallel to those enclosures is found in a Soviet law, on which Stalin reported to the sixteenth congress, a law which allowed the collective farms to 'enclose' or 'round off' their land so that it should comprise a continuous area. In this way the individual farmers were either compelled to join the collective farms or were virtually expropriated.[2] Marx recalls 'the bloody discipline' by which the free peasants of England were made into wage-labourers, 'the disgraceful action of the state which employed the police to accelerate the accumulation of capital by increasing the degree of exploitation of labour'.[3] His words might apply to many of the practices introduced by Stalin. Marx sums up his picture of the English industrial revolution by saying that 'capital comes [into the world] dripping from head to foot, from every pore, with blood and dirt'. Thus also comes into the world—socialism in one country.

In spite of its 'blood and dirt', the English industrial

---

[1] K. Marx, *Capital*, vol. i, pp. 740-66.

[2] The law was adopted in January 1930 (J. Stalin, *Leninism*, vol. ii, p. 343). K. Marx, op. cit., p. 761: 'Thus were the agricultural people first forcibly expropriated from the soil, driven from their homes, turned into vagabonds, and then whipped, branded, tortured by laws grotesquely terrible, into the discipline necessary for the wage system.'   [3] K. Marx, op. cit., p. 766.

revolution—Marx did not dispute this—marked a tremendous progress in the history of mankind. It opened a new and not unhopeful epoch of civilization. Stalin's industrial revolution can claim the same merit. It is argued against it that it has perpetrated cruelties excusable in earlier centuries but unforgivable in this. This is a valid argument, but only within limits. Russia had been belated in her historical development. In England serfdom had disappeared by the end of the fourteenth century. Stalin's parents were still serfs. By the standards of British history, the fourteenth and the twentieth centuries have, in a sense, met in contemporary Russia. They have met in Stalin. The historian cannot be seriously surprised if he finds in him some traits usually associated with tyrants of earlier centuries. Even in the most irrational and convulsive phase of his industrial revolution, however, Stalin could make the claim that his system was free from at least one major and cruel folly which afflicted the advanced nations of the west: 'The capitalists [these were his words spoken during the Great Depression[1]] consider it quite normal in a time of slump to destroy the "surplus" of commodities and burn "excess" agricultural produce in order to keep up high prices and ensure high profits, while here, in the U.S.S.R., those guilty of such crimes would be sent to a lunatic asylum.'

．　　．　　．　　．　　．　　．　　．　　．　　．

It is easy to see how far Stalin drifted away from what had hitherto been the main stream of Socialist and Marxist thought. What his socialism had in common with the new society, as it had been imagined by Socialists of nearly all shades, was public ownership of the means of production and planning. It differed in the degradation to which it subjected some sections of the community and also in the recrudescence of glaring social inequalities amid the poverty which the revolution inherited from the past. But the root difference between Stalinism and the traditional Socialist outlook lay in their respective attitudes towards the role of force in the transformation of society.

Marxism was, as it were, the illegitimate and rebellious offspring of nineteenth-century liberalism. Bitterly opposed to its parent, it had many a feature in common with it. The prophets

[1] J. Stalin, *Leninism*, vol. ii, p. 369.

of *laisser faire* had deprecated political force, holding that it could play no progressive role in social life. In opposition to liberalism, Marxists stressed those historic instances and situations in which—as in the English and French revolutions, the American War of Independence and the Civil War—force did assist in the progress of nations and classes. But they also held that the limits within which political force could effect changes in the outlook of society were narrow. They held that the fortunes of peoples were shaped primarily by basic economic and social processes; and that, compared with these, force could play only a subordinate role. Much as the Marxist and the Liberal ideals of society differed from one another, both trends shared, in different degrees, the optimism about the future of modern civilization, so characteristic of the nineteenth century. Each of the two trends assumed that the progress of modern society tended more or less spontaneously towards the attainment of its ideal. Marx and Engels expressed their common view in the famous phrase that force is the midwife of every old society pregnant with a new one. The midwife merely helps the baby to leave the mother's womb when the time for that has come. She can do no more. Stalin's view on the role of political force, reflected in his deeds rather than his words, oozes the atmosphere of twentieth-century totalitarianism. Stalin might have paraphrased the old Marxian aphorism: force is no longer the midwife—force is the mother of the new society.

CHAPTER IX

The Gods are Athirst

Introduction: Bolshevism and Jacobinism.—Stalin watches Trotsky's activities abroad.—Trotsky's influence in Russia.—Two generations of Bolshevik oppositionists.—Stalin wavers between repression and Liberal gestures (1934).—The assassination of Kirov (December 1934) and the end of the quasi-liberal spell.—Zinoviev's and Kamenev's new recantations.—Stalin sends Zhdanov to 'purge' Leningrad.—Bukharin and Radek the chief authors of the 'Stalin Constitution' of 1936.—A digression on Stalin and Dostoyevsky's Grand Inquisitor.—The outlook of the Politbureau.—Stalin's literary and cultural influence.—His friendship with Maxim Gorky.—The 'purge' trials (1936–8).—The defendants and the charges.—Why did the defendants make their 'confessions'?—The timing of the trials.—Tukhachevsky's conspiracy.—Stalin promulgates the new Constitution (November 1936).—The end of the purges, in the beginning of 1939, and their consequences.—The assassination of Trotsky (Mexico, August 1940).

IN the middle thirties begins the most obscure chapter in Stalin's career, the series of purge trials in which he destroyed nearly the whole Old Guard of Bolshevism. This period has often been compared with the closing phase of the Jacobin revolution— the rule of the guillotine—in France. In many respects the similarity was indeed so close that some of the chief actors of the drama as well as many outsiders were tempted to overlook the differences. In Stalin's as in Robespierre's 'reign of terror' there was the same macabre quality, the same black hues of irrational cruelty, the same mythological horror that the sight of a revolution devouring its own children never ceases to evoke. Up to a point even the sequence of events was identical. Robespierre first defeated the Jacobin left which was led by Hébert and Clootz, and he did so with the help of the Jacobin right led by Danton. Then he destroyed Danton and his associates, too, and secured for a short time the undisputed rule of his own Jacobin centre faction. We have seen Stalin as the leader of the centre faction in Bolshevism. We have seen him assisted at first by the Bolshevik right in defeating the left and then turning against the right. We have seen him finally as the triumphant leader of his faction in sole possession of power.

But the differences are not less striking. The mutual slaughter of the Jacobin leaders took place at an early stage of the revolution. The intervals between the various phases of the revolution, its climaxes and anti-climaxes, were extremely short; and all its phases seemed to be governed by the same blind but still fresh passion. Early in 1793 the Mountain and the Gironde appeared to stand united against the King. Ten months later, on 31 October, the leaders of the Gironde ascended the scaffold. Then came the Feast of Reason, the climax of Jacobinism. Barely five months later, in March 1794, the leaders of the Jacobin left were beheaded. Within a fortnight the hangman showed Danton's enormous head to the watching crowd of Parisians. Robespierre's undivided dictatorship lasted less than four months, until 27 July (9 Thermidor) 1794. Against the spontaneous, frenzied tempo of the events human reason, self-discipline, and any instincts of self-preservation seemed helpless. Leaders and followers, factions and individuals, all seemed to perform their historical function, that of undoing feudal France, and to exhaust themselves to death in a single fit of delirium.

The chain of events looked vastly different in the Russian revolution. The Bolshevik régime was nearing the close of its second decade without showing signs of Jacobin-like insanity. To be sure there was no lack of terror in the years of the civil war, from 1918 to 1921. But that terror was still a measure of war against an armed and militant counter-revolution. Its methods and objectives were defined by the nature of that war. Unlike the Jacobins, the Bolsheviks did not execute their Girondists. The most eminent spokesmen of Menshevism, Martov, Dan, Abramovich, were either allowed to leave or were exiled from Russia after their party had been banned. A handful of those who stayed behind were imprisoned, but most Mensheviks, reconciling themselves to defeat, loyally served in the Soviet administration and even on the staffs of the leading Bolsheviks.

It seemed therefore natural to expect that the Russian Mountain, having spared the lives of its Girondists, would not wallow in the blood of its own leaders. In the early thirties the story was still current among Bolsheviks that at the outset of the struggle their leaders had taken a secret and solemn vow never to set the guillotine into motion against one another. Whether this was true or not, it is certain that Stalin did ponder over the horrifying French precedent; and that for some years this deterred him from resorting to the most drastic means of repression. More than once he said so. This is, for instance, how he countered Zinoviev's and Kamenev's demand for reprisals against Trotsky: 'We have not agreed with Zinoviev and Kamenev, because we have known that a policy of chopping off [heads] is fraught with great dangers. . . . The method of chopping off and blood-letting—and they did demand blood—is dangerous and infectious. You chop off one head to-day, another one to-morrow, still another one the day after—what in the end will be left of the party?'[1] The revolution of the twentieth century, he seemed to say, may spurn its children but it need not devour them. In 1929 he made up his mind to exile Trotsky from Russia. It was still inconceivable that Trotsky should be imprisoned, let alone put before the firing squad. It was not until several years later, after the lava of the revolution seemed to have cooled down completely, that the new eruption of terror occurred. This circumstance, no less than the confessions and self-condemnations of Stalin's rivals, which contrasted so sharply with the proud and defiant behaviour of most of the Jacobin leaders in the dock, made Stalin's purge trials appear even more mystifying than were Robespierre's 'amalgams'.

The French revolution was entirely spontaneous. Its parties and factions sprang into being in the process of the upheaval. They had had no fixed programmes or clear-cut ideas. They were part of the great flux of the revolution, from which their policies and slogans emerged as the movement was passing from phase to phase. The strength of Jacobinism was in its determination to smash the feudal structure of France. Its weakness lay in its utter incapacity to give French society any new and positive organization. Robespierre offered France the Utopia of social equality based on small property, while France was only prepared to pass from feudal to bourgeois inequality. He strove to transform the whole of France into a virtuous lower middle-class community; and he sent his bourgeois and quasi-proletarian opponents to their death. France, breaking out of the Procrustean bed into which he tried to force her, rid herself of the Utopian dictator who had freed her from her feudal

[1] J. Stalin, *Sochinenya*, vol. vii, p. 380.

chains—in this way she secured her recovery and her bourgeois progress. The staying power of Jacobinism was so slight because none of its factions possessed any realistic and positive view of the social needs and possibilities of the nation.

The staying power of Bolshevism was incomparably greater. Far from itself being part of the revolutionary flux, Lenin's party entered the revolution as a closely knit body determined to dominate the spontaneous movement. The broad lines of the Bolshevik programme had crystallized long before 1917. Even when the tide began to ebb, the party, though it was torn by inner strife, still offered the nation a constructive programme of social development. In the course of nearly two decades its rational outlook protected it against the irrational urges inherent in a despotism issued from revolution. For nearly two decades Bolshevism resisted the gods that were athirst. But when it succumbed to them its prostration was even more frightful than that of Jacobinism.

It was more frightful but less complete. Unlike Robespierre, Stalin himself was not caught by the guillotine he had set in motion.

.   .   .   .

Having expelled Trotsky from Russia, Stalin must have sighed with relief. Even in his Siberian exile Trotsky had kept in touch with those of his followers who had not 'capitulated'; and left in Russia, amid all the discontents and tensions of the first five-year plan, he might still have inspired an effective opposition. Stalin had obtained the agreement of Kemal Pasha's Government for Trotsky's deportation to Turkey. He hoped that there, cut off from the world, Trotsky would be reduced to inactivity. But the exile continued to fight with the one weapon left to him, his pen. From the isle of Prinkipo, where he settled, he arranged for the publication of a small periodical, *The Bulletin of the Opposition (Bulleten Oppozitsii)*, which he himself filled with his running commentary on Soviet and Communist policies. This inconspicuous publication, at first, exercised a considerable influence upon Soviet officials who travelled abroad, read it, and often carried it in their luggage back home to pass it on to friends. Stalin himself carefully studied every copy.[1]

¹ J. Stalin, *Problems of Leninism*, p. 507.

The paper was well informed about happenings inside Russia; and Trotsky was not a critic to be ignored. Quite a few of Stalin's own moves may be traced to suggestions which were first made in the *Bulletin*.[1] Apart from this, the *Bulletin* enlightened Stalin better than the reports of his own political police on the moods and hopes of the opposition.

He was not inclined to take lightly the influence which Trotsky unexpectedly began to exercise from abroad. He remembered that Lenin's *Iskra* (Spark), a sheet not more impressive than Trotsky's *Bulletin*, had once 'kindled the flame of revolution'. Trotsky, it was true, now preached reform, not revolution. Unlike the old clandestine Bolshevik papers, his *Bulletin* probably never reached workers in Russia; but it circulated all the more freely among high officials and influential members of the party, many of whom had served under Trotsky and preserved a sentiment of loyalty towards him. Soon after his banishment one of the chiefs of the political police itself, Blumkin, during a trip abroad, visited Trotsky in Prinkipo. Stalin was determined to put an end to such contacts. Blumkin was shot, *pour décourager les autres*. This seems to have been the first instance in which a sympathizer of the opposition suffered capital punishment. Some time later Trotsky and his family were deprived of Soviet citizenship. From now on anybody who put himself in touch with the founder of the Red Army was liable to be charged with contact with a 'foreign conspirator'.

Nevertheless, Trotsky continued to exercise some influence from afar, especially during the critical years 1932–3. At the height of the crisis, about the time when Stalin's wife committed suicide, his *Bulletin* published a detailed survey of the economic situation, containing a wealth of statistical data of the sort that was available only to members of the Soviet Government.[2] The anonymous article concluded: 'In view of the incapacity of the present leadership to get out of the economic and political deadlock, the conviction about the need to change the leadership of the party is growing.' The author of the survey was I. N. Smirnov, the victor over Kolchak, an adherent of Trotsky who had 'capitulated' and was now back in office. Trotsky himself, protesting against being deprived of Soviet

---

[1] This is especially true of economic policy in 1932–3. See, for instance, *Bulleten Oppozitsii*, no. 33, March 1933. [2] Ibid., no. 31, November 1932.

nationality, once again reminded his former colleagues of the advice to 'remove Stalin' that Lenin had given them in his will.

The opposition in Russia stirred; but it did not move. The leaders who had returned from Siberia and surrendered to Stalin could not suppress their uneasiness over Stalin's policies, but they did not and could not openly come out against them. Trotsky himself, sparing Stalin no criticism, vacillated in his practical conclusions: 'At present', he wrote in the autumn of 1932,[1] 'the upsetting of the bureaucratic equilibrium [that is of Stalin's rule] in the U.S.S.R. would almost certainly benefit the forces of counter-revolution.' This amounted to advising the opposition to do nothing other than abstract propaganda. On another occasion, however, he claimed that 'the very near future will show that the left and the right oppositions have been neither routed nor annihilated and that, on the contrary, they alone have a true political existence'.[2] In 1932 Zinoviev, Kamenev, and many others were once again expelled from the party and exiled to Siberia. 'The greatest political mistake of my life was that I deserted Trotsky in 1927', Zinoviev now said.[3] Smirnov, the author of the revelations in Trotsky's *Bulletin*, was arrested. So were Riutin, chief of propaganda, around whom malcontents had begun to rally, and Uglanov, secretary of the party in Moscow. Rykov, Tomsky, and Bukharin renounced those of their followers who had sought agreement with the left opposition, and once again denounced their own views. A few months later, however, in May 1933, Zinoviev and Kamenev were, after a new recantation, allowed to return from exile. 'Stalin, like Gogol's hero, is collecting dead souls for lack of living ones', Trotsky commented on the new 'capitulations'.[4] Yet the repeated deportations and recantations served Stalin's purpose: the deportations terrorized the opposition, the recantations confused it. Trotsky's irony was not, however, altogether groundless. Discontent was rife in the party. The number of members expelled in 1933–5 ran into hundreds of thousands; many more were expelled from the Komsomol. What was even more important was that the discontent began to express itself in new forms. A cleavage appeared between two generations of the opposition, a schism between fathers and sons, which was

---

[1] *Bulleten Oppozitsii*, no. 36/7.   [2] Ibid., no. 31.
[3] Ibid., no. 33.   [4] Ibid., no. 35.

not unlike the schisms in the Russian intelligentsia of the nineteenth century.

By now the old men of the opposition had long been not only defeated but spiritually broken. Even the indomitable Rakovsky, former Ukrainian Premier and Ambassador in London and Paris, who had held out in exile and prison longer than the others, surrendered and returned to Moscow in 1934. Like all the other penitents he, too, signed a statement containing as much flattery of Stalin as self-accusation. The gist of all such statements was that Stalin's conduct of policy was the only correct one, and that any of the courses advocated by the oppositions would inevitably have brought disaster. The 'capitulators' did not admit yet that they had striven towards a restoration of capitalism. Nor were admissions to that effect demanded from them. The gravamen of their self-accusations was that their policies, if adopted, would have, against their best intentions, exposed the country to the danger of capitalist restoration.

That they agreed to indulge in such 'self-criticisms' was due not merely to the hard blows which Stalin dealt them. The fact itself that they yielded proved that they were politically weary or else only half-hearted in their opposition. Their age alone would account for the weariness: most of the 'capitulators' had behind them thirty or forty years of incessant struggle, the greater part of it waged in the underground. Their half-heartedness was growing with the realization that the changes accomplished by Stalin, no matter what they thought of his methods, could not be reversed without detriment to the revolution. For all the horror with which his methods filled them, they felt that they were all, Stalinists and anti-Stalinists, in the same boat. Self-debasement was the ransom they paid to its captain. Their recantations were therefore neither wholly sincere nor wholly insincere. On returning from the places of their exile they cultivated their old political friendships and contacts, but carefully refrained from any political action against Stalin. Almost till the middle of the thirties nearly all of them kept in touch with the members of his new Politbureau. Some of the penitents, Bukharin, Rykov, Piatakov, Radek, and others, were either Stalin's personal advisers or members of the Government. If they had wanted to assassinate either Stalin or his close associates they had innumerable opportunities to do so.

One of Trotsky's correspondents in Russia thus described the mood of these men in 1933: 'They all speak about Stalin's isolation and the general hatred of him. . . . But they often add: "If it were not for that (we omit their strong epithet for him) . . . everything would have fallen into pieces by now. It is he who keeps everything together. . . ." '[1] Among themselves the 'fathers' of the opposition grumbled, sighed, and talked their troubles off their chests. They continued to refer to Stalin as the Genghiz Khan of the Politbureau, the Asiatic, the new Ivan the Terrible. The grumblings and epithets were immediately reported to Stalin, who had his ears everywhere. He knew the real feelings of his humiliated opponents and the value of their public eulogies. But he was also confident that they would not go beyond violent verbal expression of their political impotence.

The veterans of the opposition, it is true, gave themselves to vague hopes about the future. Perhaps after the second, perhaps after the third five-year plan, so they thought, prosperity and political contentment would come; and then the rigours of Stalin's régime would not be needed or tolerated. Meanwhile, they bided their time and curbed their younger and more impatient followers. Even Trotsky, who thundered at the 'cowardly capitulators', wrote in March 1933: 'Within the party and beyond, the slogan "Down with Stalin" is heard more and more widely. The reasons . . . need not be explained here. Nevertheless, we think the slogan to be wrong. What is at issue is not Stalin's person but his faction. . . . It goes without saying that the Bonapartist régime of a single leader, compulsorily adored by the masses, should be and will be brought to an end as the most shameful distortion of the idea of a revolutionary party. But we are concerned not with the expulsion of individuals but the change of the system.'[2] Trotsky even offered Stalin his co-operation against the dangers of counter-revolution during the critical period when the régime would be liberalized.

The waiting attitude of the veterans could not and did not satisfy the discontented elements among the younger men. That the 'sons' should try to react against the stifling atmosphere of the dictatorship with greater vehemence than the weary 'fathers' was natural and inevitable. The new generation could certainly not begin where the old one had left off—with nauseating

---

[1] *Bulleten Oppozitsii*, no. 34.   [2] Ibid., no. 33.

recantation and self-humiliation. It still looked with some respect to the 'grand old men' of Bolshevism, hoping to re-habilitate them and to return them to power. Not only did the 'sons' feel that the 'fathers' were superior to them in education and political experience, they also accepted from them their main idea: 'Back to pure Leninism', whatever that meant. It was in the choice of the means that they differed. The old Bolsheviks had in their young days been opposed to assassinations of Tsarist satraps, as practised by Narodniks and Social Revolutionaries; they had, as Marxists, relied upon the growth of a mass movement against Tsardom. They still remained true to that political tradition and hoped that a change in the attitude of the working classes, and not a conspiracy of individuals acting behind the backs of the people, would lead to a reform of the régime. The 'sons' knew no such inhibitions. They saw that the industrial working class now consisted mainly of raw peasants, just drafted from the country-side, whose political consciousness was very poor and whose capacity for action was almost nil. If reform were to be achieved through the political action of that working class, then the country would be condemned to endure Stalin's rule for many years. This was precisely the prospect to which the most ardent young oppositionists would not reconcile themselves. At school and in the cells of the Komsomol they had learned the stories of those lonely Russian revolutionaries who in the nineteenth century, supported by almost no class of Russian society, attacked autocracy with bombs and revolvers. Was not Lenin's brother among the conspirators who attempted to kill Tsar Alexander III? The text-books surrounded those martyrs and heroes with a romantic halo; and so the sacred shadows of the past seemed now to press bomb and revolver into the hands of some impatient anti-Stalinist Komsomoltsy.[1]

. . . .

Parallel to this cleavage in the opposition, a new dissension arose in the Politbureau. Its members, though they had all been hand-picked by Stalin and were pledged to defend the existing state of affairs, differed on means and methods. Some urged

[1] It was for this reason that Zhdanov later demanded that the text-books should cease to glorify the revolutionary terrorists of the nineteenth century.

Stalin to give his autocracy a more Liberal tinge, while others advocated the strong hand. It seems that Kirov, Voroshilov, Rudzutak, and Kalinin were the 'Liberals'. Voroshilov had to reckon with the effects of collectivization on the army's morale. The commander in the Far East, General Blücher, declared that he would not shoulder responsibility for the defence of the Far Eastern frontier if collectivization was enforced on the borderlands.[1] Voroshilov supported Blücher's view before the Politbureau and obtained the exemption of farmers in the Far East from collectivization. Kirov, who had gone to Leningrad to suppress the Zinoviev opposition, willy-nilly became a mouthpiece of the restive mood that prevailed in Russia's most European and most revolutionary city. He pleaded with Stalin for leniency towards the opposition; and in his own domain he did his best to restrain the political police.[2] Rudzutak, vice-Premier and leader of the trade unions, exercised his influence in the same direction. Molotov and Kaganovich were the chief advocates of the strong hand.

The devotion of all these men to Stalin was beyond doubt. They were the leaders of his praetorian guard. The public, who saw them always marching in step closely behind Stalin, had no idea of the tug-of-war. Stalin himself watched it calmly; he had nothing to fear from it. The antagonists appealed to his wisdom and awaited his verdict. He gave his support now to this and now to that faction. Throughout 1934 he wavered between intensified repression and Liberal gestures. In the spring he ordered a limited amnesty for rebellious *kulaks*. In June, however, he authorized a decree which proclaimed the collective responsibility of every family for treason committed by one of its members. People who failed to denounce a disloyal relative to authority were made liable to severe punishment. A month later he abolished the G.P.U. and replaced it by the Commissariat of Internal Affairs. The powers of the political police were limited; and the Attorney-General—an ex-Menshevik lawyer Andrei Vyshinsky was soon to be appointed to that post—was given the right to supervise its activities and to veto them if they conflicted with the law. The leaders of the oppositions were allowed to address public meet-

---

[1] E. Wollenberg, *The Red Army*, p. 258.
[2] A. Barmine, *One Who Survived*, pp. 247-8 and 252.

ings and to write for the press, though not to criticize the powers that be. Hopes for further Liberal measures rose high. The idea of a constitutional reform was vented in the Politbureau; and the main leaders of the opposition were invited to co-operate on the projects for a new constitution.

The quasi-Liberal spell was suddenly interrupted when, on 1 December 1934, a young Communist, Nikolayev, assassinated Sergei Kirov in Leningrad. Stalin rushed to Leningrad and personally interrogated the terrorist in the course of many hours. The assassin had belonged to a small group of young Communists embittered by the oppressive atmosphere in the country and spellbound by ideas of revolutionary terrorism. Such moods were fairly widespread among the young. Nikolayev and his friends regarded themselves as followers of Zinoviev, with whom, however, they had had no direct or indirect connexion. Probably it was Kirov's liberalism that enabled the terrorist to gain access to his offices in the Smolny Institute, for Kirov had objected to being heavily guarded by the political police. At any rate, the G.P.U. of Leningrad had known about the planned attempt and had done nothing to prevent it. Had Stalin also known about it and connived? Nothing is certain; but he used Kirov's death to justify his conclusion that the time for quasi-liberal concessions was over. His victory over the opposition had been far from complete. He had only succeeded in driving discontent underground. He would now strike deeper and harder.

Events now follow a pattern familiar from the history of Russian autocracy. Almost in every generation under the Tsars there was a latent tug-of-war between the gendarmes and the semi-Liberals in the Tsar's *entourage*, corresponding to the split in the opposition between the moderate 'fathers' and the radical 'sons'. Even in its spells of relative mildness, autocracy was never liberal enough to satisfy the opposition; it was just mild enough to enable the revolutionaries to strike at it. The moderate 'fathers' tried in vain to prevail upon the radical youth to wait patiently until the Tsars granted further concessions. Each revolutionary attempt at autocracy had the same results. Among the ruling groups the semi-Liberals were defeated, and the gendarmes came to the fore. The gendarmes were not satisfied

¹ *Short History of the C.P.S.U.*, p. 327.

with suppressing the revolutionaries. They held the moderate opposition responsible for the deeds of the radical youth. The Liberals protested and charged autocracy, which had not allowed open and legal opposition, with the moral responsibility for the 'excesses' of the youth. Thus, the reign of Alexander I abounded in semi-Liberal reforms. The Decembrist rising of 1825 was the prelude to the reign of Nicholas I, the Iron Tsar, the Tsar of the gendarmes. The semi-Liberal Alexander II was killed by revolutionary conspirators, whom his successor Alexander III suppressed with a mailed fist. The policy of the last Tsar swayed between the two courses. Under Stalin these traditional features of the political struggle in Russia were thrown into even sharper relief by tensions characteristic of an unconsolidated, post-revolutionary society.

Nikolayev and his associates were executed. They were tried *in camera*, under a decree issued *ad hoc*, which denied the terrorists the right of defence and appeal. Stalin would not allow them to use the dock as a platform from which to state their views and fling accusations at the rulers. He did not stop at that. Like the old gendarmes, who used to take the Liberal 'fathers' to task for the deeds of the radical 'sons', he charged Zinoviev and Kamenev with responsibility for the assassination of Kirov. Their trial, too, was secret. Both denied any connexion with the assassin. Condemning the deed, they admitted that the young terrorists might have drawn inspiration from the criticisms of Stalin they had once made; but they claimed that, by suppressing open criticism, Stalin had driven the Komsomoltsy to acts of despair. Zinoviev was sentenced to ten and Kamenev to five years' penal servitude. But Stalin was now least of all interested in keeping the two old Bolsheviks in prison, which would have made of them martyrs and, in a sense, re-established them as claimants to power. His main aim was to extract from them an admission of guilt, by which they would with their own hands destroy their halo of martyrdom.

What followed was a grotesque process of bargaining over a formula of recantation, bargaining that went on between Stalin's offices in the Kremlin and the prison cells of the Lubyanka, where Zinoviev and Kamenev were held. Stalin agreed publicly to exonerate the prisoners from all connexion with the assassins; but he demanded from them an admission that they had aimed at the restoration of capitalism. This the prisoners refused. Then Stalin seized upon the one point which they had already admitted, namely, that the terrorists had drawn their inspiration from the opposition's old propaganda.[1] Whether by threat or argument, he got Zinoviev to make that admission in public. 'The former activity of the former opposition could not, by the force of objective circumstances [so Zinoviev stated], but stimulate the degeneration of those criminals', that is of Kirov's assassins. Sincerity was mixed here with diplomatic evasiveness. The condemnation of the terroristic act was sincere; and Stalin was able to extract it from Zinoviev because he, too, wished to counteract the tendency towards terrorism. But Zinoviev took care to stress that he was prepared to shoulder only indirect moral responsibility—it was, in his words, only the 'former activity of the *former* opposition' that might have inspired the terroristic trend. The formula also implied an accusation of Stalin, for it said that terrorism had been bred by 'objective circumstances', i.e. by the oppressive atmosphere in the country. At this stage neither Zinoviev nor Kamenev was prepared to say more in self-accusation; and Stalin left matters at that. To the public the subtle qualifications by which Zinoviev hedged off his 'admission' meant nothing; the admission itself mattered. The leaders of the opposition had moved farther down the slippery slope that led to the great purge trials.

The assassination of Kirov alarmed Stalin. Had not conspirators penetrated into his own office? In the spring of 1935 nearly forty men of his own bodyguard were tried *in camera*. Two were executed. The rest were sentenced to various terms of penal servitude. No mention of that trial was made in the press.[2] A feverish search for terrorists followed in all branches of the party and the Komsomol. Stalin now acted on the principle that it was not enough to hit his real opponents; he rooted out the environment that had bred them. He vented his wrath on Leningrad, whose *genius loci* had seemed to defy him for the last

---

[1] See *Bulleten Oppozitsii*, nos. 42, 47, 52/3. The course of events can be recontructed from reports in *Pravda* for the second half of December 1934 and beginning of January 1935.

[2] Most of these facts were disclosed by A. Ciliga, ex-leader of the Yugoslav Communist party, who had met the defendants of those trials in prison. See *Bulleten Oppozitsii*, no. 47.

ten years. He appointed Andrei Zhdanov to succeed Kirov as the governor of Leningrad. Zhdanov was a young, capable, and ruthless man, who had purged the Komsomol of deviationists and distinguished himself in arrogant attacks on Tomsky during the fight in the trade unions. Stalin could rely upon him to destroy the hornets' nest in Leningrad. In the spring of 1935 tens of thousands of suspect Bolsheviks, Komsomoltsy, and their families were deported from Leningrad to northern Siberia. Multitudes of 'Kirov's assassins', as those deportees were called, from other cities, too, filled prisons and concentration camps.

The treatment of the political prisoners underwent a radical change. Hitherto it had not been different from that accorded to them in Tsarist days. Political offenders had enjoyed certain privileges and been allowed to engage in self-education and even in political propaganda. Oppositional memoranda, pamphlets, and periodicals had circulated half freely between prisons and had occasionally been smuggled abroad. Himself an ex-prisoner, Stalin knew well that jails and places of exile were the 'universities' of the revolutionaries. Recent events taught him to take no risks. From now on all political discussion and activity in the prisons and places of exile was to be mercilessly suppressed; and the men of the opposition were by privation and hard labour to be reduced to such a miserable, animal-like existence that they should be incapable of the normal processes of thinking and of formulating their views.[1]

While Stalin was thus betraying the hopes of Liberal reform, he still pretended that he was willing to satisfy them. He offered the people a diet mixed of terror and illusion. He acted shrewdly, for if he had fed them with terror only, they might have revolted in such desperation that even the most powerful political police might have been helpless. But popular illusions would not have protected a government like Stalin's if it had

---

[1] While trainloads of 'Kirov's assassins' were moving east and northwards from many corners of Russia, Stalin thus justified his action: '. . . these comrades did not always confine themselves to criticism and passive resistance. They threatened to raise a revolt in the party against the Central Committee. More, they threatened some of us with bullets. Evidently, they reckoned on frightening us and compelling us to turn from the Leninist road. . . . We were obliged to handle some of these comrades roughly. But that cannot be helped. I must confess that I, too, had a hand in this. (*Loud cheers and applause.*)' (J. Stalin, *Problems of Leninism*, p. 522.)

not been shielded by terror. Two months after Kirov's assassination, on 6 February 1935, the seventh congress of the Soviets passed a motion on the need for a new constitution and elected a commission which was to draft it. The commission, headed by Stalin, included men like Bukharin, Radek, Sokolnikov, as well as their future prosecutor Vyshinsky. In the course of the next year and a half the commission frequently met in Stalin's presence. Bukharin and Radek were the chief authors of the new constitution, which they often discussed in the columns of *Pravda* and *Izvestya*. The constitution was to be adopted by the next congress of the Soviets, in November 1936, several months after the execution of Zinoviev and Kamenev. It was to be called the 'Stalin Constitution', 'the most democratic in the world'.

. . . .

Describing the situation before and after the assassination of Kirov, we have referred to the traditional pattern of politics under Tsarist autocracy. This comparison may seem far-fetched, because of the gulf that separates Bolshevik from Tsarist Russia. Yet it was none other than Lenin who first hinted at the comparison. In one of his last speeches he reminded his followers what happened in history to conquerors whose civilization was inferior to that of the conquered. The vanquished nation imposed its civilization upon its conquerors. Something similar, Lenin said, might happen in the struggles between social classes. The Bolsheviks had defeated the landlords, the capitalists, and the Tsarist bureaucracy. 'Their culture [i.e. the culture of the defeated classes]', Lenin said, 'is at a miserably low and insignificant level. Nevertheless, it is higher than ours. Miserable and low as it is, it is still higher than that of our responsible Communist administrators.'[1]

Lenin saw only the beginnings of the process by which defeated Tsarist Russia was imposing her own standards and methods upon victorious Bolshevism. The past took a cruel revenge upon a generation that was making a heroic effort to get away from it; and that revenge reached its climax precisely in the course of the second revolution. This paradox of Russian history became embodied in Stalin. More than anybody else

[1] *The Essentials of Lenin*, vol. ii, p. 789.

he represented those 'responsible Communist administrators' whose 'culture' was still inferior to that of Russia's old rulers, and whose overwhelming inclination it was therefore to imitate, often unknowingly, the old rulers' customs and habits. This, historically inevitable, process was reflected in the changing expressions of Stalin's own political physiognomy: the features of not one but of several great Tsars seemed to revive in the Georgian Bolshevik who now ruled from their Kremlin. At one time he showed a trait of family likeness to the Iron Tsar, Nicholas I. At another he looked more like Peter the Great's direct descendant: was he not building industrial Russia in a way similar to that in which Peter the Great built his St. Petersburg, on the swamps and on the bones of the builders? Again, in the years of the Second World War, he would assume the postures and imitate the gestures of Alexander I. Now, in the period of great purges, as he suppressed his opponents, he more and more resembled Ivan the Terrible raging against the *boyars*. His political police, in charge of industrial enterprises as well as of prisons, were not unlike the *oprichnina*, that landed praetorian guard, through which Ivan had secured his ascendancy. In his dispute against Trotsky there might be detected faint echoes of the fierce controversy between Ivan and Prince Kurbsky, the rebellious leader of the *boyars*. As in the sixteenth century, the people of Moscow now 'prayed in terror that the day may pass without execution'. In this revenge of history, it was not so much the recent past as the remote one that seemed to chase and overtake the forward-moving nation. What was reasserting itself was the ferocious spirit of the early, pioneering, empire-building Tsars rather than the later, milder, more 'liberal' spirit of Tsardom in decay. The cruelty with which the past oppressed the present was proportionate to the determination with which the revolution had set out to repudiate the past.

Yet in Stalin the revolutionary elements, especially features inherited from Lenin, combined strangely with the traditional ones; and this combination made of him the most puzzling and elusive personality of his age. The past did not efface the revolution. It rather imprinted its own pattern on a new social substance. Like Cromwell as Lord Protector or Napoleon as Emperor, Stalin now remained the guardian and the trustee of the revolution. He consolidated its national gains and extended them. He 'built socialism'; and even his opponents, while denouncing his autocracy, admitted that most of his economic reforms were indeed essential for socialism. The revenge of the past thus bore not on his social programme but on his technique of government. It was mainly in that that the 'low and miserable' tradition of Tsardom came to predominate.

His technique of power, we know, revealed his distrustful attitude towards society, his pessimistic approach to it. Socialism was to be built by coercion rather than persuasion. Even where he attempted some sort of persuasion he more readily resorted to propagandist stunts than to enlightening argument. He drew, in other words, on that wide assortment of chicanery and trickery by which rulers of all ages and countries had held their peoples in subjection. As the revolution had proclaimed confidence in the people, that is in the working classes, to be its guiding principle, and as it had denounced political deception as serving class-oppression, the revenge of the past inevitably entailed a great conflict of ideas, a veritable spiritual crisis, which finally transformed the face of communism in this generation. This was the epilogue to the protracted conflict between authority, bent on moulding society exclusively from above, and society longing for freedom of self-determination.

The conflict was not peculiar to the Russian revolution. It reappears in every revolution and, indeed, in every religious creed. It forms the essence of the profound, gloomy, and passionate controversy between the Grand Inquisitor and Christ in Dostoyevsky's *Brothers Karamazov*. Stalin, like Dostoyevsky's Grand Inquisitor, represents the Church in revolt against the Gospel. Christ, so argues the Grand Inquisitor, based His teaching on the belief in Man, in Man's dream of freedom, and his proud and courageous ability to live in freedom. He had, therefore, rejected Satan's temptations and refused to convert Man by an appeal to the slave in him. But Christianity could not live up to Christ. When Christ reappears on earth, the Grand Inquisitor addresses Him thus: 'We have corrected Thy deed and based it on Miracle, Mystery, and Authority. . . . And men were delighted that they were led again, as a herd, and that there had been lifted from their hearts, at last, so terrible a gift, the gift [of freedom] that had brought them so much torment. Were we right in teaching and acting like that? Speak! Surely, indeed, we loved mankind, when, realizing so humbly its impotence, we lovingly lightened its burden, and allowed its feeble nature even to sin, provided it was with our permission? Why then hast Thou now come to hinder us?

'I repeat to Thee [the Inquisitor goes on], this very morrow Thou shalt see that obedient herd which, at a mere sign from me, will rush to heap up hot coals against that stake at which I shall burn Thee for having come to hinder us. For if ever there was one who most of all deserved our fire it is Thou. To-morrow I shall burn Thee.' In the prison cell of the Inquisition Christ 'approaches the old man and gently kisses him on his bloodless ninety-year-old lips', as if He, Himself, had acquiesced in the conversion of His Church from freedom and respect for Man to Miracle, Mystery, and Authority.

Many a creed has undergone the conversion; and Bolshevism has not escaped it. If Stalin were ever to expound his esoteric philosophy, he would speak out openly of Russia's inescapable need to 'correct the deed' of the October revolution and to purge it of its original belief in the proletarian, in his freedom and progress and solidarity. 'Only the elect and the strong act on this belief, but mankind is weak and craving for bread and authority', he would say, paraphrasing the Grand Inquisitor. He would look grimly and uneasily into the faces of the founders of socialism and ask them: 'Why have you come to hinder us?'

.   .   .   .

He knew that the old generation of revolutionaries, though weary and humiliated, would, with very few exceptions, never be whole-heartedly converted to Miracle, Mystery, and Authority; and that it would always look upon him as a falsifier of first principles and usurper. He disbanded the Society of Old Bolsheviks, the Society of Former Political Prisoners, and the Communist Academy, the institutions in which the spirit of the old Bolshevism had had its last refuge. These moves indicated the stretch of the road he had travelled since he had begun his struggle against the 'ex-Menshevik' Trotsky in the name of the Old Bolshevik Guard. He now appealed to the young generation, not, of course, to its restive spirits, but to its more timid and yet very important mass which, though eager to learn and advance socially, knew little or nothing about the pristine ideas of Bolshevism, and was unwilling to be bothered about them. This younger generation, as far back as it could remember, had always seen the leaders of the various oppositions in the roles either of whipping-boys or of flagellants. It had been accustomed from childhood to look up to Stalin wrapped in Mystery and Authority. He had long ceased to be the easily accessible, patient, and helpful spokesman of the party secretaries, the Stalin of the early twenties. He could no longer be seen patiently listening to their grievances on the staircases of party offices. He now appeared in public only on very rare occasions, always surrounded by a large suite, the members of which, like courtiers, followed him at a distance, in a carefully fixed order of precedence. To the public he spoke rarely; and every statement of his was made to appear as a milestone in history. As a rule these statements, which were in the nature of an autocrat's orders, did, indeed, have a practical significance for people in every walk of life. The contrast between the remoteness of his person and the omnipresence of his influence did invest his figure, especially in the eyes of the younger generation, with something of that awe-inspiring quality by which oriental rulers used to impress their peoples.

. . . .

The suite by which he was surrounded was, of course, his Politbureau. It was his in every sense, for the men he had picked for it corresponded to his idea of what a leader should be. The 'new type' of a leader, so he wrote as early as 1925, should be no man of letters; he should not be burdened by the dead weight of social democratic habits; and he should be feared as well as respected.[1] Molotov, Kaganovich, Voroshilov, Kuibyshev, Kossior, Rudzutak, Mikoyan, Andreyev—nearly all of them suited that ideal. Nearly all were practical administrators, devoted to their jobs. None had any knowledge of foreign countries; all had, like Stalin himself, been home-bred Bolsheviks.[2] Most of them were small men raised up by

[1] J. Stalin, *Sochinenya*, vol. vii, pp. 42-7.
[2] It had been a stock argument against the leaders of the opposition, one that was used especially by Molotov, that they had been émigrés uprooted from the Russian soil. Stalin dwelt on this in his interview with Emil Ludwig.

Stalin. But as the years went by their knowledge and experience grew with their responsibilities. In a sense the Politbureau was a unique school of government. All the affairs of the country, from the major diplomatic and political decisions to the minor troubles of provincial authorities, came up for debate before that body, which was in almost permanent session. The Politbureau had the last word in all the interminable inter-departmental squabbles; and Stalin had the last word in the Politbureau. He did not even preside over its sessions. Usually he listened silently to the arguments and resolved most of the issues by a plebeian sarcasm, a half-jovial, meaningful threat, or a brusque gesture of impatience. The few men who, in the course of many years, had to make personal decisions on measures to be taken in this or that industry, in this or that branch of agriculture, on educational matters, on the types of weapons that were to be introduced into the army and so forth, eventually accumulated so enormous a knowledge of the tech-nical details of a great variety of jobs as could rarely be obtained by administrators working in a less centralized system. No wonder that in the years of the Second World War foreign statesmen and generals were impressed by Stalin's extra-ordinary grasp of the technical details of his gigantic war machine. But this over-centralized method of government also had its fatal drawbacks. It instilled a grotesque fear of initia-tive and responsibility in all grades of the administration; it reduced every official to a cog; it often brought the whole machine to a standstill, or, worse, by sheer force of inertia it made the machine move in the wrong direction whenever the man at the top failed to press a button in time. Thus the whole administrative machinery was clogged by such red tape and bureaucratic hypocrisy as would have given material to a great pleiad of satirical writers, if the satirical writers, too, had not been paralysed by the fear of responsibility.

Not satisfied with dictating his will in all matters affecting the body politic, Stalin also aspired to be sole spiritual leader of his generation. He did so in part because his vanity had been hurt by the fact that the intellectual *élite* of Russia had hardly noticed him before he had brought them under his tutelage; and that even then they had at first treated his pronouncements on science, philosophy, and art with some irony. Apart from this, he had banished heresy from politics and economics only to find that the philosophical and literary journals bristled with heretical allusions. To venture out into these fields became for him a political necessity. Marxism had, in fact, shortened the distance between politics, philosophy, and literature. Stalin crudely over-simplified the Marxist view of their interconnexion, until he degraded science, history, and art to the point where they became handmaidens of his politics. Every time he issued a new economic and political directive, the historians, the philosophers, and the writers had to check carefully whether in their latest works they were not in conflict with the leader's last word.

The historians fared worst of all. As early as 1931 he rebuked them sharply in his famous 'Letter to the Editor of *Proletarskaya Revolutsia*'. The journal, specializing in the history of the revolution, had permitted 'Trotskyist contraband' in its columns. Recent history had to be rewritten so as to show his opponents in the light that suited Stalin. This was done. As the struggle grew fierce, the versions of history dictated from the General Secretariat proved to be not derogatory enough of Stalin's opponents; and one new version after another had to be composed. As, for reasons of expediency, the official attitude towards the more remote past was also changing, the histories of old Russia, too, had to be rewritten. Trotsky had exercised a strong influence upon literary criticism, not by his official authority, but as a literary critic in his own right. The whole Trotskyist school of literary criticism had to be uprooted. The philosophers had taught Marxist dialectics on the basis of Plekhanov's writings, of which Lenin had, in spite of his political controversies with the leader of the Mensheviks, thought very highly. Stalin summoned the professors and lecturers of philosophy to his office and inveighed against their 'rotten liberalism'. The dean of the philosophers, Professor Deborin, and many of his pupils were barred from the universities and the periodicals. Instances of this rule of club over pen can be multiplied at will. In the end literary critics, historians, and philosophers extolled the 'beloved leader' as the greatest literary critic, historian, and scientist of their age and of all ages. Disraeli once flattered Queen Victoria: 'Your Majesty is the head of the literary profession'; but neither Macaulay nor

Carlyle was required to write in Queen Victoria's style. Now that the General Secretary had been proclaimed the head of the literary profession it was the duty of Soviet writers 'to write like Stalin'.

What followed was a grim page in the annals of Russian literature: Stalin's personal style became, as it were, Russia's national style. Not only was it a daring deed for any publicist or essayist to compose a paragraph or two including no direct quotation from Stalin. The writer took great care that his own sentences should, in style and vocabulary, resemble as closely as possible the quoted text. An indescribably dull uniformity spread over the Russian press and most periodicals. Even the spoken language became 'Stalinized' to a fantastic extent, at least when people talked on ideology and politics. It was as if a whole nation had succumbed to a ventriloquial obsession.

This anomaly, by which the style of the ruler became the ruling style of the nation, would perhaps have been less intolerable if the ruler had possessed literary talent. As it was, the national style degenerated into a peculiar lingo characterized by stiff, boring repetitiveness, plebeian coarseness mixed with pseudo-scientific pretentiousness, and grammatical and logical incongruity. After his ascendancy Stalin's style became even more uncouth than it had been before. The contrast between the great, dramatic role of the man and the dull, plodding style of his speech and writing, which he only now and then enlivened by a quotation from popular Russian satire or by a crude joke, is indeed astonishing. Here is a specimen of his style, chosen at random:

Our Party alone [this is one of the closing passages of Stalin's speech to the seventeenth congress] knows where to direct the cause; and it is leading it forward successfully. To what does our Party owe its superiority? To the fact that it is a Marxian Party, a Leninist Party. It owes it to the fact that it is guided in its work by the tenets of Marx, Engels, and Lenin. There cannot be any doubt that as long as we remain true to these tenets, as long as we have this compass, we will achieve successes in our work.

It is said that in some countries in the west Marxism has already been destroyed. It is said that it has been destroyed by the bourgeois nationalist trend known as fascism. That is nonsense, of course. Only people who are ignorant of history can say such things. Marxism is the scientific expression of the fundamental interests of the working class. If Marxism is to be destroyed, the working class must be destroyed. And it is impossible to destroy the working class. More than eighty years have passed since Marxism came into the arena. During this time scores and hundreds of bourgeois governments have tried to destroy Marxism. But what has been the upshot? Bourgeois governments have come and gone, but Marxism still goes on. (*Stormy applause.*) Moreover, Marxism has achieved complete victory on one sixth of the globe—has achieved it in the very country in which Marxism was considered to have been utterly destroyed. (*Stormy applause.*) It cannot be regarded as an accident that the country in which Marxism has fully triumphed is now the only country in the world which knows no crises and unemployment, whereas in all other countries, including the fascist countries, crisis and unemployment have been reigning for four years now. No, comrades, this is not an accident. (*Prolonged applause.*)

Yes, comrades, our successes are due to the fact that we have worked and fought under the banner of Marx, Engels, and Lenin.

Hence, the second conclusion: we must remain true to the end to the great banner of Marx, Engels, and Lenin. (*Applause.*)[1]

Historians will wonder how a nation which had had Tolstoy, Dostoyevsky, Chekhov, Plekhanov, Lenin, and Trotsky as its intellectual guides could have allowed the lights of its language and literature to be so thoroughly blacked out. They will perhaps draw some analogy between this phenomenon and the striking decline, in the years of revolution, empire, and restoration, of another literature that had given the world Rousseau, Voltaire, and the Encyclopaedists. In France as in Russia, an extraordinary exertion of spiritual energy and literary genius is followed by a condition of lethargy and torpor. However, the cultural significance of Stalinism cannot be judged merely by the way it ravaged letters and arts. It is the contradiction between Stalin's constructive and his destructive influences that should be kept in mind. While he was mercilessly flattening the spiritual life of the intelligentsia, he also carried, as we have seen, the basic elements of civilization to a vast mass of uncivilized humanity. Under his rule Russian culture lost in depth but gained in breadth. The prediction may perhaps be ventured that this extensive spread of civilization in Russia will be followed by a new phase of intensive development, a phase from which another generation will look back with relief upon

---

[1] J. Stalin, *Problems of Leninism*, pp. 517-18.

the barbarous antics of the Stalinist era. It will then perhaps be said that Stalin's style was peculiarly adapted to the tasks of a ruler himself not well educated, who had to dragoon the *muzhiks*, and a bureaucracy issuing from the *muzhiks*, out of their anarchic poverty and darkness.

We shall only approach the same problem from another angle if we say that culturally all this meant a relative eclipse of European Russia in favour of the backward Asiatic and semi-Asiatic periphery. The standards of European Russia were levelled down and those of the Asiatic periphery were levelled up. The intelligentsia of Leningrad and Moscow, who once distinguished themselves by their independent mind, and often surpassed their western European counterparts by the earnestness and *élan* of their intellectual pursuits, were now forced to give up many of their sophisticated aspirations and to meet half-way their much younger and cruder brothers as they came flocking into the universities straight from the Kirghizian or Bashkirian steppes. Under a leader who had himself come from the border of Europe and Asia, European Russia thus became more than half-assimilated to Asia, while Asiatic Russia was achieving a considerable degree of europeanization. In part, this mutual assimilation was inevitable and fruitful. But only too often it was carried to the point where it impoverished the nation intellectually. Paradoxically enough, Stalin, who fostered inequality and social differentiation on the basis of a collectivized economy, was, in matters of the spirit and the intellect, a crude and tyrannical leveller, not by conscious design—in his own way he patronized science and art—but because of his distrust of intellectual and artistic originality: for in that he always scented unorthodoxy.

Thus it came about that even Russian poetry and fiction lost its old lustre. 'Give us a Soviet Tolstoy', official literary critics clamoured for years. The Soviet Tolstoy failed to appear, perhaps because life was too much in a flux to lend itself to epic artistry or perhaps because a Tolstoy is not bred in an atmosphere in which he is not free to say: 'I cannot keep silent.' The two most original poets of contemporary Russia, Yesenin and Mayakovsky, committed suicide. Some of the best writers sought refuge in silence, others were silenced. Like a reminder of past glories, Maxim Gorky, acclaimed as the patriarch of proletarian culture and as Stalin's close friend, lingered on during the first half of the thirties. The friendship between Stalin and Gorky was hardly a true meeting of minds. Stalin needed his intellectual and moral authority to be endorsed by somebody whose authority was commonly recognized. Gorky had been Lenin's intimate friend back in the days of the underground; and Stalin thought it wise to inherit that friendship together with many other attributes and titles of leadership. Gorky, on the other hand, had more than once violently quarrelled with Lenin, who endured from him things he would never have endured from any politician. The old writer, emotionally attached to Bolshevism and somewhat remorseful because of his old attacks on Lenin, resolved not to quarrel with Lenin's successor, who was, anyhow, not prepared to tolerate any quarrel. Occasionally Gorky tried to soften Stalin's temper and gently to shield an old Bolshevik or an erratic man of letters. He even made an attempt at reconciling Stalin and Kamenev. But in the end he had to desist. He died in 1936. With him the great line of pre-revolutionary writers came to an end.

After Gorky's death, at the height of the purges, two poets were for a time most celebrated in Moscow: the Kazakh Djambul Djabayev and the Caucasian Lezghin Suleyman Stalsky. Both were the last of the oriental tribal bards, illiterate nonagenarians, long-bearded, picturesque, composers of folk-songs, belated native Homers. From their highland and steppe they came to Moscow to sing, to the accompaniment of their harps, Stalin's praise at the Lenin Mausoleum.

The assimilation of European to Asiatic Russia led to the spiritual isolation and detachment of Russia, as a whole, from Europe. This was only partly due to the antagonism between communism and capitalism—in the twenties, when that antagonism was no less strong, the Russian mind was wide open to progressive influences of European thought and art. The isolation was conditioned by the peculiar climate of the thirties; and it became complete during the great purges.

.   .   .   .

After the trials and deportations which followed the assassination of Kirov, the régime seemed to relax once again. In the second half of 1935 and the first half of 1936 the successes of the second five-year plan and the forthcoming constitutional reform had the main share of public attention. Stalin was more frequently seen in the limelight, all smiles, surrounded by Stakhanovite workers, successful *kolkhoz* farmers and their womenfolk, who were all busy thanking him for their 'new and joyous life'. He appeared at popular festivals, handed out prizes to successful athletes, accepted bouquets of flowers from children, and postured in all sorts of idyllic scenes for the camera. Everything seemed to promise a long spell of political mildness. Of the former opposition chiefs Zinoviev, Kamenev, and Smirnov were held in the prison of Verkhne-Uralsk; but they hoped to be released once more. Bukharin, Radek, and Sokolnikov continued to rub shoulders with Stalin at the sessions of the constitutional commission. Bukharin was editor of *Izvestya* and Radek was the chief journalistic interpreter of the Kremlin's foreign policy. Piatakov was deputy Commissar for Heavy Industry and its real organizer. The former Premier Rykov was Commissar of Posts and Telegraphs; Rakovsky, Krestinsky, Karakhan, Raskolnikov, Antonov-Ovseenko, Rozengolz, Yureniev, Bogomolov, and many, many others who had long made peace with Stalin were abroad as ambassadors, special envoys, heads of trade missions. Even in Georgia, Stalin's old opponents, who had come out against him in Lenin's lifetime, seemed to have been pardoned. Their chief leader Budu Mdivani was back in office, as vice-Premier of the Georgian Government. The relations between Stalin and the leaders of the army seemed unruffled. In 1936 the army was reorganized from a predominantly territorial into a standing force; the old pre-revolutionary discipline, complete with the old officers' ranks, was reintroduced. Five of the military chiefs, Tukhachevsky, Yegorov, Blücher, Voroshilov, and Budienny, were appointed Marshals.

In the lower grades of the party and the administration, however, the purge went on unabated. Towards the end of 1935 *Pravda* and *Izvestya* were full of stories about the discovery of secret opposition cells in nearly all Russian and Ukrainian cities. The newspapers also reported opposition among workers to the fostering of Stakhanovite methods: that is, to the increase in the intensity of factory work and to payment by results.

Here and there workers assaulted and even assassinated Stakhanovites and smashed machines. *Muzhiks*, newly drafted into industry, often damaged or broke their tools by clumsy or child-like handling: impatient over a hitch the *muzhik* would, not rarely, try to knock his machine into motion with hammer or axe. Industrial accidents were very numerous. This was the 'sabotage' by which Russian backwardness, illiteracy, and despair obstructed the forcible industrial revolution. It did not then occur to anybody to charge with sabotage Piatakov, for many years the chief organizer of industry, or any other ex-leader of the opposition.

Commenting on the reports of *Pravda* and *Izvestya* about the never-ending expulsions of Trotskyists and Zinovievists, Trotsky, then engaged in an attempt to build up a fourth international opposed to Stalin's third, wrote in his *Bulletin*: 'It can be said with confidence that in spite of thirteen years of persecution, slander, unsurpassed in wickedness and savagery, in spite of capitulations and defections, more dangerous than persecution, *the fourth international possesses already to-day its strongest, most numerous and most hardened branch in the U.S.S.R.*'[1] Trotsky's assertion was in part an empty boast, for in the course of the seven years of his exile he had lost all personal contact with Russia.[2] Nevertheless, Trotskyism did in fact remain a great potential trend of opinion inside Russia. Trotsky's self-confident assertions could not but intensify Stalin's already acute suspicion. On reading it he must have said to himself: *nous verrons*. Six months later Russia and the world were aghast at the trial of Zinoviev and Kamenev.

This is not the place to describe the long series of trials. We are concerned here with Stalin's role in them and with his motives. Not once did he appear personally in the courts. The man who was alleged to be the chief victim of so many wide-spread sinister conspiracies was not even called into the witness-box. Yet throughout the macabre spectacle one could feel his presence in the prompter's box. Nay, besides being prompter he was the invisible author, manager, and producer as well.

[1] *Bulleten Oppozitsii*, no. 48, February 1936.
[2] *The Case of Leon Trotsky*, pp. 264-5.

Of the endless trials, public and secret, four were of the greatest importance: 'the trial of the sixteen' (Zinoviev, Kamenev, Smirnov, Mrachkovsky, and others) in August 1936; 'the trial of the seventeen' (Piatakov, Radek, Sokolnikov, Muralov, Serebriakov, and others) in January 1937; the secret trial of Marshal Tukhachevsky and a group of the highest generals of the Red Army in June 1937; and 'the trial of the twenty-one' (Rykov, Bukharin, Krestinsky, Rakovsky, Yagoda, and others) in March 1938. Among the men in the dock at these trials were all the members of Lenin's Politbureau, except Stalin himself and Trotsky, who, however, though absent, was the chief defendant. Among them, moreover, were one ex-Premier, several vice-Premiers, two ex-chiefs of the Communist International, the chief of the trade unions (Tomsky, who committed suicide before the trial), the chief of the General Staff, the chief political Commissar of the Army, the Supreme Commanders of all important military districts, nearly all Soviet ambassadors in Europe and Asia, and, last but not least, the two chiefs of the political police: Yagoda, who had provided the 'evidence' for the trial of Zinoviev and Kamenev, and Yezhov, who had done the same for the trials of all the others. All were charged with attempting to assassinate Stalin and the other members of the Politbureau, to restore capitalism, to wreck the country's military and economic power, and to poison or kill in any other way masses of Russian workers. All were charged with working from the earliest days of the revolution for the espionage services of Britain, France, Japan, and Germany, and with having entered into secret agreements with the Nazis by which they were to dismember the Soviet Union and cede vast slices of Soviet territory to Germany and Japan.[1] If these charges, which accumulated from trial to trial, had been true, it would be impossible to account for the existence and survival of the Soviet state. Having infiltrated the whole machinery of the administration to its very top, the alleged terrorists managed to kill only one of Stalin's dignitaries, Kirov. In the course of the trials the prosecution alleged two more victims of the conspiracy:

---

[1] See the official verbatim reports of the trials: *Sudebnyi Otchet Po Delu Trotskistskovo-Zinovievskovo Terroristskovo Tsentra* (1936); *Sudebnyi Otchet Po Delu Antisovietskovo Trotskistskovo Tsentra* (1937); and *Sudebnyi Otchet Po Delu Antisovietskovo Pravo Trotskistskovo Bloka* (1938).

Kuibyshev, the chief of the State Planning Commission, and Maxim Gorky.[1] The allegations only emphasized the incongruous disproportion between the all-pervading character of the 'conspiracy' and its negligible results. It was as if the whole power of the Niagara Falls had been harnessed in order to move a toy boat.

The unreal nature of all this was further underlined by the phantom-like behaviour of the defendants, at least of those tried in public. Many prominent men, all the military and many civilian leaders, were tried *in camera*; many were executed without trial because they could not be brought to admit and recant crimes of which they had not been guilty. But all those unfortunates on whom the limelight was turned appeared in sackcloth and ashes, loudly confessing their sins, calling themselves sons of Belial and praising *de profundis* the Superman whose feet were crushing them into dust. A horrified and stultified nation was made to echo in one voice the refrain: 'Shoot the mad dogs!' with which the prosecutor Vyshinsky invariably wound up his denunciations. The confessions of the defendants were the only basis for the proceedings and the verdicts. Not a single piece of evidence that could be verified by means of normal legal procedure was presented. In those few cases where the defendants did refer to specific circumstances of their alleged meetings with Trotsky abroad, circumstances that could be verified, the falsehood of their confessions was immediately plain. A hotel in Copenhagen where three defendants, Holtzman, David, and Berman-Yurin, had allegedly had an appointment with Trotsky, had ceased to exist many years before the date of the appointment. The authorities of an aerodrome near Oslo, where Piatakov claimed to have landed in a German plane for a meeting with Trotsky, testified that at the time indicated (and during several months before and after) no foreign plane had landed there. Trotsky and his son produced evidence, some of it bearing the signature of Edouard Herriot, the French Prime Minister of the day, known for his friendly disposition towards Stalin, to show that physically they could not have

---

[1] Stalin's chief secretary, A. Poskrebyshev, in his reminiscences (published in Voronezh in 1940) intimates that Gorky died a natural death. See A. Poskrebyshev i B. Dvinsky, 'Uchitel i drug chelovechestva' in *Stalin (Sbornik Statey)*, p. 194.

been present at the places where, according to the accusation, they should have been present at certain dates.[1]

In the light of the story of the struggle inside the party, the recantations of the men in the dock are far less surprising than they might have been otherwise. They did not come like a bolt from the blue. Ever since the middle twenties recantation had been something like a ritual habit, an accepted routine, with the broken men of the opposition. They had begun with the admission of ordinary offences against discipline and they ended by confessing apocalyptic sins. In between there was a wide gamut of gradations which they had gone through slowly, like sleepwalkers almost, hardly perceiving the direction of their movement. Each time they made a recantation, they agreed to confess some sin only slightly graver than the one confessed before. Each time they hoped, of course, that this would be the last sacrifice demanded of them for the sake of the party and for their own redemption. It is doubtful whether even at the end of the journey they saw clearly that what awaited them now was the holocaust.

Throughout they had been oppressed by the insoluble conflict between their horror of Stalin's methods of government and their basic solidarity with the social régime which had become identified with Stalin's rule. Yet this feeling alone would not have sufficed to make them behave as they did. In his exile Trotsky, too, wrestled with the dilemma, without bending his knees. They were preyed upon by their own scruples and remorse; but they were also terrorized by Stalin's terror. The stories that they were hypnotized or given mysterious drugs may be safely dismissed. But it cannot be doubted that they were subjected to physical and moral torture of the sort that is used in third-degree interrogation in Russia—and elsewhere. In addition, the political police, as we have seen, had been given the right to take the defendants' relatives as hostages; these hostages did, indeed, appear in the witness-box. Even the most indomitable, those most ready to sacrifice their own persons for their cause, cannot feel that they have the right to sacrifice their parents or children in the same way. The defendants certainly hoped that their confessions would save their families; and they may also have had a glimmer of hope

---

[1] *The Case of Leon Trotsky*, pp. 109–227.

to save themselves. After the assassination of Kirov, terrorists had been deprived by decree of the right of appeal; but, a few days before the opening of the trial of Zinoviev and Kamenev, the right of appeal was restored, as if to keep that glimmer of hope alive to the very end. A few of them, Radek and Rakovsky, were not indeed brought before the firing squad; and one man's escape from death would induce ten or twenty to hope that they, too, might escape. They certainly believed that their self-accusations were so absurd and so obviously made under duress as not to blot their reputations. (Similarly, in Nazi concentration camps men were drilled by their guards to shout at themselves: *Ich bin ein Schweinhund* or some other insult, in which no sane person would believe.) Thus, the pressures and motives that brought so many eminent men to file past Stalin with the terrible cry: *Ave Caesar, morituri te salutant,* were manifold and complex.

. . . .

But why did Stalin need the abominable spectacle? It has been suggested that he sent the men of the old guard to their death as scapegoats for his economic failures. There is a grain of truth in this, but not more. For one thing, there was a very marked improvement in the economic condition of the country in the years of the trials. He certainly had no need for so many scapegoats; and, if he had needed them, penal servitude would have been enough, as was the case in the earlier trials of the so-called Industrial Party and the Mensheviks. Some of the people convicted in those earlier trials re-emerged in the forties as celebrated personalities and bearers of high honours (e.g. Professor Ramzin). Stalin's real and much wider motive was to destroy the men who represented the potentiality of alternative government, perhaps not of one but of several alternative governments. It is, naturally enough, impossible to quote chapter and verse from Stalin's own speeches and writings for this. It is in the whole preceding story, in the setting of the trials and in their consequences, that the motivation for his deeds is found. From the outset he had identified any attempt at creating an alternative government, and even the thought of this, with counter-revolution. The destruction of all political centres from which such an attempt might, in certain circumstances, have emanated, was the direct and undeniable consequence of the trials.

The question that must now be answered is why he set out to reach this objective in 1936. Considerations of domestic policy can hardly explain his timing. Widespread though popular dissatisfaction may have been, it was too amorphous to constitute any immediate threat to his position. The opposition was pulverized, downtrodden, incapable of action. Only some sudden shock, some convulsive disorder involving the whole machine of power, might have enabled it to rally its scattered and disheartened troops. A danger of that kind was just then taking shape; and it threatened from abroad. The first of the great trials, that of Zinoviev and Kamenev, took place a few months after Hitler's army had marched into the Rhineland; the last, that of Bukharin and Rykov, ended to the accompaniment of the trumpets that announced the Nazi occupation of Austria. German imperialism was rearming and testing its strength. The diplomatic dispositions which Stalin made to meet that threat will be discussed in the next chapters. This much may be said here: he had no illusions that war could be altogether avoided; and he pondered the alternative courses —agreement with Hitler or war against him—that were open to him. In 1936 the chances of agreement looked very slender indeed. Western appeasement filled Stalin with forebodings. He suspected that the west was not only acquiescing in the revival of German militarism but instigating it against Russia.

The prospect of a single-handed fight between Russia and Germany seemed grim. In the First World War the strength of the German military machine, involved as it was then in a struggle on two fronts, sufficed to deal a shattering blow to Russia and to sap Tsardom.[1] The shadow of the last Tsar must have more than once appeared before Stalin, as he viewed Hitler's preliminaries to war. One might sketch an imaginary conversation between the living man and the ghost. 'Your end is approaching,' the phantom whispers; 'exploiting the chaos of war, you destroyed my throne. Now the chaos of another war

---

[1] 'The recollection of German strength in the world war is everywhere still lively', so the German Ambassador in Moscow, Count von Schulenburg, reported to Ribbentrop on 6 September 1939. *Nazi-Soviet Relations*, pp. 88-9.

is going to engulf you.' 'You dethroned monarchs, you really learn nothing', the living man replies. 'Surely you were defeated not by the war itself, but by the Bolshevik party. To be sure, we used the conditions created by war to our advantage, but. . . .' 'Are you quite sure', the ghost interrupts, 'that no opposition is going to use a new war for its advantage? Remember the terrible turmoil in Petersburg when the news came that the Germans had captured Riga? What if the Germans appear in Riga again, or in Kiev, in the Caucasus or at the gates of Moscow?' 'I am telling you, you had the formidable Bolshevik party against you, while I have exiled Trotsky and crushed all my other opponents.' The phantom roars with laughter: 'In 1914-17 did not I keep you in Siberia and were not Lenin and Trotsky in exile? . . .'

In the supreme crisis of war, the leaders of the opposition, if they had been alive, might indeed have been driven to action by a conviction, right or wrong, that Stalin's conduct of the war was incompetent and ruinous. At an earlier stage they might have been opposed to his deal with Hitler. Did not Trotsky foreshadow this sort of action against Stalin in his famous 'Clemenceau thesis'? Let us imagine for a moment that the leaders of the opposition lived to witness the terrible defeats of the Red Army in 1941 and 1942, to see Hitler at the gates of Moscow, millions of Russian soldiers in German captivity, a dangerous crisis in the morale of the people such as had developed by the autumn of 1941, when the whole future of the Soviets hung by a thread and Stalin's moral authority was at its nadir. It is possible that they would have then attempted to overthrow Stalin. Stalin was determined not to allow things to come to this.

His charges against them were, of course, shameless inventions. But they were based on a perverted 'psychological truth', on a grotesquely brutalized and distorting anticipation of possible developments. His reasoning probably developed along the following lines: they may want to overthrow me in a crisis— I shall charge them with having already made the attempt. They certainly believe themselves to be better fitted for the conduct of war, which is absurd. A change of government may weaken Russia's fighting capacity; and if they succeed, they may be compelled to sign a truce with Hitler, and perhaps even agree to a cession of territory as we once did at Brest Litovsk.[1] I shall accuse them of having entered already into a treacherous alliance with Germany (and Japan) and ceded Soviet territory to those states.

No milder pretext for the slaughter of the old guard would have sufficed. Had they been executed merely as men opposed to Stalin or even as conspirators who had tried to remove him from power, many might still have regarded them as martyrs for a good cause. They had to die as traitors, as perpetrators of crimes beyond the reach of reason, as leaders of a monstrous fifth column. Only then could Stalin be sure that their execution would provoke no dangerous revulsion; and that, on the contrary, he himself would be looked upon, especially by the young and uninformed generation, as the saviour of the country. It is not necessary to assume that he acted from sheer cruelty or lust for power. He may be given the dubious credit of the sincere conviction that what he did served the interests of the revolution and that he alone interpreted those interests aright.

.   .   .   .

It was inevitable that the imaginary conspiracy that haunted him should, amid the orgy of the purges, begin to assume flesh and blood. As the vicious circle of terror widened, few men of importance felt safe. Some of them were driven to take action in order to stop the horrible *perpetuum mobile*. Such action did not come from the helpless leaders of the old oppositions, but from men who had hitherto been beyond suspicion, whose spirits had not been broken in endless recantation and whose hands still gripped some of the levers of power. The reaction against the terror began in Stalin's closest entourage soon after the trials of Radek, Piatakov, and Sokolnikov at the beginning of 1937. A conflict apparently arose between Stalin and Ordjonikidze, the old Bolshevik who had been at Stalin's side in the prisons of Baku, who in 1912 had sponsored him to the Central Committee, who had helped him to subdue Menshevik Georgia ten years later, and who had then zealously co-operated with him in the struggle against all the oppositions. Ordjonikidze now reacted against the victimization of his deputy Piatakov and many other industrial leaders. The conflict ended with Ordjonikidze's sudden death, the circumstances of which remain unexplained.

[1] It was indeed by reference to Brest Litovsk that Stalin's propagandists later tried to justify the Russo-German pact of 1939 (see *Falsifiers of History*, p. 45).

Then Rudzutak, hitherto one of the chiefs of the Stalinist faction, vice-Premier and leader of the trade unions, turned against Stalin.

But the real conspiracy was begun by the leaders of the army, Tukhachevsky and his associates. It is not certain whether the vice-Premier and leader of the trade unions, turned against Stalin, as did also Mezhlauk, another Vice-Premier. But the real conspiracy was said to have been begun by the leaders of the army, Tukhachevsky and his associates. The exact circumstances are not known, and some deny the existence of any plot, and maintain that Hitler's secret services planted the story of a conspiracy and forged evidence of it, on President Beneš of Czechoslovakia who transmitted it to Stalin. According to this version, the real forger was in the G.P.U. in Moscow and designed the whole plant with Stalin's connivance. But quite a few non-Stalinist sources maintain that the generals did indeed plan a *coup d'état* and did this from their own motives, and on their own initiative, not in contact with any foreign power.[1] The main part of the *coup* was to be a palace revolt, following an assault on the headquarters of the G.P.U. and culminating in Stalin's assassination. Tukhachevsky was regarded as the leader of the conspiracy. A man of military genius, the real modernizer of the Red Army, surrounded by the glory of his feats in the civil war, he was the army's favourite, and was indeed the only man among all the military leaders of that time who showed a resemblance to the original Bonaparte and could have played the Russian First Consul. Generals Yakir, commander of Leningrad, Uborevich, commander of the western military district, Kork, commander of Moscow's Military Academy, Primakov, Budienny's deputy in the command of the cavalry, Gamarnik, the chief Political Commissar of the army who presently committed suicide, and other officers were supposed to have been in the plot. On 1 May 1937 Tukhachevsky stood by Stalin's side at the Lenin Mausoleum, reviewing the May Day parade. Eleven days later he was demoted. On 12 June the execution of Tukhachevsky and his friends was announced. The conspirators showed no remorse and made no confessions. The plot was allegedly discovered by the political police.

[1] Among all the documents of the Nuremberg trial of the Nazi leaders not a single one contains as much as a hint at the alleged Nazi fifth column in the Soviet Government and army. Could there be a more eloquent refutation of the purge trials than that amazing gap in the otherwise abundant evidence of Hitler's preparations for the war?

Tukhachevsky was wounded while he was being arrested and then brought on a stretcher to Stalin. After a long and violent exchange of words with Stalin, the Marshal was carried back to prison. His death warrant was signed, at least nominally, by the other four Marshals, Voroshilov, Budienny, Blücher, and Yegorov—the last two were to be purged soon afterwards.[1]

Even the most complete account of the trials would give only a very inadequate idea of their consequences. The real mass purges were carried out without the thunder and lightning of publicity, without confessions of the victims, and often without any trial whatsoever. Commenting on the strange assizes in Moscow, Trotsky wrote: 'Stalin is like a man who wants to quench his thirst with salted water.'[2] He sent thousands to their death and tens and hundreds of thousands into prisons and concentration camps. The very nature of his design compelled him to do so. He had set out to destroy the men capable of forming an alternative government. But each of those men had behind him long years of service, in the course of which he had trained and promoted administrators and officers and made many friends. Stalin could not be sure that avengers of his victims would not rise from the ranks of their followers. Having destroyed the first team of potential leaders of an alternative government, he could not spare the second, the third, the fourth, and the nth teams. All the party-men who had been raised up by Zinoviev, Kamenev, Bukharin, Rykov; the diplomats who owed their careers to Rakovsky or Sokolnikov; the officers in whose dossiers at the Military Academy could be found a favourable testimonial signed by Tukhachevsky; the business managers who had worked with Piatakov—all were dangerous, suspect, and doomed. Refugee Communists from Nazi Germany, from Pilsudski's Poland, and Horthy's Hungary, who had in the past been connected with the one or the other faction or coterie in the Bolshevik party, were automatically caught in the net.[3] The number of the victims will perhaps

[1] Official Soviet sources have given no specific account of the plot. Anti-Stalinist versions can be found in E. Wollenberg, *The Red Army*, pp. 232–64; M. Borbov, 'Zagovor ili Revolutsia' in *Sotsialisticheskii Vestnik*, no. 10, 1947; and in V. G. Krivitsky, *I was Stalin's Agent*.   [2] *Bulleten Oppozitsii*, no. 64.

[3] Among the best-known foreign Communists who then perished were: Bela Kun, the leader of the Hungarian revolution in 1919, Remmele and Neumann, the most important Communist spokesmen in the Reichstag before Hitler, nearly all members of the Central Committee of the Polish Communist party, and many others.

never be known. According to some sources, in the army alone about 20,000 officers, 25 per cent. of the entire officers' corps, were arrested and several thousands shot.[1] The whole structure of the state was shaken.

In the middle of this earthquake, in November 1936, Stalin promulgated the new constitution in an address to the eighth congress of the Soviets.[2] He drew a veil of liberal phrases and promises over the guillotine in the background. The new constitution was to replace Lenin's electoral system, which had openly and frankly favoured the industrial working class, and give equal suffrage to all classes, including the hitherto disfranchised former *bourgeoisie*. Indirect elections were to be replaced by direct, open ballot by secret. Such an advance, Stalin said, was possible because the structure of society had changed: the first phase of communism had been achieved; the working class was no longer a proletariat; the peasantry had been integrated in the Socialist economy; and the new intelligentsia was rooted in the working classes. Opposing what he claimed to be someone's amendment to the draft of the constitution, he insisted that the constitution must guarantee to constituent republics the right to secede from the Soviet Union. Opposing still another amendment, which aimed at investing sovereignty in the President of the Republic instead of in the many-headed Presidium of the Supreme Soviet, Stalin warned his audience that a single President might become a dictator —the constitution should leave no such opening. He even insisted on the enfranchisement of the former White Guards and priests. But what was real in these Arabian nights of democracy was the constitutional ban on any opposition. 'Freedom for several parties', these are Stalin's words, '. . . can exist only in a society in which there are antagonistic classes, whose interests are mutually hostile and irreconcilable. . . . In the U.S.S.R. there is ground for only one party.'[3]

Another enterprise on which he now embarked was the *Short History of the Communist Party of the Soviet Union*, which

---

[1] E. Wollenberg, *The Red Army*, p. 253.

[2] J. Stalin, *Problems of Leninism*, pp. 540–68.

[3] The argument made little sense even from Stalin's viewpoint. He regarded the British Tories and Liberals or the American Republicans and Democrats as capitalist parties not representing 'interests mutually hostile and irreconcilable'. Thus, a two-party system could be built on the basis of a single-class interest.

purported to be the first accurate and doctrinally reliable work in this field. In it, the whole history of the party was rewritten in the light of the trials. All previous text-books, even those composed by Stalin's closest followers, like Yaroslavsky, were declared to be apocryphal and withdrawn from circulation, since they all presented a history of the party which could not be squared with the latest 'findings'. The new book, which was at once declared to be the Bible of the party, was written by Stalin's secretaries under his personal guidance. Only its philosophical part, a crude digest of the Marxist theory of dialectics, was composed by Stalin himself. As the prompter of the trials he remained invisible to the public—he appeared before it in the role of philosopher, historian, and constitution maker.

. . . .

While the guillotine was in motion, it seemed to many that in the end Stalin, too, would be caught by it. He was destroying the old guard; yet he himself had been one of them. On whom could he rely for support once that prop of the Bolshevik régime was gone? 'Stalin is nearing the completion of his tragic mission', Trotsky wrote in September 1937; 'the more it seems to him that he needs nobody any longer, the nearer is the hour when he himself will be needed by nobody. If the bureaucracy succeeds in changing the forms of property and if a new possessing class crystallizes from its ranks, the latter will find new leaders without a revolutionary past and more educated ones. Stalin will hardly hear a word of thanks for the job he has accomplished. The open counter-revolution will settle accounts with him, very probably charging him with Trotskyism.'[1] A few months later Trotsky made a different forecast: 'Stalin is preparing his "coronation" on the ruins of the revolution and the corpses of revolutionaries. Stalin's Bonapartist coronation will coincide with his political death for the labour movement.'[2] None of these prophecies came true; and, as to Stalin's 'coronation', it took place before and not after the trials. The truly astonishing aspect of the purges, astonishing in view of their scope and vehemence, is how little they changed the surface of Soviet Russia, how little the structure of the régime seemed, after all, to be affected by the heavy axe that

[1] *Bulleten Oppozitsii*, nos. 58–9.   [2] Ibid., nos. 60–1.

had cut into it. After as before the trials, Russian society seemed to be on the one hand feverishly intent over its economic pursuits and on the other languishing in a condition of moral and political torpor. Before and after, Stalin was hailed as the father of the peoples, and the beloved leader.

Robespierre, having destroyed his opponents, appeared one day in the Convention to be suddenly confronted by the rebellion of the Thermidorians. The Convention was still full of that turbulent impulsiveness that had marked all its existence. In a body of that sort, people whom the reign of terror had inspired with the courage of despair, could get up, arraign the dictator, and bring about his downfall. In the course of the two decades that elapsed after 1917 all the spontaneous impulses in the Soviet body politic had withered away. No deliberating body like the Convention issued writs against the 'enemies of the people'. Stalin himself pulled the wires that ran from his office to the headquarters of the political police, the prisons, and the court rooms, wires that were insulated against unforeseen interference. At no stage did he have to justify his deeds before any audience from which a cry of protest could have been raised. The Thermidorians were backed by a people which, in all its sections, was sick of terror. They publicly appealed to that people. If any men, like Tukhachevsky and his associates, tried to put an end to Stalin's rule, they acted behind the back of the people, as a small, strictly secret group of conspirators. Therein lay their fatal weakness.

The deeper reason for Stalin's triumph lay, as we have said, in that, unlike Robespierre, he offered his nation a positive and new programme of social organization which, though it spelt privation and suffering to many, also created undreamt-of openings for many others. These latter had a vested interest in his rule. This, in the last resort, explains why, after the slaughter of the old guard, Stalin did not find himself left in a vacuum. For nearly three years his iron broom had furiously swept every office in state and party. Not more than a handful of that mass of administrators who had held office in 1936 could be found there in 1938.[1] The purges created numberless

---

[1] Not a single one of the secretaries of the provincial committees of the party, the *Obkoms*, who had held office in 1936 was reappointed in 1937. *Bulleten Oppozitsii*, no. 70.

vacancies in every field of public activity. In the five years from 1933 to 1938 about half a million administrators, technicians, economists, and men of other professions had graduated from university schools, an enormous number for a country whose educated classes had previously formed a very thin layer of society.[1] This was the new intelligentsia whose ranks filled the purged and emptied offices. Its members, brought up in the Stalinist cult from childhood, were either hostile to the men of the old guard or indifferent to their fate. They threw themselves into their work with a zeal and enthusiasm undimmed by recent events. Their qualifications, it is true, were very modest. They had almost no practical experience. The nation had still to pay an exorbitant price for the practical apprenticeship of its civil servants, industrial managers, and military commanders; and that apprenticeship was to last well into the Second World War.

By the beginning of 1939 the public purges had come to an end. In March Stalin announced this to a Party Congress, convened after an interval of five crowded years. The statutes of the party were amended in a quasi-Liberal spirit. Purges, even in the mild form they had taken in Lenin's day, were abolished. 'Undoubtedly', said Stalin, 'we shall have no further need of resorting to the method of mass purges.'[2] He mocked at foreigners who thought that the trials of 'spies, assassins and wreckers' had weakened the Soviet state. But he publicly asked himself: 'Is it not surprising that we learned about the espionage and conspiratorial activities of the Trotskyist and Bukharinist leaders only quite recently, in 1937 and 1938, although, as the evidence shows, these gentry were in the service of foreign espionage organizations and carried on conspiratorial activities from the very first days of the October revolution? How could we have failed to notice so grave a matter? How are we to explain this blunder?'[3] How, indeed? By insufficient vigilance, he answered, and by the 'under-estimation' of the importance of the Soviet intelligence service. One of the last acts of the purge was the execution of Yezhov, the chief of the political police, the direct organizer of all the trials that had taken place since Yagoda's dismissal. Yezhov's successor was L. Berya,

[1] J. Stalin, *Problems of Leninism*, p. 620. [2] Ibid., p. 625.
[3] Ibid., p. 632.

Stalin's countryman and one of his biographers, hitherto the chief of the political police in Georgia.

The real epilogue took place not in Russia, but in Mexico, where Trotsky settled down, after much wandering. In 1936, while Trotsky was staying in Norway, Stalin, through his diplomatic envoy in Oslo, exercised pressure upon the Norwegian Government in order to deprive him of asylum. The Norwegians were threatened with commercial boycott, a threat that was effective enough, for the Norwegians were anxious to maintain trade with Russia. Their Minister of Justice, Trygve Lie, agreed to intern Trotsky until the latter found asylum in Mexico. From Mexico Trotsky continued to thunder at Stalin's policies, effectively exposing the trials and endeavouring, without success, to breathe life into the Fourth International. He was harassed by repeated attempts on his life. All his children had died in mysterious circumstances, which led him to accuse Stalin as their revengeful murderer. Finally, on 20 August 1940, while he was engaged in writing an accusatory biography of Stalin, an obscure individual, posing as his supporter, smashed his head with an axe. Thus the verdict of the Moscow tribunal, which sentenced Trotsky to death, was carried out. Having mercilessly uprooted Trotskyism in Russia, Stalin now achieved his last dark triumph over the man himself, whose name, like Lenin's, had stood for the great hopes and the great illusions of the October revolution. There was a tragic symbolism in the fact that the blood of Trotsky's head spattered the sheets of paper on which he had written down his account of Stalin's career. But in the whirlwind of that year—the summer of 1940—this epilogue to the Moscow trials passed almost unnoticed.

CHAPTER X

Foreign Policy and Comintern. I

(1923–33)

Stalin presents no strict doctrine of foreign policy.—A poetic sidelight: Alexander Blok's 'The Scythians'.—The revolution breaks with imperialism.—Bolshevism opposed to the Peace of Versailles.—The Russo-German Pact of Rapallo (1922). Débâcle of German Communism in 1923.—Stalin's role in the Comintern.—The Comintern tries moderation (1925–6).—The ultra-radical turn of 1928.—Stalin on Fascism and Nazism.—A pointer to future policy: Stalin's secret speech (of 1925) on Russia's position in a new war.—He condemns ideas about a condominium of Great Powers and spheres of influence.

To most people outside Russia the internal struggles in the Bolshevik party, the five-year plans, and the purges sounded like incoherent noises off, not connected with the main plots that were being acted on the stage of world politics. Stalin's figure seemed a shadowy shape stirring on a remote periphery. Only when the danger of the Second World War had become imminent did it dawn on many that the noises off might have portended a crucial act in the drama and that the shadow in the background might reveal itself as one of the principal actors. In the year of tension that followed Munich the question was asked with ever-increasing urgency: 'What is Russia going to do?' or, more simply still, 'What is Stalin's policy?'

Part of the answer could be found in Stalin's speeches and in the 'theses' and resolutions on foreign policy adopted by the party. But these public pronouncements were not quite satisfactory. As a rule Stalin's utterances presented a jumble of dry and contradictory formulas, assembled according to the needs of the moment and the demands of orthodoxy. And the jumble revealed no systematic development of ideas, no distinct doctrine of foreign policy. Even more inscrutable seemed to be the mood of the people behind him.

A clue to that mood, to the instinctive attitudes of the Russian people, is hardly contained in the official records of party conventions and Soviet congresses. It may rather be found in the

words of a great symbolist and poet, Alexander Blok, the author
of the famous mystical revolutionary poem, 'The Twelve'. In
another poem of his, 'The Scythians', which was also written
in the early days of the revolution and which made a great
impression on the Russian intelligentsia, Blok gives a visionary
anticipation of the attitude of Soviet Russia to the world. In
a flash of poetical genius, he reveals the inner springs of
national emotion with that sort of intuitive directness which is
very rare in political formulas.

His vision spans the remote, almost prehistoric past, the
present, and the future; and it shows atavistic urges and new
revolutionary impulses woven into a single historic pattern.
The Scythians, who lived on the Russian steppes, long defended
the Greek and Roman west against the pressure of the Huns
from the east; but they themselves lived under the constant
threat of invasion from the Roman west. Not until they had
been worn down in the unequal fight against east and west did
the Roman civilization collapse under the impact of the Huns.
In the poet's vision ancient Scythia and contemporary Russia
are one. Russia, aware of her inferiority *vis-à-vis* the west and
yet proud of her mission, is still the semi-barbarous, vigorous
fringe of western civilization. She continues to fight for the
survival of that civilization, even though the west has so far
repaid her with hostility. The October revolution was the
supreme act of that defence. Is the west going to respond to the
message of the revolution or is it going to meet it with hereditary enmity? On this depends the modern Scythians' attitude
to the world:

> There are millions of you; of us, swarms and swarms
>   and swarms.
> Try and battle against us.
> Yes, we are Scythians; yes, Asiatics,
> With slanting, greedy eyes.
> . . . Oh, old world
>
> .   .   .   .
>
> Russia is a Sphinx. In joy and grief,
> And pouring with black blood,
> She peers, peers, peers at thee,
> With hatred and with love.

Yes, love, as only our blood can love,
It is long since any one of you has loved.
You have forgotten there can be such love
That burns and destroys.

Come to our side. From the horrors of war
Come to our peaceful arms;
Before it is too late, sheathe the old sword.
Comrades, let us be brothers.

And, if not, we have nothing to lose.
We, too, can be perfidious if we choose;
And down all time you will be cursed
By the sick humanity of an age to come.

Before comely Europe
Into our thickets and forests we'll disperse,
And then we shall turn upon you
Our ugly Asiatic face.

.   .   .   .

But we ourselves henceforth shall be no shield of yours,
We ourselves henceforth will enter no battle.
We shall look on with our narrow eyes
When your deadly battles rage.

Nor shall we stir when the ferocious Hun
Rifles the pockets of the dead,
Burns down cities, drives herds into churches
And roasts the flesh of the white brothers.

This is the last time—bethink thee, old world!—
To the fraternal feast of toil and peace,
The last time—to the bright, fraternal feast
The barbarian lyre now summons thee.

.   .   .   .

'Constantinople must remain in the hands of the Mohamme-
dans.' 'We announce that the agreement on the partition of
Persia [concluded between Great Britain and Russia in 1907]
is torn up and annulled.' 'We announce that the agreement on
the partition of Turkey [the secret Anglo-Russian pact of 1915]
and the seizure of Armenia is torn up and annulled.'[1] This was

---

[1] L. Fischer, *The Soviets in World Affairs*, vol. i, p. 29. The quotations are from
a proclamation to the 'Moslem Toilers of Russia and the East'.

one of the early proclamations of Soviet foreign policy, signed by Lenin and Stalin. The Bolsheviks had just opened the archives of the Tsarist diplomacy, published all secret treaties, renounced the advantages Russia had gained from them, proclaimed an irrevocable break with imperialism, and a new era of open and honest relations between the peoples of the world. Only a just and democratic peace 'without indemnities and annexations' was acceptable to the revolution. Underlying that unique act of revolutionary idealism was the Bolsheviks' hope that other nations, too, would soon establish a Socialist order and renounce domination over colonial peoples. The Bolsheviks, no doubt, believed that in the long run their renunciation of the conquests of the Tsarist empire would bring no real loss to Russia, because the material and moral advantages of an international Socialist order would heavily outweigh the meretricious profits that any nation might derive from the exploitation of weaker peoples. Immediately, the loss to Russia was real enough; but the Bolsheviks were determined to set the example for the Socialists of other countries. The 'Scythians' called upon the west: 'Before it is too late, sheathe the old sword.'

Even through the years of civil war, intervention, and famine the call continued to resound. The Comintern at first embodied the hope that the working classes of the west would, of their own accord, find their road to socialism.

Very soon, however, the Soviet leaders were compelled in self-defence to resort to some of the conventional methods of diplomacy. They improvised a diplomatic doctrine which aimed at restoring a temporary European balance of power that would strengthen their position vis-à-vis the capitalist world. By the peace of Versailles the victors, and especially France, dominated the Continent. In the French system of alliances, Poland, Rumania, and Czechoslovakia were assigned a double role: they were to be the ramparts against the revolutionary menace from the east as well as against the pressure of any reviving German militarism. That system of alliances worked at first much more directly against Russia than against Germany. The Russian objective was to create a counterbalance to it. Soviet diplomacy achieved this by a partial alinement with the vanquished against the victors, with Germany against the Allies, especially against France. Curiously enough, British and Soviet policies, for all their ideological conflicts, developed in part along parallel lines. For different reasons, from opposite fringes of Europe, both Britain and Russia sought to counteract the domination of the Continent by a single military power. The parallelism can be found even in the attitudes of public opinion in the two countries towards the peace of Versailles. Both in Britain and Russia Versailles was denounced. The main arguments of J. M. Keynes's *Economic Consequences of the Peace* were expounded in the Marxist idiom by Soviet economists. But, unlike Britain, Bolshevik Russia was not encumbered by commitments to France and had a freer hand in playing for a balance of power. In 1922 Chicherin signed the Russo-German treaty of Rapallo. Even before that Russia had achieved friendship with Turkey, another vanquished country.

The Bolsheviks at first regarded their manœuvres in the diplomatic field as temporary half-measures. They still expected social upheaval in the west. The Comintern was the main lever of their foreign policy; diplomacy was a poor auxiliary. The Politbureau sternly instructed the diplomats to say and do nothing that might embarrass the Communist parties abroad. Ambassadors were as a rule instructed to disregard etiquette and to speak like revolutionary agitators; at the most they were to engage in 'sober, business-like' commercial deals with the capitalist states.

This trend had prevailed in foreign policy some time before Stalin stepped to the fore as one of the triumvirs. Lenin had shared the direction of foreign policy with Chicherin, the Commissar for Foreign Affairs, Kamenev, Trotsky, and Chicherin's assistants Karakhan and Litvinov, all former émigrés with a good knowledge of the western countries. Stalin had not been concerned with the conduct of foreign policy. It seems that the only time that he had been involved in a diplomatic incident was when Lord Curzon protested against one of his messages to Moslems, interpreting it as incitement of colonial peoples against His Majesty's Government. His role in the Comintern, too, had been altogether insignificant.

When, as one of the triumvirs, he became active in these fields also, he at first did nothing to alter the set course of foreign policy. Russia was then reaping the first fruits of Rapallo and widening the breaches in the *cordon sanitaire*. In 1923, 1924, and 1925 many countries resumed diplomatic and commercial relations with her. Every sign of an abatement in capitalist hostility was received in Moscow with genuine joy. The Soviets were gaining breathing space.

This hopeful development, however, demanded a new balance between the Soviet diplomacy and the Comintern. The two objectives, world revolution and normal or friendly relations between Russia and the capitalist countries, were *au fond* incompatible. One of them would have to be sacrificed or, at any rate, subordinated to the other. The choice emerged from the answer that events were giving to two questions: 'What are the chances of world revolution?' and 'Is stable peace between the Soviets and the capitalist world possible?' The dilemma did not arise suddenly. It was pressed home gradually by successive changes in the international situation. Nor did the solution take the form of a deliberate decision, adopted and recorded at any definite date. It was implicit in a series of shifts, now imperceptible and now dramatic.

After four years of Lenin's and Trotsky's leadership, the Politbureau could not view the prospects of world revolution without scepticism. Its scepticism, to be sure, was qualified by the Marxist conviction of all its members that it was as certain that socialism would in due course replace capitalism as it was that capitalism had already replaced feudalism. But Stalin was not content with broad historical perspectives which seemed to provide no answer to burning, topical questions. The process by which European feudalism was abolished lasted centuries. How long would capitalism be able to resist? Lenin had counted its lease of life in the major European countries first in weeks, then in months, and then in years. Prudence now seemed to counsel counting in decades. During all that time the fate of the Soviets would hang in the balance. Could Bolshevism hope for decades of peace? Recent successes of Soviet diplomacy induced Stalin to take the optimistic view. Thus extreme scepticism about world revolution and confidence in the reality of a long truce between Russia and the capitalist world were the twin premisses of his 'socialism in one country'.

Trotsky relates how contemptuously Stalin dismissed the potentialities of foreign communism. The Comintern, he allegedly held, would carry out no revolution for many decades. Lominadze, one of Stalin's close associates in the twenties, later attributed to Stalin the saying that 'the Comintern represents nothing. It exists only because of our support.'[1] Stalin himself denied having made the remark. Lominadze may have referred to loose talk at a session of the Politbureau. But most of Stalin's public statements in the middle twenties abound in broad, though much more cautious, hints to similar effect.[2] The most illuminating of these can be found in his discourse to the students of the Sverdlov University on 9 June 1925.[3] He described the domestic policies that Soviet Russia would have to adopt 'if she was not backed by the social revolution of the western proletariat within the next fifteen years'. Elaborating his point he then made the assumption of a peaceful isolation of Russia lasting twenty years, that is until 1945.[4] Nor was this one of several alternative premisses: it was the main premiss of his policy. His listeners were ardent young Communists, many of them sympathetic towards the left opposition, to whom the mere assumption of so long a hiatus in international revolution was shocking. The perspective of so long a peace also sounded incredible. The speaker had to take the mood of his audience into account and expound his views with caution. In his own mind he almost certainly reckoned with an even longer period of Russian isolation.

His attitude demanded the gradual subordination of Communist policies to the needs of Soviet diplomacy. In the Leninist period diplomacy had been, as it were, an auxiliary detachment of the Comintern. That relationship was to be reversed. From the 'vanguards of world revolution' the Communist parties became, in Trotsky's words, the more or less pacifist 'frontier guards' of Soviet Russia. From Stalin's viewpoint it would have been utter folly to risk the substance of socialism in one country for the shadow of revolution abroad. The main thing for the Bolshevik leaders was to make up their minds on how much substance there was in socialism in one

---

[1] *Bulleten Oppozitsii*, no. 33, 1933.

[2] J. Stalin, *Sochinenya*, vol. vii, pp. 21, 25, 26, 52, 95–8, 123, 262. The writer heard the foremost European leaders of the Comintern in the early twenties, and Trotsky's opponents, attributing to Stalin remarks in substance identical with those quoted by Lominadze and Trotsky.

[3] Ibid., pp. 126 ff. [4] Ibid., p. 166.

country and whether international communism represented a mere shadow. Over these issues they split. To his last day Trotsky believed that there was more reality in international communism, despite all its weakness, than in socialism in one country, despite all its achievements. Most of the other leaders who vacillated between Stalin and Trotsky hesitated over this crucial issue. As to Stalin, this, the major premiss of his policy, remained unchanged throughout the period between the wars.

The peculiar point to be considered is that he was never free to lay bare his main premiss. The view that the world had entered into the era of Socialist revolution had been the main-spring of Leninism. The need for Stalin to pay lip-service to the expectation of revolution was the more pressing the more he was involved in the fight against the left Bolsheviks, who charged him with abandoning the Leninist heritage. It was mainly in the first phases of that struggle, in 1925 and 1926, that he could allow himself to argue publicly from the assumption that no Socialist upheaval in the west would occur for about twenty years. Then, pressed by his opponents, he either sought refuge in ambiguity or vied with them in prophesying the nearness of revolutionary events. Such prophecies represented the exoteric aspect of his policy, the coating without which a large section of the party would not have consented to swallow his ideas. His esoteric view he kept to himself: at the most, he discussed it with the leaders of his own faction; but it was always implied in what he did. The contradiction between the two sides of his policy gave to his behaviour that touch of insincerity and even duplicity which made his anti-Bolshevik critics accuse him of plotting for world revolution, while his Bolshevik critics charged him with plotting against it.

. . . .

The débâcle of German communism in 1923 decisively speeded up the crystallization of the set of ideas associated with Stalinism. In the summer of that year the Politbureau and the Executive of the Comintern hotly debated the German crisis provoked by the French occupation of the Ruhr and the galloping devaluation of the German currency. Some of the Bolshevik leaders saw the approach of the 'German October'. Heinrich Brandler, the leader of the German Communist party, arrived in Moscow to consult the Executive of the Comintern on strategy and tactics. It was on that occasion that Stalin for the first time intervened with the weight of his growing influence in a major decision of the Comintern. His view on the German situation, which he set out in a letter to Zinoviev and Bukharin, was marked by a strong disbelief in the chances of German communism. He listed all the exceptional circumstances that favoured the Bolsheviks in the revolution of 1917 and concluded: 'At the moment the German Communists have nothing of the kind. They have, of course, a Soviet country as neighbour, which we did not have. But what can we offer them? ... Should the government in Germany topple over now ... and the Communists seize hold of it, they would end up in a crash.'[1] He warned the Politbureau against encouraging any risky Communist demonstrations in Germany, which the *bourgeoisie* and the right-wing Social Democrats ('at present all the odds are on their side') would turn into a general battle that might end in the extermination of the Communists. 'In my opinion the Germans [that is the German Communists] should be restrained and not spurred on.' The difference between the chances of the Bolsheviks in 1917 and those of the German Communists in 1923, as Stalin saw it, was that the Bolsheviks had the support of a people longing for peace and of a peasantry eager to seize the landlords' estates. What his argument implied was that the German Communists could not hope to seize power either in 1923 or in any foreseeable future, because they could never obtain backing from the peasantry comparable to that received by Bolshevism, and that, at best, only a German defeat in another war might give them a chance. To the one circumstance that might have favoured them, the much greater role of the industrial working class in Germany than in Russia, Stalin paid no attention.[2]

Later in the year, as the turmoil in Germany mounted, the

---

[1] L. Trotsky, *Stalin*, pp. 368–9. The authenticity of this letter is confirmed by the two rival leaders of German communism, Heinrich Brandler and Ruth Fischer. It has not been published in Stalin's *Works*, although Stalin has never denied its authenticity. A. Thalheimer, *1923: Eine Verpasste Revolution*, p. 31.

[2] The letter contained a characteristic remark about German fascism, a pointer to future Communist tactics: 'Of course, the Fascists are not asleep. But it is to our advantage to let them attack first: that will rally the entire working class around the Communists.' (Ibid.)

Russian advocates of revolutionary action gained ground and began to 'spur on' the Germans. Stalin ceased to air his scepticism and kept in the background. He let Trotsky, Zinoviev, and Radek, who did not see eye to eye with one another, commit themselves. Brandler returned to Germany with a set of incoherent and contradictory instructions: he was to organize a revolution against the Social Democrats and at the same time to enter the Social Democratic government of Saxony; he was to start the revolution in Saxony, not in the capital or any other decisive centre, &c.—instructions that would have made any insurrectionist party miss its best opportunities. The enterprise ended in a series of unco-ordinated moves, and in failure. The effect of the failure on Moscow was very great: the isolation of Russian communism was now sealed.

In the next few years the fate of the Comintern remained unsettled. Although Stalin believed the organization to be more or less useless as the instrument of revolution, he could not dissociate Russia's ruling party from it—the ties between Bolshevism and the Comintern had been too strong for that. The Comintern, on the other hand, was inspired by a sense of its mission. It spoke for only a minority of the European working classes; but that was a large and important minority comprising the most idealistic, active, and ardent elements of the western proletariat. Its activity could not but embarrass Soviet diplomacy. This was one motive which compelled Stalin to try to tame the unruly organization. Another was the influence which the Comintern might have on the internal struggles in Russia. In those years the European Communist leaders, though accepting guidance from the successful Bolshevik experts on revolution, still talked to them as equals and took for granted their own right to have a say in Russian affairs. Most of them at first sided with Trotsky against Stalin, with the European-minded Bolsheviks against the self-centred Russian hierarchy of secretaries. Thus, for domestic as well as diplomatic reasons, Stalin could not but extend to the Comintern, still accustomed to the interplay of various trends, traditions, and views in its midst, the methods by which he was remoulding the Russian party into a 'monolithic' body.

He acted from behind the scenes, mainly through his

lieutenants who sat on the Executive of the International. Unlike Lenin, who had addressed every congress of the Comintern and, though the official head of the Government, had publicly shouldered responsibility for its policy, Stalin, holding no post in the Government, never addressed any congress of the Comintern. During ceremonial meetings he sat silently on the platform to be acclaimed by multi-national crowds of delegates. Only the initiated knew that the public debates and votes were of little significance, and that no major decision of the Comintern had any validity unless it was approved by Stalin. He looked with disdain upon the great ideological debates, in which Lenin had indulged with eagerness and gusto, and he regarded the regular congresses as a waste of time. During the four years of Lenin's leadership, four fully fledged international congresses were convened; during the twenty-five years of Stalin's leadership only three: one in 1924, which endorsed the denunciation of Trotskyism, another in 1928, at which the influence of Bukharin and the right Bolsheviks was eliminated, and a third in 1935, which proclaimed the policy of Popular Fronts. The centre of gravity of the organization shifted to its Executive Committee. As in the Russian party so in the Comintern, the caucus gained absolute predominance over the whole body of the movement.

Naturally most of the work that Stalin did in setting up that caucus was hidden in obscurity. He squeezed out the men who had independent minds, the rebels, the theoreticians, the radical *literati*, the leaders of European communism in its period of revolutionary spontaneity. Almost every one of them was involved in the reverses of the early twenties and therefore vulnerable; and Stalin made the most of their 'errors' and 'deviations' to discredit them. The emotional attachment of European Communists to the much-maligned and attacked Russian revolution was so great that almost any leader was undone if it was known that he had against him the authority of the Russian party. Stalin rarely used that authority directly. The verdicts and condemnations were passed by the Executive of the Comintern. The Executive was democratically elected at international congresses. But it was almost always swayed by the Russian delegation, on whom the views of the Russian Politbureau were binding. And inside the Politbureau Stalin swayed the majority.[1] This was the mechanism through which he controlled the International. The Russian members of the Executive nominally had no prerogatives other than those possessed by representatives of foreign parties; but their moral pull was decisive. Where this was not enough, various forms of pressure were used to crush opposition. Rebellious foreign leaders were assigned with all honour to work at the headquarters of the International in Moscow, where they were easily controlled and cut off from their followers; public opinion in other Communist parties was mobilized against them; and their opponents and rivals in their own countries were encouraged and raised up. When, in spite of all the campaigning against them, in which calumny had its part, the 'deviationists' still enjoyed authority in their own party, the cashiers of the Comintern withheld their subsidies from that party. But the effectiveness of this, the crudest means of pressure, was secondary.[2] It was the legend of the Russian revolution, its solid and permanent substance as well as the transitory myths woven into it, that gave Stalin his power over a vast agglomeration of foreign parties, in whose ranks the idealistic seekers for a new way of life were incomparably more numerous than the timeservers. And even the time-servers were time-servers only in a relative sense: they were ready to obey any master, but only if that master spoke with the authority of revolution. Over the years Stalin succeeded in drilling his hosts according to his own

---

[1] Stalin himself was nominally a member of the Russian delegation to the Executive of the Comintern. But only very rarely did he act in this capacity; and when he did so it was always in order to dispose of this or that foreign 'heretic'. See *Sochinenya*, vol. viii, pp. 1–10, 100–8, 109–15.

[2] The subsidizing of the various branches of the Comintern was innocuous at first. Every section was to contribute its share to the treasury of the organization and to draw on it according to needs. In varying degrees this had also been the custom in the previous Internationals, the second and the first, without producing corruption. As the financial resources of the Russian party were incomparably greater than those of the other sections, the Comintern became up to a point dependent on them. Foreign parties with a large following could, of course, easily support themselves. But Moscow encouraged them to spend on organization and propaganda beyond their means; and the more they did so the bigger grew their bureaucratic establishments and their need for subsidies. Accustomed to easy money they then tended to neglect the collection of their own dues, which had a demoralizing effect on them. While the role of 'Moscow gold' in fostering communism abroad has very often been melodramatically played up, it is true, nevertheless, that the subsidies did much to make the Communist hierarchies amenable to Stalin's guidance.

ideas, primarily because those hosts were willing to serve a great cause, a cause which, rightly or wrongly, they identified with the Soviets, a cause which seemed to them to be of much greater simplicity and magnitude than either the feuds in the Russian Politbureau or the shifts in the Comintern, than either the manœuvres of Russian diplomacy or even the dim shadows of a remote Russian reality.

Thus it came about that the Comintern not only shone with the reflected light of the Russian party, but that it reflected each of its internal alinements in turn. This was so much the case that anybody who would try to comprehend the history of any Communist party merely in the context of its own national environment would fail. He would not be able to account for the manifold changes of line, for the fading of some leaders and the emergence of others, or for the reforms in organizational structure. The origin of all these must most often be sought in the issues which preoccupied the Russian General Secretariat rather than in the social struggles on the spot. While the trium-virs were confronting Trotsky, Trotskyism haunted the Comin-tern. Then the leaders who by their views or sentiments had been tied to their President, Zinoviev, either joined in denouncing him or were effaced. During the years of his alliance with Stalin, Bukharin was the leading light of the International. He proclaimed the new policies and picked his staffs from among those foreign Communists who sympathized with the *bloc* of the centre faction and the right in the Bolshevik party. After that *bloc* had fallen asunder, the International laboured under new pangs of 'Bolshevization'.

. . . .

Here, then, was Stalin struggling to recondition an organiza-tion, inherited from the revolution, for a period which he believed to be one of stagnation in the revolutionary process. The International had, in the full tide of revolution, sprung into being from a schism in the Socialist movement and had hoped to defeat the reformist wing of labour. What could have lain nearer Stalin's present view about the stabilization of capitalism than the idea of a *rapprochement* between the two wings of the movement, the second and the third Internationals? If his diagnosis was correct, the two Internationals could not immediately do more than wrest, with more or less determination, reforms and concessions from the possessing classes. On this basis common action should be possible; and their collaboration might end in bridging the gulf between them. In this spirit the affairs of the Comintern were conducted while the partnership between Stalin and Bukharin lasted. In Russia the N.E.P. was flourishing; within the framework of a mixed economy the ruling party patronized private farming and trade; and the 'Fabianism' of its attitude seemed to demand a mild course abroad as well, much as this went against the grain of the Comintern.

Two issues claimed much of Stalin's attention in the middle twenties: the Chinese revolution and the attitude of the Russian trade unions towards the British unions. The Chinese revolution had, in its early days, come under the spell of the Russian. Sun Yat-Sen, the founder of the Kuomintang, urged his followers to guard the friendship between the two revolutions. After Sun Yat-Sen's death Stalin sent the following message to the Kuomintang: 'The Central Committee of the Russian Communist party believes that the Kuomintang will keep high the banner of Sun Yat-Sen in the great struggle of liberation from imperialism, that the Kuomintang will honourably carry that banner to the full victory over imperialism and its agents in China.'[1] Russian military advisers went to assist General Chiang Kai-shek in his operations. The Chinese Communists were instructed from Moscow to join the Kuomintang, 'the *bloc* of the four classes', as one of its constituent parts; and the Kuomintang itself was represented at the Executive of the Comintern with the rights of an associate member.[2]

The problem arose: what was the nature of the Chinese revolution? What should be its objectives? What role should the Communists play in it? The national aspirations of the Chinese, their desire to free themselves from western tutelage and from their own feudal particularism, were the driving power of the movement, which, at first, acted as a united force. Under the surface, however, there were the social cleavages between generals and peasants, merchants and coolies. The cleavages deepened as time went on. In the industrial and

---

[1] J. Stalin, *Sochinenya*, vol. vii, p. 50.
[2] *Protokoll Erweiterte Exekutive der Kommunistischen Internationale* (February–March 1926), pp. 12–13.

commercial cities of coastal China the working class became the weightiest political factor.

Could this be China's 1917? Stalin's and Bukharin's answer was 'no', Trotsky's—'yes'. If a precedent was to be sought in Russian history, Stalin preferred to look for it in 1905, when the Bolsheviks held that Russia, not yet ripe for socialism, could only aspire to a bourgeois revolution. A bourgeois revolution was all that the Chinese could now achieve, Stalin concluded. He went back to that 'old Bolshevism' which Lenin had so forcefully discarded in April 1917, but which he had never succeeded in eradicating completely from the minds of some of his disciples. Since the task of the Chinese revolution was to unify and modernize China and to win her national independence, not socialism, then the Chinese Communists should not, in Stalin's view, aim at the establishment of a proletarian dictatorship. They should, instead, work in harmony with the middle classes, the peasants, and the progressive nationalist generals. He prompted the Communist party of China to submit to the strict discipline of the Kuomintang of which it was now merely a faction.[1] He also directed the machine of Soviet propaganda to build up the prestige of General Chiang Kai-shek as the unchallenged leader of the national *renaissance* of China. The government that was ultimately to issue from the revolution was to be a 'democratic dictatorship of the proletariat and the peasantry'. That formula, developed by Lenin in 1905, described the peculiar situation, conceivable only in 'backward' countries, in which Marxist Socialists fight in a purely anti-feudal revolution and share power with the representatives of a revolutionary middle class and peasantry.

The old familiar semi-scholastic disputations over that formula soon broke out anew.[2] Trotsky denounced Stalin's alliance with Chiang Kai-shek and urged the Chinese Communists to strive for proletarian dictatorship *sans phrase*. Zinoviev and Kamenev, attached to the Leninist tradition of 1905, accepted 'the democratic dictatorship of the proletariat and the peasantry'; but they criticized Stalin's policy on the

---

[1] J. Stalin, *Sochinenya*, vol. viii, pp. 358, 365–7, and 373. See Bukharin's speech on the subject in *15 Konferentsya Vsesoyuznoi Kom. Partii*, pp. 27–9.

[2] See Chapter II, pp. 42–3, Chapter III, pp. 72–5, and Chapter V, pp. 135–41, *passim*.

ground that it subordinated Chinese communism to middle-class leadership. The dispute generated incredible heat and bitterness and speeded up the final split between Stalin and Trotsky.

Meanwhile, the 'bloc of the four classes' in China was also falling asunder. The growth of Chinese communism, moderate though its policies were, frightened Chiang Kai-shek and the leaders of the middle classes. Chiang brusquely rid himself of his embarrassing allies: he sent his Russian military advisers back to Russia and cruelly suppressed the Communists who had served under him. So strongly had Stalin committed himself to the support of Chiang that his position and prestige were for a time gravely shaken. He tried to save what he could from the ruins of his Chinese policy and instructed the Chinese Communists to coalesce with the leftish Liberals of the Kuomintang, who formed a government at Hankow opposed to Chiang Kai-shek. Soon that coalition, too, broke down. Communism, even while it attempted to deny its own nature and to adapt itself to middle-class allies, to train itself for the arts of moderation and compromise, to change its symbols and its language, did not cease to strike fear and panic in the leaders and parties of the middle classes. It bore the curse or the blessing of its origin, the hallmarks of revolution; hallmarks which evoked either horror or hope and which no tactical artifice could conceal and not even the most vigorous scourings efface.

Similar frustration attended the other major experiment in moderation, the Anglo-Russian council of trade unions, which was formed in May 1925. The Politbureau hoped that the British trade unions would use their influence to improve Anglo-Russian relations, at that time strained. Stalin delegated Tomsky, one of the most influential members of the Politbureau, to address the annual congress of the British trade unions at Hull. He hoped that understanding with the British would be followed by a fuller agreement between the opposed wings in the international Labour movement. Parallel with the Comintern, the *Profintern* (the International of the Red trade unions) had opposed itself to the so-called Amsterdam International, in which the reformist trade unions of the west had been organized. The failure of the Profintern had been even more striking than that of the Comintern. Moscow was now willing to acknowledge defeat and to make some sort of peace with Amsterdam. The Anglo-Russian council was to serve as a stepping-stone to this. Eminent right-wing Bolsheviks vaguely hoped that a reunion of the political Internationals would crown the work of reconciliation. Stalin, cautious as ever, did not commit himself to these far-reaching schemes. But he gave unstinted support to the course pursued by Bukharin and Tomsky and defended it against bitter criticism from the left Bolsheviks.[1]

The friendship between the leaders of the Russian and the British trade unions did not stand the strain of the general strike of 1926. The Russian leaders, hard-pressed by their own left opposition, could not refrain from criticizing now and then the moderation of their British colleagues. Their criticisms, however mild, caused irritation. The leaders of the British trade unions, on the other hand, exposed to the overwhelming pressure of Conservative opinion, felt uneasy over their alliance with the Bolsheviks. They refused to accept the money collected by the Russian trade unions in a gesture of solidarity with striking British miners. Some time later the Anglo-Russian council was dissolved; and with it faded the hope of any wider reconciliation between Bolshevism and European reformism.

The main avenues of compromise had thus been explored with disappointing results. By the end of 1923 the world had rejected the Bolsheviks as revolutionaries; by the end of 1927 it had rejected them again as conciliators. It was not only in China and in Great Britain that the Comintern had tried moderation in vain; it had done the same in most other European countries.[2] Everywhere the Communists were either abandoned or hunted down by their erstwhile allies. Disappointment with conciliatory policies provoked a revulsion in Communist ranks and paved the way for a new course, diametrically opposed to the old one. So strong was that revulsion that in his Chinese

---

[1] J. Stalin, *Sochinenya*, vol. viii, pp. 176–91. On his return from Britain, Tomsky, greatly impressed by the high standard of living of the British and other western European workers, told one of his intimate friends, a former German vice-President of the Comintern (from whom the present writer heard the story): 'I cannot see why your western European workers should be Communists. I do not see any possibility of revolution in the west.'

[2] In Poland, for instance, Communists and Socialists joined hands to help Pilsudski in his *coup d'état* of 1926. Similar tactics were adopted in Rumania and other Balkan countries.

policy Stalin tried, towards the end of 1927, to save his face by advising the Chinese Communists, already greatly weakened by savage persecution and slaughter, to stage the rising of Canton. The rising was in advance doomed to failure, and led in fact to a new massacre of the Reds.[1] Soon the whole Comintern sought to make amends for its ill-fated exercises in moderate statesmanship by indulging in a long bout of 'ultra-leftism'. That new ultra-left policy was carried to a suicidal extremity by the German Communist party in the face of rising nazism.

Another reason for the change in the Comintern, one that was certainly more decisive than the feeling in its own ranks, was the new alinement that took place in the Russian party in 1928–9. Stalin was then subduing the right-wing Bolsheviks. Not a single political concept or slogan that had originated from Bukharin, Tomsky, or Rykov withstood condemnation. All the real issues at stake were Russian issues: the N.E.P., industrialization, collectivization, &c. But the powerful 'switch over to the left' in the Russian party transmitted itself automatically to the Comintern hitherto guided by Bukharin. Some foreign Communists tended to side with Bukharin; and so Stalin could not but carry the struggle against him into the International.[2] He produced new policies for the European parties, which on the surface corresponded to the trend in Russia. In Russia co-operation between Communists and private farmers and traders had come to an end; and the formal corollary to this was that Communists abroad should cease to co-operate with the other parties, especially the Social Democrats.

That automatic transmission of every movement and reflex from the Russian to all the other parties constituted the main and the most bizarre anomaly in the life of the Comintern, an anomaly which became the norm. It was because of this that an air of unreality hung over so much of the Comintern's activity. Stalin's leftward switch in Russia was not only an earnest affair: it had the grandeur of national drama; it refashioned to its foundations the social structure of a great country. The whole power of the monster state stood behind

[1] The story of the 'Canton Commune' is told in Harold R. Isaacs, *The Tragedy of the Chinese Revolution*, pp. 352–77.

[2] J. Stalin, *Problems of Leninism*, pp. 245–9.

every swing of the party line and transformed words and slogans into lasting deeds. But what did such swings and turns in the policy of the Comintern signify? Meaningless mimicry, at best. It was as if the giant figure of an athlete engaged in a homeric fight had thrown around itself twenty or thirty shadows, each mimicking the tense wrestling and the violent gestures of the real body, each pretending to shake heaven and earth. The strange picture was made even stranger by the fact that the foreign sections of the Comintern were not mere shadows. They were half bodies and half shadows. With one part of their existence they were immersed in the realities of their national life, trying to express the aspirations of their own working classes, while with the other they participated in the hectic dance of phantoms round the General Secretary.

. . . .

In December 1927, immediately after Trotsky, Zinoviev, and Kamenev had been expelled from the party, Stalin surprised the fifteenth congress by stating that the 'stabilization' of capitalism had come to an end. 'Two years ago', he said, 'one could talk about a period of relative balance between the Soviets and the capitalist countries and about their "peaceful co-existence". Now we have every reason to say that the period of "peaceful coexistence" recedes into the past, giving place to a period of imperialist attacks and of preparation of inter-vention against the U.S.S.R.'[1] He did not try to square this new view with his previous forecast of fifteen or twenty years of 'peaceful coexistence'. His new thesis was finally accepted as the basis of a new policy at the sixth congress of the Comintern, in the summer of 1928, at which he surprised the foreign dele-gates by the virtual demotion of Bukharin, carried out behind the scenes.[2]

The congress forecast the approach of a catastrophic econo-mic crisis in the capitalist countries. (The forecast, authorized by Stalin, was strikingly confirmed, in the following year, by the great slump in the United States.) From these premises new tactics were developed. A whole chain of revolutionary ex-

---

[1] 15 Syezd V.K.P. (b), p. 34.
[2] For Stalin's own version of Bukharin's demotion see his speech on 'The Danger of the Right Deviation' delivered before the Central Committee in April 1929. Problems of Leninism, pp. 244 ff.

plosions was expected. The Communist parties in the west were to launch their final offensive against capitalism. The reformist Social Democratic parties, now labelled Social-Fascist, were to be regarded as the most dangerous enemies of communism. The left wings of the Social Democratic parties were to be regarded as even greater obstacles to Socialist revolution than the right ones—'the more to the left the more dangerous'. Any co-operation or contact between Communists and Social Democratic leaders was contaminating. The Comintern was to muster its ranks for the world-wide struggle, relying exclusively upon its own strength and pull.[1]

It is doubtful, to say the least, whether Stalin believed in the imminent eruption of all the revolutionary volcanoes, which his propagandists heralded. Though his grasp of conditions in foreign countries was poor, it was not so poor as to make him share the ultra-revolutionary illusions of the sixth congress of the Comintern. With even greater emphasis than hitherto, as if ignoring all the trumpets of the Comintern, he made 'socialism in one country' the supreme article of faith, obligatory not only in his own party but in the Comintern as a whole. He now attached incomparably more importance to a single factory newly built in Russia than to all the great expectations of revolution abroad.[2] His diplomacy was feeling its way even more cautiously than before and continued to work on the assumption of Russia's prolonged isolation. There was an undeniable contradiction between his two lines of policy, the one he pursued in Russia and the one he inspired in the Comintern. It is easy to guess which of the two policies had the greater weight.

The Comintern was now indeed engaged in a mock fight. Its ultra-radicalism was so unreal that Stalin, in all probability, countenanced it only because he attributed very little practical significance to whatever the Comintern did in those years. If this was what he thought, he was profoundly mistaken, for the ultra-radicalism of the Comintern had important, though only negative, consequences. This was especially so in

[1] *Kommunisticheskii Internatsional v dokumentakh*, pp. 769–92, 876–7, 915–30, 952–65.

[2] 'One Soviet tractor is worth more than ten good foreign Communists' was a characteristic remark heard from highly placed Bolsheviks in the days of the first five-year plan. The phrase reflected the tenor of the intimate talk about the Comintern in Stalin's entourage.

Germany, the chief testing-ground of the new policy, where the Labour movement was threatened by the rapid rise of nazism. The split between the Social Democrats who looked to Hindenburg for protection against Hitler and refused to have anything to do with Communists, and the Communists who held the Social Democrats to be a greater menace to them than the Nazis, that completely irrational split, paralysed the political strength of the German working class when it alone could have barred Hitler's road to power. This is not the place to tell the story of the collapse of the Weimar Republic, the story which ended in the surrender of the most powerful labour organizations on the Continent to the Brown Shirts, without a single shot, without a single act of real resistance. Suffice it to say that after the collapse, one of the phrases that were current among the men of the German left was that 'without Stalin there would have been no Hitler'. The saying should be taken with a grain of salt. Amid the *Katzenjammer* which befell them after 1933, most leaders of the German left were only too eager to explain away their own failure and ascribe it to Stalin's evil influence. Nevertheless, as the inspirer of the Comintern policy, Stalin must be held to bear his share of responsibility for the contribution which that policy unwittingly made to Hitler's triumph.

The point that emerges clearly from every Comintern document of the early thirties and from Stalin's own utterances is that he was completely unaware of the significance and the destructive dynamism of nazism.[1] To him Hitler was merely one of the many reactionary leaders whom the political see-saw throws up for a moment, then down and up again, another Brüning or Papen, another Baldwin or Harding. He, of all men, completely missed the totalitarian aspirations in nazism and its power to act on these aspirations. He formulated the essence of his views on fascism as early as in 1924:

It is not true that fascism is only a militant organization of the *bourgeoisie*. . . . Fascism is the militant organization of the *bourgeoisie* which bases itself on the active support of Social Democracy. Objectively, Social Democracy is the moderate wing of fascism. There is no reason to suppose that the militant organization of the

[1] Stalin consistently treated nazism and fascism as essentially identical. The two terms are used here, too, interchangeably.

bourgeoisie can achieve any decisive successes . . . without active support from Social Democracy. There is just as little ground to think that Social Democracy could achieve decisive successes . . . without the active support of that militant organization of the *bourgeoisie*. Those organizations do not contradict but supplement one another. They are not antipodes but twins. . . . Fascism is the shapeless political *bloc* of these two basic organizations, a *bloc* that has emerged in the post-war crisis of imperialism for the struggle against proletarian revolution.[1]

These words may be said to represent the fullest contribution that Stalin ever made to the understanding of fascism or national socialism. In subsequent years he vaguely repeated his view once or twice, without modifying it.[2] Hosts of Comintern theoreticians and writers chewed upon his 'not antipodes but twins' for years on end, without giving a single coherent explanation of that new force under whose impact the old political structure of Europe was crumbling. Even after Hitler had seized the reins of government, Stalin's spokesmen still forecast a 'deal' between the Nazis and the Social Democrats and an imminent decline of Hitler's influence to be followed by a Communist come-back.[3] After the first year of Hitler's government, Stalin himself, though he already correctly foresaw the risk of war inherent in nazism, vaguely assured the seventeenth congress of his party that 'the revolutionary crisis is maturing and fascism is far from being long lived'.[4] The one thing which he did not foresee, and which his spokesmen emphatically described as impossible, was that Hitler would destroy social democracy together with communism, that fascism would send its 'twin' to the concentration camp and build up a massive monopoly of power. In making this error, it should be added, Stalin was not alone. German Social Democratic leaders, too, hoped to the last to find a *modus vivendi* with Hitler; and German, British, and French Conservative well-wishers of nazism also deluded themselves that Hitler would play *his* game according to *their* rules.

No student of these affairs can overlook the striking contrast between the lack of understanding and imagination which Stalin, having at his command all the sources of information

---

[1] J. Stalin, *Sochinenya*, vol. vi, p. 282.   [2] J. Stalin, *Leninism*, vol. ii, p. 320.
[3] *Rundschau*, no. 43, 1933; *Kommunistische Internationale*, no. 14, 1933.
[4] J. Stalin, *Problems of Leninism*, p. 454.

and intelligence of a great power and a vast international organization, displayed at this momentous test and the insight and sense of responsibility with which Trotsky, from his lonely retreat on Prinkipo island, reacted to the German crisis. In a series of books, pamphlets, and articles Trotsky gave what is to this day the most exhaustive sociological explanation of nazism. He followed the development of Hitler's movement step by step, predicted well in advance every phase of it and tried in vain to impress the German left, the Comintern, and the Soviet Government with the fury of destruction about to break upon their heads.

It is [our] duty [he wrote in 1931] to sound the alarm: the leadership of the Comintern is leading the German proletariat towards an enormous catastrophe, the core of which is the panicky capitulation before fascism. The coming into power of the German National Socialists would mean above all the extermination of the flower of the German proletariat, the disruption of its organizations, the extirpation of its belief in itself and in its future. Considering the far greater . . . acuteness of the social antagonisms in Germany, the hellish work of Italian fascism would probably appear as a pale and almost humane experiment in comparison with the work of German national socialism.[1]

. . . .

Workers, Communists, [Trotsky sounded the alarm again, two years before Hitler's rise to power] . . . should fascism come to power it will ride over your skulls and spines like a terrific tank. Your salvation lies in merciless struggle. And only a fighting unity with Social Democratic workers can bring victory. Make haste, you have very little time left![2]

In those days Stalin and the other Soviet leaders still played up the bogy of a French-led anti-Soviet crusade, but missed the real anti-Soviet crusader when he appeared on the horizon. In July 1930 Stalin still described France as 'the most aggressive and militarist country of all aggressive and militarist countries of the world' which prepared for war against Russia.[3] 'None of the "normal" bourgeois parliamentary governments', this was in effect Trotsky's rejoinder, 'can at the present time risk a war against the U.S.S.R. . . . But if Hitler comes to power

[1] L. Trotsky, *Germany, the Key to the International Situation*, p. 23.
[2] Ibid., p. 44.   [3] J. Stalin, *Leninism*, vol. ii, p. 321.

and proceeds to crush the vanguard of the German workers, pulverizing and demoralizing the whole proletariat for many years to come, the fascist government will be the only government capable of waging war against the U.S.S.R. . . . In case he is victorious [in Germany] Hitler will become the Super-Wrangel of the world *bourgeoisie*.'[1] Moscow received Trotsky's alarm cries with complacent derision. The leaders of the Comintern went on obdurately repeating the incoherent slogan about the antipodes and the twins.

. . . .

Until Hitler's rise to power, Soviet diplomacy pursued, by and large, the policy of Rapallo. It gave qualified support to vanquished Germany against the victors. That support varied in form, but it did not, on the whole, extend to the German ambition to achieve a forcible revision of the peace of Versailles. The Soviets derived what benefit they could from their alinement with Germany, especially as long as the other powers confronted them with various degrees of boycott. The import of German industrial goods assisted Russia in her recovery in the twenties. The Politbureau authorized Trotsky and Tukhachevsky to enlist German military skill, the skill of unemployed officers and technicians, in the training of the Red Army. As a *quid pro quo* the Russians permitted German military technicians to continue on Russian soil experiments which they could not carry out in Germany under the Versailles treaty. In these arrangements Stalin made no change. They continued by force of inertia for some time after Hitler had seized power.[2]

For all that, the relations between the two countries did not have the character of an alliance. Their aim was, as it was said before, to counterbalance the predominance of the *Entente* and to prevent Germany from coalescing with the west against Russia. Whenever the western powers tried to mitigate the burden of reparations on Germany, as under the Dawes plan, or whenever they tried a *rapprochement* with Germany on the basis of Versailles, as in the pact of Locarno, the Soviet leaders

[1] L. Trotsky, *Germany, the Key to the International Situation*, p. 25.

[2] This was the grain of truth in the accusation that Trotsky and Tukhachevsky co-operated with the Wehrmacht. The co-operation between the Russian and the German armies went on for about twelve years, from 1922 till 1935, with the authorization of the Politbureau and under its control.

watched uneasily to see whether such moves did not conceal an anti-Soviet coalition; and they encouraged German opposition to the victors. But they had no illusions about the stability of the Versailles system. 'To think that Germany will put up with this state of affairs', so Stalin commented on the pact of Locarno in 1925, 'is to hope for miracles. . . . Locarno, which . . . sanctions the loss by Germany of Silesia, the corridor and Danzig and the loss by the Ukraine of Galicia and western Volhynia, the loss by Byelorussia of its western part, the loss of Vilno by Lithuania . . . will share the fate of the old Franco-Prussian treaty, which deprived France of Alsace and Lorraine. . . . Locarno is fraught with a new European war.'[1] Thus, in 1925, Stalin enumerated with the greatest precision the storm centres from which the Second World War was to begin.

Some of Stalin's prognostications, made in the middle twenties, are of special interest as pointers, direct or indirect, to his own future policy. That the peace was merely a truce between two wars was an axiom to him, believing as he did, like all Bolsheviks, that capitalist competition for raw materials, markets, and facilities for profitable investment leads inevitably to armed contest. What was uncertain, apart from the time at which war would break out, was how the line of future divisions would run. In the middle twenties Trotsky, grossly exaggerating the acuteness of Anglo-American antagonism, forecast a war between the United States and the British Empire. This view was accepted by the Politbureau; and as late as 1930 Stalin repeated it, saying that the competition between the two Anglo-Saxon powers overshadowed all the antagonisms between the European nations.[2] 'Britain's star is setting', he said on another occasion, 'and America's is rising.'[3] America's rising star filled him with forebodings for he saw the United States propping up the decaying European capitalism, mainly through loans granted to Germany. In addition the United States stubbornly refused, up to 1933, to recognize the Soviet Government.

What would be Russia's attitude in a war between great

---

[1] J. Stalin, *Sochinenya*, vol. vii, pp. 273–4.

[2] J. Stalin, *Leninism*, vol. ii, p. 316; L. Trotsky (Trotzki), *Europa und Amerika*, p. 43.

[3] J. Stalin, *Leninism*, vol. ii, p. 123. 'There is one force which . . . will inevitably destroy the British Empire—the English Conservatives.' (J. Stalin, *Sochinenya*, vol. vii, p. 292.)

capitalist powers, which were all by definition imperialist?[1] The Politbureau repeatedly broached this question without reaching final conclusions. The customary Bolshevik answer had been to wish a plague on both the houses of the future belligerents, to view the Second World War through the prism of the first one, and to hope that the working classes of the warring countries would revolt as the Russian working class had done. Broadly speaking, Russia's task was to consist in promoting revolutionary anti-militarism abroad.

Already in the debates of the middle twenties, however, Stalin took a different and more complex view of the future. It is still impossible to detail those debates, most of which were held in secret. It was only in 1947 that Stalin for the first time published a speech he made at a plenary session of the Central Committee in January 1925, which throws a retrospective light upon his attitude.

The preconditions for war [Stalin said in a debate over defence expenditure] are getting ripe. War may become inevitable, of course not to-morrow or the next day, but in a few years. . . . I suppose that the forces of the revolutionary movement in the west are great; that they grow; that they will grow; and that they may overthrow the *bourgeoisie* here or there. That is true. But it will be very difficult for them to hold their ground. . . . The problem of our army, of its strength and readiness, will inevitably arise in connexion with complications in the countries that surround us. . . . This does not mean that in any such situation we are bound in duty to intervene actively against anybody. . . . The banner of peace remains our banner as of old. But, if war begins, we shall hardly have to sit with folded arms. We shall have to come out, but we ought to be the last to come out. And we should come out in order to throw the decisive weight on the scales, the weight that should tilt the scales.[2]

[1] It should be remarked that the Bolsheviks used the term 'imperialism' in a sense somewhat different from that which it has in current English usage. Imperialism, in their sense, did not primarily or necessarily mean direct domination over foreign lands. The essential features of imperialism (as Lenin defined it on the basis of the works of English and German Liberal and Socialist economists) were: (a) the concentration of capital in monopolistic trusts and cartels; (b) the merging of industrial and banking capital into 'finance capital'; (c) the export of capital as well as of commodities; and (d) the division of the world between national and international capitalist monopolies. (*The Essentials of Lenin*, vol. i, p. 709.) Lenin did not seem to regard the formal possession of a colonial empire as the essential feature of an imperialist state. In the light of his formula he would class the United States among the modern imperialist states.

[2] J. Stalin, *Sochinenya*, vol. vii, pp. 13–14.

This illuminating statement should be read in its context. The phrase about the strength of the revolutionary forces in the west hardly concealed the speaker's scepticism. 'Great' and 'growing' as those forces were supposed to be, they could overthrow the *bourgeoisie* only 'here and there'; and even then they would not be able 'to hold their ground'. Stalin had no doubt that Russia's armed strength, and not the revolutionary forces abroad, would be the decisive factor in the Second World War. Would the Red Army come out to help foreign revolutions to 'hold their ground'? He evaded the issue, but insisted that it was not bound in duty to do so. He would prefer to see the warring capitalist countries fighting themselves to mutual exhaustion, though he did not say this in so many words, so that the Red Army should 'tilt the scales', perhaps in the same way in which the American army tilted the scales in 1918. For the time being he was out to establish two points: first, that Russia's interest lay in remaining for as long as possible a spectator of the future contest; and, second, that the Red Army was preeminent over any revolutionary forces, actual or potential, in the west. How far these points had become clear in his mind by 1925 is not certain. He may have been merely thinking aloud while he addressed the Central Committee. Or he may have been thinking about Russia's aloofness from the much discussed Anglo-American war. Whatever the truth, it was on these two principles that he was to act in the beginning of the Second World War.

Somewhat later in 1925 he made still another pronouncement on foreign policy which assumes special significance in retrospect. He talked to the students of the Sverdlov University about the opposition of certain diplomats—he did not mention names—to the Government's foreign policy. That opposition, he said, favoured a *rapprochement* between Russia and the former *Entente*, an abandonment of the Comintern and the re-acquisition by Russia of the spheres of influence she had voluntarily given up. These were apparently the second thoughts of Bolshevik diplomacy, regretful of its own renunciation of imperialist privilege. But these second thoughts also represented a shrewd anticipation of the method by which Stalin himself was to conduct his foreign policy from 1939 onwards, in agreement first with Hitler, and then with Roosevelt and

Churchill. There is a touch of irony in the blunt condemnation with which Stalin then met those anticipatory suggestions.

This would be the road to nationalism and degeneration [in these terms he referred to the concepts of spheres of influence in June 1925, exactly twenty years before the Potsdam conference], the road of the full liquidation of the international policy of the proletariat. People possessed of this disease see our country not as part of a whole, which is called the world revolutionary movement, but as the beginning and the end of that movement, thinking that the interests of all other countries should be sacrificed to the interests of our country. Why support the movement for the emancipation of China? Will that not be dangerous? [so they ask]. Will that not involve us in quarrels with other countries? Will it not be better for us together with other 'advanced' countries to establish 'spheres of influence' in China and to tear away something from China to our benefit? This would be profitable and safe. . . . Why back the emancipation movement in Germany? Is the risk worth while? Would it not be better to agree with the Entente on the Versailles treaty and to bargain out some compensation for ourselves? . . . Why keep friendly with Persia, Turkey, Afghanistan? . . . Would it not be better to re-establish 'spheres of influence' in co-operation with some of the great powers? Such is the nationalist frame of mind of a new type which aims at doing away with the foreign policy of the October revolution.[1]

That the yearning for spheres of influence was already then alive in Soviet diplomacy appears even more surprising than Stalin's condemnation of it. In the twenties such ideas were at any rate premature. Russia's bargaining power was too low then for either Britain or France to agree to any division of spheres. This perhaps accounts for the bluntness with which Stalin ruled the idea out of court. He had no need gratuitously to compromise the ideological purity of his foreign policy. For many years to come his diplomacy was still to confine itself to the defence of the *status quo*, in so far as it concerned Russia. 'We do not want a single foot of foreign territory', Stalin told the sixteenth congress in June 1930, 'but we will not surrender a single inch of our territory either.'[2] This was the *leitmotif* of Stalin's foreign policy until 1939.

[1] J. Stalin, *Sochinenya*, vol. vii, pp. 167–9.   [2] J. Stalin, *Leninism*, vol. ii, p. 325.

CHAPTER XI

Foreign Policy and Comintern. II

(1934–41)

Stalin's cautious silence in the first year of Hitler's rule.—The search for 'collective security' (1934–8).—Stalin receives Eden, Laval, and Beneš (1935).—Russia joins the League of Nations; the Comintern proclaims the policy of Popular Fronts.— World-revolution—a 'tragi-comic misunderstanding'.—Stalin's stake in the Spanish Civil War (1936–8).—Russia's isolation before and during Munich.—Stalin's *riposte*.—His speech at the XVIIIth Congress (March 1939).—Diplomatic manœuvres in the last months of peace.—Final preliminaries to the Russo-German Pact.—Ribbentrop at the Kremlin (23 August 1939).—The partition of Poland.— The first Russo-Finnish war.—Stalin refuses to go to Berlin at Hitler's invitation (March 1940).—Stalin surprised by the collapse of France.—Russo-German rivalry in the Balkans.—A Japanese envoy in the Kremlin.—Stalin becomes Prime Minister (6 May 1941) and makes his last attempt to conciliate Hitler.—The balance sheet of Stalin's diplomacy in 1939–41.

THE Nazi upheaval in Germany did not at once suggest to Stalin the need for some revision of his foreign policy. He at first waited to see how stable the Nazi régime would prove to be, and whether Hitler would take up the Rapallo policy of his predecessors or whether he would, in accordance with the ideas expressed in *Mein Kampf*, take up an attitude of implacable hostility towards the Soviets. Meanwhile Stalin took great care not to offer any provocation. The absolute passivity with which German communism had allowed itself to be crushed by Hitler might have been expected to facilitate continued friendly relations between Russia and Germany, so spectacularly did it seem to disprove the current notions about Russia's interference in German affairs.[1] The agreement of Rapallo and the pact of neutrality and friendship of 1926 were still in force; they had been prolonged in 1931; and the prolongation was ratified in May 1933, a few weeks after Hitler had become Chancellor.

[1] Some of Stalin's Communist opponents (Wollenberg, Krivitsky, and others) claimed that Stalin had deliberately led the German Communists to surrender to nazism in order to save the policy of Rapallo. This version has, in our view, not been supported by convincing evidence. Stalin's policy *vis-à-vis* rising nazism represents a record of rare shortsightedness and folly, but not of deliberate treachery.

Hitler's bloody suppression of all domestic opposition and his racial persecutions affected diplomatic routine business between Moscow and Berlin as little as it affected similar business between Paris or London and Berlin. Stalin undoubtedly calculated on the strength of the Bismarckian tradition among the German diplomats, a tradition which demanded that the Reich should avoid embroilment with Russia. In the first year of Hitler's Chancellorship he did not utter in public a single word about the events in Germany, though his silence was excruciating to the bewildered followers of the Comintern.[1]

He broke that silence only at the seventeenth congress of the party, in January 1934. Even then he refrained from drawing the conclusions from events which had ended so disastrously for the European left, and he vaguely fostered the illusion that fascism, 'a symptom of capitalist weakness', would prove short-lived. But he also described the Nazi upheaval as a 'triumph for the idea of revenge in Europe' and remarked that the anti-Russian trend in German policy had been prevailing over the older Bismarckian tradition. Even so, he was at pains to make it clear that Russia desired to remain on the same terms with the Third Reich as she had been with Weimar Germany:

Some politicians say that the U.S.S.R. has now taken an orientation towards France and Poland; that from an opponent of the Versailles treaty it has become a supporter of that treaty, and that this change is to be explained by the establishment of the fascist régime in Germany. That is not true. Of course, we are far from being enthusiastic about the fascist régime in Germany. But fascism is not the issue here, if only for the reason that fascism in Italy, for instance, has not prevented the U.S.S.R. from establishing the best relations with that country. Nor is it a question of any alleged change in our attitude towards the Versailles treaty. It is not for us, who had experienced the shame of the Brest Litovsk peace, to sing the praises of the Versailles treaty. We merely

---

[1] A special reason for his reserve was the simmering conflict between Russia and Japan. This led to two important results: In November 1933, sixteen years after the revolution, the United States, on President Roosevelt's initiative, at last granted official recognition to the Soviet Government. About the same time Russia ceded the eastern Chinese Railway to the Japanese puppet government of Manchukuo. The establishment of diplomatic relations with the United States strengthened Stalin's hand; but, on the whole, he then played from weakness *vis-à-vis* both Germany and Japan. His home front was labouring under the after-effects of collectivization.

do not agree to the world being flung into the abyss of a new war on account of this treaty.[1]

Subsequent events intensified his forebodings. Germany and Poland concluded a pact of non-aggression, which made him wonder whether Hitler was not playing on the old Polish ambition to dominate the Ukraine, an ambition of which Marshal Pilsudski had been the most outstanding exponent. He was partly reassured when Poland agreed to prolong her pact of non-aggression with Russia. At the same time Moscow proposed to Berlin the granting of a joint Russo-German guarantee of the frontiers and independence of the small Baltic states—these states formed a sort of a corridor for any army invading Russia. Hitler, not wishing to tie his hands, rejected the proposal. Henceforward the preoccupation with the security of Russia's frontiers was uppermost in Stalin's mind. The existing state of affairs was highly unsatisfactory. The northern Baltic route into Russia lay open; the use by an invader of the central route, through Poland, seemed to depend on the ambiguous attitude of the Polish Government; and an attack upon Russia's southern flank might be facilitated by the anti-Russian attitude of several Danubian states—it was only in the summer of 1934 that Czechoslovakia, Rumania, and Bulgaria established diplomatic relations with the Soviets. For the first time since Rapallo, the need for a thorough-going revision of Soviet foreign policy became apparent to Stalin.

The diplomatic game that now began between Russia and Germany's western adversaries, the game which was to last till the end of the decade, was perhaps the most intricate in modern history; and Stalin's role in it appeared more complex than anybody else's. Yet the complexity of the game was caused not by the diversity of the motives and moves of the parties concerned, but, on the contrary, by their basic simplicity and similarity. The many deadlocks and stalemates that ensued were very much like those that arise on a chessboard as a result of a long continuance of plain and strictly parallel moves on both sides of the board. Each of Germany's future enemies was torn between the illusion that war could be avoided and the dim awareness of its inevitability. Each was terrified by the

---

[1] J. Stalin, *Problems of Leninism*, pp. 465–7.

danger of isolation, and each made some moves towards building up a protective system of alliances. Each shirked definite military commitments, fearing that such commitments might bring war nearer or bring it nearer to his own frontiers. In every member of the future Grand Alliance the hope was alive that the impetus of resurrected German militarism might be diverted in some direction indifferent to his national interest. In each at first the weakness of German militarism induced passivity; and each began to play from weakness after Hitler has used that passivity in order to build up his war machine. Each of the future allies sold space for time and let down allies and friends, until no space was left to be sold and no time to be bought.

The parties concerned could not, of course, make their parallel moves simultaneously. At every phase somebody had to lead: somebody had to break the deadlocks; somebody had to be the first to sacrifice the pawns. Thus, in spite of all the similarity of the clever moves and tricks on all sides, each side paraded its self-righteousness at one moment and each looked like the villain of the piece at another. France and Britain floundered in appeasement while Russia bravely sounded the clarion of collective security. Again, when Britain was glorying in the proudest hour of her history, Russia was immersed in sordid bargaining with Germany. Then for the duration of the Grand Alliance there was mutual forgiveness, to be followed by a return to mutual denunciation soon after the cease fire.

.   .   .   .

In the course of 1934 Stalin set out on his search for protective alliances. Gradually, but not imperceptibly, he switched over from opposition to the system of Versailles to its defence. In September Russia joined the League of Nations. Hitherto the Kremlin and the League had boycotted each other. To Lenin the League had been the 'robbers' den', the organization designed to enforce the peace of Versailles, to perpetuate colonial domination and to suppress movements of emancipation all over the world. 'In order to join the League of Nations', Stalin, too, had argued, 'one would have, as Comrade Litvinov rightly said, to choose between the hammer or the anvil. Well, we do not want to be either the hammer for the weak nations, or the anvil for the mighty ones.'[1] But German revenge was worse than Versailles. Litvinov soon became the most ardent advocate of a 'strong' League that should be capable of curbing or punishing aggression. There was a touch of pacifist illusion in Stalin's new-found ardour for the League. The same might be said about his attempt to build up an eastern pact. Under that pact Russia, Germany, and all countries of eastern Europe were to pledge themselves to automatic mutual assistance if one of them became the victim of aggression. This Russian effort to create an eastern Locarno was strongly supported by Barthou, the French Minister for Foreign Affairs; but it was defeated by common German and Polish opposition.

By the beginning of 1935 Stalin had passed from the futile attempt at creating a regional, eastern European system of defence to plans for alliances with the west. In March 1935 he received Anthony Eden in the Kremlin. The future Foreign Secretary was then only a junior Minister. He had come to Moscow after similar visits to Prague and Warsaw. Almost simultaneously a senior British Minister, Sir John Simon, visited Hitler in Berlin. Eden was, nevertheless, given a cordial welcome at the Kremlin. He was the first of His Majesty's Ministers to pay an official visit in Red Moscow after many years of friction and hostility. The ice between the two countries seemed to be breaking; and Stalin spared nothing that might make it break more rapidly. He emerged from the obscurity of his General Secretariat and presided over the reception for the British guest. Against all Bolshevik custom he ordered 'God save the King' to be played. The visit, however, was not meant to produce and did not produce any specific results. Later, in May, just after Hitler had reintroduced conscription, two other important visitors, Laval and Beneš, arrived in Moscow. The Russo-French and the Russo-Czech alliances were concluded. Both Laval and Beneš were entertained by Stalin. Although nominally he was not a member of the Soviet Government, his participation in parleys with important foreign statesmen and in official receptions now became part of normal diplomatic procedure.

One incident of Laval's visit created a stir. On his return to Paris, Laval stated that Stalin had authorized him to say that

[1] J. Stalin, *Sochinenya*, vol. vii, p. 296.

he sympathized with France's effort to strengthen her defences. Hitherto the French Communist party, like all other sections of the Comintern, had on principle been opposed to national defence. Its deputies had invariably voted against military expenditure; and its rank and file had carried revolutionary propaganda into the armed forces. Stalin's statement sounded like a disavowal of that attitude; and there was a touch of scandal in the circumstance that he chose to convey it through Laval, whom the French left regarded as one of its most vicious renegades. For a time the Communist deputies in the French Chamber continued to vote against defence expenditure. The anti-militarist tradition was still too strong in the party to be so unceremoniously flouted. In addition Laval had no intention of giving effect to the alliance just concluded; he delayed its ratification in the Chamber and prevented the French military leaders from discussing plans of defence with their Russian colleagues. The Communists, therefore, had no inducement to vote for his military budgets. All the same Stalin's statement foreshadowed an important change in the Comintern.

This change was made public at the seventh congress of the International in the same year. All the theories, tactical recipes, and slogans that had been in use since 1928—the view that fascism and democracy were 'twins', the ban on co-operation with the Social Democratic leaders, and so on—were quietly relegated to the lumber rooms of the Comintern. The defence of democracy (the adjective 'bourgeois' was discreetly dropped) against fascism was declared to be the supreme task of Labour. Social Democrats and Communists were called upon to join hands and to form 'Popular Fronts' which were to include all middle-class parties and groups, Liberal, Radical, and even Conservative, who declared themselves willing to stand up against fascism. (This was a most radical departure not only from previous tactics but from the basic statutes of the Comintern, the famous 'twenty-one conditions of member-ship' drafted by Lenin and Zinoviev, which had explicitly forbidden Communists to coalesce with bourgeois parties.) Communists were not to 'frighten away' middle-class Liberals by unduly radical demands and anti-capitalist slogans. Soon after the congress the Communists became the most ardent and even vociferous supporters of national defence in the democratic countries. So earnestly did the Comintern enforce this new 'line' that from this point onward it pursued residual anti-militarism and pacifism in the ranks of the left as a dangerous heresy and it welcomed, as its virtual allies, the men of the traditionalist anti-German right, like Mandel in France and Churchill in Britain. Manuilsky, Stalin's mouthpiece in the Comintern, who had excelled everybody in his vituperations against the Social-Fascists, was replaced by Georgi Dimitrov, hero of the Leipzig trial over the Reichstag fire, whose name was now the symbol of militant anti-fascism. Stalin demonstrated his personal association with Dimitrov on every possible occasion—the Bulgarian leader invariably appeared at his side at ceremonies and parades.

Did Stalin sincerely seek alliance with the bourgeois democracies of the west? The events of 1939 seem to justify retrospective doubt. But even in 1936 the head of a French military mission to Russia wrote: 'La Russie cherche à rejeter vers l'Ouest un orage qu'elle sent monter vers l'Est ... Elle ne veut pas être mêlée au prochain conflit européen, dans lequel elle aspire à jouer comme les États-Unis l'ont fait en 1918, le rôle d'arbitre dans une Europe qui sera épuisée par une guerre sans merci.'[1] This view seems borne out by the speech of 1925, when Stalin spoke of Russia as a spectator of the future war, which the French general could not have known. Yet, in spite of all this, one feels justified in asserting that in those years, 1935-7 and even later, Stalin was genuinely striving for an anti-Hitler coalition. This course of action was dictated to him by circumstances. Everything then seemed to testify that the Bismarckian tradition of the German diplomacy had been utterly defeated. At the Nuremberg rally of September 1936 Hitler spoke about the Ukraine and Siberia as belonging to the German *Lebensraum* in terms so emphatic and fiery that they seemed to exclude even a transient understanding between himself and Stalin. Later in the year the leaders of the Axis came together to announce the conclusion of the anti-Comintern pact. Throughout all that period clashes, some of them serious, were occurring between Russian and Japanese frontier troops. The storm seemed

---

[1] These words are from a report by the French General Schweisguth to his chiefs Édouard Daladier and Léon Blum. See Georges Bonnet, *Défense de la Paix, De Washington au Quai d'Orsay*, p. 124.

to be gathering over Russia in Asia and Russia in Europe. If not anti-fascist virtue, then the demands of self-preservation drove Stalin to seek security in a solid system of alliances.[1]

His main endeavour now was to persuade the western powers to accept definite commitments or to manœuvre them into such commitments. In this he met with frustration after frustration. The Russo-French pact of mutual assistance remained a scrap of paper, even after Laval had gone and Daladier and Blum had been raised to power by the Popular Front. France and Britain failed to lift a finger in reply to Hitler's provocations, to his rearmament and his remilitarization of the Rhineland. Stalin would have been the last to believe that western appeasement was caused by weakness or shortsightedness. Weakness? But two or even three years after Hitler had reintroduced conscription, the Wehrmacht could not yet be regarded as a serious military force. Like most statesmen, Stalin still saw the French army crowned by its laurels of 1914–18; and, as we shall see later, he went on overrating it until 1940. His military and diplomatic advisers were telling him, and they were not wrong, that at that stage Germany's adversaries could stop Hitler, at least for a time, by the mere threat of military action. Shortsightedness? But was it not clear that the coalition of German big business, militarism, and nazism was not out merely to right the wrongs of Versailles and that Germany's imperialist ambition would grow with her military power? As we now know, weakness and shortsightedness were not absent among the many factors that favoured western appeasement. Yet Stalin apparently made no allowance for such frailties in bourgeois democratic statesmen.

He suspected that the French and the British acquiesced in the revival of German militarism because they hoped to turn its impetus against Russia, just as he, if he could, would have

---

[1] It was in 1935-6 that a great reform was carried out in the Red Army, resulting in its modernization and mechanization. A special feature was the reorganization of the infantry from the system of militias to that of a standing army. Tukhachevsky, the inspirer of the reform, reported on it to the Central Executive Committee of the U.S.S.R. on 15 January 1936. His speech was remarkable for its shrewd anticipation of Hitler's methods of warfare and for its extraordinary emphasis on the danger from the Third Reich. Tukhachevsky's emphatic warning sharply contrasted with Stalin's ambiguity. The English translation of Tukhachevsky's speech was published in the volume *Soviet Union 1936*, pp. 389-405.

turned it against the west. But even if he had thought that the course pursued by the western diplomacies should be attributed to defects of mind and character and not to any design against Russia, he could not be sure about this; and he had to act so as to meet the worst of all possible contingencies. It was undeniable that to the British and French ruling circles the thought of a coalition with the Soviets was still repugnant even though the old hostility towards the Soviets had partly worn off; that some leading western statesmen looked upon nazism as upon a reliable barrier against Bolshevism; and that a few among them did toy with the idea of turning that barrier into a battering ram; and that, finally, even among those who saw the inescapable need for an alliance with Russia, some wondered whether it would not be sound policy to let Germany come to grips with Russia first.

Behind all the diplomatic manœuvres, the gestures of friendship, the cold-shouldering and snubbing, there loomed the old ideological antagonism. Stalin tried to disarm the suspicions, the fears, and the prejudices of the west by moderation and pliability. He tried to lay the ghosts of the past, the giant ghost of world revolution first of all. 'We have never had such plans and intentions . . .', he pleaded with one of his foreign interviewers, who had mentioned world revolution to him. 'This is the product of a misunderstanding.' 'A tragic misunderstanding?' the interviewer interrupted. 'No, a comic one', was Stalin's reply, 'or rather a tragi-comic one.'[1] His assertion was a half truth. The Bolsheviks had indeed not planned to export ready-made revolutions; they had believed that every revolution must grow and mature on its national soil; but they had hoped to stimulate the processes of growth. . . . The *bourgeoisie* of the western countries now found it hard to believe that all this was merely a comic or tragi-comic misunderstanding.

Its distrust of Stalin was based not merely on memories. Even now Stalin could as little lay the ghost of revolution as he could forbid his own shadow to follow him. No matter how moderate and 'purely' democratic, how constitutional and 'purely' patriotic, were the slogans he had composed for the Popular Fronts, he could not undo the revolutionary potentialities of those 'Fronts'. Willy-nilly, he had to develop those potentialities and use them

[1] *Pravda*, 5 March 1936.

to his advantage. The electoral victories of the Popular Fronts in France and Spain almost automatically raised the anti-capitalist temper and the confidence of the working classes who vaguely believed them to be preludes to root and branch reform if not to revolution. The French and Spanish Communist leaders could not dissociate themselves from that mood of the masses. France was shaken by strikes, mass meetings, and demonstrations of unseen power. Spain was in the throes of civil war. The whole of western Europe was labouring under new social strains and stresses. Though the Communist leaders, pressed by Moscow, often did their best to put brakes upon the movement, events struck fear into the hearts of the middle classes, stirring latent sympathy for fascism and fanning distrust of Russia. Thus, by a curious dialectical process, the Popular Fronts defeated their own purpose. They had set out to reconcile the bourgeois west with Russia; they increased the estrangement. They had intended primarily to press reluctant governments into coalition with Russia; but as the strength of their pressure grew, it widened the gulf between the would-be allies. In the eyes of the French and British upper classes Litvinov's calls for collective security and appeals to British and French self-interest became associated with the sit-down strikes, the forty-hour week, the high wages, and the other social reforms which the Popular Front wrested from France's stagnant economy.

To achieve its positive objectives a revolution must actually take place. But to achieve a negative result, to provoke a counter-revolutionary reaction, it need do no more than cast a shadow. That reaction was rapidly mounting in France on the eve of Munich. The Popular Front was visibly disintegrating; and the Russo-French alliance was even less real than before. 'France has no confidence in the Soviet Union', Litvinov told a fellow diplomat in March 1938, 'and the Soviet Union has no confidence in France.'[1]

The Spanish civil war presented Stalin with similar dilemmas. He could not but wish Franco's defeat, not only because this followed from his anti-Fascist policy of the day, but because a Fascist régime on the Pyrenees was likely to increase French timidity *vis-à-vis* Germany. The civil war, on the other hand,

[1] Joseph E. Davies, *Mission to Moscow*, p. 189.

was fraught with revolutionary complications. The working classes, armed for the defence of the republican Government, might attempt to establish a proletarian dictatorship, Communist or Anarcho-Communist. The landless peasants, in a country as feudal as old Russia, might press for agrarian revolution. But if Spain were to have its 'October', western Europe would be split even more sharply; and the chances of agreement between Russia and the west would be even more slender. The Comintern therefore instructed its Spanish members to limit themselves to the defence of the legal republican Government against Franco. No demands were to be made for socialization of industry or expropriation of landlords. Stalin ordered Litvinov to join the committee of non-intervention, which was formed on Leon Blum's initiative; and for some time Russia was indeed conspicuous by her non-intervention in Spanish affairs.[1]

Stalin could not, however, persevere in this attitude. For one thing Hitler and Mussolini did intervene; and this alone made it very difficult for him, the protector of the left, to keep aloof. He, too, intervened, and, through the French Communists, urged France to follow his example. The least he hoped for, if France did so, was to frighten Hitler and Mussolini off Spain. But a bigger issue was at stake as well. If the western democracies had intervened, they would have gone a long way towards a definite military commitment against Germany. From being a European shooting-range, Spain might even have become the first real battlefield of the Second World War. It was precisely because they feared that the Spanish war might become the prelude to world conflict or because they were reluctant to help the Popular Front in defeating Franco, or for both these reasons, that the western governments persistently refused to intervene, even though Hitler and Mussolini were the beneficiaries of their inactivity. In the end the wrangle over Spain in the committee of non-intervention did much to exacerbate the relations between Russia, Britain, and France.

The contradictions in which Stalin involved himself led him to conduct from the Kremlin a civil war within the Spanish civil war. The extreme Spanish Anarchists and

[1] G. M. Gathorne-Hardy, *A Short History of International Affairs, 1920 to 1938*, pp. 430–2; Joaquin Maurin, *Révolution et Contre-révolution en Espagne*, pp. 131, 145.

Anarcho-Syndicalists fretted at the non-revolutionary tactics of the Communists. In Catalonia a semi-Trotskyist party, the P.O.U.M., tried to bring more social radicalism into the struggle. Stalin undertook the suppression of these unorthodox elements on the left. He made their elimination from the republic's administration a condition of the sale of Soviet munitions to its Government. He dispatched to Spain, together with military instructors, agents of his political police, experts at heresy-hunting and purging, who established their own reign of terror in the ranks of the republicans. As if to underline the grotesqueness of this performance, he put Antonov-Ovseenko, the hero of 1917 and the ex-Trotskyist, in charge of the purge in Catalonia, the stronghold of the 'heretics', only to purge Antonov-Ovseenko himself after his return from Spain. The prime motive behind all these doings was Stalin's desire to preserve for the Spanish Popular Front its republican respect-ability and to avoid antagonizing the British and the French Governments. He saved nobody's respectability and he antagonized everybody. Conservative opinion in the west, not interested in the internecine struggle of the Spanish left and confused by the intricacies of Stalin's policy, blamed Stalin as the chief fomenter of revolution.

One more reason why Russia's diplomatic stock dropped so strongly before Munich, the effect of the purges in Moscow, cannot be glossed over. In 1936 British and French generals had attended the manoeuvres of the Red Army and had, on the whole, been favourably impressed by its technique and martial qualities.[1] The purges inevitably contradicted that impression. They looked like ominous cracks in the whole edifice of the Soviets. Whether western statesmen and military men believed the charges levelled against the defendants to be true or not, their conclusions could not but detract from Russia's value as an ally. If so many outstanding politicians, administrators, and military men had in fact formed a monster fifth column, it was asked, then what was the morale of a nation in which this could happen? If the charges were faked, then was not the régime that indulged in such practices rotten from top to bottom? The issue, as we have seen, was not so simple; but this is how it presented itself to outsiders. Nor were the outsiders altogether

[1] Lt.-Gen. Sir Giffard Martel, *The Russian Outlook*, pp. 13–33.

wrong. The purges did have a most damaging effect upon the Red Army and the Soviet administration as a whole. But that effect was not so disastrous as to preclude a slow, costly, and yet sure recovery, even though external stimuli of a most extraordinary power were needed for that recovery; and it took nothing less than Hitler's attack to provide them.

. . . .

For a great variety of reasons, then, Russia was almost completely isolated on the international scene when German expansion took on its explosive character. The Munich crisis underlined that isolation and made it unendurable. Throughout the crisis Stalin kept an uneasy silence, as he was wont to do at such moments. But he felt alarmed and humiliated to the quick. 'One might think', he said a few months later, 'that the districts of Czechoslovakia were yielded to Germany as the prize for her undertaking to launch war on the Soviet Union.'[1] He could think of no other reason why Chamberlain and Daladier should have helped Hitler, of their own free will, in the partitioning of Czechoslovakia. Not only was all the talk about collective security now rendered ridiculous; not only was the League of Nations, and its Council of which Russia was a permanent member, by-passed and ignored; not only was Russia snubbed by Britain, with whom she had no formal compact; but France had as good as torn up her alliance with Russia in the eyes of the whole world. The alliances between Russia and France, France and Czechoslovakia, Russia and Czechoslovakia had been interlinked. France and Russia had been committed to take up arms in defence of Czechoslovakia; but Russia had been under the obligation to go to war only after France had already done so. Ignoring her ally's interests and *amour propre*, treating her future enemy like an actual ally and her nominal ally almost like an enemy, France invited Russia to repay her in her own coin. ('We, too, can be perfidious if we choose', Stalin might then have said to himself in the words of 'The Scythians'.) Formally, of course, Britain had had no obligations *vis-à-vis* either Russia or Czechoslovakia; but as Chamberlain, rather than Daladier, had been the initiator of the Munich deal, Britain, too, inflicted the insult and the injury.

[1] J. Stalin, *Problems of Leninism*, p. 604.

In the middle of the crisis Stalin ordered Litvinov to tell the Czechs that Russia was ready to go to war in Czechoslovakia's defence, provided the French, too, carried out their obligation. The Poles were warned that if they invaded Czechoslovakia they would be guilty of an act hostile to Russia. As France, committing a breach of faith, did not carry out her obligation, Russia had no need to keep to hers; but she committed no breach of faith. The Poles invaded Czechoslovakia and were told by Moscow that they had not, after all, been guilty of any act hostile to Russia. Once again, the question arises whether Stalin was really prepared to do in 1938 what he was not willing to do in 1939. Did he mean to keep the pledge which Litvinov repeated to the Czechs at the critical hour? If the west had then gone to war, would Stalin then have sensationally contracted out of it, all the same? The historian of those events may indulge in such speculation; but he has no means of knowing what were Stalin's innermost thoughts in September 1938. If Stalin is to be judged by his conduct at the time, there is nothing with which he can be reproached. To the last he demonstrated his readiness to fight, somewhat in the style of that brave soldier whom only an ill-timed cease-fire prevented from accomplishing a great feat of arms—only that this time the fire had not even been opened. It is probable that before Munich Stalin was in a different mood than after. The partition of Czechoslovakia changed the balance of forces in eastern Europe to Russia's grave disadvantage. The risk in Stalin's eyes was greater in 1939 than in 1938. His suspicion that the west was trying to unleash Germany on Russia was also stronger then; and so, correspondingly, was his desire to have his own back on the west.

The unwritten maxim of Munich was to keep Russia out of Europe. Not only the great and seemingly great powers of the west wished to exclude Russia. The Governments of the small eastern European nations as well squealed at the great bear: 'Stay where you are, stay in your lair.' Some time before Munich, when the French and the Russians were still discussing joint action in defence of Czechoslovakia, the Polish and the Rumanian Governments categorically refused to agree to the passage of Russian troops to Czechoslovakia. They denied the Red Army the right of passage not merely because they were afraid of communism; they fawned on Hitler. A characteristic incident, one of many, showed Stalin their state of mind: shortly before Munich half a dozen Russian aircraft were flown across Rumania to Czechoslovakia; and, though the Russians observed all traffic regulations, the incident provoked a protest, first from Colonel Beck, the Polish Foreign Minister, and then from his Rumanian colleague.[1] There were many such insults and pinpricks, which rankled a long time after.

It must have been shortly after Munich that the idea of a new attempt at a *rapprochement* with Germany took shape in Stalin's mind. The great hopes for peace, fostered by the authors of Munich, had quickly faded. It was obvious that Hitler would now seek to avoid a dispersal of his forces and concentrate them either against the west or against the east. This was the moment for Stalin to try to influence Hitler's decision. But the risk of any overtures was great: if Hitler rejected them, Russia's championship of the anti-fascist coalition would be compromised and no advantage gained; and the British and French Governments might have an excuse for giving Hitler a free hand in the east. The job that Stalin was now about to tackle required the utmost tactical elasticity. For a time he would have to run with the hare and hunt with the hounds, and to take care that the hare should not notice his presence among the hounds. He could, of course, try to sound Hitler by the normal diplomatic means; but these did not seem reliable. The German Ambassador in Moscow, Count von Schulenburg, a diplomat of the Bismarckian school, favoured Russo-German co-operation; but precisely because of this his views were not typical of those of the German Foreign Office, let alone of Hitler himself. The Russian Ambassador in Berlin, Merekalov, was a third-rate diplomat, to whom the men who really mattered in the Third Reich were almost inaccessible. Apart from this, secret exchanges might give rise to damaging indiscretions. Stalin decided, shrewdly enough, that it would be best for himself to make in public a veiled and yet transparent overture.

The eighteenth congress of the party, which assembled, after an interval of four years, in the first days of March 1939, gave him his opportunity. As General Secretary he was, as usual, to survey the domestic and foreign events of the preceding four years. His speech, the highlight of the congress, was certain to

---

[1] Georges Bonnet, *Défense de la Paix, De Washington au Quai d'Orsay*, pp. 121–40.

be listened to abroad with just enough attention to make sure that no important hint meant for foreign consumption was missed. On the other hand, any veiled overtures, made as if *en passant*, in a routine report of the General Secretary, were sure to sound less sensational than they would have sounded in any other context. When at last, on 10 March, Stalin delivered his address, that part of it in which he spoke about the international situation was a rare masterpiece of *double entendre*.

'A new imperialist war', he stated, 'is already in its second year, a war waged over huge territory, stretching from Shanghai to Gibraltar and involving over 500 million people.'[1] The term 'a new imperialist war' vaguely suggested that he viewed all the future belligerents as imperialists, from whom it behoved Russia to keep aloof. He went on to point to the connexion between an approaching slump and the war. But then he bluntly described Germany, Italy, and Japan as the 'aggressive countries' and said that they would soon try to escape from a very severe slump into world war. Dwelling on the economic background of diplomacy, he underlined the economic and also the potential military supremacy of the United States and Great Britain. The realism of his remarks lay not only in the correct valuation of the powers, but also in the tacit assumption that the United States would eventually join in the war, an assumption which at the time seemed far-fetched. Then followed a blunt attack on western appeasement: 'The war is being waged by aggressor states, who in every way infringe the interests of the non-aggressive states, primarily England, France, and the U.S.A., while the latter draw back and retreat, making concession after concession to the aggressors.' In a closely reasoned argument he analysed the motives of the appeasers: their fear of revolution, their attitude of neutrality towards the aggressors and their victims, and their desire to let Germany and Russia 'weaken and exhaust one another; and then when they had become weak enough, to appear on the scene with fresh strength . . . and to dictate conditions to the enfeebled belligerents. That would be cheap and easy.'[2] So far, his speech, for all its acid criticisms, still sounded like one of Litvinov's appeals for collective security. It suggested that Russia was not willing to

---

[1] J. Stalin, *Problems of Leninism*, p. 596.
[2] Ibid., p. 603.

engage in a single-handed fight but that she would join a broad anti-Nazi coalition. But then he suddenly turned round to say that there were no 'visible grounds' for any conflict between Russia and Germany, even though the west would like to egg on Russia against Germany. In coarsely sarcastic language he derided the western friends of nazism who had been tempting the Third Reich to attack Russia but had been disappointed by the Nazi leaders. The responsible Nazi leaders, he implied, were not among 'German madmen', dreaming about the conquest of the Ukraine, for whom Russia would find 'enough straitjackets'. He summed up by listing the objectives of his foreign policy, objectives that were mutually incompatible. He wanted Russia to do business with all countries, even though he himself had so emphatically argued that the time for normal business had passed and that world war was imminent. He wanted Russia to improve her relations with all her neighbours as long as they did not act 'directly or indirectly' against her interests—this was the principle of the sacred egoism of the Socialist state. At the same time he pledged Russia's support to all victims of Nazi aggression. He thus put all his irons into the fire. He pleaded with France, Britain, and the United States for determined action against the aggressors and thundered against appeasement; and he pleaded with the aggressors that they should leave Russia in peace, hinting that, if they did so, he, Stalin, would produce his own version of appeasement, his own Munich, worthy of Chamberlain's. The anti-Nazi motif of his argument was by far the more emphatic one; the appeaser's *ballon d'essai* was extremely elusive. He was still anxious to keep the door wide open for agreement with Britain and France; his other door, through which Ribbentrop was eventually to enter, he kept only ajar. A week after he had put out his feelers, he ordered Litvinov to denounce Hitler's march into Prague and to declare that Russia would not recognize the Nazi Protectorate.

Only the highlights of the story which unfolded in the following months can be recalled here. On 18 March, the day on which Litvinov denounced the Nazi occupation of Prague, the British Foreign Office asked what would be Russia's attitude if Rumania became a victim of aggression. Moscow proposed a conference of Britain, France, Rumania, Poland, Turkey, and Russia, a conference which, in the circumstances, would have amounted to an anti-German confederation, with Russia as one of its chief leaders. Chamberlain refused even to consider the proposal.[1] A few days later he announced the Anglo-Polish pact of mutual assistance, quickly followed by British guarantees of the independence and integrity of Rumania and Greece. Only after Britain had thus, against her tradition, committed herself in eastern Europe, did her diplomacy make a remote approach to the strongest power in that part of the world. On 15 April Russia was asked whether she would agree to guarantee the frontiers of Poland and Rumania. This was to be 'a unilateral guarantee'. The bear was still asked to stay in his lair, but he was also asked to come out of it and return to it according to the wishes of his small neighbours, who might be in need of his help.

.   .   .   .

On 17 April Stalin's diplomacy made two moves in opposite directions. He refused to enter, at the behest of Britain, into any one-sided commitment *vis-à-vis* Poland and Rumania. Instead he proposed the conclusion of an alliance and military convention between Britain, France, and Russia, after which the three powers were jointly to guarantee all the countries between the Baltic and the Black Sea against aggression. On the same day, however, the Soviet Ambassador in Berlin, Merekalov, on routine business in the German Foreign Office, cautiously broached the subject of Russo-German *rapprochement*. Stalin watched the reactions to his two moves. Those that came from Paris and London were utterly discouraging. The western powers, so it seemed, wished to be able to call on Russia as an ally in reserve, but were determined to avoid a formal coalition or, failing that, to deny her any real influence in shaping the fortunes of that coalition. They rated Poland's military strength as high, if not higher, than Russia's. The countries between the Baltic and the Black Sea again loudly declared that they wanted no alliance with their neighbour. The Baltic governments feared that the freedom of military

[1] Winston S. Churchill, *The Second World War*, vol. i, p. 273; L. B. Namier, *Diplomatic Prelude*, p. 83; *Istorya Diplomatii*, vol. iii, p. 673. A similar proposal made by Moscow after the Nazi conquest of Austria had also been rejected.

action in their lands, which Stalin demanded for himself, implied a threat to their independence. The threat was to prove only too real; but it was also true that Stalin had a strong case: he should not be expected to incur the risk of war if he was not allowed to defend the Baltic approaches to Leningrad and Moscow. The Polish Government stated that it had no need of the alliance, because in case of war the Polish army would be so fully engaged in defending its own soil that it would not be able to rush to the succour of the Red Army. Pointing to the objections of Russia's small neighbours, the western governments declined the Russian proposals. Stalin considered their references to the objections of the Baltic states to have been mere excuses; he held that the western powers, if they had desired the alliance with Russia, would have either overcome or disregarded those objections. Even now, he felt, he could expect nothing but obstruction and affront from London and Paris.

Meanwhile something seemed to stir in the net he had thrown into the Spree. On 28 April Hitler made a boisterous speech threatening Poland with war. Against his custom, he made not a single unfriendly remark on Russia. His newspapers refrained from the usual anti-Bolshevik tirades. Towards the end of April Stalin was becoming hopeful about his chances with Germany, but would not yet risk a break with France and Britain. On 3 May he dismissed from the Foreign Office Litvinov, the Jew and the man of western orientation, replacing him by Molotov, the home-bred Bolshevik, who as an 'Aryan' was better suited for eventual negotiations with the Nazis, and in whom he placed more trust than in Litvinov.

On 19 May the British Prime Minister made a few particularly disparaging remarks in the House of Commons about Russia.[1] On the morrow, on 20 May, Molotov acting on

---

[1] On that day Lloyd George made one of his formidable attacks on Chamberain, pointing out that as in 1914 the western powers could not go to war against Germany without Russia. Chamberlain thus tried to refute the analogy: 'At that time [1914] Russia and Germany had a common frontier, and Poland did not exist, but it is a satisfaction to think that, if we should become involved in war, there is that great, virile nation on the borders of Germany which under this agreement is bound to give us all the aid and assistance it can. . . . The direct participation of the Soviet Union in this matter might not be altogether in accordance with the wishes of some of the countries for whose benefit, or on whose behalf, these arrangements were being made.' In the same debate Churchill pressed the Government for a pact with Russia 'in the broad and simple form proposed by the Russian Soviet Government'. 'If you are ready', Churchill said,

Stalin's instructions established contact with Count von Schulenburg. The German had expressed the wish to renew trade negotiations that had previously broken down. Referring to this, Molotov remarked that a 'political basis' should first be created for such negotiations. In vain did the German Ambassador try to induce Molotov to say what he had in mind. 'Herr Molotov', von Schulenburg reported to Berlin, 'had apparently determined to say just so much and not a word more. He is known for this somewhat stubborn manner.'[1] Evidently it was Stalin who instructed Molotov 'to say just so much and not a word more'.[2] Having made the first move, Stalin expected Hitler to make the next. But Hitler, too, would not yet commit himself. Stalin now allowed only an obscure official, the Counsellor of the Russian Embassy in Berlin, George Astakhov, to sound more freely the German Foreign Office and to drop meaningful remarks. In case of failure, Stalin could easily disavow Astakhov and make him a scapegoat. In his caution Stalin went so far as to recall Merekalov, the Ambassador, from Berlin and to keep him away from his post throughout the spring and the summer. The Ambassador's prolonged absence was doubly useful: it burdened Moscow with less formal responsibility for Astakhov's contacts, and it served to camouflage their actual importance.

By the end of June Stalin's manœuvres in Berlin as well as in London and Paris had seemingly come to a standstill. In all capitals there was the same distrust and the same playing for time. But in the silent multilateral trial of nerves, Hitler's nerves seemed to give way first. By devious routes, through Ciano, Stalin learned that Germany was ready to switch to a pro-Russian attitude. He did not know that Ribbentrop was impatiently pressing his embassy in Moscow to make the Russians show their hand. 'We could not drag Molotov and

---

'to be an ally of Russia in time of war, . . . why should you shrink from becoming the ally of Russia now, when you may by that very fact prevent the breaking out of war? I cannot understand all these refinements of diplomacy and delay . . .' (L. B. Namier, *Diplomatic Prelude*, pp. 167–9). If Churchill could not understand those 'refinements', what wonder that they looked altogether sinister to Stalin?

[1] *Nazi-Soviet Relations*, pp. 5–7.

[2] In the later phases of the negotiations neither Molotov, who was then Prime Minister and Foreign Secretary, nor Mikoyan, the Minister of Foreign Trade, both members of the Politbureau, concealed from their German partners the fact that they were referring every detail of their parleys back to Stalin and that the decisions were Stalin's. *Nazi-Soviet Relations*, pp. 86 and 134.

Mikoyan through the Brandenburger Tor', the Embassy answered half apologetically.[1] On 22 July, when the clouds had already gathered thick and low over Poland, the Russians at last agreed to talk about trade, without insisting that the 'political basis' be laid first. But three days later London and Paris at last agreed to send their military missions to Moscow. Leading the double game into its decisive phase, Stalin continued to insure and reinsure his flanks. He still kept his front doors open for the British and the French and confined the contact with the Germans to the back stairs. He detailed the most important army chiefs and the Commissar of Defence, Voroshilov, to the talks with the western military missions. The main burden of the contact with the Nazis was still on Astakhov.

Even now, when so many documents on these events have been published, it is still impossible to say confidently to which part of the game Stalin then attached the greater importance: to the plot acted on the stage or to the subtle counter-plot which he was spinning in the twilight of the *coulisse*. What is certain is that, if the western governments had wanted to drive him into Hitler's arms, they could not have set about doing so more effectively than they did. The Anglo-French military mission delayed its departure for eleven precious days. It wasted five days more *en route*, travelling by the slowest possible boat. When it arrived in Moscow its credentials and powers were not clear. The governments whose prime ministers had not considered it beneath their dignity to fly to Munich almost at Hitler's nod, refused to send any official of ministerial standing to negotiate the alliance with Russia. The servicemen sent for military talks were of lesser standing than those sent, for instance, to Poland and Turkey.[2] If Stalin intended an alliance, the way he was treated might almost have been calculated to make him abandon his intention. If his objective was, on the contrary, to come to terms with Hitler, and he negotiated with the western powers in order to obtain a moral alibi and to be able to blame the British and the French for the abortion of the great and long-heralded anti-Nazi coalition, then the British and the French provided him with that alibi, gratuitously and with baffling zeal.

[1] *Nazi-Soviet Relations*, p. 31.
[2] L. B. Namier, *Diplomatic Prelude*, pp. 188–9.

Early in the summer of 1939 his mind was probably not yet made up. His old idea that it would be best for Russia to stay out of the war had certainly lost nothing of its attraction. Nothing would suit him better than to be first a spectator and then an arbiter in the contest to come. This ambition he could satisfy only by a deal with Hitler: an alliance with the west would have obliged Russia to fight from the first day of the war. This consideration, then, disposed Stalin to seek accommodation with his arch-enemy. But would Hitler, too, be willing to strike a bargain? A month before the outbreak of the war Stalin still had no answer to this question. Up to the end of July things had not actually progressed beyond vague soundings, i.e. not beyond the point reached in the early spring. Not a single specific move had since been made to prepare the Russo-German agreement. Given this situation, Stalin must, on the other hand, have feared that not only would he be unable to keep Russia out of the war, but that, isolated from the west, she might be the next victim of German aggression. True, between Russia and Germany there was still Poland, the immediate object of Hitler's threats; and the western powers were committed to come to Poland's aid. But, as Stalin told Churchill later, he supposed that the western powers might abandon Poland as they had abandoned Czechoslovakia; and that then Germany and Russia would directly confront each other.[1] His only insurance against this was, after all, an alliance with the western powers. Much as he preferred a deal with Hitler, he was probably still ready, in view of all the uncertainties, to join hands with that side that would be the first to come along and grasp his hand. He would probably have joined the anti-Hitler coalition if the terms offered by the western powers had allowed Russia to play in it the role he considered to be due to her. Less than three weeks before Ribbentrop's visit to Moscow, Schulenburg reported to Berlin: 'My overall impression is that the Soviet Government is at present determined to sign with England and France, if they fulfil all Soviet wishes.'[2]

In the first half of August a sharp turn occurred. Hitler unmistakably began suing for Stalin's friendship. The suitor

[1] Winston S. Churchill, *The Second World War*, vol. i, p. 305.
[2] *Nazi-Soviet Relations*, p. 41.

became more and more importunate with every day that passed. Astakhov reported growing impatience in the German Foreign Office for a friendly settlement with Russia. On 3 August Schulenburg conveyed to Molotov a message from Ribbentrop, almost recanting the anti-Comintern pact and promising 'respect for Soviet interests in Poland and in the Baltic states'.[1] Stalin's mind was now made up. He would, after all, be able to stay out of the war. But he was in no hurry yet to clasp hands with Hitler. His answer was still:

> If thou dost love, pronounce it faithfully:
> Or if thou think'st I am too quickly won,
> I'll frown and be perverse and say thee nay,
> So thou wilt woo . . .

Shaking his head, Molotov gravely told Schulenburg that he saw no change of heart in Germany yet. He opposed a German suggestion that a preamble about Russo-German friendship be inserted in the draft of the trade agreement to be concluded; and he continued to make broad hints to Schulenburg that Germany was making itself guilty of aggression against Poland.[2] When Ribbentrop, now really burning with impatience, begged for an appointment with Stalin, he was put off at first; and Stalin let Molotov answer Schulenburg's repeated queries with the invariable refrain that 'long preparations' were needed for the visit of Hitler's envoy. So now at last he, the pariah of diplomacy, was being courted by the man before whom Europe trembled.

. . . .

The time when Stalin finally resolved no longer to 'frown and be perverse' can be indicated with some precision—it was about 3.15 p.m. on 19 August. Early that afternoon Schulenburg once again requested Molotov to fix the date for his master's visit. Molotov, 'unaffected' by the German Ambassador's protests, again said that 'it was not possible even approximately to fix the time of the journey since it required thorough preparation'. Ribbentrop, he complained, had so far, in any case, offered him a pig in a poke. At 3 p.m. Molotov parted with the German Ambassador and hastened to report

---

[1] *Nazi-Soviet Relations*, pp. 39–41.   [2] Ibid., pp. 41, 47.   [3] Ibid., p. 64.

his conversation to Stalin. It was then that Stalin instructed Molotov immediately to call back Schulenburg, to hand him a draft of a pact, and to tell him that he, Stalin, would be ready to receive Ribbentrop in about a week. At 3.30 p.m. Molotov was again in touch with the German Ambassador. The next day Hitler personally requested Stalin to receive his envoy two or three days earlier.[1] War was imminent, and every day counted. Stalin consented. This was the first time the two men exchanged personal messages. Hitler's was grandiloquent and pompous. He declaimed about 'long-range policy', 'bygone centuries', &c. He could not refrain from shouting threats against Poland in hysterical soap-box style even while he was supposed to be whispering statesmanlike into Stalin's ear. He used abundantly the first person singular: 'I accept', 'I welcome', 'My Minister', 'this means to me'. Stalin's reply was correctly polite, concise, almost cool for the occasion and almost impersonal: '. . . The Soviet Government has authorized me to inform you that it agrees to Herr von Ribbentrop's arriving in Moscow on 23 August.'[2]

In the course of two meetings in the Kremlin, on the evening of 23 August and late the same night, the partners thrashed out the main issues of common interest and signed a pact of non-aggression and a 'secret additional protocol'. In the pact they undertook to remain strictly neutral towards each other if one of them should be involved in war. The document contained no assurances of friendship, except for the obligation of the two governments to settle their disputes 'through friendly exchange of opinion'. Stalin could not have had the slightest doubt that the pact at once relieved Hitler of the nightmare of a war on two fronts, and that to that extent it unleashed the Second World War. Yet he, Stalin, had no qualms. To his mind the war was inevitable anyhow: if he had made no deal with Hitler, war would still have broken out either now or somewhat later, under conditions incomparably less favourable to his country. He did not feel an incendiary—it was Hitler who was setting fire to the world. He, Stalin, was merely diverting the conflagration away from Russia. He expected Poland, as subsequent events demonstrated, to resist longer than she did. But he had no doubt that Poland would succumb and that the

---

[1] Ibid., pp. 65-7. [2] Ibid., p. 69.

western powers would not be able or willing to give her effective help.[1] Consequently he saw Germany shifting her jumping-off ground for possible attack against Russia several hundred miles eastwards. His task, as he saw it, was to reduce the strategic risk with which the change was fraught; and reduce it he could only by taking part in the dismemberment of Poland. This was arranged for in the 'secret protocol'. Thus he now came to drop the favourite maxim of his foreign policy: 'We want not a single foot of anybody's land.'

The era of Russia's territorial expansion had begun. Stalin's immediate motive was the search for security, the same search, *mutatis mutandis*, which, in the eighteenth century, made the Tsars, afraid of the growth of the Prussian military state, take part in three partitions of Poland. By this, the fourth partition, Russia was at first allotted the whole territory bounded in the west by the rivers Narev, Vistula, and San. Her frontier posts were to be placed in the suburbs of Warsaw, on the eastern bank of the Vistula. The secret protocol also allotted Finland, Estonia, and Latvia to the Russian 'sphere of influence', leaving Lithuania on the German side. Russia thus obtained the defensive *glacis* for her second capital, Leningrad, which had been badly exposed. In the south, her right to reincorporate Bessarabia was recognized; and Germany declared herself to be 'politically disinterested' in the Balkans.[2] The wording of the secret protocol was vague, because, as Ribbentrop explained later, the partners were still full of mutual distrust and feared disclosures and blackmail.[3] It was not stated what was meant by 'spheres of influence', but it was taken for granted that this implied any form of domination, including plain possession. The fate of the Balkan countries was not even discussed in any detail. At this stage Stalin could have dictated his terms in the Balkans, too, for Hitler, anxious to obtain a free hand, was very generous with other people's lands. But Stalin was acting only from immediate motives of security, without pursuing expansion for its own sake; and as Germany was not moving into the

---

[1] 'We formed the impression', Stalin told Churchill three years later, 'that the British and French Governments were not resolved to go to war if Poland were attacked, but that they hoped the diplomatic line-up of Britain, France, and Russia would deter Hitler. We were sure it would not' (Winston S. Churchill, *The Second World War*, vol. i, p. 305).

[2] *Nazi-Soviet Relations*, p. 78.   [3] Ibid., pp. 157-8.

Balkans, he did not move either. The exception was Russian-speaking Bessarabia, whose annexation by Rumania during the revolution had never been recognized by Moscow.

What were Stalin's ideas about the war? How solid did he think was his agreement with Hitler? It is not known whether at that stage he looked back to the historical precedent, which he was so frequently to invoke after 1941—the alliance and the war between Alexander I and Napoleon. But often he did behave as if he had that precedent before his eyes. He now had *his* peace of Tilsit, though, unlike his crowned predecessor, he had not met his partner on a raft fixed in the middle of a river. After Tilsit, Alexander I had a breathing space of four years, and he clashed with Napoleon only towards the end of a long series of wars. That Stalin hoped for a respite of similar length follows from almost every step he took before Hitler disillusioned him in June 1941. That he had little confidence in Hitler's victory is equally certain. His purpose now was to win time, time, and once again time, to get on with his economic plans, to build up Russia's might and then throw that might into the scales when the other belligerents were on their last legs.[1]

That such were his views can be inferred even from his talks with Ribbentrop. Of these we have only Ribbentrop's record, which is not very complete and may be inaccurate on some points, but which, nevertheless, reproduces Stalin's part in a fashion which seems true to character. No other version has been produced by the Soviet sources, and surely they would have hastened to point out any flagrant inaccuracies in Ribbentrop's account.[2]

Stalin and Hitler's envoy talked to each other in the specious tone of reconciled enemies who are trying to disguise with false and over-emphatic cordiality a long record of hostility. 'Tell

[1] 'Lastly we require time', Stalin had said at the congress in March. 'Yes, Comrades, time. We must build new factories. We must train new cadres for industry. But this requires time, and no little time at that. We cannot outstrip the principal capitalist countries economically in two or three years' (*Problems of Leninism*, p. 611). Both Stalin and Molotov at the congress spoke about Russia's economic achievements with relative sobriety and restraint, which strikingly contrasted with earlier over-optimism. The new tone was needed to justify indirectly extreme caution in foreign policy.

[2] Wherever this was possible, the author has checked the versions of diplomatic events in Moscow, as given in *Nazi-Soviet Relations*, with leading diplomatic personalities involved in these events.

me', says one of them in effect, 'what dirty trick did you try on me on this or that occasion? I may also tell you a few inside stories that will interest you.' The reconciled foes affect *bonhomie*, drink and laugh and let themselves go, but each is on guard and wary of letting out a single important item of information or making a single untimely move. They promise each other endless friendly services, apart from the deal they are about to conclude; but none of these promises will be kept.

Such was, indeed, the friendly gossip between Stalin and Ribbentrop. The English, says Ribbentrop, have spent five million pounds to bribe Turkish politicians. Oh, Stalin butts in, they have spent more than that, I can assure you. The conversation shifts to the anti-Comintern pact. Only the City of London and small British merchants have got excited over that, Stalin swaggeringly remarks. You know, Ribbentrop grows familiar, in Berlin they say that you, too, are going to join the anti-Comintern soon. Jokes alternate with pin-pricks. Every now and then Stalin implies that he still regards Hitler as the aggressor and that, though Hitler may want war, the German people want peace. Stalin 'comments adversely' on the British military mission in Moscow, on whom he has just sprung the surprise of his pact with Hitler, obviously relishing their bewilderment and humiliation. But he tells Ribbentrop nothing of the content of his long negotiations with the British and the French, gives him none of the military information, important or unimportant, exchanged between the military missions. He puts Ribbentrop off by the remark that the British military mission 'never told the Soviet Government what it really wanted'. Then again, Ribbentrop offers his own and the Führer's services in bringing about a *détente* between Japan and Russia, only to hear from Stalin that he, the Caucasian, knows the Asiatics better than Ribbentrop.[1] (We shall soon hear Stalin dropping again this characteristic remark: 'I am an Asiatic.') Ribbentrop has another 'friendly service' up his sleeve: he has been instructed by Hitler to tell Stalin that Germany is not interested in Constantinople and the Straits. But, although Turkey has been discussed, Constantinople and the Straits are not even mentioned, evidently because Stalin, contrary to Hitler's expectation, has not yet developed any interest

---

[1] *Nazi-Soviet Relations*, p. 251.

in the topic. He merely nods assent when Hitler's envoy complains of the unreliability of the Turks.

He tries to draw Ribbentrop out on Italy's military plans, but obtains little enlightenment. The conversation then shifts to England and France. Stalin comments on Britain's inadequate armament and vents his anti-English feelings: 'If England dominates the world . . . this is due to the stupidity of the other countries that always let themselves be bluffed. It is ridiculous, for example, that a few hundred British should dominate India'; but he adds that 'England, despite its weakness, will wage war craftily and stubbornly', a view which is obviously not shared by the Nazi Foreign Minister.[1] Nor does Ribbentrop agree with Stalin's high opinion of the French army. Here we reach the major premiss of Stalin's policy, and his major blunder: he expected Britain and France to hold their ground against Germany for a long time; he appreciated correctly Britain's military weakness and her determination to fight; he overrated France's military strength; and he underrated Germany's striking power. He was the last man to suppose that he would have to meet the second anniversary of his pact with Hitler with the cry: 'Death to the German invader.'

. . . .

Stalin's first, not very important, miscalculation was already apparent in the first days of September. He was surprised by the rapidity with which Polish armed resistance collapsed. When, on 5 September, Ribbentrop began to press the Russians to march into their share of Poland, Stalin was not yet ready to issue the marching orders.[2] He was now given over to scruples and second thoughts. He would not openly lend a hand in defeating Poland, and he refused to budge before Poland's collapse was complete beyond doubt. His second thoughts concerned the fixed demarcation line which left part of ethnical Poland on the Russian side. This he was in no mood now to annex, for that would be too flagrant a violation of the

---

[1] Ibid., pp. 72–6.

[2] Ibid., p. 91. The error about Poland, almost endemic, reflected the illusory nature of that scale of international power which prevailed between the wars. As long as Germany was disarmed and Russia half disarmed, the importance of the Polish army was naturally inflated beyond measure. But the illusory scale of power was still in use, even after the real relationship of power had fundamentally changed.

professed principles of Bolshevik policy. He now preferred to shift the demarcation line farther east, from the Vistula to the Bug, so that only lands with a predominantly Ukrainian and Byelorussian population should be left on the Russian side. The reunion of those lands with the Soviet Ukraine and Byelorussia could be politically justified.[1] It would permit the Red Army to cross the frontier not as a conqueror of Poland but as the liberator of the Ukrainians and the Byelorussians, the 'blood brethren' as he now called them, having caught a germ of racialism from his Nazi partners. While Stalin delayed action, Ribbentrop began blackmailing him with a political 'vacuum' in eastern Poland, in which 'new states' might spring into being.[2] The 'new states' could be headed only by anti-Soviet Ukrainian nationalists. Hitler also objected to a communiqué proposed by Stalin, which was to state that the Red Army had crossed the border to protect the Ukrainians and the Byelorussians from the Nazis. Meanwhile, Stalin became uneasy as he saw the Wehrmacht operating already in eastern Poland; and he asked the German Ambassador for a reassurance that it would withdraw from there.[3] For a while he reflected whether a Polish rump state should not be set up. Then he gave up the idea and issued the marching orders for the Red Army.

At the end of September Ribbentrop was again in the Kremlin, banqueting all night and listening to Stalin's second thoughts. A new bargain was made: Germany retained the whole of ethnical Poland, and Lithuania was allotted to the Soviet zone.

Impressed by Hitler's lightning victory over Poland, Stalin lost much of his self-confidence. The phoney war in the west made him apprehensive: were the British and the French not

---

[1] Poland acquired these lands under the peace of Riga in 1921. The hope of a reunion of all Ukrainian lands was always alive on both sides of the frontier. The Ukrainian nationalists strove to achieve reunion and independence from both Russia and Poland. The Communists, at times very influential among the peasantry of Poland's 'eastern marches', aimed at a reunion under the Soviets. Even among those Communists who felt uneasy over Stalin's deal with Hitler, the reunion of the Ukrainian lands was extremely popular. As recently as the summer of 1939 Trotsky could still write: 'Stalin, Dimitrov and Manuilsky . . . are ready to give away the western Ukraine to Poland for ever, in exchange for a diplomatic pact' (Bulleten Oppozitsii, no. 77–8).

[2] Nazi-Soviet Relations, pp. 93–4.

[3] Ibid., p. 98.

holding back their fire in order to encourage Hitler to attack Russia? Now it was he who was zealously offering friendly services to Hitler. The pact of non-aggression was supplemented by a treaty of friendship, which declared that it was an exclusive Russo-German task 'to re-establish peace and order' in Poland and 'to assure to the peoples living there a peaceful life in keeping with their national character'.[1] The western powers had no right to dispute German and Russian acquisitions. Gone was Stalin's cool reserve. Before the whole world he now assumed co-responsibility for the horrors of the Nazi occupation of Poland. He showed himself not merely Hitler's business partner, but also his accomplice. In a special secret protocol both governments obliged themselves to work hand in hand to suppress Polish propaganda for the restoration of Poland's independence.[2] Crowning the work was a joint declaration which called for immediate peace and shifted responsibility for the continuation of war on England and France.[3] In lending his support to this 'peace offensive' of Hitler's, Stalin surpassed himself in hypocrisy. Nobody was now praying for the prolongation of war more ardently than he. If the western powers had now concluded an armistice and acquiesced in the German conquest of Poland, Hitler would probably have attacked Russia in the summer of 1940.

This dissimulation was to characterize Stalin's behaviour towards Hitler right up to June 1941: the more acutely he distrusted the Führer and feared his aggression, the louder and the more ostentatious were his declarations of friendship. His talk grew less friendly and his gestures stiffer whenever Hitler's forces seemed to be pinned down far from Russia's frontiers. There was to be give and take in their deal. Stalin, of course, wished to give as little as possible and take as much as he could. Russia was to supply Germany with grain and raw materials and to receive German machines and machine tools. One of the first things Stalin did, after the conclusion of the pact, was to dispatch his military missions to Germany. With what avidity those missions tried, in the first flush of friendship, to ferret out the German war factories can be seen from the complaints about their 'excessive curiosity', which Göring, Keitel, and Räder were already lodging at the beginning of

[1] Ibid., p. 105. [2] Ibid., p. 107. [3] Ibid., p. 108.

October.[1] A little later the Nazi economic leaders complained that the Russians wanted too many machine tools for the production of artillery and too much other war material.

No sooner had the Polish campaign been finished than Stalin began to cast uneasy glances at the vast no-man's land that lay between Russia and Germany. Since August, in fact, the Baltic countries had ceased to be a no-man's land. In September and October Russian troops were already garrisoned in Estonia, Latvia, and Lithuania. The three countries still retained their old régimes and governments; and Stalin acted as if he had no intention of doing more than secure strategic bases. For the first time he now betrayed a passing anxiety about the Balkans, the real no-man's land. In October, Molotov asked the Bulgarians to conclude an alliance with Russia. The Bulgarians refused, and Stalin did not pursue the matter. His attention was now absorbed by the embarrassing conflict with Finland, which had refused to grant Russia strategic bases, needed for the defence of Leningrad, or to regard herself as part of the Russian sphere of influence.

The Russo-Finnish war broke out on 30 November 1939. That military expediency should impel Stalin to wage this war was one of history's malicious whims: for it was he who had, in the first month after the October Revolution, proclaimed Finland's independence. The Finns now defended themselves tooth and nail. At first the war brought them important successes. These were in part due to accidents of climate and in part to the weakness of the Russian command after the recent purges. Russia's prestige and bargaining power sharply declined for a time. The adventure threatened grave complications. In Britain and France sympathy for Finland ran high; the two allied Governments officially promised military aid; armies of volunteers were recruited in both countries; and, while an uncanny calm reigned over the Siegfried Line and the Maginot Line, the French Government announced that a numerous army under General Weygand was concentrated in the Middle East, opposite Russia's vulnerable Caucasian frontier. On 14 December Russia was expelled from the League of Nations, which had always been so indulgent towards the Third Reich and Fascist Italy. Stalin had some ground for wondering

[1] *Nazi-Soviet Relations*, p. 127.

whether the western powers were not going to 'switch' the war from Germany to Russia. The Finnish game was not worth the candle; but he was so deeply involved that he could not withdraw from it. It was in this mood of uncertainty that he celebrated his sixtieth birthday in December 1939. He used the opportunity to assure Hitler of his friendship in a manner as ridiculous as it was unworthy: 'The friendship of the peoples of Germany and the Soviet Union', he cabled Hitler in reply to a birthday message, 'cemented by blood, has every reason to be lasting and firm.'[1] How much would Stalin have given later to have this phrase deleted from the records.

In March 1940 the Finnish war was over. The prestige of Russian arms was in part restored. Hitler was now preparing his invasions in western Europe; and the fear of a 'stab in the back' from Stalin was probably not completely absent from his mind. Once again the two changed roles. On 28 March Ribbentrop cabled his ambassador in Moscow: 'The Führer will not only be particularly happy to welcome Stalin in Berlin, but he would also see to it that he would get a reception commensurate with his position and importance. And he would extend to him all the honours that the occasion demanded.'[2] Stalin was in no hurry to receive the honours or, like another Duce, to review parades by Hitler's side. Not even Molotov hastened to accept the invitation. Count von Schulenburg sweetened the pill for the Führer and explained Stalin's reserve by his 'inhibitions against appearing in strange surroundings'.[3]

Soon came the events that gave Stalin the rudest shock—the rapid collapse and surrender of France and the withdrawal of the British from the Continent. Stalin's strategic calculations, too, now collapsed.[4] Fearing a *tête-à-tête* with Hitler in Europe, he bolted the Baltic door to Russia without a moment's delay. Distrusting the Baltic governments, who looked ideologically to Berlin rather than to Moscow, he dispatched Zhdanov to Estonia, Vyshinsky to Latvia, and Dekanozov to Lithuania, with orders to overthrow the governments on the spot, to set

---

[1] *Pravda*, 25 December 1939.   [2] *Nazi-Soviet Relations*, p. 135.
[3] Ibid., p. 136.
[4] Ribbentrop was not quite wrong when later in the year he told the Japanese Foreign Minister Matsuoka 'in confidence' that 'the Soviet Union wanted the war to last as long as possible. . . . The exceedingly rapid defeat of France did not suit that sly politician Stalin very well' (ibid., p. 305).

up new Communist-controlled administrations and to prepare the incorporation of the three republics in the Soviet Union.

A new and important shift thus occurred in Stalin's foreign policy. His first move in the Baltic lands, the establishment of bases, had been dictated solely by strategic expediency. He had apparently had no intention of tampering with their social system. His sense of danger, heightened and intensified by the collapse of France, now impelled him to stage revolutions in the three small countries. For the first time he now departed, in a small way, from his own doctrine of socialism in one country, the doctrine that he had so relentlessly inculcated into a whole Russian generation. He departed from it in the same un-premeditated, pragmatic manner in which he had arrived at it. But what he did was very different from the spread of revolution of which the old Bolsheviks had dreamt. He carried revolution abroad on the point of the bayonet or rather on the caterpillars of his tanks. The Baltic working classes probably supported the socialization of industry he decreed; but what was decisive was Russia's armed power, not the popular sentiment on the spot. The old Bolsheviks had, as a rule, imagined revolution primarily as a popular movement, as the work of the toiling masses, organized and led by their own party. Now, the Red Army substituted itself for that party. The upheaval was a mechanical by-product of the strategy of a great power.

Such upheavals could hardly have been carried through in any great or even medium-sized country, whose social organism pulsated with its own life blood. The three tiny republics with their expensive, comic-opera police régimes, were simply crushed by the stirring of their great neighbour. They had owed their existence in part to Russia's weakness in 1918 and in part to early Bolshevik generosity. Stalin's Russia was neither weak nor generous; and so Stalin appeared on the Baltic coast as the collector of old Russian possessions, the claimant to a portion of the Tsarist patrimony. *Vis-à-vis* the outside world he, now, in 1940, impersonated that role for the first time. The September before he still shrank before the annexation of a slice of ethnical Poland which had belonged to the Tsars and he had contented himself with lands to which Russia's ethnical claim was at least as valid as Poland's. Now he annexed the Baltic states to which Russia neither had nor pretended to have any ethnical claim whatsoever. Yet he could not openly refer to the Tsarist title-deeds—Bolshevik orthodoxy still forbade him to do that. Nor did that orthodoxy allow him to admit that he was overruling the will of small and weak neighbours for strategic reasons, for, by Leninist standards, this smacked of imperialism. To save appearances, he falsified the popular will and staged plebiscites, in which Estonians, Latvians, and Lithuanians begged to be absorbed in the Soviet Union. His conduct was not more reprehensible than that of any other leader of a great power holding fast to or seizing strategic bases. But in appearance it was more odious, because it contrasted so sharply with the principles he professed and because he resorted to such crude tricks to cover up that contrast.[1]

Throughout the summer he watched vigilantly Hitler's reaction to the sovietization of the Baltic states. On the whole, Hitler still kept his part of the bargain and did not interfere. Nor did he put obstacles in Stalin's way when Stalin detached Bessarabia and northern Bukovina from Rumania. These were the last acts of their smooth co-operation.

Late in the summer of 1940, during the Battle of Britain, Stalin's tactics became even more tortuous than hitherto. He was still sceptical about Hitler's victories, sweeping and overwhelming as these were; but he apparently also reckoned with the possibility of Britain's surrender. At any rate, he did his best to give Hitler the impression that he, Stalin, believed Hitler's triumph to be almost final and that Russia was ready to adjust herself to, and to settle down in, the Nazi 'new order'. Soon after the French surrender, Molotov, knowing well that his words would at once be reported to Hitler, told the Italian Ambassador that his Government regarded the war as nearly finished and that Russia's main interest was now in the Balkans, where she wanted to spread her influence to Bulgaria and to deprive Turkey of

---

[1] Stalin's treatment of Finland was, of course, different. By the peace of 1940 Finland had ceded the strategic bases demanded from her, but she was not then absorbed in the Soviet Union. In part this was due to the Finns' own attitude—an attempt to absorb their country might have led to another war—and to the sympathy which the west had shown for their fight. In part, however, Stalin's exceptional 'mildness' towards Finland, now and in 1945, may have been due to the fact that he himself had proclaimed her independence. This had been his first important appearance as Commissar of Nationalities. To this feat he may have looked back with enough pride and sentiment to prevent his disavowing his own pledge.

exclusive control over the Straits. Ostensibly, Stalin was thus claiming his share in the spoils of Hitler's 'final' victory. Actually, his claims were dictated by his fear of German encirclement in the south. To Hitler they looked like Russian attempts at the encirclement of Germany. Jockeying for positions in the Balkans filled the second year of their *soi-disant* friendship.

While to Hitler Stalin was expressing confidence in a rapid conclusion of the war, his diplomatic envoys and agents abroad encouraged every sign of resistance to the 'new order'. The newspapers of Moscow, which hitherto had only disparaging remarks for the allies, began to report sympathetically the Battle of Britain and to call upon French patriots to resist the subjugation of their country. Even before this the German Foreign Office had had to protest against the anti-Nazi propaganda in which Madame Kollontai, the Soviet Minister in Sweden, had indulged.[1]

Such sallies, however, were made stealthily or by people for whom Stalin could disclaim responsibility. The dominant tone was still one of friendship for Germany. Above all Stalin carefully avoided giving Hitler the impression that he was seeking contact with Great Britain, Hitler's only enemy erect and fighting. On the other hand, he had every reason to keep in touch with the British. In the beginning of July 1940 he personally received the new British Ambassador, Sir Stafford Cripps, an honour which, since Ribbentrop's visit, he had bestowed on no other foreign envoy. The new Ambassador had distinguished himself as a champion of Anglo-Russian friendship; and his appointment was a mark of the importance that Winston Churchill even now attached to good relations with Russia. It was as awkward for Stalin to acknowledge this gesture as not to do so. He listened to the British Ambassador on the danger that German imperialism spelt to Russia, a danger of which he was only too well aware, and—this was more novel— on Russia's exclusive right to maintain the *status quo* in the Balkans and to safeguard her interests in the Straits and in the Black Sea. But he refused to show his hand. He denied that there was any German threat to Russia and rejected the suggestion of Russia's exclusive rights in the Balkans, though he

---

[1] *Nazi-Soviet Relations*, p. 147.

confirmed his desire for a new settlement in the Straits. Wary of dropping a single word that could be interpreted as an expression of sympathy, he talked in an evasive though not unfriendly manner. He held that it was natural for the British to want to embroil Russia with Germany and that a single incautious phrase of his, especially if it were reported in the British newspapers, might precipitate the Russo-German conflict. He carried his caution so far as to instruct Molotov to give Count Schulenburg an appropriate version of his conversation with the British Ambassador. In that version Stalin was reported to have talked much more harshly than he did and to have uttered flattering remarks about 'leading German statesmen'.[1]

Even before the Battle of Britain was over, the competition between Russia and Germany for the Balkan no-man's land became open. Without consulting the Kremlin, Hitler drew new frontiers for Hungary and Rumania. He also gave Rumania a guarantee of her changed frontiers, which was implicitly directed against Russia. German troops appeared in Rumania and in Finland. When Molotov protested against these breaches of previous agreements, he was told that the Wehrmacht had moved into the two countries to forestall the 'English menace'. Throughout the no-man's land points of friction multiplied. Eastern and south-eastern Europe was rapidly becoming too small to hold both Hitler and Stalin; and it was Hitler who was saying: ôte-toi pour que je m'y mette.

Stalemated in the war against Britain, Hitler could no longer look with indifference on the might of the Red Army in the east. He could now remain at peace with Russia only if Stalin agreed to join his camp and thus become his satellite. He made an attempt to reduce Stalin to that role, trying to make it as attractive as possible. 'In the opinion of the Führer . . .', Ribbentrop wrote to 'My dear Herr Stalin' on 13 October 1940, '. . . it appears to be the historical mission of . . . the Soviet Union, Italy, Japan, and Germany to adopt a long range policy' and to carry out a 'delimination of their interests on a world-wide scale'.[2] Hitler did not repeat his once rejected invitation to Stalin. Instead, he asked Molotov to come to Berlin and let Ribbentrop try to fix a date to talk with Stalin

[1] Ibid., p. 167.   [2] Ibid., p. 213.

in the Kremlin. Assuming that the proposal for a pact of four powers would be accepted, Ribbentrop informed Stalin that he was ready to come to Moscow for the great occasion, along with Japanese and Italian envoys.

To Ribbentrop's long and bombastic message Stalin replied briefly, drily, and with a week's delay.[1] He was not 'in principle' opposed to Ribbentrop's suggestions, but would not be rushed. He was willing to send Molotov to Berlin and to see Ribbentrop in Moscow, but 'joint deliberations with the Japanese and the Italians' must—the favourite excuse again!—be preceded by much 'previous examination'.[2] From the accounts of Molotov's behaviour in Berlin it is easy to infer how Stalin briefed him for the mission: Molotov was to listen attentively, with a friendly mien, to all suggestions, to accept no new commitments, and to bargain hard over Balkan stakes.

The tale with which Molotov returned from Berlin was briefly this: Hitler in person had repeated the proposal for the pact of four powers, evidently hoping that Russia's adherence might move Britain to surrender. Russia would be rewarded with a portion of the British Empire, that 'gigantic world-wide estate in bankruptcy, of forty million square kilometres'. The four powers that would partition the 'bankrupt estate' should stop quarrelling among themselves. The Führer held that in the long run, the interests of Germany, Russia, Japan, and Italy required expansion in one direction only—southward. Germany and Italy would build their colonial empires in Africa; Japan was building hers in south Asia; and Russia should expand in the direction of India. Molotov had tried hard to turn the conversation from the alluring vistas painted by Hitler to smaller matters nearer home. To him one Balkan bird in the hand was worth all the oriental birds in all the bushes of the British Empire. He tried to get Hitler to disentangle the Russian and the German spheres of influence in south-eastern Europe. In this he failed.

The step that Stalin now took was of the gravest consequence. It amounted to a rejection of Hitler's proposals. Nominally, he agreed to join in the pact of the four powers, but before he did

---

[1] In that week President Roosevelt, who had earlier in the year imposed a moral embargo upon exports to Russia, made a speech in which he referred to Russia as to a 'great friendly power'.　　　　　　　　　[2] Ibid., p. 216.

so he wanted Hitler to withdraw troops from Finland, to recognize that Bulgaria belonged to the Russian sphere of influence, to help Russia in obtaining a long-term lease of bases in the Straits, and so on. Hitler could have accepted such terms only if he had given up all plans to attack Russia and if he himself had not feared any Russian attack. Neither was the case. The idea of a four-power pact was dropped and never mentioned again. Three weeks after he had received Stalin's reply Hitler gave his chiefs of staff his first instruction on the campaign against Russia, the directive 'Barbarossa'.

In the first few months of 1941 Russia was completely squeezed out of the Balkans; and the Kremlin vented its displeasure. In January it suddenly announced that it had not been consulted about the entry of German troops to Bulgaria and had not agreed to it. In March the protest was repeated in even blunter terms. Every sign of opposition to Hitler was now encouraged. The Yugoslav Ambassador in Moscow, Gavrilovich, was received at the Kremlin 'as a brother; there he discussed, plotted and signed agreements in all confidence. Stalin . . . had himself photographed at his side and . . . discussed the friendly prospects with him throughout the night. "And if the Germans, displeased, turn against you?" . . . asked the Yugoslav Minister. . . . "Let them come!" . . . replied the dictator, smiling.'[1] On 4 April 1941 Russia concluded a pact of friendship with Yugoslavia; and Molotov told the German Ambassador that he expected Germany to keep peace with the southern Slavs, only to hear from the Ambassador two days later that the Wehrmacht was about to attack both Greece and Yugoslavia.

There was only one march that Stalin still succeeded in stealing on Hitler before they confronted one another as open enemies. On 13 April 1941 he received Matsuoka, the Japanese Foreign Minister, and negotiated a pact of neutrality. That pact freed Russia from the danger of a war on two fronts; and it also untied Japan's hands for the war in the Pacific. Matsuoka had just come back from Berlin, where Hitler and Ribbentrop had given him broad hints of the forthcoming German attack on Russia and had urged him to refrain from concluding any pact in Moscow. But Japan as well as Russia now feared war

[1] G. Gafencu, *Prelude to the Russian Campaign*, p. 192.

on two fronts; and that fear was stronger than ideological friendships and antagonisms.

During Matsuoka's visits to Moscow—the first in March 1941 and the second in April 1941—Stalin was unusually animated and even talkative. 'We both are Asiatics', he told his visitor. He took up that motif repeatedly. In part this was diplomatic cant. In part Stalin was preening himself on his descent. The Asiatic element in Russia had been exalted ever since his ascendancy; and now he himself carried that exaltation to the highest pitch. It was as if he were seeking to remind people that Russia owed her precious peace to him, who had risen from the borderland between Asia and Europe. He delighted in demonstrating his Asiatic outlook to his Japanese guest. Both had a peculiar way of wearing their hearts on their sleeves and holding their daggers up their sleeves. Matsuoka, the scion of a great feudal family, introduced himself as a 'moral communist'. Stalin listened to the stories about the heroic exploits of Matsuoka's ancestors and to his assurances that Japan was fighting in China not the Chinese, but Anglo-Saxon liberalism bent on overthrowing Japan's 'moral communism'.[1] From political philosophy the two men turned to bargaining over concessions in northern Sakhalin. They bargained hard, in oriental fashion; and Stalin gesticulated to show that Matsuoka—the heartless creature—was out to strangle him.

In his 'Asiatic' *panache* Stalin had an ulterior motive. He had just drawn his conclusions from the fact that, despite his resistance, Germany had become the master of the Balkans and had not left an inch of European land open to the expansion of Russian influence. He had had to put up with his reverse. Six months before he had sent Molotov to haggle with Hitler over Russian interests in Europe. Now he was trying, in his cryptic manner, to convey to Hitler that he, Stalin, had withdrawn from the contest and that he was ready to content himself, as Hitler had advised him through Molotov, with advantages in Asia. On the day of Matsuoka's departure from Moscow,

[1] This was during Matsuoka's first visit in March 1941. A few days later Matsuoka told the Pope that his country was fighting not the Chinese but Bolshevism which was supported in Asia by the Anglo-Saxons. Shortly before his second visit to Stalin he suggested to Hitler the revival of the anti-Comintern pact. *Nazi-Soviet Relations*, pp. 297 and 313.

18 April, he made an ostentatious gesture calculated to bring his new attitude to Hitler's notice. Quite unexpectedly, he emerged from his seclusion to see off the Japanese Minister at the railway station. In the presence of a large gathering of foreign correspondents and astonished diplomats, he embraced his 'fellow Asiatic'; and then, to quote Schulenburg, he 'publicly asked for me and when he found me came up to me and threw his arm around my shoulders: "We must remain friends and you must now do everything to that end!" Somewhat later Stalin turned to the German . . . military attaché, Colonel Krebs, first made sure that he was a German, and then said to him: "We will remain friends with you in any event." [1] Hitler and Ribbentrop could not possibly have missed the meaning of all this. Stalin was, as it were, taking up their proposals of November and indicating his desire to negotiate.

Too late! In the next few weeks Moscow and Berlin fired protests at each other against violations of the frontier. German planes were flying over Russian territory and Russian planes were reconnoitring German terrain. About 150 German divisions were concentrated on the frontier. They were confronted by a slightly superior number of Russian divisions. It was in those days, about the end of April, that Stalin received the British message, which Churchill was to mention in his speech of 22 June, warning him of the imminence of the German attack. So precise was the warning, according to some versions, that it mentioned 22 June, the anniversary of Napoleon's invasion of Russia, as the probable date of the German invasion. [2]

At least two men in Moscow refused to take the warning seriously: Stalin and von Schulenburg. The German Ambassador's mistake is understandable. He was true to his Bismarckian tradition and hoped that the friction between Germany and Russia would not lead to war. In the last days of April he went to Hitler to plead for peace, just as another Ambassador, Caulaincourt, had pleaded with Napoleon against

---

[1] Ibid., p. 324.

[2] The German naval attaché in Moscow, reporting to Berlin that that date had been mentioned by Sir Stafford Cripps, commented that it was 'absurd'. Ibid., p. 330. A similar warning about the German attack was conveyed to Moscow by the United States Government earlier in the year. See Sumner Welles, *The Time for Decision*, p. 136.

the invasion of Russia, 130 years before. Schulenburg brought with him a Russian offer of five million tons of grain to be delivered to Germany next year; and he tried to explain to Hitler the concentration of Russian troops on the frontier by the 'well-known Russian urge for three hundred per cent. security. If for any reason we sent *one* German division, they would send ten for the same purpose in order to be completely. safe. I could not believe that Russia would ever attack Germany.'[1] But Hitler was not to be moved.

That Stalin, too, hoped that the peace between Russia and Germany could still be saved may seem almost incredible. Yet this follows from his whole behaviour in these critical weeks. He now committed one of those errors to which the over-cunning are sometimes liable. He dismissed all ill omens and was confident that he, by himself, with his tactical skill and flair for sharp political turns, could retrieve the situation.

On 6 May Moscow was startled by the news that Stalin had become Prime Minister. What made him step out of the General Secretariat, for the first time since 1923, and assume direct responsibility for the Government? Grave, fateful decisions were in the balance. What were they to be? The last May Day parade had been turned into an unusual display of military power. On the eve of his appointment Stalin had attended military exercises at the War Academy and had made a long, secret speech to the graduating officers, extolling the valour of the Red Army. Was it war then? Hitler's opponents watched with bated breath the first steps of Stalin, the Prime Minister; and they were appalled. He denied the rumours of strong military concentrations on the frontier; he resumed diplomatic relations with the pro-German Government of Iraq, which he had previously refused to recognize; and—most amazing of all —he asked the Belgian, Norwegian, and Yugoslav envoys in Moscow to close their embassies and leave Russia, because their Governments had ceased to exist. This last act, and even more so the allegation by which he supported it, was obviously meant to placate Hitler; and it is difficult to say which was more astounding in them: his lack of scruple or his short-sightedness. Yet, while going out of his way to regain Hitler's confidence, he also feared that in doing so he might infect his own people

---

[1] *Nazi-Soviet Relations*, pp. 331–2.

with weakness and defeatism. He therefore kept secret from the Russian people and the Red Army his decision to wind up the three embassies. Then he waited a whole month to see whether Hitler would show any sign of appreciation. No sign came.

He made one last desperate and tragi-comic effort. On 14 June, exactly one week before the German invasion, he authorized his news agency to publish a statement which, against all diplomatic custom, violently attacked the British Ambassador for spreading rumours of an 'impending Russo-German war'. The statement, in which Stalin's hand could easily be recognized, denied that Germany had made any economic or territorial demands on Russia, and that, because Russia had rejected them, the two countries were completing their preparations for war. Contradicting several of Molotov's secret notes to Ribbentrop, Stalin now credited Germany with 'fulfilling to the letter' her agreements with Russia; and, though he no longer denied that great armies were standing on both sides of the frontier, he described as 'false, nonsensical and provocative' all suggestions that either the German or the Russian troops were there to wage war.[1]

It would be difficult to find, even in the diplomatic records of the Second World War, anything quite as pathetic. And yet this bizarre statement, where Stalin praised before the whole world those who next week were to unmask themselves as Russia's mortal enemies and taunted those who next week would be her only allies, this bizarre statement was not wholly false. It was true, as Stalin claimed, that Germany had made no demands on Russia. He evidently expected Hitler to raise demands over which it would be possible to bargain. German attacks on Austria, Czechoslovakia, and Poland had indeed been preceded by open claims and loud threats. Stalin apparently thought that Hitler would act according to precedent. Because he did not see the usual danger signals he refused to admit the imminent danger. In his statement he invited Hitler, in that devious manner which Hitler understood so well in March 1939, to put forward his claims and to start negotiations. Hitler did not take the hint.

But why did not Stalin spare the British his taunts even now? He believed, and in this he was right, that the British were

[1] Ibid., pp. 345–6.

interested to frustrate his plans for a last-minute conciliation of Hitler. He was incensed by what he believed to be the British Ambassador's indiscretion. But even if the British had been completely unselfish in the matter, they would probably still have aroused his anger: the mere forecast of the storm seemed to him to bring the storm nearer. He could well afford, on the other hand, to hurt British susceptibilities. Now, after Britain had stood alone against Germany for a year, he knew that he had no need to sue for British friendship, that the alliance between Russia and Britain would be established almost automatically once hostilities had broken out; and then bygones would be bygones.

.   .   .   .

Very few of Stalin's deeds have given rise to so many passionate disputes as his dealings with Hitler between 1939 and 1941. It was in those years, so his critics say, that, low as had been his previous record of political morality, he descended to even lower depths of treachery. His apologists retort that though his path was full of twists and turns, he acted from legitimate expediency, never losing sight of his ultimate objectives, never discarding his principles.

Stalin himself made his own apology soon after the outbreak of hostilities. 'It may be asked', he said on 3 July 1941, 'how could the Soviet Government have consented to conclude a non-aggression pact with such perfidious people, such fiends as Hitler and Ribbentrop? Was this not an error on the part of the Soviet Government?'[1] He denied the 'error' and pointed to the advantages of his policy: 'We secured to our country peace for a year and a half and the opportunity of preparing our forces.' Apart from time Russia had, of course, also gained territory, the much desired defensive *glacis*. Her moral gain consisted in the clear awareness of her peoples that Germany was the aggressor and that their own Government had pursued peace to the very end.

Of these three alleged gains—in time, space, and morale—the gain in morale was the most real. It had been a peculiar feature of Russian military history that the Russian soldier had, unlike the German, fought best in the defence of his native soil;

[1] J. Stalin, *War Speeches*, p. 8.

and the clear conviction that the fight for national survival had been forced upon Russia brought out the best qualities in him in the years that followed. The strategic value of Russia's territorial acquisitions appears far less certain. The military outposts in the Baltic states and in former eastern Poland were lost by Russia a few days after hostilities began. Yet to build up these outposts had been so arduous and ugly a job; it had caused so much resentment among so many small nationalities, especially after the mass deportations of 'unreliable' Poles and Balts into the interior of Russia; in a word, the strategic advantages of those outposts were so negligible or, at any rate, so quickly lost, and the moral and the political disadvantages arising from their acquisition were so great, that on balance the whole undertaking was a costly and dismal failure.

Nor was the gain in time more positive. To be sure, Stalin used the twenty-two months of the respite for an intensive development of Russian war industries and for retraining the armed forces in the light of fresh military experience. But Hitler, too, used those twenty-two months. Freed from the nightmare of war on two fronts, he subjugated nearly the whole of Europe and harnessed the economic resources and the manpower of a dozen countries to the German war machine. No matter how great and important was the fresh accumulation of war stocks and the expansion of armament plant achieved in Russia between 1939 and 1941, it could not match the additional power that accrued to Hitler in the same period.[1] For three long years now, the Red Army was to confront almost single-handed Hitler's forces on the land, to cede vast and most valuable territory, to bleed more profusely than any army had ever bled, and to watch in anxious and frustrating suspense for the opening of a second front in the west. Yet that second front had been there in 1939 and 1940; and it might still have been there later, had Stalin thrown Russia's weight into the struggle during one of its earlier phases.

Nor is it true that he used his respite as fully as he might have used it. Hoping till the last minute to avert the war and disregarding the omens that showed it inevitable and imminent, he refrained from mobilizing sufficient strength to prevent the

---

[1] This, too, was virtually admitted by Stalin in his speech of 6 November 1941 *War Speeches*, p. 17.

Wehrmacht from scoring its great initial victories. He met Hitler's onslaught only half mobilized. In June 1941 the number of mobilized Russian and German divisions was almost equal, but only part of the Russian divisions were ready to meet their experienced and well-equipped opponent, to whom a long succession of brilliant victories had given high self-assurance. Yet the Red Army could have had strong superiority in numbers.[1] The excessive complexity of his political game led Stalin to put himself at a military disadvantage. He had been uneasy enough to mobilize 170 divisions and to move most of these to the frontier; but he had still been too complacent, or too wary of 'provoking' Hitler, to carry out the mobilization on the scale required. For this we have his own authority: 'The fact of the matter is', he stated (3 July 1941), 'that the troops of Germany, a country at war, were already fully mobilized, . . . and in a state of complete readiness, only awaiting the signal to move into action, whereas the Soviet troops had still to effect mobilization and to move up to the frontiers.'[2] What Stalin in fact admitted was that in the last weeks before the invasion he had squandered much of that precious time, to the gain of which he still pointed as to the justification of his policy. 'Of no little importance', he added, '. . . was the fact that Fascist Germany suddenly and treacherously violated the non-aggression pact.' The world was told then that 'vizor'd falsehood and base forgery' betrayed his 'credulous innocence'.

When the balance of those strange twenty-two months is drawn, it is impossible to overlook the gratuitous service which the Comintern unwittingly rendered to Hitler. No sooner had Molotov and Ribbentrop put their signatures to the pact of August 1939 than the Comintern called off the anti-Hitler crusade to which its trumpeters had so long summoned governments and peoples.

---

[1] Cyril Falls, *The Second World War*, p. 113. Schulenburg was obviously wrong when he assured Hitler that the 'urge for security' made the Russians send ten divisions wherever the Germans sent one.

[2] J. Stalin, *War Speeches*, pp. 7–8. Stalin admitted the fact even more explicitly to Harry Hopkins. See Robert E. Sherwood, *Roosevelt and Hopkins*, pp. 333 and 335. Not only the mobilization of the army but the final conversion of industry to war was also unduly delayed. It was only in 1948 that the chief of the State Planning Commission, Vice-Premier N. Voznesensky, disclosed that the economic plans for the third quarter of 1941 had been based on the assumption of peace, and that a new plan, suited for war, had been drafted only after the outbreak of hostilities. N. Voznesensky, *Voennaya Ekonomika SSSR*, p. 37.

All the strategy and tactics of anti-fascism, all its elaborate arguments and slogans, were scrapped. The European shadows of the Russian General Secretary adopted an ambiguous pose of neutrality. Both belligerent camps, it was now said, pursued imperialist aims, and there was nothing to choose between them. The working classes were called upon to resist war and fight for peace. Outwardly, these appeals resembled the policy of revolutionary defeatism which Lenin had pursued in the First World War. The resemblance was deceptive. In Lenin's opposition to war there was revolutionary integrity and consistency, while the policy of the Comintern merely suited the temporary convenience of Stalin's diplomacy and was as tortuous as that diplomacy. At times the opposition to war had an unmistakably pro-German twist as, for instance, in October 1939, when the Comintern echoed Molotov's and Ribbentrop's call for a negotiated peace and blamed France and Britain for the war. The effect of that policy, especially in France, was merely defeatist, not revolutionary. It supplemented the defeatism that corroded the top of French society with a quasi-popular brand of defeatism coming from below. Only after the harm had been done, when Moscow, alarmed by Hitler's victories, began to encourage resistance to Nazi occupation, did the French Communist party switch over to a new policy. Less obvious, though not unimportant, was the effect of the Ribbentrop–Molotov pact upon anti-Nazi elements in Germany; it made their confusion worse confounded, it deepened their sense of defeat and induced some of them to reconcile themselves to Hitler's war.

It would be naïve to suppose that Stalin was not aware of those results of his 'friendship' with Hitler. But he almost certainly thought them of little importance in comparison with the tangible advantages he had obtained. His pragmatic mind stuck to concrete, strategic conceptions, to military bases, rivers, salients, and rounded-off frontiers, all the elements of defence, the value of which had been so greatly reduced by modern military technique. He disregarded such imponderables as the mood of the French or the German working classes or the national resentments of Poles, Finns, and other Baltic nationalities. Yet all those imponderables were to take, and some of them are taking even now, their revenge on Russia. In this, his disregard of the immaterial factors in great political processes, lay the main weakness of his strong but limited realism.

When all that is necessary has been said about Stalin's miscalculations and errors of judgement, it would still be wrong to attribute them merely to his personal shortcomings. His policy had behind it a powerful current of popular feeling, the current of which Alexander Blok had so strong a presentiment.

> But we ourselves henceforth shall be no shield of yours
> We ourselves henceforth will enter no battle!

These words of 'The Scythians', addressed to the west, epitomized the emotional strains in the Russian society of 1939. The bulk of the Russian people, wearied by years of strenuous economic construction, attached by an exalted devotion to the results of their labour, made sullen by the hostility or, at best, the lukewarmness of the outside world, feeling themselves isolated and betrayed in their idealistic pursuits—that people was at one with Stalin, when he refused to 'stir when the ferocious Hun rifled the pockets of the dead' and when he clung to peace even while the Nazis were already building the death chambers of Auschwitz and Maidanek to 'roast the flesh of the white brothers'.

This was not the only current of popular feeling in Russia. There was also an undercurrent of uneasiness and misgiving. The party had a guilty conscience. The army suffered from a vague sense of humiliation. But stronger than all that was probably the people's urge to escape the inexorable destiny of war.

CHAPTER XII

The Generalissimo

Stalin's behaviour after Hitler's attack on Russia.—His speech of 3 July 1941.—
His leadership in the war.—He saves Moscow and orders first Russian counter-
offensive (December 1941).—'Victory in 1942.'—Inter-allied fears and suspicions.
—'This is no class war.'—The Second Front.—Churchill's meeting with Stalin in
August 1942.—The battle of Stalingrad.—Upsurge of traditionalism and national-
ism in Russia.—Stalin's attempt to reconcile Leninism and Russian traditionalism.
—He disbands the Comintern and rehabilitates the Greek Orthodox Church.—
The Politbureau and the General Staff.—Stalin and Hitler compared as military
leaders.—Stalin and his Marshals.

ON 22 June 1941 Molotov broke to the Russian people the
grim news about the German attack. Stalin, as if embarrassed
by the disastrous collapse of his hopes, shunned the limelight.
He did not utter a single word in public for nearly a fortnight.
He apparently waited to see what were the results of the first
battles, what was the attitude of Great Britain and the United
States, and what was the feeling in the country. Closeted with
his military leaders, he discussed measures of mobilization and
strategic plans. He divided the enormous front into three sectors and put Voroshilov in command of the northern sector,
Timoshenko of the centre, and Budienny of the south. He himself assumed the supreme command. His chief of staff was
General Shaposhnikov, who had served on the General Staff
since before the revolution and had been reputed a scholarly,
hard-working, but not original strategist. The supreme direction of the war effort was concentrated in the State Defence
Committee, which consisted of five members: Stalin, Molotov,
Voroshilov, Berya, and Malenkov. Molotov was to conduct
diplomacy. Berya was in charge of domestic policy. Voroshilov
was to ensure liaison between the armed forces and the civilian
authorities. Malenkov, one of Stalin's assistants at the General
Secretariat, represented the party. Stalin himself presided over
the Committee.

Despite all his miscalculations, Stalin was not unprepared to
meet the emergency. He had solidly armed his country and

reorganized its military forces. His practical mind had not been wedded to any one-sided strategic dogma. He had not lulled the Red Army into a false sense of security behind any Russian variety of the Maginot Line, that static defence system that had been the undoing of the French army in 1940. He could rely on Russia's vast spaces and severe climate. No body of men could now dispute his leadership. He had achieved absolute unity of command, the dream of the modern strategist.

Those advantages were, however, offset by serious disadvantages. The Red Army was only now to undergo its real baptism of fire. Its morale was still uncertain. Only ten years had passed since the peasantry revolted against collectivization; and memories of the great purges were even fresher. First reports from the fronts gave a confused and contradictory picture. Here divisions crumbled and dissolved into chaos; and vast hauls of prisoners taken by the Germans indicated an alarming lack of fighting spirit. Elsewhere formations, surrounded and cut off, defended themselves stubbornly, delaying the enemy's advance. Elsewhere again, under overwhelming pressure, troops retreated in good order, saving strength for future battles. But everywhere, Hitler's armies advanced irresistibly. Behind the fighting lines, rumour, confusion, and panic began to spread.

On 3 July 1941 Stalin at last broke silence to offer guidance to his bewildered nation. In a broadcast address he spoke of the 'grave danger'. His voice was slow, halting, colourless. His speech was, as usual, laborious and dry. It contained none of those rousing words which, like Churchill's promise of 'blood, toil, tears and sweat', pierce the mind of a people. His style was strangely out of keeping not only with the drama of the moment, but even with the content of his speech, with his own appeals and instructions which reflected his unbreakable and unbendable will to victory.

He began by stating that 'although the enemy's finest divisions and the finest units of his air force had already been smashed and had met their doom on the field of battle, the enemy continued to push forward'.[1] He could not bring himself to tell the people the bitter truth without prefacing it by a wildly optimistic and palpably untrue statement.[2] He went on to make

[1] J. Stalin, *War Speeches*, p. 7.
[2] 'Our losses had not been heavy until the final attack on Moscow', says General

the apologia for his pact with Hitler, which we already know, and he added that Hitler had secured the advantage of surprise but that that would not benefit him long. Then he described the objectives of the enemy with deliberate *muzhik*-like crudeness: 'The enemy is cruel and implacable. He is out to seize our lands watered by the sweat of our brows, to seize our grain and oil, secured by the labour of our hands. He is out to restore the rule of the landlords, to restore Tsarism . . . to germanize [the peoples of the Soviet Union], to turn them into the slaves of German princes and barons.'[1] This was an issue of 'life and death'; 'the Soviet people . . . must abandon all complacency. . . . There can be no mercy to the enemy. . . . There must be no room in our ranks for whimperers and cowards, for panic-mongers and deserters. . . .' He called for ruthlessness, ruthlessness, and once again ruthlessness in dealing with the invader and in overcoming chaos and panic behind the fighting lines. Then he made his awe-inspiring call on the people to 'scorch the earth' that they must cede to the enemy:

In case of a forced retreat . . ., all rolling stock must be evacuated, the enemy must not be left a single engine, a single railway car, a single pound of grain or gallon of fuel. The collective farmers must drive all their cattle and turn over their grain to the safe keeping of the authorities for transportation to the rear. All valuable property, including metals, grain, and fuel, that cannot be withdrawn, must be destroyed without fail. . . . In areas occupied by the enemy, guerrillas, mounted and on foot, must be formed; sabotage groups must be organized to combat the enemy, to foment guerrilla warfare everywhere, blow up bridges and roads, damage telephone and telegraph lines, set fire to forests, stores, and transport. In occupied regions conditions must be made unbearable for the enemy and all his accomplices. They must be hounded and annihilated at every step, and all their measures frustrated.[2]

It was as if the Russia of 1812 had resurrected and spoken through Stalin's mouth. He did, indeed, recall Russia's victory over Napoleon and said that Hitler was no more invincible than Napoleon had been. He mentioned, 'with gratitude', the 'historic utterance of the British Prime Minister, Mr. Churchill,

Blumentritt (B. H. Liddell Hart, *The Other Side of the Hill*, p. 200); and Stalin spoke only a fortnight after the attack on Russia had begun.
[1] J. Stalin, *War Speeches*, p. 9.   [2] Ibid., pp. 10–11.

regarding aid to the Soviet Union and the declaration of the United States government. . . .'[1] As in 1812, Russia was fighting a 'national patriotic war', which was also a war for the freedom of all peoples. He wound up by calling upon the people to 'rally round the party of Lenin and Stalin'.[2] This unexpected reference in the third person to himself, added a touch of incongruity to his speech—a speech at once so great and so flat, so indomitable and so uninspiring.

.   .   .   .

Russia was to sell space for time; the space sold was to be made unusable to the enemy; and a merciless price was to be exacted for it. This was the only way in which, after all his errors and miscalculations, Stalin could meet the conqueror of Europe. He confronted him with superior will-power. But is it true, as it has been asserted, that he never lost his confidence, even for a moment? In the light of some of Stalin's casual remarks, made in those critical months, one may doubt whether this was so. In his speech of 3 July he spoke not only of Napoleon's defeat in Russia. He also recalled the fate of Kaiser Wilhelm, who, although he had been considered invincible, had finally been defeated 'by Anglo-French forces'. Stalin did not recall that the Kaiser's army had defeated Russia before it succumbed to its western enemies. But his mind was obviously wandering from Napoleon to the Kaiser and from the Kaiser to Napoleon. He could not help reflecting whether Hitler might not achieve what the Kaiser had achieved. Some such thought must have flashed across his mind when, on 30 July, he talked to Harry L. Hopkins, President Roosevelt's envoy. He admitted that he himself had not expected Hitler to launch the attack; he further said that the 'war would be bitter and perhaps long', that 75 per cent. of his war industries were located in and around Moscow, Leningrad, and Kharkov, all soon to be threatened by the enemy, and that he would like the President to know that he, Stalin, 'would welcome American troops on any part of the Russian front under the complete command of the American army'.[3] This is one of the most revealing statements attributed to Stalin by the memoirists of the Second World War. Throughout the war Stalin persistently refused to

[1] J. Stalin, *War Speeches*, p. 12.   [2] Ibid., p. 12.
[3] Robert E. Sherwood, *Roosevelt and Hopkins*, pp. 339–43.

admit to the front any foreign troops not under his command. He kept foreign observers away from the fighting lines; and as a rule, to which there were exceptions, he would not even allow allied pilots to fly over Russia. What then made him eager to 'welcome American troops on any part of the Russian front under the complete command of the American army' in July 1941, when the United States was not even at war and when his suggestion was completely unreal? One can only conclude that he uttered those words in a mood of flagging confidence, perhaps of despair. This would have been only natural, because, when Stalin talked to Hopkins, Hitler's troops had covered more than 450 miles in less than a month; in the north the battle of Smolensk was flaring up; and in the south the rout of Budienny's armies was beginning. In September, after Budienny's disastrous defeat on the Dnieper, two other visitors, Harriman and Beaverbrook, noticed signs of depression in Stalin; and Stalin then inquired whether the British would not send some of their troops to the Ukrainian front.[1] Later in the autumn, when the Germans were approaching Moscow, he betrayed his anxiety to Sir Stafford Cripps. He told the British Ambassador that Moscow would be defended to the last, but he also envisaged the possibility that the Germans might seize it. He went on to say that if Moscow fell, the Red Army would have to withdraw from the whole territory to the west of the Volga. He believed that even then the Soviets would be able to go on waging war, but that it would take many years before they could strike back across the Volga.

Shortly after the war Stalin himself made an oblique admission. On 24 May 1945, celebrating victory at the Kremlin, he raised a 'toast to the Russian people'. 'Our government', he said, 'made not a few errors, we experienced at moments a desperate situation in 1941–1942, when our army was retreating, because there was no other way out. A different people could have said to the government: "You have failed to justify our expectations. Go away. We shall instal another government which will conclude peace with Germany. . . ." The Russian people, however, did not take this path. . . . Thanks to it, to the Russian people, for this confidence.'[2] In the first months

---

[1] Robert E. Sherwood, *Roosevelt and Hopkins*, pp. 387–9.
[2] J. Stalin, *War Speeches*, p. 139.

of war uncertainty must have gnawed at Stalin's mind, even though to the world he showed only an iron mask.

He wore that iron mask with amazing fortitude and self-mastery. Perhaps, indeed, that mask was his most powerful weapon. It gave his will to victory an heroic, almost super-human appearance. Russia was replete with elements of weakness. The slightest sign of flagging in the man in whose hands the nation, half-coerced and half-persuaded, had wholly rested its fate, might have increased those elements of weakness with disastrous results. Stalin knew, of course, that to him personally, more than to any one of Hitler's adversaries or victims, hesitation or weakness spelt an inglorious end. Self-preservation bade him behave as he did; and now, more than ever before, his personal interest was at one with the interest of the nation. This is at once the strong and the weak point of any totalitarian régime—that at certain moments the entire fate of a mighty nation seems to depend on the nerve of its dictator, whose breakdown or effacement would create a void which hardly anyone could fill.

Many allied visitors who called at the Kremlin during the war were astonished to see on how many issues, great and small, military, political, or diplomatic, Stalin personally took the final decision. He was in effect his own commander-in-chief, his own minister of defence, his own quartermaster, his own minister of supply, his own foreign minister, and even his own *chef de protocole*. The *Stavka*, the Red Army's G.H.Q., was in his offices in the Kremlin. From his office desk, in constant and direct touch with the commands of the various fronts, he watched and directed the campaigns in the field. From his office desk, too, he managed another stupendous operation, the evacuation of 1,360 plants and factories from western Russia and the Ukraine to the Volga, the Urals, and Siberia, an evacuation which involved not only machines and installations but millions of workmen and their families. Between one function and the other he bargained with, say, Beaverbrook and Harriman over the quantities of aluminium or the calibre of rifles and anti-aircraft guns to be delivered to Russia by the western allies; or he received leaders of guerrillas who had come from German-occupied territory and discussed with them raids to be carried out hundreds of miles behind the enemy's lines. At the height of the battle of Moscow, in December 1941, when the thunder of Hitler's guns hovered ominously over the streets of Moscow, he found time enough to start a subtle diplomatic game with the Polish General Sikorski, who had come to conclude a Russo-Polish treaty. In later days the number of foreign visitors, ambassadors, and special envoys from all parts of the world grew enormously. He entertained them usually late at night and in the small hours of the morning. After a day filled with military reports, operational decisions, economic instructions, and diplomat haggling, he would at dawn pore over the latest dispatches from the front or over some confidential report on civilian morale from the Commissariat of Home Affairs, the N.K.V.D. The N.K.V.D. report might also contain, say, a detailed record of the things that the general in charge of the British Military Mission in Moscow had said, the previous day, about Russia, about her allies and their plans, and about Stalin himself in the privacy of his office, for the office of the British general was 'infested with well concealed dictaphones' which recorded every word of his.[1] Thus he went on, day after day, throughout four years of hostilities—a prodigy of patience, tenacity, and vigilance, almost omnipresent, almost omniscient.

.   .   .   .

In October Hitler formally opened the battle of Moscow, 'the greatest offensive ever known'. Leningrad had been cut off and blockaded. Nearly the whole of the Ukraine and the coast of the Azov Sea had been conquered by the Wehrmacht. Budienny's armies had been routed—the Germans took half a million prisoners on the Dnieper. Stalin dismissed both Voroshilov and Budienny from the command—the men of Tsaritsyn, the 'N.C.O.s', as Trotsky used to call them, were not equal to this motorized warfare. New commanders, Zhukov, Vassilevsky, Rokossovsky, were soon to replace them.

In November the Germans made an all-out attempt to encircle Moscow. Their vanguards advanced to within twenty to thirty miles of the capital—at one point they were only five miles away. All the Commissariats and government departments were evacuated to Kuibyshev on the Volga. In Moscow officials were burning the archives that had not been carried

[1] John R. Deane, *The Strange Alliance*, p. 154.

away. On 6 November, the anniversary of the revolution, the Moscow Soviet assembled, as usual, for a ceremonial meeting, but this time the meeting was held underground, at the Mayakovsky station of the Metro. Stalin addressed the assembly in calm words, although he made the alarming admission that Russian troops 'had several times fewer tanks than the Germans'.[1] The next day he stood at the top of the Lenin Mausoleum to take the parade of troops and volunteer divisions of people's guards, marching straight from the Red Square to the front at the outskirts of the city. He appealed to the soldiers to draw inspiration from the memories of the civil war, when 'three quarters of our country was in the hands of foreign interventionists' and the young Soviet Republic had no army of its own and no allies. 'The enemy is not so strong as some frightened little intellectuals picture him. The devil is not so terrible as he is painted. . . . Germany cannot sustain such a strain for long. Another few months, another half a year, perhaps another year, and Hitlerite Germany must burst under the pressure of her crimes.' He finished with a strange, unexpected invocation to the saints and warriors of Imperial Russia: 'Let the manly images of our great ancestors—Alexander Nevsky, Dimitry Donskoy, Kuzma Minin, Dimitry Pozharsky, Alexander Suvorov, and Mikhail Kutuzov—inspire you in this war!'[2] This was the first time he so evoked the shadows of the past which the revolution seemed to have covered with contempt and banished for ever. 'May the victorious banner', he added, 'of the great Lenin guide you.'

The news about the evacuation of the Government shook the people of Moscow. Psychologically, this was a moment of supreme danger. The decision of any government to leave its capital in the middle of a war tends to sap the moral strength of a fighting nation and to add impetus to centrifugal forces. So it was in France in 1940, when the Government, thrown out of its traditional seat of power, became as vulnerable as a snail divested of its shell. The more centralized the Government, the more is its stability and authority rooted in familiar landmarks of power, nearly all of which are in the capital. The evacuation of the Government from Moscow was followed by riots and disorders. People thought that the city had been given up. Crowds

---

[1] J. Stalin, *War Speeches*, p. 17.   [2] Ibid., pp. 25–6.

stormed foodstores. Members of the party destroyed their membership cards and badges. Anti-Communists prepared to settle accounts with Communists and to win favour with the invader. Symptoms of anarchy appeared in many places all over the area between the fronts and the Volga.

People who spent those days in Moscow described later the salutary effect which the news that Stalin had not left with the rest of his Government had on the mood of the Muscovites, who saw in it evidence that the will to victory, personified in Stalin, was unshaken. His presence in the Kremlin at this late hour was indeed a challenge to fate. It was as if the fortunes of the world had been balancing on the towers of the old fortress. To both Stalin and Hitler the Kremlin became the symbol of their ambition, for while Stalin was refusing to leave its walls, Hitler issued an order that 'the Kremlin was to be blown up to signalize the overthrow of Bolshevism'.[1] It was in the setting of the Kremlin that Stalin's figure had grown to its present stature. He had become one with that setting and its historical associations and he was as if afraid of detaching himself from it. At least part of his power had lain in his remoteness from the people. If he had left, the spell of his remoteness might have been broken. He might have appeared to the people as a dictator in flight. This is not to say that he could not have conducted the war from some retreat in the country. But to leave Moscow was for him a step awkward and humiliating enough to make him shrink from it to the end.

He was, incidentally, to remain thus voluntarily immured in the Kremlin throughout the war. Not once, so it seems, did he seek direct personal contact with his troops in the field. Trotsky in the civil war moved in his legendary train from front to front, exploring, sometimes under the enemy's fire, advanced positions and checking tactical arrangements. Churchill mixed with his soldiers in the African desert and on the Normandy beaches, cheering them with his idiosyncrasies, with his solemn words, his comic hats, his cigars, and V-signs. Hitler spent much of his time in his advanced field headquarters. Stalin was not attracted by the physical reality of war. Nor did he rely on the effect of his personal contact with his troops. Yet there is no doubt that he was their real commander-in-chief. His leader-

[1] B. H. Liddell Hart, *The Other Side of the Hill*, p. 194.

ship was by no means confined to the taking of abstract strategic decisions, at which civilian politicians may excel. The avid interest with which he studied the technical aspects of modern warfare, down to the minute details, shows him to have been anything but a dilettante. He viewed the war primarily from the angle of logistics, to use the modern expression. To secure reserves of manpower and supplies of weapons, in the right quantities and proportions, to allocate them and to transport them to the right points at the right time, to amass a decisive strategic reserve and to have it ready for intervention at decisive moments—these operations made up nine-tenths of his task.

Towards the end of 1941 it was precisely from that angle that the situation appeared to be hopeless. This is how N. Voznesensky, the director of the State Planning Commission, describes it: 'On the territory that had been occupied by the Germans in November 1941 lived about 40 per cent. of the whole Soviet population. About 65 per cent. of the whole pre-war output of coal had come from there, 68 per cent. of all pig iron, 58 per cent. of all steel, 60 per cent. of aluminium . . ., 38 per cent. of the grain, 84 per cent. of sugar . . ., 41 per cent. of all railway lines of U.S.S.R. . . .'[1] From June till November industrial output was reduced by more than a half; and the output of steel by more than two-thirds. The production of ball-bearings, so indispensable for modern machines, was less than 5 per cent. of normal. At this moment Russia's proverbial 'inexhaustible reserves' were a myth. Her material resources were infinitely inferior to Germany's. Even her manpower was not greatly superior; and it was at any rate much inferior to the combined manpower of Germany and her satellites. Thus, Russia's resistance, especially in the first year of the war, was a triumph of her superior determination and spirit, the spirit that made young Communists die at the outskirts of Moscow with the cry: 'Behind us is Moscow—there is no room left for retreat.'[2]

On 8 December Hitler announced that he had suspended all

---

[1] N. Voznesensky, *Voennaya Ekonomika SSSR*, p. 42.

[2] 'A few parties of our troops', relates General Blumentritt, deputy Chief of the General Staff of the German army, 'from the 258th infantry division, actually got into the suburbs of Moscow. But the Russian workers poured out of the factories and fought with their hammers and other tools in defence of their city.' B. H. Liddell Hart, *The Other Side of the Hill*, p. 196.

operations for the winter. Twice had his troops attempted to storm Moscow and been repulsed. They were now immobilized by an accident of the weather. A severe winter had set in several weeks earlier than usual. Hitler did not know that two days before he announced the end of the 1941 campaign, on 6 December, Stalin had issued his orders for a counter-offensive.

In later years the Russians reflected over the circumstances that compelled them to retreat in 1941-2. Immediately after the outbreak of hostilities, Stalin, as we know, explained the initial Russian defeats by the advantage of surprise which Hitler had secured. In 1946 he put a somewhat different construction on the events, suggesting that he had deliberately lured the Germans into the interior of Russia in order to destroy them there. In a letter to the military historian, Colonel E. Razin, he recalled two historic examples he had followed: 'Already the old Parthians knew this type of counter-offensive, when they drew the Roman commander Crassus and his troops into the interior of their country and then struck out in a counter-offensive and destroyed them. Kutuzov, too, our commander of genius, knew it well when he destroyed Napoleon and his army by means of a well-prepared counter-offensive.'[1] This second interpretation was calculated to stop inquisitive probings into the causes of the defeats of 1941-2—such probings could not but detract from Stalin's prestige. That the Russians were compelled to retreat by overwhelming German pressure, that it could not have been part of their strategic plan to withdraw from their wealthiest provinces is certain. Stalin did not, like Kutuzov, attempt to trap the enemy into Moscow, which was now the capital—in 1812 the capital was St. Petersburg. In 1812 the loss of territory did not impair Russia's capacity to

[1] J. Stalin, 'Letter to Colonel Razin', *Bolshevik*, 3.2.1947. Stalin's reference to the Parthians suggests that he must have studied with especial interest the history of the old states bordering his native Caucasus—the Parthian empire had covered the area of northern Persia. Incidentally, the Scythians were the warrior class of the Parthian empire. From their tribes came its commanders and some of its emperors. The study of 'Scythian military art' was almost the fashion in war-time Russia. The Historical Faculty of the University of Moscow celebrated the twenty-fifth anniversary of the Revolution, in November 1942, by a special session, at which Professor Mishulin delivered a lecture on the 'military art of the Scythians'. The lecturer summed up this strange commemoration of the Revolution with the words: 'The stubborn fight of the Scythians for their independence filled not a few heroic pages in the ancient annals of our Fatherland.' See Professor A. Mishulin, 'O voennom iskustve Skifov', *Istoricheskii Journal*, nos. 8-9, 1943.

wage war; and Napoleon's advance was confined to the roads leading to Moscow. In modern war a deliberate retreat on such a scale and involving such losses as those suffered by Russia in 1941–2 would have been stark madness, if not worse.

Yet Stalin's two explanations of his strategy are not so mutually exclusive as they might appear. Once he had been compelled to give up vast territories, he decided to make the best of a disastrous situation, to gather new forces, to avoid decisive battles, to extricate his forces from successive encirclements, to wait for the moment when Hitler's armies had overreached themselves, and then to strike back at their overextended flanks and lines of communication. With primitive, oriental, but unfailing shrewdness, he gambled on Hitler's arrogance. A long and unparalleled succession of victories had indeed made Hitler so overweening that after the assaults on Moscow he failed to take the precautions which even a mediocre general would have taken. Instead of withdrawing his troops to defensive positions, he ordered them to take up winter quarters within sight of Moscow; he failed to supply them with winter clothing; he failed to foresee that the Russian mud and frost would bring his war machines to a standstill, and that winter was the element in which the Russian soldier was superior to any opponent. Stalin, whose military mistakes so far had originated from an excess of caution and prudence, had a quick eye for that lack of prudence in the Führer; and on it he based his own plan of action. Not only did he thus save Moscow—he forced the Germans to make a long and costly retreat, the first they ever made.

After this first success of Russian arms, a feeling of confidence spread over the country. The armies in the field suddenly realized that they had achieved something of which no army had been capable so far. For a few weeks it seemed that the Wehrmacht, constantly attacked by regular forces and harassed by guerrillas, would, like the *Grande Armée*, disintegrate in the snowy wastes. This did not happen. But the Russian soldier now felt that having beaten the enemy once he would be able to beat him again.

Stalin encouraged the new mood and called for 'victory in 1942'. At the outset of hostilities he had told Harry L. Hopkins that he reckoned on a long and costly war, lasting three or four years. What impelled him now to launch the new slogan? The chances had undoubtedly improved, not only because of recent Russian victories, but also because the United States was now in the war. Against these new circumstances he had to set the fact that the success of his offensive from Moscow had been due largely to the winter; that the United States had still to translate its gigantic strength from the potential to the actual; that the British armies had not yet recovered from the shock of their defeat on the Continent. Only a 'miracle' could have brought the end of the conflict in 1942. But was not the defence of Moscow a 'miracle'? It may be that Stalin earnestly hoped for a rapid conclusion of the struggle. But it is also possible that, although he knew that he could not expect victory in 1942, he could not face the Russian people with the sober warning that their ordeal would go on for several years more. The ordeal was too terrible to allow such brutal frankness.[1]

. . . .

The duration of the war obviously depended on the attitude of the western allies. Russia had already concluded agreements with both Great Britain and the United States, obtained an American loan of a billion dollars and the promise of a steady flow of war material from the west. But Stalin was on guard against the surprises with which the war might be fraught. The allied coalition had come into being against the will of each one of its members. The bonds between them still seemed tenuous. They might snap under the pressure of failures, rivalries, mutual recriminations. Under the surface, old antagonisms and tensions were still there. Might not the west, Stalin could not help pondering, seek to conclude a separate peace with Germany and leave Russia in the lurch? In his eyes the conflict between the fascist capitalism of Germany and the liberal capitalism of

---

[1] That the slogan 'Victory in 1942' was not then as utterly fantastic as it seems in retrospect follows from the fact that at the beginning of that year Rundstedt and Leeb urged Hitler to retreat right to the Polish frontier (see B. H. Liddell Hart, *The Other Side of the Hill*, p. 203). A German withdrawal of that depth would have amounted morally to a Russian victory. This must have been the reason for Hitler's refusal to follow his generals' advice. While his generals had their eyes fixed on military strategy, Hitler was concerned primarily with political strategy; and it is by no means as certain as the German generals believe that Hitler was 'wrong' in refusing to retreat. His misfortune was that both he and his generals were 'right', each from a different angle.

Britain and the United States was much more superficial than the basic antagonism between Bolshevik Russia and either of the other two. He saw the irony of history in the fact that British Conservatives were, for the sake of self-preservation, fighting Hitler, the leader of all anti-Communist forces, the virtual head of the European counter-revolution. That paradox of history, he must have reasoned, might prove treacherous. We know how on the other side the thought that Russia might conclude a separate peace with Germany weighed upon the minds of Roosevelt and Churchill, who feared that Russia's losses and the element of kinship between two totalitarian régimes might yet induce Stalin to reconcile himself with Hitler as he had done in 1939.[1] The fears, then, were mutual; and they coloured the political conduct of the war.

Stalin carefully refrained from waging the war under the banner of proletarian revolution, believing apparently that this would have wrecked the coalition. He threw overboard the instructions and recipes that the congresses of the Comintern had worked out for the conduct of Communist parties during the war. According to those instructions, the Communists were to propagate the overthrow of the capitalist order and to use for that purpose all opportunities created by war.[2] Instead, they now accepted the leadership of the allied Governments and supported the war effort in order to help Russia. In most Nazi-occupied countries they recognized the bourgeois leadership of the resistance: de Gaulle's in France, Beneš's in Czechoslovakia, Queen Wilhelmina's in Holland, and so on. Even their propaganda addressed to Germany, Italy, and the Balkans did not call for the overthrow of capitalism. It called on the peoples of those countries to resist their rulers in the name of democracy, not of proletarian dictatorship. (It was only towards the end of the war that the very term 'democracy' was to become the object of conflicting, 'eastern' and 'western', interpretations.) Moscow now spoke to every nation with the voice of national

Robert E. Sherwood, *Roosevelt and Hopkins*, pp. 400, 466, 495, 734 and *passim*; ...nowski, *Defeat in Victory*, pp. 167–8; Lt.-Gen. Sir Giffard Martel, *The ...k*, p. 76; *The Memoirs of Cordell Hull*, vol. ii, p. 1171 and *passim*.
Stalin repeatedly stated in the thirties, 'is sure to unleash revolu-... the very existence of capitalism in a number of countries, as ... of the first imperialist war.' (J. Stalin, *Problems of Leninism*,

interest, sentiment, and even prejudice, not with that of Marxist internationalism. 'This is no class war', Churchill declared on the day Hitler attacked Russia; and Stalin seemed to echo Churchill. He studiously cultivated the appearance of a single anti-fascist interest and democratic ideology, common to the whole coalition. To that appearance he sacrificed the Comintern, when, in May 1943, he decided to disband it. This was his political contribution to the coherence of the Grand Alliance.

It was not only the fear of a separate peace that haunted Stalin. Only slightly less grave, but much more real, in his eyes was the danger that the western allies would remain inactive and let Russia and Germany mutually exhaust themselves. In this suspicion he was confirmed when, in the first days of the Russo-German war, a member of the British Government, Lord Brabazon of Tara, publicly urged the allies to adopt such an attitude. Lord Brabazon of Tara had to resign from the British Government, and both Churchill and Roosevelt spoke with great feeling about Russia's fight and Stalin, their ally. But in the inner councils of the Kremlin the words of the indiscreet Minister were well remembered. It was undoubtedly Stalin's view that the Minister had been disavowed because he had been imprudent enough to utter what most of his colleagues had at the back of their minds. To Stalin everything seemed to point that way: the class antagonisms, barely hushed up, the old Russo-British rivalry, in which Britain invariably appeared to Russians as 'perfidious Albion' using the *muzhik* as cannon fodder, and, last but not least, the logic of his, Stalin's, own attitude in 1939–41, which now seemed revengefully to rebound upon him. He began to press the western allies that they should at once join battle with Germany on the Continent, and he strove to obtain from them a formal commitment to that effect.[1]

At the same time he kept his eye on a diplomatic issue of infinite intricacy. In co-operation with Hitler he had extended the frontiers of the Soviet Union. He had changed the social structure and the political outlook of the incorporated lands and had sealed their incorporation by appropriate entries in the

[1] As early as November 1941 Stalin said in his speech at the Mayakovsky station of the Metro: '. . . there are still no armies of Great Britain or the United States on the European continent to wage war against the German fascist troops, with the result that the Germans are not compelled to wage war on two fronts.' (J. Stalin, *War Speeches*, p. 16.)

Soviet Constitution. He was now out to save his acquisitions from the wreckage of his partnership with Hitler; and he urged the western allies to recognize the legitimacy of the gains he had derived from what they had considered an altogether illegitimate bargain. Neither Britain nor the United States hastened openly to recognize the incorporation of the Baltic states. But this was not a major problem. The Polish issue was much more difficult. Poland had been the oldest member of the anti-German coalition. She had lost her eastern marches to Russia through the same act which had prepared her subjection to Germany. The decorum of the Grand Alliance, if nothing else, demanded that Poland should be given satisfaction, not because her title-deeds to her Ukrainian and Byelorussian marches were un-challengeable, but because she had been deprived of those possessions in so indecent and brutal a manner. Yet, Stalin could not return those lands to Poland without arousing bitterness among the Ukrainians, whose resistance to the German occupa-tion he had to maintain; without exposing the plebiscites which he had ordered in eastern Poland in 1939, and which served him as his title-deeds to those lands, for the fraud which they were; without exposing as a hollow formality the entries which he had made in the Soviet Constitution; and without himself losing face in the process.

He therefore made a gesture towards the Poles, suggesting that he gave them satisfaction without actually giving it to them. In the first days of the war his Government declared, in general terms, that the Ribbentrop-Molotov pact on Poland was null and void. General Sikorski, the head of the Polish Government in exile, interpreted this as meaning that Russia had agreed to return the eastern marches to Poland. But this was not what Stalin meant. At the height of the battle of Moscow he asked Anthony Eden, who was then in the Russian capital, for British recognition of Russia's frontiers as they had been at the moment of Hitler's attack. The British Foreign Secretary pre-ferred to leave the issue in suspense.[1] Stalin then proposed talks to Sikorski. The Polish Premier replied that the Polish Constitution gave him no right to negotiate over his country's frontiers. Thenceforward Stalin, too, would refer to his Con-stitution and say that it forbade him to cede any part of the

---

[1] *The Memoirs of Cordell Hull*, vol. ii, pp. 1166–7.

Soviet territory.[1] Thus began a new phase of the protracted Russo-Polish conflict, a conflict which was exacerbated by the sufferings of great masses of Polish deportees in Russia.

. . . .

It was with a view to the attainment of these three objectives— guarantees against a separate peace, the speeding up of the second front, and allied recognition of Russia's 1941 frontiers —that Stalin sent Molotov to London and Washington in May 1942. Molotov's mission was ostensibly successful. He concluded the Anglo-Soviet treaty of alliance—Stalin had first suggested it to Lord Beaverbrook in September 1941. The alliance was to be valid for twenty years. Moreover, the British publicly stated that they agreed with the Russians 'on the urgent need for the opening up of a second front in Europe in 1942'. Both Churchill and Roosevelt, the former not without reluctance, assured Stalin privately that their troops would actually invade France across the Channel in September. Molotov failed, however, to secure British or American recognition of Russia's frontiers of 1941. On the face of things, Stalin had ground for satisfaction. All members of the coalition had declared an equally strong determination to defeat Germany; and Russia's position was greatly enhanced. In the first months of the war the west had been inclined to take a poor view of Russia's powers of resistance. After the battle of Moscow the British and American appreciation of her military strength rose; and Russia at once took a leading place in the coalition. The old anti-Soviet feeling in the west was quickly giving place to a naïve but sincere popular admiration for all things Russian and for Stalin personally. Roosevelt and Churchill spared him no flattering words; and something like popular affection began to surround his figure, hitherto remote, incomprehensible, or even repulsive to western eyes.

The swing of public opinion was not one-sided. In Russia, too, people were made to forget old grievances and suspicions. The propagandists no longer divided the world into capitalists and proletarians, into imperialists and their colonial victims, but into fascists and democrats. Not only Roosevelt, leader of the New Deal and promoter of friendly Russo-American

[1] J. Ciechanowski, *Defeat in Victory*, pp. 88–9.

relations, but even Churchill, ex-leader of the anti-Bolshevik crusade, was hailed as a symbol of progressive mankind, ally, friend. This mood rose to a climax with the announcement about the second front in 1942. Such was still the mood when in July 1942 Stalin invited Churchill to come to Moscow to discuss common military action.

Churchill arrived in August, but his visit was a bitter disappointment. He had come to tell Stalin that the Anglo-American Chiefs of Staff had decided to cancel the planned invasion of France and to prepare instead an invasion of North Africa. The meeting between Stalin and Churchill was acrimonious and stormy. A semi-official Russian account contains the following dialogue:

Churchill: . . . we have reached the conclusion . . .
I find it difficult to talk about this, but . . .
Stalin: There are no people with weak nerves here, Prime Minister.
Churchill: The invasion of Europe is impossible this year . . .
Stalin: That is to say that the English and American leaders renounce the solemn promise made to us in the spring . . .
Churchill: We propose an invasion of Sicily.
Stalin: This will be a political rather than a military front . . .
Churchill (assures that the invasion of western Europe will take place in 1943).
Stalin: Where is the guarantee that this solemn promise, too, will not be broken?
Molotov: The British Prime Minister will once again prove to us that his country is not in a position to sacrifice men.[1]

It may be doubted whether Stalin's language was quite as rude as that. But that such was approximately the content and the tenor of the conference is confirmed by British and American sources.[2] In a memorandum for Churchill Stalin said that the postponement of the second front was 'a moral blow to . . . Soviet public opinion' and that it 'prejudiced the plans of the Soviet command for the summer and the winter operations'.[3]

[1] N. Virta, *Stalingradskaya Bitva*, pp. 21–3.
[2] R. E. Sherwood, *Roosevelt and Hopkins*, pp. 590, 617; John R. Deane, *The Strange Alliance*, p. 17; Lt.-Gen. Sir Giffard Martel, *The Russian Outlook*, pp. 113, 157, 158.
[3] It was probably in connexion with this that Stalin took an extremely risky decision. He threw into the battle of Stalingrad part of his Far-Eastern Army, which he had hitherto kept intact and in readiness against Japan. After the battle of Stalingrad he brought his Far-Eastern reserve back to its complement. See John R. Deane, *The Strange Alliance*, pp. 223–4.

The situation on the Russian front was indeed dangerous once again. The Germans had advanced into the Caucasus and almost reached the Volga. The battle of Stalingrad had just begun. The armed forces were in danger of losing the Caucasian oil. Although Russia could no longer be defeated by a knock-out blow, Stalin had reason enough to fear a war of attrition, which would immobilize his tanks, planes, and transport. He attached especial importance to the fighting at Stalingrad, 'the city of Stalin', his old Tsaritsyn, whose fall might have had the worst possible effect upon the morale of the people. No wonder that he reacted to the news Churchill had broken to him with the angry reproach that Russia had been let down. He, who had so often repeated that he would not 'pull chestnuts out of the fire for others', now felt as if he had, after all, been manœuvred into performing that distasteful job. In the Russian account of Churchill's visit Stalin is quoted as saying, after Churchill's departure: 'All is clear. A campaign in Africa, Italy. They simply want to be the first in reaching the Balkans. They want us to bleed white in order to dictate to us their terms later on. . . . Nothing will come out of this! The Slavs will be with us. . . . They hope that we shall lose Stalingrad and lose the springboard for an offensive. . . .'[1]

This account appears to be in part coloured by afterthoughts. It is doubtful whether in August 1942 Stalin in fact attributed to Churchill the plan for the invasion of the Balkans, a plan which had by then hardly matured in Churchill's own mind. But the reasons for the postponement of the second front that Churchill gave him—the main one was the lack of landing craft—certainly failed to convince him. He held that Germany's armed forces had been so overwhelmingly engaged on the Russian front that Hitler had not enough men to defend the Atlantic coast.[2]

Churchill later confessed that he was puzzled by the capriciousness of Stalin's behaviour. After the squall over the second

---

[1] N. Virta, *Stalingradskaya Bitva*, p. 26.

[2] This view was shared by leading American generals, including General Marshall, and also by some British experts. (R. E. Sherwood, *Roosevelt and Hopkins*, pp. 526, 568–70, 589–91 and *passim*.) Lt.-Gen. Martel claims in his *Russian Outlook* pp. 157–62) that in 1942 the Germans could spare less manpower for the defence of the Atlantic coast than they could in 1944. 'Here was our golden opportunity', says Gen. Martel, 'but the landing craft were not there.' General Martel's view is confirmed by Field-Marshal Rundstedt and other German generals. See *The Other Side of the Hill*, pp. 237–40 and *passim*.

front, Stalin showed him unexpected kindness, listening with much friendly attention to Churchill's exposition of the scheme for the African invasion and expressing exuberant delight over British plans for the ruthless bombardment of German cities. Stalin's 'capriciousness', it is easy to guess, reflected a contradiction in his attitude: he could not help venting his ill temper over the second front, but he was too much concerned over Russia's alliance with the west and too much haunted by the fear of a separate peace not to try to humour his guest after the row was over. The world could, of course, be told nothing about the grave dissension. It learned that the talks between the two Premiers 'were carried on in an atmosphere of cordiality and complete sincerity'. The Russian soldier, nevertheless, sensed that something had gone awry; and in his ordeal he grew more and more impatient and disillusioned with the western Allies. It would be difficult to exaggerate how strongly the fact that it was to take another two years before the Allies invaded western Europe affected the popular mind. It was with an oppressive feeling of its isolation that the Red Army fought the battle of Stalingrad.

. . . .

The opening of the battle was preceded by a sharp slump in the morale of soldiers and civilians. 'In the south', writes the head of the British Military Mission in Moscow, 'by Rostov the Russian morale seems to have fallen to a low level, and they almost ceased fighting. It is believed that Marshal Stalin himself visited that part of the front. In any case it seems clear that a widespread purge was immediately carried out. . . . It was very successful and the Russian morale in the south responded at once.'[1] Stalin allegedly presided over a court martial which tried several generals charged with neglect of duty.[2] Yaroslavsky, the head of the propaganda department of the party, charged the civilian authorities in the Caucasus with complete failure to prepare the defence of their cities. German attempts to play off Caucasian nationalities and tribes against one another and to recruit collaborators among them were not without

[1] Lt.-Gen. Sir Giffard Martel, *The Russian Outlook*, p. 43.
[2] About that time, Marshal Timoshenko, who had replaced Budienny and had won much distinction, disappeared from the command, but it is not clear whether he was deposed or whether he left because he had been wounded in battle.

success—the fact was to be officially admitted after the war, when several hundred thousand Chechens and Ingushs, as well as Crimean Tartars, charged with helping the enemy, were punished with deportation to Siberia. Thus the omens for the battle of Stalingrad were not good. But this was a contest which for personal, perhaps even more than for purely military, reasons Stalin could not afford to lose. Throughout the six months of its duration he directed and watched the course of the battle and of the counter-offensive that developed from it.

From the outset the fortunes of this campaign were extraordinary. The Germans had at first not considered the city to be of prime importance. The Russians began to deploy their troops for its defence only in the middle of July. There was, indeed, no compelling military reason why Stalingrad should have become the site of this greatest battle of the Second World War. The Germans probably could much more easily have cut the Volga lifeline at any point to the south of Stalingrad, between Stalingrad and the Caspian Sea. It was mainly a psychological motive that now impelled Hitler. 'By the time that the more deliberate bid for Stalingrad began, in the second half of August' (so runs the story told by the German generals), 'the Russians had collected more reserves there. . . . It was easier for the Russians to reinforce Stalingrad than the Caucasus, because it was nearer their main front. Hitler became exasperated at these repeated checks. The name of the place—"the city of Stalin"—was a challenge. He drew off forces from his main line, and everywhere else, in the effort to overcome it—and exhausted his army in the effort.'[1] The previous year the ambition of both, Hitler and Stalin, had been focused on the Kremlin—now it was equally strongly focused on Stalingrad.

By the second half of August the Russians had retreated into the middle of the Stalingrad defensive area. Stalin sent Zhukov, his ablest commander, and Vassilevsky, who had replaced Shaposhnikov as Chief of Staff, and Malenkov to the danger spot. 'Not a step back' was his famous order to the garrison of Stalingrad. This was no piece of martial rhetoric such as is often indulged in by commanders of retreating armies. Nor was Stalin obsessed with the idea of static defence, as Hitler was to be after the tide of war had turned against him. On the

[1] B. H. Liddell Hart, *The Other Side of the Hill*, p. 215.

contrary, skilful withdrawals and evasions had so far been the main elements of Stalin's 'defence in depth'. But to stem the German advance at the city that bore his name was to him a matter of supreme importance. His legend was at stake.

The German advance continued, but it was very slow and very costly. In the first half of September the fighting shifted to the close approaches to the city; in the second half it raged in its suburbs and its centre. Chuikov's 62nd army was joined by workers of the Stalingrad factories, among whom were the veterans who had fought here under Stalin and Voroshilov twenty-two years ago. The defenders were squeezed right to the Volga; all their ways of retreat were cut off; reinforcements and supplies reached them only across the river, through heavy German fire; and ice-floes were soon to obstruct traffic on the water. On 5 October Stalin again addressed the besieged garrison: 'I demand from you to take every measure to defend Stalingrad. . . . Stalingrad must not be yielded to the enemy, and that part of it that has been captured by the enemy must be liberated.' From 27 September till 13 October the battle was fought in the sheds of three factories, the Stalingrad Tractor Plant, the Red October, and the Barricade. From 14 October till 19 November the fight was for single houses—the conquest of a single street now cost the Germans as much time and blood as they had hitherto spent on the conquest of entire European countries. In the middle of November the defenders held only a few scattered positions, hard by the banks of the river. At that moment, in his order of the day of 7 November, Stalin tried to lift their hearts: 'There will still be', he promised, 'rejoicing in our street.' On 19 November, when the Germans seemed to be engaged in a last effort to gain complete mastery of the city, he ordered the counter-offensive.

He had begun to plan it in September, at the moment of the great confusion. 'We are fighting single-handed', thus he summed up the situation to Vassilevsky. 'Our counter-attacks do not yield the expected results. Divisions perish. Some [generals] want us to do one thing, others another. Some insist that we limit ourselves to expelling the Germans from Stalingrad. Others want to persuade us to wait for allied help. And all are asking us for reserves.' He held that the crisis could be overcome only by a great counter-offensive, and that the time for that was ripe. He asked Vassilevsky (or was it Zhukov whom he asked?) to work out the operational plan.

Stalin's idea of the counter-offensive was based on the same psychological premisses and the same insight into Hitler's mentality which underlay the scheme for the battle of Moscow, although the operational aspect of the present campaign was to be much more complex, mature, and effective. Once again Stalin banked on his foe's blind arrogance. He took it for granted that Hitler was considering the Russian forces in the south to have been so upset and disorganized in the summer as to be incapable of rallying for a counter-offensive. Stalin further assumed that the Germans would once again fail to redeploy their troops from offensive to defensive formation. In his order of 14 October Hitler did in fact explicitly assure his men that a Russian counter-offensive was out of the question. The task Stalin assigned to the defenders of Stalingrad was to pin down and wear out the *élite* of the southern German armies inside the Stalingrad bag. Meanwhile he was building up a strategic reserve, and was utterly insensitive to the desperate cries for reinforcements that came from hard-pressed commanders in the field. 'No matter how they cry and complain', he instructed his Chief of Staff, 'don't promise them any reserves. Don't give them a single battalion from the Moscow front.' He did not commit the mistake of dissipation which was to be Hitler's undoing—Hitler was just then aimlessly shifting his reserves between Stalingrad and the Caucasus. Stalin put the whole operational reserve under the orders of Zhukov,[1] who distributed it, in complete secrecy, between the three armies that flanked Stalingrad from the north, the north-west, and the south. Vatutin, Rokossovsky, and Yeremenko were in charge of the three armies; and Voronov was in command of the great

[1] In the histories of the battle of Stalingrad, written after the war, Vassilevsky, not Zhukov, is named as the commander of that reserve and of the counter-offensive at large. This must be regarded as part of that 'revision' of history which was undertaken after the war with the distinct purpose of playing down Zhukov's role. The official communiqué of the Soviet Information Bureau, published in *Pravda* on 31 December 1942, in the course of the battle, stated that the operation was 'under the over-all direction of the representatives of the Supreme Command: Army General G. K. Zhukov, Colonel General A. M. Vassilevsky and Army General of Artillery N. N. Voronov'. Since Zhukov, as Army General, was the senior of the three officers, he and not Vassilevsky must have been in supreme command.

mass of artillery, the master weapon of this battle. The three commanders of the sectors were to strike concentric blows at the rear of the German besiegers of Stalingrad and cut them off from the German armies in the west. The first blows were to fall upon the weak joints of the German front, at those parts of it which were held by half-hearted Rumanian, Hungarian, and Italian troops—this was another instance of the psychological and political insight on which the plan was based. On 19 November Vatutin struck from the north. He was followed by Rokossovsky next day, and then by Yeremenko, who struck from the south. On the fourth day the German besiegers of Stalingrad were themselves besieged.

Stalin now ordered his generals to pay no attention to von Paulus's surrounded divisions, but to strike instead at the outer German forces and to drive these back from the Volga to the Don and beyond. Presently, a German army group under Manstein rushed from the south to relieve von Paulus; and Hitler ordered his aviation to keep open an air corridor to Stalingrad, by which his blockaded divisions were to be supplied with food and ammunition. Stalin threw his air force reserve into the battle and blocked the 'corridor'. Then when his generals could not agree among themselves whom to tackle first, von Paulus or Manstein, he decided that Manstein be attacked first. The attack was successful; and by the end of December the main German force had been thrown back 120 miles from Stalingrad. On 1 February von Paulus and twenty-three German generals and their troops surrendered. Soon afterwards the Caucasus was cleared of Germans. Thus ended the campaign, in all respects so closely linked with Stalin's name, in which the flower of the German army perished. It was against the background of this battle, fought where he had a quarter of a century before made his first stumbling steps as a military leader, that Stalin now rose to almost titanic stature in the eyes of the world.[1]

.   .   .   .

The events of 1941 and 1942 wrought significant changes in

---

[1] This account of the Stalingrad battle is based on Soviet reports, published in *Pravda, Izvestya, Krasnaya Zvezda*, the official communiqués (vol. iii, *Soobshchenya Sovetskovo Informbureau*), the collection *Velikaya Bitva pod Stalingradom*, and a very clear summary and analysis of the campaign by B. Telpukhovsky, 'Velikaya Stalingrad-

Russia's outlook. Stalin himself often pointed out that the war had put the Soviets to the most severe test possible and had provided the final justification for the ideas and principles that inspired them. It is true that the régime stood the test much better than its opponents, and even some of its admirers, had expected. The supreme crisis revealed its basic strength. But it is also true that the war tended to upset some of those habits of mind on which the régime, as it had evolved in the-thirties, was based; and that it compelled Stalin to make open and veiled political adjustments, designed to overcome cleavages existing in the nation and to create the unity of purpose that was essential for victory.

Twice had the morale of the nation been strained to breaking-point: on the eve of the battle of Moscow and on the eve of the battle of Stalingrad. Some of the critical symptoms, acts of panic and desertion, were inherent in the situation and would have appeared under any comparable circumstances. Others, such as mass collaboration with the enemy, especially in the Ukraine and the Caucasus, resulted from grievances and resentments lingering on since the thirties. Stalin realized that the country needed some sort of internal truce. He could the easier arrange such a truce because this implied no reconciliation on his part with any battleworthy political opponents—these he had destroyed. All he had to do was to try to dissipate an indefinite *malaise*, an inarticulate resentment, in some sections of the people. It is wellnigh impossible to say just how large or important were those sections. It should not be imagined that a majority of the nation was hostile to the Government. If that had been the case no patriotic appeals, no prodding or coercion, would have prevented Russia's political collapse, for which Hitler was still confidently hoping.[1] The great transformation that the country had gone through before the war had, despite all its dark sides, strengthened the moral fibre of the nation. The majority was imbued with a strong sense of its economic

skaya Bitva', in *Voprosy Istorii*, no. 2, 1948, M.Vodolagin, 'Narodnoye Stalingradskoye Opolchenye' in *Istoricheskii Journal*, no. 3, 1945. N. Virta's *Stalingradskaya Bitva* is of limited documentary value; in some points its reliability is highly doubtful. The German view of the battle is given in B. H. Liddell Hart's *The Other Side of the Hill*.

[1] B. H. Liddell Hart, *The Other Side of the Hill*, p. 182. 'Hopes of victory were largely built on the prospect that the invasion would produce a political upheaval in Russia', says Field-Marshal von Kleist.

and social advance, which it was grimly determined to defend against danger from without. A minority was certainly sullen and bitter; and, judging by the scope of the pre-war upheavals and by the range of interests adversely affected, this could not have been an insignificant minority. Between the satisfied elements and the dissatisfied ones there were those who doubted and vacillated. Amid terrible defeats the mood of the nation might have fluctuated, risen, and fallen and swung this way and that so suddenly and so rapidly as to upset the political balance. The Government had to exert itself to steady the nation's temper. Only then could it hope that its exacting demands on the people would be met. Only then could it arouse the country to that pitch of enthusiasm without which the great victories of the coming years would have been impossible.

Before the war the whole propaganda machine incessantly harped upon the story of strife in the party. Not for one moment was the nation then allowed to forget the evils of Trotskyism, Bukharinism, and other deviations or to relax in its 'vigilance' vis-à-vis the 'enemies of the people'. During the war this theme was discreetly dropped. In the face of Hitler's all too real conspiracy, the bogus conspiracies of previous years were as if forgotten. Survivors of the crushed oppositions, who could be useful in the war effort, were brought out of concentration camps and assigned to important national work. Tukhachevsky's disciples, who had been cashiered and deported, were rushed back to military headquarters. Among them, according to one reliable report, was Rokossovsky, the victor of Stalingrad, a former Polish Communist, who had served as liaison officer between Tukhachevsky's staff and the Comintern. Professor Ramzin, the head of the 'Industrial Party', who, in the early thirties, had been charged with conspiracy and compact with a foreign power, was released, acclaimed for his services, and awarded the highest prizes and medals. Professor Ustrialov, who had in fact advocated the transformation of the Soviets into a nationalist-bourgeois republic, reappeared as a contributor to leading Moscow newspapers. These were the most spectacular cases which illustrated the indefinite domestic truce. It was indefinite because it was not based on any formal act of reconciliation or on a general amnesty, but merely on Stalin's allusive gestures, which, though their meaning was clear to those for whom they were meant, committed him to nothing, and amounted to no 'self-criticism'.

. . . .

The most significant new development, however, was an upsurge of nationalism, such as would have been thought incompatible with Bolshevism only a short time before. The upsurge was in part spontaneous. The mass of the people reacted with an outburst of anger and national pride to the news, which filtered through from German occupied territory, about the sadistic ill-treatment of their kinsmen by the Nazis, and to the Hitlerian propaganda about the racial inferiority of the Slavs, especially of the Russians. The anger and the pride were further intensified by the nation's sense of its isolation, which deepened with the delays of the allied invasion of western Europe. That sense was expressed by poets, writers, and journalists. Russia saw herself, in the words of Alexei Tolstoy, as 'Atlas, alone carrying the whole burden of the world'. To some extent, however, Stalin artificially boosted the nationalist emotion as a matter of policy. We heard him conjuring up the spirits of Kutuzov, Suvorov, Minin, and Pozharsky in the first months of the war. Hosts of propagandists followed him with a grotesquely immoderate glorification of Russia's imperial past. Then he showered upon the country a long series of decrees, reforms, or counter-reforms, all designed to whip up the new mood.

The nation was in need of something, a slogan or an idea, that would fire its imagination and sustain its valour. In the civil war the ideas of international socialism and world revolution animated the Red Army. Later the mass of Bolsheviks took it for granted that, if attacked, Russia would turn the war into a struggle in which the lines of division would run not between nations but between classes within each nation. This belief in revolutionary internationalism had gradually slumped; and little life was left in it after the prolonged cultivation of a self-centred socialism in one country and the victimization of the exponents of internationalism in the great purges.[1] Stalin's

[1] The old Bolshevik idea still echoed in Molotov's words, spoken on the first day of the war: 'This war has been forced upon us not by the German people, not by the German workers, peasants, and intellectuals, whose sufferings we well understand, but by the clique of bloodthirsty fascist rulers' (*Soviet Foreign Policy during the Patriotic War*, vol. i, p. 75). This sweeping exoneration of the German people, even of the intellectuals, was never afterwards repeated.

present anxiety to maintain the coalition between Russia and the western powers was the decisive deterrent to any revival of the old revolutionary internationalism. Nationalist exaltation was the reaction from it; and the exaltation, naturally enough, rose to the pitch of intensity in the armed forces.

It was in the armed forces that the most startling changes, conceived in the new spirit, were made. Most of the customs, habits, and institutions that had remained in the army as a legacy of the revolution and the civil war were swept away. In the middle of the battle of Stalingrad, in October 1942, a special decree did away with the political commissars, who had hitherto controlled the officers on behalf of the party—the political commissars in fact remained, but were subordinated to the military commanders. The measure was militarily justified—it created unity of command and enhanced discipline. But its political implications were no less important. It was the signal for a zealous return to pre-revolutionary military traditions. Commenting, in November 1942, on a decree which abolished 'socialist competition' in the army, *Pravda* bluntly stated that the soldier had no Socialist obligations whatsoever and that his job was simply to serve his fatherland, as his forebears had done. The army regulations of Peter the Great were recalled as a model for imitation. Guards regiments and guards divisions—their very names recalled Tsarist days—were created. Orders of Suvorov and Kutuzov were instituted. Cossack formations, once despised as symbols of Tsarist oppression, were brought back to life and to the old glamour. Finally, on the eve of the twenty-fifth anniversary of the revolution, epaulettes were re-introduced as part of the officer's uniform, the epaulettes that had in one of the first Bolshevik decrees been banned as marks of a reactionary caste system in the army. Saluting was made obligatory and strictly enforced. Exclusive officers' clubs and strictly separate messes for junior and senior officers were opened. As if to sanction this whole trend, by which the standing and the privileges of the officers' corps were enhanced, and to underline his personal connexion with it, Stalin himself assumed the title of Marshal—his first military rank at the age of sixty-four—in March 1943, after the conclusion of the battle of Stalingrad. He had just covered his officers' corps with honours and laurels. In December alone he had promoted 360 commanders to the rank of general; and in the following weeks the pages of the newspapers were daily filled with long lists of promotions. He had just handed marshals' batons to his most brilliant commanders; and now he was eager to demonstrate that he was one with his officers' corps.

The traditionalist and nationalist trend was not confined to the army; it permeated the political climate of the whole country. Stalin was careful not to commit himself personally too directly to the new line—old Bolshevik inhibitions were apparently too strong in his mind for that. But he authorized the new line in his own, curiously elusive, manner. During the battle of Moscow he made this remark on national socialism: 'Can the Hitlerites be regarded as *nationalists*? No, they cannot. Actually, the Hitlerites are now not nationalists but *imperialists*.'[1] He went on to argue that as long as Hitler was collecting German lands he had some right to the title of a nationalist, but that he forfeited it when he began to annex non-German countries. This was a strange argument in Stalin's mouth, for never hitherto had the Bolsheviks, including Stalin, denied their enemies and opponents the label of nationalism which had for them, the disciples of Lenin, a derogatory meaning. In denying Hitler that label now, he stripped it of the derogatory connotation and said, as it were: 'It is *we*, not our enemies, who are the real nationalists.' His propagandists grasped the hint and acted upon it. He himself uneasily balanced between residual internationalism and an inclination to fan the nationalist emotion. Thus he once said: '. . . if the Germans want to have a war of extermination they will get it. From now on . . . our task will be . . . to exterminate every single German who has set his invading foot on the territory of our Fatherland.'[2] This was widely used by Hitler's propagandists, who told the German soldiers that the Red Army did not spare the lives of prisoners, and thereby induced them to fight with savage despair. Stalin then corrected himself, describing the interpretation given to his words as a 'stupid lie and a senseless slander against the Red Army'. 'It would be ludicrous', he added, 'to identify Hitler's clique with the German people, with the German state. The experience of history indicates that Hitlers come and go,

[1] J. Stalin, *War Speeches*, p. 18.
[2] Ibid., p. 20.

but the German people and the German state remain.'[1] His propagandists, as a rule, failed to make this distinction until the final phase of the war. Like many of their colleagues in the other allied countries, they aroused the people against the German nation as a whole, not merely against Nazis. Stalin's own orders of the day invariably ended with the words: 'Death to the German invaders!' This grim refrain, repeated day after day and serving as the text for poems and journalistic articles, at once reflected the fury of the embattled nation and sustained that fury, reducing, as it were, the intricate and many-sided business of war to the primeval physical element of slaughter.

Hitler's racial barbarity, on the one hand, and the nationalist vehemence of Stalin's propaganda on the other, left almost no room for any genuine Russian appeal to the rank and file of the German army, for any attempt to drive an ideological wedge between the National Socialists and the rest of the German people, for any effective political warfare that might have reduced the scale of the horrible slaughter. It was the strength of the nationalist message that it did not allow the Russian soldier to flag or falter. It was its weakness that, because of it, Russia could buy victory only at the highest and the most terrible of prices. It is, indeed, difficult to say which was greater: Russia's misfortune in having a leadership incapable of winning the war at a price involving less destruction and bloodshed, or her good fortune in having a leadership which, once the course of history had left her no other way out, apart from surrender and subjection, was capable of paying the most prodigious price any nation had ever paid for victory.[2]

On 4 September 1943 Stalin startled the world by his sudden rehabilitation of the Greek Orthodox Church, which, identified with the *ancien régime*, had been half-suppressed since the revolution. Stalin received the Metropolitan Sergius, the actual head of the Church, and after a long and friendly interview with him, decreed the restoration of the Holy Synod. The reason he gave for this act was that the Church had co-operated in the war effort and thereby proved its loyal devotion to the fatherland.

---

[1] J. Stalin, *War Speeches*, pp. 29–30.

[2] 'It is very fortunate for Russia in her agony', this was Churchill's wartime verdict, 'to have this great rugged war chief at her head. He is a man of massive outstanding personality, suited to the sombre and stormy time in which his life has been cast.'

This was true enough, although it was also true that bishops and priests in the occupied territories collaborated with the Germans. The fresh zeal for the old Russian tradition demanded the rehabilitation of the Church, which had held a central place in that tradition. As religion had by no means lost all its hold on the *muzhik*, and as some revival of religious sentiment had made itself felt amid recent trials and tribulations, the new deal for the Church was likely to pull down a barrier between the Government and religious people. It enhanced the political truce.

Stalin had in mind wider considerations as well. In the course of its summer offensives the Red Army had just liberated most of the Ukraine; and Stalin looked forward to the day when it would cross the frontiers into the Balkans, where eastern Christianity was the dominant religion. Russia's influence in the Balkans is worth a Greek Orthodox Mass, he might have said to himself. The Tsars had used the Church as an obedient tool of their policy; and from cool opportunistic calculation Stalin now followed in their footsteps. That he, the *élève* of a theological seminary, should have staged the half-real and half-spurious come-back of the Church was one of those little coincidences of history into which romantic historians might read a special meaning. But that he should have rehabilitated the Church so soon after he had disbanded the Comintern was a coincidence to which more political importance was attached. The two acts were consonant with one another; and their consonance was made even more emphatic when the Internationale, the hymn of the Labour movement of the world, composed by a French Communard, hitherto the anthem of the Soviet Republic, was replaced by another anthem of greater patriotic respectability.[1]

It was also in keeping with the whole trend that Stalin sponsored a new Slavophil movement. Slavophilism, with Panslavism as its extreme, had been part and parcel of pre-revolutionary Russia. One of its varieties had been an instrument of Tsarist diplomacy which, in its struggle against the Ottoman and Habsburg empires, appealed to the racial solidarity of their Slavonic subjects—Bulgars, Serbs, Slovenes,

---

[1] The new anthem begins with the following words: 'An indestructible union of free republics *Great Russia* has rallied for ever . . . .'

and Czechs—with Russia. Another variety of Slavophilism had a revolutionary, 'populist' tinge—it proclaimed the solidarity of the Slav peasant nations against both feudal autocracy and western capitalism. Russian Marxism, including Bolshevism, had renounced Slavophilism in all its versions because the Marxists despised any appeal to racial solidarity. The now resurrected Slavophilism combined the features of its two earlier varieties—it was an instrument of diplomacy and at the same time it hinted at a common, peculiarly Slav, revolutionary interest.

Although Stalin patronized the new traditionalism, he could not but realize that fundamentally the two outlooks, the one harking back to All the Russias of the Tsars and the other deriving its inspiration from Lenin, were antagonistic to each other. He could not completely identify himself with either. He had left the shores of Leninist Russia far behind, but he could not lay anchor at the shores of Mother Russia—he was the wanderer between the two. There could, of course, be no question of any open controversy between the two outlooks, for the régime and its ideology had to remain 'monolithic'. It cannot even be said which of the members of the Politbureau were more expressive of one principle and which of the other, or whether there were such differences between them at all, because almost nothing is known about the inner life of the Politbureau in those years. Nevertheless, two parties, a party of revolution and a party of tradition, only half-conscious of themselves, led a silent existence in the thoughts and feelings of the people and in the mind of Stalin himself. The careful reader of his wartime speeches can trace, through his successive ideological inflections and shifts of emphasis, the instances in which now this and now that party takes precedence of the other, and the instances in which they keep each other in check. The duality of Stalin's outlook was strikingly reflected, for instance, in his behaviour during the celebration of the anniversary of the revolution in 1943. On the eve of the anniversary he was decorated with the Order of Suvorov. He appeared before the Moscow Soviet to make his customary commemorative speech, but for the first time he now appeared there in Marshal's uniform, wearing epaulettes embroidered with gold and with stars adorned with diamonds and jewels. While out-

side salvoes of artillery fire and fabulous displays of fireworks
were greeting the news of the liberation of Kiev, he stood before
the Soviet like the very embodiment of the Russia of the
Suvorovs and Kutuzovs. But in his speech he completely
ignored the exalted symbols of Imperial Russia. Instead he
recalled the 'behests of the great Lenin', and dwelt at length
on the Socialist achievement of the revolution. As if to counterbalance the cult of the army, which had been mounting in
preceding months, he now said: 'As in the years of peaceful
construction so in the days of war, the leading and guiding force
of the Soviet people has been the party of Lenin.'[1]

.   .   .   .

His behaviour, and, indeed, the whole situation, suggested
that he was trying to alleviate some latent tension between party
and army. There was enough ground for such tension. The
nationalist emotion was focused on the army. The army was
garnering the laurels and overshadowing the party. The two
bodies were not necessarily engaged in any sensational intrigue
or struggle for power. The links between them had so far been
too strong for that—many of the officers had been members of
the party; and peril from without made for unity. A degree
of rivalry was, nevertheless, inevitable. In peace the party
zealously guarded its supremacy *vis-à-vis* all other organizations.
The war tended to weaken that supremacy. It gave new weight
to the army. The force of circumstances made of the General
Staff the Politbureau's equal, and invested the officers' corps
with more authority, not to speak of glamour, than that which
the civilian hierarchy of the party secretaries enjoyed. The party
had to put up with that, but it could not help being fretful.

Hitler, exasperated by disagreements with his own generals,
once told his friends how much he envied Stalin, who could
deal much more ruthlessly with obstinate generals than he could
himself.[2] In this, as in many of his 'intuitions' about Russia,
the 'Bohemian corporal' was superficial and wrong. He probably had in mind the purge of Tukhachevsky and his group,
which, incidentally, took place three years after Hitler's show-
down with General Schleicher. The truth is that the officers'

---

[1] J. Stalin, *War Speeches*, p. 78.
[2] B. H. Liddell Hart, *The Other Side of the Hill*, p. 207.

corps of the Red Army had been the only organization in the state upon which Stalin had not brought to bear the full measure of totalitarian pressure. To be sure, he kept the armed forces under his control. But he also took care not to involve them too closely in all the controversies and intrigues which shook party and state. He encouraged the non-political general, devoted to his job and bent on making the best of it, as long as that officer paid lip service to the party on one or other rare occasion. The general who had in the past been sympathetically inclined to this or that opposition but had not been politically active was not required to go through these humiliating motions of contrition, which no civilian with a similar blot on his political conscience was allowed to dodge. Military art was one of the few politically important domains in which Stalin encouraged the original and experimenting mind, in which he did not impose the do's and don't's of his pseudo-dialectical catechism. Until 1937 he had allowed Tukhachevsky a free hand in matters concerned with strategic and tactical conceptions and with the modernization of the armed forces. Thus, the officers' corps largely escaped that oppressive spiritual drill which, over the years, maimed and crushed the civilian character. True enough, the purge of 1937 led to a grave worsening. But it was significant that not one of the indicted military leaders was brought to recite the usual confessions and self-accusations. All faced their judges and executioners like men. That circumstance alone indicated that the officers' corps had acquired a distinct mentality of its own, an independence of mind and a moral staying power quite exceptional in the climate of totalitarianism.

In the first phase of the war the army paid a heavy price for, among other things, the loss of self-reliance which its commanding staffs had suffered as a consequence of the purges. The warning was not, however, wasted on Stalin. He had the sense to give back to his generals their freedom of movement, to encourage them to speak their mind, to embolden them to look for the solution of their problems by way of trial and error, and to relieve them from the fear of the boss's wrath, a fear which weighed so heavily on Hitler's generals. He punished his officers with draconic severity for lack of courage or vigilance; he demoted them for incompetence, even when the incompetents happened to be Voroshilov and Budienny; and he promoted for initiative and efficiency. Hitler's generals had a shrewder appreciation of Stalin's method than Hitler himself when they said that the top rungs of the Russian ladder of command 'were filled by men who had proved themselves so able that they were allowed to exercise their own judgement, and could safely insist on doing things in their own way'.[1]

It is nevertheless true that, like Hitler, Stalin took the final decision on every major and many a minor military issue. How then, it may be asked, could the two things be reconciled: Stalin's constant interference with the conduct of the war, and freedom of initiative for his subordinates? The point is that he had a peculiar manner of making his decisions, one which not only did not constrict his generals, but, on the contrary, induced them to use their own judgement. Hitler usually had his preconceived idea—sometimes it was a brilliant conception, sometimes a bee in his bonnet—which he tried to force upon a Brauchitsch or a Halder or a Rundstedt. For all his so-called dilettantism, he was a doctrinaire in matters of strategy, impatient with those who could not see the merits of his particular dogma or plan. Not so Stalin. He had no strategic dogmas to impose upon others. He did not approach his generals with operational blue-prints of his own. He indicated to them his general ideas, which were based on an exceptional knowledge of all aspects of the situation, economic, political, and military. But beyond that he let his generals formulate their views and work out their plans, and on these he based his decisions. His role seems to have been that of the cool, detached, and experienced arbiter of his own generals. In case of a controversy between them, he collected the opinions of those whose opinion mattered, weighed pros and cons, related local viewpoints to general considerations and eventually spoke his mind. His decisions did not therefore strike his generals on the head—they usually sanctioned ideas over which the generals themselves had been brooding. This method of leadership was not novel to Stalin. In the early twenties he came to lead the Politbureau in an analogous way, by carefully ascertaining what were the views of the majority and adopting these as his own. Similarly, the generals were now receptive to his inspiration, because he

[1] B. H. Liddell Hart, *The Other Side of the Hill*, p. 232.

himself was receptive to their thoughts and suggestions. His mind did not, like Hitler's, produce fireworks of strategic invention, but his method of work left more room for the collective invention of his commanders and favoured a sounder relationship between the commander-in-chief and his subordinates than that which prevailed at the *Oberkommando der Wehrmacht*.[1]

This is not to say that Stalin simply followed the majority of his commanders. Even that majority was, in a sense, of his own making. In the depths of defeat he radically renewed and rejuvenated the high commanding staffs. He brushed aside all sterile pretensions of seniority and paid attention only to performance in battle. Nearly all his famous marshals and generals held subordinate positions or were juniors when war broke out. The basic selection of the new military *élite* took place during the battle of Moscow, when Zhukov, Vassilevsky, Rokossovsky, and Voronov came to the fore. It continued with the battle of Stalingrad, in which Vatutin, Yeremenko, Malinovsky, Chuikov, Rotmistrov, Rodimtsev, and others made their names. It was nearly completed during the battle of Kursk, the turning-point in the meteoric career of the young Cherniakovsky, who within three years rose from major to army general. These men, nearly all in their thirties or forties, unhampered by the deadweight of routine, avidly learned in the hard school of battle until they became their enemies' equals and then superiors.

[1] Stalin's method of work is quite well illustrated in the following quotation which describes—in a too popular and simplified manner but correctly in substance —his intervention in one of the more important episodes of the Stalingrad battle, the disagreement between Vassilevsky and Rokossovsky over whether they should strike first at von Paulus or at Manstein. The disagreement had been referred to Stalin. Rokossovsky protested against the diversion of Malinovsky's army, which had been placed under his orders, for the operation against Manstein. Stalin sounds the views of other generals:

Moscow G.H.Q.

Stalin (speaks over the phone): What is your opinion? Turn against Manstein? Thank you. *(Puts down the receiver and calls again)*. Hallo . . . There is a proposal from Vassilevsky that we should dispose finally of Manstein. It is proposed that Malinovsky's army be used for that. What is your opinion? To leave it with Rokossovsky? Thank you. *(Puts down the receiver and calls again.)* Vassilevsky proposes to shift Malinovsky's army and to assign it to Yeremenko in order to rout Manstein. Your opinion? *(Listening)* No, that's no answer. Yes or no? You would like to think it over? All right.

In the end Stalin sides with Vassilevsky and orders the attack on Manstein (N. Virta, *Stalingradskaya Bitva*, pp. 230-1).

The regeneration of the army, of its morale, and of its commanding staff was one of Russia's most remarkable achievements, for which credit was due to Stalin. But the political implications of this could not have been quite to Stalin's taste. His marshals and generals began to steal the limelight. He, Stalin, had hitherto towered so high above even his associates of the Politbureau that, in the eyes of the people, not one of them had held the position of his second in command. Not one of them had had any hold on popular imagination or affection. On top of the pyramid of power Stalin had stood alone; only far below had appeared the almost impersonal characters of Molotov, Kaganovich, Mikoyan, Zhdanov, Andreyev. The political life of the country had been enveloped in a grey atmosphere of anonymity. That atmosphere was now largely dispelled. New names, coupled with great and glorious victories, were on everybody's lips. They represented a potential force which, although not in any way opposed to Stalin, did not suit his political style. We have seen how the fear of a Bonapartist deformation of the revolution had haunted the Bolsheviks since early days. Although Stalin himself had since been accused of being a sort of a Bonaparte, he could not but look askance upon the military legend that was growing around his marshals.

CHAPTER XIII

Teheran—Yalta—Potsdam

Stalin's diplomacy in 1943.—Preliminaries to the Teheran Conference.—Stalin, Churchill, and Roosevelt; their personalities compared and contrasted.—The controversy over the 'second front'.—'Friends in fact, in spirit, and in purpose.'—The 'ten blows' of 1944.—Stalin rejects western mediation between Russia and Poland.—Delimitation of spheres of influence (June–October 1944).—Stalin's policies in eastern and western Europe.—His behaviour during the Warsaw rising of August 1944.—Stalin at the Yalta Conference (February 1945).—His interest in the Pacific war.—Two strands in his policy.—1815 and 1945; Alexander I and Stalin (similarities and differences).—The story of the 'people's democracies'.—Stalin's view on Communism in Germany.—His frustrated hope for a condominium of the Great Powers.—Stalin at Potsdam (July 1945).

AFTER the summer offensive of 1943, in which the Red Army recaptured nearly two-thirds of the lost Soviet territory, Stalin could have had no doubt about the outcome of the war. For the first time now General Winter had no share in his victories. The Russian forces in the field had not yet obtained that numerical superiority over the Germans with which they were to overwhelm them later. As Stalin himself was to tell Roosevelt and Churchill at Teheran, he had only sixty divisions more than the Germans, and these he rapidly shifted between the various sectors of the front in order to have superior striking power at selected places and at decisive moments.[1] Nor had his troops yet had the advantage of fighting with more and better weapons than those possessed by the enemy. In 1942 Russian industry, slowly recovering from dislocation, produced very little. Only in 1943 did the newly built factories and those that had been 'leap-frogged' from the west to the Urals and beyond begin to pour out great quantities of tanks, planes, and guns. These had to be transported to the fighting lines over a distance of 1,000–2,000 miles, over bad roads and scarce railway lines. The full weight of those weapons would not be felt in battle before 1944. Similarly, supplies of war materials from the western powers were to swell to their maximum only in 1944. Stalin therefore

[1] John R. Deane, *The Strange Alliance*, p. 87.

knew that he had scored his great successes by using only part of the strength he would soon be able to marshal. Although he still warned his people against complacency and slackness, his utterances reflected growing confidence. 'The Red Army', he could now state, 'has become the most powerful and steeled of modern armies.'[1]

His fear of a separate peace between Germany and the western powers, if it had not been altogether dispelled by his pacts and agreements, must have decreased very considerably. Hitler had already thrown 80 or 90 per cent. of his land forces against Russia, and, whatever happened, he could not add to his striking power in the east enough to defeat Russia.[2] It may even have occurred to Stalin that a favourable combination of circumstances, among which Hitler's blundering strategy was not the least important, might enable Russia to win the war without an Anglo-American invasion of the Continent.[3] He would not gamble on such a chance; but he knew that his bargaining position *vis-à-vis* his allies was unusually strong: it was they who now had the stronger reason to fear a separate peace, and who would be more anxious to preserve the alliance. He also knew that they were eager to secure Russia's participation in the war against Japan, the prospects of which were still dim. Rarely had any statesman held so many trumps in his hand.

For all that, he still failed to achieve the objectives he had set himself in 1941: the British and the Americans had not so far recognized the incorporation of the Baltic lands and of Poland's eastern marches in the Soviet Union. Roosevelt and Churchill urged him to postpone a settlement with Poland until after the war. Stalin resolved to force the issue now. Since the Polish émigré Government in London claimed back every inch of land that had been Polish before 1939, it was his obvious interest to prevent the establishment of that Government in Poland. In the spring of 1943 an obscure incident helped him in the matter. The Germans announced that they had

---

[1] J. Stalin, *War Speeches*, p. 85.

[2] Hitler guarded the Atlantic coast with 59 second-rate divisions, while 260 of his divisions, including the best, fought on the Russian front, a force twice as large as that which defeated Russia in the First World War. See the account of the German generals, which in all essentials confirms Stalin's own statements on the subject, in Liddell Hart's *The Other Side of the Hill*, p. 247.

[3] This is the view which Russian military writers were to express after the war.

discovered a mass grave of Polish officers, prisoners of war, at Katyn, near Smolensk, whom, they said, the Russians had done to death. The Poles in London asked for a neutral investigation of the Katyn graves, suggesting that they gave credence to the German version. They had in fact been uneasy about the fate of those officers for some time; and when Sikorski visited Stalin in 1941 he asked questions about them to which Stalin gave no satisfactory answer. It was, nevertheless, impolitic on the part of the Poles to support indirectly the German accusation, especially when there were reasons to suspect that the Germans themselves, who were then putting millions of people to death, might have been guilty of the deed. If Stalin was looking for a pretext that would allow him to declare the Polish Government to be worthless, as he certainly was, then he had found one. None of the allies defended the action of the Poles. Moscow severed relations with the Polish Government in London and began to prepare for the setting up of a Polish administration friendly to Russia. The allies had now come to disagree not only over Poland's frontiers but even over her government; but Stalin obviously believed that they would have to put up with whatever he did. He was confident that the Russian, and not the British or the American, armies would drive the Germans out of Poland, and that consequently he, not Churchill or Roosevelt, would call the tune on the Vistula.

His ambition was rising with the certainty of victory. He was no longer content with safeguarding the gains he had obtained in partnership with Hitler. He was out to secure gains which had eluded him because of Hitler's opposition. In 1940 he had claimed predominance for the Russian interest in Rumania and Bulgaria. He now staked out that claim again. His idea of the peace to come had taken shape—it linked up with those concepts of spheres of influence which had lured some Soviet diplomats in the twenties and which he himself had then so bluntly denounced.[1] It is still impossible to trace with much precision the various phases of this development. The division of Europe into zones of influence was broached at the conference of allied foreign ministers in Moscow in October 1943.[2] The discussion was vague and the issue was left open.

---

[1] See Stalin's speech at the Sverdlov University quoted in Chapter X, pp. 412–13.
[2] *The Memoirs of Cordell Hull*, vol. ii, p. 1298.

It may be assumed that, through Molotov, Stalin then sounded the allies, but that in his inner councils the issue had already been thrashed out.

It was also about this time, in the second half of 1943, that Stalin began to be strongly preoccupied with the peace that was to be imposed on Germany. A guiding principle of policy had been pronounced by President Roosevelt at Casablanca in January 1943: Germany was not to be allowed to negotiate a peace—she would have to 'surrender unconditionally'. In putting forward that formula Roosevelt was influenced by reminiscences of the American Civil War, in which the Northern States refused to parley with the South on the terms of surrender.[1] Roosevelt launched his policy, fraught with grave consequences, without consulting either Stalin or Churchill. Stalin accepted the formula with mixed feelings. He saw in it an additional guarantee that the western powers would seek no accommodation with Germany to Russia's detriment— when Roosevelt announced the policy of unconditional surrender the tide had not yet turned so strongly in Russia's favour that Stalin could afford to despise that additional guarantee. In his order of the day of 1 May 1943, he, too, spoke about unconditional surrender, making the formula his own. But he also realized that Roosevelt's policy tended first to stiffen and prolong German resistance and then to burden the allies with the sole responsibility for the peace. He tried to prevail upon the President to modify his policy or at least to mitigate it by a general definition of peace terms. Similar representations, incidentally, were made to Roosevelt by the British. But Roosevelt stuck to his viewpoint.[2]

The slogan of unconditional surrender soothed nationalist emotion in every allied country. Everywhere the idea of a punitive 'Carthaginian' peace with Germany gained much ground. Even as late as September 1944 both Roosevelt and Churchill were still to favour plans for the 'pastoralization' of Germany which were to deprive Germany of her heavy industry.[3] Stalin's views were of the same pattern. In September 1943 his economic adviser Professor Varga, who in the twenties criticized so severely the economic clauses of the peace of Versailles, publicly advocated the view that Germany should

[1] Ibid., p. 1574. [2] Ibid., pp. 1572–3. [3] Ibid., pp. 1602–5.

be made to pay heavy reparations to the allies. That demand was the more popular the more the Russian armies advanced and saw that the Germans had, in a fury of wanton destruction, turned the lands they had occupied into a desert. It was about this time also that Stalin spoke his mind about re-drawing Germany's frontiers. In July 1943 he authorized Maisky, then on a special mission in London, to state that Russia would favour the incorporation of East Prussia and Danzig in Poland, a plan to which President Roosevelt consented; but Stalin did not yet propose that Poland's frontiers be extended farther west to the Oder and the Neisse.[1] The incorporation of the German provinces was to 'compensate' the Poles for their eastern marches; but it was also to expose them to such danger of German revenge in the future as to make them absolutely dependent on Russia's protection. Thus far, roughly, had Stalin's ideas about the peace and his ambitions evolved when, in November 1943, he met Churchill and Roosevelt at Teheran.

. . . .

The preliminaries to the Teheran conference were strange. Stalin avoided meeting his partners as long as he could. Earlier in the year he refused to attend their conference at Cairo on the ground that, since Chiang Kai-shek was taking part in it, his, Stalin's, participation might offer untimely provocation to Japan, with whom Russia had been anxious not to embroil herself. He refused to meet Roosevelt alone, when this was suggested to him.[2] In October 1943 Cordell Hull, attending the conference of foreign ministers in Moscow, pressed him hard to agree to a meeting. Stalin yielded, but insisted that the conference should take place at Teheran, then occupied by Russian and British troops. He stubbornly refused to go to any other place farther away from Russia; and in reply to Roosevelt's repeated suggestions to that effect he proposed to postpone the conference till the spring of 1944, when he would be ready to meet his partners at the Russian war-time base of Fairbanks in Alaska.[3] He excused himself on the ground that the course of military operations demanded his presence in Moscow and that he could leave only for a place from which he could keep in

[1] J. Ciechanowski, *Defeat in Victory*, pp. 198, 213.
[2] Robert E. Sherwood, *Roosevelt and Hopkins*, pp. 671, 733–4.
[3] *The Memoirs of Cordell Hull*, vol. ii, p. 1294.

direct touch with his general staff. He may have been reluctant to leave the Kremlin, where, surrounded by his trusted guards and secretaries, he had the full sense of his security and power; or he may have hoped to induce his partners to meet him in Russia, which would have added lustre to his already elevated position. He also had his political motives for being so evasive. He demonstrated his ill temper at the failure of the allies to invade western Europe. He used every opportunity to show them that he considered their efforts in southern Italy to be negligible in comparison with his great campaigns in Russia. He may also have wished to avoid disclosing to his allies his military and political plans. In the end both Roosevelt and Churchill agreed to meet him at Teheran.

One can think of very few instances in which men of such contrasting temper, background, and interests came together, as allies or partners, to decide issues of the greatest moment and gravity. What different worlds, what different outlooks and aspirations were embodied in these three men confronting one another across the conference table! The extreme antipodes were Churchill and Stalin, the descendant of the Duke of Marlborough and the son of serfs, the one born in Blenheim Palace, the other in a one-room hovel. The one still breathed the spiritual climate of Victorian and Edwardian England, whose imperial heritage he was guarding with the full vigour of his romantic temperament. The other had in him all the severity of Tsarist and Bolshevik Russia, whose storms he had ridden in cool, icy self-possession. The one had behind him four decades of parliamentary debate; the other as long an activity in clandestine groups and secretive Politbureaux. The one—full of eccentric idiosyncrasies, a lover of words and colour; the other —colourless and distrustful of words. Finally, the one had an empire to lose; the other something like an empire to win.

Roosevelt stood between the two, but much closer to Churchill. The environment in which he had grown up, the family of landowners and big industrialists, and the influences which moulded him, the political traditions of the Roosevelts in all their variety, the New York Bar, and the Navy Department, were extremely remote from those that had moulded Stalin. But Roosevelt's traditions were as much younger and more popular than Churchill's as the American middle class was younger than the English aristocracy. This perhaps brought Roosevelt nearer to Stalin. At times he shared Stalin's impatience with Churchill's rhetorical performances; but more often he relished them, while Stalin, following Churchill's words with the help of an interpreter, was left cold or ironically amused. Stalin and Churchill represented two opposed types of class-consciousness. To both, Roosevelt, the prophet of leftish bourgeois progress, must at times have appeared as an illogical middle-of-the-roader. Stalin, despite his evolution, would still have expressed his outlook in the words of the *Communist Manifesto*: 'The history of all society hitherto has been the history of class struggle.' Churchill had epitomized his outlook in an epigram of his own, as if designed to dispute the Marxian axiom: 'The story of the human race is War.'¹ Roosevelt, the Puritan and the leader of a nation that had so far been spared the worst violence of class struggle and the worst calamities of war, would hardly have adopted either of these generalizations.

Stalin looked upon both his allies as representatives of the capitalist class. He would have attached little importance to their professions of democracy, even if he had not doubted their sincerity. To him their democracy was a sham, for what meaning had the façades of government by the people, on which they so prided themselves, if these served to conceal gigantic mechanisms of exploitation, factories for the production of surplus value? He watched his partners with the cool curiosity with which a scientist may observe elements of nature, convinced that he knows their structure and can reasonably foresee their reactions to certain circumstances. Here they were—two living specimens of alien society, two great leaders of the 'other world'. That 'other world' was now, by a paradox of history, strangely split: one part of it was locked in mortal struggle with the Soviets, while the other was tied to them by bonds of alliance. The gulf between the allies might be bridged—it was very important to bridge it—but it had not disappeared, whatever might be said in solemn declarations of friendship and unanimity addressed to the peoples of the world. Some such ideas almost certainly crossed and re-crossed Stalin's mind.

The thoughts that crossed Churchill's mind could not have been very different, though they started from the opposite

¹ Winston S. Churchill, *The Aftermath*, p. 451.

extreme. On 22 June 1941 Churchill had said: 'No one has been a more persistent opponent of communism than I have been for the last twenty-five years. I will unsay no word that I have spoken about it, but all this fades away before the spectacle which is now unfolding.' It is enough to know some of the words about the Bolshevik revolution which Churchill refused to 'unsay'—words of fear, hate, and contempt—to realize that 'all this' could not really have faded from his mind. But it may be guessed that Churchill's attitude towards Stalin was in some ways more complex than Stalin's towards him, if only because Churchill could not but view his partner with the historian's and artist's eye as well as with the eye of the politician. The politician was preoccupied with the tactical handling of the man whom he regarded as a dangerous ally. The imagination of the historian was probably stirred by the curious changes which the successor to the Great Repudiator, as Churchill had called Lenin, was bringing about in Russia. The recent upsurge of Russian traditionalism could not but make him feel that Stalin had half-embraced his, Churchill's, principle, that he had been infusing the Conservative spirit in a revolutionary society. This, as much as the common military interest, may have accounted for those flashes of genuine sympathy that often gleamed through Churchill's references to Stalin. The artist in Churchill must have been fascinated by the sombre drama of the man and his life, though the excess of its sombriety filled him with revulsion which at times he found hard to conceal.

While Stalin's attitude towards the two western leaders was fixed and rationalized, while Churchill's sympathy for the Russian 'war horse' was mingled with antipathy, Roosevelt seems to have been completely baffled by the strange phenomenon with which he had come face to face. To him Russia, especially Bolshevik Stalinist Russia, was *terra incognita*. He modestly admitted this to his assistants. 'I don't know', he said, 'a good Russian from a bad Russian. I can tell a good Frenchman from a bad Frenchman, I can tell a good Italian from a bad Italian, I know a good Greek when I see one. But I don't understand the Russians.'[1] Stalin was obviously beyond all his ideas of 'good' and 'bad'.

[1] Frances Perkins, *The Roosevelt I Knew*, p. 72.

They had hardly met when Stalin invited Roosevelt to stay with him in the Russian embassy, saying that a plot had been afoot in Teheran. Stalin himself moved to a small cottage in the embassy grounds to make room for his guest. Despite this gesture of solicitude, he remained, as Roosevelt said later, 'correct, stiff, solemn, not smiling, nothing human to get hold of'. The President made a desperate attempt to 'cut through this icy surface'; and he thought he had succeeded when he contrived to amuse Stalin by a few pin-pricks at Churchill.[1] The truth was that any sign, even the slightest, of disharmony between Roosevelt and Churchill had a soothing effect on Stalin. In all probability he had invited the President to be his guest to prevent him from keeping in closer touch with Churchill than would have suited Stalin's tactical convenience.

Doubtless to his surprise he soon found that he had had no need to resort to the petty stratagem, because Roosevelt and Churchill did not see eye to eye on the main issue they were to debate. Ostensibly, that issue was the further course of military operations. In truth it was much wider, for on those operations depended, up to a point, the political outlook of post-war Europe. Churchill laid before the conference his plan for an Anglo-American invasion of the Balkans, which was to delay still further the invasion of France. At once the animosity between Stalin and Churchill, which had lingered on since their meeting in August 1942, burst forth with new intensity. In 1942 Stalin suspected that the motive behind the postponement of the second front was the intention of the allies to let Russia and Germany mutually exhaust themselves. He may still have harboured that suspicion when the invasion of France did not take place in the summer of 1943 either. But now, towards the end of 1943, he himself no longer feared attrition. Nor could he have supposed that Churchill banked on it. His present suspicion must have been that Churchill reckoned with Russia's strength, not weakness; and that the purpose of his new plan was to forestall a Russian occupation of the Balkan lands. Churchill did, indeed, link his proposal for the new Mediterranean venture with a scheme for a joint British, American, and Russian occupation of the Balkans.[2]

---

[1] Frances Perkins, *The Roosevelt I Knew*, pp. 70-1.
[2] John R. Deane, *The Strange Alliance*, pp. 42-4.

Stalin stiffly opposed the scheme and asked for landings in France. Neither he nor Churchill nor Roosevelt touched the underlying political issues, although those must have been on everybody's mind. The talk was all about the military pros and cons. Stalin was in the advantageous position that the balance of the military arguments was strongly in his favour. Churchill proposed to land allied troops at selected points along the Mediterranean: in northern Italy, whence they were to relieve the allied forces blocked by the Germans in southern Italy; on the Adriatic coast, whence they were, with the help of Tito's partisans, to force their way into the valley of the Danube; and in the Aegean area, where Turkey was to join in an attack northwards. Stalin pointed out that those operations could not be decisive and that they might fritter away much of the allied strength. In contrast, in an invasion across the Channel, the allies would have the benefit of a short and well-protected line of communication; they would bring their concentrated pressure to bear upon the enemy; they would, in liberating France, inflict an irretrievable moral blow on Germany; and they would, finally, have in front of them the shortest and the most direct route to the Ruhr, the hub of German industrial power. Stalin put his argument bluntly and tersely, interspersing it with caustic remarks, which made Churchill growl and redden in the face. The argument went on during three plenary sessions of the conference and two private sessions of the heads of the Governments. All the time Stalin alone spoke for the Russian delegation, which consisted only of himself, Molotov, Voroshilov, and an interpreter.

His arguments carried the day. The American chiefs of staff agreed with him. Even some British generals were opposed to Churchill. Roosevelt, at first hesitant, accepted Stalin's view. To win the war, to win it as rapidly as possible and at the least cost to the invading armies—this was Roosevelt's main preoccupation. From this viewpoint, the invasion across the Channel offered much greater promise than the Mediterranean campaigns. In Roosevelt's pragmatic, non-class-conscious mind, the importance of this, the immediate purpose, overshadowed the aftermath of the war, with its possible antagonisms and tensions that were already perplexing his British friend. Another circumstance which must have influenced his decision was the statement that Stalin had made at the opening of the conference that Russia would join in the war against Japan as soon as she was relieved from the struggle in Europe. Whatever Roosevelt's reasons, his decision settled the matter. It was agreed that 'Operation Overlord'—this was the code name for the invasion of France—should be carried out next May.

This was a moment of Stalin's supreme triumph. Perhaps only he and Churchill were aware of its implications. Europe had now been militarily divided in two; and behind the military division there loomed the social and political cleavage. Against a vastly different social background, an old dream of Russian diplomacy—the dream about bringing the Balkans under Russian influence—was coming true.

Having scored this success, Stalin relaxed and mellowed. He took a lively part in the argument which followed over the way in which the invasion across the Channel was to be made. He assumed an attitude of benevolent superiority, the attitude of the veteran victor towards allies who were only now about to start on their first really big venture. He offered helpful advice and drew readily on his own fund of experience. He insisted on the need for the British and the Americans to attain unity of command and urged them to appoint at once their commander-in-chief. His promptings, says General Deane, 'certainly hastened the selection of General Eisenhower'.[1] Repeatedly he warned them against the faults of delay and omission; and when Churchill dwelt on the need for secrecy, camouflage, and manœuvres of diversion—'a bodyguard of lies that was to protect truth'—Stalin disclosed some of his own *ruses de guerre*: he had 5,000 dummy tanks, 2,000 false aircraft, and so on which he used as decoys for the enemy. Most important of all, he promised to launch strong supporting offensives when the western armies would be descending on the Continent.

The rejection of Churchill's military plan was not Stalin's only success. The other was a private agreement of the 'Big Three' over the Russo-Polish frontier. The foreign ministers, who had just conferred in Moscow, had reached no conclusion on this. But both Churchill and Roosevelt felt that it was now pointless to advise, as they had done before, that the Russo-Polish feud should await settlement by a peace conference. The

[1] John R. Deane, *The Strange Alliance*, p. 43.

Red Army was fast approaching the former eastern marches of Poland; and it was sure to reincorporate them in the Soviet Union. Unable to forestall this act of reacquisition, Churchill apparently preferred to put the stamp of allied approval upon it. It was he who now came forward with a proposal that the 'Big Three' should recognize the so-called Curzon Line as the new frontier between Russia and Poland. To this Stalin readily agreed. Apart from minor rectifications, the Curzon Line, so called after the British foreign secretary on behalf of whom it had been proposed in 1920, left the debatable land with the Soviet Union. Roosevelt approved the proposal but still tried to secure the city of Lvov for the Poles.

The advantage which Stalin now secured could not but give him ironical satisfaction. He must have probed with some curiosity into Churchill's motives. It was true that he had confronted Churchill with a case which it was not easy to refute: in 1941 the western powers welcomed the Soviets as an ally, such as they were, within the frontiers they then possessed, and the western powers could not expect Stalin to agree to the shrinkage of Soviet territory after a victory so dearly bought. But this exactly was also the Polish case. The Poles argued that Britain had tied herself by an alliance to a Poland that possessed the eastern marches, that they had the right to demand from the British that they should not lend a hand in depriving them of their possessions, and that, in addition, Poland had been an older ally than Russia. The Polish claim carried little weight compared with the massive shift in the balance of power that had just been revealed on the eastern front. Nor did Churchill merely bow to power. His idea was to stop the spread of communism at the Curzon Line. That was to be the new frontier between the opposed social and political systems. He retreated before Stalin in order the better to hold him on what at that time seemed to him a fairly solid line of defence. He hoped that west of the Curzon Line the Polish Government of London, which was sure to oppose communism, would establish itself, and he pressed Stalin to resume relations with that Government now that the western powers no longer disputed Russia's gains. Churchill also hoped that by persuasion and pressure he would prevail upon the Poles in London to agree to the new frontier, for otherwise Stalin would not even parley with them. Stalin was apparently convinced that in this Churchill would not succeed, and that he, Stalin, would then be free to sponsor another Polish Government, and that the western powers, having once committed themselves to the Curzon frontier, would, by the logic of their own position, be compelled to accept the Polish Government that accepted that frontier. Shortly before the Teheran meeting he had already indicated to Polish Communists in Russia that he would welcome the formation of a political body in Poland which, although not yet a rival government, would dispute the claim of the London émigrés to speak on behalf of Poland. That body, the Polish National Council, was in fact formed in German-occupied Poland a month after Teheran. The intricate game over Poland was not yet played out.

Having agreed on the second front and on the Curzon Line, the 'Big Three' informally exchanged views, *inter alia*, on the future of Germany. The exchange was vague and hazy, so hazy indeed that none of the participants seemed to have any real foretaste of the great controversy to come. The three heads of the Governments seemed broadly to agree on a 'Carthaginian' peace, although in advocating it Stalin was undoubtedly more determined than the others.

Towards the end of the conference the tensions and animosities that had marked its beginning seemed dispelled. At a celebration of Churchill's sixty-ninth birthday Stalin toasted him as his 'great friend'. At another ceremony he received from Churchill's hand a sword of honour sent by the King for the city of Stalingrad. Roosevelt related afterwards that he saw tears in Stalin's eyes, when Stalin, in a strange posture of chivalrous romanticism, bowed to kiss the sword.[1] The tears may seem out of character, but perhaps Stalin was overwhelmed with emotion. This was a strange moment in his career, for who would have foretold that a day would come when His Britannic Majesty would honour a Russian city named after the son of Georgian serfs, a former inmate of the prison of Baku, a Siberian exile, a disciple of Lenin? And who would have foretold that the disciple of the 'Great Repudiator' would not repudiate such an honour?

On 1 December the heads of the three Governments left

---

[1] Frances Perkins, *The Roosevelt I Knew*, p. 71.

Teheran. Before parting they issued a joint declaration about their complete agreement. The world was given no hint of the acrimonious controversy that had preceded the agreement—such indiscretion was unthinkable in the middle of war. The 'Big Three' solemnly stated: 'We came here with hope and determination. We leave here friends in fact, in spirit and in purpose.'

. . . .

The year 1944 brought Stalin one military success after another. At its beginning the Russians were still fighting to break the German blockade of Leningrad; towards its end they blockaded the German garrison of Budapest.

In the course of the year the Red Army was engaged in a continuous series of offensive operations—'the ten blows' Stalin was to call them—and in its middle the western allies landed in France. Enormous masses of men were locked in battle on the eastern front, from the northern to the southern extremities of Europe, and the front irresistibly shifted westwards. The pattern of the campaigns emerges from a simple enumeration of the main offensives: in January Leningrad was relieved, and the Russians thrust out by way of Novgorod towards the Baltic coast. In February and March, having already captured Kiev, they advanced from the Dnieper to the Bug and the Dniester. In the early spring the fight shifted far to the south—the Germans were ousted from the Crimea and Odessa. In June, simultaneously with the invasion of France, the fighting shifted back from the southernmost to the northernmost fringe of the front, and Finland was to all intents and purposes knocked out. In June and July the Red Army freed Vitebsk and Minsk and swept forward to the Niemen and the Vistula. In July and August it continued to advance in southern Poland, along the Carpathians. In August it occupied Rumania and, helped by an internal upheaval in that country, advanced upon Bulgaria and Hungary. In September and October the main fighting once again shifted back to the north, to Finland, Estonia, and Latvia. Then the centre of operations moved back south, to the Carpathians and beyond, to Hungary and Slovakia.

By the beginning of the year the Red Army had already secured considerable superiority in numbers and weapons, and that superiority grew progressively. It was characteristic of

Stalin that even now he was not given over to the illusions of *blitzkrieg*, as Hitler had been before. He did not attempt any of those sweeping, spectacular offensives which might have confused the enemy and struck him off his feet but which might also have dangerously extended the attacker's own lines and exposed his flanks. Even now, when victory was so obviously coming his way, he remained stolidly cautious. Throughout the year he shifted the centre of the fighting from the north to the south, backward and forward, with astonishing regularity, power, and circumspection, like a boxer who systematically covers his opponent with telling blows without expecting that one single blow will knock him down. He kept Hitler constantly guessing, constantly rushing his reserves to plug ever new breaches, constantly trying to meet new threats and constantly expending his strength in the process. The 'ten blows' were co-ordinated and timed with clockwork precision, proof of the organizing ability and systematic work of Stalin's present general staff, so radically contrasting with the inefficiency and the confusion of 1941.[1]

[1] A few words must be said here to explain the material aspect of the Russian superiority. Throughout the war Russia was confronted with German armies roughly twice as numerous and strong as those that had defeated her in the First World War. The Russian achievement was made possible primarily by the rapid industrialization of the eastern provinces, much of which took place in the course of the war on a basis prepared in peace. The industrial output of the provinces that escaped German occupation was normally about 40 per cent. of the total Soviet output. It was doubled between 1942 and 1945. The production of the armament factories in the east went up by 500–600 per cent. On the average, 30,000 tanks and fighting vehicles and nearly 40,000 planes were turned out every year between 1943 and 1945—almost none of these had been manufactured in Russia in the First World War. The annual output of artillery guns was now 120,000, compared with less than 4,000 in 1914–17. The Russian army was supplied with nearly 450,000 home-produced machine-guns annually—only about 9,000 had been produced under the Tsar. Five million rifles and tommy guns, five times as many as in the First World War, were produced every year. (See A. I. Notkin, *Ocherki Teorii Sotsialisticheskovo Vosproizvodstva*, pp. 272–3.) The Red Army fought its way from the Volga to the Elbe mainly with home-produced weapons. The weapons which the western powers supplied were a useful and in some cases a vital addition. But the lorries which carried the Russian divisions into Germany were mostly of American, Canadian, and British make—more than 400,000 lorries were supplied to Russia under Lend-Lease. So were most of the boots in which the infantry proper slogged its way to Berlin, through the mud and snow and sand of the eastern European plain. Much of the army's clothing and of its tinned food were supplied under Lend-Lease. One might sum up broadly that the fire-power of the Red Army was home produced, whereas the element of its mobility was largely imported.

New York Times

WITH RIBBENTROP, AUGUST 1939

Imperial War Museum

WITH CHURCHILL AND ROOSEVELT AT TEHERAN, 1943

Imperial War Museum

PRESENTATION OF THE STALINGRAD SWORD, 1943

STALIN WITH HIS MARSHALS, 1945

Every major success of the Red Army brought new political issues to the fore; and it was to these that Stalin now devoted himself, leaving with ever greater confidence the conduct of the military campaigns to his marshals and generals. In the first days of January the Red Army crossed the old Russo-Polish frontier; and the Polish crisis became acute. The Polish Government in London loudly claimed that it was entitled to administer the territories that were now coming back under Soviet control. Moscow equally loudly refuted the claim. Eager to compose the public row between the two allied Governments, the American Secretary of State, Cordell Hull, offered American mediation. The offer apparently incensed Stalin, who held that after Teheran the western powers should neither themselves question his right to control Poland's eastern marches nor allow the Poles to dispute it—there was no room for any mediation.

He vented his irritation in a curiously devious manner. An obscure report was published in Moscow which charged the British with negotiating a peace with Germany behind Russia's back.[1] The charge, made so soon after Teheran, was the more insulting to the British, since they had only a few weeks before rejected 'peace feelers' thrown out by Himmler, the chief of Hitler's police; and Stalin could hardly have been unaware of this.[2] The insult was, in all probability, meant to make the British and the Americans wonder whether the Russians themselves were not looking for an excuse to negotiate a separate peace. Stalin confronted his allies with the hint of a threat. Faint as this was, it cannot be said with certainty that Stalin would not under any circumstances have contemplated carrying it out. As his armies were approaching the frontiers of 1941, it was natural that he or somebody in his entourage should have reflected for a while whether this was not the time to halt, to stop the terrible carnage and to make peace. Did not Kutuzov urge Alexander I to stop pursuing the *Grande Armée* at Russia's frontier instead of continuing the war for the benefit of that 'accursed British island', which he, Kutuzov, wished to see disappear under the sea?[3] On the other hand, Stalin, like Alexander, was burning with the ambition that his troops

---

[1] This report appeared in *Pravda* on 17 January 1944.
[2] *The Memoirs of Cordell Hull*, vol. ii, p. 1573.
[3] E. Tarlé, *Napoleon*, p. 248; and *Istorya Diplomatii*, vol. i, p. 373.

should march triumphantly into the enemy's capital; and, like Alexander, he was loath to give the enemy any respite. It is not known whether any man either in his General Staff or in the Politbureau dared to whisper to him Kutuzov's advice. But it is conceivable that his determination to destroy the Third Reich might have slackened if he had reason to think that he could gain more through a separate peace than through victory obtained in common with the western powers. That he had no reason so to think—the western powers had repeatedly to provide the proof.

He rejected the offer of western mediation between Russia and Poland not merely because the issue of the Polish frontier had, in his view, been settled at Teheran. He insisted on the principle that the allies should not interfere with matters that, in his view, concerned Russia and her neighbours only. Eastern Europe was to be Russia's zone of influence.

It was at this stage, in the months that followed the Teheran conference, that the plans for the division of Europe into zones were becoming more and more explicit. The idea had been in the air even before Teheran. Politicians and journalists in the allied countries had discussed a condominium of the three great allied powers, each of whom was to wield paramount influence within its own orbit, since the great powers alone possessed enough might to win the war and guard the peace. At Teheran Roosevelt put to Stalin a not dissimilar project, the project of the 'Four Policemen'—the United States, Russia, Britain, and China—that were to keep order in the world.[1] The minds of allied diplomats wandered back to the Holy Alliance which ruled Europe after the Napoleonic wars and to the more recent experience of Versailles, for, despite all its democratic trappings, the last peace conference, too, had been dominated by the concert of the great powers. Stalin's diplomats looked up the secret treaties that had been concluded by Russia's pre-revolutionary rulers and then published and denounced by Lenin. There was the Anglo-Russian treaty of 1907, under which the two powers had divided Persia into separate zones. There was the Treaty of London of 1915, in which the British had agreed that Russia should annex Constantinople, the Turkish Straits, and Thrace, and that she should in effect dominate the Balkans. If the

---

[1] Robert E. Sherwood, *Roosevelt and Hopkins*, p. 785.

British, so Stalin's diplomats now apparently reasoned, had been willing so to reward Tsarist Russia for her far less effective contribution to a common war, why should they begrudge Stalin's Russia the same prize or the major part of it?

The concerts of victorious powers in the past had owed their relative unity to the fact that the rulers of those powers had belonged to the same social class or had represented parallel social interests; that they had spoken in the same or a similar idiom and had consequently been bound to one another by ties of some solidarity. What was new and startling in the present experiment was that it was undertaken by men who represented antagonistic interests and conflicting principles. More paradoxically still, it was the British Prime Minister, the sworn enemy of communism, who acted as the chief sponsor of the scheme.

The first more or less formal arrangement about zones of influence was apparently proposed by the British Government in June 1944.[1] The British suggested that Rumania and Bulgaria should be treated as part of the Russian zone and that British influence should be supreme in Greece. Stalin readily consented to this. Now as in 1939 it was not he but his partner who took upon himself the odium of carving out the zones. He wanted to know whether Churchill acted on his own initiative and responsibility only. Would Roosevelt, he asked, endorse the arrangement? Roosevelt was now non-committal. He refused in fact to face the consequences of his own attitude at Teheran, which helped the Russian army to become the sole master of the Balkans, while Churchill was now drawing the conclusions from his defeat at Teheran and doing his utmost to keep Greece out of Russian reach. But Roosevelt raised no explicit objection, and so Stalin took it for granted that under the agreement of June 1944 Britain and the United States had assigned the greater part of the Balkans to Russia. In October 1944, when Churchill and Eden came to Moscow, the arrangement was confirmed and extended. An almost absurd tone crept into their talks when the two Prime Ministers and their ministers fixed the percentages of their respective shares in the Balkans. As the American Ambassador in Moscow wrote to the Secretary of State, they agreed that Russia should have a 75–80 per cent. predominance in Bulgaria, Hungary, and

[1] *The Memoirs of Cordell Hull*, vol. ii, pp. 1451 ff.

Rumania, while the British share was expressed in 20–25 per cent. In Yugoslavia the two countries were to exercise their influence on a fifty-fifty basis.[1]

In June 1944 it was still claimed that the division of zones was to have no political significance—it was to be a strictly military arrangement. In October the partners made no bones about its political character. They agreed confidentially that 'if the British found it necessary to take military action to quell internal disorders in Greece, the Soviets would not interfere. In return, the British would recognize the right of the Soviets to take the lead in maintaining order in Rumania.'[2] Stalin could have had no doubt what sort of 'internal disorders' Churchill anticipated. The British had just landed in Greece and found the Communist-led partisans of E.L.A.S. in virtual control of the country. Churchill was anticipating civil war and preparing for it. Stalin declared in effect his *désintéressement* in the fate of the Greek left. The *quid pro quo*—the promise that the British would not interfere in Rumania—amounted to Churchill's disinterest in the fate of the Rumanian right.

This was a perfect (some may say a perfectly cynical) bargain if there ever was one; and it involved, of course, other countries as well. Having clinched it, Churchill and Stalin surprised the world by the zeal with which they defended each other's actions and by the indubitable admiration with which they spoke of each other. 'The surprising thing', Stalin said shortly after Churchill's visit, 'is not that differences [between the allies] exist, but that they are so few, and that as a rule in practically every case they are resolved in a spirit of unity and co-ordination.' 'A still more striking indication', he added, 'are the recent talks in Moscow with Mr. Churchill . . . and Mr. Eden . . ., held in an atmosphere of friendship and a spirit of perfect unanimity.'[3] Churchill returned the compliment: 'Marshal Stalin and the Soviet leaders', he told the House of Commons, 'wish to live in honourable friendship and equality with the western democracies. . . . I feel also that their word is their bond. I know of no government which stands to its obligations even in its own despite, more solidly than the Russian Soviet government. I decline absolutely to embark here on a discussion

---

[1] *The Memoirs of Cordell Hull*, vol. ii, p. 1458.
[2] James F. Byrnes, *Speaking Frankly*, p. 53.   [3] J. Stalin, *War Speeches*, p. 111.

about Russian good faith.' Churchill had good reason to make this statement, for when, in December 1944, the civil war broke out in Greece, the Soviet Press and radio had not a single word to say in sympathy with the Greek left-wing partisans. That 'enigmatic', persistent silence testified that Stalin had washed his hands of the affair. This was the real heyday of his amity with Churchill. 'A good plot, good friends, and full of expectation; an excellent plot, very good friends.'

It should not be imagined that the terms of the agreement were clearly defined, that Stalin ever frankly expressed his assent to the suppression of communism outside the Russian zone or that he declared his intention to establish communism inside it. The issue may not have been quite so clear either in his or in Churchill's mind; and, in spite of everything, the partners still distrusted each other enough to avoid being too explicit. Even the term 'zone of influence' seems hardly ever to occur in the official records. Their language was all hint, suggestion, intimation, insinuation. Almost every declaration of their policy contained the sacramental clause about 'non-interference in the internal affairs' of other countries. Yet throughout the war every power had interfered in the domestic affairs of every country in which it had had any military interest. The British and the Russians had jointly interfered in Persia and overthrown its pro-German Government. The British had interfered in Egypt and Iraq, the Russians in Poland and every other country in which they had solemnly pledged themselves not to interfere. The Americans had intervened in France in the controversies between Darlan, Giraud, and de Gaulle, in Italy in the disputes between Victor Emmanuel, Badoglio, and the opposition, and elsewhere: 'I hoped . . . to persuade Russia', wrote Cordell Hull, 'to adopt the policy of co-operation and non-intervention'; and for that reason he opposed the Act of Chapultepec of March 1945 'whereby the American Republics agreed in effect to intervene militarily in any of their number in certain circumstances. Once we had agreed to this new position on intervention, Russia had more excuse to intervene in neighbouring states, and we had less reason to oppose her doing so.'[1] But, despite Cordell Hull's

---

[1] *The Memoirs of Cordell Hull*, vol. ii, pp. 1466–7.

opposition, the Act of Chapultepec was American policy. Stalin, 'the man without illusions', reckoned with the intervention of each of the 'Big Three' in the domestic affairs of their spheres as with a certainty, intervention that was in part dictated by military necessity and in part exploited military necessity as an excuse.

Stalin was eager to show that he was keeping his hands off the spheres of British and American influence. Yet he was in no position to keep off altogether. In western Europe, especially in France and Italy, the Communist parties had, in the course of the war, gained enormous prestige and authority, largely because of the creditable part they had played in the resistance. Although the Comintern had been disbanded, Moscow was still their Mecca. Thus Stalin continued to command a potent and growing influence within the orbit of the western powers.[1] Soon after the liberation of France he used that influence in a manner calculated to satisfy Conservative opinion and to set at rest any fears or suspicions that Churchill and Roosevelt may have had. It was undoubtedly under his inspiration that the French and Italian Communist parties behaved with extraordinary, selfless moderation. For the first time in their history, disregarding their own programmes, which forbade them to take part in bourgeois administrations, they joined in governments based on broad national coalitions. Although they were then the strongest parties in their countries, they contented themselves with minor positions in those governments, from which they could not hope to seize power either now or later and from which they were eventually to be ousted, almost without effort, by the other parties. The army and the police remained in the hands of Conservative or, at any rate, anti-Communist groups. Western Europe was to remain the domain of Liberal capitalism.

At times Stalin demonstrated his attitude with so little regard to appearances that he shocked the palest of the pink Socialists and the most moderate Liberals. This was the case when, in March 1944, even before the agreement on spheres was made, he recognized the Italian Government of Marshal Badoglio.

[1] Stalin himself must have been surprised by this growth of Communist influence in western Europe. During the war he expressed the view that the French people stood behind Pétain. See Robert E. Sherwood, *Roosevelt and Hopkins*, p. 777.

The Italian parties of the left and the centre still clamoured for the dismissal of Badoglio, the conqueror of Abyssinia, the henchman of King Victor Emmanuel. Stalin enhanced Badoglio's position *vis-à-vis* his opponents. Shortly afterwards *Izvestya* counselled the Italian left, which had pressed for the abdication of the discredited King, to postpone their dispute with the dynasty. Even much later, the Communist deputies in the Italian Constituent Assembly voted for the renewal of the Lateran Pacts which Mussolini had concluded with the Vatican; and so, against Socialist and Liberal opposition, they ceded to the Catholic clergy a dominant position in the spiritual life of the country. In France the Communist party, with hardly more than the softest murmur of discontent, lined up behind General de Gaulle, whose dictatorial ambition, anti-Marxist attitude, and clerical associations had long since been manifest.

Nor did Stalin yet give any clear impression that he would sponsor revolution in the countries of the Russian zone. Communist propagandists there spoke a nationalist and even clerical language. King Michael of Rumania was left on his throne; and he was even awarded one of the highest Russian military orders for his part in the *coup* in consequence of which Rumania had broken away from Germany. The Soviet generals and the local Communist leaders did honour to the Greek Orthodox clergy in the Balkan countries. In Poland they courted the Roman Catholic clergy. There was no talk yet of socialization of industry. Only long overdue land reforms were initiated.

In the spring of 1944 Stalin made a queer attempt at reconciliation with the Pope, an attempt with which a truly farcical episode was connected. On 28 April 1944 he received in the Kremlin a strange visitor, an American Roman Catholic priest of Polish descent, the Reverend S. Orlemanski from Springfield, Massachussets. The priest, a simple devout soul, unaware of the pitfalls of high politics, had left his quiet parish and come to Moscow with a sense of a mission to perform. He was out to make a personal contribution to two 'historic' reconciliations, one between the Kremlin and the Vatican, the other between Russia and Poland. For a few days the good man was in the limelight. To everybody's amazement, Stalin not only received him, but was twice closeted with him for long hours. Orlemanski, whom no authority in his Church had empowered to parley on its behalf and who had even left his parish without his bishop's permission, obtained from Stalin a solemn written declaration, signed in Stalin's own hand, in which he, the master of the Kremlin, offered collaboration to the master of the Vatican.[1] What use should be made of the offer he left to Orlemanski's discretion; and Orlemanski, with the momentous document in hand, returned to his parish. There his bishop pounced upon him, charging him with a breach of ecclesiastical discipline and threatening excommunication. The hapless priest suffered a nervous breakdown and removed himself to a cloister to do penance for his vagaries. Thus the great attempt at reconciliation between the Kremlin and the Vatican came to an end. The incident throws a comic light on the streak of naïve maladroitness which so often appeared in Stalin, despite all his shrewdness, cunning, and occasional far-sightedness. Here he was, the great dictator, remote from his own people, not easily accessible to the important diplomats in his own capital, one of the three men, at this moment almost their senior, who decided the future of the world—here he was, in the middle of his great offensives, closeting himself with an unknown crank to make through him an important political statement to the world. Stalin could have approached the Pope, if he wanted to, through any prominent Catholic politician; he could have used the good offices of the allied Governments. It may be that he was more eager to advertise his own respectable moderation than to seek peace with the Vatican; but even then he had no need to resort to a stunt which for a few days made him the laughing-stock of the world. The incident was, nevertheless, characteristic of the opportunistically rightist colouring of Stalin's policy in those days.

At the same time, however, Stalin managed to establish and to obtain his allies' sanction for two principles, both very hazy, by which political life in the Russian zone was to be guided. One was that he should be free to intervene against pro-Nazi and Fascist parties and groups and to establish a democratic order in the countries neighbouring Russia. The other was that the Governments of those countries should be 'friendly to

[1] *Vneshnyaya Politika Sovietskovo Soyuza*, vol. ii, pp. 129–32.

Russia'.[1] For the first time Stalin applied these principles to the Polish issue, which stood at the centre of allied diplomatic activity throughout the last year of the war. His purpose was to prevail upon the western allies that they should abandon the Polish Government in London, on the ground that it was neither democratic nor friendly to Russia. The manner in which he, the dictator *par excellence*, was now granting or refusing to grant testimonials of good democratic conduct to other people was extremely grotesque. So were the grave mien and the solemn gestures with which his allies participated in the strange show, in order to keep up the appearance of the common democratic interest of the Grand Alliance. Yet it would be wrong to describe Stalin's action as mere trickery, strong as was the element of trickery in it. Apart from the fact that he undoubtedly believed that what he did served a profoundly democratic purpose, the strength of his argument was in the fact that the Polish Government in London had indeed been a motley coalition of half-Conservative peasants, moderate Socialists, and of people who could not by any criterion, 'eastern' or 'western', be labelled democrats. The core of its administration consisted of the followers of the Polish dictators Pilsudski and Rydz-Smigly. More important still, the members of that Government, democratic and anti-democratic, were, with very few exceptions, possessed by that Russophobia which had been the hereditary propensity of Polish policy, a propensity enhanced by what the Poles had suffered at Russian hands since 1939. In truth, of all Polish parties, only the Communists were 'friendly to Russia'.[2] Stalin used that Russophobia as the justification for sponsoring, as soon as the Red Army had entered Poland proper, a Polish National Committee of Liberation, in which Communists and leftist Socialists wielded the decisive influence. Even then Stalin's relations with the Poles were ridden with

[1] On his return from his October visit to Moscow, Churchill said in the House of Commons: 'We have never weakened in any way in our resolve that Poland shall be restored and stand erect . . . free to model her social institutions . . . in any way her people chose, provided, I must say, that these are not on fascist lines, and provided that Poland stands loyally as a barrier and friend of Russia. . . .'

[2] It was characteristic of the attitude of the Polish Government in London, especially of its complete unawareness of the change in the balance of international power, that it protested to the allied Governments against the march of Russian armies into Rumania, Hungary, and Slovakia. J. Ciechanowski, *Defeat in Victory*, p. 227.

anomalies, as can be seen from the following episode. Among his Polish protégés were men who had been released from Russian prisons and concentration camps only after 1941. At a reception he once gave for the Committee of Liberation, Stalin turned to one of its leaders, an old left Socialist, who had suffered persecution in pre-war Poland, and asked him: 'How many years, comrade, have you spent in prisons?' This was the typical question that one former political prisoner would ask another. 'Which prisons', said the Pole, 'do you have in mind: the Polish or the Soviet ones?' 'The quicker we forget about the Russian prisons', Stalin rejoined, 'the better will it be for both our nations.'

In sponsoring the Committee, Stalin confronted Churchill and Roosevelt with an awkward choice. They either had to acknowledge that Committee, if they were to be guided by the principle that only a government friendly to Russia should be tolerated in Poland, or they had to disregard that principle and go on supporting the Poles whom they had supported so far. At first they tried to evade the dilemma and to prevail upon Stalin to negotiate with Stanislaw Mikolajczyk, the Conservative peasant, who had, since Sikorski's death, headed the Polish Government in London. Mikolajczyk was one of the very few Polish émigré politicians who were inclined to bargain over, if not to accept, the Curzon Line. Towards the end of July 1944, indeed, Mikolajczyk went to Moscow, only to find on his arrival that the Russian Government had just officially recognized the so-called Lublin Committee. Having, by a most radical act of intervention, installed a government of his choice in Poland, Stalin now disclaimed any intention of meddling in Polish domestic affairs; and he advised Mikolajczyk to come to terms with the 'Lublin Poles'.

Right in the middle of that haggling a tragic event occurred, in which Stalin's role appeared extremely ambiguous and even sinister. On 1 August 1944 armed insurrection against the Germans broke out in Warsaw. The insurgents were led by officers who took their cue from the Polish Government in London. The Red Army had rapidly approached Warsaw, and the commanders of the rising mistakenly believed that the German garrison was about to evacuate the city. The mass of the insurgents were animated by the desire to liberate their capital through their own efforts. Their commander, however, was himself guilty of a gross political mistake—he gave the order for action without trying to establish contact and to co-ordinate the rising with the command of the advancing Russian army. Incidentally, the commander of that Russian army was a Pole, Marshal Rokossovsky. That mistake sprang, of course, from the political situation. The leaders of the rising hoped that they would either be in control of the Polish capital before the entry of the Russians, or that, failing this, they would exert moral pressure on the Russians to acknowledge the political claims of those who had helped them to expel the Germans.

It soon turned out that the timing of the insurrection was disastrous. Rokossovsky's army had been stopped by the Germans at the Vistula and then thrown back. The German garrison, far from evacuating the capital, turned all its might and fury against the insurgents. A sombre and desperate battle developed, in which the Poles fought with unique romantic heroism, and the Germans revenged themselves by burning and pulling down street after street and house after house, until the city of Warsaw virtually ceased to exist. The Poles begged for help. Mikolajczyk appealed to Stalin. Stalin's behaviour was extremely strange, to say no more. At first he would not believe the reports about the rising and suspected a *canard*. Then he promised help but failed to give it. So far it was still possible to put a charitable interpretation upon his behaviour. It may be, it is indeed very probable, that Rokossovsky, repelled by the Germans, was unable to come to the rescue of Warsaw, and that Stalin, just conducting major offensives on the southern sector of the front, in the Carpathians and in Rumania, could not alter his strategic dispositions to assist the unexpected rising. But then he did something that sent a shudder of horror through the allied countries. He refused to allow British planes, flying from their bases to drop arms and food to the insurgents, to land on Russian airfields behind the fighting lines. He thereby reduced British help to the insurgents to a minimum. Then Russian planes appeared over the burning city with help, when it was too late. It is not easy to see what Stalin hoped to gain from his demonstration of callousness. The tragedy of Warsaw added new bitterness to the anti-Russian feeling in Poland, and it shocked even Stalin's admirers in the west. It is difficult to think what political calculation, be it even the most cynical one, accounted for his attitude. He was moved by that unscrupulous rancour and insensible spite of which he had given so much proof during the great purges.

.   .   .   .

When Stalin, Churchill, and Roosevelt met at Yalta, in February 1945, victory was within their grasp. They knew that it could elude them only through their own discord. This was, indeed, the only hope of Hitler, reading and rereading the story of Frederick the Great, who miraculously escaped defeat in the Seven Years War when his enemies fell out with one another. The three allied leaders, eager to inflict their last blows on the enemy, were therefore busy shelving the issues that divided them.

Stalin was no longer the only victor, as he had been at Teheran. The British and the Americans stood on the Rhine. But Russian military preponderance was still marked. On the Oder the Red Army was preparing its assault on Berlin. A fortnight or so before the Yalta conference something happened that seemed to throw the Russian preponderance into even sharper relief. The Germans launched their last counter-offensive in the Ardennes, and for a time it seemed that they might split the British–American front. On 14 January General Eisenhower's deputy, Air-Chief Marshal Tedder, went to Moscow to request Stalin for Russian offensives to divert German pressure from the west. Stalin acceded to the request. Three days later the Red Army entered Warsaw and swept forward from the Vistula to the Oder. When he met his guests at Livadia, the Tsar's summer residence, near Yalta, amid the ruins and the desolation of recent battles, Stalin had therefore a strong sense of the Russian contribution towards victory; and his guests could not but show gratitude.

In their thoughts the 'Big Three' still tended to project their present unity into the peace and to see the future in terms of their condominium and of spheres of influence. But the nearer the war drew to an end the stronger grew their mental reservations, doubts, and fears. Each side made concessions to the other, but sought guarantees for itself. To every act of agreement, each was anxious to add an escape clause. At every step military considerations overlapped or conflicted with social interests and ideological principles. As if by some fatality, the 'Big Three' were driven to adopt one military expedient after another; and every expedient contained seeds of future discord and rivalry.

Their state of mind is curiously illustrated by a dialogue between Stalin and Churchill which took place at Yalta, in the course of a discussion on the statutes of the United Nations Organization. The debate centred on the clauses dealing with the right of veto, which the great powers wished to reserve for themselves in the Security Council of that organization. Stalin, more emphatic in this than his partners, wanted to make the right of veto absolutely rigid, proof against any attempt at obviating or weakening it. Churchill had said something to the effect that the organization should be able to act against a great power that might aim at world domination. 'I would like to ask Mr. Churchill', was Stalin's rejoinder, 'to name the power which may intend to dominate the world. I am sure Great Britain does not want to dominate the world. So one is removed from suspicion. I am sure the United States does not wish to do so, so another is excluded from the powers having intentions to dominate the world.' 'May I answer?' Churchill interrupted. 'In a minute', Stalin was impatient to clinch his argument. 'The danger in the future is the possibility of conflicts among ourselves.' He brought out the implications of Churchill's attitude—Churchill had apparently been suspicious of Russia and had wished to make the statutes of the United Nations as vexatious to her as possible. Churchill, somewhat embarrassed by Stalin so dotting the i's, answered that as long as they, the three men who had jointly conducted this great war, were alive, there was no danger of conflict; but would their successors remain united? Stalin was not to be set at ease. He reminded his guests of a rankling Russian grievance: in 1939, during the first Russo-Finnish war, the League of Nations pilloried Russia and expelled her from its midst—the same League that had never lifted a finger against Hitler and never done anything against any act of aggression. . . . No, Russia would not allow herself to be so treated in the future.[1]

It is curious to watch how throughout this phase of the war Stalin, on the one hand, advocated with the greatest perseverance the world condominium of the 'Big Three', resenting

[1] James F. Byrnes, *Speaking Frankly*, pp. 36–7.

any suggestion that tended to weaken it, and how, on the other, he at every step betrayed his fear and suspicion of Russia's would-be partners in that condominium. When Churchill and Roosevelt proposed that France be given a share in the control of Germany he objected, because 'France had opened the gates to the enemy'. It was his stock argument that the place any nation was to be allowed to keep in peace should be proportionate to the strength it had shown and the sacrifices it had borne in war. That the principle favoured Russia more than any other nation goes without saying, for no other nation had borne sacrifices comparable to hers. When Churchill ironically remarked that the 'Big Three' were 'a very exclusive club, the entrance fee being at least five million soldiers or the equivalent',[1] Stalin must have bitterly reflected that the entrance fee that Russia had paid was many more than five million *dead* soldiers. He stubbornly opposed any suggestion that would allow the small nations to speak up against the great powers in the future league of nations. What he apparently feared was that the great powers might incite the small ones against Russia. At one time he insisted that the United Nations must have armed forces of their own, especially an international air force with bases in various small countries.[2] The proposal, although it was rejected by the United States, seemed to testify to his confidence in the solidarity of the 'Big Three'. But then again, prompted by the fear that Russia might be outvoted in the United Nations, he asked that the Ukraine and Byelorussia be recognized as members of the United Nations with their own vote. It was mainly in order to be able to substantiate that demand that in February 1944 he carried out a constitutional reform, by which he abolished, at least nominally, the main principle of his own Constitution of 1924, and replaced the *Union* of Soviet Republics by a sort of a federation, under which each of the constituent republics was to have its own foreign ministry and its own army.[3]

---

[1] James F. Byrnes, *Speaking Frankly*, p. 25.

[2] J. Stalin, *War Speeches*, p. 114; and *The Memoirs of Cordell Hull*, vol. ii, p. 1682.

[3] A secondary motive for the reform may have been Stalin's desire to placate the nationalist mood in the outlying republics, especially in the Ukraine. As the Red Army advanced into those republics, the specific Russian patriotic propaganda was toned down in favour of a broader Soviet patriotism, embracing all the nationalities of the Soviet Union. Nevertheless, the upsurge of Russian traditionalism stimulated similar nationalist trends among the smaller nations of the Soviet Union.

One can hardly help reflecting on the contrast between the gravity of the underlying issues and antagonisms and the futility and pettiness of the bargaining to which they gave rise. Heads of governments, ministers, ambassadors had haggled for months over the Ukrainian and Byelorussian votes, as if the future of the peace had really hung on them. At Yalta, Stalin obtained what he wanted. But even from his own viewpoint he gained nothing except perhaps the satisfaction of a capricious ambition, because, as a *quid pro quo*, he agreed that the United States should also have three votes in the United Nations, a right of which the United States was not to avail itself. Finally, with a singular lack of sense of humour, the 'Big Three' called from Yalta on all neutral states of the world to declare war on Germany before 1 March 1945, that is after the war had practically been won, in order to gain admittance to the founding conference of the United Nations at San Francisco. After 1 March the box office was to be closed.

The complex and fascinating story of all the deals and bargains that were concluded and of all the controversies and squabbles that went on at Yalta and Potsdam cannot be told or even summarized here. The nature of the solidarity of the 'Big Three' was such as to enable them to take joint decisions and carry them out with comparative ease whenever a major and immediate military interest was involved; but as they moved away from that interest they invariably found less and less common ground. At Yalta they laid plans for the continued advance of their armies and delineated the portions of Germany that were to be occupied by each of them; but they did not even try to work out the implications of the division of Germany into four zones; and they only broached its constitutional and economic aspects. In addition, their solidarity was now less and less due to their common military interest in Europe, and more and more to the new partnership which they were planning in the war against Japan. As early as 1943 Stalin had promised to join in that war. At Yalta he pledged himself to do so three months after the termination of hostilities in Europe. Neither Roosevelt nor Churchill was yet confident of the outcome of the experiments with the atomic weapon, experiments that had been kept strictly secret even from the Russian ally; they were not sure that they could easily vanquish

Japan without Russia's help; and so they conceded to Stalin things, not only in Asia but in Europe, which they would otherwise hardly have conceded.

What was Stalin's interest in the Pacific war? By her alliance with Britain and her agreements with the United States, Russia had not been bound to come out as their ally in Asia. Nor was the war against Japan popular with the Russian people, to whom Japan was their enemy's ally but not their enemy, and who were far too weary of one war to desire another. If Stalin nevertheless decided to embark upon the new venture he did so because he was convinced that the risk was extremely low. While Roosevelt and Churchill supposed that they might yet have to wage a long and costly campaign in the Far East, Stalin assumed that his troops would have to fight for three months at the most.[1] He played for definite stakes. His purpose was to regain for Russia all the ground she had lost to Japan since the Treaty of Portsmouth, concluded after the Russo-Japanese war of 1904–5. At Yalta he struck a most secret bargain with Roosevelt, by which Russia was to receive back not only the Eastern Chinese Railway, ceded to Japan about ten years before, but the southern part of the island of Sakhalin, the Kuril Islands, and Port Arthur as well.[2] To his people and to the world Stalin depicted this war as Russia's revenge for 1904–5: '. . . the defeat of Russian troops in 1904 . . .', so he stated in his proclamation on Japan's surrender, 'left bitter memories in the mind of the people. It lay like a black spot on our country. Our people believed and hoped that a day would come when Japan would be smashed and that blot effaced. Forty years have we, the people of the old generation, waited for this day.'[3] Stalin's words flew in the face of historical facts, for the men of the old generation, Bolsheviks, Mensheviks, and even Liberals, had rejoiced over the defeat of Tsardom in 1904. 'The European *bourgeoisie* has its reason to be frightened. The proletariat has its reasons to rejoice', so Lenin had commented on the Russian defeat at Port Arthur. 'The disaster that befell our worst enemy means not only that

---

[1] John R. Deane, *The Strange Alliance*, p. 264.

[2] It was thus the lot of Franklin D. Roosevelt to undo the work of Theodore Roosevelt, under whose auspices the Treaty of Portsmouth was negotiated in 1905.

[3] *Bolshevik*, no. 16, August 1945.

Russian freedom has come nearer. It foreshadows a new revolutionary upsurge of the European proletariat.'[1] In those days Stalin himself had addressed the workers of Tiflis in the same spirit though less explicitly in his proclamation 'Workers of the Caucasus, the time for revenge has come!'[2] His new view of history, his newly found sorrow for Russia's past humiliation, nevertheless fitted in well with that traditionalist spirit in which he was framing his policy. He now appeared on the Pacific coast, as he had previously done on the Baltic, as the collector of old Russian possessions, the inheritor of the Tsarist patrimony. In such terms he presented his aspirations to Roosevelt and Churchill, disclaiming any revolutionary ambition in Asia. Not only was he to put up with the United States' virtually exclusive control over Japan. At Potsdam he went so far as to disavow the Chinese Communists opposed to Chiang Kai-shek and to say that the Kuomintang was the only political force capable of ruling China.[3]

To whichever fragment, Asiatic or European, of Stalin's policy we turn, we always find in it the strange interplay of the traditionalist and the revolutionary strands which puzzled his allies and enemies alike. What is Stalin, after all? The architect of an imperial restoration, who sometimes exploits revolutionary pretexts for his ends, or the promoter of Communist revolution, camouflaging his purpose with the paraphernalia of the Russian Imperial tradition? British and American statesmen pondered the question as they tried to penetrate Stalin's motives. The question presupposed that only one of those characters in Stalin was genuine, that the other was sham and pretence. Yet both characters seem to be equally real. So much so, that one may venture the guess that at times Stalin himself would have been at a loss to identify himself, even in his own mind, with only one of them. That duality was too universal—Tradition and Revolution did actually lead a silent existence, side by side, in

---

[1] Lenin, *Sochinenya*, vol. viii, p. 32.

[2] J. Stalin, *Sochinenya*, vol. i, pp. 74–83.

[3] James F. Byrnes, *Speaking Frankly*, p. 228. Pursuing his aims in the Far East, Stalin inevitably came into conflict with Chinese aspirations. Shortly before the Potsdam conference he negotiated with the Chinese Foreign Minister, T. V. Soong. Under combined Russian and American pressure, and in the hope that this would strengthen his hands *vis-à-vis* the Communist opposition, Chiang Kai-shek accepted Stalin's demands.

the thoughts and feelings of the Russian people; and it appeared too consistently in every sphere of Stalin's activity, domestic and foreign, to be explained away as sheer artful camouflage or artificial posture, although Stalin sometimes undoubtedly camouflaged his actions to mislead his enemies or his allies.

In the closing phase of the war it became almost impossible to disentangle the two strands of his policy. The traditionalist one was often so much to the fore that Stalin's conduct, aspirations, methods of action, even his gestures and caprices, vividly resembled the behaviour, the aspirations, and gestures of Alexander I at the conclusion of the Napoleonic wars. The similarity was largely genuine; but there must have been a dose of deliberate imitation in it as well—this was apparent when Stalin officially called the war the 'Fatherland war', the name by which the epic of 1812 had gone down in Russian history. After the defeat of the *Grande Armée*, Tsar Alexander sought to aggrandize his empire at the expense of Russia's own and Britain's allies, Prussia and Austria, whose Polish lands he wanted to unite to his Kingdom of Poland. Prussia was to be 'compensated' by the acquisition of Saxony. It is enough to substitute in this tale Poland for Prussia to obtain a description of Stalin's policy. In the reports of British and American diplomats on their talks with Stalin there was more than one passage recalling the words from Castlereagh's reports on his talks with Alexander:

The Emperor insinuated [wrote the British foreign secretary of 1815] that the question [of Poland] could only end in one way, as he was in possession. I observed that it was very true, His imperial Majesty was in possession, and he must know that no one was less disposed than myself hostilely to dispute that possession; but I was sure His Imperial Majesty would not be satisfied to rest his pretensions on a title of conquest in opposition to the general sentiments of Europe.

Both Alexander and Stalin were concerned with Russia's influence in the Balkans; and both strove to bring the Turkish Straits under their control. The tension between Russia and her western allies was as acute in 1945 as it had been in 1815.[1]

---

[1] '. . . almost everywhere in Europe during these three years, their [Britain's and Russia's] policies apparently conflicted. [Thus C. K. Webster describes Russo-British relations in 1815–18 in *The Foreign Policy of Castlereagh*, vol. ii, p. 88.] The Tsar, or at least some of his servants, engaged in multifarious activities which

The secretiveness of the diplomacy of both rulers, their tactics of taking their allies by surprise, and their alternation of conciliatory and strong-arm attitudes caused the same confusion and embarrassment among their allies. The foreign ministers of the one and the other were equally afraid of making their own decisions, equally waited for their master's word, and equally taxed the patience of their allies by the bizarre dilatoriness of their dealings. The complaints of British and American negotiators about Stalin's capriciousness may still be best expressed in Byron's words about Alexander:

> Now half dissolving to a liberal thaw
> But hardened back whene'er the morning's raw
>
> . . . .
>
> How nobly gave he back to Poles their Diet
> Then told pugnacious Poland to be quiet.

It is curious how the analogy can be extended from major issues down to details. Alexander, eager to uphold the Russian prestige, wished to be fêted as the chief victor in Paris. Similar motives impelled Stalin to order Marshal Zhukov to stage a special ceremony of Germany's surrender in Russian-occupied Berlin, after the German representatives had signed the act of surrender at the British and American headquarters at Rheims. A strange episode of the Potsdam conference suggested another peculiar reminiscence. On his arrival at Potsdam Stalin expressed the view that Hitler was alive, hiding outside Germany. To the astonishment of the British and the Americans he repeated that assertion with apparent conviction many days later.[1] It was as if the thought of Napoleon's return from

were in almost all cases hostile to Britain. There was a kind of diplomatic duel between the two countries which extended over a large area. At Paris they appeared to be rivals for the favour of Louis XVIII, at Madrid there was a fierce contest on which large issues hung, in Italy and Germany Britain supported Austrian influence against Russian, at Constantinople there were almost openly confessed divergencies of view; the contest extended into Asia; and the struggle over Persia had already begun. It must be remembered that this was an entirely new part for Russia to play. Before the French Revolution she had appeared as a half-barbarous Power who had no relations with western Europe . . . . Now her influence was supreme and apparently increasing at half the Courts of Europe, and her agents were engaged in stirring up strife all over the West. No wonder, therefore, that many men accused the Tsar himself of hypocrisy and trickery. His professions of Christian principles were thought to be merely designed to cover his far-reaching schemes of European domination.'

[1] James F. Byrnes, *Speaking Frankly*, p. 68.

Elba and of the Hundred Days had crossed Stalin's mind—would not Hitler perchance try a similar come-back? Since Napoleon's reappearance restored the unity of the victors at the Congress of Vienna, Stalin seemed to use Hitler's phantom at Potsdam in order to recapture something of that allied unity which had been of the living Hitler's making.

Yet, for all that similarity, Stalin was not and could not have been just another Alexander. The world situation would not have allowed him to keep within that role. Alexander's army, even though it had been the strongest on the Continent, did not march into a Europe so unsettled and disintegrated and so reduced to a vacuum as was the Europe into which Stalin's armies advanced. At the Congress of Vienna the Tsar had to contend with an opposition coming not only from the British, but also from the Austrian Empire, Prussia, and the Ottoman Empire, all present in central, eastern, and southern Europe. Even the voice of vanquished France carried great weight in the councils of the nations. In 1945 the vanquished nation, Germany, was politically crushed into dust; and all other continental nations, victors and vanquished, had almost no breath in them. Because of the contrast between that extraordinary vacuum and Russia's newly revealed might, Stalin's figure loomed incomparably larger on the European horizon than did Alexander's, a larger menace to some and a bigger promise to others.

Nor was the political horizon now limited to Europe. The world had just witnessed the astonishing polarization of power between the United States and Russia. In abstract statistical terms, Russia's economic strength was much less than that of the United States. But because of Russia's proximity to the European scene, her pressure was much more effective than her economic strength might have suggested. By the end of the war Stalin may have reckoned with a more or less rapid withdrawal of American power from the Continent and consequently with the further growth of Russian predominance. But this is not certain. Against the fact of Russia's increased power must be set that element of her weakness which was due to the prodigious losses and the ravages of war she had suffered; and this tended to limit the spread of the Russian influence.

To all these differences between 1945 and 1815 must now be

added the revolutionary element in Stalin's diplomacy. Only after the war was the Bolshevik in Stalin to reassert himself so strongly as to efface Alexander's likeness, but his presence was felt even earlier, in the period of Yalta and Potsdam. It was in the last months of the war that the pattern of the revolution that was eventually to embrace nearly all countries within the Russian orbit began to develop.

In all those countries governments were set up which nominally represented coalitions between several parties: Communists, Socialists, Peasants, Clericalists, and even quasi-Fascists. But in each of those governments the Communists were in charge of at least two decisive departments: police and army. They used those departments to establish control first over their country as a whole, and then over their partners in the government, until they were able either to oust their partners or to compel them to co-operate in the revolution. In carrying out this design the Communists were assisted by the fact that each of those governments was under the obligation, stipulated in armistice terms or in special declarations, to purge its civil service and its political institutions from those who had worked against Russia, from Nazis, Fascists, militarists, and so on. They were further under the obligation to ensure the security of the lines of communication which the Russian army maintained in all those countries. Those clauses, endorsed by the western allies, were enough to enable Stalin to initiate and direct, without flagrantly offending against inter-allied conventions, a process by which the old ruling classes of eastern Europe were thrown into complete disarray, deprived of organization, and rendered politically impotent. The bulk of those classes had in fact consisted of anti-democratic elements and had compromised itself by its pro-German, or at any rate by its anti-Russian, attitude in the war. The elimination of the old ruling classes prepared the ground for the ascendancy of the Communist parties. Intermediate groupings, which might have stood for parliamentary government, lacked any substantial tradition and were extremely weak or ineffectual. When their ranks swelled, in part by the adherence of members of the old ruling groups and parties, it was their turn to be subjected to the purge. It was rarely possible to say when Stalin, or the local Communists, really acted on the clauses endorsed by the western allies and when they used those clauses as excuses for settling accounts with parties and groups whom they were only too eager to suppress. In actual fact they did both.

Through this chain-process of purges, which were to drag on into the late forties, was to be built up the monopoly of the Communist parties, without spectacular Russian interference. Only when real hitches occurred, especially in the initial phase, did Stalin authorize direct, drastic Russian intervention. Thus, when King Michael of Rumania refused, in the spring of 1945, to dismiss his courtier General Radescu from the post of Prime Minister, Vyshinsky, now vice-minister of foreign affairs, appeared at the Rumanian court, ordered the King to change the government within two hours, and threatened that refusal would be treated by Russia as a breach of the armistice. Grozea, a pro-Communist politician, replaced Radescu; and Stalin personally sought to strengthen the hands of the new Premier by announcing that Transylvania, which Hitler had awarded to Hungary, would be returned to Rumania. After one such act of Russian intervention, the local Communist party could take charge of the further transubstantiation of the government.

The world was thus treated to the spectacle of a social upheaval that was unlike any previous revolution. At the beginning of the Russian revolution there was the Word. The revolution began from a mighty popular movement. For the purposes of self-defence it then built up its own police and invested it with enormous power. Then the new state succumbed to its own instrument—it turned into a police state. In the revolution which Stalin now carried into half a dozen countries, the whole process was as if reversed. The first acquisition of the revolution, its first base, was the police. Captured or built up by the Communist party, the police appeared to be the demiurge of social transformation. To be sure, the masses, the people— they, too, appeared on the stage and played a part. But it was never quite clear what they thought and what they felt, whether they acted of their own accord or whether they had been marshalled and drilled to act as they did by the demiurge in the background.

This revolution hesitated to proclaim its principles and define its aims. Its story was one succession of manœuvres, stratagems, and tricks, which in the end fell into the pattern of a revolution, but which in themselves were petty and wicked. Of these tricks none was quite as wicked as the falsification of the popular vote —sooner or later 99 per cent. of the voters must vote for the powers in being. In Russia the Bolsheviks had at first described their rule as proletarian dictatorship; they had disfranchised the members of the former ruling and possessing classes; they had made an electoral law so designed as to ensure the predominance of the industrial workers over the peasant majority; but within these avowedly narrow limits the vote had been a vote. Friend and foe of the Bolshevik revolution knew where they stood; and even its foes had to acknowledge with some respect the frankness with which it had proclaimed its class principle. The eastern European offspring of the Russian revolution pretended much higher democratic respectability; they indignantly denied that they had anything in common with dictatorial rule; they produced with superior airs the overwhelming votes they had allegedly obtained in universal and secret ballot; and even their friends were irritated by the crude hypocrisy of their pretensions.

Yet, by sponsoring that strange revolution, Stalin rendered the peoples of eastern Europe 'services, of which it is difficult to overrate either the wickedness or the utility', to paraphrase Macaulay's verdict on an English statesman. Between the two wars nearly all those peoples had been stranded in an impasse; their life had been bogged down in savage poverty and darkness; their politics had been dominated by archaic cliques who had not minded the material and cultural retrogression of their subjects as long as their own privileges had been safe. That whole portion of Europe had emerged from the Second World War and from the hideous 'school' of nazism even more destitute, savage, and helpless. It may well be that for its peoples the only chance of breaking out of their impasse lay in a *coup de force* such as that to which Stalin goaded them. In Poland and Hungary the Communist-inspired land reform fulfilled, perhaps imperfectly, a dream of many generations of peasants and intellectuals. All over eastern Europe the Communists, having nationalized the main industries, vigorously promoted plans for industrialization and full employment such as were beyond the material resources and the wit of native 'private enterprise', notoriously poor in capital, skill, and enterprise. With fresh zeal and ambition they took to hard educational work, trying to undo the age-old negligence of previous rulers. They did much to calm nationalist vendettas and to promote co-operation between their peoples. In a word, they opened before eastern Europe broad vistas of common reform and advancement. It was as if Russia had imparted to her neighbours some of her own urge for trying out new ways and methods of communal work and social organization. It ought perhaps to be added that, considering the vastness and the radical character of the upheaval, it is remarkable that Stalin and his men brought it off not without terror, indeed, not without indulging in a long series of *coups*, but without provoking in a single country within the Russian orbit a real civil war, such as that waged in Greece.

The question must be asked whether Stalin, while he was bargaining for his zone of influence, already contemplated putting it under exclusive Communist control. Had the scheme of revolution been in his mind at the time of Teheran or Yalta? Had it finally taken shape at the time of Potsdam? His detractors as well as his apologists concur on this point, for both want us to see an extremely shrewd and far-sighted design behind his actions. Yet Stalin's actions show many strange and striking contradictions which do not indicate that he had any revolutionary master-plan. They suggest, on the contrary, that he had none. Here are a few of the most glaring contradictions. If Stalin consistently prepared to instal a Communist government in Warsaw, why did he so stubbornly refuse to make any concessions to the Poles over their eastern frontier? Would it not have been all the same to him whether, say, Lvov, that Polish–Ukrainian city, was ruled from Communist Kiev or from Communist Warsaw? Yet such a concession would have enormously strengthened the hands of the Polish left. Similarly, if he had beforehand planned revolution for eastern Germany, why did he detach from Germany and incorporate in Poland *all* the German provinces east of the Neisse and the Oder, of the acquisition of which even the Poles themselves had not dreamt? Why did he insist on the expulsion of the whole German population from those lands, an act that could not but further embitter the German people not only against the Poles but also against Russia and communism. His claim for reparations to be paid by Germany, Austria, Hungary, Rumania, Bulgaria, and Finland, understandable as it was in view of the devastation of the Ukraine and other Soviet lands, could not but have the same damaging effect on the Communist cause in those countries. This was even truer of Stalin's demand for the liquidation of the bulk of German industry. Already at Teheran, if not earlier, he had given notice that he would raise that demand; at Yalta he proposed that 80 per cent. of German industry should be dismantled within two years after the cease fire; and he did not abate that demand at Potsdam.[1] He could not have been unaware that his scheme, as chimerical as ruthless, if it had been carried out, would have entailed the dispersal of the German working class, the main, if not the only, social force to which communism could have appealed and whose support it might have enlisted. Not a single one of these policies can by any stretch of the imagination be described as a stepping-stone towards revolution. On the contrary, in every one of those moves, Stalin himself was laboriously erecting formidable barriers to revolution. This alone seems to warrant the conclusion that even at the close of the war his intentions were still extremely self-contradictory, to say the least.

Mikolajczyk reports a curious conversation with Stalin in August 1944. Not without peasant-like slyness, the Polish politician tried to sound Stalin on his plans for Germany, and told him that German prisoners, captured by the Poles, allegedly expressed the hope that after the war Germany would embrace communism and, as the foremost Communist state, go on to rule the world. Stalin, so Mikolajczyk reports, replied indignantly that 'communism fitted Germany as a saddle fitted a cow'. This contemptuous aphorism undoubtedly reflected his mood. It harmonized so perfectly with the whole trend of his policy *vis-à-vis* Germany, it was so spontaneous, so organic, so much in line with what we know of his old disbelief in western European communism, and it accorded so much with all that he said and did in those days, that it could not have been sheer tactical bluff.

It was, indeed, in Stalin's approach to Germany that the conflict between his nationalism and his revolutionism was

[1] James F. Byrnes, *Speaking Frankly*, pp. 26–7.

sharpest, and that the nationalist, one might say the anti-revolutionary, element predominated longest. 'It would be naïve to think', he said shortly before Yalta, 'that Germany will not attempt to restore her might and launch new aggression. . . . History shows that a short period—some twenty or thirty years —is enough for Germany to recover from defeat and re-establish her might.'[1] He had used the same argument at Teheran, only that there he had forecast Germany's come-back within a much shorter period.[2] He repeated the same thing to nearly every one of his many visitors in the Kremlin. He appeared almost obsessed by the thought of future German revenge. When he spoke about the need for the unity of the great allied powers in peace, he pointed to that danger. He did the same when he proposed to cripple German industry, to change Germany's frontiers, to detach Austria from Germany, or to establish a pro-Russian government in Poland, 'that corridor through which the Germans march into Russia'. In this preoccupation with Russia's security vis-à-vis Germany, he used the language that Foch, Clemenceau, and Poincaré had used after the First World War, the language of the Conservative who projects the past into the future and sees that future in terms of competition, struggle, and war between nations. His warnings about German revenge 'in twenty or thirty years' were in his mouth identical with the firm assumption that 'in twenty or thirty years' Germany would still remain a capitalist, imperialist nation, obviously because 'communism fitted her as a saddle fitted a cow'. Had he reckoned on the chance of a Communist revolution in Germany he would have seen no need for the punitive peace he advocated.

In speaking as he did, he undoubtedly spoke for Russia. It is not an exaggeration to say that the whole of Russia hoped that the day of victory would be the day of judgement for Germany and that the judgement would be conducted by Germany's victims. Internationalist ideas and sentiments of solidarity with foreign working classes, in so far as such sentiments had not been swamped by the nationalist tide, had no validity vis-à-vis the enemy nation, for the German working classes appeared to have done nothing either to prevent Hitler's

[1] J. Stalin, War Speeches, p. 113.
[2] Robert E. Sherwood, Roosevelt and Hopkins, pp. 786–7.

aggression, to obstruct it, or to revolt against it. It is true that the nationalist feeling in Russia had been violently kindled by the propagandists and by Stalin's own grim, inexorable 'Death to the German invaders' repeated day after day. Without that the national temper might not have risen quite to the pitch of fury which it reached in the end. But cause and effect were highly confused. Even if there had been no nationalist propaganda, the German atrocities, the methodical mass-slaughter of women and children, the slave-labour, and the cold-blooded devastation of town and country spoke louder than any propagandist. The soldiers who marched from Stalingrad to Berlin saw all that—they had marched through a German-made desert. As victors they vented their fury upon the vanquished; they expected their Government to rebuild Russia with the help of German industry and labour, and to destroy Germany's capacity to wage war. When, at last, they hoisted the red flag over the ruins of the Reichstag, this was to symbolize the triumph of revolutionary Russia over Germany, not the triumph of revolution in Germany.

This fearful Russian hatred of Germany, however, was turning out to be a great political liability as the war drew to a close. It inspired panicky fear in Germany and prolonged German resistance. To the end, Hitler's troops fought with much greater tenacity in the east than in the west. Stalin had striking evidence of this when, in March 1945, Field-Marshal Kesselring, the German commander-in-chief in Italy, made his first proposal for the surrender of his whole army to the British and the Americans. Stalin was 'seething' when he learned about British and American negotiations with Kesselring—this was a belated reflex of his old fear of a separate peace between the western allies and Germany.[1] Soon afterwards, in April, he called a halt to the nationalist hue and cry and ordered his propagandists to re-publicize his own almost forgotten saying that 'Hitlers come and go, but the German nation and the German state remains'.[2] This attempt to allay the German fear of

[1] John R. Deane, *The Strange Alliance*, p. 164; James F. Byrnes, *Speaking Frankly*, p. 56.

[2] It was in connexion with this that George Alexandrov—he was then the head of the party's propaganda department—attacked in *Pravda* the writer Ilya Ehrenburg for failing to discriminate in his articles between Nazi and non-Nazi Germans. Ehrenburg had been the soldiers' favourite writer and his articles appeared daily in the *Krasnaya Zvezda*, the organ of the Red Army.

Russia came too late to be effective. In the last days of the war masses of German soldiers, stricken with guilt and panic, fled from the Russians into British and American captivity, while German representatives sought to arrange an armistice with the western powers, but not with Russia. Bristling with suspicion, Stalin watched these manœuvres; and when at last he was able to announce the German surrender, he could hardly suppress his own surprise and relief at the fact that the Wehrmacht had capitulated to Russia, too.[1] The events of the last few weeks of the war revealed the terrible gulf between Germany and Russia, which both Hitler and Stalin, each in his own way and each in a different degree, had dug, a gulf that neither ordinary diplomacy nor revolutionary policy would be able to bridge for many years after the war.[2]

Stalin's foreign policy thus appears to have been not the result of any preconceived plan but the resultant of contradictory domestic and foreign pressures. Now, as so often in the past, the control of events over him was much stronger than his control over events. We have seen some of the domestic pressures at work. As to the foreign ones, these were evident in the long series of inter-allied conflicts and squabbles which filled the months between Yalta and Potsdam, and in acrimonious controversies at Potsdam itself. Despite the agreement on the zones of influence and despite Stalin's silence over the civil war in Greece, the western powers protested against Russian intervention in Rumania and against developments in Poland and Yugoslavia. Disagreement over the United Nations, patched up at Yalta, came to light once again. Stalin showed his displeasure by refusing Roosevelt's request that Molotov should attend the founding conference of the United Nations at San Francisco. (Only after Roosevelt's death, on 12 April 1945, did Stalin, wishing to make a friendly gesture

[1] J. Stalin, War Speeches, p. 136.

[2] It was largely for that reason that the Free German Committee, formed in Moscow after the battle of Stalingrad, was utterly ineffectual in its propaganda. The role which Stalin assigned to that Committee, at first headed by General Seydlitz and then also by Field-Marshal von Paulus, was the object of much anxious speculation among the western allies. It was thought that the Committee was the nucleus of a Russian sponsored German Government. Actually, it was merely an abortive propagandist venture. It attempted to appeal primarily to German conservative opinion, and for that reason it not only spoke in the non-revolutionary idiom, but used the old banner of the Hohenzollern Empire as its own.

towards the new American President, consent that Molotov should by his presence add splendour to the San Francisco conference.) In those days Stalin undoubtedly felt that his allies were trying to manœuvre him out of positions previously conceded to him; and it was with genuine resentment that he told Harry L. Hopkins, when the latter came to see him for the last time, that 'even though the Russians were a simple people, the West often made the mistake of regarding them as fools'.[1]

The condominium of the 'Big Three' was toppling even before it had taken solid shape. It would be futile to try to establish which of the allies made the first decisive move away from it. Through the labyrinth of conflicting versions and recriminations it is hardly possible to trace the first 'broken pledge'. The pledges of the allies had, anyhow, been so vague and contained so many loopholes that by reference to the text each side could justify its conduct. The point is that the fundamental cleavage between the allies could not but lead the one side or the other, or both, to abandon mutual commitments. In this *mariage de convenance* the thought of the inevitability of divorce had been in the back of the mind of each partner from the beginning; and almost from the beginning each side had to think about the advantages it would secure and the disadvantages from which it would suffer at the moment of the divorce.

The arrangement about the zones of influence, although some of its features looked very attractive to its authors, was unnatural enough to provoke regrets and second thoughts. It was unnatural for the leaders of Liberal capitalism to concede so much new ground to the Soviets. Even if Churchill or Roosevelt had completely overcome their own scruples, they could not ignore those important sections of public opinion at home which, either from Conservative hostility to the social revolution in eastern Europe or from democratic aversion to the police state with which that revolution was identified, strongly objected to the deals with Stalin. Those deals must also have seemed unnatural to important sections of Soviet opinion, which, however inarticulate, did exercise their pressure in many devious ways. The editorial silence of the Moscow Press about the civil

---

[1] James F. Byrnes, *Speaking Frankly*, p. 62; Robert E. Sherwood, *Roosevelt and Hopkins*, p. 894.

war in Greece and the extraordinary moderation of the French and Italian Communists may have puzzled many a Bolshevik; but these were still relatively remote affairs. What was going on nearer home, in the Russian-occupied countries, was much more vital. To the occupying troops, at least to many politically minded officers and men, and to active members of the party and the Komsomol at home, it must have been an intolerable thought that the capitalist order should survive in the lands that the Red Army alone had freed—and at what prodigious cost!—from the Nazis. Should they, the people who had, in spite of all recent traditionalism, been bred on and for socialism, now become the guardians of capitalism there?— they asked themselves. Of that same capitalism which had ushered Europe into the Nazi era and which, if allowed to recover, would again lead Europe to nothing better, because nazism and fascism had not been just accidental aberrations of European history, but had expressed the very nature of capitalist society *in extremis*. That they, the victors, should now preserve an order from which they had experienced nothing but hostility, and could expect nothing but hostility, was not only unnatural to them—it would have been the most miserable anti-climax to their great 'war of liberation'.

Stalin could not ignore such moods. At first he apparently wished to meet them half-way only. He sponsored the idea of the 'people's democracy'. The order to be established in the countries neighbouring with Russia was to have been neither capitalist nor socialist, it was to stand between the two. In the light of later events it has often been assumed that the slogan was but dust thrown in the eyes of the *bourgeoisie*, and that Stalin had from the outset aimed at sovietization. Yet the concept of a people's democracy, as distinct from the Soviet system and the proletarian dictatorship, was for a time taken very seriously by the leaders of the Communist parties; and it was earnestly discussed by leading Russian political theorists *pro foro interno*.[1] Stalin himself, it will be remembered, had been brought up on the notion of a system that was to have been neither fully capitalist nor socialist. This had been the idea

[1] See the discussions on that subject in *Gosudarstvo i Pravo*, 1947; *Mirovoye Khozyaistvo i Mirovaya Politika*, no. 2, 1947 (Special Supplement) and in E. Varga, *Izmenenya v Ekonomike Kapitalizma*, pp. 14, 291.

behind the formula of the democratic dictatorship of the proletariat and the peasantry, to which he had stuck until 1917, and which he had put forward again in 1925-7, in the debate over the Chinese revolution. Towards the end of the war and some time later that idea was apparently back in his mind.

From his viewpoint, the main justification for the intermediate system, with which he was experimenting, was the chance that this would help him to preserve the condominium of the 'Big Three'. This hope was to be dashed. The 'people's democracy' had too much of the revolutionary flavour and it bore its maker's stamp all too distinctly to win the approval of the western powers. It generated all the tension and friction which Stalin wanted to prevent. This suggested to him that the western powers were out to reinstal the old anti-Russian parties and groupings on Russia's borders and eventually to squeeze Russia out of Europe. That this should be their intention appeared equally plausible to the Russian traditionalist and to the Bolshevik. Exactly so had the western powers after the Napoleonic wars been eager to deny Russia the position of influence she had just gained. Exactly so had they combined against her after the treaty of San Stefano and deprived her of mastery over the Balkans at the Congress of Berlin in 1878. It was Stalin's ambition not to allow Russia to be so thrown back once again. In the past the spread of her influence into Europe had been more or less ephemeral, and her influence in the Balkans had flowed and ebbed with the political tide, because under the Tsar that influence had not and could not have been anchored in the social structure of the countries where Russia had wanted to see her interest supreme. Slavophilism and Greek Orthodoxy had not been enough to create permanent bonds. This time Russia's ascendancy could assume a lasting character if it was based on revolution, on a transformation of the social structure of eastern Europe such as no diplomatic pressure or intrigue could reverse. As the controversies between Russia and her allies widened and grew bitter, Stalin inclined more and more to give up his experiments with the intermediate régimes and to reduce the 'people's democracy' to a mere façade for the Communist monopoly of power. Every step of his in that direction heightened, of course, the tension between Russia and the western allies still further.

At Yalta Stalin pressed Churchill to explain his hints about the power that might seek world domination, and Churchill spoke about the conflict that might arise between the successors to the three war-time leaders. At Potsdam the partners used less allusive language. It was there that Churchill, complaining about the position of British representatives in Bucharest, threw in Stalin's face the words: 'An iron fence has come down around them!' The iron fence was later to become the 'iron curtain', the *leitmotif* or the shibboleth of a much greater controversy. 'All fairy-tales!' Stalin snapped back. When he was assailed for his policies in Rumania, Bulgaria, and Yugoslavia, he retorted with an attack on the British for their pro-royalist policy in Greece, on which he had hitherto kept silent. But he dropped his charges as soon as the British desisted from their attacks on Russian policy. Yet the field of controversy continued to widen. Shortly before Potsdam Stalin had raised the demand for a Russian base in the Turkish Straits—the never-fulfilled dream of the Tsars. At Potsdam he could see that he, too, would in this striving be thwarted by his allies, especially the British, who had frustrated the Tsars' aspirations. Then, during the discussion on allied trusteeship over Mussolini's African empire, he surprised his partners by the demand that one of the Italian colonies be put under Russian trusteeship. Churchill, taken aback by this new demand, exclaimed that it had not occurred to him that Russia might wish 'to acquire a large tract of the African shore'.[1] This, of course, appeared to be a menace to British control over the Mediterranean. It seems that Stalin did not hope for the satisfaction of this particular claim, for his best time for bargaining was over. Nevertheless, in the sum total of his demands there were the makings of a crisis over the old Eastern Question that had bedevilled Russia's relations with Britain in the nineteenth century.

However, it was not even on the new version of the Eastern Question that the conflict between the allies was focused. The greatest single problem for which they could find no agreed solution was Germany. Most, if not all, of their acute disagreements on Germany sprang from the one point on which they did agree, namely, from their joint determination to keep the country under military occupation for many years. The actual

[1] James F. Byrnes, *Speaking Frankly*, p. 76.

term of the occupation was never defined—ten, twenty, thirty, even forty years had been mooted. This alone was enough to drive the policies of the allies in diametrically opposite directions. The longer they were to stay on, performing the functions of a German government, which in the absence of any German government they had to do, the more would each occupying power be inclined to mould in its own image the economic and political life of its part of Germany. It was as unnatural for the officers of the Soviet military administration to administer a capitalist economy in eastern Germany as it was for their counterparts of the American military government to reorganize western Germany on Socialist lines. Thus, the prolonged presence of the allied armies in Germany tended to split the country economically and politically as well as militarily.

Yet the victors pledged themselves to maintain the unity of Germany and to exercise for that purpose joint control over her affairs. They pronounced that pledge with much emphasis at Potsdam; and they actually set up the Allied Control Council, in which the theoretical sovereignty over all parts of Germany was invested. But already at Potsdam it was, or should have been, clear to those concerned that their joint control over Germany would be a pull-devil-pull-baker business. Neither the east nor the west really wanted the other side to have any say in the affairs of its own part of Germany. Stalin confronted his partners with an accomplished fact when he transferred the whole area east of the Oder and the Neisse to the Poles. Nominally the Poles were merely to administer those provinces; and Stalin so presented the case to the western allies. But in the circumstances the administration of those provinces by the Poles amounted to their incorporation into Poland. The western powers acknowledged this, at least implicitly, when they agreed to Stalin's proposal for the expulsion of the whole German population from those lands. True enough, the western powers accepted the accomplished fact with the proviso that only a peace conference should draw the final frontier between Germany and Poland; but, as they agreed in advance to the expulsion of the whole German population that had lived east of the Oder and the Neisse, that proviso sounded fictitious. The conclusion which Stalin must have drawn from the behaviour of the allies was that they had reconciled themselves to a position in which they were to have no influence on matters concerning eastern Germany. That Russia was to have no influence on western Germany became evident when the western powers categorically rejected the proposals, repeatedly made by Stalin and Molotov, for Russia's participation in control over the economy of the Ruhr.

The division of Germany was further deepened by an ambiguous compromise on reparations. At Yalta Stalin had sought to obtain British and American endorsement of the Russian claim for reparations amounting to ten billion dollars. He obtained a vague promise from President Roosevelt that that figure would serve as a basis for further discussion. At Potsdam the western powers refused to consider it again. In part this was due to the circumstance that the Russians were already dismantling industrial plant in eastern Germany and transferring it to Russia, and that the British and the Americans had no control over the scope of the process. But a deeper cause underlay this new disagreement. Stalin still stuck to his plans for a Carthaginian peace. The British, and in a lesser degree the Americans, were already shrinking from the destruction of Germany's industrial strength. This conflict of views was veiled by an agreement, reached at Potsdam, that each occupying power was free to dismantle industrial plant and to satisfy its claims in its own zone.[1] This arrangement placed, actually if not nominally, on each power the sole responsibility for the manner in which it managed the economic and social affairs of its own zone. It made of eastern Germany the domain of Stalin's 'revolution from above'. Shortly after Potsdam that revolution began. Its first act was the expropriation of the Prussian Junkers, the landlord class that had formed the backbone of Germany's bureaucracy and had been the mainstay of her militarism. With one stroke of the pen, or perhaps with only a wink, Stalin destroyed a powerful reactionary social force, with which the German left had wrestled unsuccessfully for over a century. The second act was the nationalization of some industries in eastern Germany. The third was the actual suppression of the Social Democratic party, a suppression veiled

[1] According to the Potsdam agreement Russia and Poland were, in addition, to receive 10 per cent. of 'surplus' industrial plant from western Germany, and 15 per cent. more in exchange for food and raw materials.

as a merger of Communist and Socialist organizations in the Socialist Unity party.

The area of the social revolution was thus extended from the Oder to the Elbe. This was not the first time in German history that the Elbe marked the boundary between different social and political systems. But in the past the ramparts of German conservatism had lain east of the Elbe, while impulses for reform and revolution used to come mostly from the west. The social influence of the French revolution and of Napoleon's reforms had not spread across that river. As if to compensate for this, another revolution now came from the east and swept the country up to the Elbe. But now the river separated not merely two Germanys. It became the frontier between 'two worlds'. The longer the representatives of those two worlds were bent on confronting one another with their armed forces on either side of it, the more was that frontier likely to turn into a potential front line.

A significant episode of the Potsdam conference foreshadowed new strains and stresses within the victorious coalition. On 24 July, after a session of the 'Big Three', President Truman told Stalin, in an almost casual manner, about the discovery of the atomic weapon. 'Stalin's only reply', according to James F. Byrnes's report, 'was to say that he was glad to hear of the bomb and he hoped we would use it.'[1] He showed no further interest in the matter and asked for no information, which led the American Secretary of State to conclude that he either had not grasped the importance of the discovery or that he had thought it improper to ask questions about a matter kept in so great secrecy. Maybe the Russian intelligence services had known more about it than Truman and Byrnes supposed, and that Stalin's show of indifference was due to the fact that he had not been greatly surprised. That he should not have grasped the importance of the discovery seems improbable, in view of his own sustained and detailed interest in technical weapons and of the interest that Soviet scientists, like their colleagues in other countries, had long since shown in the splitting of the atom. Even if he had not grasped the significance of the event at once, he must have been aware, towards the end of the conference, of the extent to which the new

[1] James F. Byrnes, *Speaking Frankly*, p. 263.

weapon, abruptly tilting the scales of military power in favour of the United States, was likely to intensify and dramatize the conflict between the allies.

At Yalta Churchill had dropped the remark that perhaps not they, the allied war-time leaders, but their successors might confront one another in enmity. At Potsdam this was already coming true, at least in part. In the first half of the conference only two of the war-time triumvirate, Stalin and Churchill, participated. In the second Churchill and Eden were replaced by Attlee and Bevin as a consequence of the return of a Labour Government at the British General Election. This is not to say that the further course of the drama would have been very different if the cast had remained unchanged. It was Churchill, after all, who was soon to become Stalin's most outspoken antagonist; and if Roosevelt had been alive, he might not have been at all that patron saint of Russo-American friendship that some people saw in him. Nevertheless, the change of cast was probably not without immediate adverse effect upon the Potsdam performance. And although the causes of the appearance of new actors lay outside the sphere of inter-allied policy, there was a symbolic significance in the fact that in the residence of Frederick the Great, amid the ruins of Hitler's capital, Stalin alone of the war-time leaders remained to make the peace. The Grand Alliance was dissolving.

CHAPTER XIV

Dialectics of Victory

Grandeur and misery of the Russian victory.—Nationalism and Revolution in Stalin's policy.—From 'Socialism in one country' to 'Socialism in one zone'.— Stalin as the promoter of *revolution from above*.—The 'iron curtain', its story and significance.—The impact of the west upon Russia.—Stalin and Zhukov.—The Leninist revivalism.—The dilemma: 'One World or Two?' in the atomic age.— A general appreciation of Stalin's role.

ON 24 June 1945 Stalin stood at the top of the Lenin Mausoleum and reviewed a great victory parade of the Red Army which marked the fourth anniversary of Hitler's attack. By Stalin's side stood Marshal Zhukov, his deputy, the victor of Moscow, Stalingrad, and Berlin. The troops that marched past him were led by Marshal Rokossovsky. As they marched, rode, and galloped across the Red Square, regiments of infantry, cavalry, and tanks swept the mud of its pavement—it was a day of torrential rain—with innumerable banners and standards of Hitler's army. At the Mausoleum they threw the banners at Stalin's feet. The allegorical scene was strangely imaginative, yet almost familiar: for so had Kutuzov's soldiers once thrown French standards and banners at Alexander's feet. The next day Stalin received the tribute of Moscow for the defence of the city in 1941. The day after he was acclaimed as 'Hero of the Soviet Union' and given the title of Generalissimo.

These were days of undreamt-of triumph and glory. Yet rarely had triumph and frustration been as close neighbours as they were in Russia in 1945; and never perhaps had any victory been so chequered with grandeur and misery as was this one.

Stalin now stood in the full blaze of popular recognition and gratitude. Those feelings were spontaneous, genuine, not engineered by official propagandists. Overworked slogans about the 'achievements of the Stalinist era' now conveyed fresh meaning not only to young people, but to sceptics and malcontents of the older generation. The nation was willing to forgive Stalin even his misdeeds and to retain in its memory only his better efforts. Since nothing succeeds like success, even his errors and miscalculations, including those of 1939–41, now looked to many like acts of prudent statesmanship. Even the cruelties of the thirties appeared in a new light, as salutary operations to which the peoples of the Soviet Union owed their survival.

This new appreciation of Stalin's role did not spring only from afterthoughts born in the flush of victory. The truth was that the war could not have been won without the intensive industrialization of Russia, and of her eastern provinces in particular. Nor could it have been won without the collectivization of large numbers of farms. The *muzhik* of 1930, who had never handled a tractor or any other machine, would have been of little use in modern war. Collectivized farming, with its machine-tractor stations scattered all over the country, had been the peasants' preparatory school for mechanized warfare.[1] The rapid raising of the average standard of education had also enabled the Red Army to draw on a considerable reserve of intelligent officers and men. 'We are fifty or a hundred years behind the advanced countries. We must make good this lag in ten years. Either we do it, or they crush us'—so Stalin had spoken exactly ten years before Hitler set out to conquer Russia. His words, when they were recalled now, could not but impress people as a prophecy brilliantly fulfilled, as a most timely call to action. And, indeed, a few year's delay in the modernization of Russia might have made all the difference between victory and defeat.

Against this must be set the price Russia had paid for victory: the seven million dead, officially counted—the losses may in fact have been much larger; the uncounted millions of cripples; the devastation of most cities and towns, and of much of the country-side in European Russia; the destruction of industry, exemplified by the total flooding of the coal-mines of the Donets; the complete homelessness of twenty-five million people, living in caves, trenches, and mud huts, not to speak of the latent homelessness of many more millions of evacuees

---

[1] Incidentally, collectivization had made it easier for the Government to build up stocks of food and raw materials, by which the townspeople were saved from famine, and industry from paralysis, when the country was cut off from its granaries and transport was disrupted.

in the Urals and beyond. Last but not least, the cost of victory included the utter weariness of a people that had, in the interests of industrialization and rearmament, for many years been denied the most essential necessities of life.

The nation was crippled and hungry. It probably expected miracles from its victory and miracles from its government. It wanted to see its cities rebuilt and its industry and agriculture rehabilitated as rapidly as possible. It craved for more food, more clothing, more schools, more leisure. But these could not be obtained quickly from Russia's own depleted and disorganized resources. Misery flushed with victory was doubly impatient; and Stalin could not risk disappointing it. To speed up reconstruction and to raise the standard of living he had to draw on the economic resources of other nations.

In theory he could do that in three different ways. He might have asked the western allies, especially the United States, for assistance. In the heyday of the alliance there had been much talk of American loans to Russia and of Russo-American trade. But amid the tensions and conflicts that developed later, the vistas of economic co-operation faded. Stalin must, anyhow, have been reluctant to bring his country to that position of relative dependence in which any debtor inevitably finds himself *vis-à-vis* his creditor. His choice was practically limited to two methods, one essentially nationalist, the other revolutionary. The nationalist method consisted in the imposition of tribute on the vanquished nations, the dismantlement and transfer to Russia of their industries, the levying of reparations from their current output, and the direct use of their labour. The revolutionary method, promising to bear fruit more slowly but more permanently, consisted in the broadening of the base on which planned economy was to operate, in an economic link-up between Russia and the countries within her orbit. The gradual integration into the system of planned economy of several small and medium-sized countries, most of which had been industrially more developed than Russia before the thirties, promised to quicken the tempo of Russia's as well as of their own reconstruction. The first condition of that integration was that communism should be in power in the countries concerned. In treading this path Stalin tacitly admitted that the productive forces of the Soviet Union revolted, to use

Trotsky's favourite expression, against its national boundaries. Russia's economic organism was in such a state that its recovery and further growth could not be secured merely by its internal strength, unless that recovery was to be slow, painful, and accompanied by so much misery that the victor nation was not likely to put up with it.

We have seen that the two policies, the nationalist and the revolutionary, clashed on crucial points. Stalin did not, nevertheless, make a clear-cut choice between the two; he pursued both lines simultaneously; but whereas the nationalist one predominated during the war, the revolutionary one was to gain momentum after the war.

This development constitutes by far the most striking paradox in Stalin's political evolution, so rich in paradox. For more than two decades he had preached the gospel of socialism in one country and violently asserted the self-sufficiency of Russian socialism. In practice, if not in precept, he had made Russia turn her back upon world revolution—or was it Russia that had made him turn his back upon it? Now, in his supreme triumph, he disavowed, again in practice if not in precept, his own gospel; he discarded his own canon of Russia's self-sufficiency and revived her interest in international revolution. Bolshevism appeared to have run full circle and returned to its starting-point. Such, indeed, was the strange dialectics of Stalin's victory that it seemed to turn that victory into Trotsky's posthumous triumph. It was as if Stalin himself had crowned all his toils and labours, all his controversies and purges, by an unexpected vindication of his dead opponent.

Yet such a view would represent a half truth only. Doubtless, the Stalin of 1945-6 was no longer quite the same Stalin whom we had known in 1925 and 1935. The tide of events carried him away from a position which he had claimed to be, and which had in fact been, peculiarly his. But it did not carry him back to his starting-point, to the conception of world revolution he had once shared with Lenin and Trotsky. He now replaced his socialism in one country by something that might be termed 'socialism in one zone'. In Lenin's and Trotsky's conception, the Socialist revolution was essentially a continuous, global process, admitting no durable truce between the hostile forces of capitalism and socialism. In that conception there was no room for any deliberate division of spheres of influence between the two systems. The idea of a condominium of the great powers based on that division would have appeared, from the pristine Bolshevik viewpoint, to be a negation of every Socialist principle. In the Stalinist conception, in so far as this can be inferred from Stalin's policies, the process of world revolution is still a global one, for the antagonism between capitalism and socialism is, like the earlier one between capitalism and feudalism, inherent in all modern civilization. But their struggle is continuous only in the broadest historical and philosophical sense. It is likely to extend over the lifetime of many generations. In the reality of practical politics, the discontinuity of the revolutionary process matters as much as, if not more than, its continuity. War-like collision between the opposed systems is, or may be, followed by a durable truce, lasting perhaps a few decades, in the course of which the antagonism of the two systems assumes the character of peaceful rivalry. The nature of the process not only allows but positively presupposes compacts and transactions between the Socialist and the capitalist states. It even allows the Socialist state to adhere to such international pragmatic sanctions as the division of zones of influence, by which the Socialist state strengthens the position of capitalism in one part of the world, provided that, as *quid pro quo*, it is allowed to strengthen its own position and expand in another.

Connected with this is another difference of approach, which the events of the forties have thrown into the boldest relief. In the old Bolshevik view the real *terra firma* for socialism was 'the highly industrialized west'. Russia had *begun* the revolution; the west was to *continue* it, to bring it to fruition, and to *react* back in the Socialist spirit upon 'backward Russia'. This scheme of things was now, in the Stalinist view, ridiculously obsolete, in part because the west was still incapable of making its revolution, and in part because the importance of the west for socialism had, in consequence of Russia's progress, so much diminished that western Europe could safely be ceded to capitalism in the great share-out of the zones. Lenin and Trotsky had their eyes fixed on the German, French, and British working classes as the main agents of the revolution of the twentieth century; Stalin's eyes were fixed primarily on revolutions in Warsaw, Bucharest,

Belgrade, and Prague. To him socialism in one zone, in the Russian zone, became the supreme objective of political strategy for a whole historical epoch.

The most important difference, however, lies in the method of the revolution. Broadly speaking, the old Bolshevism staked its hopes on the revolutionary momentum of the international Labour movement. It believed that the Socialist order would result from the original experience and struggle of the working classes abroad, that it would be the most authentic act of their social and political self-determination. The old Bolshevism, in other words, believed in *revolution from below*, such as the upheaval of 1917 had been. The revolution which Stalin now carried into eastern and central Europe was primarily a *revolution from above*. It was decreed, inspired, and managed by the great power predominant in that area. Although the local Communist parties were its immediate agents and executors, the great party of the revolution, which remained in the background, was the Red Army. This is not to say that the working classes on the spot did not participate in the upheaval. Without their participation the venture would have been only a flash in the pan. No revolution can be carried out from above only, without the willing co-operation of important elements in the nation affected by it. What took place within the Russian orbit was, therefore, semi-conquest and semi-revolution. This makes the evaluation of this phenomenon so very difficult. Had it been nothing but conquest it would have been easy to denounce it as plain Russian imperialism. Had it been nothing but revolution, those at least who recognize the right of a nation to make its revolution—a right of which every great nation has made use—would have had no scruples in acclaiming it. But it is the blending of conquest and revolution that makes the essence of 'socialism in one zone'.

As an inspirer of revolution from above, Stalin does not stand alone in modern European history. He takes his place by the side of Napoleon and Bismarck, from whom in other respects he differs so much. This role of his results from one peculiar parallelism between the bourgeois and the Socialist revolution in Europe, a parallelism that has come to light only since the Second World War. Europe, in the nineteenth century, saw how the feudal order, outside France, crumbled and was replaced by the bourgeois one. But east of the Rhine feudalism was not overthrown by a series of upheavals on the pattern of the French revolution, by explosions of popular despair and anger, by revolutions from below, for the spread of which some of the Jacobins had hoped in 1794. Instead, European feudalism was either destroyed or undermined by a series of revolutions from above. Napoleon, the tamer of Jacobinism at home, carried the revolution into foreign lands, to Italy, to the Rhineland, and to Poland, where he abolished serfdom, completely or in part, and where his Code destroyed many of the feudal privileges. *Malgré lui-même*, he executed parts of the political testament of Jacobinism. More paradoxically, the Conservative Junker, Bismarck, performed a similar function when he freed Germany from many survivals of feudalism which encumbered her bourgeois development. The second generation after the French revolution witnessed an even stranger spectacle, when the Russian Tsar himself abolished serfdom in Russia and Poland, a deed of which not so long before only 'Jacobins' had dreamt. The feudal order had been too moribund to survive; but outside France the popular forces arrayed against it were too weak to overthrow it 'from below'; and so it was swept away 'from above'. It is mainly in Napoleon's impact upon the lands neighbouring France that the analogy is found for the impact of Stalinism upon eastern and central Europe. The chief elements of both historic situations are similar: the social order of eastern Europe was as little capable of survival as was the feudal order in the Rhineland in Napoleon's days; the revolutionary forces arrayed against the anachronism were too weak to remove it; then conquest and revolution merged in a movement, at once progressive and retrograde, which at last transformed the structure of society.

· · · · · · · ·

Another 'dialectical contradiction' in victorious Stalinism relates to the 'iron curtain', that is the extremely rigid isolation from the outside world in which Stalin brought up a whole Soviet generation. That isolation has in fact been essential to the political and cultural climate of Stalinist Russia, and Stalin may be described as the chief architect of the 'iron curtain'. Yet the reasons for the isolation and the elements that went into its making were diverse and manifold; and it was their combination that made the 'iron curtain' so solid, so thick, so impenetrable.

The first of those elements was the self-defensive attitude of Bolshevism after the frustration of its hopes for world revolution. Bolshevik Russia shut herself off from a hostile world. In this respect she was not very different from Cromwellian England or Jacobin France. Puritan England lived in suspicion and fear of 'French intrigue' and 'French gold' working against her. The spectres of 'English intrigue' and 'English gold' haunted Jacobin France. In each case the revolutionary nation had real reasons for suspicion—the hostile 'intrigue' and 'gold' had not been just figments of its imagination. All the same, in each case the suspicion of and the reaction against the outside world assumed that extraordinary intensity which is characteristic of popular feeling in any revolutionary epoch.

This frame of mind in Bolshevik Russia was tremendously enhanced by native Russian tradition. As in so many other respects, so in this the national custom and habit reasserted themselves the more easily and the more potently, because they harmonized with the real and the apparent needs of the revolution. Russia's age-old seclusion from the west had been dictated by military considerations—the Russian plain had no natural barriers to stop invaders—by the hostility of Greek Orthodoxy to Roman Catholicism and, in later times, by the anxiety of autocratic Tsardom to defend itself against the infiltration of Liberal and Socialist ideas from the west. It is true that in the nineteenth century the Russian intelligentsia partly succeeded in breaching the wall; but even this success, achieved not without a bitter struggle, underlined the basic fact of isolation. Breached, the wall was still there. Russia's Bolshevik rulers tried at first to pull it down; then they found it useful not merely to let it stand, but even to close its breaches.

Seen from another angle, the 'iron curtain' has been a variety of economic protectionism. No great modern nation, with the peculiar exception of the British, has developed its industry without defending itself by high tariff walls and a variety of other prohibitive measures against the competition of older industrial nations. Shielded by protectionism, the United States and Germany grew to their industrial maturity. Socialism in one country could not but resort to the same method. Other nations had in their industrial development been favoured by the assistance of foreign capital or, in the case of the United States, by the geographic 'protectionism' of two oceans. Bolshevik Russia had no comparable advantages. Foreign capital did not help her to develop her wealth. She had hardly started her industrialization in real earnest before she was confronted with the threat of new, total war and was compelled to divert much of her wealth to armament. This made her industrial revolution infinitely more painful than it might otherwise have been; and this invested her protectionism with extraordinary severity and harshness.

That severity, that harshness, was felt in the first instance by the ordinary working man. The Government and the planning authorities had to allocate the national resources to the development of industry and transport, the mechanization of agriculture, armaments, and private consumption. The larger the resources allocated to industry and armament, the less, relatively or even absolutely, was left over for private consumption. This was the plain economic logic of the situation, a logic which all belligerent nations were to learn or re-learn, in different degrees, in the years of the Second World War, but with which Russia had been uncomfortably familiar many years before. The standard of living of the mass of the people, traditionally very low, was sacrificed to higher purposes of national policy. In spite of all that, it began appreciably to rise in the late thirties. But the rise was ephemeral. War once again depressed the standard of living to a terribly low level.

The mass of the Russian people saw how rapidly the nation grew wealthier and wealthier, while the overwhelming majority of its members remained individually poor or even grew poorer and poorer. True enough, the economists knew that this had been roughly the position of almost every nation engaged in an industrial revolution. The essence of protectionism in the nineteenth century was that it withheld cheap foreign goods from the mass of consumers in order to shield and stimulate the growth of the nation's industrial strength. But in no other country had the contrast between the accumulation of national wealth and individual poverty been as sharp as in Russia under Stalin; and, what is perhaps more important, in no other country had that contrast been identified with socialism and a classless society. Stalin asked the working classes not only to make the effort they were making and bear the sacrifices they were bearing, but also to believe that they had an easier and better life than the peoples of the capitalist countries. This was not and could not have been true; and this was not the fault of socialism. Nor was it, by and large, the fault of Stalin or of his Government, although some of their mistakes aggravated the situation. But it was Stalin's fault, if this be the right word, that he presented to the Russian people their miserable standard of living as the height of Socialist achievement.

This misrepresentation was the source of an astounding system of hypocritical deception. Its first consequence was that the mass of the people was not to be allowed to make real comparisons between the Russian and the foreign standards of living. The second was that over many years the propagandists not only gilded the conditions of life at home, but persistently set up an absurdly exaggerated picture of the misery of the working classes abroad. The third was that as few Soviet citizens as possible were allowed to study social life in foreign countries either through personal observation or through reading foreign books and newspapers. To maintain the 'iron curtain' became Stalin's major economic and political interest.

Russia's isolation from the world became hermetic, and turned into a morose psychosis during the great purges. The picture of a sinister, all-pervading foreign conspiracy, which Vyshinsky, the general prosecutor, drew, and which the defendants through their confessions made even blacker, the fact that the conspiracy was alleged to have had its agents in almost every cell of the body politic, the terrible punishment inflicted upon the 'conspirators'—all that spread a neurotic horror of all things foreign. Every contact, be it ever so casual, with foreigners and foreign affairs was deemed contaminating. Old people suspected, of course, that it was all a frame up; and, from fear, they accepted the isolation. But the young took things at their face value. Their horror of foreign vice coupled with domestic heresy was genuine. It was part of their normal state of mind, part of their character. They had almost from the cradle been moulded by the monolithic state; they had been indoctrinated not with Marxism indeed, but with one crude

Byzantinesque version of it. They had not been allowed to acquire the habit of questioning accepted truth; they had not been afforded the experience of any real clash of conflicting views and principles, the experience of independent formation of opinion. The purges finally insulated the mind of the young generation from any disturbing outside influence.

Made up of so many diverse elements, the 'iron curtain' performed in effect a dual function, 'progressive' and 'reactionary'. Behind that curtain the revolution found a degree of safety and the Government could go ahead with the job of industrialization and modernization. (The strictly military value of the 'iron curtain' was up to a point demonstrated in the war, when Hitler's generals, on invading Russia, found that what they had known about their enemy was next to nothing.[1]) At the same time, the 'iron curtain' shielded Stalin's autocracy, his uncanny despotism, his legends and deceptions. In both its functions the 'iron curtain' had become to Stalinism the indispensable condition for its very existence.

It was of that condition, of that *sine qua non* of its self-perpetuation, that victory now threatened to rob Stalinism. Russia suddenly found herself involved in a thousand ways in the life and the affairs of the outside world. Millions of Russian soldiers marched into a dozen foreign lands. They were, in more than one sense, *l'état en voyage*, as Napoleon had called an army marching into a foreign country. Millions of former forced labourers returned home from a long sojourn in Germany. Multitudes of Russian officers sat on inter-allied commissions, in daily contact with an alien world. The 'iron curtain' was pierced, breached, almost shattered.

The impression that the capitalist west made on the Russians was by no means as uniformly favourable as some people in the west, given to self-flattery, were inclined to think. The Russians saw Europe in ruin. Millions of their men and women had lived for years behind the barbed wire of German concentration camps or in the shadow of gas-chambers. They saw the hideous diseased rump of European civilization, not its old noble face. To many of them the picture of the outside world must have looked even blacker than the propagandists at home had painted it. Even those who had been spared such gloomy

[1] B. H. Liddell Hart, *The Other Side of the Hill*, pp. 184, 187, and 196.

experiences were by no means converted to the capitalist way of life. To most of them any society in which the means of production were not publicly owned was social injustice itself, a baffling or ridiculous anachronism. Nevertheless, in this contact with the outside world, habits of thought, formed in the years of isolation, began to weaken, if not to crumble. Russians noticed that, even amid the ravages of war, foreigners had a higher standard of living than they themselves. They were dazzled by the amenities of life which even the vanquished still enjoyed.[1] They observed, not without envy, that Poles, Hungarians, Czechs, and Yugoslavs were less constrained than they themselves, that they were suffering from fewer inhibitions in speaking their minds; in a word, that they were enjoying a measure of freedom.

The contact with foreign countries generated moral ferment. The scope of that ferment can be gauged from the fact that it affected millions of people who, on their return home, could not be prevented from conveying something of their experience to their relatives and friends. No sensational political developments could immediately result from this. Nor could the ferment crystallize into any definite political ideas—no independent groups or organizations capable of formulating such ideas, had been left in being. The nation could not quickly re-learn those habits of forming its own opinion, from which it had been so forcibly dissuaded. What had begun in its mind, so it seems, was an imperceptible process of transvaluation of values, the duration and ultimate outcome of which nobody could prophesy. The recent experience gave new urgency to the nation's desire for a betterment in the material conditions of its life, a desire which Stalin's Government probably met half-way by levying reparations from the vanquished and by an energetic rehabilitation of the domestic economy. Beyond the sphere of material interest a new vague yearning for freedom and a novel curiosity about the outside world made itself felt; a yearning and a curiosity which the Government was ill

---

[1] In the twenties Trotsky argued that the 'pressure of cheap goods' produced by the capitalist countries would defeat socialism in one country. Stalin's economic protectionism kept that pressure at bay. The 'flood of cheap foreign goods' was not allowed to break into Russia. But, advancing into Europe, Russia had come to feel the moral pressure, as it were, of the 'cheap goods', that is of the higher standard of living that had been produced by capitalism. L. Trotsky, *The Real Situation in Russia*, p. 83.

equipped to satisfy.[1] Victory could not but impart to the nation, at least to its intelligent, forward-looking elements, the feeling that it had stood its supreme test, that it had attained maturity and outgrown the tutelage to which it had owed and from which it had suffered so much. While it is true that in the mood of victory the nation was willing to forgive Stalin his past misdeeds, it is probably even truer that it was not willing to see a repetition of those misdeeds.

We have said that no groups or organizations existed to translate the new ferment into political ideas. This statement needs to be qualified. Towards the end of the war the officers' corps represented the germ of such an organization. In a previous chapter we have analysed the circumstances which had half exempted it from the totalitarian pressure and allowed it to acquire a distinct identity of its own. Towards the end of the war the officers' corps was morally on top of the nation. It had a leader to look up to in Marshal Zhukov, the defender of Moscow and the conqueror of Berlin, whose popularity was second only to Stalin's. It may have been by one shade more genuine, because it had owed less to official publicity. This is not to say that Stalin's personal position was in any danger or that Zhukov could have assumed the role of his rival. Much time was probably needed before any political opposition could evolve; and it was highly doubtful whether it could do so while Stalin was alive. But although his own position was not imperilled, Stalin was only too anxious, just as he had been in the thirties, to suppress once more, though in much milder fashion, the potentiality of an alternative government, or rather of a successor to his government whom he himself had not designated. He may have recalled the sequel to the ferment which arose in the army of Alexander I from its contact with Europe. Barely a few years after the victory over Napoleon the Tsar's officers' corps was riddled with secret societies, formed by men whom the observations of life abroad had induced to fight for reform at home. After Alexander's death those secret societies prepared and staged the Decembrist rising of 1825, the forerunner of a long series of revolutionary convulsions.

---

[1] This probably accounts for the abolition of capital punishment, the quasi-Liberal modification of the criminal code, the emphasis on habeas corpus and on the rule of law, and a number of other post-war reforms.

Stalin's main endeavour was therefore to lift the party back to its old exalted status, which it was to share with no other body. The celebrated marshals and generals suffered eclipse. A few months after the cease fire their names and deeds were hardly ever mentioned by the propagandists. It might be said that this was normal and sound and that it would have happened in any nation which was not under the thumb of a military dictator. Yet there was more to it than that. The eclipse of the officers' corps had its political significance. It was staged with deliberation and consistency. This became clear when in 1946 Marshal Zhukov completely disappeared from the public eye. From then on his role in the defence of Stalingrad and even Moscow was gradually blurred in the official accounts of the war, until, on the third anniversary of the battle of Berlin, Pravda managed to commemorate the event without mentioning Zhukov even once.[1] His name was being deleted from the annals of the war, as so many names had been deleted from the annals of the revolution.

Stalin's effort to restore the moral supremacy of the party was coupled with his endeavour to re-establish the party outlook as against the nationalist mood of the preceding years. In the tug-of-war between Revolution and Tradition, the former was strikingly reasserting itself, though it did not completely suppress or eliminate the latter. Peace, like the war before it, entailed many ideological adjustments in every sphere of public life, in politics, in economics, in the writing of philosophy and history, in fiction, and in the arts. From everywhere, the household deities of Mother Russia, only recently re-installed with so much unction, were quietly removed to the lumber rooms, if not cast out altogether. It was no longer good patriotic style to evoke the names of Kutuzov, Suvorov, Minin, and Pozharsky. It was no longer fashionable to glorify the great Tsars, Ivan the Terrible and Peter the Great, whom historians and writers had just treated with more reverence than discretion as Stalin's spiritual forebears. Even Slavophil propaganda was damped down. It was, generally speaking, no longer regarded as desirable that the mind of the people should be turned too

---

[1] Pravda, 9. 5. 1948 claimed that the author of the plan for the storming of Berlin was Stalin himself. The writers of the anniversary articles mentioned many of the generals who took part in the battle, but not Zhukov.

much towards its past.[1] The new task was to revive 'Bolshevik consciousness'. The young were now to be taught to value the things in which modern Russia differed from the old, rather than those in which she resembled her. They were to be made aware how much the Soviet Union owed to socialism, to class struggle, and to Marxism-Leninism as interpreted by Stalin. Something like a Leninist revivalism was now sponsored and encouraged.

In part, the new turn was probably a genuine reaction from the surfeit of wartime nationalism. In part, it may have been dictated by Stalin's personal considerations. In 1941–3 he could still be flattered by comparisons between himself and Peter the Great and take pride in analogies drawn between the two Fatherland wars of 1812 and 1941. Mounted on ancestral shoulders he gained in stature. As victor he had no need for all that. The Peters, the Kutuzovs, the Alexanders looked like pygmies in comparison with him. It was a different thing for him to present himself once again as Lenin's successor, for Lenin's stature had, after all, remained what it had been. But apart from such considerations, about which one can only speculate, Stalin had a broader motive in fostering the Leninist revivalism. Through it he hoped to counter the new impact of the capitalist west upon Russia. Nationalist propaganda had been good enough to arouse the people to its bitter struggle for survival. But it was not good enough when the people had to be braced against the 'corrupting' influence of the outside world and given new hope. Only in the light of the Bolshevik doctrine, which preached that capitalism was bound to disintegrate and socialism to triumph, could the people be made to see that the things by which the west had impressed them were so many pleasant appearances, concealing incurable decay. Stalin tried to stir the old half-extinct ideological zeal and fervour of communism in order to hold his ground against the west, not only outside but even inside Russia. By appealing to that zeal and

[1] In the beginning of 1945 the Central Committee of the party decided to close down the *Istoricheskii Journal*, the journal of the Russian historians, and to replace it by another one called *Voprosy Istorii*. 'In our historical research in the last few years there were also distortions . . . tending towards great power chauvinism, there was a tendency to rehabilitate, in summary fashion, the colonial, annexationist policy of Tsardom, to bring back bourgeois conceptions into the presentation of the growth of the Russian state, to deny the revolutionary significance of the peasant movements, to idealize the men of the autocratic order and to give up the class analysis of historical phenomena' (*Voprosy Istorii*, no. 1, 1945).

fervour he hoped, in particular, to restore the morale of the intelligentsia and to re-reconcile it to the rigours of his rule. By one of history's many ironies Leninism was now called upon to stop the breaches in Stalin's 'iron curtain'.

There was a Sisyphean touch about these labours, which was due to an obvious contradiction between Stalin's foreign and domestic policies. His foreign policy was to keep Russia in Europe. His domestic policy was to keep her mind out of Europe. His purpose was to re-isolate Russia not only from that part of the Continent that was under American and British influence, but even from that portion of it that had come under Russian influence, for the way of life and the spiritual climate of the 'people's democracies' was very different from the Russian. In part this was due to the dissimilarity of the national traditions of Russians, Poles, Czechs, Hungarians, Serbs. Even in Russia the formative processes of Stalinism had lasted many years and had necessitated many economic upheavals, political shocks, and slow changes. The end product of that long painful evolution could not be exported ready made to the countries in the Russian orbit. Meanwhile, their economic systems, with private ownership still predominating in farming, with diverse methods of industrial work and varying degrees of efficiency, would be different from the Russian. The standards of living of the Czechs or Poles, traditionally higher than those of the Russians, could not be so depressed for the sake of industrialization as they had been in Russia. All this was likely to produce 'deviations' from orthodoxy. Genuine contact between Russia and the 'people's democracies'—free travel and free exchange of ideas—could easily have become another source of ferment inside Russia. Stalin had therefore to keep in being two 'iron curtains', one separating Russia from her own zone of influence, the other separating that zone from the west. Public opinion in the west was more preoccupied with the latter, but it was the former that was the more impenetrable of the two. Yet it is questionable whether even this double wall can effectively serve a policy that aspires to keep Russia in and out of Europe at the same time.

. . . .

The chief drama of victorious Stalinism lies, however, in a wider and much more dangerous dilemma. Stalin has staked everything on revolutionizing the whole of the Russian zone of influence. He apparently believed that, having achieved this, he would be able to secure the great truce, the 'peaceful coexistence', to use his own term, between the capitalist west and the communist east. These two objectives, revolution within the Russian orbit and the peaceful coexistence of the two systems, have tended to militate against each other. The truce between capitalism and communism, which lasted through the twenties and thirties, was based on a precarious balance of power, which can hardly be restored. Among its essential elements were Russian weakness and American isolationism. Both belong to the past. Any new balance would require that the United States should reconcile itself to Russian ascendancy in the east and Russia to American ascendancy in the west. It would require that the powers should perpetuate the division of the world into zones of influence. Even if they could bring themselves to do that, the new balance would still be highly unstable, because of the extreme polarization of power in the world and the friction on the borderlines of the two systems. More important still, the outcome of the Second World War has posed the question whether the world, on the threshold of the atomic age, has not become too small for the two antagonistic systems. This is not an entirely new question. The advance of industrial technique has long since tended to render nation-states and empires obsolete. But the sudden expansion of both the American influence and the Soviet system, coinciding with the new revolution in industrial technique, has re-posed the question with baffling insistence and unendurable acuteness. Before that question victorious Stalinism, like the rest of the world, seems to stand defeated.

. . . .

Here we suspend the story of Stalin's life and work. We are under no illusion that we can draw from it final conclusions or form, on its basis, a confident judgement of the man, of his achievements and failures. After so many climaxes and anticlimaxes, his drama seems only now to be rising to its pinnacle; and we do not know into what new perspective its last act may yet throw the preceding ones.

What appears to be established is that Stalin belongs to the breed of the great revolutionary despots, to which Cromwell, Robespierre, and Napoleon belonged. It is only right to place equal emphasis on each part of this description. He is great, if his stature is measured by the scope of his endeavours, the sweep of his actions, the vastness of the stage he has dominated. He is revolutionary, not in the sense that he has remained true to all the original ideas of the revolution, but because he has put into practice a fundamentally new principle of social organization, which, no matter what happens to him personally or even to the régime associated with his name, is certain to survive, to fertilize human experience, and to turn it in new directions. It has, indeed, been one of Stalin's triumphs to see how many other governments have tried to steal his thunder, claiming that they, too, have adopted the methods of planned economy. Finally, his inhuman despotism has not only vitiated much of his achievement—it may yet provoke a violent reaction against it, in which people may be prone to forget, for a time, what it is they react against: the tyranny of Stalinism or its progressive social performance.

The complexity of Stalin's character and of his role becomes most apparent when a comparison is attempted between him and Hitler. Their similarities are numerous and striking. Each of them suppressed opposition without mercy or scruple. Each built up the machine of a totalitarian state and subjected his people to its constant, relentless pressure. Each tried to remould the mind of his nation to a single pattern from which any 'undesirable' impulse or influence was excluded. Each established himself as an unchallengeable master ruling his country in accordance with a rigid *Führerprinzip*.[1]

Here the similarities cease and the differences begin. Not in a single field has Hitler made the German nation advance beyond the point it had reached before he took power. In most fields he has thrown it back far behind, terribly far behind. The

[1] There is, however, a difference between the Nazi and the Stalinist versions of the *Führerprinzip*. Hitler was worshipped by his followers as a demi-god, without any inhibition, because hero worship suited only too well a racialist mystique. The cult of Stalin, on the other hand, could never be made to fit in properly with the realism of Marxism-Leninism. Stalin has been worshipped not as the mythical hero but as the guardian of the doctrine, the trustee of the revolution, the symbol of authority. The Marxist inhibition has compelled him to cloak his personal authority with the collective authority of the Politbureau or of the Central Committee.

Germany he took over in 1933 was, despite economic depression and social strains and stresses, a wealthy and flourishing country. Its industry was the most efficient on the continent. Its social services were the most modern that any European nation had had. Its universities were great centres of learning, priding themselves on famous men of science. The better part of the German youth was serious, alert, and idealistic. The German theatre was the object of the highest admiration and of imitation. The best German newspapers were the most intelligent and the best informed of the continental press.

The Germany that Hitler left behind was impoverished and reduced to savagery. We are not speaking about the effects of Germany's defeat, but about the state of the nation, regardless of defeat. The material apparatus of production which the country possessed under Hitler was, apart from special armament plants, not essentially greater than that which it had possessed before. Its social services were half destroyed. Its universities became drilling grounds for a generation of horrible brutes. Its famous men of science were compelled either to emigrate or to accept the guidance of S.S. men and to learn racialist gibberish. Its medical men were turned into specialists on the racial purity of blood and into the assassins of those whose blood was deemed impure. In the sanctuary of national philosophy Alfred Rosenberg sequestrated for himself the niche that used to be occupied by Immanuel Kant. Twelve years of 'education' by a nazified press, radio, cinema, and theatre left the collective mind of Germany stultified and ruined. These terrible losses were not redeemed by a single positive acquisition or by a single new idea, unless one chooses to regard as new the idea that one nation or race is entitled to dominate or exterminate the others. Nor was the social structure of the nation essentially changed by national socialism. When the Nazi façade was blown away, the structure that revealed itself to the eyes of the world was the same as it had been before Hitler, with its big industrialists, its Krupps and Thyssens, its Junkers, its middle classes, its *Grossbauers*, its farm labourers, and its industrial workers. Sociologically, although not politically, the Germany of 1945 was still the Germany of the Hohenzollerns, only thrown into terrible disorder and confusion by a tragically purposeless riot.[1]

[1] 'More terrifying than the spiritual legacy is the economic aftermath of

What a contrast, after all, Stalinist Russia presents. The nation over which Stalin took power might, apart from small groups of educated people and advanced workers, rightly be called a nation of savages. This is not meant to cast any reflection on the Russian national character—Russia's 'backward, Asiatic' condition has been her tragedy, not her fault. Stalin undertook, to quote a famous saying, to drive barbarism out of Russia by barbarous means. Because of the nature of the means he employed, much of the barbarism thrown out of Russian life has crept back into it. The nation has, nevertheless, advanced far in most fields of its existence. Its material apparatus of production, which about 1930 was still inferior to that of any medium-sized European nation, has so greatly and so rapidly expanded that Russia is now the first industrial power in Europe and the second in the world. Within little more than one decade the number of her cities and towns doubled; and her urban population grew by thirty millions. The number of schools of all grades has very impressively multiplied. The whole nation has been sent to school. Its mind has been so awakened that it can hardly be put back to sleep again. Its avidity for knowledge, for the sciences and the arts, has been stimulated by Stalin's government to the point where it has become insatiable and embarrassing. It should be remarked that, although Stalin has kept Russia isolated from the contemporary influences of the west, he has encouraged and fostered every interest in what he calls the 'cultural heritage' of the west. Perhaps in no country have the young been imbued with so great a respect and love for the classical literature and art of other nations as in Russia.[1] This is one of the important differences between the educational methods of nazism and

Hitler. Even the most ruthless implementation of socialist and communist economic doctrines would not have been more devastating in its consequences than was Hitler's complete ignorance in matters of economic policy. . . . Hitler's four year plan had nothing in common with constructive planning in the style of the Russian five year plans.' This statement comes from so uncompromising an opponent of communism and socialism as Hjalmar Schacht, Hitler's one time 'financial wizard'. Dr. Hjalmar Schacht, *Abrechnung mit Hitler*, p. 41.

[1] In the years of the Soviet régime, up to the war, the total editions of foreign classics were: Byron's works half a million copies, Balzac nearly two millions, Dickens two millions, Goethe half a million, Heine one million, Victor Hugo three millions, Maupassant more than three millions, Shakespeare one million two hundred thousand, Zola two millions, &c.

Stalinism. Another is that Stalin has not, like Hitler, forbidden the new generation to read and study the classics of their own literature whose ideological outlook does not accord with his. While tyrannizing the living poets, novelists, historians, painters, and even composers, he has displayed, on the whole, a strange pietism for the dead ones. The works of Pushkin, Gogol, Tolstoy, Chekhov, Belinsky, and many others, whose satire and criticism of past tyranny have only too often a bearing on the present, have been literally pressed into the hands of youth in millions of copies. No Russian Lessing or Heine has been burned at an *auto-da-fé*. Nor can the fact be ignored that the ideal inherent in Stalinism, one to which Stalin has given a grossly distorted expression, is not domination of man by man, or nation by nation, or race by race, but their fundamental equality. Even the proletarian dictatorship is presented as a mere transition to a classless society; and it is the community of the free and the equal, and not the dictatorship, that has remained the inspiration. Thus, there have been many positive, valuable elements in the educational influence of Stalinism, elements that are in the long run likely to turn against its worse features.

Finally, the whole structure of Russian society has undergone a change so profound and so many sided that it cannot really be reversed. It is possible to imagine a violent reaction of the Russian people itself against the state of siege in which it has been living so long. It is even possible to imagine something like a political restoration. But it is certain that even such a restoration would touch merely the surface of Russian society and that it would demonstrate its impotence *vis-à-vis* the work done by the revolution even more thoroughly than the Stuart and the Bourbon restorations had done. For of Stalinist Russia it is even truer than of any other revolutionary nation that 'twenty years have done the work of twenty generations'.

For all these reasons Stalin cannot be classed with Hitler, among the tyrants whose record is one of absolute worthlessness and futility. Hitler was the leader of a sterile counter-revolution, while Stalin has been both the leader and the exploiter of a tragic, self-contradictory but creative revolution. Like Cromwell, Robespierre, and Napoleon he started as the servant of an insurgent people and made himself its master. Like Cromwell he embodies the continuity of the revolution through all its phases and metamorphoses, although his role was less prominent in the first phase. Like Robespierre he has bled white his own party; and like Napoleon he has built his half-conservative and half-revolutionary empire and carried revolution beyond the frontiers of his country. The better part of Stalin's work is as certain to outlast Stalin himself as the better parts of the work of Cromwell and Napoleon have outlasted them. But in order to save it for the future and to give to it its full value, history may yet have to cleanse and reshape Stalin's work as sternly as it once cleansed and reshaped the work of the English revolution after Cromwell and of the French after Napoleon.

CHAPTER XV

Postscript: Stalin's Last Years

Stalin's fulfilment and undoing.—The post-war Five-Year Plan.—The twenty million dead.—The new terror.—Zhdanov's control over the intelligentsia.—The opening of the cold war.—Stalin rejects 'Marshall Aid'.—The Cominform.—Revolution in Czechoslovakia.—The blockade of Berlin.—The U.S.S.R. breaks the American nuclear monopoly.—The Chinese revolution: Stalin and Mao Tse-tung.—The excommunication of Tito.—The Korean war and its consequences.—The upsurge of Great Russian chauvinism.—Stalin and the Jews.—Did he suffer from paranoia?—His last pronouncements on linguistics and economics.—The XIX Congress.—'The Doctors' Plot'.—Stalin's role re-assessed.—His death.

STALIN's last years brought him his fulfilment but also his undoing. The drama of his career was re-enacted in the epilogue; and the stage, so huge from the beginning, on which he played his role was enlarged to dimensions which might have dwarfed even a greater man. The conflict between the Soviet Union and its wartime Allies had already involved half the world; now the Chinese revolution achieved its triumph, putting a final end to the isolation of the Soviet Union and to 'Socialism in One Country'. It overshadowed all the dubious revolutions Stalin had stage-managed in eastern Europe. It changed at a stroke the balance of power in the world. And it turned Stalinism, with its national self-sufficiency and sacred egoism, into an offensive anachronism.

At the same time, changes in the Soviet Union were slowly but surely eroding Stalinism from within. The nation was reliving some of its experiences of the nineteen-thirties, for the war had thrown it back and retarded its growth and development. Stalin reinitiated the processes of 'primitive socialist accumulation'. He could not allow the people any respite from the exertions of the war. He had to mobilize them again and extract from them every ounce of energy so that they should rehabilitate the wrecked or overworked industries, and rebuild the scores of cities and towns reduced to ruins. He met the people's utter weariness with his unwearying ruthlessness. He disciplined and regimented them anew, reimposed on them the harshest emergency decrees and labour codes, subjected them to all-pervading police control, and stamped out every spark of resistance and heresy.

Yet history was not simply repeating itself. The nation did not lapse back into a bygone phase of its existence. Though it had lost much through the carnage and devastation of war, it had also gained new ground and new advantages; and it was making a rapid and vigorous recovery. The industrialization of the eastern republics and provinces had been accelerated; the lands beyond the Volga and the Urals, where the Red Army's arsenals had lain since the German invasion, served as the base for the rehabilitation of the national economy, which was also assisted by reparations from Germany and other defeated countries. Above all, culturally and politically the nation was not what it had been. We have seen how its moral fibre had been enriched by the experiences of 1941–5, and what ferments these had set up in its mind. The continuing modernization of society and education of the masses intensified those ferments, even though the popular mood was, in the calamitous aftermath of the war, sadly subdued.

True to character, Stalin sought to intercept and deaden the stirrings of a new social consciousness. Driven by his own insecurity and anxious to perpetuate the 'monolithic' shape into which he had forced the nation's life, he tried to revive and bring back the nightmares of the great purges. He could not see that by fostering the modernization of society and mass education, he himself was 'poisoning' the popular mind and preparing Russia for a break with Stalinism. Failing to grasp the obsolescence of his methods of government and dogmas, and surrounded by ever thicker and ever more blinding clouds of incense, he was in his last years more and more estranged from the realities of his time and even of his own rule.

Stalin's heirs, his meek servants in his life-time, after his death depicted in the darkest hues the gloom of his closing years, and dwelt on his callousness to the people's sufferings, his lack of comprehension, and his ineptness. There is much truth in these testimonies; but they also contain an element of parody designed to throw into relief the presumed virtues of his successors. In the aftermath of the war Stalin still acted with that mixture of courage and cowardice, statesmanship and folly, acumen and myopia that had been characteristic of him throughout his career; and in many respects his tasks were now more daunting than ever.

On 9 February 1946, in an 'electoral' speech, he proclaimed the first post-war Five-Year Plan and outlined the major purposes of 'three or more Five-Year Plans'. He pointed out that only after the objectives of these Plans had been achieved would the peoples of the U.S.S.R. at last attain genuine prosperity and security. They must go on building up their economic power so that within fifteen years or so they would be producing 60 million tons of steel annually, 500 million tons of coal, 60 million tons of oil, and so on. 'Only then', he said, 'shall we really be guaranteed against any surprises.' Speaking only a few months after the first atom bombs had exploded over Hiroshima and Nagasaki, he hinted at the new insecurity to which the American nuclear monopoly had exposed Russia; he urged the people to meet the American challenge.[1]

To many, this ambitious programme seemed unreal. The workers to whom Stalin was appealing were hungry—urban consumption had shrunk to about 40 per cent. of what it had been in the very lean year of 1940. In the coal-mines of the Donetz Basin men were still pumping water out of the shafts; every ton of coal brought up to the pithead had to be cherished. The steel mills, rattling with wear and tear, turned out only 12 million tons of ingot, a fraction of the American output. Engineering plants were worked by adolescent semi-skilled labour. People were dressed in rags; many were barefoot. It seemed almost a mockery to urge them to 'catch up' with the United States. Yet the U.S.S.R. was to attain the major industrial targets Stalin had set; and it was to do so ahead of time. The coal-mines yielded 500 million tons a year after twelve years only. The output of oil was stepped up to 60 million tons after nine years. And the steel industry produced its 60 million tons at the end of the nineteen-fifties. Within the same period the production of cement, and industrial construction, expanded more than four times; the industrial use of electricity per worker increased three times; and the output of

[1] *Pravda*, 10-11 February 1946; Stalin, *Rechi na Predvybornykh Sobrannyakh* . . ., pp. 22–3.

machines and machine tools was raised seven or eight times. The greater and the most difficult part of this advance was made in the last years of the Stalin era.[1]

Simultaneously, the foundations of Russia's nuclear industry were laid. This undertaking claimed a large part of Russia's reduced resources. The capital invested in all branches of industry between 1946 and 1950 was as large as all the investments made in the thirteen years of the pre-war investment drive, from 1928 up to the moment of the Nazi invasion. As always, Stalin was bent on developing heavy industry and armament plants; he set extremely modest targets for consumer industries; and even these were not attained. And it was once again on a most shaky agricultural foundation that the huge construction rested. During the war, after the enemy had seized the nation's richest granaries, farm output in the rest of the country fell to less than half of normal. The first post-war harvest yielded in the whole country not more than 60 per cent. of pre-war crops. The reserves were exhausted; many cattle had been slaughtered; machines and tractors were in poor repair; and there were not enough of them; and even the stocks of seed had been either depleted or completely eaten up. Nor was there enough labour available to bring under the plough fields that had lain fallow for years.

Such was the situation when, in 1946, a terrible drought hit the country. This was, as an official announcement put it, the worst disaster agriculture had suffered for over half a century, since 1891. It was far more widespread than the droughts and storms of 1921 that had destroyed all crops in the Volga lands and had brought to 36 million peasants a famine that led to outbreaks of cannibalism.[2] People listened to this announcement with a shudder, for the calamity of 1891—an event which hastened the decline of Tsardom—had haunted popular memory ever since. The crisis of 1946 revealed and aggravated the rickety condition of the entire agricultural structure. The collective farms were in a state of semi-dissolution.[3] The peasants cared more for the tiny plots they still owned privately than for

[1] *Promyshlennost SSSR (Statisticheskii Sbornik)*, pp. 35, 39 ff., 151, 154, 157, 161–3; *Bolshaya Sov. Encyclopaedia*, vol. 50, 1957 (*SSSR*), pp. 290–6.

[2] P. I. Lyashchenko, *Istorya Narodnovo Khozyaistva SSSR*, vol. iii, pp. 578–9.

[3] *KPSS v Rezolutsyakh*, vol. ii, pp. 1038–44.

the fields they owned in common; by the help of the produce of those plots, which they were selling at high prices, they supplemented their meagre earnings from the *kolkhoz*. During the war the farming population had slaved to keep itself alive, to supply the armed forces, to subscribe to war loans, and to send food parcels to fathers, brothers, and husbands at the front. When the war ended few families saw their menfolk return to the villages. The peasantry had lost the most vigorous and productive age groups of its manpower; during the post-war decade old men, cripples, women, and children tilled the land.

This was the most tragic aspect of Russia's military triumph: 20 million of her people had lost their lives in the war. Stalin carefully concealed the magnitude of the loss: the official death roll gave the number as 7 millions. Every family knew, of course, how much it and its neighbours had suffered from the carnage. Every village knew how many dead it was mourning. What Stalin did not allow the nation to do was to add up the lists of casualties. He was afraid of the effect on the national morale; and he sensed here a danger to himself: if he had allowed the people to know how huge the blood-letting had been, they might have inquired far more insistently than they did into all the circumstances that had brought it about, including his own errors and miscalculations. Nor did he wish his war-time allies, who were now potential enemies, to know just how weak and exhausted Russia had emerged from the holocaust—even his successors hesitated many years before disclosing the data: the country had to wait for nearly a decade and a half, until 1959, for the first post-war population census. This showed that in the age groups that were older than eighteen years at the end of hostilities, the age groups that had borne arms in the war, there were only 31 million men left compared with 52 million women.[1] Among the survivors were millions of cripples and invalids; and there were, of course, millions of old men. An entire generation had perished: and its shadow darkened the peace for Russia.

[1] *SSSR v Tsifrakh v 1961 g.*, pp. 34–5. A certain lack of balance in the population had already resulted from the loss of manpower in the First World War, the Civil War, and in the years of the purges and mass deportations. Before the year 1941, however, the ratio of male to female in the age groups discussed here was 9 to 10; in 1946 it was approximately 6 to 10, although many women had perished in the war and under Nazi occupation.

To extract from the nation's shrunken labour force the maximum of productive energy was bound to be the first purpose of any policy determined to prevent the nation from slumping into helpless contemplation of its wounds. The danger was all too real. Stalin's Government proceeded to keep in employment the millions of women and adolescents drafted into industry during the war, and to draft further millions. Western travellers visiting Russian and Ukrainian towns, the scenes of recent battles, reported, sometimes with misplaced indignation, that everywhere they saw elderly women engaged in the back-breaking toil of clearing with bare hands acres of rubble from streets and public squares. In fact, women provided nearly one-third of the labour employed in building; in branches of the economy more congenial to them, they formed two-thirds or even four-fifths of the labour force, and on the average 51 per cent. of those employed in the urban economy, and 57 per cent. of those in farming were women. All legal restrictions on the employment of juvenile labour were disregarded. The long working hours introduced just on the eve of war, with a 48-hour week as the minimum, remained in force, together with the draconic industrial discipline, under which workers were liable to be deported to concentration camps for the most trivial offences. Only in this way was it possible to increase urban employment in the first five years of peace by nearly 12 millions, so that in 1950 the number of workers and employees was higher by 8 millions than in 1940.[1] No one was free to choose or change a job—the state retained unlimited power for the direction of labour. To the end Stalin kept up the campaign against 'petty-bourgeois egalitarianism', fostered Stakhanovite competition, and enforced differential wage rates and piece-work so as to maintain or widen discrepancies between rewards.

It was not easy to gauge the mood in which the people responded to his exacting demands; nor was it easy to say which of these were justified by national needs and which were arbitrary impositions. What was remarkable was how much heroic courage and how much cowed meekness coexisted in the Soviet character side by side. The survivors of the Battle of Moscow and the siege of Leningrad and the victors of Stalingrad and Berlin had returned home feeling equal to any task or

<hr />

[1] *SSSR v Tsifrakh v 1961 g.*, pp. 310, 313.

predicament that lay ahead. Amid their recent ordeals many had reflected on the miseries of their national existence, the poverty and the oppression they had had to endure in peacetime; and many had vowed not to submit to these again but to exert themselves to the utmost and to make Russia a happier and freer country. They did not now find it easy or even possible to act on this resolution. Viewing the ruins of their cities and the scorched earth of their villages, they saw that they had to accept a poverty even more oppressive than that to which they had been accustomed, and that only in back-breaking toil could they rebuild the very foundations of their national existence. And often they were indeed not in a position to discern which of Stalin's decrees served the common interest and which served only his autocracy. Thus the most creditable and even noble motives sometimes moved brave men to become once more Stalin's compliant servants. The instincts and habits of obedience worked powerfully, for the memories of the great terror of the nineteen-thirties still oppressed the minds of all, except the very young. Stalin did all he could to keep alive or revive those memories. Wherever his suspicious eye discerned the slightest challenge to his authority, he punished. The concentration camps in the Far North and Siberia were filling up again. Their new inmates were officers and soldiers who had, as prisoners of war, spent dreadful years in German camps. No sooner had they crossed the frontier of their country than they were subjected to interrogation; and without being allowed even to see their families, they were imprisoned and deported. So were many of the civilians whom the enemy had mobilized in the occupied provinces for forced labour in Germany. They were all branded as traitors: the soldiers for having disobeyed Stalin's orders, according to which they should not have allowed themselves to be taken alive by the enemy; the civilians for having collaborated with the enemy. It did not matter that Stalin's orders had been impracticable, that millions of soldiers had been forced to disregard them, and that they had amply redeemed the 'breach of discipline' by the torment they had suffered in captivity. Even on the most cynical calculation, the punishment Stalin meted out to them was absurd, for it made further inroads into the nation's manpower. Yet even before the end of hostilities Stalin had ordered the deportation of entire nationalities accused of treason: the Crimean Tartars, and the Ingush-Chechens, had all, like the Volga Germans before them, been forced to leave their homelands and settle in Siberian deserts. 'The Ukrainians,' Khrushchev claims, 'escaped this fate only because there were too many of them ...' Yet many of them who collaborated, or were suspected of collaboration, with the enemy were sentenced to long-term servitude.[1]

Stalin's raging wrath burst over the people's heads not merely to punish past transgressions but to stifle any new impulse to disobedience. The severe sentences and mass deportations were meant to deter those who had returned from the war with bold ideas about changes and reforms needed at home. And Stalin again 'acted on the principle that it was not enough to hit his real opponents; he rooted out the environment that had bred them'. Yet even his political police were at times unable to control the flux and chaos, to penetrate the human streams on the move, the millions of evacuees and demobilized soldiers returning to their old homes or searching for new ones. Nor were they always able to get the better of the courage of despair that would suddenly flare up in violence. In the provinces that had been under German occupation, Nazi propaganda had made an impression, even though the occupants had made themselves hated. In the Western Ukraine, re-annexed from Poland, armed bands of Ukrainian nationalists operated from the mountains and forests of the Carpathians, obstructed the re-establishment of Soviet authority and spread terror. There was turmoil in the eastern parts of the Ukraine as well. Gangs of ex-collaborators and marauders roamed the steppe; and even the settled and peaceful population vented anti-Russian and anti-Jewish emotions. Moscow's shrill Great Russian chauvinism exacerbated the never dormant local chauvinisms of the outlying republics. To stem these, Stalin from time to time toned down the Great Russian propaganda, but never for long. His self-contradictory attitude corresponded to divisions in his bureaucracy and in the people at large, divisions which he prevented from crystallizing and which he blurred as well as he could. The conflict between Tradition and Revolution

---

[1] Many novels and dramas of the post-Stalin years describe these moods and conditions.

outlasted the war and was growing in intensity. The 'two parties' still coexisted within the Stalinist monolith—one sensitive to the Leninist tradition and its proletarian internationalism; the other responsive to Great Russian pride and prejudice and even to the traditions of the Black Hundreds and the pogroms.[1]

The ideological malaise was most acute among the intelligentsia. Even under a monolithic-totalitarian régime, the creative urges of writers, artists, philosophers, and historians must come to the surface and clash with official conformism and must express, however faintly, the actual diversity of the national thinking and feeling. Hence the tragic and tragicomic tug-of-war between Stalin and the intelligentsia which fills these years. However much the intelligentsia tried to keep in line with orthodoxy, they were often overwhelmed by the tension between the contradictory elements of Stalinism; and they failed to combine these in accordance with the master's mysterious and elusive prescriptions. A celebrated Ukrainian poet would suddenly be found guilty of voicing 'local chauvinism'; authoritative historians would be castigated for underrating the progressive nature of Tsardom's conquest of the Caucasus and Central Asia; a popular satirical writer would be charged with nihilism; philosophers would be accused of glorifying unduly the German Hegelian ancestry of Marxism; great composers would be denounced for their haughty and insensitive disregard of folk music, beloved by Stalin; literary critics would be charged with offending against the canon of socialist realism; and so on. The intelligentsia had to walk a narrow path between the precipices of nationalism and 'rootless cosmopolitanism'. Stalin appointed Andrei Zhdanov, a member of his Politbureau and Governor of Leningrad, to keep order in the ranks of the ideologues and to chastise stragglers. The brief period of Zhdanov's censorship over the arts and literature—he died in the summer of 1948—was to be long remembered by the intelligentsia as one of the worst visitations they had to endure.'[2]

[1] See Chapter XII, pp. 487–93; and E. Yevtushenko, *Autobiographie Précoce*, pp. 108–15 and *passim*.

[2] The Zhdanov campaign began in the summer of 1946 with attacks on Leningrad's literary periodicals, on Zoshchenko, Akhmatova, and other writers, and

Zhdanov's *ukasy*, however, affected directly only the uppermost layer of society. Down below, the workers and peasants were quite inarticulate. Would they have been so if the war had not torn so huge a gap in their midst? Within thirty years the Soviet people had repeatedly lost, through war, civil strife, purges, and famines, their most active, intelligent, and selfless elements, those that might have striven to safeguard the heritage of the revolution against autocratic despotism. Now one half of the working class consisted of middle-aged and old men who had experienced and suffered too much to have any militancy left in them; the other half was made up of adolescents who had experienced and understood too little to have a political mind of their own. The silence of the generation lost in the war lay like a pall upon the consciousness of the whole class. The peasantry was even more depressed and passive. Intimidated, absorbed in the labour of re-creating the most elementary material conditions of their existence, the mass of the people abdicated all political aspiration and withdrew into their private lives. The loss of the young, mature, and virile age groups had other consequences as well, which are hardly ever mentioned—for how is one to describe the effect which the deficit in the balance of population, the absence of 21 million men, had on family relations, and on the sexual life of a huge segment of society? This upset in the nation's biological structure was yet another source of its psychological instability and socio-political atrophy.

.   .   .   .

Such was the state of the U.S.S.R. during the first phases of the Cold War. In March 1946, in his famous Fulton speech, Winston Churchill had raised the alarm about the 'growing challenge and peril to civilization' from the 'Communist fifth columns', the peril of 'a return of the Dark Ages, the Stone Age'. Nobody knew, he stated, 'what Soviet Russia and its Communist International organization intends to do in the future, or what are the limits if any, to their expansive and proselytizing tendencies'. And when Churchill called upon the United States to guard its superiority in nuclear weapons and uphold

with a resolution of the Central Committee castigating the directors of the major theatres for producing 'improper' plays. *Pravda*, 21 August 1946; *Bolshevik*, nr. 16, 1946; *VKP v Rezolutsyakh*, pp. 1028–37.

the peoples of eastern Europe in their resistance to Communism, waves of fear and panic began to sweep the world. The image of Red hordes ready to swoop down upon the free peoples of the West was held out before the imagination of Europeans and Americans. In Russia ordinary people felt 'as if atom bombs might start dropping on them before midnight'.

Stalin, playing from terrible weakness, decided to bluff his way out by a show of calm, self-assurance, and power. He had already withdrawn, under Anglo-American pressure, from northern Persia which his troops had occupied on the basis of a war-time agreement with Britain. He had failed to obtain a naval base in the Turkish Straits, the prize that Russia's western Allies had always promised her in war and denied her in peace. It now looked as if those Allies were seeking to reduce or to eliminate Russian influence from the Balkans and eastern Europe as well. In the summer of 1946, the Paris Peace Conference turned into a political battle over the control of the Danube Basin. Stalin's diplomacy fought tenaciously and won, because the Russian armies were in occupation, and western diplomacy was not yet quite ready to respond to Churchill's battle-cry. And when, in September, Churchill openly called for a reversal of alliances urging the 'Germanic races' to stop 'tearing each other to pieces', and exhorting France and Germany to establish a 'partnership' while they were 'dwelling strangely and precariously under the shield and . . . protection of the American atomic bomb'—even then Stalin replied that in his view 'the possibilities of peaceful co-operation' between Russia and her former allies 'far from decreasing may even grow'. To refute Churchill's talk about 'Communist expansion', he assured the West that he, Stalin, believed that it was possible to build not merely Socialism but even Communism in a 'single country'.[1] Early in 1947, he still hesitated whether he should carry to its conclusion the 'revolution from above' in eastern Europe, where he still tolerated non-Communist parties in the governments and allowed some scope to capitalist interests. Having agreed with the western powers over peace treaties with Italy and the Balkan States, he imagined that he might yet agree with them on a German settlement as well. This issue was

[1] See Stalin's answers to Alexander Werth's questions, *The Sunday Times*, 24 September 1946.

on the agenda of a Foreign Ministers' conference that met in Moscow on 10 March 1947.

The conference had been in session for only two days when at a stroke the hope for agreement was shattered. On 12 March the President of the United States read, at a joint session of the two Houses of Congress, a message that was to become the text of the so-called Truman Doctrine. This was the formal American declaration of the Cold War, which had so far gone on intermittently and undeclared. The occasion was the crisis in Greece, where after two and a half years of civil war, a Royalist Government, backed by British arms and subsidies, was unable to prevail against Communist guerrillas fighting on in the country. The British, whose economy was in a severe crisis, were unable to continue intervention and were about to withdraw; and President Truman announced that the United States was stepping into the breach to ensure that Greece should not succumb to Communism. If this had been all, the American decision might not have greatly troubled Stalin who had, at Yalta, washed his hands of Greece, had neither aided nor encouraged the Greek insurgents, and had even frowned on the Yugoslav Communists who assisted them.[1] President Truman, however, had spoken also against Russia's coveting a base in the Turkish Straits and undertook to subsidize and arm the Turks as well. Moreover, he proclaimed that henceforth his Government would support any nation resisting Communism, and that it was the duty of 'nearly every nation' to resist. Thus, the Government of the United States committed itself to intervene against any Communist revolution anywhere in the world, and it branded in advance the Soviet Government as the instigator of any such revolution.

The effect was instantaneous. The conference of the Foreign Ministers dispersed amid loud recriminations. Within a few weeks the French and Italian Communist parties were ousted from the coalition governments in which, following Stalin's instructions, they had sat as meek junior partners, eagerly subduing the revolutionary mood of the working classes in their countries. It was an open secret that American influence had been active and decisive in bringing about the exclusion of the Communists. Presently, General Marshall, the American

[1] Dedijer, *Tito Speaks*, p. 331.

Foreign Secretary, launched his Plan, offering American economic assistance to all governments whose countries were struggling with the poverty and chaos bequeathed by war. The Plan appealed greatly even to Communists in eastern Europe. Stalin himself must have hesitated for a moment; and before the end of June he dispatched Molotov and a large number of experts to Paris to ascertain what benefit, if any, the Plan might hold out to Russia. It turned out that to obtain aid the Soviet Union was required, in the first instance, to draw up a balance sheet of its economic resources; and, according to the Soviet experts, the Americans attached to the aid conditions that would hamper the U.S.S.R. in its economic planning, and the governments of eastern Europe in nationalizing their industries. Moreover, the Americans were now determined to rehabilitate the economy of western Germany and to disregard Russian, Polish, and Czechoslovak claims to German reparations.[1]

Stalin could not but reject these terms. He could not agree to submit to the West a balance sheet of Soviet economic resources, in which he would have had to reveal Russia's appalling exhaustion and the frightful gap in her manpower that he was concealing even from his own people. And he was not only bent on disguising Russia's weakness; he was afraid of American economic penetration into eastern Europe and even into Russia which might have given an impetus to all anti-Communist forces there and promoted counter-revolution. He decided to close eastern Europe to western penetration. Consistent though his motives were, his moves were abrupt and clumsy: he rejected the American offer summarily, failing to demonstrate that its terms were really unacceptable to any anti-capitalist government; and in his anxiety to conceal the weakness of his position, he behaved with such offensive brutality that in the eyes of most people in the West it was he who bore the odium not only of refusing aid but of driving the war-weary world to the brink of new war.

The contrast between America's immense wealth and Russia's utter destitution cast another deep shadow upon these years,

---

[1] See Walter Bedell Smith, *My Three Years in Moscow*, chapter x; V. M. Molotov, *Voprosy Vneshnei Politiki*, pp. 345–63 and *passim*; George F. Kennan, *Russia and the West*, chapter xxv and *passim*; and D. F. Fleming, *The Cold War*, vol. i, chapters xiv–xvii.

and determined Stalin's policy. That the American Government was throwing its economic power behind its anti-Communist campaign was far more important than were its acts of military intervention. Yet the Truman Doctrine had also immediate military consequences. The threat of war implied in it was rendered incalculable by the American nuclear monopoly. If the threat did not materialize, this was partly because it was not easy to arouse against Russia the peoples of the West, who still remembered the fulsome tributes their statesmen had so recently paid to their Russian ally, and who had themselves not yet cooled off from their admiration for the defenders of Moscow, Stalingrad, and Leningrad, and from the gratitude to them for what they had done to tie down Hitler's forces in the East and relieve the West. It was to take time before a succession of crises, alarms, and scares, in which Communism was invariably presented as the villain disturbing the peace of the world, was to sway the popular mood in the West and turn it against Russia. Meanwhile, the United States had demobilized; its people had clamoured for a return of the troops from Europe; and its generals and diplomats had relied on their nuclear monopoly to assure them lasting superiority *vis-à-vis* Russia. The assumption that Russia, unable to break that monopoly in the near future, would have to yield to American pressure also underlay the Truman Doctrine. Stalin countered by his determination to break the American monopoly at any cost and as soon as possible. But before he could achieve this, he had reduced his armed forces from $11\frac{1}{2}$ million men to less than 3 millions. From the beginning of 1948 he began to increase the size of this military establishment until he had in the early nineteen-fifties, more than $5\frac{1}{2}$ million men under arms.[1] That this mobilization was a tremendous drain on the Soviet economy and its manpower is obvious. But Soviet superiority in conventional arms was the only answer Stalin could give to American nuclear supremacy. He staved off any possible threat of a nuclear attack on Russia by an implied counter-threat of a Soviet invasion of western Europe, an invasion the powers of the North Atlantic Alliance would not be

---

[1] *Malaya Sov. Encyclopaedia*, 1960, vol. viii, p. 922. These figures were published seven years after Stalin's death, when they were certainly not produced to serve his propaganda.

in a position to stop. Thus the bogy the West had invoked to justify the Truman Doctrine—the Red hordes threatening Europe—assumed some reality; but it did so only in consequence of the proclamation of the Truman Doctrine. Stalin had no intention of moving his armies beyond the agreed demarcation line in Europe. But he established a relative equilibrium of power, or, to use a term that became fashionable later, a balance of deterrents. At this early stage the balance was attained between two different elements of military force, nuclear weapons on the one hand and conventional ones on the other.

Behind his military shield Stalin accelerated the revolution in eastern Europe. If America's economic power enabled Washington to exercise an indirect and discreet political control over its western European allies, Russia could prevail in eastern Europe only by means of direct political control and naked force. The impression which the offer of Marshall Aid had made even in eastern Europe showed how favourable the ground there was for American penetration. The remnants of the Polish, Hungarian, and East German *bourgeoisie* and large parts of the individualistic peasantry were praying for the nuclear annihilation of Russia and Communism. The working classes were starving. Counter-revolution could still rally considerable strength. True, in Yugoslavia, Czechoslovakia, and Bulgaria Communism was still overwhelmingly popular; but in the rest of eastern Europe it was weak or, at least, unable to hold its ground by its own strength. Stalin now resolved to establish it irrevocably; and so, while the Communists were being ejected from the governments of Italy and France, he saw to it that the anti-Communists should be squeezed out of the governments of eastern Europe and—suppressed. He installed the single-party system all over the Soviet sphere of influence. And he sent out his plenipotentiaries, administrative experts, generals, and police agents to instruct and supervise the local Communist parties and governments, and to impose on them a single policy and a single discipline.

While he was engaged in this political reorganization, he decided to galvanize the rump of the old Communist International, which he had disbanded in 1943. He founded the so-called Cominform, in September 1947, in order to unify Communist action in eastern Europe and give a new turn to the policies of the western European parties. As in the days of the Comintern, he himself kept in the background. He delegated Zhdanov and Malenkov to guide the foundation conference of the Cominform, at which only the Soviet, the East European, and the French and Italian Communists were represented. So little did Stalin think of turning the Cominform into any genuine instrument of international revolution, that he did not ask the Chinese and other Asian parties to join the new organization. His chief concern, outside the Soviet 'sphere of influence', was to adjust the policies of the French and Italian Communists to the new needs of his diplomacy. At the foundation conference Zhdanov castigated the French and the Italians for allowing inertia to govern their conduct, for collaborating with the *bourgeoisie* of their countries and for meekness towards the Catholics and the Social Democrats, policies and attitudes which, in Moscow eyes, were admirable as long as the Grand Alliance lasted, but pernicious in the Cold War.

Ironically, it was the Yugoslavs, Kardelj and Djilas, who most vehemently advocated Stalin's and Zhdanov's new line. 'If workers' parties plunge into parliamentarianism, all is finished. . . . We have seen in the international labour movement a tendency towards a new revision of Marxism–Leninism, a new deviation . . .' Kardelj admonished the French and the Italians. The new revisionism, he explained, could be found in Togliatti's and Thorez' hope for a new epoch of peaceful parliamentary action and in their subservience to the Vatican and Gaullism. 'The Italian Communist party,' Kardelj went on, 'has been too slow in grasping the sense of the American policy. Hence its slogan: 'Neither . . . Washington nor Moscow.' Yet it is clear that without Moscow there can be no liberty, no national independence.' Djilas was even more categorical: 'The essential fact . . . is the American ambition to dominate the world. This constitutes . . . a menace even greater than fascism . . . The French Party has yielded step by step to reaction and has permitted the disbandment and disarmament of the *Resistance*.' Yet the Cominform did not offer its western European members any plan of revolutionary action, for which, after they had missed their opportunities in 1944–6, it was too late anyhow. The French and the Italian parties were expected merely to obstruct the implementation of the Truman Doctrine and the Marshall Plan; and even this they did feebly and incoherently.[1]

In the meantime Stalin was imposing a state of siege upon the countries of eastern Europe. Through special agencies such as the Soviet-Hungarian, Soviet-Rumanian, and Soviet-Bulgarian Joint Stock Companies he obtained control of their economies. Poland, East Germany, Hungary, Czechoslovakia, and Rumania delivered to Russia their coal, machines, bauxite, oil, and wheat either as reparations or at extremely low prices, while their own peoples suffered want and poverty. As the parties of opposition were suppressed one after the other, popular discontent found no mouthpieces. A reign of terror stifled any cry or murmur of protest. Soviet administrators and engineers were supervising the industries of eastern Europe, Soviet generals commanded some of its armies, and Soviet policemen managed its security forces.

At the beginning of 1948 Czechoslovakia alone of all these countries was not yet conforming to the new pattern. Ever since 1945 Moscow had insisted that the Czech Communists should refrain from revolutionary action. Yet Czechoslovakia had emerged from the war in a truly revolutionary condition, its working class armed and clamouring for socialism, and its Communist party polling, in free elections, nearly 40 per cent. of the national vote. The pro-Russian sentiment of the Czechs was genuine, rooted in national tradition, and, since the Munich crisis, enhanced by a revulsion against the West. Nevertheless, for nearly three years, although it was ruled by a government of which Gottwald, the Communist, was Prime Minister, the country still lived in a *bourgeois* democracy. Edouard Beneš was still Czechoslovakia's President; Jan Masaryk was Foreign Minister; and the Government depended on the parliamentary vote of Communists, Liberals, and Social Democrats. This régime could not survive the blast of the Cold War. Beneš and Masaryk tried hard to maintain a neutral attitude; but they were essentially 'men of the West' and had shown themselves, as had even Gottwald, eager to accept the American offer of aid.

[1] See Eugenio Reale, *Avec Jacques Duclos au banc des accusés*, an Italian participant's account of the foundation conference of the Cominform. Reale summarizes Kardelj's and Djilas's speeches from notes taken on the spot (pp. 129–50). His version is confirmed by Yugoslav sources: Dedijer, op. cit., pp. 302–6, and Djilas *Conversations with Stalin*, pp. 100–1.

Here was clearly a gap in Stalin's defences; and the Czech Communists had to close it. In the last week of February 1948 they carried out the long-delayed revolution and seized power. Unlike other East European upheavals, this bore the marks of a revolution from below, even though it was timed to suit Stalin's convenience. The Communists accomplished the revolution by their own strength, supported by the great majority of the workers; they had only to parade their armed militias in the streets to block any counter-action. The Soviet occupation troops had long left the country; and the mere fear of their return was enough to paralyse the *bourgeois* parties. Gottwald could even afford to observe the rules of the parliamentary game: the *bourgeois* Ministers, hoping to forestall or prevent the revolution, had rashly resigned their posts and left the administrative machine in Communist hands; then Gottwald and his comrades managed to cajole the hesitant and divided Social Democrats, who rejoined them and formed with them a new parliamentary majority. Beneš and Masaryk, overwhelmed and depressed by the evidence of popular support for the revolution—the streets of Prague were full of armed workers marching towards the seats of government—bowed to the victors. A few days later, however, Masaryk was found dead on a pavement below an open window in his Ministry; and it was never established whether he had jumped from that window or had been thrown out of it.

No sooner had this upheaval been accomplished than Stalin had to deal with another, more dangerous, breach in his defences. Nowhere was the conflict of the powers more intense than in Germany; and nowhere was it more sharply focused than in Berlin. There the contrast between American affluence and Russian destitution was brutally exposed for everyone to see. While the United States and Britain were already pumping economic aid into western Germany, Russia was still draining the resources of East Germany which she needed for her reconstruction. It was only too easy for anti-Russian propagandists to present this outcome of the war, and of long and complex preceding historic developments, as the test of the opposed socio-political systems; and to claim that western capitalism brought prosperity and freedom while Russian Communism could live only by spoliation and slavery. No people were likely to swallow such crudities of propaganda as readily as the Germans, who resented the reparations they had to pay and their humiliations at Russian hands and who were now eager to escape the worst consequences of defeat by joining the western camp. Stalin, impatient to put a stop to the constant confrontation of Russia's economic weakness and unpopularity with America's wealth and its attractions, had already drawn the 'iron curtain' across Germany. Yet 125 miles behind that curtain, in the Reich's old capital, the confrontation went on from day to day; every day it became rougher, more blatant, and more explosive. It was galling enough for Stalin, as it must have been for most Russians, to see his power and prestige constantly deflated and ridiculed in the city which his armies had conquered unaided, and into which he had admitted his western allies in those far-off days when they were all contemplating a joint condominium over Germany.

Of that condominium hardly a trace was now left: Stalin had refused the western powers any say in the conduct of East German affairs just as they had denied him any share in the control of western Germany. The Americans, the British, and the French were already forming the Federal German Republic, which was to be ruled by Adenauer's conservative and avowedly anti-Russian Government. In these circumstances the original motive for the presence of western representatives and garrisons in Berlin had lost meaning; the western powers now held Berlin as an enclave in enemy territory. It was only natural that Russian policy should seek to eliminate that enclave—Stalin's successors were to be preoccupied by this problem even a decade later. In the spring of 1948 the issue was brought to a head. The western powers, anxious to hasten the economic rehabilitation of their parts of Germany, proposed to introduce a currency reform under which the old depreciated Mark was to be replaced by a new one. The reform put a seal upon Germany's division; and it posed at once the question of Berlin's currency. Russia could not allow the city to become financially incorporated in West Germany; nor could the western powers permit it to be financially absorbed by East Germany. If two different currencies were to circulate in Berlin, the result would be a chronic conflict, for while a growing volume of goods in the West was bound to assure the stability of the new Mark, the value of the eastern currency would be undermined by a continued scarcity of goods. To forestall this, Stalin ventured a desperate gamble. He ordered a blockade of those sectors of Berlin that were held by the Americans, the British, and the French. Soon all traffic heading for West Berlin, whether by land or by water, was brought to a standstill.

By ordering the blockade Stalin hoped either to force the western powers out of Berlin, or at least to induce them to give up their plan for using the Federal German Republic as their ally against Russia. The blockade, however, failed to achieve the first objective; and it only prompted the western powers to carry the reversal of alliances to its conclusion. In his gamble Stalin again relied on bluff. He lost through a miscalculation which reflected his curiously old-fashioned way of thinking. He threatened to paralyse Berlin's industries and starve its garrisons and population into submission. He was not deterred by intimations that American armoured trains would fight their way through. He disregarded loud threats uttered by American generals that they would drop atom bombs on Moscow. He tried to win over the people of Berlin by offering to feed them; and he provoked the British and the Americans into rejecting this offer. He was prepared to go on with the blockade until he wore down all resistance. He was confident that time was on his side; that the blockade was hermetic; and that his opponents could not breach it because he held all the roads leading to the city. What he overlooked was that, under an inter-Allied agreement, the western powers still held narrow 'air corridors' leading from their zones in Germany to Berlin; and that by using those corridors they would be able to supply the city's garrisons, its population, and even its industries. He made no allowance for western air strength and the capacity of the Americans and the British—and this after a war in which they, unlike the Russians, had long fought primarily in the air.

On 28 June 1948 the Americans and the British opened their 'air-lift' to Berlin. Surprised by this move, yet not daring to deny his opponents the air corridors, Stalin personally opened negotiations with the western ambassadors in Moscow. Then he broke these off again, convinced that with the onset of the winter Berlin would be at his mercy. The western air-lift, however, steadily expanded and kept Berlin supplied with food, fuel, and raw materials throughout the critical months. The blockade was defeated. Nearly a year after it had begun, it was brought to an end by an agreement discreetly negotiated in the United Nations; and the *status quo* was restored in Berlin.

However, the blockade had wide effects which could not be undone. The *status quo* was not to be restored on the international scene. While the city was besieged, the Federal German Republic had come into being and the North Atlantic Alliance had been proclaimed. The blockade had provided grist to all the mills of anti-Russian propaganda; and the American and the British peoples, outraged by Stalin's action, acclaimed their governments for the reversal of alliances, the very idea of which had until quite recently been abhorrent to them. Thus, while the Truman Doctrine had imparted some reality to the dangers and threats it was supposed to forestall, Stalin's blockade in its turn provided something like a *post factum* justification for the Truman Doctrine, and intensified the Cold War.

. . . .

While western capitalism was drawing vigour and confidence from Stalin's reverses, communism gained a momentous victory in the East. On 22 January 1949 Mao Tse-tung's armies had entered Peking. The event almost escaped the attention of Europeans and Americans, whose eyes and ears were full of the flash and roar of the air-lift over Germany. For decades, amid changing fortunes, Mao's partisans had been fighting against Chiang Kai-shek's forces, which were armed since the war with American weapons and occasionally supported by American marines. At times the partisans seemed in danger of succumbing. They survived and fought on; but hardly anyone outside China reckoned with the imminence of their total triumph. As late as 1948 Stalin still advised Mao, as he had advised Chen Tu-hsiu twenty-odd years earlier, to make peace with the Kuomintang; and when he was informed of Mao's plans for an all-out offensive, he dismissed them as unrealistic and reckless. The victorious Generalissimo of the world's largest army was contemptuous of partisans, sceptical of the chances of communism in China, and distrustful of any revolution asserting itself without his *fiat* and beyond the range of his military power.[1]

---

[1] See Stalin's statements on his 'mistake in China' made to Kardelj in Dedijer, op. cit., p. 331 and Djilas op. cit., pp. 141–2.

He was also afraid that Mao's venture might provoke massive American intervention and bring American forces close to Russia's Far Eastern frontiers. The Chinese Communists, nevertheless, pressed home their offensives until the Kuomintang, rotten inside, collapsed. In April, just when the western powers were proclaiming the Atlantic Alliance, Mao's troops held victory parades in Nanking and Shanghai; and before the summer was out the whole of the Chinese mainland was theirs. On 24 September Mao proclaimed the People's Republic of China. A new epoch had opened for communism and the world. Russia's long-lasting isolation had finally come to a close; and the October revolution, contrary to so many expectations, found its much delayed sequel and continuation not in Europe but in Asia.

We shall see later how this event was to affect the fortunes of Stalinism. Its immediate effect was to strengthen Stalin's position *vis-à-vis* the western powers, who suddenly found themselves out-flanked in Asia, where the colonial and semi-colonial peoples were in uproar and rebellion. Discomfited in the West, Stalin could play from strength in the East. And by a curious coincidence it was in the week that the People's Republic of China was formed that the world also heard the detonation of Russia's first atom bomb.

The spread of revolution was destroying some of the circumstances in which Stalinism, the product and epitome of Bolshevik isolation, had flourished. The consolidation of new revolutionary states was bound to undermine Stalin's—and indeed Moscow's—unique authority over the Communist movement throughout the world. That authority, we know, had rested on the double foundation of ideology and force, on the willingness of Communists in all countries to identify themselves with the Soviet Union as the 'workers' first state' and to subordinate their own aspirations to Stalin's *raison d'état*; and on the pressure or coercion which Stalin employed to eliminate his critics and opponents. This double foundation was now shattered. Foreign Communists, who from being persecuted agitators had now become rulers in their countries, were not likely to remain for long as overawed by their great oracle in Moscow as they had been or as easily bullied. They no longer felt the same moral compulsion to sacrifice their own aspirations and ambitions to the real or pretended needs of the Soviet Union. They had increasingly to represent their own ambitions and the needs and interests of their own revolutionary states. The epoch of 'polycentric communism' had imperceptibly begun long before Palmiro Togliatti coined the term.

No sooner had Stalin founded the Cominform, in order to re-centralize and rediscipline the Communist parties, than his authority was challenged by the Yugoslav members of the new organization. We have seen with what zeal the latter assisted at the Cominform's inaugural meeting, supporting Stalin's and Zhdanov's latest turn of policy. No wonder that Tito and his comrades were, up till 1948, considered to be the most dog-matic and fanatical of all European Stalinists. This reputation was to some extent based on their record. It was not for nothing that Tito had been promoted to his party's leadership during his stay in Moscow at the time of the great purges. The party's previous chiefs had just perished in those purges; and his orthodoxy and bigotry had to be quite exemplary to earn him, precisely at that moment, Moscow's confidence. His con-duct over Spain during the Civil War, while the *G.P.U.* was exterminating many Communists and anti-Fascists, was little better than that of any of Stalin's puppets. The years of armed revolutionary struggle in his own country, however, had trans-formed the puppet into a man and a leader. Stalin sensed the change, and grew suspicious. He wanted the Yugoslavs to wage a 'patriotic and anti-Fascist' war, not to make a social revolution; they disobeyed his injunctions. He reproached them with endangering Russia's alliance with the United States and Britain and 'stabbing the Soviet Union in the back'. The dis-cord grew after the end of the hostilities. The Yugoslavs, who were ultra-radical and intensely nationalist, strove to annex Trieste in the teeth of Anglo-American and Italian opposition; Stalin, wary of exacerbating his conflict with the western powers, curbed them. They deprecated his 'opportunism and cynicism'. They winced at the arrogance with which Stalin's envoys and generals treated them; they protested against the misbehaviour of Soviet troops in Yugoslavia; and they ex-ploded with anger when they discovered that Stalin's secret services were recruiting agents in the Yugoslav Army and police. Stalin, infuriated by so much unaccustomed resistance, resolved to deal with them as he had dealt with all his Communist opponents: he branded them as Bukharinists and Trotskyists, traitors and agents of imperialism; and he denounced Titoism as a heresy. 'I shall shake my little finger,' he boasted, 'and there will be no Tito', The Yugoslavs still swore allegiance to Stalin and displayed his portraits at meetings and demonstrations; but they protested against the denunciations and defended themselves vigorously. Stalin retorted with an economic and military blockade, which was quite as savage as the blockade of Berlin, and just as ineffective.[1]

For the first time in his career Stalin was now helpless against a Communist opponent. Tito was succeeding where heretics of far greater stature, Trotsky and Bukharin, had failed. His own state, his own army and police, protected him from Stalin's blows; and the national enthusiasm and devotion which he aroused by his defiance of Moscow shielded him even more securely. His action did irreparable damage to Stalin's authority and prestige. Many eastern European Communists found in Tito's behaviour an example worthy of imitation. Their grievances against Stalin were even more bitter than Tito's; and they, too, longed to be able to assert their national dignity and so to rehabilitate themselves in the eyes of their own people from the odium of being Russian stooges. And it was not to be ruled out that the Yugoslav defiance might stir a sympathetic echo even in Stalin's own entourage.

Frightened of the 'Titoist' contagion, Stalin fought back with all his sanguinary cunning tested in so many heresy-hunts. He declared it to be treason for Communists to show sympathy with Titoism and maintain contact with Belgrade. As Moscow was withdrawing all its advisers and special envoys from Yugoslavia, the eastern European governments had to follow suit. Stalin also moved them to carry out threatening military manoeuvres on the Yugoslav frontiers. Yet it was not easy to suppress sympathy with Titoism, for what Titoism represented was not any new doctrine or programme but an elementary impulse of brave men and fighters to assert their national and

---

[1] See Yosip Broz–Tito, *Political Report at the Fifth Congress of the Communist Party of Yugoslavia* (1948); *Correspondence between Central Committee of CPY and Central Committee of CPSU*, published in Belgrade in 1948; and Djilas, op. cit., pp. 98–144.

Communist self-respect against a great power and a master who had over-exploited their devotion and recklessly insulted them. This impulse was alive in internationally minded party members as well as in the 'national communists'. Stalin's agents kept a close watch on all of them and noted carefully every sign of the 'Titoist' disposition that any of them might show.

The hallmark of such a disposition was a Communist's propensity to expatiate on the legitimacy of 'various national roads to socialism'. Stalin himself had dwelt on this theme in the first post-war years, while he was working to disarm the various nationalist oppositions to Russian supremacy all over eastern Europe. The Yugoslavs now invoked the slogan against him; and in every eastern European capital there were men prominent in the Stalinist hierarchy, Gomulka, Clementis, Rajk, Kostov, and others, who had taken the slogan at its face value. The new course initiated by the Cominform did not suit them. They had identified themselves with the 'rightist', 'moderate', and nationalist policy which they had in previous years pursued with Stalin's encouragement; and they clung to it even after Stalin had changed the line. This was their undoing. They were accused of collusion with Titoism, branded as wreckers and spies, imprisoned, subjected to blackmail and torture, and made to confess their sins, as the defendants in the Great Moscow Trials had confessed theirs. After more than a decade the terrible spectacle of the years 1936–8 was restaged in nearly every eastern European capital. In September 1949 Rajk and other Hungarian leaders were tried and executed; in December Kostov and a number of prominent Bulgarian Communists met the same fate. In the course of the next three years a pandemonium of show trials and mass terror raged all over eastern Europe. Only exceptionally did a heretic like Gomulka survive to emerge in triumph after Stalin's death. And the purge had its obscure ramifications in the U.S.S.R. as well: N. S. Voznesensky, a member of the Politbureau and its chief economic planner, who had marshalled the nation's economic resources during the war, M. Rodionov, Premier of the Russian Federal Republic, Kuznetsov and Popkov, organizers of Leningrad's defences during the siege in 1941–3, and other members of the so-called Leningrad group, were the victims. Nearly twenty years after the event it was still not known why Stalin's suspicion fell on these men, whether they had been opposed to any of his policies or whether they had merely been involved in a murderous scramble for power, such as the rivalry between Zhdanov and Malenkov, that was going on in Stalin's entourage. Their trials and executions were closely guarded secrets. In these years Stalin did not dare to re-enact in Moscow and Leningrad the show-trials with public confessions that were being staged in Budapest and Sofia.[1]

While Stalin was thus fiercely hitting out at Titoism, a heresy far more potent and dangerous was rearing its head in Peking. The Chinese Communists, proud of having risen to power despite Stalin's obstruction, were conscious of their historic role as the architects of China's independence, as the makers of a revolution which embraced a huge segment of mankind and was sure to reverberate in decades and centuries to come. They looked up to Mao Tse-tung as to an outstanding innovator of revolutionary strategy and a leader and theorist of genius. Even though they grossly over-advertised Mao's contribution to theory, he was indeed the greatest and most original practitioner of revolution since Lenin and Trotsky. He was certainly a man of far richer personality and of far greater courage and *élan* than Stalin. Yet Stalin had treated him superciliously, had never found a word of appreciation for his deeds, and viewed distrustfully his unorthodox behaviour. As early as 1927–8, when Mao first shifted the centre of his activities from town to country, the Stalinized Comintern disowned him and endorsed his demotion from the Central Committee of his party. Even after reinstatement, and after he had consolidated his Red armies and his Yenan government, Moscow still treated him with embarrassed reserve. He was contending that the Chinese revolution, unlike the Russian, must base itself primarily on the peasantry, and must be carried from country to town rather than from town to country. This was heresy indeed. To avoid an open breach with Moscow Mao took on the protective colour of Stalinist orthodoxy. Stalin was aware of the intricacy of

---

[1] *László Rajk and his Accomplices Before the People's Court*, Budapest, 1949; *The Trial of Traïcho Kostov and his Group*, Sofia, 1949. An incomplete account of the Gomulka case is in *Nowe Drogi*, October 1956, containing the report of the session of the Central Committee at which Gomulka returned to office. The East German repercussions of the anti-Tito campaign are related by Wolfgang Leonhard in *Child of the Revolution*, pp. 386–94, and *passim*.

Mao's game; and he would not have tolerated anything like it in any Communist party situated in a sphere of world politics which he considered vital to his interests. But almost until 1949, China occupied a subordinate place in Stalin's calculations; and Mao's behaviour seemed to him so quixotic—and outwardly so submissive—as not to call for excommunication.[1]

Even so, the Chinese partisans never, during their long ordeal, benefited from any Soviet help. They felt a deep grudge, but smiled and concealed their disappointment. Since the war Stalin had given them cause for fresh and bitter resentment. Soviet troops occupying Manchuria after Japan's surrender treated that country as if it were conquered enemy territory, not part of China. The Japanese, it may be remembered, had detached that vast province from China and had placed it under the rule of the Manchurian dynasty, which was their puppet. To that dynasty Stalin had, in 1935, sold the Manchurian railway which the Soviet Union had held as a concessionaire —in this way he hoped to appease Japan. Then, in 1945, he recovered the railway for Russia, instead of allowing China to obtain it. In addition, he extended Soviet control to Port Arthur and Dairen, the two great Manchurian harbours. All this hurt the Chinese. They were then shocked to see that the Russians treated Manchuria's industries as war booty, dismantled many factories and plants and shipped them to the Soviet Union. As the Japanese, who had deliberately denuded China proper of its industries, had for their own convenience promoted Manchuria's heavy industry, the Chinese saw in Manchuria the industrial base for the economic development of the whole of China. Mao's Government could not but convey to Moscow something of the outrage the Russian actions had caused; and it was anxious to recover the installations and the machinery the Russians had appropriated.

Here were the makings of a tremendous discord—a foretaste of the conflict that was to trouble Stalin's successors a decade later. Any reckless gesture or indiscretion might have led to an explosion forthwith. In these circumstances Stalin acted with remarkable caution and cool-headedness. No sooner had the

---

[1] Edgar Snow, *Red Star over China*, pp. 377–88, and *The Other Side of the River*, pp. 201, 646–72; and Isaac Deutscher, 'Maoism, its Origins and Outlook' in *Ironies of History* (1966).

People's Republic of China been proclaimed than he invited Mao to Moscow.

In December 1949 he received him in the Kremlin with every honour and every sign of friendship and respect. These were the days of the great hunt for the Titoists and of the Leningrad affair. Voznesensky had been disgraced only a few months before, and the Kostov trial was just on in Sofia. Yet amid all his frenzy of persecution, Stalin assumed, with seeming effortlessness, the role of affable host and wise and helpful senior comrade towards the one truly great and dangerous heretic in the Communist world. He had learned from his mistake about Tito. He knew he could not afford to shake his 'little finger', let alone his fist, at Mao. He was all sweetness and light.

Yet the situation was delicate: Stalin had to reconnoitre, and he was reluctant to yield up his Manchurian booty. He dragged Mao into long unhurried explanations and slow bargaining; and he frequently interrupted these with state banquets and private talks, given over to mutual confidences such as the heads of two revolutions might be expected to exchange. Yet in personal contact the two men could only become more aware of the contrasts in their characters and positions. Stalin was now every inch the 'world statesman', the bemedalled Generalissimo, and the head of an immense bureaucratic establishment, as remote from his own people as any Tsar had ever been. About Mao there was still the air of the twenty years he had spent in the mountains and caves whence he conducted the longest civil war in modern history—he had lived all those years amid the poorest peasants, had fought and marched together with his partisans, had allowed no differences in food rations and uniforms and no social estrangement between his officers and men. If in Stalin so much of Tsardom and Greek Orthodoxy had superimposed itself on Marxism, in Mao Leninism was refracted through oriental *jacquerie* and the cultural heritage of a Confucian mandarin. Both men had inexhaustible cunning, but in Mao this was held in check by a character more humane than Stalin's and a more cultivated mind. To Mao the Chinese revolution was his whole life and his mission. To Stalin it was a gigantic windfall, but potentially also a gigantic danger. He had, at the height of the Cold War, suddenly acquired a great ally. Henceforth, China would protect Russia's immense frontier in Asia; and he would be able to concentrate his military resources in Europe. And, although China's new rulers might one day defy Moscow, they were for the time being dependent on Stalin and anxious not merely to recover Manchuria's industrial plant but to obtain Soviet economic, military, and diplomatic aid and protection.

It took Stalin and Mao nearly three months to strike their bargain and to conclude, on 14 February 1950, a formal alliance. Stalin undertook to return his 'war booty' and to relinquish the Manchurian Railway 'not later than by the end of 1952'. He yielded Port Arthur as well, the acquisition of which, by a secret agreement with Roosevelt, he had celebrated as Russia's revenge for her defeat by Japan in 1905 and as an act of historic justice.[1] He still maintained control over the strategically important port of Dairen and Manchuria's communication lines. But he committed himself to assist China generously in economic development. In this way he prevented open rivalry between himself and Mao, and a conflict between their parties and between their governments.

. . . .

Only four months later the Korean war began: and many assumed that Mao and Stalin must have planned it in Moscow. For some time clashes and skirmishes between the Northern Communist troops and the Southern anti-Communist forces had been occurring along the 38th Parallel which had since Japan's surrender separated the two parts of the country. In June 1950 Kim Il Sung, the head of the Communist Administration, charged Synghman Rhee's Government of the South with aggression and ordered a general offensive across the 38th Parallel. The rapid initial success of the Northern troops indicated that the blow had been well prepared, so well, indeed, that it seemed plausible that Stalin and Mao had been consulted beforehand or that they had even issued the marching orders. That Mao should have favoured the venture would not be surprising. To him the Communist attempt to obtain control over the whole of Korea must have seemed a natural sequel to the Chinese revolution; its success promised to make it impossible

<hr>

[1] See Chapter XIII, pp. 528–9.

in the future for any hostile power to use Korea, as it had been used in the past, as a base for an invasion of China. Stalin's motives were less clear. He was anxious to avoid armed conflict with the West; and his strategic interest in Korea was only slight. (Korea has a ten-mile frontier with the U.S.S.R., whereas her frontier with Manchuria stretches over 500 miles.) He probably acted with an eye to his latent rivalry with Mao. Having so recently and so scandalously misjudged the chances of the revolution in China, he may have been anxious to dispel the impression of political timidity he had given, and to prove himself as daring a strategist of revolution as Mao.

The risks seemed negligible. It was about two years since the Soviet occupation armies had left Northern Korea; and by the end of 1948 the American troops had withdrawn from the South. Moreover, the Americans had declared that they had no vital interest to defend in Korea and hinted that they considered the country 'expendable'. Stalin had, therefore, some reason to assume that Kim Il Sung was starting a local war which would not turn into a major international conflict. He discovered his error when the United States decided to intervene and called upon the United Nations to do likewise. He committed another blunder when the Americans brought the issue before the Security Council. The Soviet member of the Council could easily have blocked the American action by making use of his right of veto, to which he had had frequent recourse even on trivial occasions. Instead, he demonstratively walked out of the Council during its critical session, as Moscow had instructed him to do; and so the United States and its allies, taking advantage of his absence, passed a vote obliging all members of the United Nations to send troops to Korea to fight against the Communists. The local war grew into an international conflagration. In the course of three years it threatened to lead to regular hostilities between America and China, or even to turn into a world war. Having blundered into this situation, Stalin took his precautions: although he armed the North Koreans, and the Chinese 'volunteers' who confronted the Americans on the 38th Parallel, he did not allow Russian forces to become involved. And he kept the door ajar for negotiations.

.   .   .   .

The Korean war and its perils overshadowed the last three years of Stalin's rule. He was still playing from grave weakness. The Soviet Union had detonated its first atom bomb less than a year before the outbreak of the war; the United States had been piling up nuclear weapons for over five years. Its Supreme Commander in the Far East, General MacArthur, was clamouring for the bombardment of Manchuria; this would have obliged the Russians to come to China's aid, under the newly concluded alliance. Stalin could not rely, as he could a few years earlier, on American popular pacifism and sympathy with Russia to avert the spread of war, for the popular mood in the United States had in the meantime swung to grim hostility.[1] And, even though involvement in Korea hampered American freedom of movement in Europe, Stalin had to keep up the mobilization of his conventional forces, to prod his nuclear industry to extraordinary efforts, to keep the Soviet economy on a near-war footing and to tighten the state of siege in the Soviet Union and eastern Europe. He achieved some of his vital objectives. He resisted western pressures firmly enough to deter any American design for spreading the war; and Soviet nuclear industry progressed by leaps and bounds and produced its first hydrogen bomb in 1953, shortly after the Americans had achieved the feat. The basic sectors of the Soviet economy, having reached their pre-war level of output in 1948–9, rose 50 per cent. above it in Stalin's last years. The modernization and urbanization of the Soviet Union was accelerated. In the early fifties alone its urban population grew by about 25 million. Secondary schools and universities were giving instruction to twice as many pupils as before 1940. Out of the wreckage of the world war the foundations had been relaid for Russia's renewed industrial and military ascendancy, which was presently to startle the world.

Yet the miseries of Russian life remained almost as shocking as they had been during the primitive accumulation of the nineteen-thirties and were even more unbearable. The mass of the people were living on cabbage and potatoes; were dressed

---

[1] It was characteristic of the change that a popular American magazine, *Collier's*, devoted a special issue to imaginary stories of a victorious American war against Russia and to a description of Moscow under American occupation written by Arthur Koestler.

in rags; and were housed in wretched hovels. While the most advanced machine-tool plants of the U.S.S.R. were as efficient as those of the U.S.A., its grossly under-developed consumer industries were at least half a century behind. The Soviet citizen consumed less than one-third, perhaps even less than one-quarter, of the goods the American enjoyed. With the continuous swelling of the urban population, the housing situation was desperate. It was quite common in capital cities for several families to share a single room and kitchen. The Government did little to relieve their plight: the destroyed towns were being rebuilt too slowly; and against the background of ruins and huge slums Stalin ordered grandiose public edifices and monuments to be erected, which were unsurpassed in their ornamented gracelessness and were to become the symbols of bureaucratic pomp and bad taste.

Worst of all was the condition of agriculture. In the last four years of Stalin's rule the average grain harvest amounted to only 80 million tons—it was 95 millions in 1940 and 86 millions in 1913. The cattle stock was also less than in 1913. And so, although the Government confiscated or bought at less than nominal prices nearly half the grain crops, the feeding of the urban population was exposed to terrible hazards. The city-dweller consumed less than half a pound of meat and a quarter pound of fat per week. The farms lacked manpower, tractors, machinery, transport, and fertilizers. The *kolkhoz* remained an economic hybrid, semi-collective and semi-private; beside the commonly owned fields there were the residual tiny smallholdings to which the peasants clung, cultivating them industriously while neglecting the fields collectively owned. The Government sought to secure food supplies by means of bureaucratic regimentation: it prescribed to the peasant what he was to grow and how much he should reap on every patch of soil. Legions of supervisors and taskmasters turned every farming operation which should have been a matter of simple routine, every sowing, ploughing, and harvesting, into a tense 'battle on the food front'.

Finally, in 1950, rural Russia was once again in the throes of an upheaval, which can be described as the supplementary collectivization. About 240,000 collective farms, each comprising a thousand acres on the average, were merged into

120,000 and finally into 93,000 larger units. The peasantry reacted to the merger with resigned apathy, not with the desperate resistance it had put up to the initial collectivization. But agriculture remained unsettled; and a controversy about what was to be done next divided the ruling group. N. S. Khrushchev proposed that the farms should be reorganized into grain factories and that the farmers be resettled in 'Agrotowns'. Stalin disowned the idea. In the midst of a tense international situation he was afraid of exposing the country to so drastic a change.

With so much weakness and turmoil within and so much adversity without, Stalin kept Russia more hermetically isolated than ever from the world. He decreed it a crime for a Russian to marry a foreigner, treason for an official to reveal any data, no matter how trivial, about any aspect of Russian life, and espionage for a foreigner to show curiosity for such data. Soldiers returning from occupation duty in Germany, Austria, or any other country were forbidden to talk about their experiences. Newspapers depicted social conditions in the West, including the United States, in the blackest of colours so that the Soviet citizen should see in a rosy light even the wretchedness of his existence. All of Russia's windows and doors to the world were slammed; and behind them went on an orgy of national self-glorification. The grandeur of Tsarist Russia was trumpeted more stridently than it had been even during the war. The historians exalted every feat of imperial conquest: they presented every act of violence once inflicted upon Russia's subject nations as an act of emancipation and progress, for which the oppressed nations should have been grateful. They hailed Catherine the Great and Nicholas I as the benefactors and protectors of the peoples of the Caucasus and of Central Asia; and they portrayed the leaders of those peoples, who resisted Tsardom and struggled for independence, as reactionaries and British or Turkish stooges. Schoolchildren were given a view of history as a single sequence of wicked foreign conspiracies invariably foiled by their ancestors' vigilance and valour. No one was to doubt that Russia, and Russia alone, was the salt of the earth, the cradle of civilization, the fount of all that is great and noble in the human spirit. The Russians became the pioneers, discoverers, and inventors of all those feats of modern technology which an ignorant or malicious world attributed to Britons, Germans, Frenchmen, or Americans. Day in day out, the newspapers filled their pages with stories of miraculous Popovs or Ivanovs who had been the first to design the printing press, the steam engine, the aeroplane, and the wireless. What was lacking to render this self-adulation complete was that *Pravda* should divulge that the prehistoric man who had built the first wheel had lived on the banks of the river *Moskva*, or that even Prometheus had been a Great Russian, for who but a Great Russian would have been capable of his heroic deed?

Thus (to quote from a contemporary essay of mine on 'Mid-century Russia'[1]),

Russia is taught to distrust and despise the world outside, to glory in nothing but her own genius, to care for nothing but her own self-centred greatness, to rely on nothing but her own selfishness, and to look forward to nothing but the triumphs of her own power. Stalinism tries to annex to Great Russia all the feats that the genius of other nations has had to its credit. It declares it to be a crime for the Russian to entertain any thought about the greatness, past or present, of any other nation—to 'kow-tow to western civilization'—and a crime for the Ukrainian, the Georgian, and the Uzbek not to kow-tow to Great Russia.

Megalomania and xenophobia were to cure the people of their sense of inferiority, render them immune to those attractions of the western culture by which generations of the intelligentsia had been spellbound, protect them against the demoralizing impact of American wealth, and harden them for the trials of the Cold War and, if need be, for armed conflict. The heat of the chauvinistic agitation was a measure of the war fever in which the country lived.

. . . .

It was not surprising that while so much crude national arrogance was being fostered, the old only half-hidden prejudices of anti-Semitism also surged up. Despite all that the Bolshevik Governments had done, in their better years, to combat those prejudices, enmity towards the Jews was almost unabated. Anti-Semitism drew nourishment from many sources: from Greek Orthodoxy and the native tradition of pogroms; from the population's war-time contacts with Nazism; from the fact that

[1] I. Deutscher, *Russia in Transition*, pp. 83–100.

Jewish traders and artisans, unadjusted to a publicly owned economy, were conspicuous in the illicit and semi-illicit commerce flourishing amid a scarcity of goods; from the great number of Jews among the early Bolshevik leaders; and from their relative importance, even after the extermination of those leaders, in the middle layers of the Stalinist bureaucracy. The simple-minded Communist often looked upon the Jews as the last surviving element of urban capitalism; while the anti-Communist saw them as influential members of the ruling hierarchy.

Stalin's attitude was equivocal. Personally free from crude racial prejudice, he was wary of openly offending against the party canon which was hostile to anti-Semitism. Jews were quite prominent in his entourage, though far less so than they had been in Lenin's. Litvinov stood for over a decade at the head of the Soviet diplomatic service; Kaganovich was to the end Stalin's factotum; Mekhlis was the chief political Commissar of the army; and Zaslavsky and Ehrenburg were the most popular of Stalin's sycophants. Yet he was not averse from playing on anti-Jewish emotions when this suited his convenience. During the struggle against the inner-party oppositions his agents made the most of the circumstance that Trotsky, Zinoviev, Kamenev, and Radek were of Jewish origin—in the trials of 1936-8 Vyshinsky again and again referred to them as 'people without a fatherland' and creatures devoid of any native Russian feeling. Then, during the war, when Hitler's propaganda vituperated against the 'Jewish war' and the Jewish Commissars who battened on it, and called the Russians and the Ukrainians to rise against them, Stalin's propagandists countered with nothing better than embarrassed silence. He forbade them to reply with a counter-blast that would expose the dreadful inhumanity of Hitler's anti-Semitism. He feared that such a counter-blast might suggest to the mass of the people that there was some truth in what the Nazis were saying and that it would make him appear in the role of the Jews' defender, a role which at this time nothing in the world would make him assume. He was frightened of the popular appeal of anti-Semitism, and the eagerness with which Russian and Ukrainian Jew-baiters had, in the occupied areas, responded to Nazism confirmed him in his fear.

Yet, while Hitler's armies were advancing, the Soviet authorities did their best to evacuate the Jews from the threatened areas, even though in some towns—the case of Taganrog was notorious—the Jews, disbelieving the warnings about what awaited them under Nazi occupation, refused to budge. With Stalin's authorization, a Jewish Anti-Fascist Committee, headed by well-known personalities, was formed; it called upon the Jews of the West to support the Soviet Union. (The Committee, however, began its work under grim auguries; as early as 1942 two of its members, Henryk Erlich and Victor Alter, leaders of the Jewish-Polish *Bund* and members of the Executive of the Socialist International who had sought refuge in Russia, were arrested and executed as 'Nazi agents'.) Jews serving with the armed forces fought bravely, were decorated, and promoted even to the highest ranks. But *qua* Jews they were not accorded any merit. As a nationality they were virtually obliterated. Press and radio were silent about the destruction of European Jewry behind the enemy lines. They mentioned only rarely the death camps of Auschwitz or Majdanek, or else mentioned them in such a manner that no one could guess that the Jews provided the main contingent of victims. After the war Soviet citizens guilty of collaboration with the Nazis and of Jew-baiting were punished as traitors. But even then the truth about the martyrdom of the Jews remained suppressed; and the symbol of the suppression was Babyi Yar in Kiev, where fifty or sixty thousand Jews had been done to death while the city was held by the Germans, but no monument or other sign was allowed to honour their memory.

Yet so tortuous, so completely governed by expediency, was Stalin's conduct that in 1948 he acted as godfather to the new state of Israel. His representative in the United Nations pleaded for its recognition when many governments still disputed its legality. (It should not be forgotten that not only the Communists but the entire Left in Russia and in eastern Europe, including most Jewish Socialists, had traditionally been anti-Zionist.) Stalin encouraged some of the governments of eastern Europe to allow the Jews who had survived in their countries to emigrate to Palestine, and even to supply the weapons with which the Zionists fought their war of independence. The motives of his policy were not far to seek: the Zionist revolt in

Palestine marked a stage in the dissolution of the British Empire; it hastened the British withdrawal from the Middle East. As the United States was also backing Israel, Stalin hoped that by his policy he might mend Russo-American relations. This hope proved vain. Moreover, Israel soon became a western outpost in the Middle East; and Stalin blamed its leaders for their ingratitude. Meanwhile, the renascence of a Jewish state impressed those Russian Jews who were still steeped in the Biblical tradition, and were agonized by the ordeal of their people and hurt by the surreptitious discrimination from which they suffered. When Israel's first ·diplomatic envoy, Mrs. Golda Meir, made her appearance in Moscow, she became the object of tumultuous ovations on the part of her co-religionists. This occurred just at the time when Stalin was whipping up the national megalomania and xenophobia that were to make the people impermeable to foreign influences. The sudden revelation of the depths of feeling that some Soviet Jews had for Israel could not but alarm Stalin. The spontaneity with which they were expressing their sentiment defied the mechanical discipline under which he kept the whole of society. He could not tolerate it. In his monolith the most minute fissure was a danger to the whole structure. If the Jews were to be permitted to vent unlicensed emotions in unauthorized demonstrations, how could he forbid the Russians or the Ukrainians to do likewise? He prohibited the demonstrations and ordered some of the Jews to be arrested and deported. The party agitators began to denounce the state of Israel as a tool of western imperialism; and they upbraided those Soviet Jews who by showing friendliness towards it had shamefully failed to give their undivided loyalty to the Soviet fatherland.

This was not all. The Jews were deprived of the right which as a nationality they had hitherto enjoyed; the right to cultivate, within limits, their Jewish consciousness; to send children to state schools, where they received instruction in Yiddish; to publish their own periodicals and newspapers; and to develop their own literature and theatre. In this way Stalin reversed the policy which he himself had once initiated when as Commissar of Nationalities he worked under Lenin's guidance. The pretext he used was that the Soviet Jews, enjoying complete equality with other citizens, had become 'assimilated' with the

Russians and had no need to cling to an obsolete separatism. There was some truth in this; but, as the response of the Jews to Israel had shown, their 'assimilation' was far from being general or thorough: even in the most Russified Jews a new sense of Jewishness had been stirred by the recent tragedy of their race; and the measures of compulsory assimilation to which Stalin now resorted could only make that sense more poignant and persistent. His officialdom invoked the principle of racial non-discrimination to justify acts of discrimination which were all the more shocking because they were perpetrated so soon after the extermination of millions of Jews by the Nazis.

As the Jewish theatres, periodicals, and publishing houses were closed down, their personnel was purged. Men prominently connected with the Jewish Anti-Fascist Committee were also victimized. Among them were Lozovsky, once the head of the International of Red Trade Unions and then Vice-Minister of Foreign Affairs; David Bergelson, Itzik Pfeffer, and Peretz Markish, popular Yiddish writers and poets—all imprisoned, sentenced to death, and executed. Mikhoels, a Yiddish actor of genius, perished in mysterious circumstances. The terror, surrounded by deep secrecy, then hit Russian writers of Jewish origin. The world got an inkling of it only from allusions in the Press, which, castigating 'rootless cosmopolitans' and men of 'uncertain allegiance', revealed systematically the Jewish names of writers who had been known to the public under Russian pseudonyms. Stalin, it was later said, even intended to deport all Jews to Birobidjan, the 'Autonomous Jewish Region' formed near the Manchurian frontier in the nineteen-twenties, just as he had deported the Volga Germans, the Crimean Tartars, and the Ingush-Chechens. If he did entertain the idea, it was impracticable. The Jews were to some extent protected by their prominence in vital spheres of the national life, in the management of industry, in nuclear research, in the party machine, in the academic world, and in the armed forces. (Nearly twenty thousand Jews held teaching posts in the Universities.) But though the state could not dispense with their services, they found themselves under a cloud, distrusted by superiors, envied by subordinates, uncertain of the future, stigmatized as aliens, yet deprived of the protection that aliens normally enjoy in any civilized society. They felt that they were the object of an obscure and ominous intrigue; and just before the end of Stalin's rule, the cloud hanging over their heads grew huge and black.

. . . .

For many years not even an outward show of 'collective leadership' had restricted Stalin's autocracy; and the 'cult of his personality' had assumed unimaginably absurd forms. He was addressed as Father of the Peoples, the Greatest Genius in History, Friend and Teacher of All Toilers, Shining Sun of Humanity, and Life-giving Force of Socialism. Poems and newspaper articles, public speeches and party resolutions, works of literary criticism and scientific treatises—all teemed with these epithets. In the apostolic succession of Marx–Engels–Lenin–Stalin he seemed to dwarf his predecessors. If absolute monarchs had ruled by the Grace of God, he ruled by the Grace of History; and he was worshipped as the demiurge of history. The nation which in its proud nobility was supposed to tower above the rest of mankind lay prostrate at his feet. Day in and day out, *Pravda* carried on its front pages adulatory 'Letters to Stalin'; and its example was faithfully followed by the rest of the Press. On the occasion of his seventieth birthday, in December 1949, the flood of congratulatory messages was so immense that *Pravda* went on publishing them in almost every copy for years thereafter—the tributes to the septuagenarian were still appearing in its columns shortly before his death. The famous Museum of Revolution in Moscow was transformed into an exhibition of the birthday gifts which poured in from every factory, coal-mine, *kolkhoz*, trade union, party cell, and school in the land. It was as if the Chinese revolution, the grave conflicts with the West, the Korean war, and even the feats of industrial construction at home mattered but little in comparison with the dictator's 'historic birthday'; as if the only purpose that the 200 million Soviet citizens had in life was to worship him and shower gifts on him. In order that this massive adulation should not defeat itself by monotonous repetitiveness, the sycophants had to strike ever new flatteries from their arid imaginations and startle the public with ever new and ever more bizarre superlatives.

According to Khrushchev, 'Stalin himself used all conceivable methods to promote the glorification of his own person'. He edited an official account of his own life, and into its 'most dissolute flattery', which he found inadequate, he himself inserted *inter alia*, these phrases: 'Stalin is the worthy continuer of Lenin's work . . . the Lenin of today'; 'the advanced Soviet science of war received further development at Comrade Stalin's hands . . . At the various stages of the war Stalin's genius found the correct solutions . . .'; 'Stalin's military mastery was displayed both in defence and in offence. Comrade Stalin's genius enabled him to divine the enemy's plans and defeat them.' And finally, this incomparable touch: 'Stalin never allowed his work to be marred by the slightest hint of vanity, conceit, or self-adulation.'[1] Like a drug addict, he craved the incense burnt for him and administered it to himself in ever-increasing doses. He seemed to be still trying to escape from the sense of inferiority that had so long gnawed at him, from inner uncertainty, from loneliness at the pinnacle of power and from a horror of the distance that separated him from the people below. The effect of the adulation upon minds ceaselessly subjected to it was to impress on them the image of him as a force almost supernatural and immovable, a force which it was vain to resist even in one's most hidden thoughts and feelings.

Khrushchev has left us a vivid description of Stalin's entourage in these years. No decadent Caesar, no Borgia, had treated his flunkeys more contemptuously and whimsically than Stalin treated the highest dignitaries of the state and the members of his Politbureau. He 'acted in [their] name . . . not asking for [their] opinion . . .; often he did not even inform them about his . . . decisions [on] very important matters of party and state . . . during all the years of war not a single plenary session of the Central Committee was held. . . . True, there was an attempt to call a Central Committee session in October 1941. From all over the country members were called to Moscow. They waited two days . . . but in vain. Stalin did not even deign to meet them and talk to them.' Khrushchev points out that Stalin had become especially wilful and tyrannical since the liquidation of the Trotskyists and Bukharinists (in which Khrushchev and his like had eagerly assisted him). 'Stalin thought that henceforth he could decide all things alone; he now needed only extras; he treated all in such a way that they could only listen and praise him'. In fact, after he had des-

---

[1] N. Khrushchev, *The Dethronement of Stalin*.

troyed the anti-Stalinist opposition, Stalin proceeded to suppress his own faction, the Stalinists. Khrushchev's revelations bear precisely upon this, the last stage of the great purges, when Stalin suspected his own adherents of crypto-Trotskyism or crypto-Bukharinism. Consequently, he ordered the arrest and execution of the great majority—1,108 out of 1,966—of the delegates to the Seventeenth Party Congress, held in 1934, and of 70 per cent.—98 out of 139—of the members of the Central Committee elected at that Congress.[1] These were all Stalinists —the textbooks referred to the Seventeenth Congress as the 'Victors' Congress', because at it the Stalinists had celebrated their final triumph over all inner-party oppositions. After the annihilation of over two thirds of the leading Stalinist cadres, the survivors trembled for their lives. 'In the situation which then prevailed,' Khrushchev relates, 'I often talked with Nikolai Alexandrovich Bulganin; once when we two were travelling in a car, he said: "It happens sometimes that a man goes to Stalin, invited as a friend; and when he sits with Stalin he does not know where he will be sent next, home or to jail." ' 'Stalin was a very distrustful man, diseased with suspicion. . . . He could look at you and say: "Why are your eyes so shifty today?" or "Why are you turning so much today and trying to avoid looking me directly in the eyes?" ' 'He indulged in great wilfulness and choked one morally and physically.' After the war 'Stalin became even more capricious, irritable, and brutal. . . . His persecution mania reached unbelievable dimensions.'

Since Khrushchev made these statements it has become common to refer to Stalin's paranoia. Yet it is not necessary to assume that he became insane in the strict sense. His quasi-paranoiac behaviour followed from his situation; it was inherent in the logic of the great purges and in their consequences. The suspicion with which he treated even his own adherents was not groundless. They had been with him and had abetted him during the persecution of the Trotskyists, Zinovievists, and Bukharinists; but as the persecution turned into the great massacre of 1936-8, many of the most faithful Stalinists were shocked and became remorseful. They had accepted the premises of Stalin's action, but not the consequences. They had agreed to the suppression of the oppositions, but not to physical

---

[1] Khrushchev, op. cit.

annihilation. Postyshev, Rudzutak, Kossior, and others dared to express their remorse or doubts and to question Vyshinsky's procedures. In doing so they at once incurred Stalin's suspicion of disloyalty; and, in truth, they were becoming 'disloyal' to him. Questioning the need for the extermination of the Trotskyists and Bukharinists, they were not disputing any of Stalin's ordinary political decisions; they were impugning his moral character and suggesting that he was guilty of an unpardonable enormity. If they were to behave consistently, they were bound to work henceforth for his overthrow. In that case, they could become more dangerous to him than the Bukharinists or the Trotskyists, for they could use against him the influence and power they still exercised as the leading men of his own faction. He had to assume that their actions would be consistent with their words. He could not afford to wait and see whether they were actually going to use their power against him. For the sake of self-preservation he had to forestall them. And he could forestall them only by destroying them.

He was moving within the vicious circle of his terror, where his mind, even if it were perfectly sane, was bound to become gripped by persecution mania. The more realistic, sober, and sound the view he took of the men around him, the more acute became his distrust and fear of them. The more he was free from self-delusion, the worse were the nightmares he saw. He could not keep himself in power and destroy the whole of his own faction; he had to save part of it, keep it alive, and use it as the instrument of his rule. But with what feelings did the survivors serve him? Did men like Molotov, Khrushchev, Malenkov, Kaganovich, Berya, and Mikoyan not mind the execution of Rudzutak, Kossior, Postyshev, and Eikhe, who had been their closest comrades in the Stalinist Old Guard? If they did not mind it, they were scoundrels without a shred of con-science—how, then, could Stalin count on their loyalty? If they did mind, then, no matter how carefully they concealed their feelings, they could not but nurture a deep resentment and a hatred of their heartless master. In either case, Stalin could not take their obedience or obsequiousness at its face value. He had to distrust them, watch them, and be on his guard against them. Sometimes, as when he was growling 'Why are your eyes so shifty today?', he tried to penetrate into their hidden thoughts and feelings. But these were impenetrable; he himself had made them so. Having forced his lieutenants and underlings to feign boundless admiration and devotion, to dissemble and wear masks, he could not now induce them to show their faces. And so he could not know what evil thoughts and conspiracies they might be harbouring behind their masks. That they should be hatching plots of some kind would be only natural. No one is more inclined to see in the autocrat the source of all evil than are the tyrant's courtiers, the closest witnesses of his omnipotence, who know best how often their own fortunes and the conduct of public affairs depend on his whim or conceit. The idea of a conspiracy comes to them quite naturally; the palace revolt is their characteristic method of action.

Were no attempts at a palace revolt made in the Kremlin during these years, when the Kremlin was the sole centre of political activity in the country? All the inside stories Stalin's successors have told us contain no answer to this question: what they do reveal, however, is that in Stalin's last years there were the makings of an almost permanent conspiracy in his entourage. His closest lieutenants lived in constant fear of him, hovering ceaselessly between office and disgrace, and between life and death. If nothing else, self-preservation must have prompted them to take some action; and if Khrushchev and other party leaders could burst out with so much loathing and rage against Stalin in 1956, then surely these emotions must have stirred in them in his life-time as well, and tempted them to try and free themselves from the incubus. Stalin could not fail to sense this or guess it.

Why, then, did no plot against him ever materialize? Clearly, the would-be plotters were held back by strong inhibitions. Their Marxist habits of thought, however residual and perverted, were against the use of 'individual terror'. Far more powerful was the inhibition rooted in collective guilt and responsibility. Malenkov, Khrushchev, Berya, Molotov, Bulganin, and their friends, had been privy to so many of Stalin's misdeeds and were bound to him by so many ties that it would have been suicidal for them to try and break those ties with violence. (Even when, after his death, they tried to cut the ties without violence, they found themselves drifting into disgrace.) It should be recalled that the terror first hit Stalin's own adherents shortly before the Second World War, when they had reason to fear that a palace revolt might ruin the country's morale and defences. The war adjourned the crisis at the top. After the war Stalin was protected by his victory—who would dare to lift a hand against the Generalissimo in his glory? It took time before the new miseries, the new terror, and new disillusionments tarnished the glory and once again drove men to despair. Thus, it was only in Stalin's last years that the crisis at the top was reopened. Voznesensky's fall and the Leningrad affair were its first manifestations. The new purges had not been preceded, as were the purges of the Trotskyists and the Bukharinists, by protracted and partly open conflicts over issues of ideology and policy. And so no one could say what men like Voznesensky or Kuznetsov had stood for and what their disgrace portended. Perhaps no fundamental political issues were at stake. It was now enough for a member of the Politbureau or for a Secretary of the Central Committee unwittingly to irritate the *Vozhd*, or to get caught in an obscure court intrigue, for his fate to be sealed; and his fate was a warning to others.

Khrushchev relates that shortly after Voznesensky had vanished, he, Malenkov, and another member of the Politbureau came to Stalin to intercede on behalf of their colleague. 'Voznesensky,' Stalin snarled at them, 'has been unmasked as an enemy of the people; he has been shot this very morning. Are you telling me that you, too, are enemies of the people?' After such a dictum Khrushchev and his comrades either had to demand an immediate session of the Politbureau (or of the Central Committee) to consider the matter, which would have amounted to starting a revolt; or they had to reel back. They reeled back. They knew that they would be undone before they even tried to convene the Politbureau. Stalin would be informed of their intention before they had managed to communicate with the other members; every one of them was spied upon and overheard even in the intimacy of his bedroom or bathroom. And the Politbureau, not to speak of the Central Committee, was incapable of action anyhow. Stalin, by instigating the most furious rivalries among its members, kept it divided against itself. Fearing a plot from the men of his entourage, he himself relentlessly plotted against them.

.   .   .   .

The health of the septuagenarian was declining, and his strength was rapidly waning. He did not at all resemble, Ehrenburg notes, his public portraits, but looked 'an old small man, with a face ravaged by the years'. Yet no one seemed to think, and no one dared even to whisper a word about what would happen after his death. 'We had long forgotten', the writer adds, 'that Stalin was a mortal. He had changed into an omnipotent and mysterious deity.' 'I could not imagine him dead,' says Yevtushenko, the poet of the young generation, 'he was part of myself and I could not grasp how we could ever separate.'[1]

His will was omnipresent, as it were, and he himself almost invisible. Muscovites caught a distant glimpse of him only very rarely, on a national holiday, when he stood at the top of the Lenin Mausoleum and took the salute, or on the occasion of the funeral of some dignitary, when for a few moments, he walked by the side of the coffin to the burial place at the Kremlin wall. For about five years he made not a single public utterance (apart from a few trite interviews accorded to foreign journalists; but the journalists were hardly ever admitted to his presence; they received his answers to their questions in writing). When in the anxious early days of the Korean war, he chose to make a pronouncement, it was on—linguistics. In a series of letters, filling many pages in an enlarged edition of *Pravda*, he attacked the academic school of N. Y. Marr, which had for nearly three decades been the authorized Marxist interpreter of language.[2] Stalin, uninhibited by the scantiness of his own knowledge—he had only the rudiments of one foreign language—expatiated on the philosophy of linguistics, the relationship between language, slang, and dialect, the thought processes of the deaf and dumb, and the single world language that would come into being in a remote future, when mankind would be united in communism. Sprinkling his epistle with a little rose water of liberalism, he berated the monopoly the Marr school had established in Soviet linguistics and protested against the suppression of the views of its opponents. Such practices, he declared, were worthy of the age of Arakcheev, the ill-famed police chief of Alexander I. He appeared to stand aloof from

---

[1] I. Ehrenburg, *Memoirs*, vol. iii; E. Yevtushenko, op. cit.
[2] Stalin, *Marxism i Voprosy Yazykoznaniya*.

the drive for conformism that was raging in the Press, from Lysenko's attacks on unorthodox biologists, from the Zhdanovist baiting of 'decadent modernists' in the arts, and from the campaign against 'rootless cosmopolitans' and 'rotten liberals'. He, the instigator of all these witch-hunts, presented himself to the public as the nation's intellectual arbiter, nay, the guardian of academic freedom. However, he wound up with an argument against those who were saying that since the Soviet Union was no longer living in a hostile capitalist encirclement, but among friendly socialist nations, it was time for the state to 'wither away', that is for political coercion to be discarded. No, Stalin replied, the state cannot begin to wither away before socialism has won in most—and not just in a few—countries. Couched in dogmatic terms this was his *'Pas de Rêves!'* thrown at the intellectuals.

His edict on linguistics was hailed as an epoch-making event; and for a few years the party hacks, denied any fresh texts from their silent master, quoted again and again his lucubration on the thought processes of the deaf and dumb (in articles pretending to enlighten people about current political affairs). Not until October 1952 did he come forward with a new and more significant pronouncement on the 'Economic Problems of Socialism in the U.S.S.R.' and a series of letters he had written to various Academicians in connexion with a discussion on a textbook on economics.[1] Amid meditations on the U.S.S.R.'s supposed 'transition from socialism to communism', he discussed the cleavage in the Soviet economy between the socialized industry and the semi-collective and semi-private agriculture. He pointed out that the peasantry's private interests and trade were impeding the nation's progress; and he sounded this alarm: 'It would be unforgivable blindness not to see that . . . these phenomena are already beginning to act as a brake . . . they hamper state planning in its striving to encompass the whole of the national economy . . . the further we proceed the more will these phenomena act as a brake on the continued growth of our country's productive forces'. He thus gave the country an inkling of the controversy in the ruling group over agricultural policy—a previous indication had been the official disavowal of Khrushchev's idea of 'Agrotowns'. Stalin now

---

[1] Stalin, *Ekonomicheskie Problemy Sotsializma v SSSR.*

repudiated a proposal coming from some economists—the proposal on which Khrushchev was to act five years later—that the state should sell its Machine Tractor Stations to the collective farms. Stalin was against it on the ground that the farmers could not be relied upon to renew and modernize agricultural machinery as the state was doing; and that the sale of the Machine Tractor Stations to them would enhance the non-socialist trends in the rural economy that were already impeding national planning. He proposed to restrict rural trade gradually and to introduce a direct exchange of industrial goods and agricultural produce between government and collective farms. But he insisted that this could be only a long-term solution; and he offered the party no advice as to how it should cope immediately with the stagnation of agriculture. He was bequeathing this predicament, the crushing legacy of his forcible collectivization, to his successors.

On 4 October 1952, a day after the publication of these remarks, the Nineteenth Congress opened; and for the first time since 1923 Stalin did not address the delegates as chief *rapporteur*. Instead, Malenkov appeared in this role, just as Stalin had done for the first time in Lenin's last year; and Khrushchev submitted proposals for changes in the party's statutes. The party was thus given to understand that the problem of the succession was on the order of the day. Stalin sat on the platform, withdrawn and remote, the object of interminable ritualistic tributes and ovations. Speaker after speaker quoted from his 'Economic Problems'; but there was no real debate. The delegates voted in 'one-hundred-per-cent. unanimity' for a new Five-Year Plan and for the changes in the party's statues. Only at the closing session Stalin rose to utter a few words about the Soviet Union's position in the world. Gone was the epoch, he said, during which the Soviet Union stood alone as an isolated rampart of socialism. Now it was surrounded by the friendly 'shock brigades' of new socialist states; and in solidarity and co-operation with these it would find it much easier to carry on with its tasks. He also called on the Communist parties in the capitalist world to 'raise the banner of *bourgeois*-democratic freedom' and to struggle for the independence of all nations. He spoke with optimism, even warmth. Yet what he pronounced was a funeral oration on his own doctrine of Socialism in a Single Country. This was his last message to the party and the nation he had ruled for three decades.

Despite Stalin's reassuring words, the Congress sensed the approach of enigmatic and ominous events. Malenkov and other speakers dwelt on dangers ahead, on the aggravation of social conflicts and class struggle, and on the need for the utmost watchfulness. Just as on the eve of the pre-war purges, a cry for vigilance was mounting on all sides.[1] As if anticipating a new break with the past, the Congress decided that the party should no longer call itself 'Bolshevik'. The new Central Committee, to which 240 members were elected, was twice as large as the old one. The Committee, in its turn, elected a Presidium —the Politbureau had been abolished—two or three times larger than its predecessor. Both the Committee and the Presidium were too numerous and top-heavy to function as the party's leading bodies. Why had Stalin made them so? Khrushchev later maintained that Stalin got the Congress to elect so large a Central Committee because he was planning to reduce its size by means of a bloody purge—he had introduced understudies for the men he had marked for destruction. At the first session of the new Committee, Khrushchev further relates, Stalin venomously assailed Molotov and Mikoyan, against whom he levelled unspecified charges—he had already expressed a suspicion that Voroshilov was a 'British agent'. Stalin again, according to Khrushchev, was bent on 'finishing off' the old members of the Politbureau in order to remove the witnesses of his crimes, who could testify against him to posterity.[2] Whatever the truth of the matter, immediately after the Congress the air grew heavy with terror. In November the great trial of Slansky, Clementis, and other Czechoslovak Communists, branded as Trotskyists, Titoists, and Zionist–American spies, opened in Prague. This was the last of the series of trials in eastern Europe and the prelude to the new purges in Moscow. Hardly a day passed without mysteriously inspired vicious attacks on men eminent in the party and the professions; without allegations of a criminal lack of vigilance in the highest places; without dark hints about the infiltration

---

[1] See *Pravda* for the first half of October 1952.
[2] Khrushchev, op. cit.

of 'enemies of the people' and spies; and without an ever louder clamour against the 'rootless cosmopolitans' of Jewish origin. *Pravda* was grimly reminding readers that any Soviet citizen was responsible for crimes committed by his relatives— the warning was all too familiar from the days of Yagoda and Yezhov. Few knew to whom it applied. But two of Mikoyan's sons had just been arrested; and Molotov's wife, a party veteran and political figure in her own right, had been deported from Moscow. The year ended with the demotion of Fedoseev, the editor of *Bolshevik*, whom Suslov, one of the secretaries of the Central Committee, denounced as Voznesensky's accomplice.

Finally, on 3 January 1953, it was officially announced that nine Professors of Medicine, all serving in the Kremlin as house doctors to the men of the ruling group, had been unmasked as agents of the American and British Secret Services, on whose orders they had murdered two party leaders, Zhdanov and Shcherbakov, and had tried to assassinate Marshals Vassilevsky, Govorov, Koniev, Shtemenko, and others, so as to weaken the country's defences. Most of these 'assassins in white blouses' were Jews and were accused of acting at the instigation of 'Joint', an international Jewish organization with headquarters in the United States. The country was given to understand that the conspiracy had had many still undetected ramifi- cations; and the cry for vigilance, with its anti-Jewish under- tones and overtones, rose to a pitch of fury.

The incrimination of the Kremlin doctors could only be a curtain-raiser. By themselves the medical men were of little or no political importance: they could not be presented as people striving to seize power for themselves. If it came to a trial, the prosecution would have to characterize them as cats'- paws of men with more obvious political ambitions, and as accessories to other conspirators, whose interest in power was credible and, so to speak, professional. These conspirators could be found only high up in the party hierarchy; and the sensational unmasking of the 'real' directing centre of the plot was to be the climax of the doctors' trial. No hint was as yet given who the chief culprits might be. For the time being, the stage managers of the trial were busy forcing the doctors to make 'confessions' and preparing them to act their prescribed parts. The doctors were confronted with a false witness, a certain Doctor Timashuk, who testified against them in a letter to Stalin (and was rewarded for this with the Order of Lenin just on the anniversary of Lenin's death). Khrushchev describes how Stalin himself supervised the interrogation and ordered the prisoners to be put in chains and beaten. 'If you do not obtain confessions from them', he said to Ignatiev, Minister of State Security, 'we will shorten you by a head.' He then distributed protocols of the doctors' confessions among members of the Presidium, whom, however, he did not allow to go into the case and verify the allegations. Sensing their incredulity and unease, he scoffed at them: 'You are blind, like young kittens. What will happen here without me? The country will perish— you do not know how to recognize an enemy.'

The members of the Presidium had every reason to feel perplexed and alarmed. Although the case was so reminiscent of the old purge trials, it had one startlingly novel feature. In the old trials the defendants were invariably charged, *inter alia*, with attempts on the lives of Voroshilov, Kaganovich, Molotov, and other party leaders. To the latter this circumstance was of great importance. The list of the would-be victims of the 'conspirators' was Stalin's List of Honours, as it were. During the trials prosecutor, judges, and the Press were telling the nation: 'These are our irreplaceable leaders, with whose services we cannot dispense. The enemy knows it—that is why he seeks to destroy them.' A Politbureau member whose name was omitted from this peculiar Honours List was virtually disgraced, for if the 'enemies of the people' did not try to destroy him, then he was either unworthy of his high office or perhaps even in collusion with them.

The astonishing novelty of the doctors' case was that the defendants were not accused of trying to assassinate a single one of the *living* party leaders—only Zhdanov and Shcherbakov, who had long been dead, figured as their victims. The accusation stressed with deliberate emphasis that the doctors aimed exclusively at the heads of the armed forces. This strange circumstance, the fact that the enemy was alleged to have chosen only the marshals and generals as his targets, gave the party leaders food for much anxious thought. They had to reflect what moral the tale was intended to convey. Clearly, whoever concocted it was out to place the military on a pedestal and by implication to disparage the civilian leaders. Who had invented the tale? Its text bore the trademark of military Intelligence rather than that of State Security. The rivalry between these two Secret Services was notorious; and, obviously, Ignatiev, the Minister of State Security, was a reluctant executant of orders, if Stalin had to threaten him that he would 'shorten' him 'by a head'. Berya, the Minister of Interior, was hardly among the initiators—later in the year, when Stalin's successors 'liquidated' him as Stalin's evil genius and a traitor, they did not charge him with complicity in instigating the doctors' case. But if the initiative came from the military, why did Stalin support them? Was he—with an eye to the succession—encouraging the generals to make a bid for power? If so, what did this portend for the party leaders? Were they to be stripped of office and wiped out? Was this the meaning of Stalin's attacks on Molotov, Mikoyan, Voroshilov, and Andreev? Was this perhaps to be his last and final purge, his ultimate break with the party he had degraded and bled white? Was he, with one foot in the grave, setting the stage, or helping the generals to set it, for the Bonapartist *coup*, the fear of which had so long haunted the Bolsheviks? But what interest had Stalin in acting in this way? He was to take his secret with him to the grave; and in the meantime the party leaders could no more unravel the tangle of his intentions than can posterity—his motives and actions seemed to have lost all coherence.

The struggle was over fundamental issues of policy as well as over claims to power. The differences between Stalin's successors that were to come to the surface in 1953 and after, divided them even earlier. The divergencies between the groups of Molotov and Kaganovich and of Malenkov and Berya—with Khrushchev sitting on the fence and the military keeping in the background—were already there; although as long as Stalin's presence blocked any free exchange of views, the groups could not work out the differences and give them definite form. Most members of Stalin's entourage knew and felt that the cauldron of the state was dangerously overheated and that it was necessary to open safety valves. With the last remnant of his fitful energy, Stalin was choking the valves and screwing them tight. The preparations for a repetition of the Witches' Sabbath of 1936-8 were heightening the pressures in the cauldron and the tension between Russia and the West. The feverish search for American spies under every bed in the Kremlin, in every office, research establishment, Jewish home, and intellectual circle, was admittedly insane; but a method could be found in the madness on the assumption that the country was being prepared for war. In that case, Stalin's decision to exalt the marshals and generals, and to turn all the limelight on them, might make some sense. So might his obsession with secrecy, unusually intense even for him, his insistence on steep rises in military expenditure, and his other measures—all designed to turn the country into an armed camp and to impress on it that it must be ready to repulse an enemy attack at any moment.

In this way the stiffness and rudeness of Stalin's diplomacy might also be accounted for. The hostilities in Korea dragged on; and Stalin prevented the conclusion of protracted negotiations for an armistice on the flimsiest of pretexts, such as the belligerents' disagreement over the treatment of prisoners of war. Stalin appeared to be reluctant to allow the United States to disengage its forces from Korea and gain freedom of manoeuvre in other theatres of the Cold War. His diplomacy was, in fact, fixed in an immobility which resulted from a deadlock between conflicting policies. It was as if a 'war party' and a 'peace party' were at loggerheads in the Kremlin and for the time being in a stalemate. This is not to say that influential elements in the Government really favoured war and that Stalin patronized them. With the nation still so terribly debilitated by the carnage of the last war, not even the most cynical, or the least realistic, of policy-makers could indulge in designs for military aggression. The differences centred rather on an appraisal of the enemy's intentions—on the question whether the Western Powers were likely to attack Russia or Eastern Europe in the foreseeable future. This was the perennial issue that had underlain the disputes of the nineteen-twenties and that was to loom again in future Russo-Chinese controversies. Stalin himself had defined this as the debatable question when, in his essay on 'Economic Problems', he went on record with the view that wars between the imperialist powers and the countries of socialism were no longer 'inevitable'.

On this crucial point Stalin, regardless of this optimistic statement, prevaricated. Ostensibly dismissing the threat of an

American attack, he initiated, or connived in, courses of action predicated on the reality and the immediacy of the threat. Only if it was assumed that Washington was planning war was there—in Stalinist terms—any reason for the ceaseless and strident denunciations of the American warmongers, for presenting the Kremlin doctors as assassins in the service of an American-Jewish organization, for the mobilization and the hysterical incitement of the nation, for keeping American forces tied down in Korea, and for maintaining the Soviet Union and its satellites in a state of permanent alertness and military preparedness.

The dilemmas of foreign policy had, of course, their bearing on domestic affairs. Those who held that the nation must be kept, materially and morally, on a war footing could not favour any reform at home that would relax political discipline or re-allocate the nation's economic resources in favour of civilian needs. Any advocates of domestic reform, on the other hand, were led by the logic of their attitude to bank on the possibility of peaceful accommodation with the Atlantic powers, to call for more diplomatic initiative and flexibility, and to hope for an 'international *détente*' that would enable them to pacify and normalize the atmosphere at home. There was and there could be no question among these men of any reform that would restore civil liberties to the nation, pave the way for representa-tive government, and so safeguard the heritage of the revolution. They aimed at something far more modest yet important enough: at freeing the nation from the insanity of the Stalinist terror and rationalizing the method of government. In foreign policy, too, their objectives were, of necessity, limited, for they knew that the Cold War, unlike any armed conflict, could not be brought to an end by *parlementaires* going out with a white flag and arranging for a cease-fire. Yet, even in the Cold War, there was scope for more genuine contact and bargaining between Russia and the West, and for fruitful mutual con-cessions. (More sweeping plans and ambitions, however, were also entertained: Berya, for instance, contemplated the idea of a Soviet withdrawal from Berlin and East Germany, the idea that presently cost him his head.[1])

[1] These differences crystallized, however, only after Stalin's death. Khrushchev attributed the plan for a Soviet withdrawal from East Germany to Berya, after the

However, as long as Stalin was at the helm, all avenues of change and reform were blocked, and with every week that passed the situation was becoming more explosive and incalculable He liked to preen himself on his tactical shrewdness and realism. He spoke contemptuously of the 'greedy conquerors' who, like Hitler, were unable to 'apportion their aims to their capacity' and did not know 'where to stop'.[1] He was not Hitler, he was saying; he knew where to stop. The boast was not quite groundless. Stalin had repeatedly halted at the very brink of armed conflict with his ex-allies. He had stopped at the Turkish Straits; he had stopped in Persia; he had stopped before attacking Tito with armed force; he had stopped before turning the blockade of Berlin into ultimate disaster. It was not so clear how far he was prepared to go in the conflict engendered by the Korean war. 'Does he still know where to stop?' the men around him now wondered.

.   .   .   .

One thing is certain: he no longer knew where to stop in offending and outraging his own nation. He was completely unaware of the moral crisis into which he had thrown it. He did not realize that it was impossible either for himself, or anyone else, to continue with his methods of government, and that his ideas and conceits were in irreconcilable conflict with the country's needs and the realities of the age. The nation had outgrown his tutelage and could not endure it much longer. His mind seemed fixed in the twenties and thirties. His image of his own people was still that of the primitive pre-industrial and largely illiterate society over which he had established his rule. He was unable to adjust himself to the mid-century Russia, the Russia that had, partly despite him but partly under his inspiration, industrialized herself, modernized her social structure, and educated her masses. The transformation was still in progress; the nation had a long way to go yet before it would truly benefit from its results. Yet it is a fact that 'Stalin

latter's execution. A circumstantial corroboration of this version and a description of Berya's moves in Berlin were given independently by Heinz Brandt, Secretary of the S.E.D. in East Berlin in 1950–1953, who later escaped to Western Germany. See H. Brandt, 'The East German Popular Uprising, 17 June 1953' in *The Review* (October 1959), a quarterly published by the Imre Nagy Institute in Brussels.

[1] See, e.g. Stalin's remark to the British Foreign Secretary, made during the war. *The Eden Memoirs, The Reckoning*, p. 413.

found Russia working with a wooden plough and left her equipped with atomic piles',[1] even though the epoch of the wooden plough still persisted in lingering on all too many levels of her national existence. This summary of Stalin's rule is, of course, a tribute to his achievement. But in Stalinism, too, the wooden plough and the atomic pile grotesquely coexisted— just as primitive barbarism and Marxism did; and as the nation advanced, the retrograde factors of Stalin's régime increasingly impeded progress and threatened to bring it to a halt.

Stalin's whimsical despotism had drawn its strength from the sloth and torpor of the old peasantry, from which even the new working class had been recruited; but it was in utter discord with the huge urban and industrial society that had come into being. The over-centralized control which he and his minions were exercising from the Kremlin over the entire economy might have had its uses in the early phases of 'primitive accumulation', when it was necessary to marshal the country's extremely meagre resources and to watch that every ton of steel, coal, or cement should be channelled to the proper pro- duction site and employed in the prescribed manner. But this method was becoming absolutely detrimental when it was applied to a vast, technologically advanced, and complex industrial system. Similarly, the coercion by means of which Stalin's Government transplanted millions of *muzhiks* to the factories, trained them in productive skills and tied them to their jobs, might have been partly excused as long as labour and productive skills were desperately short. Something might have been said then even for the determination, though not for the callousness, with which Stalin fostered inequality by means of differential wage rates and Stakhanovism. But as industrial skills were becoming less and less scarce, the coercion and the excesses of inequality hampered economic growth; they kept the vast majority of workers apathetic and sullen. Generally speaking, the terror, justified originally by the need to defend the 'conquests of October' from counter-revolution, was grow- ing more and more pernicious as the new social structure became consolidated and the possibility of a capitalist restora- tion grew more remote. The recurrent witch-hunts and purges

[1] The quotation is from my obituary of Stalin published in the *Manchester Guardian* on 6 March 1953.

crushed all social initiative and responsibility in the bureaucracy as well as in the masses. And the cult of the Leader which had offered to masses of benighted *muzhiks* the 'father figure', a substitute for God and Tsar, insulted the intelligence of a nation that was diligently modernizing itself, avidly absorbing modern science, and reaching cultural maturity.

We have said earlier that Stalinism drove barbarism out of Russia by barbarous means.[1] We should now add that it could not go on doing this indefinitely. In Stalin's last years the progressive impact of his régime was increasingly nullified by the means he employed. In order to go on civilizing herself, Russia now had to drive out Stalinism. Nothing made this more urgent than the interference of Stalinist dogma with biology, chemistry, physics, linguistics, philosophy, economics, literature, and the arts—an interference reminiscent of the days when the Inquisition decided for the whole Christian world which were the right and the wrong ideas about God, the Universe, and Man. In Soviet universities Einstein's work was taboo until 1953-4—Freud's ideas still are. Such intrusion of theological or bureaucratic dogma on the working of the scientific mind belongs essentially to a pre-industrial epoch. In mid-century Russia it amounted to a sabotage of science, technology, and national defence. Not even the narrowest sectional interest was served by that sabotage; and all educated people were eager to break it. To do this they had, first, to dispel the stifling fog of Great Russian chauvinism and xenophobia which, in an era of a tremendous technological revolution, was cutting off their country from the world-wide movement of ideas and feeding it on the exclusive feats of Muscovy's native genius. The Stalinist isolation which had seemed to many so plausible and realistic in the nineteen-twenties and nineteen-thirties now revealed itself in its ultimate absurdity: from Socialism in One Country it had passed to Science in a Single Country. Such national self-centredness was an unbearable anachronism when Russia's destiny had become inextricably bound up with that of the rest of the world. Even from the Stalinist viewpoint, preposterous glorification of old Mother Russia could not be reconciled with the spread of revolution in recent years. One-third of mankind already lived

[1] See p. 568.

under Communist governments, and Stalinism spoke as if its realm had been confined to the old Tambov *Gubernia* or the Tula district. All account of time was lost in the Kremlin.

The scandal of the 'doctors' plot' finally exposed a moral gangrene. This was not one of the many instances of Stalin's equivocal treatment of the Jews. The tale about the anti-Soviet conspiracy of world Jewry had the odour of the Protocols of the Elders of Zion and of the concoctions of Goebbels' Ministry of Propaganda. If the intrigue had been allowed to run its course—if the trial of the doctors had been held—it could have only one sequel: a nation-wide pogrom. Yet the Government that had instigated the intrigue was still professing Marxism–Leninism, was still ordering the writings of the founders of the proletarian Internationals to be printed in millions of copies, and was still including a study of these in the educational curricula obligatory in its schools. Stalin now struck at the very roots of the idea by which the revolution, the party, and the state, had lived; he was destroying the birth certificate and the ideological title-deeds even of his own régime. By this act Stalinism was committing suicide even before its author was dead. The party, despite its degeneration and stultification, could not follow Stalin on this self-destructive course. Nor could the numerous advanced elements in the intelligentsia and the working class do so. The scandal served only to hasten the decomposition of Stalinism and to prepare a revulsion. It was to be wound up less than a month after Stalin's death; and the complete rehabilitation of the doctors was to be one of the first manifestations of the country's break with Stalinism.[1]

. . . .

Summing up Stalin's rule in 1948 I said that 'Stalin cannot be classed with Hitler, among the tyrants whose record is one of absolute worthlessness and futility. Hitler was the leader of a sterile counter-revolution, while Stalin has been both the leader and the exploiter of a tragic, self-contradictory, but creative revolution.'[2] This remains true if the whole of Stalin's career is assessed. 'The better part of Stalin's work,' I went on, 'is as certain to outlast Stalin himself as the better parts of the work of Cromwell and Napoleon have outlasted them.' This,

---

[1] I. Deutscher, *Russia After Stalin*, chapter vi; 'The Moral Climate'.
[2] See pp. 569–70.

too, may stand; but it must be added that in Stalin's last years the worst features of his rule were aggravated and magnified. This circumstance only adds point to our conclusion that 'in order to save the better part of Stalin's work for the future and to give it its full value, history may yet have to cleanse and reshape Stalin's work as sternly as it once cleansed and reshaped the work of the English Revolution after Cromwell and of the French after Napoleon'. We now know that history began this cleansing and reshaping on the very day Stalin yielded up his ghost—and here 'history' stands not for any Supreme Will, *Zeitgeist*, or abstract Law, but for the effective action of human beings, impelled to act by their needs and ideas. It was the needs of Soviet society at the close of this great and sombre epoch, and the ideas which that society had inherited from the October revolution that moved its forward-looking elements towards the break with Stalinism. In the late nineteen-forties it may have seemed a sanguine hope that 'in the long run the many positive valuable elements in the educational influence of Stalinism will turn against its worse features'. This expectation, too, has now been fulfilled, although the conflict between the discordant elements of the Stalinist legacy was not yet finally resolved even in the middle nineteen-sixties. The main characteristic of Soviet society in the first decade or so after Stalin lay in the contradiction between its progressive socio-economic *élan*, awakened by the revolution and stimulated by victory in the Second World War, and its moral and political atrophy, brought about by decades of totalitarian rule and the extermination of all independent centres of political thought and action. A radical change in the government and the way of life of the Soviet Union became a national necessity, while no organized political forces capable of bringing it about, or pressing for it in an articulate manner, yet existed in the mass of the people. There was therefore no immediate possibility of a revolutionary overthrow of the bureaucratic despotism. Nor did any organized movement for gradual reform surge up from the depths of society. Reform could come only from above, from the ruling group itself, from Stalin's adherents and accomplices. This circumstance determined beforehand the hesitant, contradictory, and opportunist nature of the so-called de-Stalinization.

This was, incidentally, not the first time that a vital and long overdue change in Russia's mode of existence was carried out from above by purely bureaucratic means. A hundred years earlier, after the death of Tsar Nicholas I, it was his son Alexander II who decreed the abolition of serfdom, the greatest single reform in the whole history of pre-revolutionary Russia. When the dismayed serf-owners, who felt that the Tsar was betraying them, protested, he replied: 'It is better to abolish serfdom from above than to wait till it begins to abolish itself from below.' Similarly, in Stalin's last days his successors decided that it was better to abolish the worst features of Stalinism from above than to wait till they were abolished from below. But just as the Tsar's half-hearted emancipation of the peasants had left Russia with her immense land problem unresolved, so Malenkov's and Khrushchev's de-Stalinization was to leave the Soviet Union with its socialist aspirations still unsatisfied and its longing for freedom frustrated. History has still to complete the 'cleansing and reshaping' of Stalin's work.

Stalin's death was announced on the morning of 6 March 1953. According to the official medical bulletins, he had, six days earlier, suffered a brain haemorrhage and a stroke of paralysis and lost speech and consciousness. On the night of 4 March a second stroke affected his heart and respiratory organs; he died—at the age of 73—the next day at 9.30 p.m.

His brief illness gave his successors just enough time to consider how they should face the country and to agree on a provisional redistribution of the highest offices in party and state. According to all accounts, the nation reacted to the event with the contradictory moods which Stalin's complex and ambiguous personality inspired: some wept in anguish, others sighed with relief; most were stunned and afraid to think of the future. His successors walked warily. They had been Stalin's mere shadows; they could not now rule the country as his shadows. They were not inclined to pay the dead man the fulsome tribute they had paid the living; and they were terrified of not paying it. Even those among them who longed to free themselves from the encumbrances of his cult, the cult of which they had been the high priests, were alarmed at the thought of the turmoil they might provoke by any act that would look like Stalin's desecration. At his funeral, therefore, Malenkov, Molotov, and Berya, spoke about his merits in muffled voices, with unwonted restraint. While the ceremony was on, immense multitudes moved of their own accord towards the Red Square; and as the authorities had not foreseen so huge an irruption, the militiamen failed to cope with it; the crowds stampeded; and many people, women and children, were trampled to death. Such disasters had occurred in the past at the funerals or the coronations of the Tsars.

The bier with Stalin's body was carried down to the crypt of the Mausoleum in the Red Square, and placed there by Lenin's side. At night Stalin's name was painted next to Lenin's on the outer wall of the Mausoleum. But presently the body was to be ejected from the shrine and the name to be wiped off. Posterity, haunted by Stalin, perplexed by the legacy of his rule yet still unable to master and transcend it, for the time being sought merely to cast him out of its memory.

Bibliography

This list includes only such sources as have been quoted or directly referred to by the author.

ALLILUYEV, S., *Proidennyi Put.* Moscow, 1946.

ALLILUYEVA, A. S., *Vospominanya.* Moscow, 1946. (This book of memoirs by Stalin's sister-in-law was warmly received in the Russian press in 1946; but in 1948 it was severely censured by *Pravda* and apparently confiscated on the ground that Alliluyeva had treated her brother-in-law and the other leaders of the party with 'impermissible familiarity'.)

ARKOMED, S. T., *Rabocheye Dvizhenie i Sotsial-Demokratya na Kavkaze.* Fore-word by G. Plekhanov. Moscow–Petrograd, 1923.

BADAYEV, A. E., *Bolsheviki v Gosudarstvennoi Dumie.* Moscow–Leningrad, 1930.

BARMINE, A., *One who Survived.* New York, 1945.

Batumskaya Demonstratsya 1902 goda (a collection of memoirs and records). Moscow (?), 1937.

BAZHANOV (BAJANOV), B., *Stalin, der Rote Diktator.* Berlin, no date.

BERYA (BERIA), L., *On the History of the Bolshevik Organizations in Trans-caucasia.* (English translation from the fourth Russian edition.) London, no date.

Bolshaya Sovetskaya Encyclopaedia, vol. 50, *SSSR,* Moscow, 1957.

BONNET, G., *Défense de la Paix, de Washington au Quai d'Orsay.* Geneva, 1946.

BUKHARIN, N., *Kritika Ekonomicheskoi Platformy Oppozitsii.* Leningrad, no date.

—— *Dengi w Epokhe Proletarskoi Diktatury.* Moscow, 1920 (?).

—— *Historical Materialism.* London, 1926.

—— and PREOBRAZHENSKY, E., *The ABC of Communism.* London, 1922.

BYRNES, J. F., *Speaking Frankly.* London, 1948.

CHURCHILL, W. S., *The Aftermath.* London, 1944.

—— *The Second World War,* vol. i. London, 1948.

CIECHANOWSKI, J., *Defeat in Victory.* London, 1948.

DAN, F., *Proiskhozhdenie Bolshevizma.* New York, 1946.

DAVIES, J. E., *Mission to Moscow.* London, 1942.

DEANE, J. R., *The Strange Alliance.* London, 1947.

DEDIJER, V., *Tito Speaks,* London, 1953.

DJILAS, M., *Conversations with Stalin,* London, 1963.

EASTMAN, M., *Since Lenin Died.* London, 1925.

EDEN, A., *The Eden Memoirs, The Reckoning,* London, 1965.

EHRENBURG, I. *Memoirs,* vols. i–iii, New York, 1964–5.

FALLS, C., *The Second World War.* London, 1948.

FISCHER, L., *The Soviets in World Affairs.* London, 1930.

FLEMING, D. F., *The Cold War and its Origins,* vols. i–ii, London, 1961.

GAFENCU, G., *Prelude to the Russian Campaign*. London, 1945.

GATHORNE-HARDY, G. M., *A Short History of International Affairs*. London, 1938.

History of the Civil War in the U.S.S.R., The. Edited by M. Gorky, V. Molotov, K. Voroshilov, S. Kirov, A. Zhdanov, J. Stalin. (English edition.) Moscow, 1946.

History of the Communist Party of the Soviet Union (Bolsheviks). Short Course. Edited by a Commission of the Central Committee. (Authorized English edition.) Moscow, 1943.

HULL, CORDELL, *The Memoirs of Cordell Hull*, vols. i–ii. New York, 1948.

ISAACS, H. R., *The Tragedy of the Chinese Revolution*. London, 1938.

Istorya Diplomatii, vols. i–iii. Edited by V. P. Potemkin. Moscow, 1941–5.

Istorya Klasovoi Borby v Zakavkazi, vol. i. Tiflis, 1930.

KENNAN, G. F., *Russia and the West under Lenin and Stalin*, London, 1961.

KHACHAPURIDZE, G. V., and MAKHARADZE, F., *Ocherki po Istorii Rabochevo i Krestyanskovo Dvizhenya v Gruzii*. Published by the Society of Marxist Historians and the Institute of History of the Communist Academy. Moscow (?), 1932.

KHRUSHCHEV, N. S., *The Dethronement of Stalin* (The 'secret speech' at the 20th Congress) Published by *The Manchester Guardian*, Manchester, 1956.

—— Speeches in *Reports of 20th, 21st, and 22nd Congresses* of CPSU.

KIROV, S. M., *Izbrannye Stati i Rechi*. Moscow, 1944.

KOLLONTAI, A. M., *The Workers' Opposition in Russia*. London, 1923.

KOSHELEV, F., PROFESSOR, *Stalinskii Ustav — Osnovnoi Zakon Kolkhoznoi Zhizni*. Moscow, 1947.

KOSTOV, *The Trial of Traïcho Kostov and his Group*, Sofia, 1949.

KOT, St. *Rozmowy z Kremlem*, London, 1959.

KPSS v Rezolutsyakh, vols. i–ii, Moscow, 1953.

KRASIN, L., *Leonid Krasin, his Life and Work*. London, no date.

KRASIN, L. B., *Dela Davno Minuvshykh Dnei*. Moscow, 1930.

KRITSMAN, L., *Geroicheskii Period Velikoi Russkoi Revolutsii*. Moscow, 1924 (?).

KRIVITSKI, W. G., *I Was Stalin's Agent*. London, 1939.

KRUPSKAYA, N., *Memories of Lenin*. London, 1942.

Lenin (Official biography by Marx–Engels–Lenin Institute in Moscow). London, 1943.

LENIN, V. I., *Sochinenya*. Moscow, 1935 and 1941–8. Quotations from vols. i–xx are from the fourth Russian edition unless otherwise stated; quotations from vols. xxi–xxx are from the third Russian edition.

—— *Collected Works of V. I. Lenin*. Vols. xx–xxi authorized English edition. London, no date.

—— *Letters of Lenin*. London, 1937.

—— *The Essentials of Lenin*, vols. i–ii. London, 1947.

LENIN, W. I., *Briefe an Maxim Gorki 1908–13*. With foreword by L. Kamenev. Vienna, 1924.

LENIN and STALIN, *Sbornik Proizvedenii k Izucheniu Istorii VKP (b)*, vol. ii. Moscow, 1936.

Leninskii Sbornik, vols. ii and xviii. Moscow, 1931.

LEONHARD, W. *Child of the Revolution*, London, 1957.

LIDDELL HART, B. H., *The Other Side of the Hill*. London, 1948.

LYASHCHENKO, P. I., *Istorya Narodnovo Khozyaistva SSSR*, vols. i–ii. Moscow, 1948.

MAKHARADZE, F., and KHACHAPURIDZE, G. V., *Ocherki po Istorii Rabochevo i Krestyanskovo Dvizhenya v Gruzii*. Moscow (?), 1932.

Malaya Sovetskaya Encyclopaedia, Moscow, 1960.

MARTEL, SIR GIFFARD, *The Russian Outlook*. London, 1947.

MARX, K., *Capital*, translated by S. Moore and E. Aveling, vol. i. London, 1938.

—— and ENGELS, F., *Perepiska K. Marxa i F. Engelsa s Russkimi Politicheskimi Deyatelami*. Moscow, 1947.

MAURIN, J., *Révolution et Contre-révolution en Espagne*. Paris, 1937.

MOLOTOV, V. M., *Voprosy Vneshnei Politiki*. Moscow, 1948.

NAMIER, L. B., *Diplomatic Prelude*. London, 1948.

Nazi-Soviet Relations, 1939–41. Documents from the Archives of the German Foreign Office, edited by R. J. Sontag and J. S. Beddie, Department of State. Washington, 1948.

NOTKIN, A. I., *Ocherki Teorii Sotsialisticheskovo Vosproizvodstva*. Moscow, 1948.

Nowe Drogi, The Review.

PERKINS, F., *The Roosevelt I Knew*. London, 1948.

PILSUDSKI, J., *Rok 1920* (Pilsudski's polemic against Tukhachevsky). Warsaw, 1931.

POKROVSKY, M. N., *Brief History of Russia*, vols. i–ii. London, 1933.

POPOV, N., *Outline History of the Communist Party of the Soviet Union*, vols. i–ii. English translation from the sixteenth Russian edition. London, no date.

Prazhskaya Konferentsya RSDRP (collection of memoirs and documents, editor O. Pyatnitsky). Moscow (?), 1937.

Promyshlennost SSSR (Statisticheskii Sbornik), Moscow, 1964.

Rajk, László, and his Accomplices Before the People's Court, Budapest, 1949.

Razkazy o Velikom Staline (memoirs by Stalin's Georgian friends and schoolmates), vol. ii. Tbilisi (Tiflis), 1941.

REALE, *Avec Jacques Duclos, Au Banc des Accusés*, Paris, 1958.

REED, JOHN, *Ten Days that Shook the World* (3rd edition). London, 1934.

SCHACHT, DR. HJALMAR, *Abrechnung mit Hitler*. Hamburg–Stuttgart, 1948.

SCOTT, JOHN, *Behind the Urals*. London, 1942.

SERGE, VICTOR, *Portrait de Staline*. Paris, 1940.

SHERWOOD, ROBERT E., *Roosevelt and Hopkins*. New York, 1948.

SHLYAPNIKOV, A., *Semnadtsatyi God*. Moscow–Leningrad, 1925.

SIKORSKI, W., *Nad Wisłą i Wkrą*. Lvov (?), 1928.

Smiena Vekh (Essays by N. N. Ustrialov, V. V. Kliuchnikov, and others). Prague, 1922.

SMITH, WALTER BEDELL, *My Three Years in Moscow*, New York, 1950.

SNOW, E., *Red Star Over China*, London, 1963.

—— *The Other Side of the River*, London, 1963.

SOUVARINE, B., *Stalin*. London, no date.

Soviet Foreign Policy During the Patriotic War, vol. i. London, no date. (References to vol. ii are to the Russian edition: *Vneshnyaya Politika Sovietskovo Soyuza v Period Otechestvennoi Voiny*, vol. ii. Moscow, 1946.)

Soviet Union 1936 (Collection of statements by Stalin, Tukhachevsky, Molotov, and others). Authorized English edition. London, no date.

SSSR v Tsifrakh v 1961 g., Moscow, 1962.

STALIN, J. V., *Sochinenya*, vols. i–viii. Moscow, 1946–8.

—— *Problems of Leninism*. Authorized English translation from eleventh Russian edition. Moscow, 1945.

—— *Leninism*, vol. ii. London, 1933.

—— *The October Revolution*. London, 1936.

—— *War Speeches, Orders of the Day*. London, 1945 (?).

—— *An Interview with the German Author Emil Ludwig*. Moscow, 1932.

—— *Rechi na Predvybornykh Sobrannyakh*, Moscow, 1946.

—— *Marxism i Voprosy Yazykoznaniya*, Moscow, 1950.

—— *Ekonomicheskie Problemy Sotsializma v SSSR*, Moscow, 1952.

—— *Perepiska Predsedatelya Soveta Ministrov SSSR s Prezidentami SSHA i Premierministrami Velikobritanii* vol. i–ii, Moscow, 1957.

—— and LENIN, *Sbornik Proizvedenii k Izucheniu Istorii VKP (b)*, vol. ii. Moscow, 1936. (Other sources for Stalin's statements include the reports and records of Congresses and Conferences of the Communist Party, various periodicals, &c.)

J. Stalin (A collection of articles on his sixtieth birthday). Voronezh, 1940.

Stalin i Khashim. With a foreword by N. Lakoba. Sukhum, 1934.

Stalin, Kratkaya Biografya (Official biography by Marx–Engels–Lenin Institute). Moscow, 1944.

SUKHANOV, N., *Zapiski o Revolutsii*, vols. iii–iv. Berlin, 1922.

Sverdlov, Y. M., Sbornik, Vospominanya. Leningrad, 1926.

TARLÉ, E., *Napoleon*. Moscow, 1942.

THALHEIMER, A., *1923: Eine verpasste Revolution?* Berlin, 1931.

TITO, Y. Broz, *Political Report at Fifth Congress of CPY*. Belgrade, 1948; and *The Correspondence between C.C. CPY and C.C. CPSU*, Belgrade, 1948.

TROTSKY, L., *Sochinenya*, vol. iii. Moscow, 1924.

—— *Europa und Amerika*. Berlin, 1926.

—— *Germany, the Key to the International Situation*. London, 1931.

—— *Kak Vooruzhalas Revolutsya*, vols. i–iii. Moscow, 1924–5.

—— *Mein Leben*. Berlin, 1930.

—— *Permanentnaya Revolutsya*. Berlin, 1930.

—— *Stalin* (2nd edition). New York, 1946.

—— *The History of the Russian Revolution*, vols. i–iii. London, 1932–3.

—— *The Real Situation in Russia*. London, no date.

—— *The Revolution Betrayed*. London, 1937.

—— *The Stalin School of Falsification*. New York, 1937.
—— *The Third International after Lenin*. New York, 1936.
The Errors of Trotskyism (A symposium by Krupskaya, Kamenev, Stalin, Trotsky, Zinoviev, and others). London, 1925. (Other sources for Trotsky's statements include reports and records of Congresses and Conferences of the Communist party, various periodicals, *The Case of Leon Trotsky*, &c.)
TROTSKY, N., *Nashi Politicheskiye Zadachi*. Geneva, 1904.
Trudy Pervoi Vsesoyuznoi Konferentsii Istorikov-Marksistov, vols. i–ii. Moscow, 1930.
TUKHACHEVSKY, M., *Voina Klassov*. Moscow, 1921.

U Velikoi Mogily (a collection of articles, memoirs, and obituaries on Lenin). Moscow, 1924.

VARGA, E., *Izmenenya v Ekonomike Kapitalizma*. Moscow, 1946.
VIRTA, N., *Stalingradskaya Bitva*. Moscow, 1947.
VOROSHILOV, K., *Lenin, Stalin i Krasnaya Armya*. Moscow, 1934.
VOZNESENSKY, N., *Voennaya Ekonomika SSSR*. Moscow, 1948.
—— *Economic Results of the USSR in 1940*. Moscow, 1941.

WEBSTER, C. K., *The Foreign Policy of Castlereagh*, vol. ii. London, 1934.
WELLES, SUMNER, *The Time for Decision*. London, 1944.
WOLLENBERG, E., *The Red Army*. London, 1940.

YAROSLAVSKY, E., *Landmarks in the Life of Stalin*. London, 1942.
Yevtushenko, E. (Evtushenko), *Autobiographie Précoce*, Paris, 1963.

ZETKIN, KLARA, *Reminiscences of Lenin*. London, 1929.
ZINOVIEV, G., *Sochinenya*, vol. xv. Moscow, 1926.

The following protocols and verbatim reports of Conferences, Congresses, and collections of resolutions have been quoted:
2 Syezd RSDRP. Moscow, 1932.
Protokoly Obyedinitelnovo Syezda RSDRP v Stokholme v 1906 g. Moscow–Leningrad, 1926.
Prazhskaya Konferentsya RSDRP. Moscow (?), 1937.
6 Syezd RSDRP. Moscow, 1934.
8 Syezd RKP (b). Moscow, 1933.
10 Syezd RKP (b), Stenograficheskii Otchet. Moscow, 1921.
13 Syezd VKP (b), Stenograficheskii Otchet. Moscow, 1925.
14 Syezd VKP (b), Stenograficheskii Otchet (2nd edition). Moscow, 1926.
15 Syezd VKP (b), Stenograficheskii Otchet. Moscow, 1928.
15 Konferentsya VKP (b), Stenograficheskii Otchet. Moscow, 1927.
3 Syezd Profsoyuzov. Moscow, 1920.
VKP (b) v Rezolutsyakh i Reshenyakh, vols. i–ii. Moscow, 1936.
Kommunisticheskii International v Dokumentakh (edited by Bela Kun). Moscow, 1933.
Protokoll der Erweiterten Exekutive der Kommunistischen Internationale (February–March 1926). Hamburg–Berlin, 1926.

The following official reports of the purge trials have been used by the author:

Sudebnyi Otchet po Delu Trotskistskovo-Zinovievskovo Terroristskovo Tsentra. Moscow, 1936.

Sudebnyi Otchet po Delu Anti-Sovietskovo Trotskistskovo Tsentra. Moscow, 1937.

Sudebnyi Otchet po Delu Anti-Sovietskovo i Pravo-Trotskistskovo Bloka. Moscow, 1938.

Also:

The Case of Leon Trotsky (report of hearings on the charges made against him in the Moscow Trials by the Preliminary Commission of Inquiry). London, 1937.

Miscellaneous documentary sources:

Batumskaya Demonstratsya 1902 goda. Moscow (?), 1937.

Falsifiers of History, communiqué of Soviet Information Bureau, English version. London, 1948.

Kratkii Otchet o deyatelnosti Narodnovo Komisariata Raboche-Krestyanskoi Inspektsii za 1921 g. Moscow, 1921.

Soobshchenya Sovietskovo Informbureau, vol. iii. Moscow, 1943.

Newspapers and periodicals:

Bolshevik, Bulleten Oppozitsii, Gosudarstvo i Pravo, Istoricheskii Journal, Izvestya, Krasnyi Arkhiv, Krasnaya Zvezda, Kommunistische Internationale, Mirovoye Khozyaistvo i Mirovaya Politika, Planovoye Khozyaistvo, Pravda, Proletarskaya Revolutsya, Rundschau, Sotsialisticheskii Vestnik, Voprosy Istorii, Strany Mira (Statistical Yearbook for 1946).

Index

Rapallo, Russo-German Treaty of, 390, 409; prolongation of, ratified in 1933, 414.

Raskolnikov, 370.

Razin, E., Colonel, Stalin's letter to, 471.

Red Army, founded, 192, 197–8; Tsarist officers in, 196–8; its strategy and tactics in civil war, 210–11; in Russo-Polish war, 215–17; Zinoviev opposition in, 308–9; and collectivization, 354; reformed in 1936, 370, 421; its condition in 1936, 425; and purge trials, 372, 379–81, 425–6, 494; and Wehrmacht, 409; and revolution abroad, 412; crosses Polish frontier in 1939, 442; as agent of revolution, 446, 554; Hitler's fear of, 449; and Russo-German pact of 1939, 455, 460; its strength in defence, 456–7; retraining of, in 1939–41, 457; only half-mobilized in June 1941, 458; not hampered by one-sided strategic dogma, 462; its experiences in 1941, 462; Stalin contemplating withdrawal behind Volga, 465; after Dnieper defeat, 467; Allied view of, 477; disillusioned with western Allies, 480; on eve of Stalingrad battle, 480; internationalism and nationalism in, 487–9; war-time changes in, 488; mass promotion of generals in, 488–9; and prisoners of war, 489; and party in World War II, 493; German generals' view of, 495; selection of new commanders in, 496; recaptures two-thirds of Soviet territory, 498–9; marches into Poland, 500, 511, 523; conducts ten offensives in 1944, 511–12; its equipment from home production and Lend-Lease, 512 n. 1; and Warsaw rising, 522–4; enters Warsaw 524; marches into European vacuum, 532; reacts emotionally to German atrocities, 539; and eastern European capitalism, 542, 545; its 1945 victory parade, 549; and rise in standards of education, 550; its experience of western Europe, 559–61; potential opposition of, 561–2; during cold war, 584–5.

Red Guards, in 'July days', 150; inflicting defeat on Kornilov, 156; absorbed by Red Army, 198.

Reed, J., 177–9.

Reparations:
after World War I, 409–10, 501.
after World War II, 501–2, 537, 546; and dilemmas of Stalin's foreign policy, 551–2; at close of Stalin era, 572, 587–9, 597.

Resistance (to Nazi occupation), Russia begins to encourage, 448, 459; under bourgeois leadership, 474; Communist influence in, 518–19.

'Revolution from above', its first phases in Russian sphere of influence, 533; technique of, 533–4; compared with 1917 revolution in Russia, 534–5; its negative and positive aspects, 535–6; and People's Democracy, 542–3; in eastern Germany, 546–7; Napoleon and Stalin as makers of, 547, 554–5; and Russia's economic needs, 551–2; and 'revolution from below', 554; after French and Russian revolutions, 554–5; completed in eastern Europe, 585–9.

Revolution, permanent (Trotsky's theory), 120, 283–93 passim.

Revolutions:
English Puritan, 327, 344; haunted by fear of French intrigue and gold, 556; its work outlasts Cromwell, 570.
French Great, and Russian, 76, 173–6, 192, 220; as prototype, 273, 345–8, 382–3; its repercussions in western Germany, 547; followed by 'revolution from above', 554–5; haunted by fear of English intrigue and gold, 556; its work 'reshaped' after Napoleon, 570.
Russian, of 1905, 44, 62–4; its prospects discussed, 72–5; its ebb, 86–7.
Russian, of 1917, 129–72; and 'revolution from above', 534–5, 554.
Chinese, see China.

Ribbentrop, J., 430; his impatience for deal with Russia, 433–4, 436; received by Stalin, 437–41; his second visit to Stalin, 442; invites Stalin to Berlin, 445; on Stalin's calculations, 445 n. 4; proposes four-power pact to Stalin, 449–50; and Stalin's last overtures, 453; Molotov's secret protests to, 453; called 'fiend' by Stalin, 456; his 1939 'peace offensive' echoed by Comintern, 459; –Molotov Pact on Poland declared null and void, 476.

Riga Treaty, 442 n. 1.

Riutin, 333, 350.

Robespierre, M., 53, 145, 152; and Lenin, 220; and Stalin, 340, 345–8, 382–4, 566, 569.

Rodionov, M., 595.

Rodymtsev, General, 496.

Rodzianko, M., 123.

Rokossovsky, Marshal, 467, 496; in Stalingrad battle, 483–4; alleged to